LIFE AND CORRESPONDENCE

OF

THEODORE PARKER.

THEODORE PARKER.

Eng.ᵈ by F. Halpin, from a Daguerreotype taken in 1853.

LIFE AND CORRESPONDENCE

OF

THEODORE PARKER,

MINISTER OF THE
TWENTY-EIGHTH CONGREGATIONAL SOCIETY, BOSTON.

BY

JOHN WEISS.

IN TWO VOLUMES.
VOL. I.

NEW YORK:
D. APPLETON & COMPANY, 443 & 445 BROADWAY.
1864.

Select Bibliographies Reprint Series

 BOOKS FOR LIBRARIES PRESS
FREEPORT, NEW YORK

Reprinted 1969

LIBRARY OF CONGRESS CATALOG CARD NUMBER:

69-16854

PRINTED IN THE UNITED STATES OF AMERICA

PREFACE.

Soon after this Memoir was commenced, in the spring of 1861, it became evident that the original plan of publishing a single small volume would serve to present hardly a sketch of Mr. Parker's varied and useful life. At the same time, the biographical material, principally in the form of letters, began to increase in such a way that the plan was insensibly enlarged, and the publication from time to time postponed. These delays fortunately coincided with a season of great dulness in the literary market, when the events of the War were absorbing every mind.

As the mass of letters which existed among Mr. Parker's papers became slowly reduced to a sequence of time and to alphabetical order, so that the subjects discussed and the names and qualities of the writers could be seen, it was plain how much important matter from his own hand remained yet uncollected from every part of the country and from the Old World. This index of correspondence registered, by the surest and most delicate of tests, his diffused and latent life. It was worth while to spend a good many months in obeying such directions —to bid the man rise from beneath these sumptuous epitaphs of love, reverence, and human dependence.

This has been done to the extent which these volumes will show. No friend of Mr. Parker will regret the laborious delay which has recalled so many expressions of his mind upon such varied themes.

The distribution of these letters conforms to the method of the memoir, which could not be a chronological one without greatly confusing the subjects covered by his life. To do justice to each subject, and develope his thought thereon, and to preserve distinctness of effect, the memoir remands into groups, as far as possible, the elements of his manifold career. The order of time is preserved in the narrative of his material and mental growth to full manhood and consciousness of the work he had in hand, and wherever else it can be done without running together too many themes.

The Journal is a collection of a dozen manuscript volumes, some of them bulky ledgers, which are thickly sown with extracts, analyses of books, notifications of thinking. They would be called commonplace-books were it not for the vein of his private life which occasionally appears at the surface, and for the fact that his book-reading and note-making are really personal ; for they grow with his growth in a most simple and organic way. The diaristic matter makes a small portion of the whole contents of these volumes. I have given all of it that contributes to a knowledge of his life.

Besides the collection which I have called " The Journal," there are several little pocket note-books, out of which something has been gleaned, principally from those which he used during his last journeyings. But the few passages that are found in a condition to print appear as from " The Journal."

Wherever a citation occurs from his printed works, it is made from the only uniform American edition that has appeared. Many of the foot-notes would be trivial or superfluous except for the English and foreign reader, for whose benefit they were inserted. It is difficult to anticipate where a foreign reader might need a note or explanation ; sometimes I may have exceeded, sometimes fallen short of, the natural requisition.

His brother, Isaac Parker, his nephew, Columbus Greene, and other persons, have most kindly furnished recollections of different portions of his life, chiefly of his boyhood. And his friends have freely rendered up the precious letters which they had in keeping ; and distant and unknown, as well as famous, persons, in both hemispheres, whose names and habitat were discovered only by a sifting of the correspondence, have, with hardly an exception, responded to the call for the letters in their possession. Mrs. Parker would publicly return thanks to all these. It is hardly necessary for me to add how much the memoir is indebted to such contributions.

But it is indebted greatly to that devoted heart, that delicate disposition, and that good sense, which has been left to recall how loving a husband was this champion of oppressed thoughts and people, and to build, with most careful and assiduous hands, a memorial to the dear one, so illustrious to her by private sweetness as by public service. It is from her that I have derived all my authority and opportunity to undertake this work.

Only three years have passed since another ministry called the noble and variously gifted man, whom my pen, at a long interval and with many an imperfect movement, has been striving to recal, hoping, at least, not greatly to mar the character which is now perceived to have been bone of the bone and flesh of the flesh of America. But the consideration which is paid to him, in all quarters where it is worthy to be well remembered, through most diverse theological and political confessions, is a tribute which hastens very early to his grave. In England alone, the simultaneous publication of two distinct editions of his Works,* though both of them are quite unauthorized, and neither respects the duty and wishes which rule in his late home, sufficiently attests the importance of his writings to the popular mind, to develope therein free and manly thought.

The soil of no grave was ever more fertile. Men, who ex-

---

* One, edited by Miss F. P. Cobbe, and published by Trübner and Co., entitled "The Collected Works of Theodore Parker," &c. ; the other, published by Barker and Co., 4, Thanet Place, Strand, and called "The Works of Theodore Parker, Minister of the Twenty-Eighth Congregational Church, Boston, U.S." The latter edition, the price of which is but two shillings per volume, has the merit of cheapness, with good type and paper.

pected that his influence would become extinct, and that he had no gifts incisive enough to write his name upon the heart, acknowledge even now that he was a representative man, with conscience and humanity enough to feed a generation, to warn and to save, to build up with healthy tissue, to repair the degenerate waste of a noble people, and to pull down and trample on their crimes alone. He has been missed during these three years. The best men have asked for him, because they wanted New England granite to build with a breakwater, to have firm words to put in slippery places, that the country might be helped across into purpose and a definite policy of freedom. Men have said, at home and abroad, in various tongues, He grows upon us : he was healthy as immortality, he was as unconventional as a period of revolution always must be——a strong soil full of seeds : the more you till it, the better it nods with wheat, and corn, and all the substantial elements of human food. Foreign thinkers are very quick to perceive the drift of his mind, and very enthusiastic to recognize his capacity for entertaining righteousness. They see from afar, what we are now beginning to see close at hand, that he was a pioneer of this America which has been sending her dreadful columns over roads of his surveying and which he helped to clear.

It would be surprising to see how readily everything which is now happening connects itself with his sincerity and indignation, if we did not know that God's hand holds nothing but things that are sincere, and that His earth must grow the things that are planted. It is the test of the symmetry of a great mind ; its anticipations Providence seems to have overheard, so readily do its thoughts, its just wrath, its salutary hatred, its heavenly hopes, become converted into history.

His Life appears at the very moment when the great struggle which he anticipated is going against the wickedness which he smote so valiantly. The sound of victorious cannon is a salvo of recognition over his distant grave——a thundering welcome paid, so soon after those mutterings of hatred and contempt, to the great sense of liberty which he represented. The Lexington blood is cold ; flowers cover that simple and manly presence, and divert our thoughts from its decay ; he is absent upon some ministry that requires a brave and unselfish heart. But look through the hearts of the common people who supply this redness and are blushing so frankly at Gettysburg and Charleston, —what American ever had so good a right as he to say, as for himself, " There is a day after to-day " ?

Through three-and-fifty years of his I have been wandering— for the last words of this Preface pass under my hand upon the anniversary of his birth—fifty, almost, of his faithful life, three of the proud tears and keen recognition of the noblest minds. As I must at length commit this imperfect memorial to the gentleness of all readers, can I help recollecting that my hand has been held by a stalwart nature, whose thought and affection have passed, to thrill and enrich me ? He has confirmed and guided me. He has befriended the conscience and the will ; he has been munificent with suggestion. He drops my hand, and leaves me for the host of friends and lovers to whom his presence has so long been due.

August 24, 1868.

CONTENTS OF VOL. I.

ILLUSTRATIONS TO VOL. 1.

LIFE AND CORRESPONDENCE

OF

THEODORE PARKER.

CHAPTER I.

IT is surprising to find how many farmers of Eastern Massachusetts can still trace their lineage directly back to ship-board,
whence their ancestors descended to possess the new soil. These
sturdy men draw a straight furrow across two hundred years,
but the waters of the bay obliterate it, and its course can be
seldom resumed beyond. Of the English annals of the Parker
family, only a few disconnected scraps exist. Names and places
are confused, and many Parker families are scattered over the
kingdom.* As nearly as can be now determined, our branch of
the Parkers came from the parish of Browsholme, in the county
of York, and this family appears respectable and flourishing early
in the sixteenth century. A coat of arms, profusely blazoning
leopards' heads, stars, and a stag pierced by an arrow for a crest,

---

* The name is as old as the word *Parcarius*, park-keeper or shepherd; *Parcus* meant
a picketed enclosure for domestic animals, and also a preserve for game. *Parcarius* and
De Parco are mentioned in Doomsday Book. They are found in "Liber Feudorum,"
and one Samuel Parker is noted in the reigns of Henry III. and Edward I. A James le
Parker turns up in Norwich in 1261 ; the "Taxatio Ecclesiastica" yields the name, and
we find the following in mediæval Latinity of 1205: "Johannes le Parker tenet dimid.
hidam terrae, per servantiam custodiendi Parcum Domini Regis et Riesam forinsicum et
valet hoc annum dimidiam marcam": John the Parker holds half a hide of land for
the service (sergeantry) of keeping the King's park and pasture-ground, and receives
this year half a mark. Fifty acres, and 6*s*. 8*d*. per annum for folding the royal sheep and
driving them to pasture.

2

has the motto *Semper aude,* which many of the descendants did their best to vindicate. Our business begins with Thomas Parker, who brought over the spirit which earned a better blazon than the family arms which were afterwards discovered for his descendants. The name occurs so often among the enemies of the Church of England, that we may suppose Thomas had very good Puritan reasons for his emigration. Many Quakers and two non-conforming clergymen, bear the name. A Rev. Thomas Parker, of Newbury, brought over a company from Wiltshire, and settled Newbury and Newburyport.

Thomas Parker came over, in 1635, in a vessel fitted out by Sir Richard Saltonstall, who was then in London. There was some connection between the Parkers of Browsholme * and the Sir Richard Saltonstall who was Lord Mayor of London in 1597. Thomas Parker settled at Lynn, and he was made freeman in 1637. In the division of the town among its early settlers, forty acres of land were allotted to him. A lineal descendant occupied, not long ago, if a statement made by Alonzo Lewis be correct, the old homestead which has been in the family for seven generations. It is now, since a division of the township, in Saugus, on the west bank of the river, about eighty rods below the Iron Works. Thomas removed to Reading in 1640, and was one of seven who founded the first church of Reading, of which he was a deacon in 1645. Here he died, August 12, 1683, having been the father of six sons and four daughters. In the course of a century and a half, many of the stones which marked the resting-places of these early settlers had crumbled away, and when a new place of burial was opened, the town let out the old place as a mowing lot. The lessor was bound not to swing his scythe beyond the line marked by a few gravestones, already half-buried in the dust which they professed to celebrate. The scythe, however, slipped gradually over the whole ground, and the thrifty descendant illustrated scriptural views of

---

* Edward Parker, born 1602, married Mary, daughter of Richard Sunderland, of Yorkshire, whose wife was Mary, sixth daughter of Sir Richard Saltonstall. He had a coat of arms, displaying three bucks' heads and a buck for the crest, with the motto, *Non fluctu nec flatu movetur.* A seal engraved with this motto was sometimes used by Mr. Parker.

There is a Thomas Parker registered by Burke as belonging to this family, who was a son of John Parker of Little Norton and Jordenthorpe, and he was baptized March 31, 1609. The Thomas Parker who emigrated was 74 years old when he died at Reading in 1683. This age refers his birth to 1609. This is the only coincidence of date which can be discovered, and of its value we know nothing.

mortality through the grass which his ancestors were nourishing. *Hoc est veré monumentum patris colere.* Later still, in building a Town-house, where it was supposed no graves had ever existed, old ones were broken into accidentally ; the stones thus recovered were piled in a row against the wall, with Thomas Parker's at the head. So that the upright and sturdy old Puritan, who began life in America with forty acres in Lynn, ends with nothing this side the grave except the fame of his descendant.*

In the Massachusetts recórds we find the sumptuous prefix of *Mr.* to his name in the list of freemen : that was more charily pronounced in 1637 than to-day.† He and his posterity were flourishing and reliable men : wherever they settled, we trace them by the offices they filled, the claims they adjudged, the boundaries they assisted in defining. They viewed land, reviewed the militia, and were lieutenants and captains of companies. The military spirit was very strong among them in days when fighting was often the final cause of training. The " dying words " of one Jonathan Parker, a discoloured sheet, with only the date 1680, and no other note by which his age or work in this life can be fixed, is a most tender and God-fearing document. He had passed through perils of the field in King Philip's war : perhaps he was one of the 150 volunteers under Turner, or one of Lathrop's picked company. This was in 1675–6 : but he was spared to die at home.

Then he was heard to say that he desiered, and that if it wear the will of God, that this cross might pass from him, but if not he did desier to submit, allso he desiered that God would soport his parents, and make them wiling to submit, if he must dey, that God would be pleased to make his pasing easy into glory, and if that he did dey he hopt to go to a heavenly Father.

He did entreate his father and mother to forgive him all his ofencis, telling of them that he would entreate them to submit to the will of

---

* From his grave-stone, as it stood in the yard of the Centre School-house, South Reading, this epitaph was transcribed:—

Memento Mori !
Fugit Hora !
Here lyeth within
This sacred place
The body of Deacon
Thomas Parker
who was won of
the foundation of
the church, who dyed
yᵉ 12 of August,
1683, aged about 74.

frey's New England, II. 67.

God. In parting with them, saying that he had cometted his case to God, and if it may make most for God's glory and youer comfort, I desier to live, if not I am willing to dey.

Being asked if he wars not afraid of deth, he sayed noe, for Christ had taken away the sting of deth, tho Sathon had a thrust at him to make him fall, but he said he had no foothould, and had not yet prevailed, and he hopt that he never should, for he was a coward. Then his mother said that it was a great merci that God did coop him in the sins of the wars and brought him home to die by his parents—there was notice taken of him that he prayed, for had nothing els to do—he did desier to be remembred to his two sisters, and tell them that if they do see him no more, they should not see him sinn.

This Jonathan belonged to the family before its removal to Lexington, which was then called Cambridge Farms. John, a grandson of Thomas, left Reading in 1710, carrying with him all his children and grandchildren but Hananiah. This one, a son of John, junior, had already enlisted in the Massachusetts Regiment, which shared in the various operations against Port Royal from 1707 to 1710. A letter of his is preserved, dated March 8th, 1708, from *Annapolis Royal;* for the soldiers in the camp before that place already called it by the name which it received after its capture, in honour of Queen Anne. Passages from this letter, showing his grave and virtuous bringing-up, are worth transcribing. Grahame * speaks of the great sickness and mortality among the troops. Hananiah's spelling is more than obsolete, but here it is as he penned it in the wet trenches, the Yankee spelling and disposition for 1708 :—

Honored Father and Mother,—After my Deuty Remembered to you and to my Grandfather and Grandmother, and my love to my brothers and all my friends. Hoping theas few lines of my Love Will find you in as Good health as I am at this present Writting, Blessed be god for it. And this is to let you understand that i Receaved youer Second letter, and that it is a werey sickly time with us, and we have Lost above Three scor men that belong to New England. Sr. Charles † has lost 11 men out of his Redgement. Coronal Whiting has lost 16 or 17 and he has 24 men sick. One man Dyed out of our Company : he belonged to Wobone, his name was Robert Peirce. But we hope to see you in a litle time, they that are living, but if we stay hear much Longer thair will but few of us se New England, but Sr. Charles saies he will cary us home as soon as y⁰ govenor coms : we hope to see you

---

* History of the United States, III., 39–43.

† Four regiments were raised in New England, two of which were commanded t Charles Hobby and Colonel Tailer, of Massachusetts.

in a month or six weaks, if we live—for Sr. Charles is a wearey of this place and amost Discouraged, and wants to git home as much as we do.

Out of all New England men thair is but about 40 men fit for Deuty, and thair is hardly men enough to berrey y⁰ dead and look after y⁰ sick, for we berrey 2 or 3 men everey Night : for we berrey them in night becaus y⁰ french Should not know how many men we loos, and we berrey them out of the buring place down by y⁰ water side below y⁰ fort and spread y⁰ ground leavel over them that they might not be seen.

But i desire youer prayers for me that i may be kept from sin and sickness, beaing in a dangerous place for them both : for thair is nothing but wickedness carried on hear, cursing and swearing for every man's mouth.

We hear that thair is men a coming from New York to Releaive us. But No mor At Present, for i have No News to send you. So i

Remain your Deutyfull Son.

Hananiah was eighteen when he wrote this letter. We fancy him eager to return that he might share in the family removal to Lexington ; and the father was longing to recover so much helpful muscle from the barren trenches, to plant the fresh acres, and bring in wood for that new hearth which blazed afterward so clear for freedom. But he was kept in garrison at Port Royal after the capitulation, and died there of the prevailing sickness, sometime during 1711.

The rest of the family (nine children), one or more of whom were married, went with the father to Lexington in 1710, leaving many of the name in Reading, whence they went to settle in various neighbouring towns. A Nathaniel had fourteen children ; Bethiah, the mother of these, was ninety when she died. Each generation lost many children ; but also reared many, who were strong and prolific, cleared many a good acre, and ploughed sinew into the soil of the coming commonwealth. They lived long and well, loved peace, and abated rural acrimonies ; but always, from the time of landing, kept a musket for the frontier, against Pequod, King Philip, French, and Ojibways ; they never shrunk from pain nor fainted at the inevitable blood-lettings of discomposed times, and always made a solemn business of militia drill, as old family almanacs and account books attest, in which the phrases of field manœuvres and words of command alternate with the price of hay and lumber and the settlement of a neighbour's bill. Take, for instance, this specimen, from " Josiah Parker's book, 1738,' of the terms used in the manual by all the fighting men of Lexington : —

> Joyne your right hand to your F.*
> Present your F.
> Rest your F.
> Cock your F.
> Present—fire.
> Recover your F.
> Half-cock your F.
> Handel your primer.
> Prime.
> Shut your Pan.
> Cast about to charge.
> Handel your carthrige.
> Open your carthrige.
> Charge with carthrige.
> Draw your rammers.
> Shorten your rammers.
> Put them in the barrels.
> Ram down your carthrige.
> With-draw your rammers.
> Shorten your rammers.
> Return your rammers.
> Cast off your F.
> Your right hand under the lock.
> Poise your F.
> Shoulder your F.
> Rest your F.
> Ground your F.
> Take up your F.
> Rest your F.
> Club your F.
> Rest your F.
> Secure your F.
> Shoulder your F.

May ye first, 1744.

Then setled yᵉ Dignity of Officers in Colonol Phip's Ridgement.

Captains.	Lieutenants.
1. Saml. Green.	John Tainter.
	Saml. Hendly.
2. Benj. Reed.	Josiah Parker.
3. Saml. Livermore.	John Baal.
4. Capt. Hayes.	Thom. Symms.
5. Capt. Codman.	Wm. Hide.
6. Capt. Fuller.	Jos. Bryant.
7. Capt. Kendrick.	Robert Mardock.
8. Capt. Brooks.	Benj. Blany.
9. Capt. Dana	Stephen Hall.

* In the corner of the page is written, "N.B.—that F. stands for firelock."

And here is a note made by some painstaking captain, ambitious of perfecting his company drill :—

Reare half files, double the depth of your right flank. Left half files of left flank face to the left about. Front half files of left flank face to the left. Reare half files of right flank face to the right—march 10 paces—the whole face to the right—march 10 paces—face to the right.

Such matter as this lies confusedly mixed with charges made for mechanical labour and farm produce ; for the Parkers knew how to wield a good many kinds of tools :—

1752. To a harrow and exeltreeing your cart—to mending your Cyder-mill—to a chees mill—to making 3 keelers and a churn—to making a coffin—to 3 days and ½ work Stoning your Seller—to 3 Doz. of Compas boxes—6 pair of Bed Screws at £7 10s. a pair old tenor— to a beetel and how handel and sithe sneth—to my oxen to Cambridge and 3 Cartouch boxes—to whetting and setting your hand-saw—to my oxen to plough in your Rie—to shoeing your sled—to making your leading staff—to 23 pound of Veal at 15d. per lb.—to mending your Chimney back—to Cutting 19 lbs. of tobacco—to a tobacco tub and mending a brine tub lid.

But the pens which noted down rather laboriously the proceeds of meadow and garden land, and the number of planks which were rafted down the Mystic for ship-building, have left no trace of the early sufferings and sorrows. Hananiah's homesickness was, I fancy, an achievement of garrulity uncommon in the family. Like all the pioneers of New England, they minded their business, and never hinted at their feelings. Their diary is their fair and lawful portion of the history of the plantation as it stands to be read in all authentic books.

Reminiscences of military life and border suffering came also into the family on the mother's side subsequent to 1754, when Hannah Seger was married to Benjamin Stearns, of Lexington. One of their daughters was the mother of Theodore Parker. His grandmother's ancestor, Thomas Seger, or Seager, came to Newbury before 1637. The descendants seem to have had a taste for frontier life. Nathaniel, of uncertain date, was one of the earliest settlers of Bethel, Maine ; the Indians carried him off into Canada, as they did many another man and woman, when they could surprise them in the fields, driving them thence through the desolate gaps in the White Mountains, to make a bloody trail where now the summer streams of fashion and invalidism so easily flow.

Nathaniel had a very hard time of it, which he must needs write about afterwards.   Another member of this family enlisted during the Revolutionary war, was a sergeant in Capt. Bryant's company of artillery, and went through many an engagement. His captain lay mortally wounded after the battle of Brandy-wine, within the enemy's lines, whence he brought him away by night upon a litter, with two or three comrades helping, though he, too, had sustained a severe wound that day.   Stories of the wilderness and of battle were told into greedy ears at the winter firesides of the Lexington families.

Toryism did not flourish among the descendants of Thomas Parker of Browsholme.   "*Semper aude*" was the creed of five generations of them, who knew small Latin, but kept alive an instinct for supporting the weak against the strong, the wronged against the wronger.   By-and-bye the doctrine was heard from the pulpit of Lexington Green, where Jonas Clark made sincere and earnest application of it, not to judges, tax-gatherers, and governors, who were groping in Sheol some time before the settlement of the Old Testament canon, but to flesh-and-blood Britishers waiting at Boston to carry Tory mandates up the country.   Jonas believed in preaching directly to the point, in days when political sermons were not dictated by the nice distinction constructed for the benefit of the Fugitive Slave Bill, that the oppressing power, in '75, resided in England and not at Washington; they were inspired by the plain circumstance that there was oppression in America.   Mayhew, Clark, and other brave pre-revolutionary preachers, did not withhold their word because Tory countrymen sat in the pews and helped support the minister.   A divided opinion, a country tardy or irresolute, a prospect of irreconcileable divisions, were so many arguments for quickly reinforcing the spirit of liberty with words of pro-testing truth.   This they did, seeing the green fields beyond the swelling flood.

The plain people hungered for these appeals, and their repre-sentatives knew how to use the great influence which a faithful pulpit then possessed.   Here is a trace of it :—

In Provincial Congress.   Watertown, May 22, 1775.

The Congress having requested the Rev. Dr. Langdon to deliver a sermon before the next Massachusetts Congress, at their meeting in this place, on the last Wednesday of this month, and he having signified that he will comply with such request,

Resolved, that it is the desire of the Congress, that the Reverend Ministers of the Gospel in this Colony would assemble at that time, agreeable to their ancient custom, and hold a convention, as usual (if they think proper) ; as, in the opinion of this Congress, the cause of religion *and the political interest* of this Colony may be served by such meeting.*

Old Dr. Byles, of Hollis Street Church, was 'singular in this respect, as in many others, and held out against the expressed desire of his own parish that he would consider the condition of the Colony in the pulpit, and against the enthusiasm of all of his Congregational brethren in Boston. The sermons of the time abounded, except in Western Massachusetts, with eager discussion of public affairs. Clergymen responded to invitations to preach by taking the popular side, not in veiled generalities, but with the plainest exposition of the doctrine for which Massachusetts rose in arms. "If it be," said one of them,† "in the nature and reason of things lawful for a people to enjoy their lives, liberty, and property, it must be also, in the same nature and reason of things, lawful to preserve them ; for to suppose a right to them, and no right to preserve or defend them, is manifestly absurd."

Treason was levied in these terms in the house of God : the commonwealth sat wakeful in the high-backed pews of the old fireless meeting-houses, warmed by hearts that glowed in the pulpits, feeling Religion place the sword of the Lord and of Gideon into every hand. What wonder that the green before the church became wet with blood ! What wonder that the drops sowed heart's love for liberty, fresh from praise and prayer, in the spring soil !

In the old meeting-house sat Capt. John Parker (born, 1729 ; died, 1775), Jonathan Harrington, his nephew, and fifer of his company, and Jonas Parker, who fell upon the Green. Captain Parker had been a sergeant in the French war, 1749–59, and was at the taking of Quebec. Jonas Clark, then forty-five years of age, had for some time discussed the successive points of the great controversy as it became developed. He drew up the instruc-

---

* Find the sermon itself reprinted in J. W. Thornton's "Pulpit of the American Revolution," and on page 255, the following note : "Governor Gage, in his proclamation of June 12, 1775, a few days after Dr. Langdon's sermon was preached, said 'To complete the horrid profanation of terms and of ideas, the name of God has been introduced in the pulpits to excite and justify devastation and massacre.'" It sounds like a modern Tory newspaper denouncing the introduction of "exciting topics" into the pulpit, and predicting that strife will be stirred up by the ministers of a Gospel of peace.

† Elisha Fish, minister of Upton, preaching at the invitation of the Committee of Correspondence for Worcester County, March 28, 1775

tions which his people desired to have presented to the Provincial Legislature by their delegate. This is a model paper, which simply and strongly sets forth the views often urged before in public and private by the revolutionary clergyman. He was more dangerous than all the military stores at Concord or in the Colony, and had so infected the whole district with his calm and deep indignation, that, when the regulars came marching up the old turnpike in the gray dawn of the 19th of April, after powder and flour, they found all the farmers converted to a doctrine of liberty which armed and provisioned a young nation for seven years of war. In the meeting-house and town-house, ringing with Clark's religious convictions, filled with his enlightened points and improvement, was the history of that glorious morning slowly prepared.

What a speech it gained at two o'clock, when the little belfry-tower opposite his meeting-house rang the inhabitants together for the action which had been foreshadowed in prayer and sermon ! One hundred and fifty men gathered to the call, and waited quietly for the reports brought in by riders who had been despatched a few miles down the road. The pastor was there, encouraging and reminding the flock that the opinions which they accepted in their pews must be advanced upon the Green. About one of the clock, their captain, John Parker, had been summoned, who was then ill with troubles which grew, by neglect and exposure, into the disease of which he died in September of the same year. He resided about three miles from the meeting-house. Being informed " that there were a number of regul? officers riding up and down the road, taking and insulting people,"[*] he issued the orders which assembled his company, and hastened to his minister's side. He concluded " not to meddle or make with said regular troops, unless they should insult or molest us." At the approach of this body of regulars, which was 900 strong, he formed his own little troop of 70 men into the first line of the Revolution, and bade them charge their pieces with powder and ball. A scattering and ineffective fire was their response to the three volleys which the British delivered ; after this he told them to disperse and take care of themselves. Fifteen men had fallen ; seven of these were killed, including Jonas Parker, " the strongest wrestler in Lexington, pierced with both ball and bayonet." The men dispersed for a

---

[*] Affidavit of Capt. Parker, April 23, 1775. MS. copy.

time, to join in a few hours the great uprising of the country, which followed the regulars to Boston, with Jonas Clark's Sunday doctrine practically administered all along the road.

Captain Parker was not too ill to engage far and well in this pursuit. He was also at the battle of Bunker's Hill, in command of troops, but not engaged. The King's arm, which he took from a grenadier of the 43rd Regiment (the first weapon captured in the Revolution), and his own light fowling-piece which he had carried at Quebec, stood by the door of Theodore's study in Boston till the executors of his will consigned them to the keeping of the State. In the Senate Chamber they hang, and Massachusetts still yields children worthy to take them down who have not degenerated from those who first bore arms for her. The rusted pattern is still symbolical of the old spirit tried again in the same old cause, whose minute-men are again first in the field, and have drawn the first shot upon the same April date.* Jonas Clark and Theodore Parker are in array against a tyranny whose forms are various, but whose intention is evermore the same.

This letter, addressed to Mr. Bancroft, after the publication of the seventh volume of his History, contains some interesting notices :—

Boston, 10th September, 1858.

MY DEAR BANCROFT,—Last May came your beautiful volume on the Revolution. I was ill, and yet obliged to work. I read it with enthusiasm in the pauses of my toil. It ran into the night, and was soon in my head. I rejoice in it greatly. You confirm my suspicions that George III.—miserable old wooden-head!—was the real cause of the mischief. But you shed a deal of light I had no suspicion of on many matters; of course you do. It is thoroughly *democratic*, in the best sense of the word. This volume has more of the *Life of the People* in it than any of the last three. It seems to me history has been hitherto the life of kings, priests, nobles, soldiers, and the like—not the *Life of the Million*, as it should be. " *Les gens des salons partout se ressemblent*," but the people are every where different. I am glad to find a historian who cares for " the rest of mankind."

One fact or two let me give. At the battle of Lexington, when Capt. P. drew up his men as the British were nearing, he ordered " every man to load " his piece with powder and ball. " Don't fire unless fired upon ; but if they mean to have a war, *let it begin here!*" I think these significant words ought to be preserved. They were kept as the family tradition of the day, and when the battle was re-enacted

---

* Written just after the Massachusetts three-months men had passed through Baltimore, April, 1861.

in 1820 (or thereabout), his orderly sergeant took the Captain's place, and repeated the words, adding, " For them is the *very words* Captain Parker said." Besides, some of the soldiers, when they saw the flash of the British guns, turned to run : he drew his sword, and said, " I will order the first man *shot* that offers to run !" Nobody ran till he told them, " Disperse, and take care of yourselves." Prince Estabrook, who was killed at the second fire, was a *negro.**

Thankfully yours,

THEODORE PARKER.

And here is an extract from Mr. Parker's journal, written on occasion of a visit to Lexington to attend the ordination of Jason Whitman. The Jonathan Harrington herein mentioned was the grandfather of John W. Harrington, master's mate of the *Cumberland*, who was killed during the fight with the *Merrimac* in Hampton Roads :—

Jonathan Harrington was a fifer in my grandfather's company, and is the last survivor (1845), now 87 years old. He was then in his 17th year. I asked him how he felt as he marched on to the spot. He said he felt well enough then ; but when they saw the reg'lars march up, he felt kind o' queer. Some offered to run away, but Captain Parker drew his sword, and said he would run through the first man that offered to run away. He said Captain P. looked as if he could face anything, and so he could. He was a large-boned man ; his face longer than my father's, but in other respects built like mine (*i. c.*, stout, a stocky man.) His (Jonathan's) uncle, Wm. Munro, had been out in the French war. He showed me a pistol that belonged to him, and which he used there. Jonathan H. was in the American service at Prospect Hill, as one cf the guard of Burgoyne's troops, but never had a pension. His father (Uncle Harrington) dealt in ship timber. He often had trains of it that reached more than half a mile, and great quantities at his *bank* (depôt) in West Cambridge, whence he rafted it to Boston down the Mystic River. He was a patriot, but the Revolution ruined his business, and " kind o' broke it up." He lost great quantities of timber ; the British plundered his house at the battle—carried off his clock, leaving the weights and the case ; the pendulum was afterwards found dropped in the fields half a mile off, &c. Jonathan then went to school to Mr. Pitt Clark, " a pretty man." He taught on the Common. Jonathan studied Latin, but the soldiers took away his Latin books— all of them but the dictionary, which he still keeps (Young's Dictionary). He went to school no more. He would, perhaps, have gone

---

* This is a mistake, according to information kindly furnished by Hon. Charles Hudson, who is preparing a history of Lexington. He was wounded, but recovered and served in almost every campaign of the war. '' He is represented, by those who knew him, as a fine specimen of a man, tall, well-built, and muscular, having a carriage which fully justified the name of Prince.'' Estabrook was his master's name. He, with other negroes who served in the Revolution, obtained his freedom as a reward for military service ; but it was also secured to them by the Constitution of 1780, which entirely abolished slavery.

to college but for this. He remembers my grandfather as well as if he saw him now before his eyes.

John, Theodore's father, was born Feb. 14, 1761, and married Hannah Stearns, a daughter of Benjamin Stearns of Lexington and Hannah Seger. He was more of a mechanic than a farmer, and during his life the farm was mainly carried on by the boys, while he worked in the little shop just above the house, making and mending wheels, pumps, and farming-gear. He taught his children the use of tools, and Theodore became very handy with them. The cradle which he made (while he was preparing for college), for his sister-in-law's first child, is solid and shapely. He learned to hoop barrels and mend the plough. But his father was a great reader also, and thus many a book found its way into the house, borrowed of friends or hired from the little circulating library upon the Green, which Theodore would not have otherwise obtained ; they filled the long evenings, when all the children gathered around the table, in front of the fire, and the father read, sometimes aloud, when a passage pleased him, till eight o'clock struck, and with a wave of his hand he dismissed them to bed.

We gather from some rude notes which Mr. Parker made concerning his father, that he was a stout and able-bodied man, "uncommon strong," very ingenious and industrious. He had studied algebra and geometry, was particularly fond of mathematics, and was "great at figures." He was a good talker, and might have been an orator. If he ever got into an argument, which was seldom, as controversy did not suit him, he was very effective. He liked metaphysics, psychology, and all departments of intellectual and moral philosophy, and he had read all the English books upon philosophy. "He was a great reader, rising before day in the winter to study, sleeping but about five hours ; nice and acute in metaphysical analysis, jovial and funny," but not so exuberantly mirthful as Theodore was, nor so grotesque in his fun. He was well-mannered ; no clownishness, profanity, or indecency marred his humour. In religious matters he thought for himself, and hated Paley and Jonathan Edwards. "Paley left us no conscience," he used to say. He did not believe in eternal damnation, nor in the more extravagant of the miracles in the Old and New Testament, but he was a great reader of the Bible, and taught the younger children the

ten commandments every Sabbath evening, and Sunday prayers
and hymns.

"He did not like poetry, but read Pope, Dryden, Milton,
Shakspeare, Trumbull, Peter Pindar, and Abraham Cowley. In
the later years of his life he was fond of novels."

In theology he was a Unitarian, in politics one of the five
Federalists in Lexington. "He was eminently just and magnanimous, fearless in the expression of opinion, often arbitrated
in quarrels, was guardian of widows, orphans, &c., and administered estates, for there was no lawyer in town. He was not
thrifty, and so, not rich. Devoted to education," he took great
interest in the common schools, and was influential in bringing
into them a better breed of teachers. He took great pains with
the intellectual and moral culture of his children.

Mr. Parker described his mother as "a handsome woman,
delicate and slightly built, industrious, thrifty, charitable to the
poor." She was fond of hearing the father read aloud while
she sewed. She loved ballads and popular tales, could repeat a
great many of them, and had her favourites among the hymns.
She knew the Old and New Testaments thoroughly, "was ima-
ginative, delicate-minded, poetic, yet a very practical woman;
far-sighted, and so nice in her perceptions and judgments that it
used to startle me sometimes in the body, and does now as I
think of it. She took great pains with the religious training of
her children, but cared little for doctrines; no bigotry, no cant,
no fear. Religion was love and good works. She had what I call
piety, the ideal part of religion, love of God as well as morality."
She had a critical eye to the religious reading of her household,
and not much bigoted literature was allowed.

Her manners were grave and gentle, not hard, but touched, I
surmise, with the old Puritan state, which made the frank blue
eyes sometimes austere. She had a lofty soul; conscience and
piety kept it both unbending and tender. The conscience
beamed full, as the sun at eastern windows, and pervaded all the
life of the house. Nothing could lay shadowy, yet a mellow
warmth fell everywhere with its exacting light.

The phrases of religion had not tampered much with her
heart : her spiritual sense knew to perceive the things appropriate to it, and it never occurred to her to question the soul's
capacity for this immediate perception, or to be content with its
mental and social simulations. Before her children she was not

eager to explain or refute, and never tried to skim her religious life for their luncheon and nooning. The young minds breathed unconsciously her mountain air of trust and reverence. In this influence of a fine soul Theodore became filled with piety at a very early age ; he throve as much under her reticence as he did in her timely speech : for he learned few religious terms, and no formal habits. So buds seem aimlessly to unfold, while Nature really makes a point of soliciting each in her private and un-announced way.

When the children took their light and went to bed, the day had still one grace in store for them, as they listened till their mother came up to see that they were well tucked in, and to share the sweetness of their homely prayers.

Theodore learned many a nice moral distinction from this clear-judging mother. Her position in the world was whole-some ; her intelligence shared the fair country chance of every-thing that grew on the farm. Popular views of life and man-ners were within sight, but too far to become familiar. The father's thirst for knowledge and the mother's spiritual longing were satisfied in unconventional ways. And the children, in acquiring this independence, found faith and earnestness besides ; for to live in the country is not merely to riot in freedom from the constraints of the town, but to obey nature's simple regu-larity, which always surprises and stimulates. This was the health which Theodore brought at last to Boston from those inland acres. His tribute to the mother of a great New-Englander can now be paid also to his own. "When virtue leaps high in the public fountain, you seek for the lofty spring of nobleness, and find it far off in the dear breast of some mother, who melted the snows of winter, and condensed the summer's dew into fair, sweet humanity, which now gladdens the face of man in all the city streets." *

Theodore was the youngest of eleven children. He was born August 24, 1810, when his father was over 50 and his mother was 47 years old. Sweet and sound is the last apple, ripen-ing high up in the tree, through the late golden days, discovered after the leaves begin to fall.

* Discourse on Daniel Webster.

[The Battle of Lexington was preceded by the famous midnight ride of Paul Revere, who escaped from Boston and warned the towns as far as Concord. While these sheets are passing through the press, the news comes that his grandson, Col. Paul Joseph Revere, of the 20th Massachusetts Regiment, died on July 4th (1863) of wounds received while leading his command at the Battle of Gettysburg, which was fought the day before.

The little Belfry, to which allusion is made later, in connection with the homestead of Mr. Parker, stands on the right of the Meeting-house.]

THE BATTLE OF LEXINGTON, APRIL 19TH, 1775.

CHAPTER II.

A FRAGMENT of an Autobiography, which was commenced at
Rome, is printed here in its original condition, except that a
few pages of botanical matter have been corrected and arranged
by Rev. John L. Russell, of Salem, in conformity with a request
transmitted by Mr. Parker to his old friend. When he found
that he could write no more, he closed the manuscript with a
caveat to the reader, which is here transferred to the commencement.

N.B. Caveat Lector.—This will require careful re-writing, and, as it
stands, may contain many errors of detail,* for I write it when too ill
to read, and with no memoranda to aid me. I should like to consult
the deeds of the early settlers in my neighbourhood, to learn the
original ownership of land, the date of the houses, and the names of
places like "the great meadow." Few men, if any, now living will
remember the name, but I have found it in old deeds.

I began this at Rome, March 16th, 1860. It is not likely I shall
get far in it. I have waited more than a year for strength to begin it,
and now commence at my weakest point.

The material and human circumstances about a man in his early life
have a strong and abiding influence upon all, especially on those of a
sensitive disposition, who are both easily affected by such externals and
rather obstinate in retaining the impression made on them.

OF THE MATERIAL SURROUNDINGS.

About 1710, my grandfather's grandfather, John Parker, then somewhat advanced in life, with a part of his grown-up children, removed
from Reading, where a family of Parkers had settled about 1640, to
the Cambridge Farms, since called Lexington, where he had bought a
considerable quantity of land, with one small house upon it, probably
of logs. The next year he built him a large and commodious house,
and furnished it with the usual out-buildings necessary for a farmer's
business. The situation was pleasant; a considerable valley a mile
or more in length and half a mile wide, with a fresh meadow at the

---

* Much may be omitted that he would have noted under favourable circumstances,
but all blanks have been filled, and only one or two errors of commission needed
attention. This Autobiography was commenced by Mr. Parker with the object of en-
trusting it, when finished, to his friend Mr. Lyman, to be used by him some day: the
fragment, accordingly, was sent to him.

bottom, called in deeds of the time "the great meadow," wound among hills tall and steep on the western and northern side, while on the south and east the hills were of less height and more gradual in their slope. Indeed, it is the general character of the hills in that part of the country to be steep on their southern and eastern side, and of gradual ascent on the opposite side. A brook stole through the valley or percolated through the soft, spongy meadow; following a continuation of the valley, it falls into Charles River at length. The stream was then much larger than at present; for now the hills have nearly all been stripped of their trees and the meadows drained, and the brook is proportionally shrunk, except when a sudden melting of snow floods the meadow and restores it to more than its original size.

Near the upper end of this valley, in about the centre of his farm lot, the old settler built his house, in which children to the fourth generation were to be born to him. It stood about 80 or 100 feet above the present surface of the great meadow, on the south-east side of a high hill, which, gently sloping in front of the house, rose steep and abrupt behind. It faced as near the south as the rude science of the owner or builder could make it, and so was a perpetual sun-dial. It had but one chimney, that a huge one in the centre of the building. The large bricks, made half-a-mile off, were laid in clay as far as the ridge-pole, while the part of the chimney above the roof was *pointed* with mortar. Limestone was not found within many miles, and the want of it was a serious inconvenience in building. The house, like all the others in that neighbourhood, was two storeys high in front, and only one in the rear. The rooms were few, but large and airy; the windows not numerous, of various size, but all small: originally all the latches, except that of the "fore-door," were of wood, with wooden thumb-pieces, but these had nearly all passed away before my recollection. The house, as it stood in my day, had been built at different times, the eastern end being considerably younger than the western, and not furnished with the massive oak-beams which everywhere stuck out in the older part. A New England farmer of " comfortable estate " would hesitate a good deal before setting up his household in such a cheerless shelter; but three generations of stout and long-lived men were born and grew up there; and if the fourth be more puny and sink quicker to the grave, it is from no fault of the old house, but from the consumption which such spongy meadows in New England seldom fail to produce in the course of time; even children, who have removed to healthier situations, carry with them the fatal poison in their blood, and transmit it to their sons and daughters.

As the old man at sunrise stood at the front or south door of his new house on some fine October morning of 1710, he could see but a single house, and that half or three-quarters of a mile off, the other side of the valley: two other columns of pale blue smoke in that direction might tell him of other neighbours, while not far off in the same valley were two others, hid by wooded hills; in a different direction one more house had been built earlier than his own, but on the north side of the hill which sheltered him.*

---

* Childs: in the Snake Hill lot.

Agriculture was at a low stage; that part of the country was covered with thick woods, and when the farmer cut down or girdled the trees and run the ground over with fire, the land must have looked as we see it now in parts of New Hampshire and Vermont, like "the abomination of desolation." However, he planted many apple-trees, importing them from England; but they had not been grafted, and so many of them bore sorry specimens of fruit. Many of those which it is said he set out were standing in my boyhood. He, or his son Josiah, who succeeded to his lands at Lexington, planted also locust-trees, whose white blossoms used to fill the air with sweetness in June. He also brought lilac-bushes, a common ornament about the houses of New England in the last century, and planted a barberry-bush, which in my boyhood had grown to prodigious dimensions, besides having increased and multiplied and replenished that part of the earth with its descendants.

In the rear of the house was a monstrous elm which endangered the building and was removed as a nuisance; that was a full-grown tree in the days of my grandfather's grandfather: other huge oaks and elms once stood close by, but they had all perished before my birth, and only a white ash with a great round top stood at the north-west corner of the house. It was planted by my grandfather, and was the largest tree of the kind I remember ever to have seen in New England.

Huge boulders lay scattered about along the valley and its tributaries; some were of the hard blueish greenstone which forms the skeleton of all the hills in that neighbourhood, but others were of whitish granite, brought many miles from their original site to the north-west of that locality. Loose stones abounded; indeed, a more unattractive piece of land for a farmer to work could scarcely be found than that whole region for miles around in all directions. There were stones enough within a foot of the surface to fence all the land into acre lots, each surrounded with a strong "balance wall."

The most common trees were the numerous species of oak, the white pine, the pitch pine, and a variety of it called the yellow pine, the hemlock, and spruce; on the rocky hill-sides the juniper or red cedar; and in the swamps the cypress or white cedar; maples, the white or grey, black and yellow birches, the elm, white and black ashes, poplars, buttonwood, walnuts, chestnut, beech, sassafras, and wild hop or hop-hornbeam, willows; three species of sumach occurring on the homestead; indeed, most of the trees of New England grow within a few miles of my home.

The handsomest flowering shrubs and plants of New England could mostly be found in the immediate neighbourhood, the shadbush, the rhodora, the viscous or white azalea—the pink-flowered species was further off; the numerous cornels, though only a single instance of the large-flowering cornel; the several viburnums and the andromedas, the narrow-leaved kalmia, and even the broad-leaved kind, grew in a thicket in the vicinity; the choke-cherries, the spiræas, both pinkish-white flowered, and the other with steeple-shaped purple spikes; wild roses and sweet briars, the clethra, blossoming from July to October. In the meadows, spongy with soft mosses, were the arethusas and the cymbidium, and the rarer painted cup, successively disclosing their native beauties; while a little later the pitcher-plant offered its curious flower and leaf to the most careless eye. The cranberry bore in midsummer its rich pale red flowers and covered whole acres from whence the farmer hoped, often vainly, to win as fair a harvest in autumn to season his winter food. The beautiful water lily grew abundantly in a shallow pond not far off, and also in many brooks of sluggish water; nay, it did not refuse the benediction of its presence in some of the ill-formed ditches whence peat had been cut for fuel or for manure. Here the fringed gentian, not then to be seen, has happily since taken up its abode; the soap-wort gentian was uncommon, the trilliums rare; but along the brook-sides the cardinal flowers hung out their brilliant colours.

On the hard land saxifrages and columbines grew on the sunny sides of all the great rocks, blue violets and white were to be had every-where, the yellow species was rarer, and anemones nodded their hand-some heads on the south side of every wall where nature had her own way.

In the woods, the ladies' slipper hung out its mysterious beauty, the several pyrolas opened their blossoms; they, with the ground pine, the partridge-berry, and the boxberry, or Mitchella, kept a green life in the woods under the snow all winter through. What need to mention the humbler beauties of the New England flora, such as the meadow-pride and the sweet cicely, the craneflower and the buttercups? There were also red lilies and yellow, some of them stately and queen-like plants—on a single stalk I have seen forty-nine buds and blossoms; nor should the humbler-named dog-tooth violet be forgotten in the list of its liliaceous sisterhood.

My sisters cultivated the crimson peony, daffodils, white and yellow narcissus, white and red roses of the most delicious fragrance. Camo-mile, saffron, and the odorous balms were herbs for medicine, not flowers for sport.

In the thick, dark swamps, huge, corky fungi grew on the trunks of old maples, but more especially of the white birches; and curious puff-balls shot up in the hot, muggy nights of summer, and in two days became mysteriously as large as a quart bowl; while the usual variety of other fungi sprung up in their appropriate places, and the Indian pipe of seeming make and mould; while lichens, some as large as a modern Kossuth hat, covered the north side of rocks and trees.

My ancestors had planted the white locust not far from the house, and a beautiful grove had grown up; some of the trees were very large, and sweetened the air for a week or two in June, and the grass all the summer through. When the autumn came—

" Every bush did put its glory on,
Like a gemmed bride."

How red the maples were, how yellow the birches and the walnuts, and what richly tinted leaves did the chestnut shake down!—last of New England trees to blossom, and bearing the richest, sweetest fruit the savage found in the austere land. Even the ivy and the poison dog-wood were clad in more glory than the Queen of Sheba, intent on wooing the King of Israel's son; nay, Solomon himself, in all his glory, was not arrayed like one of these.

From the middle of May when the introduced trees, the plum, peach cherry, apple, and pear, began to bloom, till the middle or end of October, the eye need not seek a landscape of humble, quiet New England beauty more attractive than this, and all winter long the white pines, which seemed so cool and attractive in July and August, had a warm, motherly look, and told of life still sleeping in them, around them, everywhere.

OF THE HUMAN SURROUNDINGS.

At the age of 45, my grandfather, Captain John Parker, died on the 17th of September, 1775. He was sick on the day of the Battle of Lexington, but did his duty from 2 A.M. till 12 at night. On the 17th of June he was too ill to be allowed to enter the turmoil of the Battle of Bunker-hill, so he discontentedly commanded troops who did no fighting that day. He was never well afterwards, and an epidemic dysentery in September found him an easy prey; he died at an early age for his long-lived family, and left three sons and four daughters, with a widow, who died at the respectable age of 92, passing a portion of the last 47 years of her life in a second marriage, which both she and her children had bitter cause to repent. The respectable property of Captain Parker was wasted, the relict obliged to take her new husband and his children home, to be supported on " the widows' thirds." When my father married Hannah Stearns, the daughter of a neighbouring farmer, he went back to the original homestead to take care of his mother, while he should support his handsome young wife and such family as might happen. It was the day of small things—he wore home-made blue yarn stockings at his wedding, and brought his wife home over the rough winding roads, riding in the saddle his tall grey horse, with her upon a pillion. The outfit of furniture did not bespeak more sumptuous carriage—the common plates were of wood; the pitcher, mugs, tea-cups and saucers, were of coarse earthenware; while the great carving dishes were of thick well-kept pewter. The holiday service " for company " was of the same material. Yet, a few costly wine glasses were not wanting, with two long-necked decanters, a few china tea-cups and saucers, of the minutest pattern, and the pride of the buffet, a large china bowl. Besides, the young bride could show patch-work bed-quilts and counterpanes, and a pretty store of linen towels, and a tablecloth of the same, white as the snow, and spun, woven, and bleached by her own laborious hands; and her father raised the flax which her brother pulled, and rotted, and broke, and swingled, and hackled, and combed. Hannah made their work into linen.

In the course of many years, ten children had been born to John and Hannah (one had slipped out of life an infant), when their fourth son and eleventh child came into the world, on 24th of August, 1810, lagging a little more than five years after his youngest, and afterwards his favourite sister. I think I was the last child born in the old house, which then numbered just 100 years.

1. In my earliest childhood the family at home consisted (to begin in the order of age) of my father's mother, more than 80 at my birth. A tall, stately, proud-looking woman: she occupied an upper chamber,

but came down-stairs to dinner—other meals she took in her own room—and sat at the head of the table on the woman side thereof, opposite my father, who kept up the ancient Puritan respect for age—always granting it precedence. She busied herself chiefly in knitting and puttering about the room, but passed the Sundays in reading the large Oxford quarto Bible of her husband, bought for the price of more than one load of hay, delivered up at Boston. She had also the original edition of the Puritan Hymn Book, printed at Cambridge, which was much in her hands. She read the newspapers, the *Columbian Centinel*, which then appeared twice a week; but common mundane literature she seldom touched. It was a part of my childish business to carry the *drink* to my venerable grandmother—twice a day, at 11 A.M. and 4 P.M.; this was *flip* in cool weather, and in spring and summer was *toddy* or *punch*—the latter was, however, more commonly reserved for festive occasions.

2. Next were my father and mother: grave, thoughtful, serious, and industrious people. From an ancestry of five generations of his own name, who had died in New England, my father had inherited a strong and vigorous body; in his youth, there was but one man in town who could surpass him in physical strength, and few who were his equals. He could endure cold and heat, abstinence from food and rest, to a degree that would be impossible to men brought up in the effeminate ways which so often are thought to be the curses of civilization. He was a skilful farmer; though, as he lived not on his own land, but on "the widows' thirds," which his mother had only a life-estate in, he was debarred from making costly improvements in the way of buildings, fences, and apple-trees, which are long in returning profit to him that plants. But he yet contrived to have, perhaps, the best peach orchard in the county of Middlesex, to graft valuable kinds of fruit upon the old trees, and to adopt nearly all of the improvements in farming, as they were tested and found valuable.

He was also an ingenious mechanic: his father and grandfather were mechanics as well as farmers, and did all kinds of work in wood, from building saw-mills, cider-mills, pumps, to making flax-spinning wheels, and turning wooden bread bowls out of maple stumps. He had religiously kept the tools of his father and grandfather, and like them continued to do all kinds of ordinary jobs; indeed, both he and they were such mechanics as men must be in a new country, and should not be in one where industry is more elaborate, and able-minded men are ready to turn their hand to anything. Mechanical talent was hereditary in the family for several generations, and appeared in my remote relations, and even among women, on whose slender shoulders this mantle seldom falls. My father was a thoughtful man, turning his large and active brain and his industrious hand to the mechanical and agricultural work before him; he was an originator of new and short ways of doing many things, and made his head save his hands. In this respect his father and grandfather resembled him.

His education—his schooling ended when the Revolution begun—was of course, much neglected, but he was an uncommonly good arithmetician, often puzzling the school-masters with his original problems. Works on political economy and the philosophy of legislation were

favourites with him. He had learned algebra and geometry, and was
familiar with the use of logarithms. He read much on Sundays, in
the long winter evenings, sometimes in the winter mornings before it
was light, and in the other intervals of toil. His favourite works were
history—that of New England he was quite familiar with—biography and
travels; but he delighted most of all in works of philosophy which give
the *rationale* of the material or the human world; of course he read
much of the theology of his times, and the literature of progressive
minds found its way to the farmer's kitchen. He had no fondness for
poetry. In his latter years, his reading was chiefly of novels, not to
instruct, but only to amuse the old man, whose mortal life was all
behind him. His fathers before him had been bookish men.

My mother, a woman of slight form, flaxen hair, blue eyes, and a
singularly fresh and delicate complexion, more nervous than muscular,
had less education than my father. Her reading was confined mainly
to the Bible, the hymn-book, stories of New England captives among
the Indians, of which there were many in the neighbourhood, some in
manuscript, and perhaps never printed. Ballads and other humble
forms of poetry gave her a great delight. Of course the newspapers
passed through her busy hands. My father often read aloud to her and
the rest of the family in the long winter evenings, while her fingers
were occupied with sewing or knitting, making or mending. She was
industrious, as indeed were all the women of the neighbourhood, but
like them found opportunities, though too rare, for social enjoyment
with them. Dinner was always at noon, and after that was over and
its paraphernalia put in order, the household work was done, and a more
comely dress took the place of the blue check of the morning.

She was eminently a religious woman. I have known few in whom
the religious instincts were so active and so profound, and who seemed
to me to enjoy so completely the life of God in the soul of man. To
her the Deity was an Omnipresent Father, filling every point of space
with His beautiful and loving presence. She saw him in the rainbow
and in the drops of rain which helped compose it as they fell into the
muddy ground to come up grass and trees, corn and flowers. She took
a deep and still delight in silent prayer—of course it was chiefly the
more spiritual part of the Old Testament and New Testament that
formed her favourite reading, the dark theology of the times seems not
to have blackened her soul at all. She took great pains with the moral
culture of her children—at least with mine.

3. Come the brothers and sisters, nine in number, and one in infancy
laid away in the grave. Some of these were much older than I, and
had already gone to seek their fortunes in the various trades and call-
ings of the time. There was still a houseful at home; all of them
but three had a decided fondness for literature; they read all the good
books they could lay their hands on, and copied the better parts. At
school they were always among the best scholars.

4. The uncles and aunts come next. On my father's side there
were two uncles and twice as many aunts; one of the former, a farmer
not far off, a tall, grave man; the other, a more restless character, had
served many years in the revolutionary war; he was in the battles of
Saratoga and of Yorktown, had failed in business, gone to South

Carolina, and married a woman with some property at Charleston, where he then lived, the father of one son. Of the aunts one was a maiden, an uncommonly intellectual woman; another was a widow living in an adjoining town, while two were the wives of farmers, one living in Nova Scotia, the other in Watertown not far off. On the maternal side there was one aunt, a strange, eccentric woman, and ten uncles, rejoicing in the names of Asahel, Jepthah, Noah, Ammi, Ishmael, and Habbakuk, and the like, which, if not euphonious, are at least scriptural. They were farmers and labourers, some rich and some poor.

Besides, the brothers and sisters of my grandmother still continued to live, though aged people. Other relations from the Parker side of the family dwelt in more remote towns, who occasionally paid my father a visit, in special one very old and tall man, to whom he surrendered the head of the table and invited to say grace.

5. The neighbours about us were farmers; a shoemaker lived a mile off on one side, and a blacksmith within two miles on the other. These were generally, perhaps universally, honest, hard-working men; they went to meeting Sundays, morning and afternoon. "Their talk was of bullocks, and they were diligent to give the kine fodder." In their houses, generally neat as good housewifery could make them, you would find the children's school-books, commonly a "singing-book," Billing's Collection, or some other, perhaps a hymn-book, and always a good quarto Bible kept in the best room, sometimes another Bible inherited from some Puritanic ancestor; these, with an almanack hung in the corner of the kitchen chimney, made up the family library. Perhaps a weekly or semi-weekly newspaper was also taken and diligently read. Two families not far off were exceptions to this poverty of books. I now think of no more. Yet now and then the life of some great thief, like Stephen Burrow, or some pirate or highwayman, would show itself. In other parts of Lexington, "on the great road," in "the middle of the town," perhaps there was a better show of books. I only speak of my immediate neighbourhood.

From Birth till the Age of Eight.

On the 24th of August, 1810, early on a hot, sweltering morning, I came into this world of joys and sorrows. It seems one of my sisters thought an eleventh child improbable; for she had finished the "Family Tree" with the tenth—five years older than myself. However, a place was soon found for the new-comer both in the needle-work and the hearts of the household. As the youngest child, it may be supposed I was treated with uncommon indulgence, and probably received a good deal more than a tenth part of the affection distributed. I remember often to have heard neighbours say, "Why, Miss Parker, you're spilin' your boy! He never can take care of himself when he grows up." To which she replied "she hoped not," and kissed my flaxen curls anew.

Among the earliest things I remember is the longing I used to feel to have the winter gone, and to see the great snow-bank—sometimes, when new-fallen, as high as the top of the kitchen window—melt away in front of the house. I loved, though, to run in the snow barefoot, and with only my night-shirt on, for a few minutes at a time. When the snow was gone, the peculiar smell of the ground seemed to me delicious. The first warm days of spring, which brought the blue birds to their northern home, and tempted the bees to try short flights, in which they presently dropped on the straw my provident father had strewn for them over the snow about their hives, filled me with emotions of the deepest delight. In the winter I was limited to the kitchen, where I could build cob-houses, or form little bits of wood into fantastic shapes. Sometimes my father or one of my brothers would take me to the shop where he pursued his toilsome work, or to the barn, where the horse, the oxen, and the cows were a perpetual pleasure. But when the snow was gone, and the ground dry, I had free range. I used to sit or lie on the ground in a dry and sheltered spot, and watch the great yellow clouds of April, that rolled their huge masses far above my head, filling my eye with their strange, fantastic, beautiful, and ever-changing forms, and my mind with wonder at what they were, and how they came there.

But the winter itself was not without its in-door pleasure, even for a little fellow in brown home-spun petticoats. The uncles and aunts came in their sleighs full of cousins, some of whom were of my own age, to pass a long afternoon and evening, not without abundant good-cheer and a fire in " the other room," as the humble parlour was modestly named. They did not come without a great apple, or a little bag of shag-barks, or some other tid-bit for " Miss Parker's " baby ; for so the youngest was called long after he ceased to merit the name. Nay, father and mother often returned these visits, and sometimes took the baby with them ; because the mother did not like to leave the darling at home, or perhaps she wished to show how stout and strong her eleventh child had come into the world.

I must relate one example to show, as well as many more, the nice and delicate care she took of my moral culture. When a little boy in petticoats in my fourth year, one fine day in spring, my father led me by the hand to a distant part of the farm, but soon sent me home alone. On the way I had to pass a little " pond-hole " then spreading its waters wide; a rhodora in full bloom—a rare flower in my neighbourhood, and which grew only in that locality—attracted my attention and drew me to the spot. I saw a little spotted tortoise sunning himself in the shallow water at the root of the flaming shrub. I lifted the stick I had in my hand to strike the harmless reptile ; for, though I had never killed any creature, yet I had seen other boys out of sport destroy birds, squirrels, and the like, and I felt a disposition to follow their wicked example. But all at once something checked my little arm, and a voice within me said, clear and loud, " It is wrong !" I held my uplifted stick in wonder at the new emotion—the consciousness of an involuntary but inward check upon my actions, till the tortoise and the rhodora both vanished from my sight. I hastened home and told the tale to my mother, and asked what was it that told me it was wrong ? She wiped a tear from her eye with her apron, and taking me in her arms, said, " Some men call it conscience, but I prefer to call it the voice of God in the soul of man. If you listen and obey it, then it will speak clearer and clearer, and always guide you right ; but if you turn a deaf ear or disobey, then it will fade out little by little, and leave you all in the dark and without a guide. Your life depends on heeding this little voice." She went her way, careful and troubled about many things, but doubtless pondered them in her motherly heart; while I went off to wonder and think it over in my poor, childish way. But I am sure no event in my life has made so deep and lasting an impression on me.

Thus it closes, but not abruptly, with the incident which marked the opening of his religious consciousness ; for the life itself flows naturally on, drawing in both experience and education to make the whole of his career an amplification of the story, as he set free and vindicated in himself and others, the Life of God in the Soul of Man.

THE HOMESTEAD.

CHAPTER III.

OF the old homestead furniture Theodore possessed an oaken table, which once belonged to John Parker, his grandfather's grandfather. It was a substantial piece of work, and always stood in the library. Two new legs were made for it out of the oaken frame of the old rude farm-house, of which, excepting these, scarcely a vestige remains. The old barn, however, is still in existence. This farm-house faced towards the south, and stood nearly in the centre of the farm which had been in the family for 150 years. A cart-path led up to it from the turnpike and went no farther. Now there is a road passing in front of the new house, which faces to the east. The old workshop still stands on the spot to which it was moved in 1794 from Lexington Green. A workshop indeed! What work it did on that April morning, when it was the little belfry of Lexington Church, and stood alone on the right hand of the Boston Road; in the early light it gathered well-seasoned timber from the country side, to make therefrom a cunning piece of American joinery. When, in 1794, the new meeting-house put forth a steeple of its own, and the bell was raised to its loft, this old belfry was sold to Theodore's father, who moved it to his farm, and made spokes and felloes, cider presses and screws in the space where the voice vibrated for the divine service of liberty. But that reveillé never got out of the rafters. It got into Theodore, chipping and chiselling, planing and bevelling, wasting a good deal, but learning at last not to spoil his work; it was the old sound which afterwards rang in the sentences of his manly indignation as he strove to rouse a new generation to complete the father's labour.

Near the workshop stands a white ash tree which Theodore planted thirty-six years ago from a seed, and which until the year of his death always bore two crops of leaves, but has now

lost the singularity.   Gentle critics of his theology are hereby
furnished gratis with this fact that they may extol Nature's fine
irony of his hatred for the exceptional and preternatural.   The
present garden was formerly a piece of scrub-oak which covered
a rocky ledge as far as the top of the little hill behind the
house, where he used to go for undisturbed study.   The view
from it is over a fine peat meadow, past a gently-rolling country,
still liberally wooded ; and in a clear day the blue hills in
Milton make the horizon.   Stonybrook straggles southwardly
through the meadows.   Across the fields, in fair sight from the
topmost rocks, where Theodore loved to read and dream, stand
two great pine trees which his boyish regard had selected from
the wood, one for himself and one for a favourite sister ; when
the proprietor cleared the lot, his promise given to Theodore
years before saved these trees from the axe.

Now their evergreen, more deep and balsamic with all the
memories of the house, waves to the family across the changing
fields.   Just beyond them, on the turnpike, where a smart
district school-house now stands, was the little old brown school-
house, clinging like a lichen to the brown ground beneath the
pines, whither Theodore went, three-quarters of a mile perhaps,
across lots, in his first pursuit of letters.   Around the farm-
house was about half an acre of peach trees, now rather run out,
which used to yield in fine fruit years 500 bushels of peaches.
Very little produce was sold from the farm ; for the father was
absorbed in his mechanical pursuits, and had turned the acres
over to the boys.   Theodore sometimes went to Boston to sell
the peaches ; and people remember the bloom in the down of his
young cheeks competing with the fruit, as he jogged down the
road with it, unconscious of the ripeness he was one day to
carry from the country into those streets.   Elms stood like urns
in the meadow.   A great elm, which threatened the old house
with its weight of years, has disappeared.   A peach orchard is
planted in front ; oaks and the ledge clothed with vines and
columbines are in the rear.   Half a mile farther west rises the
hill called in those parts Mount Tabor ; what was once a cart-
path is now a cross-road ; a simple one-story house with door
in the middle of its front, out-houses scattered about at random,
a stone wall built by Theodore, near to the famous old belfry
which keeps all its first oak framing unimpaired—such formed
the landscape and surroundings of his youth.

DOUBLE-HEADED PINE TREE AT LEXINGTON.

The Parkers, for several generations, used to love to go to church; they were the best of hearers of the Word, and faithful doers too, but they had their own thoughts, and resolved as well as listened. Only one of these Parkers, so far as is discoverable now, ever joined the Church. He married the daughter of an orthodox deacon, and is suspected of a weakness for his wife's conventionalities. A strong digestive apparatus was hereditary in the family; but it was content with plain fare readily convertible into sinews and nerves. Theological side-dishes and hot sauces never seemed to agree with them. If the preaching on Lexington Green touched life at any point, it was welcomed; but the healthy appetite grew testy over mysteries. One can imagine the language of a sturdy countryman, disappointed of a righteous meal, and solemnly waved in to partake of the impossible. Tertullian's creed was instinctively rejected; the family was Unitarian long before the partizan phrase became known. It always wanted to stand upon the ground, though it would look beyond the stars; honest reverence, loyalty and trust, a scrupulous sense of duty, a love for neighbours, a hatred of all meanness and grossness, were never wanting. Hannah Stearns brought, with all a woman's tenderness and delicacy, a rare devoutness, itself unfettered, into this liberal family.

She belonged to the Church; and all her children had been christened, neighbours duly standing surety. Theodore, the last, and the mother's darling, must be christened in his turn. This ceremony was performed at home, when he was about two and half years old. Great was the gathering of friends and neighbours! As the water was sprinkled on his head, he entered his first protest against ceremonies, by lustily fighting off the clergyman, and ejaculating, "Oh, don't!" His curiosity about the whole affair did not speedily die out; and as he was always terrible for asking "Why?"—except when asked to do something for love—he "wanted to know" about being wetted, and what object the participators had in view. We have no doubt he received a sensible answer. But he did not struggle against the baptism of his mother's spirit, who led him through all his childish misgivings, though she did not discover the depth of all of them, into a tranquil recognition of the Divine Love.

Religion was the inheritance my mother gave—gave me in my birth —gave me in her teachings. Many sons have been better born than I, few have had so good a mother. I mention these things to show you how I came to have the views of religion that I have now. My head is not more natural to my body—has not more grown with it than my religion out of my soul and with it. With me religion was not carpentry, something built up of dry wood, from without; but it was growth—growth of a germ in my soul.*

There was an interval of five years between Theodore and the tenth child, so that he had no playmate for a time but his mother.

"Miss Parker, I reckon you're spilin' that boy." She used to smile, and hope not. We are not sure that his theological troubles would have begun so early if this gentle mother had mustered courage to chase him out among the boys; and, quick-witted as she was, he did not betray to her how a mob of notions hustled and bullied him.

"When a very small boy," he says, "there was no character in history that I knew so well as Jesus." For this he was in the mother's debt. But he "remembered with horror and a quivering of the flesh," the torment he underwent when he first found, in a copy of the Westminster Catechism, the doctrines of eternal damnation and a wrathful God. He was a little over six when he fell out with them.

I can scarcely think without a shudder of the terrible effect the doctrine of eternal damnation had on me. How many, many hours have I wept with terror as I laid on my bed and prayed, till between praying and weeping sleep gave me repose. But before I was nine years old this fear went away, and I saw clearer light in the goodness of God. But for years, say from seven to ten, I said my prayers with much devotion, I think, and then continued to repeat "Lord, forgive my sins," till sleep came on me.†

Either he kept the doctrine to himself as something horrible he had stumbled over in his play, the one black corner in the sunny house, or else father and mother had no idea of the way in which it haunted him. This experience was destined to be the first one of the many in which he had to feel his way alone. The child instinctively hugged the bitter moment of his opening consciousness, though it tore him. But his mother's influence was unimpaired; she never weaned him. He was not thinking of his own early life when he said, many years later, "Some parents have a strange way of educating their children; they

* MS. Sermon: on leaving West Roxbury.
† Journal, Jan., 1839. See also his story in "Sermons of Theism," p. 126.

take the breast from them spiritually as well as corporeally ;
they do not train them up in love but in fear."

His early troubles on the subject of immortality are thus
described in a letter to an Irish lady :—

When I was a large boy, and had felt more than I had reflected, I
heard a minister preach on the immortal life. He told the arguments
for it, said they were all of no value, guesses, but hardly *at* truth, only
after it : the only sufficient proof was the resurrection of Jesus Christ.
Boy as I was, I saw the folly of that as an argument to prove a universal proposition; but, boy as I was, I could not reason the matter out,
and in default of understanding prove my immortality ; so I felt constrained to doubt, almost to deny it. Some weeks passed over, weeks
of torment ; at last spontaneous nature came to my help ; and I settled
the question, not intellectually and by philosophy, but sentimentally—in
the child's way, not the man's. It was not till years after that I found
a philosophy that satisfied the intellectual demands and helped me to
prove it to myself.

I have no more doubt of my eternal life—eternally *conscious*, eternally
progressive, than of my present and mortal condition. But I do not
pretend to know anything about the *form* of that life or its conditions.
Since I believe the entire *goodness of God*, which you so beautifully
speak of, I have no fear—no desire to know more about the form of the
next life, or rather of the next stage of this life. If I had only reason,
which cares little about persons and deals more with ideas, I should not
think, I suppose, or care about meeting my friends in the next stage of
life ; but as I have affections, more powerful, too, than reason, I cannot
doubt that I shall see and know my friends in heaven. Once I did
not think so ; but at the grave's mouth, as it closed on a sister, I could
not doubt where my logic had failed me. Nature came in and completed her work.*

Nature has a marvellous faculty of turning to account the
"mumps and measles" of childhood. Her aim is to develope or
to restore the spiritual health. Theodore was saved from drugs
and quacking ; pure air, simple habits, and a loving home kept
the catechism at bay ; while the sensitive soul, which had its
crises almost before the body could dispose of its own, threw off
the maladies which so seldom recur. He grew thus in power
and sensibility ; and, succeeding these keen trials of his natural
vigour, how simple and comely was his growth.

In the traces made by these trials awe and confidence sprung
up, a profound conviction that a divine life pervaded all things,
and an unassailable willingness to trust in it. No child was
ever so loyal to its parents as his soul to this Father whom he

* May 5, 1848.

found caring for the country, for the farm and all its creatures, for himself among them. This was the ground of his future life. This positive spiritual enjoyment was so great in him, that his mind was active for a long time before it criticised and rejected the ordinary Unitarian theology. The religion of his boyhood grew more and more absorbing, the experience of successive years deepened it, gifts and acquisitions fell sparkling into its clearness and were seen through it, all the while theology touched him but lightly and did not trouble him. His views at that time of the Old and New Testaments, of miracles and inspiration, when pronounced at all, were not given with much emphasis, and were of the ordinary kind, as we shall shortly see.

No child ever had a purer piety. His soul was open night and day to heavenly influences. He and his visitant knew no frontier; and he lived so honestly, without tricks and lying, infested by no habits, untempted even by simple country dissipations, so homely and brotherly, yet so remote, that his soul never seemed to suspect that men could have other homes. Nothing stole in and slammed the door in his face. It was wide open, through all the strife and bitterness which beset his maturity; but the dust of the battle never rolled up to dispute the light on that threshold. In 1858, preaching to the Progressive Friends, he can say :—

I have swum in clear, sweet waters all my days; and if sometimes they were a little cold, and the stream ran adverse and something rough, it was never too strong to be breasted and swam through. From the days of earliest boyhood, when I went stumbling through the grass, "as merry as a May bee," up to the grey-bearded manhood of this time, there is none but has left me honey in the hive of memory that I now feed on for present delight. When I recall the years of boyhood, youth, early manhood, I am filled with a sense of sweetness and wonder that such little things can make a mortal so exceedingly rich! But I must confess that the chiefest of all my delights is still the religious. This is the lowest down, the inwardest of all—it is likewise highest up. What delight have I in my consciousness of God, the certainty of His protection, of His infinite love? God loves me as my natural mother never did, nor could, nor can, even now, with the added beatitudes of wellnigh two-score years in heaven. How the religious disposition inclines the little boy or girl to veneration and gratitude, virtues which in the child are what good-breeding is in the full-grown gentleman, giving a certain air of noble birth and well-bred superiority! There is a Jacob's ladder for our young pilgrim, whereon he goes up from his earthly mother, who manages the little room he sleeps in, to the dear Heavenly Mother, who never slumbers nor sleeps, who is never careful nor troubled about anything, but yet cares continually for the great housekeeping of all the world, giving likewise to her beloved even in their sleep. In the child it is only the faint twilight, the beginning, of religion which you take notice of, like the voice of the blue bird and the Phœbe, coming early in March, but only as a prelude to that whole summer of joyous song which, when the air is delicate, will ere long gladden and beautify the procreant nest.

This is a form of piety, springing up, like a form of polity suitable for a new world, with the wild flowers at Lexington. In its incense there is no smell of scented ambergris, but rather the smell of the fresh ground. No haggard and yellow-skinned mysticism, fed on parchment and the air of cells, loving God with passion, and Christ like a bridegroom, straining body and language to the point of tenuity to make out an artificial rapture : no doting on phrases and abnormal ecstatic conditions. The free west-wind on our hill-sides sweeps off this calenture— the east-wind, strong with iodine from the sea-weed, sweeps it out of the healthy boy while he is gathering New-England flowers.

It freshened what it swept through, and whirled nothing really tender away. When still quite young, he never went to a new place, or found himself in a wood or field or street striking to his sense, or not visited before, without indulging in quiet prayer ; " for the unknown was to me doubly holy." A natural ascription connected places and incidents with the great life over all. He said, " My Father in heaven," at every moment of awe, joy, or pain. Finding a scarce flower in the wet meadow, inhaling the piny odours, seeing first the spring blades in the garden, weeping at stories of Indian captivities, basking in the May sun at the top of the ledge, feeling the mother's heart in every room of the house,—no trick of consciousness shut up the word he had with God about it all, or hinted that a word would be highly proper.

We have seen that he tried at first, by asking the Lord to forgive his sins when he had none "to speak of," to pray himself into the conviction that his nature was depraved, and that damnation was a thing to be remembered in the days of his youth. This came from a catechism that was lying about the house. These old bundles of rags which emigration brings over will carry infection for a long while. Quarantine and a thorough smoking out is the only remedy. Few people were ever less depraved than he, or carried from birth a will and temperament more sympathetic for pure and noble things. A hasty temper, almost always the characteristic of sincere and morally indignant persons, but sometimes in the end mistaken for sincerity by them, was the only grave fault he had to struggle with. No kind of physical indulgence ever seemed to tempt him for a moment. He caught no habits from coarse boys, and his imagination was chaste as a girl's. Nothing crept into him through the loop-hole of an idle moment. When he was not at work in the field, or tinkering in the shop, he was deep in a book. In his day-dreams he looked down through a cool well: there was the blue sky at the bottom. He was very ambitious to perform all his tasks, to find out all that was learnable, to put the best foot foremost; but the gifts of others only stimulated his immense energy. Later he has been accused of envying distinguished men; but the root of envy was never in him. Not a trace of it can be found in the recollections of school-mates and kindred; but, on the contrary, all the intimates of his boyhood testify how naive and kind he was. Wrestling is a favourite rural fashion of testing back and wind: he wrestled with every mind, and openly emulated all his mates. "We love to measure ourselves," he said, afterwards, "that we may know our power, and approbation is welcome as assuring us of success; but the true test of the purity of our feeling is whether we are also rejoiced to see another receive greater approbation for a better thing. A desire of future fame is only better than that of present applause as it is an appeal to mankind in its sanity and wisdom. To a great soul the presence of a superior is the greatest of blessings." * Men would call him envious because he did not worship their superiors as his own, and withheld his consent from the vicious estimate which made intelligence more loveable than righteousness.

But as a boy he was bashful, painfully conscious of a certain awkwardness; and would underrate himself so far as to ask his teacher not to say that he wrote a composition, for fear that his name would reduce its appreciable value. He honestly felt it was good for something, and honestly doubted that he was esteemed. A burning flush and a suffused blue eye showed how sensitive he was to praise or blame. His simple delight in

* Saturday Afternoon Conversations, held with members of his parish. Feb. 24, 1849.

praise was as distant from ordinary egotism as sincere praise itself is. Here is something to the point, of his own record :—

I went to Boston—lectured before the men of colour upon the Signs of the Times. I have not been so much gratified with any applause received this long time as to-night. When Mr. Nell announced me, and that, too, as *a friend of mankind*, the negroes applauded. I was never so much gratified but once before ; that was years ago, when I was a little boy, at an examination of the district school. A spectator, one of the general committee of the town, asked my father, "Who was that fine boy who spoke up so smart ?" My father said, "Oh, that is one of *my* boys, the youngest." When my father told it at home that John Murray had asked so, I felt a deep joy, not so much for my own sake as for the satisfaction it seemed to give my father. I like this applause that comes up in the deep ground-tones of humanity ; all other I care little for—"it plays round the head, but comes not to the heart." I don't think I could withstand a righteous condemnation —not I.*

This simple disposition, content with sympathy, and influenced only by the glory of knowing true things and of being true to them, never changed. The boy never told a lie or committed a meanness. He grew hot all over at hearing of wrongs, at witnessing slights ; so he did sometimes when contemptuously slighted. He was combative to defend, but never known to be aggressive. His courage was above suspicion, being the frankness of his moral sense in action. He was a rigid boy, but never took airs among freer companions ; no one was more tolerant of infirmities and angry with malice and chicane. His worst ambitions were proud motions which his mind made in the first self-consciousness of its great energies, as it were, like a young athlete, with short, scornful lip, superbly testing his symmetry and power. Then he thought he might become what he pleased, and visions of legal and political renown enchanted him for awhile. But such dreams could not for long beguile his manly and unselfish heart. He shrank from seeking anything for himself but a place to work in, though he was early conscious that he had a great capacity for work, and lofty aims that would chafe in any low or dull routine. He sometimes said what he thought about this, as about everything else ; . and there is no doubt that his strength often surged within him like a passion, and shook his temperate bounds till they trembled. In no respect did the man change from this, excepting that the controversies, which might be expected to unmask his testy

* Journal, Nov. 19, 1844.

humour, brought out instead his warlike disposition, and woke up an indignant sincerity; but there was no place for mere touchiness in his formidable wrath.

He could not pray himself into the belief that he was a great sinner for a boy. The first hypocrisy which surprised him in the venerable garb of religion was the only one of his life, and in disposing of it his soul began its free, organic growth. If we know what a boy is, we can anticipate how he will talk about sin when he is a man; for whatever sin itself may be, the human statements of the fact will always betray a diversity in the mode of contemplating it. The practical contrast between a virtuous and a vicious life is plain enough : virtue seems normal and appropriate to man, and vice is constantly threatening the general health and order; but what is the essential ground of vice, and what is its purpose? There must be some reason for the contradictory theories which try to answer those questions. The disputants mutually accuse each other of ignorance of spiritual laws : those who japan their systems with scriptural phrases, complain that their opponents will not accept the Bible theory of sin; but the scripturalists themselves agree only in a liberal use of the japanning. Human nature is intrinsically bad, because the divine nature premeditated sin; yet it is not inconsistent to declare that sin is enmity towards God, who predestined it—something devilish. Man has altogether gone astray; his nature is a corrupt root, his will is not normally inclined to health; there is no good in him, or, if there is, it is continually at the mercy of a lower law. This is scene-painting, and not definition. When compelled to weigh in nice scales these phrases, that their essential value may be tested and represented in spiritual equivalents, believers in depravity quarrel about their favourite word, because they really estimate moral evil by their own temperament and moral condition. The scriptural agreement is merely forced by the preconception of an infallible and supernaturally-inspired Book; so that many a liberal disposition goes up and down yelling in war-paint, and flourishing tomahawks of texts. Especially if pantheists and naturalists are suspected to be settling in the neighbourhood, and threaten to encroach upon their hunting-grounds, every shade of orthodoxy rallies, and vermillion uniforms the league. If anybody is found who speculates a way of escape for the Infinite Goodness from complicity with moral evil, the dull texts rain upon his head. The effort is attributed to depravity itself, seeking for immunity. He has personal reasons for surmising that every bad act is only an inchoate good one; or, that evil is goodness underdone; or, that it is the schoolmaster bringing men to knowledge and self-consciousness; or, that the Divine Impartiality digests all actions into healthy history; or, that a developing God feels his way from stage to stage of matter, choosing thus gradually to eliminate its coarseness, clearly seeing the end of beauty; or, that all creating is but a coming to self-consciousness of the primæval mind through difficulties. But the feeling which invents such statements is a pure one; the conviction that human nature is intrinsically good because the divine nature is absolutely perfect, goes masquerading in them all.

In the meantime, both orthodox and liberal will show the colour of the leaf on which they feed. The black and passionate temperament will speak of moral evil in the Bible's most sombre language—the fair transparent disposition will borrow the most innocent and optimistic texts. Some natures grow with all the simplicity and fragrance of a flower, drawing only limpid sap from the black earth, conscious of passion by report alone. The pulse is even, the flesh is always cool, the eyes serene. Their faults have no malignity, the will is always disposed to deference, the imagination secretes no acrid and petulant images. The poisonous elements of life seem unconsciously rejected by this frank and florid organization. It never can recollect any crisis such as the theologians call a change of heart, and never desires it, except when infected sentimentally by a revival. Nothing may be very deep, but everything has been natural—a sense of dependence, a preference for cleanly and honest ways, a love of duty. There was nothing insurrectionary in the primitive motive.

But other natures have inherited the element of an internal conflict. They always have a great deal of trouble in learning to tell the truth, to keep the peace, to repress envious feelings; their fancy is precocious, and curiously anticipates the secrets of life, and is tormented with day-dreams of love or ambition. They fall into bad habits; have wretched seasons of remorse, which alternate with indulgence; they are secretive, and have a touch of the demoniacal. They are selfish, or hypocritical, or vindictive, or treacherous, or sensual, or proud, or all of these,

according to the quantitive relations of their passions and affections. But their growth is more like the campaign of two
armies than the silent ripening of summer nights and days.
They have to fight for every inch of ground they occupy.

The first class speaks of sin blandly, except when horror-
stricken at the sight of it, or conventionally taught to use the
scripture terms. Clergymen of this kind are sometimes intellectually committed to human depravity and the concurrent doctrines; but their inmost feeling never preaches it. Both the
pure and the passionate who live where the doctrine has its full
traditional sweep, and is not vigorously criticised, will accept it.*
Gentle young people will sometimes appear to suffer under conviction of sin. It is the sin of a traditional theology rioting in
morbid conditions of the mind or body. If they become clergymen, and continue their bad health, they will continue to use bad
language and defame human nature. But their sweet and blameless life totters under the ponderous phrases and shoots naive
glances at the listeners.

The people who have a great deal of trouble with their passions
will remember their personal discomfort when they speak of moral
evil. If they change their whole course of life, clean out their
fancies, and banish their ambitions, they will estimate sin at the
rate of effort and suffering they have endured. A clergyman
who has lived a rather stormy youth will, if he has talent and
dramatic power, astonish an audience with his knowledge of the
demoniacal element, and convince them for a while that neither
in himself nor in them is there one good thing. And how many
good things he will say ! Whatever faithfully repeats a personal experience is useful to men. But if a bad experience sets
up to be a system of the universe, and to represent a divine intention that omits no soul, it is a hideous idol, and the pulpit its
lumbering car in which it overrides all natural distinctions.

Now, between talking about moral evil, making one's personal

---

* After reading Miller's Life of Jonathan Edwards, Mr. Parker records his impression.
"A most remarkable child, youth and man, mild, gentle and most lovely. How such a
person must have revolted, naturally, from the stern, sour doctrines of Calvinism. How
his heart must bleed before it could admit the dreadful doctrines—total depravity and
eternal damnation, and the like. Oh ! if they wrung his soul as they have wrung mine,
it must have bled." Edwards's account of the developing of his spiritual life, which he
calls his conversion, has hardly a trace of these doctrines, though there is a free use of
the conventional phrases. With animal spirits and a robuster frame, his sense of his
own wickedness would have considerably diminished.

Mr. Parker copied, for his own use, many of the resolutions which Jonathan Edwards
wrote down before he was 20.

experience a subject of rhetoric, and defining the fact itself, there is a vast difference. The latter can only be approximately done by knowledge, as it subsidizes physical and moral science, and their analysis of human actions. The phenomena of moral evil are, like all other phenomena, subjects for a scientific investigation, that is, a complete observation of the inner and the outer man —including his locality, climate, culture, and circumstances. But anybody can talk about moral evil, from tradition and from feeling. The contradictory language which people equally sincere make use of in their attempts to speak of moral evil, is owing to their want of precise inductions from a sufficient number of facts ; in other words, to their want of knowledge. And believers of every shade of liberality think that they furnish a portable definition of sin, when in reality they are only expressing themselves ; their phrases are the net result of all their characteristics, or else a mere repetition of the tradition current in their circles. Allowing for disturbances, such as artificial teaching, and the truculent sentimentalism of conferences and revivals, it is true that the bias of a man's youth will decide his conception of the fact of sin.

Mr. Parker was healthily built, within and without, open to the air and sun, with no uncanny corners to catch dirt and vermin, and not a single rat-hole in the whole house. He shrank from vicious and slatternly habits, but knew perfectly well that he had neither. So that he could not pray against the whole sincerity of his nature in favour of any dogmatic statement of evil. At first he tried to force a conviction that in sin did his mother conceive him ; but the ingenuous boy learned, through much weeping, a holier feeling concerning himself and his mother. The unnatural attempt at last gave way to a sense of the Infinite Love, which kept his mind and heart bathed in health until maturer knowledge opened the question again, as we shall see, when the facts of evil challenged his youthful sentiment, and the understanding and the moral disposition came to terms. But a temperament undisturbed by the grosser impulses, full of warmth at feeling or perceiving wrong, neither secretive nor selfish, but magnanimous, indignant, plain-spoken, ruled by a very fastidious conscience, and penetrated by a tender piety,—this controlled his future treatment of evil and his views of sin.

But he was very early sensitive to the qualities of actions and feelings. It was almost a morbid delicacy, such as we find in weaker natures the cause of a precocious mysticism or ultra-Calvinistic views. Examples of this disease are sometimes paraded, in the interest of a preternatural theology, as evidences of early conversions from nature to grace. If this spiritual sensibility in the little Theodore had not been vigorously matched by a promising digestion, or if the family inheritance of consumption had developed earlier, the catechism might have done him some damage, and his clear strong soul might have had a harder conflict. Stalwart trappers will sometimes get debilitated by swamp mists, scurvy fare, and Indians. But Theodore came off embrowned, elastic, far-sighted, tenacious on the war-trail. The early trial taught him betimes the great secret of successful warfare, to reduce your baggage to its effective minimum. He was trained to dispense with the doctrinal impediments, and went into life carrying rations sufficient for the march.

Here he records an opportunity he had to attempt shouldering innate enmity and a perverse will. It is from a letter to a friend.

Did I ever tell you of the earliest fact of consciousness I ever felt pained at? When in my 4th year my father had a neighbour, Deacon Stearns, come to kill a calf. My father would not do it himself, as other farmers did. I was not allowed to see the butchery; but after it was all over, the Deacon, who had lost all his children, asked me who I loved best? "Papa." "What! Better than yourself?" "Yes, sir." "But," said my father, "if one of us must take a whipping, which would you rather should have the blows?" I *said* nothing, but wondered and wondered why I should prefer that he should have the blows and not I. The fact was plain, and plainly selfish, and, it seemed to me, wicked. Yet I could not help the feeling. It tormented me for weeks in my long clothes.

Long clothes are certainly embarrassing, especially in the pursuit of truth. Many a seeker trips himself up and lies a mere heap of clothing by the way; but Theodore soon got out of long clothes, and had a suit of lasting, for all work, comfortable to the sturdy limbs and delicate perceptions.

Here is a reminiscence which finds its place in this period of childhood. It is an extract from a letter written to a divinity classmate in 1839.

Death is no more to a man than the change from the infant's "long-clothes" to the "frock and trousers" of the boy. I understand, therefore, why Swedenborg found men in the other world who had forgotten all about their death; in a word, did not remember they had ever died. Perhaps most men do not remember anything about their change from baby-clothes to the boy's dress. I have not forgotten all about my change of dress. I remember that I cried, and struggled most lustily against the new dress; and when my legs were squeezed into their new envelopes, I was so ashamed that I went into the fields to hide myself. I doubt that I should complain half so much if death were to come with the new suit, and tell me to lay aside my rags.

Out of school there were various jobs for him about the house; he became a working member of the family as soon as he could steady himself upon two stout legs. All the chips must be picked up, to begin with; then he had wood to bring in, pretty soon to drive the cows to pasture, carry grain to the horse, and "*nubs* of corn to the oxen." His father was very fond of animals, a close observer of their habits; he had a respectful way of treating them, which taught his children to show kindness to every animated form. He always prevented them from witnessing any slaughtering operation. In the workshop Theodore learned to hold the chalk-line, to know the different tools and fetch them. He loved to make things, and became very expert; for he had a fitting and joining faculty not eventually to be limited by glue and scantling.

Across the meadow he went to that little brown district school-house; for he did not fancy following the cart-path into the turnpike, but saved time by putting stepping-stones across the brook. School was kept for the smallest children twelve or sixteen weeks in spring and summer; the winter term was twelve weeks long. For a year or two Theodore went to school both summer and winter, but after 1817–18 only in winter. He trudged off alone, or in bad weather was carried round, with a well-conned lesson, and a heart full of the new surmises of his conscience.

He was about six years of age when he begun to go to this public school. Oliver Locke was the male teacher, and "Aunt Pattie" (Mary Smith) the female. He was in Aunt Pattie's department. John Hastings succeeded in 1818. Theodore, then eight years old, dearly loved play, and was never left out of any game. Bat and ball, bows and arrows, and pop-guns, were successively rages. When pop-guns came in, he got his elder brother to construct one of the largest calibre, which he took to school. Till its range and effect were tested, he was very miserable; his young idea refused to shoot. Promptly, to solve the pain of a divided duty, he let it off. "Who fired that gun?"

Theodore's lips were spelling words with prodigious abandonment. Presently, however, his desire again overcame him—for such a sonorous pop-gun who would not brave the ferule—off it went, just as John Hastings happened to look up. Alas ! the reckless gunner, with his own hands, must consign his piece to the stove, where it crackled pitilessly to a reprimand.

His pop-gun was always of the biggest, for his mark was far and high.

He was never unpopular with his schoolmates, but they stood somewhat in awe of him, partly on account of his quantity of character, and partly because he was so keen for the ridiculous, and had such overwhelming powers of mimicry ; the gait, gesture, tone of voice and pet phrases, even the habit of thinking, and the average opinions of a person, were all faithfully reproduced by him. This talent was afterwards the delight of intimates in the study at West Roxbury and in Exeter Place, where politicians, professors, and clergymen slid, without extenuation or malice, through the dissolving views of his hilarious hours.

His weight of character was once well shown when he was hardly nine ; an old farmer came to the school-house to complain of some trick which the boys had played with his horse and wagon. His rage was not to be appeased without a victim. But the master, after asking one or two, came to Theodore, and said, " Theodore, do you know anything about this ? " Theodore got up and quietly remarked, " I don't know anything about it, sir." There was gravity enough in the reply for a complete outfit ; all the little fellows, culprits included, received their allowance, and the old man went away impressed with the collective innocence.

He was apt to be rough at play, and to tumble his comrades about in a shaggy fashion, as if with great, humorous paws ; but he never bullied or wilfully vexed them. All his strength was awkward then, but not unkind. And there was always in the school a wholesome sense that he could not bear to see anybody " put upon." Still we do not hear that he had lovers ; and if there were any who looked at him through devoted eyes, his glances repaid only protection and humanity. The little eyes did not meet his at a level, yet his never ceased to go hungering for their mates.

When Theodore was only eight, he was called one of the

greatest readers in the town. His father owned a share in the "Social Library," and was a devourer of books. Instead of visiting his neighbours when work was done, he sat down with his family around the dining table, where all quietly read. The women mended and darned the stockings at the same table, and the father read aloud what struck him. The old grandmother sat in the flickering fire-light—the past flickered in her mind. Much was learned in these winter evenings. Father and mother taught far beyond the school ; they taught Theodore to be curious about human affairs, and the characters of famous men. He became such a glib expositor of the current politics, that older people liked to draw him out by pretended opposition ; then his opinion grew ardent enough. But he also had books of his own to read, which his father brought him from the library.

When a little boy, an old man overtook me going to school, and walked a mile with me. He told me what it was possible for a bright boy to *do* and to *be*—what I might do and be ; it had a great influence on me. I began to think I " might be somebody."

Homer and Plutarch I read before I was eight; Rollin's Ancient History about the same time ; and lots of histories, with all the poetry I could find, before ten. I took to metaphysics about eleven or twelve.

We had in the family some MS. histories of the Segur family, and their captivity among the Indians ; also Mrs. Rowlandson's adventures. Mother knew by heart many family histories of the old New-England times, and used to tell them to me. We had also a folio volume of travels in the Levant, which interested me much, as soon as I could read, and to this day ; father and mother always read the books first, and examined me in every book I read. If I could not give a good account of it, I must not have another till I could satisfy the rigorous demands of father.

I began to write verses at eight, and could repeat at ten a poem of 500 or 1000 lines after a single reading, or a song from hearing it once. I used to commit the hymns which the minister was reading, and before the choir began to sing.

At ten I made a catalogue of all the vegetable productions, trees, and shrubs, which grew upon the farm ; there were many of which I could not find the names, so I invented them—fanciful enough.

We had a copy of Morse's large Geography, which helped me a good deal, and a folio copy of Evelyn's celebrated Sylva. It was a great treasure to me; it contained bits of poetry too, which delighted me, passages from Tusser and Chaucer, which I had not seen before.

Mr. Lyman's garden, at Waltham, filled me with admiration at the rare trees, plants, and shrubs, which I did not know. I went there when twelve or thirteen. Then the foreign fruits which I saw at my first visit to Boston, the tropical husks and leaves which came wrapped around bales of merchandize, tea-chests, and other boxes, stimulated my love of nature still more.

I used to inquire after the conformation of the hills in other parts of the country, which I had never seen. In my neighbourhood they all had their steep sides towards the south and east. I always asked boys—and men when I dared—who came from a distance, if it were so in their country. I commonly got the answer, "*I den know.*" An Englishman told me about the peat mounds in Britain, which I could not account for. I got together all the odd stones, &c., I could find. A neighbour once brought me in my fourteenth year a bit of brown oxide of manganese, which abounded on the farm of his son in Vermont, and wanted to know what it was. It took me a day or two to find out, with the rude chemical apparatus I had made; but I did —and told him, to the amusement of the neighbours.

At ten I began to study Latin. This continued five winters, in which time I read the usual elementary books, with Virgil, Cicero's Select Orations and Sallust. I began Greek at eleven. Natural Philosophy, Astronomy, Chemistry and Rhetoric I studied by myself. Astronomy had always interested me much. When twelve years old I once saw the crescent form of Venus with my naked eye. It amazed me. Nobody else could see it; father was not at home. Nobody knew that the planets exhibit this form. So I hunted after a book on Astronomy, and got it from the schoolmaster, and found out the fact and its reason.

His first school composition was on "The Starry Heavens;" the teacher found fault with it—that it was too short.

In the summer "nooning," when the hands were lolling in the shade, Theodore took out his book, and kept tilling and sowing while others slept. He never shirked his chores of work, but the book came into all lawful intervals.

The father was too poor to buy many books. Theodore must find his own methods to appease this ravening for knowledge. He early began to help himself to what he wanted. Nothing was strong enough to dull for a moment this instinctive necessity of his mind—no amusement, no accomplishment. Dancing cost too much to learn, though it was thought highly of, and country balls were courtly occasions. But money must be saved for books. With the proceeds of a whortleberrying campaign in 1822, he bought his first book. He had to carry the berries to Boston for sale; so the city purchased the incunabulum of the noble library of 11,000 volumes, which he bequeathed to it at last.

In 1820, William H. White, afterwards a highly-esteemed Unitarian clergyman, took the South District school at Lexington, and taught there two winters. He saw the ambition and capacity of Theodore, and led him along with the tenderest sympathy. Nothing but English studies were pursued in the school ; but Mr. White volunteered to teach him Latin, and afterwards Greek.

The " Historia Sacra " was his first Latin book, with Smith's Latin Grammar and Young's Dictionary for help, all of them long out of print, and replaced by better books. He became very much attached to Mr. White, and years after used to write him tender and grateful letters.

I shall never cease to thank you for starting me in Latin,* and in Greek too, nor shall I ever forget how I hid my head in the bed-clothes and cried—for I was sick then, and could not rise—when they told me that you would not keep school next winter, but a stranger was coming.

The stranger was Mr. George Fiske, who kept it for three winters, and of whom it is told, that happening to misquote scripture one morning, Theodore rose in his seat and put him right, much to the edification of the school. The boy's memory already promised the vigour and capaciousness which afterwards brought home and warehoused such varied spoils. The teachers used to extol his memory first, and his rapid acquisition next.

Now let us see how much schooling he received. Eleven weeks each winter, from 1817 to 1827, and two summer terms, from 1817 to 1819. At 16 years of age, he had one quarter at the Lexington Academy. That was all. Algebra was added to Latin and Greek at the Academy. He mastered Colburn's Algebra in 20 days. In the winter of 1827, being then 17, he began to teach : the first winter, a district school in Quincy, the second in North Lexington, the third in Concord, and the fourth in Waltham, working on the farm and in the shop the rest of the year. The farmers used to reckon that the work their boys could do in the winter season was about equal to the cost of their board ; there was no objection, then, if they wanted to

---

* He was ready enough to learn Latin ; for a Catholic cradle-hymn, which he found in an old magazine when he was hardly seven, had tormented him a good deal. Nobody around him could unlock the mystery, only his brother told him it was Latin. The word "Jesu" filled him with an intense desire to know the meaning. Almost forty years after he fell in with it again, and thus translated it :—

Dormi Jesu—mater ridet	Slumber, Jesu—mother smileth
Quæ tam dulcem somnum videt ;	As sweet sleep her babe beguileth,
Dormi, Jesu, blandule !	Darling Jesu, go to sleep !
Si non dormis mater plorat,	If art waking mother mourneth,
Inter fila cantans orat,	Singing, as her spindle turneth,
Blande veni somnule.	"Gently, little slumber creep."

leave home. But if Theodore taught school during any other weeks of the year, or left home to make a visit, he hired a man to take his place and work on the farm. So he did when he left home finally, at the age of 19 : for two years, till he was 21, he furnished his father with a labourer.

At 17 he began to *train*, with what recollections of Lexington Green and Captain Parker we may imagine. He was very active and punctual in the discharge of his military duties, was clerk of the company, and rose even to the grandeur of a lieutenancy, or, as some say, he was ensign. If he ever did bear the colours at muster or May-training, it was with gravity, no doubt, and certain private thoughts of the value of the symbol. As clerk, he called the roll of the company ; the famous names were still upon it.*

So he trained, ploughed, built stone-walls, made spokes, bored pumps, mended farm tools, filled each crevice with a book, and lifted the varied toil with generous and aspiring thought. If from the school teaching he had any money left, after sumptuously paying his substitute, it went for books, long anticipated, dearly cherished as the blossoming of all his labour. He pushed his way to Greece and Rome, and far outread the average for his years. If he made an evening visit, he would study till two or three o'clock in the morning. At Waltham, he began to teach French, after taking a few lessons ; a little later we find him mastering Spanish.

In the summer of 1830, the day before his birth-day, he went away from home, and was absent till near midnight. He had received permission from his father to be gone for a day, but was unwilling to say wherefore ; so nobody knew where he had gone. Returning, he went up to his father's bed-side, and said, " Father, I entered Harvard College to-day." He had spent the whole day in undergoing examination at Cambridge. The perplexity of the old man at his mysterious absence was not lessened when he heard the cause. " Why, Theodore ! you know I cannot support you there." " I know that, Father ; I mean to stay at home, and keep up with my class." He had quietly prepared to enter the freshman class. He remained at

---

* He did not like to see any popular indifference to the militia-system, and used to say that the time would come when we should depend upon it, and regret that it had not been vigorously sustained. He thought it one of the best things in Governor Banks, that he cherished the militia and strove to renew its effectiveness.

home another winter, doing all his work, carrying on his studies, and going down to Cambridge to participate in the examinations. He was not entitled to a degree, because he had been a non-resident, and had not paid tuition fees. But afterwards, at the kindly representation of his friend, Mr. Francis, of Watertown, the usual degree of A.B. was offered to him on payment of the usual fees of instruction for four years. But this amounted to a considerable sum, altogether beyond Theodore's ability ; and he could not buy his degree. The degree of A.M. was afterwards bestowed upon him (*honoris causâ*) in 1840.

Here is an entry in his journal for August 23, 1850 :—

It is this day twenty years since I entered Harvard College! What misgiving I had at that time. Yet how joyfully I went home and told my father—a-bed, but not asleep—that I had entered Harvard College. How joyfully I went to work again the next day! But what changes since! Then I had a father and three sisters—a few friends whom now-a-days I never see. What sad times have I passed through since —not without the Star of Faith to guide me.

After making the above record, his prayer follows ; for on all days set apart in any strong or tender way by memory his heart flowed forth in supplication :—

Father, who hast been my Help and my Reliance hitherto—in the dangerous period of passion, and my trial of poverty—be with me now in the more dangerous period of ambition. Help me to be one with Thee, obedient to Thy will in my heart, and faithful to all the monitions of thy guiding Spirit. If other twenty years pass by me, make me by so much a nobler, greater, better man.

The following extract is made from his journal for 1840 :—

I went a Sunday or two ago to preach in my native village. It was with no small emotion I ventured into the old pulpit, filled with so much holiness in my youth—a place so sacred that I scarcely dared place my unholy feet therein when a boy. But once, I remember, a Sunday noon, putting up a prayer in it, as a place peculiarly holy. How well has that prayer been answered! Great God, I thank Thee ; for the recollection of that hour is warm within me. I prayed for wisdom ; for the means of learning. Certainly, I have found the latter. I had the beginning of wisdom then—the fear and love of God.

The next spring, he left his father's house, never to return to it, save at long intervals and for hurried visits. Devout mother and downright simple-minded father had done their best for him. He had done the rest, finding help in every furrow of the farm, in the flowers of the meadow, the cool sincerity of midnight skies, the health of the wide country.   His own hands had culled this harvest in the fields.   Both mental method and religion had grown standing in an open lot.   Self-denying, hard-working, homely boy, blooming with ambition and hope, refined by clean and pious thoughts—another wild-flower of New England's soil—with all the self-reliance and sturdiness of Franklin, and all the religion and moral delicacy which Franklin had not, he goes wandering after his work in life.   He never changed. Meadow, wood, and sky went with him, everywhere looking after their dear child, lending fragrance and independence to the last.   Not toned in a conventional atmosphere, having the politeness which is unstudied motion, and more sincerity than taste, grasping strongly things rather than phrases—a smooth spade-cutter, a liberal pruner, a broadcast-sower, and judicious with the harrow—the old farm sends him forth an Emancipator, and not an Amateur.

THE LEDGE.

CHAPTER IV.

THEODORE never forgot those winter evenings, nor the father and mother who were not abashed in their homespun though all the worthies came. It was a perpetual house-warming, with Plutarch and Milton for guests, and Rollin, Shakespeare, Homer, and New,-England's Iliad in tradition. The gods repaid the hospitable instinct by making the rude fare ambrosial and perennial. What culture is like an inartificial welcome to such a company! The youngest child put fresh lips to this farm-bucket dripping with wonder and delight.

Now he must leave the richly-endowed college which Nature extemporized for him. The farm, with its cottage-house, and the ledge, more liberally roofed, behind, and the parental love overarching all, cannot shelter the young student more. But Theodore took the Faculty along with him.

On the 23rd of March, 1831, he went to Boston, having accepted an engagement to become assistant in a private school. Eleven octavos, the *dii majores* of his little library, were not difficult to transport. Among them were Virgil and Horace, which he had read some twenty times each, and could repeat all their finest pages. He was stimulated to pursue his mathematical labours by becoming acquainted with Mr. Francis Grund, who had then hours for instruction in several of the Boston schools: also, the *sight* of Newton's "Principia," which he could neither borrow nor buy, increased his ardour. The whole of Homer was read this year, a good deal of Xenophon and Demosthenes, Æschylus, and many books of metaphysics and physics. The study of German was added to French and Spanish, and he learned to write as well as read these languages.

5

He boarded at first in Blossom Street. Of his life at this time we have a trace in a letter written from Rome, March 23, 1860, to his friend Dr. Howe.

It is twenty-nine years to-day since I left my father's house and home and sought a new in Boston. A raw boy, with clothes made by country tailors, coarse shoes, great hands, red lips, and blue eyes, I went to serve in a private school, where, for fifteen dollars a month and my board, I taught Latin, Greek, subsequently French (!), and Spanish—both which I could read and write, though not speak—the mathematics, and all sorts of philosophy. I was not twenty-one, and hired a man for eleven dollars a month to take my place for five months at home and do the farm work. My father refused to accept this, but I insisted that it would be unjust to use me better than the other boys before me. I taught in the school six hours a day, and from May to September seven; but I always had from ten to twelve hours a day for my own private studies out of school. You may judge what sort of a boy I was from the kind of man you have known since. Life lay before me then (it is all behind me now), and I had hope where now is only remembrance. Judge if I did not work: it makes my flesh creep to think how I used to work, and how much I learned that year, and the four next. Had not I a constitution for a scholar? Oh, that I had known the art of life, or found some book or some man to tell me how to *live*, to *study*, to *take exercise*, &c. But I found none, and so here I am.

No doubt in this way he planted deep in his organization the weakness and dejection which subsequently appear from time to time, long indeed before any definite illness took hold of him. In consequence, it is not always easy to separate his physical from his spiritual condition, to decide when his melancholy was the tax which all powerful men pay while the soul is struggling to know itself, to repose in God, to acquire pre-eminence of will, or when it was the mood of an overworked brain, an eye that is just turned from gazing at the sun. Both causes marked themselves together before he reached a full and conscious maturity. After that nothing but the invalidism can be traced. Yet his friends and followers who sunned themselves in his warmth, little knew how often it had struggled through malign fogs of a neglected body to fall upon them. It could not have been suspected; there was never a trace of illness on the broad, fair countenance of his thought—neither sadness nor indigestion ever went so deep. The body often drooped in private, but every idea walked forth erect, its bloom untouched by care or physical liabilities.

But another cause sometimes threw a shadow over his day. Equal with his thirst for truth was his thirst for affection. No man ever lived so resolute as he, so competent to tell the truth and to defend it, with such power of concentration, and such a sense of luxury in buffeting the great waves of knowledge, who was at the same time so insatiable for sympathy and friendship. " I want some one always in the arms of my heart, to caress and comfort ; unless I have this, I mourn and weep." While he was at home this craving was too sumptuously fed ; the youngest had the whole favour of the house. A dear sister, who had shared his tastes and was his heart's sworn companion, returned to the old farm a few years after Theodore had left it, and died there while he was living in Boston, in 1831. "Dear Sister Emily ! How I longed for her recovery—how gladly I could have lain down my life for her—how, in my boyish way, I asked the Father of All to spare her, though He took my life instead." How pitiless the streets of Boston seemed to this yearning heart —ten hours a day of glorious study could not hive up all he wanted ; on the contrary, there was a sting left in that spoil, pricking him in jaded moments with home and its artless delights. He sometimes threw himself almost with frenzy upon this breast of knowledge, that it should soothe him while it nourished. But companions, mentors, muses, all the stately train, swept by his secret door. Later still, after the great trials of his life commenced, when old friends grew very cool, and new ones were slow to take their place, many words—yes, and tears !—fell from this defeated sympathy. For he would be loved by men, as well as love and worship truth. He was never frigid enough to undertake the rôle of serene indifference. Great learning could not isolate him, great labours could not beat down his childish delight in human society : he longed to know men and women more intimately. He would pour out all his riches, and yet seem to forget that he knew anything, or had any great command, if a friend came near, so controlled was he by desire for sympathy, so instinctively did his passion to feel and lavish kindness break through and domineer at the touch of a faithful hand. Toss a flower into the bosom of this burly image-breaker, he caught and held it tenderly for your sake and its own. There never was a man of the heroic protesting sort more troubled with the anxieties of love. Those who stood before him, counting the grand, firm steps he took, could not see the ensanguined tracks from which the resolute foot was lifted. Nor need they now. Occasionally, surprise broke forth ; for he could not understand why a man who was seeking neither fame nor money,

but truth alone, should be found so repellant.   He desired love
so much, that he did not readily accept the category of being
hated so thoroughly ; and when a little feeling mingled with the
surprise, it betrayed his eagerness for human recognition.   So
earnest was he, and so absorbed in his high motive, that he always
underrated the effect of his thorough speech and contempt.   He
was unconsciously performing his work before he saw that enmity
as well as love must needs bear testimony to its vigour and sincerity.   By-and-bye, he accepted the eminence of being the best-
hated man in America ; but it was with a great anguish that
supplicated for more human sweetness in the cup of truth.   Who
would have thought it who listened to his unpitying delinea-
tions, or stood by when his mailed glove rattled on the pavement, in prompt challenge to the oppressor ?   It was man whose
love he longed to share ; but it was humanity which forbade
him unduly to conciliate.   It would be very wonderful if no
effects of this noble incompatibility could be found in his private
or public thought.

   There was reason enough, then, for melancholy moods.   His
eighteen hours' daily work in Boston and elsewhere, pursued for
half-a-dozen years, with very scanty resources either of friendship or of money to supply an hour of recreation, just impaired
a little the perfect tone of a feeling which was in youth sprightly,
gamesome, elastic with spirits and humorous perception.   He had
no mercy on his body ; it always seemed to him capable of unlimited endurance.   He threw himself upon the tree of knowledge, almost fierce to feed and to assimilate : he never knew
when to leave off.   He derived from his tough and simple
paternal ancestors a great ambition of health : it tyrannized for a
long time over the fatal legacy of his mother.

   Here are excellent " canons of self-discipline," which were
drawn up when he was in the Divinity School, after his ill-
treated body grew revengeful.

   I. Avoid excess in meat and drink.
   II. Take exercise in the air at least three hours a-day.
   III. Always get six hours' sleep—more is better ; seven hours' cer-
        tainly ; eight hours' very often, and always would be more
        suitable and proper.

   Rule No. 3 shows plainly that his daily average of sleep was
less than six hours, with daily virtuous intentions to increase

the amount. The "intellectual canons" were more strictly obeyed; they show how ill the other canons must have fared in practice.

I. Exhaust a subject when curiosity is awake. Sometimes this is impossible. Note the subject in a book, and examine as soon as possible in this manner:—
    1. By finding out what I really know upon the subject.
    2. Obtaining clear and distinct notions in some way.
    3. By stating in words the result of my study, and repeating till it has made a deep impression. Sometimes write them in this book.
    4. If historical, settle time; writers who relate it, their character.
    5. The cause.
    6. The effect.

II. *Keep the mind obedient to the will*, so as to be independent of external affairs. This cannot be completely effected, but may be in a great measure, by the use of certain *intermedia, e. g.,* "words of poets," &c.

In other words, he had a regular posse recruited from all ranks of letters, which he employed to break up his reveries and distractions. While he was engaged in long investigations these were mustered, in readiness to march in and carry off all rude or dissolute disturbers.

Here are the other canons, moral and affectionate.

I. Preserve devoutness, by
    1. Contemplation of nature,
    2. Of the attributes of God,
    3. Of my own dependence;
    4. By prayer, at night and morn, and at all times when devout feelings come over me.

II. Preserve gratitude by reflections upon God's mercies to me.
    1. In giving blessings unasked.
    2. In answering prayers.

III. Restrain licentiousness of imagination, which comprehends many particulars that must not be committed to paper, lest the paper blush.

This is the old monastic foe which infests an ill-ventilated and over-studious solitude. The petulant body began to miss the old farm-ledge, "sun-blanched the live-long summer," and the expeditions of his guileless heart after things of its own kind in the woods and fields.

Here are words recorded later, but referrible to these earlier causes.

> I know not why, but heavy is my heart;
>   The sun all day may shine, the birds may sing,
> And men and women blithely play their part;
>   Yet still my heart is sad. I cannot smile
> As I could smile all day in long past youth!
>   There is no art my sorrows to beguile.
> Daily from utmost heaven descendeth truth,
> I look upon her with an unmoved face,
> And feel no leaping heart when fixed in her embrace.

It is plain that these accesses of sadness may be credited to a jaded spirit.

The other morning I arose and one side was numb; both hands were so, the left mainly. The right soon recovered, and I shaved, but the left kept mainly numb all the morning, with pricking pains from time to time.

These symptoms he had also when he was only 18.

I did not know how ill I was till I came here and find that all my *life* is *gone*. I care for nothing save my duty, and that is not so desirable as once. I feel like a heart-broken and ruined man, and think sometimes it was a mercy if Providence would take me back: not less a mercy to others than to me. Still I will not murmur, but hopefully bear up.

Here is a health-gauge which he invented.

Scale of health. When able to write the sermon Monday morning $= A$. Evening $= \frac{A}{2}$. Tuesday morning, B. Evening, $\frac{B}{2}$; and so on, C, D, E, F. If not all $= O$.

Have done little all the week. Health $= \frac{F}{2}$. This is too near an approach to O for this season of the year (September). I have not begun this month so ill for some years. If I had any of the usual humdrum parishes, I would leave it for a year and go off to Europe. But this is a parish which I cannot leave. I feel as if I had squandered a fortune; for at the age of 39 I am ill, and lose more than half my time, while my father lived a hale man till 77. For the next six months I will take especial care of my health, making all else bend to that, and that to nothing.

But he plunges straightway into researches for his work on the Development of Christianity, and with lecturing and preaching still carries the load of two or three men.

In 1842, he writes, during June, a little heart-touched as well as ill :—

I have done nothing for a month—am stupid beyond measure—was never in such a state before—never knew till now the sadness of that perpetual disappointment of hoping, hoping, and finding nothing come of that hope. But I submit. I think I should complete the Δραμα of my life well by dying next autumn, after the book is ended, but can't tell if it will then end. External sadness is in store for me, no doubt, but the light is all bright and beautiful within me.

Here is a glimpse of some experience whose root is obscurer than the body. It seems at first a shallow mood, but deepens rapidly to the whelming point.

This whole week I have had few thoughts and few sentiments. I am sorry to end and begin a year (1840-41) in this way, but I can't help it. Oh, how our life is streaked with sadness! I shall begin to believe, with some weeper, that all the birds sing in the key of grief, for the stars look melancholy now to me.

My thoughts have been low. I know not why; for I am well in body and temperate in meats and drinks. Vae mihi, quantus dolor in corde—dolor nunquam oculis humanis spectandus. Sed nunc, etiam nunc, Deus, speram in Te. Speram! dico? Non—Tibi meipsum committo, tuâ in manu recubans, molliter. Haud metuam quod mihi vir potest facere. De profundis clamavi.*

But a few months after, the old health blooms again :—

There is no end to the development of the soul. I feel the bird element is wakened in me anew. Wants of my nature never satisfied, but drugged to sleep by the will, open now their beaks, flutter their wings, and try the thin air. I feel a new development of youth. I thought once it would never return . . . there is a resurrection of myself. Last night, for the first time these many months, the lyric inspiration of joy came over me. My prayers ascend—home has a new charm. I start and tremble, and a new depth of Christian feeling opens to my eyes. Blessed be God for all!

Confinement and over-study, with deficiency of friendship, were causes which exaggerated a sentimental tendency of his mind. If he could have found his peer to live with in these early days, one earnest and strong, capable of invading his tired and dissatisfied moments with healthy confidence, he would have spoiled less paper with unquotable verses. Writing does not drain off these humours ; like tapping, it promotes secretion. A hearty slap on the back from a friend's hand would have shaken all the ink from his pen. A friend might have harmlessly received and dissipated these flamboyant moods, which grew to self-consciousness on paper. In default of a friend he

---

* Ah me ! what pain in my heart—pain never to be seen by mortal eyes. Yet now, even now, O God, let me hope in Thee. *Hope*, did I say ? No ; rather I commit myself to Thee, in Thy hand gently lying. Let me not fear what man can do. Out of the depths have I cried.

associated with the moods. I think he never quite recovered from this effect of his scholarly isolation ; a lively fancy and a great affectional instinct went sometimes wandering into vague places. The noblest objects had occasionally a wavering outline, as palms and temples seen through the trembling columns of tropical heat. But a true friendship always went through him, like a breeze blowing landward which dissipates the flickering scene. His friendships were of the manliest and simplest kind, honoured by duty and worship, and vitalized by all a woman's sensibility. Friendship, humanity, and truth always startled the brooding sentiment, and broke up its momentary rest. But it was sometimes built in high places, on the "coigns of vantage" of his finest thoughts.

For the sake of connecting these moods with their physical and moral causes we have travelled beyond our dates.

His early predilection for the profession of minister had never really been impaired by an occasional aspiration for some other career. Echoes of distinguished names stirred his imagination, a developing capacity offered success wherever he might choose to seek it. But the whole course of his thought had already consecrated him to the service of truth and humanity ; nothing could overcome this original bias. It was in his simple disposition, in his exacting moral sense, in the joy of his piety. His powers asserted their capability for any work which he chose to cut out for them ; but the quality of his motives made him fastidious.

He writes in 1848 :—

Several persons of late—as well as formerly—have talked to me about going to Congress, as Representative or Senator. To which there are two objections :—I. *Nobody would send me.* I don t believe any town in Massachusetts would give me any post above that of *Hog-Reeve*, and I don't feel competent for that office—a man in spectacles would not run well after swine. II. Politics are not my vocation, nor yet my desire. I mean to labour for ideas—to set men a-thinking. I feel as if born for a pulpit, if for anything. If I could be *well*, well enough to *work*, and do a man's duty, I should be glad ; yet that is not a thing I ever mention in my prayers. I am content, yes, content to pay the price of violating the laws of the body in struggling for an education, though I knew not what I did.

Father! help me to live better : more useful, more acceptable to Thee. As the years go by me, may I grow in manliness and all noble qualities. Teach me Truth, Justice, Love, and Trust. Let me not be idle, nor unfaithful. Give me a clean and holy life, and may each year bring me nearer to the measure of a man.

That was always the shaping prayer of his practical and ideal life. In Boston he commenced his first open preparation for this future work, in his studies which looked towards the Theological School. He must first get money enough to carry him there. But as he managed to save only three or four dollars out of each month's earning, the prospect was not bright. The Boston experiment only lasted till April, 1832 : then he would venture one of his own at Watertown. During the winter, he gave his first lecture, before the Lexington Lyceum ; the subject was the History of Poland, selected on account of the enthusiasm for the Poles which was then travelling through New England.

His life in Boston was desolate enough that winter. No friends—" nothing but thoughts, and books, books, books." But he records, in his letter from Santa Cruz [1859], one benefit which he derived from being in the city at that time.

For a year, though born and bred among Unitarians, I had attended the preachings of Dr. Lyman Beecher, the most powerful orthodox minister in New England, then in the full blaze of his talents and reputation, and stirred also with polemic zeal against " Unitarians, Universalists, Papists, and Infidels." I went through one of his " protracted meetings," listening to the fiery words of excited men, and hearing the most frightful doctrines set forth in sermon, song, and prayer. I greatly respected the talents, the zeal, and the enterprise of that able man, who certainly taught me much; but I came away with no confidence in his theology. The better I understood it, the more self-contradictory, unnatural, and hateful did it seem. A year of his preaching about finished all my respect for the Calvinistic scheme of theology.*

He took great pains, then, to understand the scheme which afterwards he attacked so unsparingly, and as its disciples aver, so ignorantly. Certainly it was an able advocate of Calvinism who indoctrinated him with disgust for it. He remembered also the great features of revival meetings ; and in his sermons " On False and True Theology," and " The Revival of Religion which we need," preached in 1858 during the great revival, he spoke from the confidence of personal experience.

The idea of going to Watertown to open a private school was probably suggested to him by relations, who were farmers living

* "March 31, 1852. Old Dr. Beecher came to see me, and spent an hour and a half. ' Tell me who you are,' he said, ' where you came from, and how you got so far from the common track.' I did so, and we had a quiet talk. He is genial, generous, activeminded, and expressed a strong sympathy for me, and a good deal of feeling of kindliness towards me."

in the north part of that town.   Thither he went in April, 1832, without a pupil engaged, and without money enough to make the few needed preparations.   He found a boarding-place at Mr. Nathaniel Broad's, who lived about half-way between the village and Newton-Corner, opposite the estate of Dr. Morse.   Part of the inducement to lodge there lay in an old bakery, the second story of which he leased of the proprietor.   He assisted in flooring it, made a rude wainscot, constructed a dozen desks, and shortly opened school with a force of two pupils, one of whom he asked to come gratis.   Collegiate and theological studies were going on all the while.   Pupils came slowly, dropping in till he had enough to divide into an upper and a lower class.   Members of the former paid each five dollars a quarter, and of the latter four dollars.   If he found a boy or girl in the town too poor to pay him anything, he invited such to come in.*   But he did not wait long for a full school, and the number rose, the first year to 35, afterwards to 54.   Most all of them were paying scholars. He was a child with all of them, and dearly beloved, for he had sweet and gentle ways.   But he felt great responsibility in undertaking to teach, and sometimes he doubted if he had the talent of imparting anything.   It fairly oppressed him, and he took endless pains with the young minds ; it touched him to see their confidence in him.   But he was grave too, and looked after justice strictly ; he had authority—only the children did not know it.   He managed to govern with little demonstration.

They brought him flowers, and welcomed him to their out-of-school games ; he loved to watch all their ways.

In one thing he had unlimited confidence—the ability of the children to learn any task he chose to set.   This sometimes startled them, and it appeared as if he went too fast.   Then he would draw them out, and restore courage by skilful questioning. In this way, too, he would make them answer their own questions, till he had an assistant in the awakened power of each one's reflection.   He had a great aversion to the text-books of Natural Theology, declaring that they were attempts to prove what no child ever thought of doubting ; and he would often bring the books to shame before the children, by drawing out their intuitions.   He loved to teach by means of objects ; and

* But after he had admitted a coloured girl who had been sent to him, he consented to dismiss her in deference to the objections of some of his patrons. This he always confessed with mortification.

when he took his class abroad, the fields seemed expressly provided with illustrations and representatives of some fair thought. All the flowers and plants of the country round were familiar to him, and the ways of birds and animals ; he tried to cultivate the observing faculty in the children. One of them remembers his lesson when the wind blew a trumpet-flower to his feet from the vine that overran her father's porch.

A letter from Rev. Charles Briggs, of Lexington, introduced him to Dr. Francis, who was then minister of the first parish in Watertown. In that red brick house, near the Charles River, were many books in many languages, a genial and liberal-minded host, a kind and cheerful wife. All these extended hospitality to the brave young student. Dr. Francis was among the earliest of New England scholars to read and appreciate a German book. His Latin, Greek, and Hebrew, were in admirable condition. Modern languages were not neglected, but among them German was especially cultivated. Here, then, were *Dogmatik*, *Metaphysik*, and *Hermeneutik* for Theodore, with a competent guide to hold the clue for him. The two years spent with these advantages were always gratefully remembered by him. Theodore's questions accumulated frightfully when he found such a hospitable ear for them. He never forgot to say that he was in debt to the free and scholarly minister, who made a friend of the bashful student and favoured the generous unfolding of his mind,* and to the wife who soothed him with home-like associations.

The preaching of Dr. Francis must also be reckoned among the things which helped Theodore on his way. His sermons were the liberal efforts of a mind constantly studying and inquiring, welcoming light, and bold to speculate. They were free from dogmatism, perhaps disinclined to definite and final statements. The tendency stimulated Theodore to form his own opinions. But, above all, Dr. Francis was a humane preacher.

Theodore soon became superintendent of the Sunday school. Up the aisle of the old meeting-house he ventures on this new mission, very awkward and diffident, a little uncertain whether people would like him, in a suit constructed on the very frontiers of economy, which appeared so often and so long that a good many persons pretend to recollect it. But when he began to speak, in his gentle and pious way, everybody was glad.

* In his Journal of a later date he says : "Then I walked long days in the strength of the meat I ate."

He also undertook a Bible-class, in a Socratic style, making the pupils themselves discover what they had to learn. The doctrine of plenary inspiration was not held by Unitarians, but they had a vague opinion that everything of consequence in the Bible was suggested or preserved in no ordinary way. Theodore would read portions to his class, and invite them to exercise their common-sense upon them—" Must a man be supernaturally inspired to say or do this—did this require a special suggestion ?" But he did not yet carry this to the criticism of a supernatural element in the nature of Christ and the Apostles, or in the prevailing spirit of the New Testament.

Mr. Broad, his landlord, died ; and Theodore, very tender and helpful, was of great use at home. Several of his pupils lived in the same house, and he undertook the general charge of their manners and morals. He sat up very late—there was never a drop of oil in his lamp the next morning ; " not that there was any scrimping in Mrs. Broad's house "—her lamps emulated her name—but Theodore could hold out to burn the longest. He was up at daylight, sawed and split the wood for the school and family, swept out and dusted the school-room, and took a walk of three or four miles.

His Cyclopean wall began each evening to the sound of music, for he had a chum, who was unhappily seized about the same moment after tea with a tendency to breathe his soul out through the flute. Theodore began with mild expostulations, when Amphion Sanger seized his melancholy reed, but the tenure of the chamber covered mutual privileges ; and the chum blew himself out by nine o'clock, but Theodore would sit up till the lamp went out at two. Between the strains, and while Amphion wetted the joints and called up the next melody, he could snatch moments of studious oblivion.*

This routine went on for two years. Twice a week he walked

---

* Theodore held to the Hellenistic interpretation of the word Music, which was a pursuit of all the liberal arts. The thoughts of great men built lofty harmonies in his mind. But he was heretical on the subject of Music. When Mr. Cranch, the painter, and Mr. J. S. Dwight, the musical journalist, were in the Divinity School, they sometimes met to meditate the muse upon a slender reed. Theodore bore it for a long time without flinching. " But on one occasion," says Mr. Cranch, " there was a movement in the entry just outside our door, executed upon a peculiar, and by no means musical instrument—a sort of *obligato ad libitum* bass thrown in as accompaniment to our strains. On opening the door to ascertain the nature of these strange sounds, there was Theodore, who had left his folios of the Latin Fathers, had rushed into the cellar, and brought up a wooden-horse, saw, and log of wood, on which he was exercising his vigorous sinews—see-saw, see-saw —to our utter discomfiture and amusement. As for Theodore, he barely smiled."

to Cambridge to take lessons in Hebrew of Mr. Thurston, then a member of the Theological School, and now settled at Belmont ; afterwards he walked as far as Charlestown to be instructed by Mr. Seixas, a Jew ; Greek and Latin literature, German metaphysics, as much political economy as he could find, mathematics and theology, missal reading, Hebrew, and a little Syriac, drained good Mrs. Broad's midnight lamp.

But a fairer light began to gild the old quartos, and redletter the pages of dingy German paper. For Miss Lydia D. Cabot was not only a teacher in the Sunday-school, but she boarded at the same house with Theodore ; and this gradually became of great importance to the young student, who had hitherto resented interruption. Now the flowers discovered in the fields along the birch and alder-fringed bank of the Charles were not brought home for botanizing. The walks themselves were not companionless. There is a charming view from Wellington Hill, and some old oaks of famous girth not far off, which were great favourites. Beaver Creek runs from the oaks through meadow land, till in two miles or more it finds the Charles. The river has pleasant reaches near the Waltham factories. Smooth Helmet Hill lifts its crest from a wide sweep of apple orchards, and Prospect Hill is not too far, when for some reason every step is beguiled of weariness. Mrs. Broad's oil must eke the night out further, for by day the books were less admired.

Præposito florem prætulit officio.

TO MISS LYDIA D. CABOT IN BOSTON.

Watertown, Tuesday Eve, Oct. 30, 1833.

I walked to father's ; he soon returned from church, and I caught him in the garden, and informed him of the "fatal " affair, if you will call it so.

The tear actually started to his aged eye. "Indeed," said he. "Indeed;" I replied, "and attempted to describe *some* of your good qualities." "It is a good while to wait," he observed. "Yes, but we are young, and I hope I have your approval." "Yes, yes! I should be pleased with anyone you would select ; but, Theodore," said he, and the words sank deep into my heart, "you must be a good *man* and a good *husband,* which is a great undertaking."

I promised all good fidelity ; and may Heaven see it kept !

Oct. 31.

I have attacked Mr. Herodotus with renewed vigour this week. I purchased a small volume which contains all his writings, and am not now compelled to wait for Mr. Francis to bring volumes from the college; those are, however, to be consulted at leisure. I intended to finish the work to-night, but fear I shall not be able. Now, I feel a *new* pleasure in the discharge of all my duties. I love my books the more, my school the more, mankind the more, and even, I believe, my God the more, from loving *you*.

Nov. 21.

I have endeavoured to cheer your absence and enliven my spirits a little by going this afternoon to Uncle Clark's, though I shall still find ten hours for study, reading, and writing.

Dec. 5.

What shall I say to you for sitting until ten o'clock to write ? Why, ten is as bad for *you* as one for *me*, and I would sometimes gladly extend my lucubrations nearer morning, but have kept my promise thus far with all good fidelity.

Dec. 27.

It has been in other times than this my highest pleasure thus to pass my time, thus to spend my nights, in " high concord with the god-like past," to collect my own thoughts and search for new. But now I find a *new* pleasure which, with a louder, sweeter voice, speaks to the heart and tells *another* tale.

Thus was planted the tender root of a happiness which, in after-years, helped him to tolerate contempt and bitterness, and to temper the dejection which they brought. When disturbed and repulsed abroad, he always hastened home to this reassuring presence ; there his wounds were touched with gentleness.

This Watertown season must have been very delightful now. The school was less oppressive, and he was led somewhat more into society. There were many fine people among the farmers in North Watertown. His cousins, the Clarks, were bright and sympathetic, and old " Uncle Peter " was Theodore's firm friend, a farmer, intelligent and fond of reading, but, better than all, endowed with a sweetness and liberality, and a real courtesy, which mere culture can never bring. These honest men and women understood Theodore, and never forsook him when his opinions were most divergent. Whoever was afterwards settled over the First Parish in Watertown, found that it was no tax upon his courage to exchange with him. The act was not dangerous there, as elsewhere, and involved no loss of position or influence. On the contrary, if the clergyman himself undertook to vindicate Mr. Parker, or to share his views, these farmers were first to countenance and welcome it. Old Deacon Stone never sat a formalist in that meeting-house ; and his heart was true to the young teacher, whose truth and innocence he remembered. The Crafts, the Barnards, the Stones, the Clarkes —Theodore would gratefully repeat their names in this connection—were the first to know what he was, and the first among New England parishes, not his own, to rejoice when they saw him standing in their pulpit. In his earliest intercourse with these warm, unsophisticated people, he used to fill their hearts with his piety and gentleness, and inspire them with his great ambition to learn the truth. The opinions were of less consequence ; they knew their man. And so it might have been everywhere else, if his beautiful disposition could have been the harbinger of his doctrine. But there was neither *diletanteism* nor dogmatism on those rich slopes where he passed his social hours, so that his pure motive was instantly discerned.

He was also recognized by some families of more wealth and cultivation, but who cherished, like the farmers, simplicity, independence and humanity—one or all of these high qualities. Among the Whites, and Thaxters, and Bigelows, and Shannons, he had always friends, and sometimes vigorous disciples. How delightful it is to inscribe all these names upon a page of his memorial ! and those, still living, who own the names, will tolerate the freedom from one who is not a stranger, for the sake of love and old companionship.

After teaching his school for two years, he reckoned he had money enough to venture with to the Theological School, where a frugal youth could live for less than 200 dollars a-year, all expenses included. He would still eke out his income with teaching, and perhaps with writing.

It was not a comfortable day for him when the leave-taking came. The scholars had devised to show their respect and love by a little presentation-scene, which was managed to surprise him. A neat speech was made by Master Briggs, and the silver cup being then revealed, Theodore seized it and vanished abruptly into the entry, being no longer fit to be seen. The scholars thought he had rushed into Mrs. Broad's, perhaps to execute one of the delotic * movements to which he was subject. He was not in condition, for some minutes, to return and dismiss the school.

* A word from the Greek is used, meaning gesture and motion demonstrative of internal feeling, to avoid applying the word dancing to Theodore's rather elephantine ballets.

He never had any trouble with his scholars, for he never stooped to coarse methods of maintaining influence. When he was afterwards Chairman of the School Committee of West Roxbury, he introduced a rule that no teacher should inflict chastisement upon a pupil without bringing in some ostensible reason for it. When asked what he intended by proposing that the reason should be "*ostensible*"—"Why don't you say *real ?*" he replied that the teacher could then say he punished for whispering, or for being out of place, while the *real* reason might be that he got up feeling very cross, or,—added he, in a whisper, "because the boy hadn't got a pretty sister." This also required explanation, and he told them that he had two pupils in Watertown, Frank and Harriett, brother and sister. Harriett was handsome, and a great favourite, with whom he used to read and take long walks. Frank was disobedient one day, and was threatened with chastisement after school, if the offence was repeated. Frank accordingly repeated it, and was told to stop after the rest were dismissed. " But upon approaching him with my ferule, he looked too much like Harriett. I had to kiss him and let him go."

During the school-keeping he read Tacitus, Cicero, Herodotus and Thucydides, and translated Pindar, Theocritus, Bion and Moschus, as well as Æschylus. He fell in with Cousin, and the new school of French philosophers, and became acquainted with Coleridge. He also pursued the literature of all the modern languages which he then knew, and made great strides in metaphysics and theology.

TO MISS CABOT.

Feb. 27, 1834.

Mr. Francis called here yesterday and lent me the necessary books, so I have commenced the great study, the criticism of the New Testament.

I spoke again to Mr. Francis of the comparative advantages and disadvantages of commencing study the first of April or next September, and he again expressed his preference for the former plan. He preached all day Sabbath, besides lecturing in the evening. How few ministers are so industrious ! but if any professional man can have an inducement to labour with all diligence, it is the clergyman.

I have been to examine a school this afternoon, and never have I seen a school better undergo an examination. This is the last of my services upon the School Committee, and glad am I.

Feb.

I consulted Mr. Francis about going to Cambridge soon, and joining the present junior class; he thought it a good plan, and gave me letters of introduction to Mr. Ware. I have walked to Cambridge this afternoon, and seen all the Faculty; have resolved to make the attempt; so I shall finish school-keeping on the first of April, and remove to Cambridge, take a room at the Hall, and commence study.

Nothing is too much for young ambition to hope, no eminence too lofty for a youth's vision, no obstacle too difficult for his exertions, and no excellence unattainable. Patience, perseverance, prayer have done something already; and when we consider that sincere desires are never neglected, and real endeavours never unassisted, we need not despair of making some *approaches* at least to the eminence Mr. Palfrey now occupies. Would not this be truly delightful? No situation can be more honourable, no task more pleasant, no prospect more celestial, than that of a virtuous, faithful clergyman.

He entered the Theological School during the last three months of the junior class, in 1834. The other members of this class were Samuel P. Andrews, Richard T. Austin, John S. Dwight, George E. Ellis, Oliver C. Everett, Abiel A. Livermore, and William Silsbee. The report of his scholarly acquisitions had preceded him, and the extent of his reading excited admiration. His talk was full of odd learning and scraps of curious information. He was crammed from books and observation, but everything lay about in undigested heaps. All the library privileges which he could find in the neighbourhood he laid hold of, and the students were frequently drafted to help him home with his bundle of folios. At one time he fancied that his memory was growing feeble: a friend found him posted before an enormous historical chart, covering one side of his room, which contained all the dates and incidents from Adam. He was committing this to memory. All real or imaginary deficiencies were attacked by him without loss of time. Everybody reproached him for taking no exercise, but he declared that it was planting-time with him, and relied upon his constitution to carry him through. He increased the bad effect of this fury for study by attempting to board himself, for a time, in his own room, a sad economy which brings expense upon later years. Classmates have said that he used to study fourteen hours a day.

He excelled in debate, but his first sermons were rather poor. Henry Ware, jun., would discuss them freely, and declare to Theodore that they were unworthy of him. This salutary candour cost the struggling student sleepless nights, broken by sobs. The next morning would find him in despair, believing that he had staked all—time, health, and hope, upon a profession, and had lost.   His talk was superior to his sermonizing ; his prayers were already full of simplicity and pious feeling.

He was very affectionate, and relied upon two or three of his classmates ; he could not be happy without the privilege of frequent sallies from his books' into their rooms, for a moment's gossip or a grotesque caper.   Once he quarrelled with a friend who was reading "Philip Van Artevelde" with him, and who could not bear the execution of Occo and Gilbert Matthew at the close of the first part of that drama.   "It is a great blemish," says the friend ; "Artevelde should have shown magnificent with mercy."   "No," cries Theodore, "it is just : it is good, it is Christian."   "It is downright murder," says the friend.   "Then get out of my room," cried Theodore, in wrath because the measure meted to two villains was not recognised.   He had to pay for that : whenever he referred to it, the tears stood in his eyes.

This letter shows that his critical tendency, which was wide enough awake upon most topics, still refused to notice the theology that he brought with him.   His statement of belief is thoroughly conventional.

TO HIS NEPHEW COLUMBUS GREENE.

Cambridge, April 2, 1834.

I came last Saturday, or rather Sunday night, and of course have scarcely had time to see how I shall be pleased; but since I am resolved to be satisfied at all events, nothing is to be feared on that account.   It is now vacation with the class, so I am alone in this great house.   Term-time commences two weeks from to-day, when I shall join the class at recitations, though I shall not be considered a member till next commencement.

You enquire about my belief.   I believe in the Bible.   Does that satisfy you ?   No, you will say : all Christians profess to the same, and how different they are.

To commence then : I believe there is *one* God, who has existed from all eternity, with whom the past, present, and future are alike present; that he is almighty, good, and merciful, will reward the good and punish the wicked, both in this life and the next.   This punishment *may be* eternal ; of course, I believe that neither the rewards nor punishments of a future state are corporal.   Bodily pleasures soon satiate, and may God preserve us from a worse punishment than one's own conscience.

I believe the books of the Old and New Testament to have been written by men inspired by God, for certain purposes, but I do not think them inspired *at all times*.   I believe that Christ was the Son of God, conceived and born in a miraculous manner, that he came to preach a better religion by which man may be saved.

This religion, as I think, allows men the very highest happiness in this life, and promises eternal felicity in another world. I do not think our sins will be forgiven because Christ died. I cannot conceive why they should be, although many good and great men have thought so. I believe God knows all that we shall do, but does not *cause* us to do anything.

The expenses at the school are 66 dollars annually; board in commons, 1 dollar, 90 cents a week; clothes, &c., will make in all about 200 dollars per annum. I shall have, when all affairs are settled at Watertown, about 150 dollars. This is too little, you will say. Well, I know it, but I have paid nearly 200 dollars for books within these two years; and clothes, you know, cost lots of money. I am now boarding myself upon dry bread; it will cost about half a dollar a week. I shall try it all vacation, and if I like it, all summer.

One scholar comes and recites once a day till commencement; the pay is 12 dollars a quarter.

I had almost forgot to mention, at the close of my school the scholars gave me a handsome silver cup, with an inscription testifying their respect, gratitude, &c. It was preceded by an address from one of the scholars. I never parted with scholars so sorrowfully in my life. I wept and so did they.

TO THE SAME.

April 28, 1834.

Let me advise you not to fear the opinion of the world. Satisfy your reason, and especially satisfy your own conscience, and all will then be well.

I hope I shall not want much money at all, and for this reason: I to-day made application to Prof. Palfrey, the Dean of the Faculty, for a benefice, and my application was successful. Of course nothing will be extended this season, but after next commencement about 110 dollars or 150 dollars will be afforded me annually. This will go a good way towards defraying my expenses; and since I have a little of my own, probably I shall not want to borrow any of you this year. This is an unexpected instance of good fortune for which I cannot be sufficiently grateful.

I tried cold bread for a fortnight, and at the commencement of the term went back again to commons; but I intend to try the old scheme again next autumn.

TO THE SAME.

July 11, 1834.

Should you be pleased to know something of our ordinary course of proceedings in this institution? We have about thirty scholars, divided into three classes; one of these graduates in about a week. Some one of the senior class preaches each Sabbath evening during the year; all the school and some few strangers attend. Prayers are performed at morning of every day by Prof. Palfrey, and at evening by one of the senior class. The junior class, to which I belong, recites in Hebrew every Monday, Wednesday, and Friday afternoon; attends a lecture upon the criticism of the New Testament, Monday and Friday, when we translate the original, ask questions, and engage in discussion with the Professor. We recite and discuss the Evidences of Christianity with Dr. Ware every Wednesday. Tuesday afternoon we have an exercise in extemporaneous speaking with Prof. Ware, jun., one of the finest men I have ever known. Some subject is proposed to the class at one meeting and discussed at the next. Saturday morning Mr. Ware delivers a lecture upon composition of sermons, subjects to be treated, &c., to the whole school. Thursday we have no recitation. One-third of the school declaims every Tuesday evening. Friday evening the whole school meet for extemporaneous speaking. Thursday evening is spent in a religious meeting.

A society for the promotion of the interests of humanity, and called the "Philanthropic Society," meets once a fortnight on Wednesday evening. A report is always read upon some interesting subject, such as "Infidelity," "Temperance," "The License Laws," by a committee previously appointed to investigate the subject. Besides this, I have a fine lad who comes every morning to recite Greek and Latin, &c., and had a young gentleman who came twice a week to recite German, but I have not seen him this fortnight.

All my leisure is devoted to translating some papers of La Fayette, which I am doing for Mr. Sparks, who is going to publish them. This is his work, and not mine. I shall be constantly occupied upon this translation during the whole of vacation.

Sunday I visit the States' Prison, where I have an interesting class in the Sunday school.

TO THE SAME.

July 8, 1835.

I have two scholars now (young men), who intend to enter an advanced class in college. They come one hour a day. Besides, you know, I have two young misses, so my time is tolerably well occupied.

He was still the bashful and sensitive boy, filled with piety and pure feelings, yet very self-reliant and ambitious. He carried into the school all the energy and purpose which his peculiar education had served to develope. He attacked every subject with enthusiasm, and extemporized his own way of mastering it. He is represented as being very eager in the debates which were held once a week in the little chapel of Divinity Hall ; there he judged everything in an independent fashion, was very reverent of truth, yet never calculated his phrases, offended the taste sometimes, but always stimulated inquiry and the deepest feelings. Dr. Ware would interrupt the ardent debater, suggesting, perhaps, that it was not quite handsome to say "old Paul," as the epithet no longer conveyed apostolic meanings. Theodore would subside, proceeding in humorous excess with allusions to the "gentleman from Tarsus." Rebuffs for want of taste, or for any disregard of conventionalisms, did not put him down, for it was in part his very eagerness which kept him so sensitive. On he went, finding his own way through everything, earnest to have a sight of genuine objects in all the fields of thought. It is singular that his colourless theology escaped so long. He still took a good many things on trust, for spiritual intuitions were very dear to him; but if a new doctrine rested upon evidence, he showed what the old doctrine might one day expect when he cross-questioned it to the extent of his critical ability. If it was developed metaphysically, each step of the process was tested by an instinctive health of all the faculties, which may be called his common-sense. It was his common-sense, and that of no other person : the most valuable result of his peculiar "bringing up." For common-sense depends upon the the personality, though in all persons it is a general soundness, or freedom from cachexy; not mere shrewdness, or ability to conduct material affairs, or perception of the best out of half-a-dozen ways, but the functional man in good condition, every part of the nature exhibiting an irreproachable digestion, and no part overnourished. A man shows his common-sense when he is seen not to be under the tyranny of any special knack or impulse; his shrewdness is not a talent, but an operative condition of his whole mind. He is too shrewd to exaggerate a single member; he promotes the fair development of all. Faith, conscience, and understanding receive their just amount of chyle; the pulse goes everywhere, touches at all the ports of entry and delivery, leaving and taking what is due. This is a sensible man, as distinguished from a commercial, metaphysical, mystical, sceptical, or sentimental man.

The common-sense which Mr. Parker began now to display had been carefully protected by his mode of life. The artifices of education injure ordinary people just where they need the greatest strengthening. Extraordinary people instinctively invent their own methods. The same drill, the same succession of text-books, the same set of theological opinions, the same clique, and neighbourhood, the same professional traditions, turn out vast numbers of conventional judgments, which for want of common-sense are considered sensible. It is said that the Flathead practice does not impair the natural capacity of the tribe ; nothing is said of the want of capacity which invented and pursues the practice.   Fortunately, nobody caught Mr. Parker when his skull was soft, to lay heavy hands on the brain's gentle respiring beat.   By-and-bye he possessed health and amplitude of organs fit for any work.   And his instinct that he must relinquish to each function its appropriate freedom and opportunities had not been taught out of him.   He, therefore, gradually and surely learned for himself how to bring all the functions to an understanding ; not thereby solving all spiritual problems, but preserving the inward health.   The healthier he grew, the more he despised all doctrines which start from a presumption of human inability. The soul seemed to him well made for its work.   It was this which made him ask for principles that are capable of promoting human welfare ; all opinions and beliefs which cannot effect this practical connection with humanity dropped gradually out of his favour.   He wanted only available truths, yet his common-sense had a high and fastidious notion of availability.   It was not a niggardly sharpness to discover the least amount that will keep alive a human being, to put men and women on famine rations of faith, thought, and feeling, but it was an instinct for the real interdependence of all these.   There naturally belonged to this a shrewd and sarcastic vein, and no little impatience with all the mystical and ecstatical luxuries which have ever corrupted honest, manly blood.   Sometimes he was disdainful, and sometimes merry, when he got into a field of these, and began to shake them out with his critical pitchfork.

After a thorough reading of the fathers, with careful notes and analyses, he breaks out one day thus :—

I am heart-weary and reason-weary of these same doting fathers. They have sense, but it is "a grain of wheat in a bushel of chaff." I shall soon be done with them, however, for the present at least.   One of the greatest proofs of the darkness of the monastic ages is the folly-admiration bestowed upon these same nonsense writers.

I will say one word about "the resolute Hierome" as an ancient has it.   He loved glory rather than truth, was superstitious, and an intro-ducer of important errors into the Church, both in doctrine and inter-pretation.   Setting aside his extensive, perhaps immense, reading and faculty of sharp declamation, and, Leclerc says, nothing but moderate faculties remain.   He was not a profound scholar in Hebrew, or even in Greek.   He *tasted* of theology rather than exhausted it.   He wrote his works in great haste.

St. Austin, we all know, introduced more error into the Church than any other man. Many of his doctrines fly in the face both of reason and virtue, to extinguish the eyes of one and to stifle the breath of the other. Everybody knows how he persecuted his opposers, Pelagius and Julian, to say nothing of others. Let him go. If anyone wishes to read an eulogy of undeserved elegance upon the Bishop of Hippo, he will find it in Maury, &c.

Tertullian I have always looked upon with considerable jealousy. He first introduced the notion that faith and reason contradict each other naturally—a doctrine so germane to the feelings of many in those unreason days. He thought faith which contradicted reason was most acceptable to God. He has regular canons of criticism; some of them are indeed good, but his application of them is faulty. Everybody knows he thought the soul material, &c.; he thought it was *sky-blue*. A sister of those days had been elevated by contemplation so high, that she saw the souls all *sky-blue*.

These patristic studies were brought to a close in the winter of 1835. But they often reappear, and in 1845 Tertullian is noticed again:

Tertullian, it seemed always to me, was one of the worst curses to the human race that has occurred since the Flood. I don't know but Africa took its revenge on the European world in advance by sending Tertullian and Augustine into it. I think, at this day, it is easier to free the negroes from their white masters than it is to deliver the human race from this wretched yoke laid on us by those two shabby Africans. I remember, years ago, thinking most of the absurdities of Christian theology came in with Tertullian; and reading a little since convinces me that he developed much iniquity that was only latent before, and brought in many wolves to the Christian flock, which have since been clothed in sheep-skins and have devoured the flock without mercy.

The Scriptures have been almost always interpreted in the interest of dogmatism, from Christ to this present; for instance, the *Regula Fidei* of Tertullian and the *Analogy of Faith* in our day. Chrysostom was better than most, but he was often absurd in his interpretations. Some of the old allegorizers equal Swedenborg—some of the Chiliasts. Irenæus, *inter alios*, was absurd as Charles Fourier.

JUSTIN MARTYR.—I admire the candour and beauty and sweetness of his *Oratio ad Græcos*, in which he shows the folly of their old mythi, if accepted as true. What is the value of his testimony to prove the fact of such acceptance? A Greek philosopher becomes Christian, and reasons as if his nation believed the stories—how much does it prove?) He urges them to accept the doctrines of one true God.

In his *Admonitio ad Græcos*, the same is done still better. Here he shows that Moses was older than the Greek teachers, and proves it from writers not Christian, after showing the folly of the Greek myths in Homer and the philosophers. Here he misunderstood both, I think, sometimes.

He says Orpheus and Homer taught some beautiful truths, and cites that fine piece of Orpheus to Musæus (which most unfortunately is spurious and of late date); the monotheistic passages from the Sybil (for he could say, " Teste David cum Sibyllâ"); and Sophocles. He speaks of the names of God, and says the name is holy for us—not for God; so each and all names are indifferent to God. The whole piece is quite noble.

The list of languages which he studied in the school included Italian, Portuguese, Dutch, Icelandic, Chaldaic, Arabic, Persian, Coptic, and a smattering of Æthiopic. He attempted Russian, but there was no one to help him master the sounds of the alphabet, and he gave it up till he lived in Boston.

In November, 1835, he began to study Swedish. At the same time, translations of Eichhorn and Ammon were going on —reading Greek comedies and German commentaries, Vico's " Scienza Nuova," and parts of Plato. Before the month was out he was translating Swedish poetry, and in the last week of it he commenced Danish. In December he undertook the modern Greek. All languages, dead or living, were mastered with great rapidity. Everything he planted grew fast, but he always seemed to have a language under glass.*

He learned not merely the vocabulary of a new tongue, as so many American students do, to get at the general sense of a book in the most economical manner, and push over the ground with smart conjectures. But he loved philology; the grammatical structure and derivation of a language attracted him first. The vocabulary came next ; in fact, his occasional mistakes in translating at a time when he was devoured by work were in the meanings of words oftener than in the idiom and structure. His knowledge of Hebrew and Syriac was so minute, that Professor Sidney Willard is said to have often applied to the young Divinity student for advices upon some nice point. And in 1843 he dropped into the middle of the course of the Arabic Professor in Paris, bringing, with entire comprehension of the subject, a capacity to criticise the lecturer's method.

To-day I made a new acquisition to my library, viz., Herder's Complete Works, in 45 volumes. I can never render sufficient thanks for God's goodness in giving me this opportunity of increasing my books, and of course my means of usefulness.

---

* "A kinsman of mine, one Thomas Parker, who lived a virgin, and 'went unto the apocalyptical virgins at death,' was such a master of the Oriental tongues that once, when some of his brother clergymen assembled to rebuke him for some heresy, he replied in Latin—they rejoined in Latin. He replied in Greek—they continued in that tongue. He answered in Hebrew—they questioned in Hebrew. He then retreated to the Arabic, where they could not follow him, when he bade them go home and study their primers before they undertook to school him."

He had in college a class of Hebrew students, which he met twice a week, and two private students ; and in 1836 he taught Hebrew to the junior class in the Divinity school, during the visit to New Orleans made by Dr. Palfrey.

Anglo-Saxon is added to the other languages before the New Year. Everything else is going on at the same time, and numerous odes and versicles are showered along the track. "A Bridal Hymn," for instance, " for the Wedding of Beauty and Truth," with choruses of earth-spirits and angels, which I forbear to disturb. He delivers a lecture in Concord during the vacation ; translates, dips into rabbinical matters, into books on Messianic prophecy, on which point he began to hold with De Wette, and asks himself some questions about the Miraculous Conception. He studies books about the Canon and the different versions of the Bible—Schrift-Erklärungs-Geschichte—translates the article " Rationalism " from the Conversations-Lexicon, and a good deal out of Eichhorn's "Ur-Geschichte." Paulus succeeds, and he writes a paper entitled " Hints upon German Theology," then goes through the " Wolfenbüttel Fragments " question, and begins to read Spinoza.

Under the head of " Horæ Platonicæ," he makes analyses and criticisms of the views in Plato's works. During the reading of the " Republic," his humanity gives significant and promising utterance.

Is a man bad, the good shall teach him *goodness*. And the teaching shall be good, not that which renders the vile doubly perverse, for that is unjust. When will this sentiment lie at the foundation of all codes of laws? Penal legislature, now-a-days, has all the effect of the purest injustice, in driving the half-guilty to increased crime, and in making *doubly deep* the hatred of the revengeful. I doubt not the angel of humanity will beat, with her golden pinions, all prisons to small dust.

On Sundays he generally went to Charlestown, where he had a class in the State prison, which greatly interested him. But occasionally we find him in Watertown.

Sunday, 22 Feb., 1836.—I heard Mr. Francis preach two very good sermons, as may be supposed, since with him good sermons are the rule, and poor ones the exceptions, and rare ones too. I dined with him, and found as much pleasure and satisfaction as usual in his varied and instructive conversation.

Then follow notes of the table-talk about Coleridge, &c. It is needless to catalogue the books which marked his course of study during the next term. Wegschieder, Staudlin, Storr, Schmidt, and better yet, Cudworth, Henry More, Norris, Descartes, Lessing, Cousin, B. Constant, Leibnitz ; also books on Magic, about which he was always very curious. Descartes furnished him with rules for studying.

April 21.—It is now the commencement of a new term—of my last term of study in college. Where shall the end of it send me—what will become of me then? What will eventually become my destiny? What preacher shall I be? And where shall I find a resting-place? All these questions come up with mighty force—they weigh heavily at times upon my soul.

A part of the decision of these great questions rests with me, a part upon something exterior to myself—upon Providence. For *my own* part alone feel I any anxiety. God has ever protected me, and even in the times when there seemed no possible way of escape from present and impending disaster, His hand has shown a way. Shall I distrust it now? Oh, no, I do not—I cannot. The Almighty will doubtless give me more than I deserve—why should I fear?

Wherever I am cast I can be happy. I will attempt to do my duty. But there are others dear to my heart. Shall I disappoint their cherished hopes? Oh, no!

Much depends upon this little term. May I improve its blessings right.

TO MISS CABOT.

Tuesday Eve.

Brother Dwight just called at my door, requesting me "to bang him up in the morning," as he elegantly calls it, which you know means it is *something like* bed-time. But bed-time is not "the witching time of night," for you nullified all late watching long ago, by an imperial decree.

TO THE SAME.

June 10, 1835.

Were I to become an idolator I should worship the stars, since they are almost a personification of ideal beauty, so bright, so clear, apparently so frail, and yet outlasting human calculation—so uncertain and yet so constant. That folly could almost be forgiven which led men to imagine them animated with celestial souls, and endowed with superhuman, and only less than supreme power, and which made them no feeble actors in the fortunes of men and fall of mighty states. But since we are no idolators, but Christians, we can look beyond the stars up to the throne of the Invisible, which they surround and adorn with their shining.

What is more beautiful than a summer's night, when the hurry and bustle of day has gone by, and calm and stillness succeeds? . . .

How happy is a mother's charge at night, when, with many a prayer, she folds up her little flowerets, and commits them to His care whose eye never slumbers nor sleeps! Perhaps you have not such associations as I have with this period; but now the days when I was a little, yes, a very little child, come up before me, when my mother taught me a prayer and a hymn, and, giving one farewell kiss, left me to repose. I cannot think of those times without a tear—a tear of regret for those days, and of sorrow that I am so little worthy of a fond parent's hopes and prayers and tears.

TO THE SAME.

June 17, 1835.

I suppose it is only by means of the imagination that we form any notion, at least any conception, of God, of the sublime, of the beautiful, the perfect. I do not mean mere fancy, which only presents us cold and lifeless pictures of things once seen, and combines them in unreal positions, but that power which acts *within*, *im-ago*, in-forms; which embodies our abstract notions, and gives them shapes, hues, and beauty, till they burn. . . .

When I was a boy I had always a world of my own, an ideal creation, where I could roam and luxuriate at random. Many a time have I strayed from the right path and gone far beyond my stopping-place, while I was brooding over some scheme not yet accomplished. How many times has my plough run upon a rock while I was expounding law, making speeches in the senate, or astonishing men with a display of intellectual power, fitly put forth, in my imaginary Utopia. . . .

It is delightful now to imagine myself a minister, to recount the duties of the station, and consider all the ways of performing them, and forefeel the glorious satisfaction of seeing God's work prosper in my hand. I turn to a home—to a home of beauty, of affection, of love! To a home where all noble feelings are cherished, and whence all jarring interests and strife are excluded. Calamities may fall upon that home; they come upon all men—each country has its own storms. But if it is built on the rock of holy affection, *it will stand:* the floods may pass over it—they can never shake its fixt foundation.

A great deal of his time in the school was spent upon contributions for the *Scriptural Interpreter*. This little magazine was commenced by Ezra Stiles Gannett in 1831. It had reached the middle of the fifth volume, in 1835, when ill-health compelled Mr. Gannett entirely to relinquish the supervision of it, and it fell into the hands of three divinity students, William Silsbee, George E. Ellis, and Mr. Parker. It was edited by them to the close of its publication in 1836, and the greater part of each number was also prepared by them. It was a little in advance of the average Unitarianism of the time on the questions of Messianic Prophecy, and of the Pentateuch, and gave the views of De Wette, Eichhorn, Astruc, and others. The subjects of miracles and inspiration were hardly yet deployed upon the field. It was only occasionally denied that the facts of miracles lent any authority to the truths of Christianity. The controversy upon the Trinity and the Atonement had subsided, and discussions upon the element of Divinity in Christ had not commenced. The Unitarians had now their position, and were recognized in a sulky fashion. The acrimony of the contest with Calvinism broke out less frequently in the religious newspapers of the day. In carrying their point, the Unitarians had gradually absorbed a great deal of the wealth, talent and influence in New England. Leading men professed the liberal faith. The old protesting impulse grew languid with this achievement of respectability. A good many generous and indignant things which the flame of battle had nourished in their minds began to fade out of the recollection. Instinctively they commenced to fortify their position as the offensive warfare slackened, and both parties stood narrowly watching each other. Decorum, regard for opinion, the habits of an established sect began to set in. A desire to be recognized as a truly Conservative and religious body, with positive faith enough left to serve the soul in living and dying, to serve education and the state, to refute practically the grave objection that they were upsetting the Bible and society with their negative criticism, prevailed so strongly that vigorous investigation nearly ceased. Tentative speculation was undertaken by the young men with little positive encouragement. They had only the advantage of a negative good-nature, which disappeared with the first serious alarm. "Whither is this tending?" and, "What will the orthodox say?" are questions which in plain language indicated the general mood. It was not so expressed, and perhaps would not be so acknowledged, but it received during the next fifteen years a good many instinctive confirmations. Thrift, housekeeping and civic propriety succeeded to adventurous exploring. After getting through swamps of Trinity and Vicarious Sacrifice in dashing style, just as the clear outlook dawned at the end of the paths cut through the matted undergrowth, and the blue lines beyond piqued the mind to gain their height and freedom, the Unitarians paused, dropped axe, rifle, and the ranging glass, and settled the flat produce-growing prairie. They have tried to deter their young men from pressing forward to penetrate the distant bold ranges, entreating them not to compromise the settlement and draw the attack of savages, and reminding them of the perils of the vast drear interval. There was a kind of sense in insisting upon content with the gently rolling fertility which they had discovered, and upon which they had stopped to plant, but this was not the highest kind of sense ; for the original squatters are sadly crowded now, and many of their young men are scattered, digging wells along a solitary trail, around which one day men and women shall gratefully cluster, and opening the green valleys where the mountain cedars stand.

The following anonymous contribution to the literature of Protestantism, shows how early the Unitarians betrayed this tendency for comfort :—

TO MESSRS. ELLIS, PARKER, AND SILSBEE, EDITORS " INTERPRETER."

April 20, 1836.

I read, in the last number of the *Scriptural Interpreter*, the article on the 52nd chapter of Isaiah, and with unmingled surprise and horror. What could possess you ? What is the object of the theologians at Cambridge ? Are they determined to break down the prophecies, and make our blessed Saviour and his Apostles impostors and liars ? Cannot our doctrines be sustained in any other way ? Must the pious Christian be compelled to give up one passage after another, one book after another, one prophecy after another, until he has nothing left to stand upon but what is in common with the Deist ? Where is it all to end ? Tell us, I beseech you, that we may quit, if necessary, the ship before it is too late ; before we have struck upon the last rock which the vessel of our faith will bear ?

This first-class passenger, so suddenly aroused, trotting up and down the quarter-deck in a minimum of clothes, with wringing hands and frantic glances, conjures the captain to alter his course, and then disappears down the companion-way for ever, thus :—

Pause then, I beseech you, before it is too late. I am a well-wisher to your work. I have always been a subscriber. I am one of the household of your faith. But another such a blow and I must quit all I value ; my religious faith above all things else. I cannot part with it. To escape, therefore, shipwreck, I must jump overboard before the last plank is taken away. And not I alone. Hundreds must do the same ; they will not bear to have the sacred records of their faith frittered all away, though it may be in a style a little more refined than that of Paine, but, nevertheless, resulting in consequences which are just the same. Mr. Noyes strikes a blow and alarms a sect. Mr. Peabody recovers the ground for a moment, by holding on to a few passages. The *Interpreter* follows to destroy one of the most essential of these few. The end cannot be far off. And then, the imposture of the New Testament and its authors will be the completion of the dreadful work.

A SUBSCRIBER.

Mr. Parker went forward, but with great deliberation ; his papers in the *Interpreter* acquiesce in the average Unitarianism ; they neither vigorously sustain nor oppose it. His understanding began to grow critical, and his intuitional beliefs looked through the accepted doctrines, but slowly at first, and not with one great gaze.

Here is a sentence from an article on the " Alleged Mistakes of the Apostles " :—

It may be urged, that even admitting they were thus mistaken, no important conclusion follows from the fact ; since supernatural instruction upon this subject was not necessary to the propagation of the Christian religion, and of course they had received no divine authority to speak on the subject. But it does appear important ; for had Paul preached to the Thessalonians, for example, that the world would soon perish—as some maintain he did—and years passed away without any approach to a fulfilment of his prediction, they must have lost confidence in his teachings. And we ourselves could scarcely place the same unbounded trust in his other doctrines.

This is the ordinary opinion, which grew into great vehemence when Mr. Parker afterwards assailed it—that if the credibility of one portion of the Scriptures be invalidated, the authority of the whole is weakened, and that if you begin to doubt you know not when to stop. Better answers to his own original fallacy can be found nowhere than in the passages of his later writings, which maintain that a true thing has the only conservative authority, which it derives from its necessary intuitive character, and that truth only is worth preserving. This is a legitimate Unitarian doctrine, but the squatters were angry when the young men ran off with the dangerous element to blow up with it fresh obstacles in the wilderness. It was very useful in the Trinitarian morass, but should be kept shut up in magazines after the country is settled.

The best thing which he wrote for the *Interpreter* was an analysis of the Laws of Moses, extending through several numbers, all remarkable for their clear and exhaustive arrangement. His notes and authorities show, of course, a great range of reading in various languages ; but it is already becoming organized by the awakening thought. Classics, commentators, travellers, Talmudic lore, lend learning and illustration ; but without parade, and never without an object. It was a very handsome piece of work for a divinity student. A more compact manual of all the details of the Mosaic law cannot be found to-day.

But it is noticeable also as betraying occasionally the transition of his mind from the ordinary interpretation of the vindictive passages of the Old Testament to his later view. Here is a passage to show it:—

Some critics think it no grave heresy to deny that the laws which command the entire extirpation of the Canaanites were inspired. They think themselves safe in referring such statutes to the difficulty of the emergency and the hardness of men's hearts, rather than to the good sense of Moses; and still less do they attribute them to the counsels of a God of love. They think, too, that such interpreters as ascribe all these *sanguinary laws* to the inspiration of the Almighty "take more upon their shoulders than Atlas could bear." They admit the inspiration of Moses, but do not suppose *every word of the law* of divine origin. We know that many of the particular statutes had no such sanction expressed. They think, too, that the Oriental custom of ascribing all remarkable events, wonderful appearances, and striking thoughts to the immediate action of God, explains the *alleged* command of the Almighty. The religion of Moses, say they, was divine; but he was left to make use of such means as he saw fit to govern the chosen people, and to bring them to the Land of Promise. When ordinary resources failed, miraculous assistance was afforded. The *position* of Moses, and not his *religion*, is to be held accountable for those edicts apparently so sanguinary.

Here he cites authorities, and continues,—

How far the above remarks are worthy of notice others will judge; but it must be remembered, the nations to be extirpated were exceedingly vicious and corrupt, and if suffered to remain, would, doubtless, have led away the Jews from their better faith. If nations are by the Divine permission visited with earthquakes and pestilences, why may not the sword be employed for similar purposes?

Both the confusion and the direction of thought in this passage are interesting. The good sense of Moses is quite sufficient to account for his policy towards the neighbouring tribes, and for the distinction which he made between dangerous and indifferent neighbours; yet it was so important that the dangerous ones should be reduced, that the necessity might rank with those evils of the physical world which depend upon Providence itself, and might be therefore divinely decreed.

But his intuitive conviction that Infinite Love cannot send to man decrees subversive of itself, and that the Christian spirit outgrows the cruelty of the Old Testament, soon began to fill his mind with abhorrence for the very phrases which attribute an exterminating message to the Lord. What just contempt he had for the ordinary interpretation which made a spirit of love responsible for old Jewish vindictiveness, and what ridicule for the doctrine which tries to escape that imputation by supposing that God was hard because men's hearts were ; that, at least, He had no alternative but to send them the revengeful messages they desired to hear.   Would anybody accept such a plea made by any abomination in favour of itself ?   No pretext of piety in making it, sincere or fraudulent, would shelter any bad passion from the hatred of our unbiassed honesty; and yet no sooner does it seem to be sanctioned by the name of Moses, and the claim to inspiration of a book, than ingenuity is exhausted to defend it, and Mr. Parker credited with a motive hostile to religion.

He was, however, slow to clear his feeling of the Divine Perfection from these dishonourable imputations, that it might become for him a reliable test of theology and practice.   It was very effective in his hands when he attacked the scriptural authority for slavery and slave-catching.   Anti-slavery orthodox men were hampered by the necessity of supposing that in old times God inspired ignorance with ignorance, and inhumanity with inhumanity, the quality of the Divine Mind being unable to transcend the moral status of the race.   A book places certain old and new iniquities under divine sanction : it would seem as if the alternative were to accept the iniquity or to deny the sanction.   Not at all ; God was merely accommodating himself to geographical and historical exigencies !   Mr. Parker shows that neither morals nor religion were saved by such a subterfuge of criticism, that they were rather put in greater danger than before, because the slaveholder was left at liberty to appeal to the traditional sanction while pleading the exigencies of his position. Mr. Parker knocked the sanction away, with unsparing strokes ; what health and liberty they released to sit in judgment on the great sin, and what a priceless advantage he thus won in dealing with it !   When he redeemed the books of the Old Testament from their critical fetters, and raised them to the simple dignity of being treated for the sake of what truth they might contain, their truth of fact and of human nature, he redeemed also religion from her bondage to political and commercial wickedness. The facts of the past and the facts of the present were cited at the bar of morality and common-sense.

Who then, were he now living, could wield with greater effect the sublime prophetic denunciations of the wicked, the Psalms which call upon God to stand at the right hand of the lovers of justice, and to scatter its enemies ?   Who would have put the chapters of ancient indignation closer than he to the great conspiracy of iniquity against which he, too, prophesied with language as sombre, as vehement, as wrathfully righteous as any page of the Old Testament affords ?   Who could more consistently thunder the old texts against the modern villainy, than he who had faithfully denied that any text could sanction, at any epoch of history, a single crime ?   He could all the more powerfully quote the justice of God against the injustice of man, because he had always scorned to make either God's love or justice seem to suggest to man one barbarous statute, or to inspire one crime of history.   Would that he lived ! to summon the old haters of iniquity to his side, that they might help him hurl the verdict of the past against the blasphemy of the present, which quotes a " Thus saith the Lord " against the Lord himself.

This he might have done, not, however, from any defection of his own.   He was fully competent to upbraid and prophesy, and needed not to borrow a single Hebrew phrase to hold his new sense of the anguish which waits upon national iniquities.

The doctrine that the moral intuition is the critic of the morality of past and present history, in books and actions, is another genuine Unitarian doctrine.   It was well applied to the moral aspects of the dogma of the Atonement, and our instinctive sense of justice and humanity was urged against its reputed scriptural authority.   But it has been applied but feebly in other directions, in the interpretation of the Old and New Testaments. There has been instead, a tendency to take refuge in doctrines of accommodation and the second sense.   The Universalists alone, as a sect, boldly put it beneath the texts which affirm eternal damnation, to dislodge them from their seats.

Mr. Parker began to write for the *Interpreter* in 1835, and wrote in all nearly forty articles.   In translating " Astruc's Conjectures upon Genesis," he hopes that it will not create any *ausschreien* (outcry) ; for the editors remembered that they had been rather sharply rebuked by somebody who had squatted very early, for their latitudinarianism on the subject of Messianic Prophecy.   Now, to-day, there is a retreating party, not content even to be settled, but who have one foot in the old evangelic

7

bog, looking about for prophecies and types, and signs, or hoping that at least some liturgy may peep.

I am in a good deal of doubt upon the subject of the prophecies relating to the Messiah. Sometimes I doubt altogether that he was ever prophesied of distinctly, with sole reference to Jesus of Nazareth. Indeed, that any inspired prophecy was ever uttered concerning him.

I do not doubt that Jesus was a man " sent from God," and endowed with power from on high, that he taught the truth and worked miracles, but that he was the subject of inspired prophecy I very much doubt.

He then proceeds to give an explanation of the allusions to prophecy in the New Testament, and adds :

I know the above would appear like blasphemy to many divines, but I must stand by my own Master, not by another *man*. My confidence in the divinity of Christ's character, of the truth and sufficiency of his doctrine, depends not at all upon prophecies, or visions, or dreams.

The miracles have little interest for him, and little value. But he takes them for granted :

Mr. Dewey gave us the Dudleian lecture this year. It was the best, perhaps, I have ever heard, though upon the least interesting part of the Evidences of Revealed Religion, viz., Miracles. He removed the presumption against them. The objections were not only met, but overturned.

Ah, me! what an infinite distance between me and such men! But what of that? My little light may still burn on.

Mark, at the same time, the gathering boldness of his mind as revealed by these extracts :

Jonathan Mayhew's discourses show a profound and bold thinker, one who feared not the truth. Some call such men rash ; but who dares say that the man who will adhere to God's truth is rash, and who will deny the presumption of one who dares depart from it ?

And here is the result of a call upon one of the Professors :

He certainly is a very urbane man, and very mild and gentlemanlike in all his deportment; but a bigot in his opinions. All the Germans are " raw " in his opinion. German scholars are *not* accurate. They make good dictionaries and grammars, which are so large that but few can use them. They are " naturally unfitted for metaphysics, and their language still more so." Schleiermacher, he supposes, was a " Pantheist," who did not believe the immortality of the soul; at least, not any *personal* immortality, only a re-absorption of the finite into the infinite. "He gave up all that renders Christianity valuable and its promises precious." His doctrines were the same with Spinoza. He said I was happy in never having read the book. He acknowledged that Schleiermacher's contemporaries did not regard him in this light.

And the next day he calls upon an eminent Doctor of Divinity, who was settled in Boston :

He found fault with my article in the *Interpreter*, upon "Servant of God." Inconsistently, as I think. He said he was sorry to see it.

Thus he went on slowly, but in perfect freedom, and never biassed by the suspicious criticism of narrow men. It was not so easy then as now for a young divinity-student to keep at arm's length the traditional authority of Boston and its neighbourhood.

A good many books on Gnosticism were read this term, and some volumes of Kant, De Wette, Ammon's " Fortbildung," * &c.; the passages which he quotes are characteristic of his developing condition. Verse-making does not slacken either— " To Sleep," " To the Logos," " Reflections at Midnight," " Spring," " To a little Flower," " To Lydia in Absence." Let the following suffice, entitled " Evening : "—

> How sweetly from the western sky,
>   Day's lingering colours fade :
> How changing features softly vie—
>   Shade deepening into shade !
>
> How softly comes the grateful calm
>   Which mellow evening brings ;
> The sweets of flowers, the breath of balm,
>   Float on the Zephyr's wings !
>
> How soft that wandering cloud appears,
>   As the last tinge of day
> Crimsons the peak it proudly rears,
>   Then slowly dies away !
>
> Now stars come forth, and one by one,
>   In the broad field of night,
> Who veiled their face before the sun,
>   Now pour emboldened light.
>
> Oh, night and stars ! your voice I hear
>   Swell round the listening pole :
> Your hymns are praises, loud and clear,—
>   Are music to my soul.
>
> Sing on, sing on, celestial band,
>   Till earth repeats your lays,
> Till the wide sea, the sky, the land,
>   Shall celebrate His praise !

* He translated the whole of Ammon's " Formation of Christianity," and found it serviceable in preparing De Wette's Introduction. But the book itself is of little value now. It was an attempt to make Reason and History account for orthodox doctrines, and was neither rational nor evangelical.

TO MISS CABOT.

Jan. 25, 1836.

Now, too, I fear,—yes, I *know*,—that you are quite too fearful of my *over*-studying. Now I tell you that I know best about these matters, and that my conscience would as little permit me to *study* too much as to *drink* too much. I am in no more danger of one of these vices than of the other: so I pray for the future you would rather urge me to study than dissuade me from it. I oftener *eat* too much than study too much. Reproach this sin as much as you please. . . . .

You have none of those stormy, violent passions that sweep, tornado-like, through my heart. . . . So I speak truth when I repeat my own unworthiness.

The month of April of this year was spent in a journey to the South, as far as Washington.

TO THE SAME.

April 13.

In the Senate, Mr. King spoke upon the bill "For Preventing the Circulation of Incendiary Papers," of course it applied only to the abolition papers. Mr. K. is a tall thin gentleman, with a long sharp Roman nose, a high but receding forehead, large black eyebrows, and a pair of keen, wicked, black eyes. Withal there is a sort of sly defiance written upon his face. I did not like his speaking much. He ranted, and has a bad voice. He implicated Mr. Calhoun, who replied to-day.

The bill alluded to was one introduced by a select committee, to whom so much of President Jackson's message as related to the transmission by mail of incendiary documents had been referred. It "subjected to penalties any postmaster who should knowingly receive and put into the mail any publication or picture touching the subject of slavery, to go into any state or territory in which the circulation of such publication or picture should be forbid by the State laws." The bill was eventually rejected.

Upon that committee was Mr. King, of Georgia, who dissented to certain portions of the bill and report after they had been brought in, and charged Mr. Calhoun with entertaining principles inconsistent with the preservation of the Union, and that he was, in fact, only striving to make a grave point of the incendiary documents in the hope to reach a dissolution of the Union. Mr. King, of Alabama, who opposed the motion to refer, was also sharply treated by Mr. Calhoun; but Mr. Parker alludes to the Georgian.

As it was expected Mr. Calhoun would reply to-day, all were anxious to get seats in the Senate gallery. I took mine half an hour before the session commenced, and found a gentleman who pointed out to me the men of distinction as they came in and strolled about, talking to one another, or writing at their desks. Mr. Calhoun came in early, and you could see from the thoughtful, restless expression of his fine face that he was meditating something. He kept aloof from almost all, and seemed lost in thought. About half-past one an opportunity offered for his reply. The whole chamber was hushed when he arose and announced his intention. There was an eager bending forward in the galleries to hear him. He began by lashing Mr. King, who had spoken of him the day before. He treated him with the most complete politeness, and yet with a severity of sarcasm which made Mr. King writhe in his seat and gnaw his lip. I could watch the changing expression of his countenance, now ashy, and now deadly pale.

I will tell you more of this when we see one another, and of many other speechifiers.

I saw the " little magician " too ; of course none can mistake his wily features. He glided about before the opening of the debate, clapping men upon the shoulders and shaking their hands. He looks very artful and naughty. I should fear that man.

Clay walks about in a dignified manner; he is tall and homely, as I think. I see no features of the great man upon him.

Plenty of negroes, of course, one sees here. I saw in the paper of to-day an advertisement offering cash for 700 negroes of both sexes. That sounds harsh to Northern ears. They are a queer set, these negroes; some of them are very merry, dancing and capering about on the sidewalk as if they had nought to do but dance. I saw two negro lovers walking arm-in-arm, cooing and billing, as if they could not restrain their joy in one another's presence. Why should *colour* prevent them ?

Before May he was at home again, and at work.

TO THE SAME.

Indeed I have felt *blue*, terribly blue, all the week. I never speculate on the causes of such chilling damps that come over the soul, like a frost in July, blasting all that the sunshine has beautified. It is enough to *bear* them without going about to analyse the nature of the complaint, and decide upon the exact quantity which was caused by an east wind, and tell how much is physical, and how much mental.

My muse has been kept upon " thin potations " and meagre diet so long that she refuses to soar to-night, otherwise she had led you such a long and lofty flight as would have quite worn down all your celestial vigour. . . .

My Aonian rill is only that very little trouting brook we have so often admired, and it is far prettier than the Helicon of old.

Here are some extracts from the journal :—

Sunday, May 8.—Preached for the last time in the chapel, once more, and all is over for school exercises ; then I hope to preach to real live men and women.

Monday, July 4.—Last night I preached *publicly* in Mr. Newell's church. This is the first time in my life that I have preached to a real *live* audience. I felt much embarrassed, though perhaps it did not show forth. Lydia, my own Lydia, and her aunt came over with me. I was less pleased with myself than they were with me. To say the truth, I did not feel the sermon so much as I usually do, for the hour usually spent in preparing for the service was consumed in " doing the agreeable," and so I did not get into the sermon so much as commonly.

May God in his mercy grant me power to improve in this holy duty. May I grow from strength to strength, increasing continually in godliness and wisdom, and thus show forth pure and holy Christianity in my life, no less than in my teachings. Oh, God, wilt thou help me to become more pure in heart, more holy and better able to restrain all impetuous desires and unholy passions ; may I "put down every high thing " that would exalt itself against the perfect law of God. Help me in the intercourse of life to discharge my duties with a more Christianlike fidelity; to love Thee the more, and those with whom I am to deal !

He had been long preparing himself for the " History of Gnosticism," which was his subject for Visitation Day. " This was a 'day of trembling,' of sad uneasiness to most of us, a day of perplexity to all."

His first sermons after graduating were preached, July 24, in the meeting-house at Watertown ; in the morning, from Matt. vi. 33, and in the afternoon, xxii. 37.

This old meeting-house acquired its first distinction in the Revolution, when it was selected as a safe place for the sittings of the Provincial Congress. The second Congress met there on the 22nd of April, 1775. After John Hancock had been chosen delegate to the Continental Congress, Joseph Warren was the presiding officer. The third and last Provincial Congress assembled in Watertown on the 31st of May. Warren was President,* and Samuel Freeman, secretary. The General Court, which succeeded the Congress, also met in Watertown, on the 26th of July, and its sessions were prolonged till the 9th of November, 1776, when it adjourned to the State House in Boston. The Council of the General Court used to hold its sittings in the old house, nearly opposite, which is now occupied by Mr. W. Russell. Here, also, it is said that a printing-press was for some time concealed. I know not whether it was the

---

* The house where Warren boarded at this time is the one across the bridge now occupied by Mr. Robinson. Here he breakfasted on the morning of the 17th of June, and before setting out for the field urged the ladies to spend the forenoon in making lint. Mounting his horse he rode slowly down towards the bridge, paused, then, galloping back to the door, with kisses bade them all again farewell.

one with which Edes escaped from Boston to Watertown, and upon which he printed his *Boston Gazette and Country Journal*, from June 5th, 1775, to October 28th, 1776.

The meeting-house was built in 1755. It stood upon land at the corner of Common and Mount Auburn Streets, surrounded by a graveyard, which now usurps the site of the church ; and the old parishioners sleep where they only nodded before. It was one of the old-fashioned square structures, called lanterns, popularly, from the two rows of windows which went all round it. In a high wind, the house was filled with the chattering of the sashes which time had loosened ; so that the clergyman, preaching in the late autumn upon the mortality of man, was never quite sure whose voice turned the drowsy ears to seasonable thoughts. Against one side rose a tower, surmounted by an open belfry, which dwindled into a thin spire. The ancient cockerel, which promised fair to Warren as he last rode by, is newly gilded, and challenges the weather still on the steeple of the Methodist church. Within, the old house had a high white-pine pulpit in the centre of one side, with a pen in front to enclose the communion table. When a Sunday-school was formed, the library was deposited in a cupboard under the pulpit. Overhead was the sounding-board, which once gathered Langdon's sermons, and Hancock's and Warren's treasonable talk. Great deep galleries ran round three sides of the house, places of mystery and sombre imaginings to the little ones, who seldom even trooped into their shadows, much less alone. Very venturous boys, however, such as play truant at school or run away to sea, had been up to gaze upon the bell.

In the choir, Thomas Larned played the double bass, and William Harrington the violoncello, when Theodore gave out his first hymns ; there was also a a clarionet, and Deacon Bailey sang bass. The body of the church was filled with highbacked pews, whose seats were lifted during prayer, and clattered down with the amen. My informant says that it was a source of great grief to him that his father's pew-seats would'nt slam. All the other boys *amened* in concert.

The meeting-house was little changed from its revolutionary aspect, excepting that a one-story addition had been made to it, to accommodate the growth of the parish, which was somewhat flippantly styled "The Kitchen." Here Theodore preached in the forenoon upon the "Necessity of a Heavenly Life," and in the afternoon upon " Religion, a Principle and Sentiment." He was not so flowery as his old friends anticipated, but more simple and direct.

These two sermons closed a fortnight of entire repose, spent in the society of the one he loved best.   At the end of that time, however, he suddenly musters together; accuses himself of indolence, and almost depreciates the joy from which he must break away.

I am not so cold-hearted as to wander among the gardens of the graces with no sense that riots, and no soul that thrills. Nay, my heart has been warmed by the sweetest, I had almost said, the noblest impulses ; but it does not advance me in the journey of life as I would wish to move. It does not allow my soul to unfold its wings in this fledging-place and trial-ground, to prepare for the lofty and dangerous flight when it must "sail with uplift wing," against tempest and storm. I have sterner deeds to *do*.   Greater dangers to *dare*.   *I must be about my work.*

In this prophetic mood he went forth to preach.

HOUSE OF MRS. BROAD, AND SCHOOL-HOUSE.

THE VILLAGE MEETING-HOUSE, SPRING STREET, WEST ROXBURY.

CHAPTER V.

A Candidate—1836–37—Marriage—Settlement at West Roxbury—Neighbours and Studies—Choice Friends—Dr. Channing—Mr. Emerson's Discourse, 1838—Strauss —Come-Outers—Doubts about Physical and Moral Evil—Thoughts and Queries— 1840.

BUT an itinerant vendor of the gospel, commonly called a candidate, is not a beautiful or heroic personage. Men hang his presageful heart on the hooks of their parochial steelyards, and narrowly scrutinize the figures. He pockets his presage, and it makes no difference in the weight.

In July Mr. Parker received an invitation to preach for four weeks at Barnstable. He started in the packet-schooner *Sappho*, and had his first marine experience.

Only one cabin, which was to serve as lodgment and lounging-room for the evening and night for more than twenty men and women. The ladies went down about half-past eight, for it was cold. Soon after, at nine, I descended, almost perpendicularly. They had gotten into their several berths, and were there lying with the curtains undrawn. I sat rather awkwardly, and chatted and laughed with them, who did not seem at all disturbed by the peculiarity of the scene. By-and-bye I, too, crept into a crib, one lady above me, another at my head, and a third at my feet.

All night long there was a noise; some getting up, and others getting down; roisterous fellows carousing, children crying, *vagitus et ingens*, and mothers attempting to quiet them. Sleep went up the hatchway, but did not find good quarters, and so came in with me, and staid till nearly five A.M.

On arriving he repaired to Mrs. Whitman's boarding-house.

TO MISS CABOT.

August 6, 1836.

We have three boarders besides myself, viz.: Mr. Drew, the school-master—*i. e.* he keeps a private academy; Mr. Brown, who keeps the store and post-office opposite; and "Squire Reed," cousin of the Hon. John Reed. He is Register of Probate, and several other things; besides, he is a good, pleasant companion, and keeps the table alive. He is about forty-five or fifty;—the others are young men. After each meal they retire to one of their rooms, and sit and smoke pipes in a right friendly and old-fashioned manner for about half an hour. This takes place regularly after each meal. It amuses me very much, for I usually join them in the conversation, though at the pipe I reluct. . . . .

I trust you will not hang the leaden collar of "be careful and not do too much," about my neck.

At Barnstable he found out the most notable people, made their acquaintance, and drew them into conversation. This he never failed to do in every new place, to satisfy his thirst for facts of every description. And he afterwards used to keep lists of people worth knowing in the various towns where he lectured, and whose acquaintance he meant to cultivate. The persons thus selected were intelligent in some calling, or attractive by moral and spiritual characteristics. He was always particularly drawn towards persons of great amiability and high conscience. If they were shrewd and full of facts, so much the better; but he seemed to love the artless man of a noble natural growth. For the society of such, he would relinquish that of scholars and cultivated men. In his list of favourites the greater number are the names of happy, unpretending, healthy people, with an unspoiled sense of right and wrong.

TO MISS CABOT.

August 10, 1836.

I felt somewhat awkward at first, as you may suppose, but I remembered the command, "Now *show what ye be*," and made an effort. I never felt in better spirits for speaking, and not only delivered the written Word, but added much that was better and more *reaching* extemporaneously. . . . .

I have been busy. I have read almost all my books—I had about a dozen—and have written two sermons. The air of the place braces one's whole soul. I could devour a whole library in a week. I think I should write three new sermons a week all the time I am here, but I have only enough of my favourite paper for two more.

TO THE SAME.

August 14, 1836.

It seems to me as if my mind had grown a-pace in some departments since I came here. I hoped it would. It seems to me I can feel a sort mental *crystallization* taking place within me, which brings order out of chaos. I hope I am not self-deceived in this regard.

TO THE SAME.

August 22, 1836.

Saturday is one of no little anxiety with me, and I am somewhat given to "jactations" on that night. This I hope to overcome, and finally to lie as stark and stiff in bed of a Saturday night as a Cape Cod fisherman . . . . .

The sermon was a new one: the greatness of Christ's character, its sources and its uses. I never felt one of *my* sermons more, nor was ever in a happier mood for delivery. Everything went right, and some of the least bad parts of the discourse were extemporaneous.

Nobody ever speaks to me about the sermons; they all have a proper delicacy about that, which is a little uncommon, too, among such people, perhaps. But to-day Mrs. Whitman said that Mr. Reed, our fellow-boarder, you know, said it was "the greatest sermon he ever heard."

This was a busy Sunday; with two funerals, a Sunday-school, two services, a visit to the sick, and calls in the evening.

This closed the labours of the day, being the seventh public prayer I had made. You may suppose I felt no little fatigue after such a variety of emotions in a single day. I went to bed quite early, but I "gat" as little sleep as King David did heat in his old age. But this morning I feel like a giant refreshed by the slumber of ages, and am gay as a lark.

TO THE SAME.

August 23, 1836.

You must tell your aunt that if I were to stay a thousand years I should not outlast that vile tremor; it is an infirmity that will cling to me. I can no more help it than a lady can keep from fainting in a crowd. Nor again do I wish entirely to avoid it, as it is a source of earnest feeling, and so of strength, for it never lets memory slip or the tongue falter.

Here is a difficulty which the style of his earlier culture helped him to overcome

TO W. SILSBEE.

Barnstable, August 21, 1836.

How disqualified we are for contact with the real world I felt when first shown a real live man ; and when brought to speak with him I was utterly at a stand, and scarcely knew what to say. Thus, indeed, we come away from our three years' studies at Divinity College, with some little knowledge of science, literature, philology ; peradventure some small inklings of theology and metaphysics,—nay, even a little knowledge of the science of things in general (*allerlei - Wissenschaft*), and with beards on our chins, but with no other marks of manhood. Now, I maintain that, besides a great deal of knowledge, one needs as much skill to make it of any use to him. *Allerlei-Kunst*, then, we need to set off our *allerlei - Wissenschaft*.

This art of things in general I hope I have made some little advances in since I came to Barnstable. Indeed, it seems to me I have *grown* in this regard, so that I can really talk to men as if I were also a man, and not a student merely. A mere student is a sort of *homunculus*, an animal not treated by Pliny, except incidentally, when he speaketh of the war they once carried on against their arch-enemies, the cranes.

TO THE SAME.

I have been called to officiate at three funerals, and it was a solemn matter. I wept,—not so much, perhaps, as the mourners, but as heartily—from very sorrow. Who could see so many weep and not join them in such a time ? I could not help it. . . . .

I know not where I shall go after the next Sabbath. I can stay here, but—*haud ego*. Touching the place and the people, I like both very much, and hate to leave them, for I " would not willingly lose sight of a departing cloud ; " but you know I have not seen *my Skyborn* these near three weeks, a separation which very ill comports with my desires.

TO MR. FRANCIS.

Barnstable, 12 Nov., 1836.

MY DEAR SIR,—I received a letter from Miss Cabot just now, stating that you mentioned that Mr. Burton would like to have me supply his pulpit for a time. I should be exceedingly happy to serve, if by so doing I do not debar myself the opportunity of preaching elsewhere with a view to a *permanent* settlement. If I supply his pulpit, and do not preach there *all* the time, I can get those to take my place who will doubtless do much better than I *can*. I shall be exceedingly happy to come upon these conditions, and if you will have the goodness to inform him of it, you will much oblige me. I would have written him, and not have troubled you, but I am but little acquainted with him, and I have other matters to speak of with you.

Sundry of my friends wish me to settle at Spring Street Church, in Roxbury. What do you think of it? I suppose it is not regarded as a *desirable* parish by most men, but there are certain reasons which make me look towards it most favourably. I should like your opinion upon the matter, and I will come up to Watertown as soon as I leave B., and confer with you upon it. I am weary of "candidating;" it is not only a "weariness unto the flesh," but unto the spirit. Men go to church when a youngster is to *hold forth*, not to hear something *good*, but something *new*, and talk of the services at home, rather that he may be criticised than that themselves may be edified. So one cannot comfort himself with the knowledge that he does any good. Besides, the frequent change of place is bad to "mind, body, and estate." One cannot pursue quiet studies; he can scarcely grow in mind or in spirit when he is so frequently transplanted. I sometimes say, with the melancholy prophet, "Oh, that I had a lodging place of wayfaring men in the wilderness, that I might turn in thither and be refreshed!" When and where I shall find it I know not. If I am at R. I shall be near you and Mr. Stetson, and the College Library, to say nothing of other persons and things which will be within hail. I hope to give you that "labour of love" I have so long intended before the month is out, but I cannot determine with certainty. I am very much obliged to you for the present of your three sermons. I trust I shall read them with as much pleasure as I listened to them, and with still more profit, for they contain matter to be chewed upon. Please to give my respects to Mrs. F., and believe me, truly yours, THEO. PARKER.

1836, August 11.—Began to translate De Wette's "Einleitung" (Introduction to the Old Testament). I cannot tell what will be the result of this. I shall leave that for another time to determine. Meanwhile I will go quietly on translating it gradually as I wish, without interrupting important studies.

He read Schelling's lectures upon Academic Study, and pronounced them too ideal; "an ideal within his own subjectivity, which is an impossible real, and contains the elements of its own destruction, since it involves a contradiction."

He went to a Barnstable tea-gathering, where among various goodly people, was a pompous old sea-captain from Boston, who had retired with a great deal of money: "*haud decet mihi facere notas, non mei peculium est. Mehercle!*"

These are notes made after attending a Methodist camp-meeting at Eastham:

The women I noticed were always the most noisy. But I was much struck with the cool indifference of one young woman, who sat very quietly munching gingerbread, while all the process of "bringing in " was taking place around her.

I always noticed, too, that the least learned were the most violent—had most of the "Spirit of the Lord," as they said. This accounts for the low opinion of learning among them, and for the great power of Whitefield, who was all *passion* and *feeling*.

The uninterested apologetic tone of one remark is amusing, when we recollect what thunder shook the Music-Hall in after years :—

There was occasionally a touch upon slavery. Who wonders at it ?

He left Barnstable at the close of his engagement, trusting that they would find such a man as they needed, but doubting that he was that man. The parish in Northfield sent for him next. He spent there a part of October, and received an invitation to settle, but declined it. Then he returned to Barnstable for the month of November, and the good people proposed to give him a call, but he intercepted their intention,

Since it would involve an entire exclusion from books and literary society. Never do I expect to find so noble and generous and true-hearted a people. But others can labour there more effectually than I, to whom absence of books is no evil. There would be a general exclamation among my books if they are carried to the Cape, from the Reimkennar of Sweden to Saadi and Ferdousi. But still, did not I know that others are to be found who will be called upon to make no sacrifices in going thither, then would I hesitate not, but instantly plant myself among these noble men of the Cape, and live, and love, and labour there.

The death of his father occurred at this time.

TO MISS CABOT.

Nov. 10, 1836.

I received your letter, my dear Lydia, as I never fail to do, with unspeakable pleasure and satisfaction ; but if the outside gave me pleasure, and the inside told me what I had long expected, yet I cannot deny that the intelligence found me unprepared. I had fondly put off the day of his departure, and when the event was told me, my sorrow was tenfold greater than I had anticipated.

After I read your letter, and sat silent and lonely by my own fire, I could almost see his fathers of other days, the wife of his youth, and his children and long-separated friends pressing gloriously around him to take him once more to their hearts. I lament not for him ; he has no sigh to stifle, no tear to wipe away. But how *can* I, who have been cradled in his arms, fed by his hands, blessed by his prayers, and moulded by his tender care, how can I forbear lamenting now he is gone ?

But enough of this. He is gone. Let *us* say no more about it; and now I entreat you to say nothing upon that subject in your letters, nor when we meet. A thousand circumstances will bring it all up before me again and again; do not let us multiply them without need.

The valley of tears, if dwelt in, hath a poisonous influence upon the soul; but if only occasionally passed through, it is full of healing waters and fountains of strength.

A list of works, comprising 320 volumes, drawn up at the close of 1836, shows his reading for fourteen months. They are in various languages, and the best books on the subjects of which they treat.

In December he went to Salem to supply the pulpit of Dr. Flint, who was ill. He spent the time very pleasantly at the house of his classmate Silsbee; some dialogues of Plato were his reading, with various books for a meditated lecture upon Etymology. The fine lines which have often been quoted were written this winter.

> Jesus, there is no dearer name than thine,
> Which Time has blazoned on his mighty scroll;
> No wreaths nor garlands ever did entwine
> So fair a temple of so vast a soul.
> There every virtue set his triumph-seal;
> Wisdom, conjoined with strength and radiant grace,
> In a sweet copy Heaven to reveal,
> And stamp perfection on a mortal face;
> Once on the earth wert Thou, before men's eyes,
> That did not half Thy beauteous brightness see;
> E'en as the emmet does not read the skies,
> Nor our weak orbs look through immensity.

Among other books, the English State Trials were carefully studied.

Very soon the following questions are put down for consideration.

I. Sundry Questions in Theology.
1. What is the extent of known supernatural Revelation made to man?
2. What is the foundation of the authority of Jesus Christ?
3. What is the meaning of Faith in Old and New Testament.
4. How is Christ more a Saviour than Socrates?
5. Why did the world need a Saviour?
6. What has been his influence?
7. Is Christianity to be a universal Religion?
8. What is the foundation of Religion in Man—the Design of Miracles—the pretence of them in other Religions?

II. Questions in Scriptural Criticism and Exegesis.
    1. The authenticity of the beginning of the Gospels of Matthew and Luke—The Miraculous Conception.
    2. The Resurrection—why was the body of Christ raised?— why "carried up?" How is the resurrection of matter proof of the Immortality of Spirit? Is not the material Resurrection of the body of Jesus Christ unspiritualizing?

It is very evident that his conventional theology is about to receive a thorough over-hauling. But these questions were not disposed of in a day.

We find him preaching in Greenfield during February, 1837, after another visit to Northfield in January.

TO MISS CABOT.

Feb. 10, 1837.

The very air of Greenfield inspires me, although you see no traces thereof in the letter, and I feel more a man; the cool wind from the north braces the outer man, and the sight of mountains and great trees and wide meadows refreshes the inner man not a little.

Besides all this I have seen little things which encourage me, make me wiser if not better.

Walking the other day in the woods—*i.e.*, in a road which goes steeply through the woods—in the midst of the snow at the bottom of the steep hill, there was a little spring of water, clear as the sky above, and as unruffled, not frozen, though winter had set her seal stiffly upon everything around. Over this beautiful spring there arose a great oak, very old and "stern to look upon," one which had mocked at many winters. Now, this great oak claspèd a young hemlock tree with its arms, and seemed to hold it in shelter from all the rude blasts of time. The younger tree had evidently grown up under its protection, and now repaid its defender by looking kindly upon him when his own leaves had all fallen away. It was beauty in the arms of strength.

All this living scene was reflected in the little spring, which seemed to smile at the tenderness of these giant plants. One would walk about the streets of Boston a thousand years without meeting such a comforter as this. But in the country there is a tale in everything, and every little object in nature hath its beauty to please by, and its moral to instruct with. Indeed, the country is a great "system of divinity," while the city is but "a commercial dictionary," a "ready reckoner," or a "cook-book."

TO THE SAME.

Feb. 13.

You know I lamented the missing of Mr. Emerson's lectures, but a single walk along the banks of the Connecticut, or among the hills, or a moment's listening to the pine's soft music, have taught me more than Mr. Emerson and all the Boston Association of Ministers.

TO THE SAME.

Feb. 24.

You do not know how delighted I have been with my quiet stay in this beautiful place—apart from the absence of Miss Lydia. I have done more in the way of reading and writing and study than in the last two months before, to say nothing of the glorious walks and comfortable chattings I have had; for Mr. Davis kindly comes in almost every night, and sometimes stays till the witching time of twelve. Without him I should have died at least once a day. Paul says he did that, and the Apostle was not engaged and away from his lady. Mrs. D. is a sweet woman, and a sensible. I almost envy them their cup of connubial happiness, but *we* will have one soon, as generous and divinely tempered. I do not know anything in contemplation more delightful than this, that we may find some place where we may receive enough of this world's treasures; may labour in the most noble and divine of employments which man can conceive of, giving a loftier action to humanity; may exercise mutually the kindliest feelings of the heart, the intellect, and the soul, founding at the same time a family which shall bear up our name, know our virtues, reflect the sunshine of our hearts, and finish our work. Can you conceive anything more noble than this? I confess I cannot.

TO THE SAME.

Feb.

Only think that after a little bit of a courtship of some four years we are at length on the very brink of Matrimony! Within a span's length of the abyss! Without a parish too! Think of that! 520 dollars a year, may be—may be much less—to support a wife. Why, I intend to commence such a rigorous system of *sparing* that I shall never cross a *t* nor dot an *i*; for I'll save ink. I dreamed last night of being at a bookstore, and when the clerk showed me some book which I had long been seeking, and at a price most villainously cheap, " Oh, no," said I; " I shall *never* buy more books; at any rate, never so cheap. I *am a-going to be married!*" and down went the corners of my mouth till they touched my stock. ·But if soft words can win hard coin, if there is any money-getting virtue in a knowledge of some twenty tongues, any talent in my mind, or any magic in the most unshrinking labour, I will take care that a wife do not beggar the soul of the means of growth and nobleness. If I can find anything to do in the literary way which will get one coin, be it never so hard, so it conflict with no duty, I will put forth my might, be it little, be it much.

TO S. P. ANDREWS.

Greenfield, Feb. 15.

Sometimes, Samuel, I fear lest I have missed it capitally in becoming a minister; that as a lawyer, or in other departments of thought and action, I might have been more useful, and at the same time free from a certain restraining bond—invincible, but strong as fate—which convention has tied up every minister withal. I do not *even think* of deserting a ministry which would dignify angels, and has been honoured by the

8

Son of God himself. No: I never think of that; for I deem it writ down in my duty to preach the Gospel, come of it what will; and although some of my dearest expectations have already been disappointed, still I shall "bear up and steer, with upright wing, right onward, nor bate one jot of heart nor hope."

Yet sometimes the thought comes mightily upon me, "Thou hast mistaken thy calling!"

One sole thing encourages me, to wit, I know that one who keeps God's "Laws of the Spirit of Life," and puts forth his might manfully in obedience thereto, be his might never so little—be it less than mine even—he has for his friend and ally and co-worker the entire almightiness and perfect virtue of God. With such a co-adjutor it is nobler to be conquered, dragged at the wheels of the enemy, yea, trodden to dust by his followers, who shout aloud, "Great is Mammon of the Yankees!" than to engage in any other warfare.

Therefore shall I go on; consequences I have nothing to do with, they belong to God—to me belongs only duty. All that I have give I to the one cause.

He spent a great deal of time in Salem in the spring of 1837, occasionally preaching; there are very meagre records of conversations with superior people, some of whom became friends for life.

On the 20th of April his marriage took place. And on the 20th of May he finished translating De Wette's "Introduction," which was the least part of the labour that preceded the publication of that work.

I now intend to revise the work diligently, to add notes from various writers, and to append divers essays and dissertations.

He had preached several times at West Roxbury, and at Waltham, and received a call from both parishes. He was also sought from Concord and Leominster, as well as Greenfield. He was awhile irresolute which to accept, but finally returned a favourable answer to the call from West Roxbury, which he received on the 23rd of May.

His ordination took place on the 21st of June. Dr. Henry Ware, sen., attended as a delegate from the college chapel, John Quincy Adams was the delegate from Quincy, Dr. Francis delivered the sermon, Henry Ware, jun., made the ordaining prayer, Caleb Stetson delivered the charge, and George Ripley gave the right hand of fellowship. His classmate, John S. Dwight, wrote for this occasion an original hymn. In 1849, recalling his ordination, he writes:—

These men had some hopes of me, that I might prove an ornament and a pillar of the Church! Now they look on me as a destroyer and a foe! Yet certainly I have been diligent and laborious. If I could have looked forward twelve years, I should have trembled, and said, "Oh, Lord, send by another hand, not mine!" Henry Ware, in his ordaining prayer, after Dr. Francis had recommended study, prayed that I might be a preacher of righteousness—"may no fondness for peculiar studies ever divert him from doing Thy work." I hope it has been as he would. Surely I have not sought *ease*, or *fame*, or *wealth*. On many things I have disappointed myself—in some things a little surpassed. I expected rather to be a scholar than a reformer—I mean, I looked to books as my means of reform. I did mean to be a reformer.

In this quiet little parish, of about sixty families, the parochial demands upon the clergyman were easily met. He interested himself in town matters, and as a committee-man regularly visited all the schools. Still there was a good deal of time for books and the garden. The pleasant white house, about a mile from the church, stood close to the straggling village street, but the study looked out through trees upon flowers, vines, and garden-beds. Two fine tulip-trees stood before the windows. The land adjoined the beautiful grounds of Mr. George R. Russell, his parishioner and friend, with whom and whose family he found such refreshment and delight. And next, going up the hill, came the grounds of another good and faithful friend, Mr. Francis G. Shaw. Mr. Parker had a right of way over the pleasantly settled hill-side. The hedges defined, but did not divide the respective places of his friends. When jaded with the old folios, he never failed to find some one at his garden limit, in whose attachment his heart recovered strength and joy. It was a gentle life, with pure friendship to lighten labour and to lift the heavy moods which sometimes came sweeping across the sky.

The Russells used to have famous visitors, those bright, fair girls, with literary and philosophic rages, who were just blooming into transcendentalism, but better yet, into womanhood. They used to hold "Olympicks," over which Theodore jovially presided. Sometimes the celestial council met in a barn, where the fresh, fragrant hay, which he had just helped toss and gather, served for the divan. Here Günderode, Bettini, and Göthe, the "Latest form of Infidelity," Fourier, Emerson's last lecture, and all kosmic questions, were discussed. The poetry in the *Dial** was somewhat lightly treated, and the Orphic sayings duly venerated. It is suspected that verses, which never

---

* The first number of the *Dial* appeared in July, 1840.

got so far as the "twi-light" *Dial* on the way to the light, were read to the blonde council, while the new hay contested for freshness and pabular availability.

He had many a "long chaffer with the fine ladies" in the next house.

TO W. SILSBEE.

July 13, 1837.

You will like to know a little of my matters, no doubt. Well, cleverly am I settled. Our neighbours are pleasant. About fifty to sixty families in the parish—a hundred to a hundred and fifty worshippers. Sunday-school teachers' meeting at the house of the pastor once a fortnight, wife's class at the Sunday-school, pastoral visits made, schools attended, calls received, baptisms, funerals. Such are my out-of-door matters. Within I have plenty of pleasant employment; De Wette done, almost; reading Jacobi and old Henry More. The life of Apollonius Tyaneus has afforded me no little pleasure of late. I have read Bulwer's "Athens;" a good book, but with mistakes, methinks. I am studying ethics, such as De Wette (a pretty good book), Fichte, Coleridge, and Descartes. Spinoza I shall take soon as I get my copy. I have a new work of Ancillon. All his *melanges* have been republished, and two more volumes added, making a fine work. I borrowed Gesenius' "Lectures on the Old Testament" of Cunningham; they are manuscripts, but will be a treasure, I doubt not. I have been reading Ovid, whom I have in a capital edition, ten volumes octavo. Seneca (and I own him in ten, octavo) I shall read with the other moral writers. The "Iliad" is a part of almost every day's reading. I have engaged to translate Ammon's "Fortbildung des Christenthums," four volumes, octavo, in the course of time. So you see I have enough to keep an idle man busy.

We have a very pleasant house, garden, "men servants and maidens," a cow, horse, and *pig!* I'm as practical as Stebbins; buy and sell, dig, lend and borrow. "To this complexion must we come at last."

TO THE SAME.

Sept. 22.

Touching things carnal, I assure you I am more disturbed than I had ever anticipated. This is between you and me. Men of the *actual*, and their name is legion, have a very cheap sort of logic, amounting to this—" My way is perfectly right :" this is the first axiom, an undisputed truth, self-evident. Then cometh the second, viz., "All important things are comprised in the actual, which alone should engross our attention." This is the theory of these worthies. Now for the practice. They see other men doing different from themselves, so they condemn them under the first axiom. They find them thinking of other matters than potatoes and turnips and railroads, specie-currency and the manners of their next neighbour, to wit, thinking of God, of duty, nature, destiny, cause, consequence, the right, the beautiful, the good, and so they condemn these under axiom the second.

Then yearn their bowels of tender mercy, and they attempt to reform the thinkers, that is, to make their talk of turnips, &c., and, failing herein, they beset me, till flesh and blood cry out, like that of Abel, for vengeance. So goes it. I feel much of this harassing.

Yet, this apart, I am very pleasantly situated; the people good, quiet, sober, church-going; capital listeners, none better; so much so, that I tell my friends I think my parishioners are as much blessed in preaching as those of even Dr. Channing; for what is wanted in preaching they make up in listening, whereas the Doctor's people depend altogether upon him. . . . .

I believe, brother William, that no good word is ever spoken in vain. I may not see it grow, but what then? As Kepler said, if God could wait four thousand years for some one to see his laws, I may wait one hundred for men to understand my sayings. I preach abundant heresies, and they all go down, for the listeners do not know how heretical they are. I preach the worst of all things, Transcendentalism, the grand heresy itself, none calling me to account therefor, but men's faces looking like fires new stirred thereat.

Old studies go on, metaphysics, theology, criticism; all that used so much to delight and instruct us flourishes and grows apace in my new situation. Thoughts high as heaven, and profound as the centre of the earth, sometimes visit me in my loneliness. Then, too, the smiles of love cheer and encourage me.

You will come and stay a week with me, at the least. I have a prophet's chamber all ready for you. You must come and stay at least a week, and as much longer as you can make it agreeable; this I shall depend upon. Remember how I stayed with you at Salem—how much delighted I was. I shall never forget the day when we walked over to Beverley; that day, as to the thoughts revealed there, was one of the brightest of my life.

I have got lots of new books—upwards of one hundred Germans! Come and see. Some of them are old friends, others new—all sorts of creatures.

The polyglott library grew fast. So grew theologic misgivings, and a dull sense that his great capacity of work and of humanity must have more room.

During August he gets hold of Palæphatus, " περὶ Ἀπιστῶν " or " On Incredible Things." Palæphatus was probably an Alexandrine Rationalist, portions of whose book on the treatment of the Greek myths survive, in various editions, of which Fischer's is the best. He attempted historical interpretations of the stories of Cadmus, Lynceus, Niobe, &c., saying, for instance, that Lynceus, who saw through the ground, was a man who discovered beds and veins of metals; that Pegasus was a clipper-privateer, and Scylla also; that the King of Lerna had a fortified town called Hydra, which was defended by fifty bow-men: and so on. He was a Greek Paulus, and equally jejune; for he did not care to let the myths bring allegorical honey to his hive, but only to extract their sting of the incredible.   Mr. Parker's opinion after reading this, betrays a mind fast becoming decided in its direction.

How the priests must have exclaimed against the "impious" book in the day of its appearance.   Such books do good.   I wish some wise man would now write a book περί Απιστων, or "On Vulgar Errors," and show up the absurdity of certain things commonly believed, on the authority of old Jews.   To be plain, I mean the Old Testament miracles, prophecies, dreams, miraculous births, &c.

Now there needs but the natural and quite logical generalization which extends the incredible element over the New Testament also.

He reads Gabler, Paulus and Bauer, and the question is first presented in the form of application of the mythical system of exposition to the New Testament: myths, not yet in the sense of Strauss, but stories merely, as of the birth of Christ, the star, the angels, &c., invented by people to give a supernatural origin to a famous man.   The history of the Temptation is a myth of this description.

About this time he wrote the two sermons upon the historical, scientific and moral contradictions of the Bible, which he kept in his desk more than a year before he dared to preach them, taking advice of various lay and clerical friends, who seemed to agree with his doctrine, but to dread having it proclaimed.   In a sermon which he preached at West Roxbury, on going to Europe, he describes the predicament.

You will have all the clergy about your ears.   An old friend, and a clergyman of high reputation in the churches, asked me what peculiar and specific thing I was aiming at.   I said: "To separate theology from religion; then to apply good sense to theology, to separate mythology from that, and so get a theology which rested on facts of necessity, facts of consciousness, facts of demonstration, &c." He said: "Then you will not stay in your pulpit seven years; no, nor three." I answered: "Then, please God, I will stay somewhere else; for this thing I will do."

So, after considering the matter for more than thirteen months after I had written, I preached the sermons.   I did not dare look you in the face while I spoke. I clutched the cushions of the pulpit, and read with a trembling heart.   To my great surprise, I found you were able to bear all that I had to say.

I did not wait thirteen months again before I ventured to preach a truth not preached before, or expose a theological absurdity.

He thus describes, in the same sermon, his conversations with the two deacons of his society :—

You did not all accept my convictions. One of your number said, with the candour and fairness which marks his whole life, that, though he thought very differently about some things in the Old Testament, and New Testament, too, yet he should be very sorry to have me refuse to preach what I thought; for it would be almost as bad as to preach what I did not think, and would soon lead to that end.

Another said: All the difficulty lies in "rightly dividing the Word of Truth;" there are things in the Bible, in the New Testament, that I am sorry to find there. But there are so many good things, that we all love it, spite of the bad. Now, if you can "rightly divide the Word," so as to leave all the truth on one side, and all the rest on the other, then you will do a great service to the Church and the World. But it is hard to do this. I don't believe it can be done without violence to the good parts. You know what Isaiah says—"As the new wine is found in the cluster, and one saith, Destroy it not, for a blessing is in it;" so I say of the Bible, Destroy it not, for a blessing is in it. But still, if you can get the blessing out of the grape-skin, that is all we want.

It was afterwards charged that he was precipitate in framing and exposing his opinions. No opinions ever grew more delibe-rately, and never was there less of light audacity in the exhibition of opinions that had fallen out of harmony with the prevailing order.

At the beginning of 1838, he is spiritless, and filled with the vague dissatisfaction which creeps so often, like a sluggish earthworm, over the hopes of many a young clergyman, who has not the excess of power which tore up Mr. Parker's ease. No routine is so disheartening, because no other one involves such high thoughts and objects, to cope with which a man is not ready at set days and hours. The theory of parish-visiting is noble, the practice is sometimes exceedingly depressing. The act of prayer is tender and sublime. To pray tenderly at eleven o'clock precisely, every Sunday morning, is a preciseness which the spirit declines to accommodate.

I often ask myself what I am doing with my one talent, and can only reply that I deem myself well nigh wasting it. Preaching to an audience of 70 or 120 souls, going about and talking little with old women, giving good advice to hypocrites, and scattering here and there, I hope, a corn-grain that will one day germinate and bear fruit. Oh, could I be satisfied that I am doing even this last! If I deemed it certain that any word of mine would ever waken the deep inner life of another's soul, I should bless God that I was alive and speaking. But I will trust. I am sometimes praised for my sermons. I wish men knew how cold those sleek speeches are. I would rather see one man practising one of my sermons than hear all men praise them.

But of this I am satisfied—I am not doing what I ought to do.

And a few days after, the mood grows very heavy, but it is not easy to decompose it and declare its physical and moral elements, or the proportion in which they mingle.

I have lost many things. The greatest was Hope. Days there have been when I saw nought else to freshen my eye, weary with looking over the dull waste of my early life. Tired with labour, I have laid down, my books beside me, the lamp at summer midnight burning low, all else silent in sleep. Hope visited me; she sat beside me, trimmed my lamp. In her sublime presence I grew calm, and composed myself by her majestic features.

Here he plays good-humouredly with the tired mood :—

TO W. SILSBEE.

November 13, 1837.

Epistola tua, O Gulielme, omnium carissime mihi, gratissima venit, instar roris vespertinæ in flores sole perustos defluentis. (Huc studium mei sanctissimum accedit conjux, in manu vilam *scopam* versans, nubes densissimas pulverûm jactura! Vae mihi!) Literas brevissimas, sic dicas, tibi scripseram! Culpam hanc gravem admitto. Pacem tuam atque indulgentiam, fortasse haud meritam, implore. Oppressus dolore, fatigatione, lassitudine corporis, multis cum malis quæ το σαρξ in vita hæreditatur in mediis hisce difficultatibus epistolam feci.

Tam sicca epistola ista, ut metui si longius protraheretur combustione spontaneâ incenderetur. Sic finem posui in metu.

Bona Dea te faveat, emens libros tam vilissimi pretii. Emens enim ab homine *Gruff* (Latinis cum literis animam suam nolo depingere), quum accedis Bostoniam, si apportabis tecum Krummacher, Twestenque, Tenneman et Wegscheider, deponens illos apud Munroe, multas gratias meritaris opus rusticum (Anglicè, yeoman-service) mihi perfungarentur.

Nunc pluma—penna stultissimæ anseris—defatigata, volitare Romano in cœlo abnegat.

But there were choice friends with whom he grew bright and happy. Mr. George Ripley, then settled over a Unitarian Society in Boston, was one of the oldest of these. Mr. Parker's debt to him was large, for counsel in all matters of the intellect, for a discriminating judgment in books, for liberal friendship of all kinds. There was strong sympathy, indeed it may be called love, between them ; a subsequent theological divergence did not impair it. If they discussed its points at all, it was done genially, and with the most perfect mutual understanding. For Mr. Ripley's convictions were held by a mind too scholarly, and a disposition too serene, to become intolerant. Mr. Parker was never tired of acknowledging the debt he owed to friends who were a few years his seniors ; and Mr. Ripley's name was among the highest on this roll of gratitude.

There was at that time in Boston, under the leadership of Dr. Channing, a Society of Friends of Progress. They met for a free and bold discussion of all current subjects of theology and social life. Here Mr. Parker found the charm of good companionship, for there came to those meetings, besides Dr. Channing, Jonathan Phillips, a dear parishioner of the Doctor's, and a man of acute and liberal mind,—occasionally Wendell Phillips, then a young lawyer, of the Suffolk bar ; Mr. Hedge, Mr. Ripley, Mr. Alcott and Dr. Follen.

To judge from some notes of these meetings which are preserved, Mr. Parker stood in little awe of the magnates. His mind willingly went down into the lists with them for a good-natured encounter. Mr. Emerson's views upon the personality of God were for discussion one evening, suggested by a late lecture of his (in the winter of 1837-38.). He was accused of maintaining that God was only an idea, formed in the mind of the individual, projected into ideas of Omnipresence, &c. Another charge was, that of Pantheism, which in those days was popularly understood to be the dread belief of a few suspected men, who were watched as jealously as Jews and witches ever were. In the last century they would have been accused of practising some diabolical ritual. Mr. Parker made a very sensible statement of what he considered the drift of Mr. Emerson's thought to be, and then nicely laid open the question of the Divine Personality.

What do we mean by the term ? Personality cannot exist without will. Suffer all my faculties to remain as they are, but annihilate the will ; I am no longer a person, an individual. I cannot say *I*—a faggot of powers has taken the place of *I*. There are attributes, but no substance to which they belong. How, then, can I conceive of God without personality ? But is will the only essential of personality ? The question is difficult. I conceive of God as a Being of infinite powers, directed by infinite love—as a Being easy of access, full of tenderness, whose character is summed up in one word—Father ! Now, the idea of God's *will* unites all these attributes into a being. Here, then, are the attributes of God united with a substance—the will. What is the essence of God ? I know not what is the essence of myself. I cannot tell. The idea of God is no more mysterious than that of self ; that of the Divine Personality is as clear as that of human personality. Men have always perplexed themselves in meditating upon this subject. And they have come to this conclusion, " He is past finding out." **This is** variously expressed by the thinkers of different ages and countries. " Search me after the essence of God and His laws," says the old Veda. God is " unrevealed light," " the ineffable," " incomprehensible," " the primal Being," say the Gnostics. " The most real of all beings," says Plato ; " Himself without being." So the mystic can only say, " I am " —" He is."

Mr. A. talks of the *progress* of God : the Almighty going forward to His own infinity—progressively unfolding Himself! An idea to me revolting, &c.

Another friend, whom he met more seldom, but always with delight and profit, was William Henry Channing, the successor of Mr. Martineau in Liverpool, and now minister of the Unitarian Society at Washington, D.C.

July 13.

Went to Boston with Mr. Ellis, and at my return found Wm. Channing at home—to my great delight. The subjects of our conversation were sundry important questions on biblical theology, embracing most of the works of the recent German theologians ; for there are no others at this day. We spoke of individuality (here follows a sketch of Mr. P.'s idea of two individualities, the phenomenal and the real ; the first being a man's peculiarities, which separate him from other men ; the second being the essential human truths and feelings, which bring all men together). I am exceedingly delighted with Mr. C. He seems true—a little diseased in the region of consciousness, but otherwise of most remarkable beauty of character ; full of good tendencies, of noblest aspirations ; an eye to see the evils of society, a heart to feel them ; a soul to hope better things, a willingness to endure all self-denial to accomplish the end whereto he is sent ; not covered by thickest wrappages, which rather obscure his worthy uncle, whom I venerate perhaps too much.

We spent all the time in conversation (to me) most profitable.

Conversations between ardent and truth-seeking friends were not confined to the theological points which agitated the denomination. The social problem attracted the same minds who sought a better authority for truth than miracles could give, in a spiritual perception of it which all mankind might share. A mutualism to secure culture and material welfare was consistently desired by those who believed in a community of the sources of moral and spiritual welfare. The social evils which result from the struggles of competitive labour seemed to outweigh all its benefits. Modern civilization was thought to be the culmination of isolated selfishness, madly struggling from bread to luxury and refined delights, which the strongest and least scrupulous only could acquire. Prisons and punishments were the defences of this artificial system, to repress instincts that were moral till they became illegal.   Hospitals and benevolent institutions were also mere defences to absorb as much misery as possible ere it became malicious, to get the social gangrene reduced to limits.   The providential impulses of the human being were forced to act in subversive ways and directions, when they might all be harmonized by their own inherent laws, and the blessing of mutualism succeed to the bane of antagonism.   Each man ought to be the guarantee to all men against disorder ;   the carefully adjusted elements of a selfishness which threatens continually to blow the social fabric to atoms, would become not only innoxious but salutary in its proper combination ;   and a new civilization might arise in fair proportion from the serial development and movement of all possible human tendencies.   Then all men and women might labour and be happy ;   all might earn with a minimum of toil a competence of culture.   Property would be the ally of the whole instead of the oppressor of the many ;   and crimes would disappear, because the instincts would no longer have motives to be criminal.

These opinions, combined with sharp and legitimate criticism of the evils of civilization and the absurdities of modern society, were presented in a scientific form by Charles Fourier, and urged with great enthusiasm by his advocates in this country, who generally had the sense to let alone some of his conclusions respecting marriage and the intercourse of the sexes.   Pure-minded men were fascinated by the idea that people could be shown and taught to work in harmony, to reduce drudgery and domestic annoyances by a skilful division of labour, to develope beauty as well as use, and to save precious time for the soul.

Mr. Ripley soon left a profession in which he seemed to be only recommending truths, to make the experiment of organizing the same truths into practical forms of use, into ideal forms of beauty.   He would show the possibility of living in a system that should not hide its roots in misery and crime.   The establishment at Brook Farm was not far from Mr. Parker's ; and Mr. Channing sometimes came there, the purest, most enthusiastic, most religious of all the speakers at those fine reunions, where the problem was discussed.

But Mr. Parker accepted the criticisms upon society, and waxed no less indignant than the rest, nor was he less warmed with the hope of a fairer future for mankind, without ever acceding to the schemes of Fourier, Considerant, or their American advocates. When afterwards the principle of association was tried at Brook Farm, he was occasionally rather sly over some of the details, and had a humorous eye for the little weaknesses of the recruits. The motive called forth his unbounded respect ; but he never could be made to see the availability of any of the plans.

R. dislikes the customs of property ; a father transmitting it to his son. But I see no way of avoiding the evil. The sin lies deeper than the transmission of property from getter to enjoyer. It *lies* in the *love of low things*, and in the *idea that work degrades*. We must correct this notion, and then all is well. Let men see there are better things than gold can buy ; that labour, *properly* pursued, gives a competence and leisure for cultivation of the man, and that labour elevates man, and the trouble is all over. How the world ever came into such a sad state it is difficult to conjecture.

Still a Phalanx seems no stranger to me than a city might have seemed to some old patriarch. Yet I suspect there has never been a time since the first settlement of this country, when morals or religion were really at a higher flood. I complain loud as others of the lowness of the common actual, and also of the common ideal ; but I will not look back on any one age, and say we are worse than our fathers, but forward to an ideal, and say we are worse than that.

There are traces of his interviews with Dr. Channing, whom he began reverently to seek while teaching in Watertown ; but no notes of this intercourse appear till later, when he had opinions of his own and felt encouraged to sustain them.

Went to see Dr. Channing last Thursday. I have not been this winter so often as usual (1838-39), though I delight to go as well as ever. We spoke of many things. The Doctor thinks the morality of Christianity as great an advance upon all previous systems as the religion itself. Praised my article in the *Examiner*,* but thought I had not quite done justice to Christianity in that respect. I should be sorry if it were true.

Afterwards we were speaking of educating the conscience, a doctrine which I rather ridiculed. But the Doctor said it must be educated, like the understanding. But upon being asked if more was needed than this, that the understanding should be rendered capable of presenting the case distinctly to conscience, he seemed to favour the hypothesis. I asked him if conscience were not an *infallible* guide. He seems to doubt it, but is going to think of the question. To me it seems that conscience will always decide right, if the case is fairly put, and old habits have not obscured its vision. This he seemed inclined to believe, yet hesitated to assent. He said conscience was like the *eye*, which might be dim, or might see wrong. But in this case it is not the eye

---

* An article for January, 1839, reviewing Ackermann's "Das Christliche in Plato."

which sees, but the soul which looks out at the eye; now the organ may be defective, and so misrepresent. But conscience, when the facts are fairly before it, acts *directly* and not *mediately*, and therefore it is not liable to the same mistakes with the eye.

He seemed inclined to admit this, yet denied that we needed any infallible guide, and said the belief in such a want had led to the theory, that the Scripture was inspired word for word. But Scripture was not an infallible guide, and if it were, it would do us no good, for we could not infallibly understand it.

He thought a man late in his life (in a case I put), who had not hitherto consulted his conscience, would, coming to that adviser, make great mistakes, and therefore be punished for his past sin of neglect. Upon the whole, he believed if a man should begin early to ask for the right, with sincere wish to find it, he never would get far out of the way. And even if he did, he was of course justifiable in the Court of Heaven.

Conscience is the last appeal. Never go beyond that; even if it says wrong, the man is degraded who disobeys it. But if a man's conscience tells him something different from other men's, he is not to forego it, but to recast its plans, examine the subject anew, but at last adhere to conscience.

19 April.—Went to see Dr. Channing. Spoke about Strauss. He observed very archly he should not be *very* sorry if some of Kneeland's followers would do it into English. He would not advise me to do it.

He said Christianity could not be separated from Christ! Jesus had a miraculous character, different in *kind* from ours. To him was made a miraculous *revelation*, different in kind from that made to other men, excepting the old prophets and apostles.

Believes the Bible miracles, not those of other people. Thinks that Paul did appeal to the Christian miracles—δυναμις is equivalent to "miracles."

May 2.—Saw Dr. Channing. Borrowed Origen of him. He is pleased with Luther's opinion on the Sabbath; says men ought to be told of these things. Why does he not tell them? He says Luther was a coarse man in the flesh. I compared him to Paul. Dr. Channing thinks the comparison favours the latter. So it does. Luther was melancholy in his latter years, because the Reformation had slipped out of his hands. He found the world ripe for his work: so it went easy.

July.—If Dr. Channing could be ground over again, and come out a young man of five-and-twenty, give all the results of his reading, experience, and life, all the insight, power, eloquence, Christianity he now possesses,—but let him hold the same religious, philosophical, political, and social opinions as now, and preach on them as he does, and let him, with such tracts as his "Letter on Slavery," &c., be all unknown to fame, he could not find a place for the sole of his foot in Boston, though half-a-dozen pulpits were vacant—not he."

TO W. SILSBEE.

August 10, 1838.

I must now say a few words of myself. I have never had a summer of more delightful study than the present, never found more satisfaction in theological and philosophical pursuits. I have solved many questions which have long perplexed and troubled me, and have grown in some small measure calmer than of old time. Tranquillity, you know, is one of my *attainable*, but unattained virtues. Some of my inquiries have been historical, others critical, but philosophy has given me most delight this season. I do not say that the greatest questions are yet solved, or will ever be. They stand now like fire-breathing dragons in my path; I cannot drive them away. But though they often heat, they never bite me. Mr. H. says, in expressing his despair of philosophy, it is better to give it all up and study the facts of nature—with Kirby and Spence, and White of Selborne! Who can do it if he would? The Sphinx will have an answer or you die. You must read the riddle. Love of philosophy may be "the last infirmity of noble minds," but I will cling to it still.

You ask me what effect my speculations have on my practice. You will acquit me of boasting when I say, the most delightful—better than I could hope. My preaching is weak enough, you know, but it is made ten times the more spiritual and strong by my views of nature, God, Christ, man and the Sacred Scriptures. In my religious conversation I tell men religion is as necessary as bread to the body, light to the eye, thought to the mind. I ask them to look into their hearts and see if it is not so. They say I tell them the doctrines of common sense, and it is true. Questions are often asked on the heretical points. I tell men that Moses and the writers of the Old Testament had *low* views of God, but the best that men could have in those times. They understand it and believe the New Testament account of God. In regard to Christ, they see a beauty in his character when they look upon him as a man, who had wants like theirs, trial, temptation, joys and sorrows like their own, yet stood higher than the tempter, overcome in every trial. They see the same elements in themselves.

I dwell mainly on a few great points, viz., the nobleness of man's nature, the lofty ideal he should set before him, the degradation of men at this time, their low aims and worthless pleasures; on the necessity of being true to their convictions, whatever they may be, with the certainty that if they do this, they have the whole omnipotence of God working for them, as the artist brings the whole power of the river to turn his wheel.

Also I dwell on the character and providence of God, and the exactness and beauty of his laws, natural, moral, and religious. My confidence in the Bible is increased. It is not a sealed book, but an open one. I consider there are three witnesses of God in creation. 1. Works of nature: these do not perfectly reveal Him, for we cannot now understand all its contradictions. 2. The words of our fellowmen: this confirms all the wisdom of all the past; it includes the Sacred Scriptures. Parts of it differ vastly in degree from other writings, but not in kind. 3. The infinite sentiments of each individual soul. Now, I lay stress on the first, but more on the second, and still more on the third; for a man may have just as bright revelations in his own heart as Moses, or David, or Paul; I might say, as Jesus, but I do not think any man ever has had such a perfect God-consciousness as he.

Men no more understand his words than they can do his miracles.
"Be perfect as God," do they know what this means? No, no. My
confidence in the Gospel is immeasurably increased. I see it has
meaning in its plainest figures. "He that is greatest among you shall
be your servant"—what meaning! It will be understood a thousand
years hence, not before. But I see the Gospel is human, but almost
infinitely above present humanity.

I feel bound to communicate my views just so fast and so far as
men can understand them,—no farther. If they do not understand
them when I propound them, the fault, I think, is mine and not theirs.
I often find it difficult to make myself understood.

We will have a long *talk* upon these points, for you know the pen
is dull and cold, while the tongue is nearer the heart. My heart and
my hand go together like two turtle-doves, who perch on the same
bough, and eat of the same food, and drop water in one another's
beaks. My religion warms my philosophy, and my philosophy gives
strength to my religion. You know I do not boast in all this.

TO W. SILSBEE.

Dec. 9, 1837.

I am reading the Phædrus. It was the first of Plato's *own* I
ever read. Several years since strolling (idly perhaps) about the
library, I took down the volume which contained the Phædrus. I
read it in a night. I was appalled by the grandeur of the thought, the
beauty of the style. The noon of night passed before I could lay it
down, and then sleep came not, for the procession of the gods,
and the ideal flight of the soul, upborne on celestial wings not yet
defiled by earthly stain, gazing upon the lofty countenance of Truth,—
all this floated in my mind and kept off the drowsy god. I shall never
forget that event in my life. How I read, and re-read, and read again,
the more delighted at each perusal. Subsequently I forgot the name
of the book, and have sought everywhere else in the mighty master for
the passage so exciting to me, but all in vain till now. I commence
with this, and all the old ideas re-awake in my soul.

Some notes of reading and conversation belong to this
period.

Bopp's Vergleichende Grammatik.—I can read almost any book
that promises instruction. This doubtless contains stores of facts
relating to comparative philology; but I can't read the book. It is
awfully written; none but a German could write such a book, none
but a German could read it; yet it is doubtless valuable.

The Germans, as Mr. Norton says, are "too raw to write books."
Certainly they have had but few good models of writing in Germany;
but they have not much improved those they have. The book belongs
to the same class with Lobeck's "Aglaophamus." It is not a book, but
a collection of valuable materials which might be put into a book. It
seems necessary to have a board of attorneys in Germany to write the
books which learned men are full of. Then a scholar like Bopp should
hie to his glib attorney, with all his facts and philosophy in his satchel;
should state its case to him, and let Mr. Attorney lay the matter before

the public in the most perspicuous and forcible manner possible. Authors might then express themselves; the public could understand them.

KARCHER'S ANALECTA.—Eichhorn's " Præfamen," as he calls it, contains a clever defence of the Masoretic text, as he calls it. The book contains the results of an immense reading of books that are not valuable, at least, not valuable to me. Karcher read all the books mentioned in Wolf's " Bibliotheca Hebraica," and added what was omitted by Wolf, if it seemed important. Of course he tells you that Rabbi Mier Hallodami Ben Job Ben . . Adam, besides the 998 ascribed to him by Wolf, wrote another called "The Fool's Way Wiser," and that one of the 998 cited by Wolf is mentioned as the " Book of Fools," and it is " The Book of Stupid Men," and the like. Doubtless the work is very valuable to those whom it concerns, but not to me.

LIFE OF SWEDENBORG.*—It seems written with the most honest intentions, but is not satisfactory to me, farther than this, it shows he was a very remarkable man. As to his wonderful deeds, I have no antecedent objection to them, though the evidence is not always sufficient to establish their actuality. If actual they are of no value to my mind as proof of spiritual inspiration. I cannot believe in his interpretations of the Scriptures, if he were to move mountains.

There is a little unfairness in giving part of the testimony of Kant, without giving the part against the credibility of Swedenborg.

CONVERSATION WITH PROF. STUART.—He says it is Emerson's doctrine, that man has in him all he attributes to the Godhead; that he has elements of religion in him; all he has to do is *to find it*. This is certainly giving up the Bible. Why ? *Ecce argumentum :* God gave man the Bible. Now this gift supposes it was God's opinion man needed it, and could not get religion or knowledge of God without it. Acting on this supposition, he made revelations of Himself, &c.

The above is beautiful reasoning, and sounds much like the following:—God gives oxen grass; therefore He supposes they need it ; therefore He thinks they would never have been hungry had He not given them grass. To say an ox would be hungry if there were no grass, is as bad as to say man would have religious wants if there were no Bible or miraculous revelation of God. Truly Jonathan Edwards was wiser than this. See his sermon on " Spiritual Light Everywhere."

But I am surprised at the general liberality of Moses Stuart. He detests littleness, and would rather give up revelation than reason. He has no notion of going back to the dark ages, as the English theologues have, with whom he has no patience, and says they belong to the fourteenth century.

CONVERSATION WITH PROF. NORTON.—Returned to Cambridge and called on Mr. Norton ; left with him Mr. Stuart's note. I found Mr. Norton in the midst of books, all neatly arranged about him. His MSS. looked as neat as a lady's album ; three pretty portfolios con-

---

* No name of author. Perhaps it was the Life prepared by Nathaniel Hobart. That contains the letter of Kant upon the alleged intercourse of Swedenborg with the spiritual world.

tained various papers. He proceeded to speak about a work lent to me when at Cambridge—Matter's work on the Gnostics. He pronounced it a romance founded on Gnosticism, and *not* a "critical history." He says M. Matter is wrong in his facts, inferences, and conclusions; is a man of considerable talent, but is hasty, and therefore inaccurate and loose in his statements. He gave me some instances.

I inquired if he had ever seen Bauer on the Gnostics—he had not; but he expressed some little dislike of the plan when told that Bauer found Gnosticism in Schleiermacher, Schelling, and Hegel. I told him Bauer found no *essence of Gnosticism*, and did not tell what was the one doctrine which showed itself in all sects, and affirmed that there was no such common doctrine. Mr. Norton differed on that head; he said the essence of Gnosticism consisted in two things:—I. A denial that Jehovah of the Old Testament was the Supreme God. II. An affirmation that the world was made by an inferior being (Demiurgos). To these he added a third tenet, scarcely distinctive, that Matter has an evil influence on Mind.

In these, he says, all the Gnostics agreed; he does not count the *Carpocratians* members of this sect. This is original with him, so he requests me to make no use of it, as he designs to use it for himself.

I am delighted to see so profound and accurate a scholar; it does one good; it sharpens attention, and is a stimulus. I wanted to ask him about the authenticity of the Pentateuch, but could not bear to trespass on his time.

During this year, 1838, he composed a treatise upon the Origin of Writing among the Greeks, Hebrews, and Egyptians, in the course of his preparation for publishing the translation of De Wette. On this, and the Homeric question, he anticipated Mr. Grote.

May 13.—To be done this week. Plant the other side the brook. Sow the garden vegetables. Plough the new land, and plant the old alleys. See about the Sunday-school. Get the benches for the vestry; and ask Mr. Ellis to be superintendent."

Following this are pages of Greek inscriptions, from tables found at Herculaneum, the two tables at Amyclæ, the Sigean Marble, &c., &c. From ploughing to Boustrophedon is not an abrupt transition.

Sunday, July 15, 1838.—Proceeded to Cambridge, to hear the valedictory sermon by Mr. Emerson. In this he surpassed himself as much as he surpasses others in the general way. I shall give no abstract. So beautiful, so just, so true, and terribly sublime was his picture of the faults of the Church in its present position. My soul is roused, and this week I shall write the long-meditated sermons on the state of the Church and the duties of these times.

9

How many generous youths were fired by the same famous sermon, which Mr. Emerson preached at the invitation of the graduating Divinity Class ; and how many, unfortunately, became infected only with certain idiomatic peculiarities : it was sometime before the neighbourhood recovered from " Ever the sun shines," &c., and all the apothecary shops were mobbed, to discover what else beside " myrrh and rosemary " Religion was. The critics used to toss and trample these phrases with great zeal, thinking they had the man in them and were punishing him well. The man was a long way off in safety, serenely viewing this taurine fury. Not critics alone, but a good many promising young men who learned better, began their career with popular satire of the idiom which clothed this pure and independent spirit. It was a mark too palpable, and the fingers could not hold the string. Some of these satirical Sauls who set out on that keen Damascus journey, were converted by the way. A noble, genial mind, in the very act of discharging its spark into such a peculiarity, is disarmed, and the man beneath the idiom holds him prisoner. How many he held fast, not by spreading the snare of a system whose definiteness chokes a little, like a noose, while it retains, but by enveloping their minds in a tranquil and poetic freedom, through which the objects of nature might be sought and into which an exacting theology could not pursue. The liberal gesture itself was worth a whole body of divinity.

Reverend doctors collected over this discourse in great alarm, declared that " what was not folly was impiety," and hoped, perhaps, to pick it to death by force of numbers. To Mr. Parker and others it imparted the lesson much needed at that moment, how salutary is the boldness of a pure and constant mind.

But with his usual good sense he set aside certain phrases which subjected the generous thought to misconstruction.

Mr. E. says, " if a man is at heart just, so far he is God." Now, it seems that he mistakes likeness for identity. My spirit is like God, but is it necessarily God ? There are ten peas in a pod, exactly alike in all things : are there not ten peas, and not one alone ? Now, if a man's spirit could become exactly like God's, would his be the same as God's ? &c.

This is very prosaic, for a mystical word does not like to be accounted for ; but it is characteristic of his love of order. Love of freedom **never** overcame that humane as well as scholarly instinct.

I begin to fear my own sermons are too speculative. Is it so? I wish to stand on the earth, though I would look beyond the stars. I would live *with men*, but think with philosophers.

The autumn of this year ripened his surmises about Inspiration. And here is the first formal reduction to words of his future doctrine.

We say a *good* man is inspired to do good deeds. Here we only mean he has *moral goodness*, which all men may have if they will. We say a *wise* man is inspired to teach wisdom, without supposing his will is interfered with, or that an unnatural (query, preternatural?) communication is made to him. We say the writers of the Scriptures were inspired, but this means the same as was meant in the other case. The inspiration of Jesus Christ could not differ *in kind* from that of Socrates, only *in degree*. He had much inspiration; Socrates little. All truth comes from God, for it is God's thought; all morality, for it is God's will (query, moral wishes?); all religion, for it is His feeling (this is afterwards changed). So far, then, as a man is *true*, virtuous, religious, so far he is *inspired*—no farther. This inspiration comes by the use of the proper faculties. Be true to your conviction, be patient, and wait for it. The inspiration will come.

In the July number of the *Boston Quarterly Review*, which commenced its career in 1838, under Mr. Brownson, there is a long article by Mr. Parker upon Dr. Palfrey's "Lectures on the Jewish Scriptures and Antiquities," which marks very clearly the progress of his mind. It is also a model of simplicity and analytic ability; the reader sees at once that the critic has a thorough knowledge of the field to be examined, the languages, the learned helps, the opinions of scholars, as well as principles of his own that are independent of theology. Upon Miracles, the immoralities of the Pentateuch, upon Revelation, the views were so decidedly liberal, that epithets not over-choice were applied to the writer. His religious motive was said to be blasphemous. The best-informed people were quite certain it was written by an atheist.

Here is a sentence upon Dr. Palfrey's treatment of the miracles of the Pentateuch, p. 269.

While he admits the abstract credibility of miracles, he seems desirous of restricting the miraculous agency to the smallest sphere possible. But when the *deus ex machinâ* is once fairly introduced, neither the frequency nor the marvellousness of his operations can produce any embarrassment. It is no relief to explain away ninety-and-nine miracles, while the hundredth is permitted to remain. If one camel may go through the needle's eye, all may.

But at this time he believed, with some exceptions, the miracles of the New Testament.

He wrote to his friend, " My hair stands up when I think of what I have written." His friend, after reading the article, gives it considerable criticism, to which the following is a reply :—

TO WM. SILSBEE.

27 November, 1838.

You think there is sarcasm. I do not think that is too strong a word, though I never intended anything like it. I hate sarcasm, yet am, perhaps, sarcastic. I wished to indulge in a little harmless pleasantry, but I fear the Dean would not share in the mirth he excited. You think I indulge the ludicrous vein too much. Such is my propensity, no doubt ; but how ought things to be treated ? Light things lightly, grave things gravely, ridiculous things ridiculously. I must think ridicule has its place even in criticism. For instance, suppose M. Poyer should write a book on the miracles of the Saviour, attempting to explain them as the results of animal magnetism, a critic might show, 1, that the attempt was not successful ; and 2, how ridiculous it was to make the attempt, and represent the Saviour as filling the 5000 with a fancy they had eaten, and letting them go off with that impression.

Mr. Parker alludes to the following sentence in his review. " He considers the religious principle as the most important element in human nature ; but at the same time so weak, that, unlike all the other principles, it cannot be trusted to shift for itself, to discover the truth and adhere to it." The letter then proceeds :—

To my mind, William, there is something strange and startling in the assertion, that man has been so constituted that he can, by the use of his faculties, on condition of obedience to their laws, achieve all the wonders of science and art, tell the dimensions of the planets and their whereabouts, and yet never be able by the use of his highest faculties—I mean the spontaneous religious sentiments—and by obedience to their laws, become able to learn religious truth, and to be certain it *was* truth he learned and not error. Is it not most of all important for man to settle the questions of duty, to possess religious truth and religious life ? Has God, so bountiful in bestowing other powers, given him none to discover those truths, the most important, the most necessary ? If I was told, by an angel from Ouranus, that the inhabitants of that planet differed much from us, that they had 70 senses for communing with the outer world, I should say with confidence, with my present views of God, then must they have 700 internal senses for communing with God, and I should expect him to add, 7000. Is it not the case, William, that, while the Almighty takes such bounteous care of all little things, that no animal can be found in utmost height or utmost deep, all of whose wants are not perfectly satisfied—none found wandering up and down, seeking rest and finding none—He lays most stress on the most important of his works ? . . . .

Truth flashes on the man. You have felt such visitations ; we labour upon a thought, trying to grasp the truth. We almost have the butter-fly in our hands, but cannot get it. Again we try ; it will not come : we walk, sit, pray, it will not come. At last in some moment it flashes on us, the crystals form, the work is all done. Whence came it ? I do not know. It is in these burning moments that *life* is lived ; the rest is all drudgery, beating the bush, ploughing, and weeding, and watering. This is the harvest hour.

These hours are few to any man, perhaps not more than two in a week ; but yet all the real thought of the man is compressed into these burning moments.

Now, I believe God is the fountain of all Truth, which overflows from Him into all minds that lie low in his power, wishing to feed these minds of theirs in a wise passiveness ; but how this influence comes, I do not know. I know nothing about the manner in which my soul is connected with God : I only know the fact. It is a matter of experience.

FROM THE JOURNAL.

Jan. 15, 1839.

The things that are around us,
  What wondrous truths they tell !
Though flesh to earth has bound us,
  The gaol's our oracle.
The sunshine in its splendour,
  The meeker moon by night,
The stars that do attend her,
  And people the broad light,
In us an open ear address,
  And tranquilly they whisper
Their Word of Holiness.

So I composed, walking along in the beautiful night from Boston, where I had attended a meeting of ministers. The stars were unusually bright and large. The pale northern lights came out, and speared up with rare and exquisite beauty. The air was clear, cool. The Great Bear looked like a constellation of suns that kept watch over the earth. I had become somewhat excited by silent meditation, when I stopped to look at the heavens more attentively. A little brook, not bound by the frost, ran beside the road, and emitted that clear tinkle so remarkable when white ice covers part of the water. As Henry More said, " My sallies towards Nature were almost ravishing ! "

1839. Visited Dr. Channing, but had only a short time to converse with him. He is in fear lest the same state of things should at length be produced in this country which now exists in England, among the manufacturing population. The cheapness and quickness of the passage to Europe will produce competition: their dense population renders wages lower there, so they will become lower here.   Then they will work fourteen or sixteen hours a-day; the same will be done here, and then—farewell, all culture, all progress, and come debauchery and ruin.   "Oh," says the Doctor, "oh, that we might be a,poor people for the sake of the highest."   He thought manufactures would not be a blessing to the nation.

We talked about great men.   He said, "Truth shines first upon great men, who slowly or suddenly communicate it to the mass.   But to produce the proper effect, the mass itself must be in a fit state. Thus for a reform is needed not only *talents*, but an *opportunity* to use them.   Had Luther been born a century before, he would only have shared the fate of Huss and Savonarola.   He was a less man than Wickliffe.   There are two errors touching the influence of great men.   One makes them simply the mouth-piece and consciousness of the people; the other calls them the makers of the people, not allowing enough for reciprocal action.   But the greatest man stands farthest in advance of his time, and so makes his thought dominant for ever.

Some enterprises are carried through without any great men.   Such was the American Revolution.   No man shot above the rest.   Dr. C. thinks Sam. Adams the greatest of those heroes.   I pitted Jefferson against Adams, and he (Jefferson) stood it best.   I have been surprised in reading his letters to notice how he foresaw the troubles that would grow out of the States-Rights question, and from difficulty in apprehending the precise meaning of the Constitution, both of which he proposed to remedy by a Bill of Rights prefixed to the Constitution.

1839.   Plato—A study.   Write an article on Plato, setting forth— 1. his Method and System; 2. the Sources of both; 3. his Influence.

Consider the relation of Platonism to Christianity.   See Ackermann, Bauer, and the reviews of these works in the *Studien und Kritiken*, and *Rohr's Bibliothek*.

Ritter's article on New Platonism in *Stud. u. Krit.*, 1838, p. 247. On the Formation of the World-Soul.   *Daub and Creutzer*, III., 7–89.

Consider Plato's own Idea.   How far did he come up to it?   His opinions on those greatest subjects — 1. God; 2. Man; 3. Their relation.

Consider his influence till Christianity.   And after Christianity, running parallel with it—sometimes streams falling from Platonism into Christianity.   Note Platonism producing mysticism in Dionysius, Scotus Erigena, the Victors, &c.   (See the various mystical articles.)

Consider Plato as one pole of thought, and Aristotle the other.

TO G. W. ELLIS, IN PARIS.

January 3, 1839.

I have often told you of the noise that Emerson's Address made. The other day they discussed the question in the Association, whether he was a Christian!   —— said he was not, and defended his position rather poorly, you may suppose.   —— maintained that he was an atheist—a downright atheist.   But nobody doubted he was a virtuous and most devout man, one who would enter heaven when they were shut out. Of course they were in a queer predicament; either they must acknowledge a man may be virtuous and yet no Christian (which most of them thought it a great heresy to suppose), and *religious*, yet an *atheist* (which is a contradiction—to be *without God*, and yet *united to God*), or else to affirm that Emerson was neither virtuous nor religious, which they could not prove. Walker and Frothingham thought he should be called a Christian, if he desired the name.

Some of the ministers think we need to have certain "*fundamentals*" fixed for us all to swear by, lest the new school among the Unitarians should carry the whole body up to the height of Transcendentalism. Now, it is notorious that the old Unitarians, in the days when there was fighting for the faith, had no such fundamentals; so Mr. Ripley showed Dr. —— that he (the Doctor) belonged to the new school, and the movement party were the lineal descendants of the old school of Unitarians.

It is quite evident there are now two parties among the Unitarians: one is for progress, the other says, "Our strength is to stand still." Dr. Channing is the real head of the first party; the other has no head. . . . .

Some day or another there will be a rent in the body; not soon, I trust, however.

TO DR. FRANCIS.

Feb., 1839.

Is Revelation at an end? Is the Bible better than the soul? The Hindoo says that of his Veda, the Mohammedan of his Koran. But if the Christian says so he *dies*; for Christianity is the religion of freedom. So the fact that we always take texts from the Bible, read its *good* passages, and pass over its objectionable clauses and allegories, or hit upon a higher sense to passages, tends to mislead men as to the true nature of the book.

Do not suppose I have any disposition to undervalue the Bible. I only want the people to understand it as it is. I remember talking with old Mr. John Richardson once about the Bible. He said he had recently read the first part of the Old Testament again, and *he was sorry he had read it*, because he could not believe it, and before he thought he believed all.

TO THE SAME.

March.

You don't know how much I rejoice at your discovery of More's Poems. I saw the announcement in your letter, and leaped up and shouted for joy; so that some men at work in the garden were boisterously mirthful, thinking I had "gone daft." I am coming to see you the last Saturday in March, if nothing prevents, to talk over 1001 things, among others about Elohim and Jehovah.

1839.—MEINER's HISTORY OF RELIGIONS is a much better book than I expected to find it, though the author sets out with wrong notions. He does not deem religion connatural with man, nor regard it as the development of an innate principle. It is quite wonderful that he does not do this, for he comes very near it, and admits the universality of religion among all the tribes of earth, and seems to be religious himself. He thinks with Lucretius (though not acknowledging the origin) that ignorance of the true causes of things is the cause of religion. Foolish man! the ox is more ignorant thereof than Abraham; but he is not more religious. Besides, as men come to understand the causes of things, they become more religious, as a thousand examples show, with their Lockes and Newtons. It is only your Diderots and Fredericks of Prussia that see no God at the end of their telescopes.

He takes the same view in regard to Polytheism, as in his "Historia doctrinæ de vero Deo," and he is mistaken, I fancy. But I admire the man's fairness. He thinks there is no little paganism in Christianity. He sets out with two fine principles, viz., that all religions agree more than they differ, and that all popular religions are false in some points; but the scholar did not look deeper and see that there can be but one religion, as there is but one kind of love, or time, or space, though various degrees, and perhaps modes thereof; nor did he see that every form of religion must at one time contain more of good than evil, of truth than falsehood—relative to the state of development in the mass of men —or it could never stand as long, or find acceptance with the mass. He does not regard religion as the standard of the development of man, nor regard it as the consciousness of man coming to himself. He would make the superficial classification of religion into Polytheistic and Monotheistic, which does not reach below the skin. It is only a cutaneous classification. The man did not know that all men saw the same religious truths at the same height of development.

I like the largeness of the man, his wide reading, his English common-sense, his cool way of stating things; but I protest against his superficial view. Poor fellow! what did you see in the great Book of Nature? Little worth seeing. But he lived in a bad time.

1839. RIMANNI, HIST. ATHEISMI, &c.—This is a very weak book; of little value, save as a guide to the other literature relating to the subject. He seems to have read few of the writers whose works are examined, but takes the opinions of Buddeus or some other writer. He often says such or such an author is accused of Atheism by this or that man, but he concludes nothing, having never seen his works. In general he seems to mean to be fair, and perhaps is not very hasty in pronouncing upon the case of scholars—certainly not so hasty as M. Leclerc in Bib. Ch., Vol. I. But the book is weak—it leaves no mark on your mind. The man wrote this mechanically, as he might have written any other book, or have made a pair of shoes. You would not look there for principles or first truths. I expected to find some curious learning, but there is none such. It is, however, curious to see how foolishly he trusts to statements of travellers alleging poor barbarians to be atheists, and how queerly he sometimes concludes a man was an atheist; for he thinks, holding this or that paradox, the man must, if consistent, be an atheist, forgetting that not two philosophers in ten centuries are consistent, logical consistency of thought being a rarer gift than genius itself. Still further, it is instructive to see how the best of men have been called atheists—Locke, Leibnitz, Socrates, Leclerc, Simon (Richard), Henry More, and Norris.

I would commend that book to the illiberal, that they may see how easy it has been for others to call names—even the worst names—and take heed to their ways. You and I may tell what is Atheism (perhaps); but God only can tell who is an atheist. There are atheists in speculation, but they are very rare—somebody says there never was *one*—but in heart there are many.

CONSERVATISM.—To hear men talk of the danger attending new things, one would fancy the world was in the best possible state, governments perfect, churches full of God's Spirit, all men contented, and the whole nation in the highest degree happy and joyful. The conservatist in Religion tells you all the world will come to an end if his old creed is left behind. He never fancies God's Spirit always takes new forms, each suited to the age, climate, &c.

To hear others, you would suppose all so bad that no man could find justice in any court, piety in any church, freedom or truth in any man, or bread in the market—that of old things all were over-old; of new things none were new enough.

Now light comes in a great tide from God down to man, it comes from him through the future, and is only reflected to us from the past. But new light is ever on the way from the primal light of all our being. Far before us, in the celestial spaces, are the stars; millions there are not yet seen, their light still loitering on the way, all the space between us and them is filled with their light not yet reaching us. So all the space between the finite and the Infinite Soul is full of truth; why not open the heart and welcome the light of truth? Each man is connected with the past; our ancestors were the first man and woman; all the vicissitudes of the universe—its eclipses of the sun and occultations of the stars, the earthquakes and famines, the jubilees of the world—all these have our parents shared in, joyfully or with sadness. So the light of experience comes to us from them. But we are connected also with the future. Why turn our backs upon it? its life is not yet lived. We also may one day be patriarchs—certainly we are all links in the great chain which winds round the two axles of the Past and the Future. They seem immeasurably distant, yet are infinitely near—the little moment called *now* being all that is between them—and that is all we are.

1839. QUESTIONS TO BE PONDERED.—MORALITY.—Is there any valid distinction between subjective and objective morality? In what does it consist? What is the value of each, separately taken? What is the result of their identity in a man's mind?

I. It is commonly supposed there is an objective standard and criterion of morality, (1), and it is shown or said to exist in the Bible; but this is not true in any practical sense; and, if it were, still it is to be found out from an examination of many passages, and the power of doing this pre-supposes an internal and subjective criterion, which renders the external useless. Besides: the Bible, taken as a whole, is progressive, and adapts itself to the rudeness of the Jew, as well as to the absolute ideal of the Christian. It is vain, therefore, to look for this criterion there. (2) We are remanded to the laws of the land, and (3) to the customs of men. But these are, many of them, arbitrary and conventional: the work of men no wiser nor better than ourselves. Here, then, is no objective standard. Nor is such an one in the lives and maxims of wise men collectively taken; for, none being perfectly wise, the aggregate of their wisdom can only be gathered by a wise eclecticism, which is only possible on the supposition that the standard is already in our bosom.

II. There can, therefore, be no objective criterion; as there is no perfect circle objective and actual in nature, and no perfectly beautiful woman objective and actual in human life. There are perfect circles *undrawn* in the air; so there are perfect men, physically and morally in life, only not actual. Yet there is an absolute circle—beauty and morality—though they exist ideally and not actually. All attempts hitherto to produce them are, in part, failures. Euclid and Newton could not draw a perfect circle, nor Phidias make a perfect beauty, though five hundred Spartan criteria stood naked before him; and Jesus of Nazareth says, " Why callest thou me good? " for the objective result was still so far below the subjective idea.

Thoughts and queries respecting Biblical matters multiply very fast. They involve all the points which were soon so vigorously made against the current theology. He wonders at the silence of Paul and Justin Martyr respecting miracles as evidence of the divinity of Christ's mission ; the Book of Acts appears to be mythological, and the immoralities of the Pentateuch are observed farther.

Notice the plea set up of the wickedness of the Canaanites, and compare the similar pleas of the Romans respecting the wickedness of the Carthaginians, of the Spaniards respecting the savages in the New World, who were murdered because they were not Christians.

The Rev. Henry Walker, of Charlestown, Massachusetts, who died at Santa Cruz, in 1838, brought home the first copy of Strauss's " Life of Jesus " which was seen in this vicinity. He studied in Germany, and, procuring there the first edition, which was published in 1835, lent it to Mr. Parker on his return in 1836 or 1837. This he studied, and it helped to mature his growing suspicions that the New Testament had a mythology, as well as the Old, and as well as all transmitted history or religion, and that the evidence upon which miracles rested was in all cases insufficient to establish clearly their claim to be facts. But the book of Strauss had no further direct influence. He saw that it was impossible to apply Strauss's definition of a myth to the New Testament. For Strauss says that a myth is the product of the average state of mind of a people, and embodies their prevailing temper and anticipations. To create a myth, nothing historical or personal is requisite. The people will take any lay-figure that happens to attract them, and drape it with their preconceptions. The Jews took Jesus in this way, and dressed him up with the Messianic and spiritual costume of their own ideas and hopes. The religion thus presented may be genuine, but was never displayed by a person, simply because it is the possession of humanity, and continent of ideas that are beyond the capacity of any one person to display. Mr. Parker shows, in his capital article * upon Strauss's book, that " if there was no historical Christ to idealize, there could be no ideal Christ to seek in history," that the effect cannot precede the cause, and that Christ is historical in the sense of actually incarnating the religious ideas attributed to him. Otherwise there would be no mythology in the New Testament, no miraculous conception, no temptation, no ascension. The person must be large enough to carry the mythology ; but according to Strauss, the myth itself is the only real thing—the essential just outgrowth of a people, which pretends a person, or catches one for ground-tackle to hold the myth in its place. Mr. Parker shows, in two or three pages of excellent raillery, how any historical event whatsoever might be dissolved, in the Straussian fashion, in a mythical solution, as preliminary to a precipitation of its " seminal ideas " in their primitive form. And he exposes the pantheistic features of the theory : and justly, too, for it is one thing to say that impersonal ideas create and exhibit themselves in history, and another and an erroneous thing to say that impersonal ideas are the only history. The boundless generality of Pantheism could never stay in Mr. Parker's field-bred and muscular mind ; but he did not sit panic-stricken in his study, and shriek to see the nebulæ blotting here and there the sky.

Perhaps Strauss's book also confirmed his growing idea of the simply human nature of Jesus, " a carpenter's son ; " but into that presentation of Jesus there flowed awe and love for the divine character, a glad recognition of every spiritual and beneficent trait of a son of God's holy soul, of a son of Man's fraternal heart. He still accepted some of the miracles, with entire indifference, however, not caring whether the evidence sufficed or not to establish them as facts.† A genuine, holy person, Jesus, containing the highest known religion and morality, was always held by him with emphasis, and prized as a guarantee, with

---

* *Christian Examiner*, April, 1840. Review of the second edition, 1837, brought home to him by Rev. George Ellis.

† His tendency at this time may be found in an article in the *Western Messenger*, Dec. 1840, and Jan. 1841, "The Relation of the Bible to the Soul."

other saintly men and women, of that which is possible to mankind.

By-and-bye he said that, although Jesus still overtopped the race, the time might arrive when a new manifestation of the Infinite Truth and Love would be made ; for it was absurd to insist that the past had exhausted in any direction the divine capability. This was, in the first place, only an injunction to restrain men from bigoted trespassing upon the Omnipotent and Infinite God: as when he said he would not declare that a miracle was an impossibility, but would wait for the evidence of its reality. But it was, in the second place, very characteristic of his hope. That was wonderfully strong. It was an intuitive expectation of more goodness, more truth, more happiness, a hunger in behalf of men, that they should be recipient for ever of an ever-amplifying love and joy. He would cast himself with ardent and generous predictions upon a future when even the pirate, the kidnapper and the adulterer should equal the manly beauty of a Christ. He would throw himself against the brazen door of a fateful theology, to hold it open for the vilest man and woman, for all men, to keep it ajar for the free communications of spirit, to let into the world era surpassing era, savior after savior, to preserve salvation for all eternity. There never was a more tender and fraternal hope ; in the interest of the miserable and profligate, and in the interest of truth, it stood in the way to forbid theology drawing finite lines against the Infinite perfection. The very bluntness of his language, when he imagined new Christs, or bade the harlot equal the old one, was honourable and worthy of respect, as when a hardy fist fights a fainting woman through a brutal crowd into air and safety. All his characteristics helped this humane hopefulness forth into the service of mankind.*

His depressing moods were no bar to it. Cheerfulness was only in favour with it, and indigestion could not thwart it. The resentment of an overworked brain did no harm to this beautiful disposition of his whole interior life.

It prompted him to seek the society of people who were in earnest to discover what was true, humane, and pure. It made no difference whether they knew much or little. John Augustus†

---

* Compare "Sermons of Theism," pp. 29, 364.

† The famous shoemaker of Boston, who devoted his time, love, and substance to youthful unfortunates of either sex, through instruction, charity, and active intervention in the Courts.

was more to him than any magnate of rhetoric or science. And where two or three came together, drawn by their hopeful seeking, he, too, was drawn to observe and sympathise. One expedition of this kind took place in the summer of 1840, when he set out, with one or two friends, to walk to Groton, attracted by the call for a Convention issued by Come-Outers and Second-Adventists. Sympathy and liberal feeling sent him that road, but good sense and knowledge of man appears also to have gone with him.

Aug .10.—At Newton we fell in with Cranch, and haled him into our brotherhood of pedestrians. We walked on to Concord, stopping ever and anon at farm-houses by the way-side. The route is beautiful, and talk of various kinds beguiled its length. At Concord, we saw old Dr. Ripley, in his 90th year, who charged us to keep the true faith, and admonished us of the evils of becoming *Egomites*, as he called certain men who claimed a divine mission for themselves (*ego, mitto*.) We all assembled and took tea with R. W. E. He and Ripley had all the talk, which turned entirely upon the *Dial*,* its merits and defects, its uses and abuses. Really it was quite too bad. The only good thing he said was, " Come and look at this print of ' Endymion,' which is very beautiful; so likewise is its rival, the ' Coming of Morning,' drawn by two dappled steeds, and attended by seven virgins, daughters of the sun." Carlyle sent it to Mrs. E. In our walk, E. expressed to me his admiration of —— and his foolish article in the *Dial*. He said it was full of life. But, alas! the life is Emerson's, and not ——'s, and so it had been lived before.

At Groton we went to reconnoitre, and find Mr. ——, the person who called the Convention which we went to attend. Our host directed us to a certain house, which we could not find, so we accosted a man in the street,—

" Can you tell us where Mr. —— lives ? "

" He boards with Brother Hall, about a mile and a half off; but his wife is up there in that house."

Ripley replied, " It is ——, sir, and not his wife we want to see."

" Oh, you will find him down at Brother Ruggs's, just behind the meetin'-house."

Thither we went, and found a body of men gathered about the door

* "*The Dial*: a Magazine for Literature, Philosophy, and Religion," was commenced this year. Margaret Fuller was the leading editor, Mr. Ripley the acting editor, and Mr. Emerson a contributor much relied on. It was designed to encourage a free speculation, to report the good things in Philosophy and Religion which the other journals considered bad, and to concentrate the genial thinking of the neighbourhood. Many crude notions crept, through its courageous invitation, into print. Some of Mr. Parker's best articles were contributed to the *Dial*: " German Literature," Jan., 1842 ; " The Pharisees," July, 1841 ; " Thoughts on Theology," a careful review of Dorner's Christology, April, 1842 ; " Hollis Street Council," a very plain-spoken review of the proceedings of a Unitarian Council called in the case of Rev. John Pierpont, who had preached against vice in his parish, Oct., 1842. Of these, the article on " German Literature" is full of learning and humour.

of the Brother. We were introduced to —— and found that dignified personage a youngster about four-and-twenty, about the middle size, with a countenance pleasant rather than otherwise. He had a cunning look, appeared designing and ambitious. His natural language was not prepossessing. It said to me, "Take care—take care!" After further introductions, we inquired as to the work to be done, and were told by the dignitary himself, that there were two questions not to be discussed —to wit, *What constitutes a Christian?* and *What constitutes a Christian Church?* Here we saw for the first time the mark of the Beast and the print of his foot. That night we were told the discourse would be very interesting. Brother Jones was to hold forth on the Millennium and the Second Coming of Christ in 1843. But thinking if Christ could not come till 1843, we could not wait so long, but would say with Sisera, "Why tarry the wheels of his chariot?" we adjourned, and had a good talk.

THE COME-OUTERS.—These are a body of men on Cape Cod, amounting to some hundreds in the several towns there, who are called by this name. They take no distinctive appellation themselves, but receive this name from the other sects, because they have come out from the churches. We had seen some of them in various places during the meeting, and asked them to come up to our room in the tavern, when they and others assembled to the number of twenty or thirty, and we had a talk.

1. NICKERSON AND DAVIS, OF BREWSTER.—These are called the "ministers" of the Come-Outers. They were two as rough-looking men as you would meet in a summer's day—rough, I mean, in their exterior, for their countenance was full of the divine. Their hands, their dress, their general air, showed they belonged to the humblest class in society. Mr. N. was asked to state his views of progress in the Christian course, which he did most beautifully. There are three stages of growth. 1. The man sees the truth and resolves to embrace it. Here he finds no great satisfaction; the longing is not appeased. He sees light, however, and goes towards it. 2. The man is in righteousness, but is not made perfect. He struggles, is *virtuous*, but not yet good; life is a battle in which he is beginning to conquer, but has not yet won the victory. 3. He gains the complete victory. He fears nothing in this life or the next; distress does not trouble him, nor success elate. He lies low in God's hand. God dwells in him, and he in God. All his thoughts are brought into subjection to Christ. He has become one with God, just as Christ was one with Him.

THEIR VIEW OF THE ORDINANCES.—The Christian ordinances, say they, we esteem most highly: they are *our daily work*. As to the Lord's Supper, they think little of that. It is rarely administered, and never except some one is moved to it by a spontaneous action of the divine feelings. They told how it was administered the last time. Several had met at Sister Nancy's house for worship one evening, and Brother Some-one said the Spirit moved him to eat the Lord's Supper; so Sister Nancy went to the pantry, and brought forth bread and wine, and set it on the table, and the Brother sat down and ate and drank. "All our meals," said they, "are the Lord's Supper, if we eat with a right heart."

CHURCH DISCIPLINE.—When one wants to become one of their number, he comes and associates with them. No questions are asked about his creed. We asked, "Then suppose some one should come who did not believe in Christ, or the Bible, or in God, what would you do ? " "Take him by the hand," said they, "and bid him welcome, and God-speed in the good course." "But would you suffer such an one to speak in your meetings like any other Brother ? " "Most certainly," said they ; " do you think we fear that error is stronger than truth ? "

PREACHING.—These ministers said they were *ministers of silence no less than of speech*, and only spoke when moved thereto ; and each who was moved spoke without restraint, *for it took the whole Church to preach the whole Gospel.*

THEIR MINISTERS.—One of them was well educated at a theological seminary before he came among them, but he cast off his doctrinal views, and became useful with them. If he wants anything, they give it him. If they want, he gives them, which is oftener the case—for the fathers ought to lay up for the children, not the children for the fathers. Mr. D. is their strongest man. He is called on to visit infidels and the like on their death-bed, and in other extreme cases. He works out for his daily bread, yet contrived last year to expend in charity 100 dollars. We asked, "Do you count your calling sacred ? " " Oh, yes, but no more so than that of the humblest Sister among us, if she be but six years old." This Brother Joshua never sleeps more than four hours in the night ; rises at four o'clock the year round. Often before daylight, the family hear him at his devotions, sending up his pious ejaculations ; and when very fervent, so that he may not disturb others, he goes out to the barn, and lets fly the torrent of his prayer.

Mr. B——, of Centreville, Barnstable, is a plain Cape-Cod fisherman, a skipper, it may be. His bright, cheerful countenance charmed me. He made a short speech, with many gestures, which troubled Brother H—— not a little. The speech was to this effect : " I see about in the land many little Babels of sectarian churches, as you call them—now I see you wish to pull down these little Babels, to take the combustible materials of which they are made, and erect one great Babel into which you may enter. You are in a fair way, and if this is not confusion of tongues already prevailing, I don't know what confusion is." Brother H—— was not a little horrified at the statement.

A good while after, Mrs. B——, or " Sister Olive," as they called her, arose and spoke, her husband cheering her on as she faltered a little, and another calling out from the distance, " Go on, Sister, Jesus is with you." She stated meekly and beautifully—that Cape-Cod saint —her religious history, her connection with an orthodox church, then with a Free-will Baptist, and her persecution in both. " Now," she said, " the Lord has set me in a large place." Her remarks showed plainly that she spoke from the divine life.

I afterwards talked with her, and saw how divine her heart appeared, and her countenance also ; for she has one of the fairest faces I have seen for many moons.

THE BIBLE.—They use the Bible, but do not worship it, nor call it master. Said B—— to me, " Men worship it now, just as the old Pagans worshipped their idols. Now the Bible is a scripture of the

Word, not the Word itself; for the Word is never written save in the living heart."

They admit that a man is inspired so far as he is obedient, and that he gets the Truth by obedience.

There was a young man of twenty-five, perhaps, who interested us much. His exterior was that of a plain working-man. Indeed, he is still a farmer, but he is a minister also, and so preaches. He has little education in the way of books, but has thought much and deep. Alcott asked him about Christ, and he said to him, "Truth was Christ, and Christ Truth." He expects salvation from the inward and living Christ, by becoming the Christ. In short, he had the same notions of Christ that Cudworth sets forth in that remarkable sermon. His idea of life and death was peculiar; if we possessed the entire truth, this body would never die, but would be caught up and spiritualized. I don't know that I understand this notion completely, but if I do it is rather weak.

MR. MANTALINI.—This illustrious person has another name. I have given him this merely as a *nom de resemblance*, on account of his striking likeness to that distinguished worthy. His air and address are the same; even his dress, his watch-chain, and all the cockney equipments are the same. His whiskers would have been the admiration of his prototype. He spoke several times, and with the most dandiacal air conceivable. Among other things, he likened the Christian Church to Samson going down to Timnath, and slaying a lion. I thought to give our friend a touch, so I replied, and said, that our brother, in a manner no less significant than touching, had compared the Christian Church. There was a resemblance, for Samson was a Nazarite from his birth. The locks of his strength were not to be shown, nor the wine of pride to pass his lips. So long he was invincible, and bore off the gates of his enemies, and slew a thousand men with the jaw-bone of an ass. So was the Church, so long as it remained as God designed, invincible. But when it relied on that Dalilah of visible organizations, she shore off the locks of its strength, delivered it into the hands of the Philistines, who put out its eyes, and made it grind in the mill of its enemies. Well for the Church if it can pull down the temple of its foes, and crush them in its own death, &c. After the meeting was over, my distinguished friend came up to me with an air of most intolerable patronage, and told how glad he was to hear me speak, and that he assented to nearly all I had said.

This man has a history. . . . Now the Christians * are fishing for the amphibious gentleman, but the draught will not be miraculous if they capture him. I should think the question would be who shall *not* have him.

RESULTS AND IMPRESSIONS IN MY OWN MIND.—1. I am surprised to find so much illiberality amongst the men who called the Convention; they were not emancipated from the letter of the Bible nor the formality of a Church. They simply wish to pull down other sects to make room for their own, which will probably be worse than its predecessors. 2. I

---

* Pronounced Christ-ians; the name of a sect in the United States, which, with unimportant differences, sympathizes chiefly with Methodists and Baptists. The more cultivated members approach the Unitarians.

am surprised and enchanted to find these plain Cape-Cod men with numerous others who have made actual my own highest idea of a Church. I feel strengthened by their example. Only let it be united with the highest intellectual culture. 3. I am surprised to find many others who have emancipated themselves from the shams of the Christian Church, and now can worship God at first hand and pray largely and like men. I don't know that I have got any new ideas; but certainly my confidence in my old ideas has been deepened, for I see they may be made actual.

10

CHAPTER VI.

Groton Convention—Letters—Speculations upon Physical and Moral Evil—Sin.

AFTER the private record of impressions, given in the last chapter, it will be interesting to have the speech which Mr. Parker delivered before the Convention. It is taken from a newspaper which existed at that time to advocate reforms in theological and ecclesiastical matters.

We have had already several definitions of sectarianism; but it is useless to attempt to define *sectarianism* until we know what Christianity is, as useless as to define a crooked line before knowing what a straight line is. To find out what Christianity is, if we go to the usages and opinions of Christ himself, the work is plain and easy. The way of Christianity, which is identical with the way of salvation, is *so* plain and easy, that none can mistake it. A young man asks of Christ, " What shall I do to have eternal life ?" The answer is very short : " Keep the commandments." And when the young man asked "Which ?" the chief moral precepts were pointed out, and the *practical duties* of love to neighbours enforced. The same question was put to him in a little different form. A scribe asked, " Which is the great commandment of the law ?" He answered, " Love God with all thy heart ; " " love thy neighbour as thyself ; on these two commandments hang all the law and the prophets." This is the Christian scheme ; here is its righteousness, its religion ; all are here. Christianity is a divine life : a life of outward goodness—a life of inward holiness. Try this by reason—reason enlightened by holiness ; there is nothing which jars with reason—nothing that conflicts with human nature. Try it by conscience—God's most intimate presence in the soul ; and when this light shines most fully into the heart, you shall find nothing wrong— nothing harsh—nothing arbitrary in this scheme of the whole duty of man. Here, among things essential to morality and religion, to Christianity and eternal life, not a word is said about belief in any dogmas ; not a word about the Atonement—the Old Testament or the New Tes-. tament—not a word about Baptism, or anything ritual. Christianity was a *divine life*, not a belief.

Now, I take it, sectarianism is a departure from this simple method of Christ. We find departures even in the New Testament, as I will show, though not in historical order. 1. At dead of night, the jailer, alarmed by an earthquake, asked Paul, " What shall I do to be saved ?" The answer was, " Believe on the Lord Jesus Christ," &c. ; *i. e.*, *believe in Christianity;* for the concrete is often used for the abstract in the New

Testament. The "word of the Lord" was soon "spoken to him," and he was baptized "the same hour of the night." Here, the only departure from the method of Christ, previously laid down, consisted in the ordinance of baptism being insisted on. Christ had caused some to be baptized, in compliance with the spirit of the times, and as a symbol of the divine life. But Paul seems to consider it as something of importance—an *essential matter*. He was not satisfied without the *sign*, though he had the *thing signified*. Perhaps, however, the great apostle did not deem it essential ; and the fact that he baptized but few would favour this supposition. Here, then, is Paul's scheme. He says not a word about the Old Testament—for he cast it behind him as a law of sin and death ; not a word about the New Testament—for it was not written save in faithful hearts ; and never, in his epistles or elsewhere, does he insist on belief in those things deemed most essential by the modern Church. He knows nothing of the miraculous birth, and proclaims no miracle but the Resurrection. Examine Paul's scheme, as that of Christ, and we can object only to the ritual observances ; and perhaps even that is, with him, but a symbol, and so is legitimate and Christian.

2. Now, Peter and the first Christians departed more widely from the simplicity of Christ. Peter, who had once denied his master during his life, misunderstanding the Old Testament, declares, "Every soul that will not hear that prophet" (meaning Christ) "shall be destroyed from among the people ;" and, with right Jewish narrowness, adds that "there is no other name given under heaven whereby men can be saved," words which seem to have a different meaning from those of Christ,—"I am the way, and the truth, and the life." It is not very easy to determine exactly what method Peter did propose ; for he taught one thing at Jerusalem and another at Antioch. This seems clear that he did not, like Christ, count a divine life as the all-in-all of Christianity ; but, while he himself lived as the Gentiles, compelled the Gentiles to accept the whole Mosaic law, for which cause Paul "*withstood him to the face.*" Peter, it seems, was inclined to go all lengths with the other Jewish Christians, and insisted that the old law,—wrathful, foolish, and absurd as it was in its form,—should be bound like a millstone on the disciples' necks. The most revolting rite of the law was selected as the point not to be given up ; for without this rite there was no salvation. Such was Christianity, according to the Jewish Christians at Antioch.

The controversy between Paul and Peter (who seem to represent the two poles of the new religion) became important, and the whole matter was brought before the council at Jerusalem. That body, like similar bodies at all times, compromised the matter, and added to Paul's list of essentials certain others of their own, viz., abstinence from blood, from things strangled, and from all food offered to idols, of which Christ said not a word. Paul did not acquiesce in this decision, except as a matter of occasional convenience, and in cases where he feared to hurt the conscience of the weak. Wonderful to tell, at this council we find inconstant Simon has shifted again, and takes sides with Paul ; or if we take a different view of the chronology, and suppose that Peter "feared them that were of the circumcision" *after* this council, then his conduct was still more inconsistent ; at any rate "he walked not uprightly according to the truth of the gospel." There was *sectarianism* in the New Testament ; sectarianism among the *very apostles,* whom my friends appeal to as infallible.   The followers of Christ did not catch the whole of his spirit, and some of the apostles became exclusive, prudish, and mechanical.

But yet they all insisted on the *divine life* as the one thing needful, though they added what suited their own caprice.

3. But in our day the departure from Christ is still more wide. Were some penitent scribe, not far from the kingdom of heaven, or some jailer in distress, to ask some of our teachers of salvation " What shall I do to be saved ? " the answer would not be so short as that of Jesus or Paul.   He would be told there was no hope for him unless he believed certain doctrines ; he must accept the Scriptures as a " rule of faith and practice ;" must believe the world was made in six days; that man was created pure, yet fell from that pureness ; that Moses out-juggled the magicians of Egypt; that prophets predicted the Messiah, who was at last born miraculously, wrought miracles, and ascended to the right hand of God.   Now, even admitting in argument that all these things insisted on were true, neither Christ nor Paul, nor even Peter ever demanded assent to them.

You go into the Catholic Church, and are told that the Church, the Scriptures, and unscriptural tradition comprise the whole sum of moral and religious truth.   You go into the Protestant Church, and the magic circle, within which all truth is supposed to be contained, is drawn still narrower.   You are told it is all in the Scriptures.   Now Christ said " Search the Scriptures."   Paul recommends them as profitable reading.   But that either tells you to believe the Scriptures against reason, I have yet to learn.   The Bible was made for man, not man for the Bible ; but men's minds have been forced into bondage to its letter.

Our teachers of commandments will give you a scheme of theology, when you ask the way to be saved.   In one church it is larger, in another less ; still all the churches trust in their creeds, and not in the divine life.   To such a pass have matters come, in this respect, that were Paul to come to us now, in New England, it is quite doubtful whether he could be admitted to our churches.   Her ministers would say to him, " Paul, what thinkest thou of the Old Testament ?" He would reply " It is a law of sin and death ; only a schoolmaster's assistant to lead us to Christ.   I settled that matter 2000 years ago." The astounded priest might proceed, " What thinkest thou of the miraculous birth of Christ, his miracles, his bodily ascension to heaven ; of the authority of the church ?"   The apostle would say, " I know them not ; I never taught them to the churches ; only the divine life and the resurrection, these were my doctrines.   Wise are you in your generation !   Festus thought much learning had made *me* mad ; but I never heard the tithe of those things whereof you are so certain, though I had visions and revelations of the Lord."   The sum of the whole matter would be that the great apostle of the Gentiles, who found the Christians an obscure Jewish sect, and left them a mighty band in all great cities, *was not up to the level of the times, and he must not sit down at the Lord's table.*   But this is not the worst ; to such a pitch has the sectarianism of the church arrived, that should Christ himself return to the earth, not stating that he was Jesus, should he live as before, and apply the truths to the time, he would be abused in our newspapers, called infidel and atheist, and only not stoned in our streets because we have another way to treat such men.

Jesus of Nazareth was the greatest soul ever swathed in the flesh; to redeem man, he took his stand on righteousness and religion; on no form, no tradition, no creed. He demanded not a belief, but a life,—a life of love to God, and love to man. We must come back to this; the sooner the better.

The Americans are marked for their good sense; they apply this to moral things, and so far are successful; they apply it to navigation, and outsail other nations on every sea; to their manufactures, and weave and spin for the antipodes; to their legislation, and have a code that comes nearer than any other to the natural laws which God has writ on man. It yet remains for us to apply good sense to religion; when this is done, it will be of very little importance what a man thinks of the Old Testament or the New Testament, so long as he loves man as himself, and God above all. Then the difference between the creed of Hopkins and Edwards, the dogmas about the Miracles, the Ascension, the Resurrection, even, and the inspiration of the apostles, will be subjects of speculation for the curious, but which have as little to do with our *religion*, as a farthing candle has with the shining of the noonday sun.

If we thus apply our good sense, Mr. President, we have but two things to fear, the flesh and the devil; but so long as we have the flesh in the world, and the devil in the Church, there is much to fear. (Expressions of agreement.)

At a subsequent stage of the discussion Mr. Parker continued his remarks. The reported interruptions and remarks of other members are here omitted.

We were invited to establish the largest Christian liberty; but this resolution* gives permission to any individual to infringe that liberty by imposing a test.

* * * * *

There is a distance heaven-wide between Christ and the apostles. If they are presented as being equally high authority, what shall we do when we recognize the difference in their teachings? Then again we find a difference between the apostles themselves: one was a thousand miles from the other. (True—amen.)

* * * * *

A gentleman who has just spoken, considers it a heinous offence for a minister of the gospel to support himself otherwise than by preaching. He will no doubt permit me also to quote "the apostle," who held a different opinion on this point. "I have coveted no man's silver, or gold, or apparel, yea, ye yourselves know *that these hands have ministered* unto my necessities," &c.

Another speaker thinks it not altogether safe or sufficient, to rely on Jesus for authority in ecclesiastical matters, but prefers the authority of the disciples to that of the master,—if I do not misapprehend

---

* Resolved—That for an individual Christian, or a church, to require more of a person, as a condition of his or her fellowship, than what they deem necessary to salvation, is an assumption unwarrantable in its nature, and schismatical in its tendency.

him. He thinks the apostles were the "foundation of the Church."
Now Paul thought otherwise, for he says, "Who then is Paul, and who
is Apollos, but ministers, (i. e. *servants*), by whom ye believed? I have
planted, Apollos watered, but God gave the increase; so then neither
is he that planteth any thing, nor he that watereth. *Other foundation can
no man lay, than that is laid, which is Jesus Christ.*" "Therefore let no
man glory in man, for all things are yours, and you are Christ's, and
Christ is God's."

Again: my worthy brother assumed that the apostles were *inspired;*
this will be granted on all hands. But he assumed they possessed a
perfect and *infallible* inspiration, which cannot be granted. It must
be denied that they had the inspiration requisite to make them masters
of conscience, reason, and faith, in all coming time. I deny that
they had this inspiration, or even claimed to have it. If they
had this inspiration, it may be proved from the New Testament,
or from some other source. But the authority of tradition, oral or
written, does *not* establish the fact. If we look at the New Testament, we find nowhere any claim set up by the apostles to such
inspiration. But supposing they were too modest to claim an honour
they really desired. Let us look at the facts.. It can be shown
very clearly that they were not thus inspired perfectly, so as to be
incapable of mistake. If thus inspired, they must have agreed in
doctrine. Now it is quite plain they did not agree. If they
were thus inspired, why was the first council at Jerusalem called to
deliberate and decide what should be done? One man *perfectly*
inspired needs no council, but is wise as a whole synod of inspired
men. I deny not that the apostles were inspired, like other good and
wise men, in various degrees. But I do deny that they were so
inspired as never to commit a fault. I do deny that Peter was inspired
by God to dissemble, or Paul to curse Alexander the copper-smith.

A worthy brother, some time ago, in a manner no less significant
than touching, compared the Christian Church to Samson going down
to Timnath, and slaying a lion. I wish he had carried out the comparison, it is quite felicitous and suggestive. Samson was a Nazarite
from his birth, as the story reads; his locks were not to be shorn, nor
was strong drink to pass his lips; so long as he obeyed God he was
invincible. So is it with the Church; so long as it was true to the
law of God, so long was it invincible; but when it yielded to that
Delilah of a Jewish organization, with a lust for power over men's
freedom, and drank deeply the wine of its pride, and forgot there was a
God, it was shorn of the locks of its strength, its eyes were put out,
itself bound to toil at the mill of its enemies, and happy will it be if
it destroys at last the temple of its foes.

I believe most fully in inspiration. There have always been inspired
men; in all times, in every land. The line of apostles reaches down
through all the ages. The tide of inspiration sets through the world,
and such souls as Numa and Solon, Moses and Solomon, Paul and
John, have drank largely in the Holy Spirit; and each, as he appeared,
was seen in conflict with the age on which he shone,—and each was
scorned and rejected of those whose selfishness obscured their vision:
yet each, in the after-age, came to be thought a demigod or an apostle
by those to whom his teachings were found to be a blessing, and then

his merest words became injunctions, from which it was heresy to dissent, and his most careless modes of life became the statute-laws for the lives of mankind. Men organized upon them; and then the spirit of a true life began to die out,—and men looked to these dead forms from the depths of human suffering for comfort, and found it not. But, still in their distress they hovered around the lifeless image as we have seen orphan girls cling to the garments of their dead mother, as if these poor relics could still give shelter and consolation. Then came Jesus; and his was a larger soul. He saw all through the conditions of humanity. He saw the poor suffering, man fallen, and the yoke of olden time pressing heavily upon him, so that he might not rise. And Jesus said to him, " Why do you not look to God? Why will you go back to Moses? Here is something greater than Moses. Why will you talk of Solomon? A greater than Solomon is here. Why cling to dead forms? Why not trust to the living spirit? Why not take religion at first-hand?" And then they cried out against him, for destroying their religion. " Why do you not fast, they said, and why do you not preach Moses?" And he replied, " Why don't you put new wine into old bottles? because the bottles will burst." He had not come to destroy but to fulfil. He had nothing to do with their organizations. He let those who would not come out of their shadows, sit there. He came not to tear down their cherished temples, but he knew that they *must* fall at the voice of teachings like his. And ever, when the true man appears, the false ones disappear before him; and when Jesus came, the dwellers in the old order of things, shrieked and fled, like owls and bats at the coming in of morning.

At only thirty years of age, they scourged him and put him to death. But his *truth* lived, and dwelt in the hearts of those poor, plain, humble fishermen, till, through their blood and sacrifice, Christianity came to be accounted a religion,—and its votaries went on spending and being spent. Men gathered themselves everywhere together in its name, at Ephesus, at Antioch, at Corinth, and at Rome; till from thence it ascended the throne of the world, and cities and broad realms bent beneath it. Then the love of power quenched its first true spirit, and now we hear men talk about its *doors!* and quote the 18th chapter of Matthew! A church! why, what does *church* mean there? Simply a gathering of men; nor can you find any mention of a church in the sense in which the word is now understood, in the whole range of Christian literature, from St. James to Hildebrand.

What is the church now? Paul says, " Where the Spirit of the Lord is, there is liberty." But where the spirit of the church is, there is slavery! The Holy Spirit says, Be a true soul! live a divine life! The church demands a *belief,* and *not* a divine life! The best men come to her, and find no life—no power; only——

The President announced that Mr. Parker's time had expired.

To go and confer with these men and women, and fraternally consider their views, required a good deal of modest humanity in those days. It was quite enough that some of them wore

their hair long ; such a symbol of radical infidelity was more
damaging to their reputation than a disregard for the Sabbath
and all scriptural ordinances.   The newspapers ridiculed those
singularities which always appear among people with little
culture who undertake a new theology.   Books and free intercourse would be fatal to these little pomposities, which are signs
of isolation oftener than of egotism.   But few people credited
that a tender and devout spirit urged many of these Come-Outers
to separate from the Church.

Mr. Parker had a native love for man.   It was not an
abstract recognition of new phrases of Equality and Fraternity.
His nature was not of the cool and serene kind which prefers
truths to people, and would never invite the latter except under
compulsion.   Every scholarly attainment only seemed to widen
the channels for his human pulse : it mantled in every gift, it
beat to shatter all doctrines which degraded or depreciated man.
He had all Dr. Channing's reverence for human nature, with a
prompt, practical friendliness, gentle to visit the humble, terrible
to defend them.   Whenever he found a truth, he placed it in
the glittering row which sits upon the rugged forehead of
humankind : there it looked handsomer to him than in
æsthetic and transcendental cabinets.   For all things look best
where they belong.

What, indeed, was the whole movement of his mind at this
time, but that act of highest and most Christ-like humanity, a
liberating of the Human from the Conventional !   As fast as his
own strong intentions struggled through scriptural views and
theological finalities, he recognized them, not as his own but as
Man's.   He possessed them in virtue of his membership in the
great society of men and women, whose hearts the Infinite
Father directly nourishes with truth and love.   No distant and
fastidious conceptions were for him.   He could not belong to a
clique any more than to a sect.   His very distinction as a
radical thinker was his conformity to absolute and universal
truths.   His unsparing criticisms were efforts to rejoin his
comrades, to level the pale-work and text-hedges, and let out
the poor huddled creatures into the common where the untaxed
food grows for all.

So he instinctively drew near whenever he saw people gather.
No pride of books, or luxury of fine thinking, held him back
from seeing what his brethren were about.   There must be

something going on, he surmised, else there would not be a crowd. Mere stupidity, folly and impiety cannot convene; some natural want makes folly cohere long enough to be marked and exposed. Yet he did not confuse movements in favor of a new theology with those in the interest of the old : it was for the sake of the human nature that is found both in a liberal convention and in a Calvinistic revival that he preferred the former. He loved to be in the company of hope, and was more tolerant of ignorance and error where he saw the work of reconstruction going on. But he had a very quick and humorous eye for the knavish little parasites who infest a growing truth ; he did not relish new hypocrisy any better than the old.

This was the human temper which he afterwards brought to the consideration of Spiritualism and Mormonism. They were new movements of sufficient magnitude to challenge the attention. He undertook a deliberate examination, to weigh their good against their evil, and especially to understand their original determining impulse. Camp meetings and revivals he and all the world knew enough about, the good and the evil which they did to the soul. The new thing deserved to be known as well, to become the object of a human observation. And when, as in the case of Spiritualism, he found a theology thoroughly anti-Calvinistic in every respect, a reassertion of the universal instinct for a life after death, and a vehement impulse to emancipate souls from degrading notions of a vindictive God, who, if He prepares immortality at all, prepares it as an opportunity for the damnation of the greater number of His own children, he bestowed his hearty sympathy upon the men and women, while he told them frankly, that their supernaturalism was no better than the old kind, and that though the evidence in favor of their miracles was as good as that in favor of any, their liberal thought and feeling would be impaired by their inclination for the marvellous.

EXTRACT FROM A LETTER.

All the world and " the rest of mankind " is talking about " spiritualism," " rappers," " tippers," " writers," " talkers," &c. There are many strange things testified to by some of the soundest and shrewdest of men; things which I cannot explain as yet. But I do not accept the hypothesis that they are the work of " SPIRITS," either the souls of dead men, or " angels " good or bad. I know nothing to justify the "spiritual" hypothesis. I am not successful in my investigations; I drive off the "spirits" by looking at the table. I once—and once only—got a *response* from a "spirit;" that was of a man whom I knew to be safe and sound on *terra firma* here below. (I have seen him since.) I got any answer that I wanted to get. If I had time I should like to look into the matter a little further. But scientific men give it the go-by—which seems scarcely right. It does not now appear in *Catholic* districts I am told. Is it so? They have enough to excite their marvellousness without tipping tables!

EXTRACTS FROM THE JOURNAL.

THE EARLY CHRISTIANS.—All I read of them convinces me more of their noble character, aim and life. But I see their limitations. They were superstitious, formal (at least after the middle of the second century, and perhaps also in the apostles' times,) the *letter* burthened them. But they were full of the noble manly spirit. Their ascetic doctrines of marriage, dress, amusement, education, I dislike, vastly. They laid too much stress on baptism, the eucharist—giving the latter to men to keep at home, carry in their pocket, &c., gave it to little children just after baptism, put it in the mouth of dead people, and the like.

But how they died—how they prayed—how they lived! We cannot yet afford to criticise these men. Certainly they were not gentlemen, but they were *men*. The wonder is that *being* so much, they *saw* no more. One thinks if Seneca could have been Christian, he would have seen truth as Schleiermacher and De Wette saw it. But who knows!

The early Christians were not literary men—none of them. They spoke because they had something they could not help saying. So the spirit found very vehement but very imperfect utterance. Culture did nothing for them (this with exceptions—Justin Martyr, Clemens, Alexandrinus, Origen, &c.) Inspiration did all, so there was no grace.

HERETICS.—They began very early. Indeed we find them in the times of the apostles. In Jesus you are in the *Pleroma* of light; step into the apostles, it is already evening, and the light is behind you. Take another step, and you are in fathomless darkness. Heretics have always been treated as the worst of men. Imaginary doctrines have been ascribed to them, immoral ceremonies; they have been charged with sins of the blackest dye. This treatment the Jews received of the Gentiles, the Christians of the Heathen, the Heretics from the Catholic Church; the Protestants—in a word, the *Come-Outers* of all ages have been abused. Jerome says the heretics, even if they lead blameless and beautiful lives, have only the image and shadow of virtue. Tertullian chides Marcion, after the fashion of Dr. South, with his God who is not to be feared; and asks him why, if he does not fear God, he does not go to the theatre, and bawdy-houses, and game and drink? Philastor and Augustine censure some heretics who would think the planets, sun, moon and stars were worlds, because they denied the resurrection of the flesh. Christ was put to death as a heretic. The treatment which the Come-Outers, and some others, Mr. Dyer, &c., have lately received, shows me how the heretics were treated in all times, and how much truth I am to expect in Irenæus, Tertullian, Epiphanius, Philastor and Jerome, when they treat of heretics.

1. A bad name is given them.

2. Some one is discovered or invented who has the same name and very dangerous doctrines and a wicked life. This is blazoned to the world, and then,

3. The heretic is charged with the same doctrines and life ; and so it goes.

Truth is unchangeable, but orthodoxy and heresy vary with each country and every age. The world seems to defend doctrines in the inverse ratio of their value, as mothers love best their weak and sickly children.

Nothing will ever save us but a wide, generous toleration. I must tolerate and comfort my brother, though I think him in error, though I know him to be in error. I must tolerate his ignorance, even his sin— yes, his intolerance. Here the only safe rule is, if some one has done you a wrong, to resolve on the spot never to do that wrong to him or any one else. It is easy to tolerate a man if you know he is a fool and quite in the wrong. But we must tolerate him when we know he is not a fool, and not altogether in the wrong.

Mr. Parker's speculative freedom brought him into suspicion as early as 1838 :—

Nov. 13.—A rare thing has happened to me to-day; simply this— a certain Mrs. —— pronounces me an *infidel* in good set speech. The reason is, that I do not think as she does of the authority of Jesus. She thinks he has a different authority from that of the truths he taught ; therefore, that we are bound to obey him, even if the doctrine in question does not seem true to us. I think Jesus Christ is to be reverenced and obeyed solely for the *intellectual, moral,* and *religious* truth which he brought to light by his doctrines and life. If sentences of his did not seem true to me, I should reject them ; for I can accept no opinion which annuls my own reason.

I honour and revere Christ more, perhaps, than she, though not in the same way. Afterwards, she retracted the offensive term, " infidel ; " but this does not mend the matter. I something doubt that my sermons breathe the spirit of infidelity.

But all this shows me—what needed no proof before—how much easier it is to censure another, and damn him with harsh names, than to amend one's own life, or even to apprehend the difference between his creed and your own.

May, 1839.—I am often struck with the great freedom and boldness of Christ's remarks. The Jews venerated manna. He told them it did not come down from heaven. They superstitiously honoured the sabbath. He said it was made for man, not man for it. He said that one greater than all the old prophets was inferior to the least of his disciples.

Consider the surpassing boldness with which he rebuked men and taught doctrines.

Here is a boldly chalked study, to serve in the composition of his mind :—

June.—How much do we idealize Christ ? Very much, I suspect; I look on the Christ of tradition as a very different being from the ideal Christ. The latter is the highest form of man we can conceive of—a perfect incarnation of the Word. The former, a man, perhaps, of passions not always under command, who had little faults and weaknesses that would offend us. His thoughts came like mine; and he was sometimes in doubt, perhaps contradicted himself, and taught things not perfectly consistent with reason, or, at best, gave utterance to crude notions. From the nature of the case, he could not do otherwise. Thought is life generalized; it arrives, therefore, only as we live—so, from year to year and day to day, Christ must have generalized better as he lived more. His plans were evidently not perfectly formed at first. He fluctuates; does not know whether he shall renounce Moses or not. He evidently went on without any plan of action ; and, like Luther at the Reformation, effected more than he designed. At first, perhaps, he meditated simply a reform of Mosaism, but finally casts off all tradition, and starts a fresh soul.

His power of miracle-working is an element of the soul. It is a vein running through all history, coming near the surface of life only in the most elevated characters, and in their most rapt states of mind. So the central rocks only crop out in mountains. We all feel this miracle-power *ideally* (A—— says *actually* likewise, and perhaps he is right; I can feel something of it, supposing it is what E—— calls demoniacal influence). Jesus, a greater man than ever lived before or since, lived it actually ; his miracles, therefore, were natural acts, not contrary to outward nature, but above it.

His inspiration I can understand still better. There can be but one *kind* of inspiration; it is the intuition of truth. And but one *mode* of inspiration; it is the conscious presence of the highest, either as beauty, justice, usefulness, holiness, or truth—the felt and perceived presence of absolute being infusing itself into me. But there may be infinite degrees of inspiration. The degree depends on the being of the man to be inspired; a noble being is capable of more, a smaller soul of less. It depends also on the faithfulness of the finite soul. It may perfectly obey the conditions on which it is obtainable, then it will have all the inspiration it is capable of at that stage of its growth ; or it may do this imperfectly, when it will have less. It depends, then, on the finite soul itself, whether or not, and to what degree it will be inspired. Hence, in all times we see instances of souls, humble by nature, obtaining a higher degree of inspiration than others, their superiors in innate capabilities, and so becoming the superior beings. Such were many prophets of the Old Testament; such was Bunyan. Now Christ, I fancy, was one of the greatest souls born into the world of time ; and did also more perfectly than any other man fulfil the conditions of inspiration ; so the spirit dwelt in him bodily. His was the highest inspiration—his the divinest revelation. But this must be said of *actualities,* not of *possibilities.* It is folly, even impiety, to say that God cannot create a greater soul than that of Jesus of Nazareth.

Who shall attempt to foreshorten God, and close the gates of time against him, declaring that no more of his spirit can be by any possibility incarnated? Jesus was cut off at an early age—the period of blossom, not fruitage. What are thirty years? How much could he have lived? All the great works of reflective genius have appeared after five-and-forty. It is only by long practice and much life that the soul's instruments—thought and language—are matured. The *reflective* had scarcely began to dawn in him; the *spontaneous* alone was active. He, then, is not a model for us in the reflective powers, only in the spontaneous. Why may we not see a soul uniting them all, and so revealing manhood in a higher form—I will not say the highest, *that* I know not of—by a revelation nobler and more perfect than his?

The Christ of tradition I shall preach down, one of these days, to the extent of my ability. I will not believe the driving beasts out of the temple with a whip;* the command to Peter to catch a fish; still less the cursing the fig-tree, and the old wives' fables about the Ascension. His predictions of his death I have reason to doubt; but I know not but they are real. He, doubtless, was mistaken in his predictions of the end of the world, or rather his disciples were; for the prediction is manifest and its failure obvious. The ideal Christ is what we are to preach; and, perhaps, we shall not need the Gospels much in delineating him. Yet I should be sorry to lose even the little they afford us, were it not for the lamentable matter they connect therewith. Christianity is much indebted to Paul. He freed it from its narrowness. Was it limited in Christ, or did its limits come from his disciples? Christ seems himself to fluctuate—once he refuses to heal a stranger-woman's child, as not being part of his mission. But he is afterwards surprised to find a greater faith than in his own nation. I doubt that he designed it to be universal; yet many passages towards the end of his life favour it.

Nov. 1839.—Saw Bancroft at his house. He spoke with delight of the intense desire of the "commonality" for spiritual truths. They will not rest their Christianity on something outside. He agreed with me that the old mode of presenting religion has ceased to have any effect, and that the Church needs to be more *democratic*, but sees not the "*how*," an important category in this connection.

He showed me a passage in Spinoza which shocked me, where he goes farther than Machiavelli, and denies the obligatoriness of a promise farther than it can allay fear or stimulate the hope of the promisee, and adds, the promiser is a great fool to think otherwise.

Bancroft thinks Jonathan Edwards was the great man of New England. The centre with Edwards, I said, was the *Bible*, and with Spinoza the *soul*. B. says no, the centre with both is *God*; the Bible does not hamper Edwards, nor does any human authority. He looks through these.

TO MISS ELIZABETH P. PEABODY

August 30, 1839.

I should make an apology, my dear Elizabeth, for not writing before, were it not contrary to my theory, and practice, also, to make apologies at any time. It has not been lack of inclination, but of leisure, you

---

* This sentimental touch disappeared in the exigencies of his own protesting, and the scourge of small cords seemed less mythological.

will do me the kindness to suppose.   Both L. and myself were highly
edified by your letter.   I am highly grateful for the advice you offer,
and doubt not it will bear fruit.   I think you have formed a very just
estimate of L.; indeed, you had done so *before*, but she will not admit
the fact.   Thinks you make her too *good*, and the like.   Touching my
becoming a martyr, as you and Miss Burley conjecture, I think I shall
have no occasion for the requisite spirit, even if I had that article in as
great abundance as John Knox or John Rogers.   I have precious little
of the spirit of a martyr; but inasmuch as I fear no persecution, I
fancy I can " say my say," and go on *smoothly ;* but if not, why—well, I
can go *roughly*.   I trust I have enough of the Spirit always to speak
the truth, be the consequence what it may.   It seems to me men often
trouble themselves about the consequences of an opinion, or action,
much more than is necessary.   Having settled the question that an
opinion is *true* and an action perfectly *right*, what have you and I to
do with consequences ?   They belong to God, not to man.   He has as
little to do with these as with the rising of the sun or the flow of the
tide.   Doubtless men said to Galileo, " Your system may be true,—but
only think of the consequences that follow !   What will you do with
them ? "   The sage probably replied, " I will let them alone.   To do
duty and speak truth is my office ; God takes care of consequences."
I am sorry you and that wise woman, Miss B., should form so high an
opinion of me, for all my subsequent life will do nothing but cancel it,
and show on what an airy base your kind feelings have erected an
imaginary character.

Dec. 4.—Mr. O. C. Everett came to see me to-day.   He said some
good things—to wit, about speaking ill of others.   He thinks one
ought never to say of another what he would be ashamed to say in his
presence.   But this is wrong.   I should be ashamed to praise as well
as to censure.   A better rule would be—1. Say nothing ill of any one
unless certain it is true ; 2. Say nothing ill, unless certain that no evil
or selfish motive animates you.

He thinks also that I confound the attributes with the *personality*
of God.   But how can it be ? where is the difference between the
two ?   Is God separate or separable from his wisdom, justice, or love ?
Surely not.

Jan. 2, 1840.—Preached the Thursday lecture on Inspiration.   After
it was over, Dr. —— came up to me, while conversing with Dr. Francis
and Mr. Cunningham, and said, " When you write about Ralph Cudworth,* I read ye and like ye ; but when you talk about future Christs,
I can't bear ye."   There was a great deal more of the same kind.   He
called me " impious," whereat I was so grieved, that I left him, not in
anger, but in sorrow, and went weeping through the street; but, at
length bethought me of Ellis, and went to see him, and so dried my
tears.

This is not the temper of an over-conscious man, who deliberately hatches new opinions, and hastens to annoy the general
convictions.   His mind worked in an impersonal manner, and

---

* Article in the January number, 1840, of the *Christian Examiner*, upon Cudworth's
Intellectual System.

he never calculated the effect of his opinions, or of the plain speech into which they flowed. He was often very much astonished at the effect of passages which slipped from his pen with no design beyond that of putting his thought into clear and strong expression. So he was surprised, and sometimes a little hurt, when his friends told him that his satire occasionally degenerated into sarcasm. It never entered his mind to be sarcastic or sneering. He vindicated the use of all legitimate intellectual weapons to defend truth and attack error. He employed the whole of his mind to enforce all his convictions, backed by health and homely vigour. He grew in a way to be plain and muscular in the performance of his function as teacher and liberator of men's minds. And he put forth his strength in such instinctive fashion, under the dominion of such an earnest motive and such absorbed convictions, that he could neither stop to think of his style nor to dilute his eagerness. There is sometimes a want of taste, but no malice, in the speech which his fiery honesty had mastered. His whole language, with its glories and its faults, is himself, in unflawed integrity, untampered with by second thoughts, the characteristic product of such education and native power as fell to him, *idiomatic*, in all the possible senses of that word. It is " a nipping and an eager air," and as little charged with malice.

His dear friend, Rev. S. J. May, of Syracuse, once urged him to abate the sarcasm ; to this he replies :—

April 1, 1845.—What you say about the sarcasm, and all that, I by no means plead guilty unto. I wonder that *you* should bring the charge. I fully sympathise with Burns in his compassion for "auld Nickie Ben," and don't like to think of hell for his sake. I wish he would " tak' a thought an' men'." But, my dear friend, I never wrote a line with any ill-will, or *sarcastic* humour, towards maid or man. I should not dare write with such a feeling, least of all in such a cause. I wonder that you can read " Pilgrim's Progress," finding nothing of the kind therein, and then discover it in my poor writings. What if I had called men a " generation of vipers," " snakes," " children of the devil," and the like ? But enough of this.

The following letter explains itself :—

West Roxbury, 22 January, 1840.

MY DEAR BROTHER,—I have just received your letter and hasten to reply, though not without deliberation. I am much obliged to the good people of Lexington for their favourable opinion, and wish I deserved it better. It is doubly delightful to learn that any one in my *native village* should be pleased with anything that I could do. But in respect to coming to Lexington as a minister I have several things to say. I think you know that I came here *against* my own consent. My friends advised this measure of settling at Spring Street, and I consented with a good deal of unwillingness, for *I neither liked the salary of* 600 *dollars, nor the small audience of* 80 *or* 150 *souls.* But I gave up my scruples, was settled—*not for life;* but can at any time leave the place, on condition of giving notice of my intention six months beforehand. The parish also can discharge me, by a majority of votes, on the same condition. Thus stands the matter between us, as settled by the contract. The parish could have no legal or common claim upon me if I wished to leave to-morrow.

But there are other considerations that have and ought to have a strong influence. This parish is small, and the people poor; their only chance of getting and keeping a minister depends on the advantages arising from their position in the neighbourhood of Boston, Cambridge, &c. Now, if I were to leave them *at this time* I fear they could not secure the services of a minister of respectable talents, who would be *really* of use to them. It is, therefore, my *duty* to stay. I could wish with all my heart for a larger sphere, a greater number of hearers, and those more intelligent and cultivated than the majority at Spring Street; but I think *they* would lose more than *I* should gain by my leaving them. Again, I intend, in the course of my life, to do more through the *Press* than the *Pulpit.* Here I can find *ten hours* a day for *five days* in the week to devote to works not directly connected with the exercises of the pulpit, and yet neglect no duty I owe to any man, or to the whole parish. I could not thus control my time in Lexington, where the people are both more numerous and more scattered. Still further, I doubt that I could long *suit* the people at Lexington. My theological opinions differ very widely from those of the Unitarians in general, and, perhaps, would not be acceptable at Lexington; though I fear very little on that ground, since I never knew men *really religious* to find any fault with them. . . . . You know my attachment to Lexington, and how much it would delight me to be near your family, and all the *good old people of the good old town,* but taking all these things into consideration, and weighing the matter fairly, I think, my dear Isaac, that you would decide as I do.

I am glad to hear you are all well. I hope the children study as well as you and I used to do at school, and wish they might profit by the *same* instruction at home, for which I shall never cease to thank you all my life. If you can do for your children what you did for your little rebellious brother, it will be better than to give them all the houses and farms in the county of Middlesex.

> Your affectionate brother,
> THEODORE.

His journal, in commenting upon this call to Lexington, has the following :—

Now, it is very pleasant to me to be thus kindly received by my old friends; the men who patted me on the head when I was a boy, and are now surprised that I am grown up. God be with you, old parish ; may you receive more men like the Clarkes and Hancocks and Easter-brooks, to freshen your souls once more.

1840.—Dr. Channing says the Universalists have the idea of Good. It is a powerful idea ; men have been governed too much by *fear*. He wishes the idea of good to be held up—not material, sensuous good—not pleasure, but spiritual good. The Universalists have only the idea of material good. Let the celestial good be held up to man. Unitarians have, perhaps, preached too much the law—morality. They make man depend on himself. Let it be shown how God, the All Good, the Altogether Beautiful, labours to diffuse Himself and spread goodness, celestial good, through all the world. This will be effective. Man does little through fear. It is negative, and leads only to defence, or offence for the sake of defence. But good is positive, the love of it creative, and not barely . critical and defensive. Consider that all creation comes from love, not fear. Notice the action of the good upon men in the arts and sciences. See how fear belittles and love magnifies.

At various periods during 1839 and 1840, the phenomena of moral and physical evil disturbed his mind, which was now so fully awakened to difficulties both in nature and theology ; and of course his intuitive beliefs had a sharper struggle to become adjusted with nature's mysteries than with man's.

He began to notice more anxiously the habits of animals, and to ponder the secrets of physical laws. Doubts of the infinite goodness besieged his mind at the spectacle of the play of brutal instincts. He still remembered, and had not recovered from, the shock at first witnessing a certain cruel trick which male squirrels practise. Nature seemed no longer innocent, an abyss of deformity opened before his guileless feet. What is the meaning of all these things ? Suspicion filled with dreadful counts an indictment against his earliest instinctive faith. The alligator devours its young till they become too large for the parental jaws. The permitted barbarity of the cat to the mouse—the eagle's injustice in robbing the fish-hawk—the destruction of young by the large black wasps in the beginning of October—the buccaneering of some birds, who steal the nests of other birds, and throw out their eggs—the reputed enslaving of the black by the red ant—the sin against nature of dogs—the vile habits of apes and of frogs—who can explain these things ? They look devilish. Is there a dark ground in the creative mind, or does matter possess properties which are not under the Deity's control ? No ! — such Gnostic notions are inconsistent with common-sense. Is the world, then, after all, the reflex and product

11

of human nature, so that the vices of men ordain the instincts of animals ?   Even if it were possible to make the evil in man accountable for the evil among animals, that would not preserve a conception of the infinite beauty and goodness.   But it is not possible ; for though man creates his environment, for better or worse, he cannot obtrude animal tendencies upon the Divine mind, which is the sole creative source.   Whence comes the power of deformity originating deformities ?   Has God delegated to man the peopling of the woods, fields, and waters, by occult moral agency ?   Besides, it remains to account for the existence of the animal tendencies in man himself.   Thus he wrestled with the problem.

He soon observed the tentative efforts of Nature on her road to man, arrested members and faculties, " the toes in a horse's hoof, the fingers beneath the skin in the manati, the singular mannishness of some monkeys, the resemblance to human limbs noticed in some plants, as the orchis and lady's slipper— the marriage and adultery of plants."   Then he frankly acknowledged the great capacity for ugliness in Nature, the strange forms by land and sea, the congenital abortions—" calves with three heads—fruits, half peach and half plum ; apples, one side early and sweet, the other winter fruit and acid."   Thus ' he gradually made his way to the speculation that there are certain " immoralities of nature, which are distinct, definite predictions and prototypes of kindred sins in man."   If at this point his understanding had been enlisted in the service of a supernatural theology, which provides a supernatural atonement for the fact of sin, he might have used these marks of divine premeditation to invent the theory of " anticipative consequences." *   For such a theology makes perennial demands upon human ingenuity, as any tremendous assumption must when it is persistently credited.   Human reason will never put up with merely crediting an assumption, it must contrive some way of making it seem reasonable.   As fast as knowledge drives it out of one statement, it hastily throws up another, which serves only to cover its retreat.   What adroitness we have seen since the developments of geology threatened Genesis and all the sacrificial schemes !   Reynard, in the mediæval poem, never saved his brush so often.   Death, sin, the federal head, the " primal, eldest curse," all the precious objects are snatched away before the

---

* Nature and the Supernatural. By Dr. Bushnell. See Chapter VII.

trained, impassive advances of science, and placed in new positions. The fetiches of the tribe must not fall into the hands of the enemy. May the day of utter rout and disenchantment end not too soon a kind of melancholy metaphysic interest we find in the shifty spectacle!

But the shiftiest thing to do is to sally forth, seize some of the hostile facts, and convert them to evangelic service. This is the theory of "anticipative consequences." Its distinction is that God foreknew that men would have to sin. His whole being was so penetrated with anticipations of this sombre exigency, that His creative skill turned itself to the preparation of abhorrent symbols, which grew gradually worse through a long course of geologic epochs, till at last the degradation was *ripe for man.* It is very possible that if a God had been in the habit of indulging such imaginations, he might originate at length a good deal of misery. Geologic epochs framed in this Dantesque conception might circle down, through subversive instinct and deepening deterioration, to man himself, "the bright, consummate" wretch of all. And he would be associated with snakes, wry-mouthed flounders, with the rage and cunning of wild beasts, with all deformed antagonistic types, that he might not forget that he was conceived in sin and disappoint parental expectations. He would be obliged to fall to sinning, because a special effort to save him, which could not take effect unless he first does his best to be lost, has also been preordained. So his rudiments are insinuated by a set of ominous pictorials; venomous reptiles, carnivorous animals, repulsive forms of life by sea and land, the bloated spider, the chattering ape, all ruthless and stealthy creatures, are mnemonics for man's life-long lesson in the business of developing the tendencies which they prefigure, that the tendencies may be overcome by grace!

What could more strikingly display the horrible necessities of that supernatural theology, which Mr.. Parker so justly hated, than this representation of an infinite Creator, seeing clearly that He must accept evil if He would go on to organize His thought; that He is confronted at the first step which he takes out of potentiality by this infamous companion, without whom He must not make the worlds. He accepts this *sine quá non,* but at the same time there occurs to Him the idea of a great supernatural remedy, into which cunning trap the cloven foot will set itself at last. He is powerless to shake off the bad condition, but is sagacious enough to make it serve a purpose. What a God is that who consoles Himself through ages of a sin-haunted imagination which deliberately invents symbols of its dreadful surmises, with anticipating that He can at last interpose Himself in person to save a ruined mankind from the consequences of His own enforced complicity with evil! How humiliating is the thought that a few words in the Bible subject men's minds to the drudgery of rearing these elaborate fantasies to imprison the stubborn facts of Nature! The facts escape, and are again at large.

Mr. Parker did not possess, and did not need, this kind of subtlety to adjust his mind to the problem which disturbed it. No adjustment, made in the interest of any theology, can answer all the questions which the intellect is capable of raising. But one mode of treatment is less fantastic than another. And every mind must make its own terms with the problem. His own broad health and common-sense, his unconquerable hope, his great humanity, and the intuitive conviction of a perfect love which ruled all his thoughts, saved him from an elaborate and tyrannizing scheme. It was a great advantage to him in exposing particular sins and sinners that he had no theory of sin to defend. He went to his reforming work uncrippled, full of faith and hope in man, full of indignation for bad men, full of pity for those who struggle in degraded conditions or in partial growth.

Now, were I to draw conclusions solely from organic nature, what attributes should I ascribe to the cause of the world? Certainly not just the same I now give Him. But, looking into my consciousness, I find there a different idea of a God; so the first witness is insufficient —the last perfectly competent.

I do not understand how all the evil which man inflicts upon another animal, or one animal upon its fellow, can consist with the ultimate happiness of that animal. But if God is infinitely just, it must be so. I know how all things may work together for the good of the extremest suffering among men, but not among brutes.

Now, in estimating the phenomena of evil, my own faith says there is a perfect system of optimism in the world; that each man's life is to him an infinite good. Of course all his physical evils must be means of progress, all his errors likewise unavoidable steps in his course to happiness. But to legitimate this in the court of the understanding, where all other truths are legitimated, I find difficult. Faith has nothing to do there. I will imagine a person who denies that all things work together for good, and suppose myself to reply to the arguments I should bring in such a case.

Here the notes end abruptly, and the mental controversy re-appears only in the statement of a few results.

The virtues of a baby are easily learned while fondling in the nurse's arms, but the virtues of a man require the stern cradling of affliction.

I think no sin can make an indelible mark on the primitive Monad—so to say—what I call the soul. I take it the atoms of matter never change, though they take the forms of gas, fluid, and solid, though they are in the form of a crystal, vegetable, or animal. So I think sin makes little mark on the soul; for, 1, much of it is to be referred to causes exterior even to the physical man; and 2, much to the man's organization. I think $\frac{99}{100}$ of sin are thus explicable—the result of the man's limitation—A, the result of his circumstances; B, of his organization. Now, I am sure that sin, the result of A or B, can make no permanent mark on the soul. God will not damn a man because his father *had bad neighbours*, nor because the man was born with a bad head, more than with a lame leg. Now, I think many struggle with both A and B, and apparently make no progress, who will yet rise in the next life far above most of us. They may make a great *inward progress*, but from defective organization or circumstances it shall not appear.

Men complain of wild beasts in the forests, of monsters in the sea, of toads and snakes, vipers, and many a loathsome thing, hideous to our imperfect eye. How little do we know! a world without an alligator or a rattlesnake, a hyæna or a shark, would doubtless be a very imperfect world.

Theologians often talk mythologically about sin, as if there was something mysterious in its origin, its course, its process, its result, and final end. They tell us that as it is a transgression against the infinite God, so it is an infinite evil, meaning an absolute evil, demanding an eternal punishment. To this scholastic folly it is enough to reply, that if sin be for this reason an absolute evil, then the smallest suffering coming from an infinite God is an infinite suffering, and cancels the sin.

That is, what the finite can do, and what it can suffer, must be of the same magnitude. You must rate both as infinite, or neither.

I am pained by every evil thing I do. In the next life I hope to suffer till I learn the mastery of myself, and keep the conditions of my higher life. Through the Red Sea of pain I will march to the Promised Land, the divine ideal guiding from before, the Egyptian actual urging from behind.*

This letter to Hon. James G. Birney gives a clear and compact statement of his belief concerning punishment:—

Boston, 3rd Oct., 1852.

DEAR SIR,—I have been so busy in removing from summer to winter quarters that I have had no time to reply to your note until this

---

* Sermons of Theism, pp. 361–62. See the sermons on the "Economy of Pain," and the "Economy of Moral Error," for his completed views on the subject of Sin.

moment. It seems to me that we should not use the word *punish* at all in reference to the action of God. The only punishment that we know is this—*the arbitrary infliction of pain from without.* Usually it is accompanied with ill-will and a desire of vengeance, but sometimes with kindly feelings and a desire to hurt for the sake of healing. Now, theological books commonly represent God as punishing men in this or the future life with ill-will and a desire for vengeance. "Hell" is for God's sake; damnation is of no advantage to the *damned,* only to the *damner.* Well, all of that language is unphilosophical, and ought to be blotted out of all decent speech, it seems to me. The trouble I believe is this—men do not believe that God is infinite, but finite and imperfect, and therefore they attribute such motives and such actions to Him. If you start with the idea of God as infinite, possessing all the attributes of a perfect and complete being, perfectly powerful, wise, just, loving, and holy (*i. e.,* self-faithful), then the difficulty is all over; for God must have created men from a perfect motive, for a perfect end, as a perfect means for the attainment of that end, and so the attainment of the ultimate end of God's design cannot fail.

Now, the infinite God must desire the ultimate welfare of each of His creatures, must have means for bringing it about—means that are adequate to the purpose. I know very little what these means are; but this is plain, that all which a man suffers by the providence of God must be for the *good of the sufferer.* It is absurd to suppose that the infinite God will allow anyone to be miserable forever in consequence of the grossest and the worst of "sins" here; for the sins are often as much involuntary as the stumbling of the child in learning to go alone. It seems to me that all the suffering of men—and in such a town as this I see enough of it—is in the end to work out a good result, not only for the race, but for the individual sufferer. Indeed, it must be so if God be infinite, and his work perfect for His purpose. I never speak of future punishment, but of *future progress,* by the justice and the mercy and the love of God.

Respectfully and truly yours, &c.

When I see the suffering of animals, the father-alligator eating up his sons and daughters, and the mother-alligator seeking to keep them from his jaws; when I see the sparrow falling at a dandy's shot, I know that these things have been provided for by the God of the alligator and the sparrow, and that the universe is lodged as collateral security to insure bliss to every sparrow that falls.*

Thus, instead of fashioning with great labour a theory that shall seem to account for all the facts, while in reality it shall fail to account for the origin of evil whence all the facts have flowed, he overcame doubt with this happy temper of his whole mind, a humane and tender optimism, which strove to embrace all the facts with something like the Divine impartiality.

The subject of the following letter gives it a place here, though it is of a later date by twenty years. It was addressed

Speculative Theism, p. 176.

to Rev. James F. Clarke, who had preached a sermon about him while he was sick at Rome, 1859-60, in which he made the criticism upon Mr. Parker's preaching, that it did not sufficiently magnify the fact of sin. Whoever has a great deal of natural piety for sin, is advised to pass this communication by :—

Many thanks for standing in my pulpit and preaching about me and mine; all the more thanks for the criticisms. Of course I don't *agree* with your criticisms—if I had I should not have given you occasion to make them.

*   *   *   *   *

Now a word about *sin*. It is a theological word, and is commonly pronounced *ngsin-n-n-n!* But I think the thing which ministers mean by *ngsin-n-n-n* has no more existence than *phlogiston*, which was once adopted to explain combustion. I find *sins*, i.e., *conscious violations of natural right*, but no *sin*, i.e. no conscious and intentional preference of wrong (as such) to right (as such); no condition of "enmity against God." I seldom use the word sin—it is damaged phraseology, tainted by contact with infamous notions of man and God. I have some sermons *of sin* and of *sins*, which I may live long enough to prepare for printing, but also may not.

Deacon Wryface, of the Hellfire Church, says, "Oh, I am a great sinner; I am one mass of sin all over; the whole head is sick, and the whole heart faint. In me there dwelleth no good thing. There is no health in me." "Well," you say to him, "for once, Deacon, I think you pretty near right; but you are not yet quite so bad as you talk."

"Why—what have *you* got against me—what do *you* know against my character?" says the Hellfire Church deacon.

"If you want a bill of particulars, here goes," say you; "just answer as I call them off.

"1. You will lie!"   "'*Tain't true.*"

"2. You cheat in your trade, and lately wronged Widow Crosby out of her house and land?"   "That's a lie—I never cheat!"

"3. You get drunk—on other men's wine—and were boosy only day before yesterday, and had to be helped up-stairs." "That's a slander."

"4. You are inhuman, and have got ships in the Coolie trade, and I think in the African slave-trade besides?"   "Well—there's no wrong in that—the niggers are the descendants of Ham, of whom God said, 'Cursed be Canaan.' I do this to bring the benighted heathen under Christian influences."

"5. You are avaricious, and dodge all the charities. You put your name at the head of subscriptions to decoy others, and then never pay up."   "That's a lie!"

"6. You are a consummate hypocrite, pretending to all the virtues of humanity, while you practise only the vices."   "It is all a lie."

"Well then," say you, "what *are* the special sins you do commit?"

"Oh, *there ain't any*. I hain't got a bad habit in the world—no, not one!"

"Then what did you mean by saying just now that you were such a sinner?"

"Oh, I referred to my *natur'* : it is all *ngsin-n-n-n.*"

That is the short of it—all men are created equal in *ngsin-n-n-n* Dr. Channing was as great a sinner—in the theological sense—as ———: it is his *fallen nature*—his will can never clean him from that o-d-i-o-u-s gall.

Oh, James, I think the Christian (!) doctrine of sin is the Devil's own, and I hate it—hate it utterly. Orthodox scholars say, "in the heathen classics you find no consciousness of sin." It is very true— God be thanked for it! They were conscious of wrath, of cruelty, avarice, drunkenness, lust, sloth, cowardice, and other actual vices, and struggled, and got rid of the deformities, but they were not conscious of "enmity against God," and did not sit down and whine and groan about non-existent evil. I have done wrong things enough in my life, and do them now; I miss the mark (ἁμαϱτανῶ), draw bow and try again. But I am not conscious of hating God, or man, or right, or love, and I know there is much "health in me;" and in "my body," even now, when it is really not worth much, there dwelleth many a "good thing," spite of consumption and St. Paul.

Here at Rome you see the odds between the old classic conception of man, and the modern Christian (!) conception. The heathen men and their gods, &c., are represented as stout able-bodied fellows, who did their work manfully, ate their dinners, married their wives, and begat sons and daughters with thankfulness of heart. But the statues and paintings of the Christian heroes hang their heads, and wring their hands, and draw down the corners of their mouth, and go without their breakfast; they don't sleep well o' nights, they make "a covenant with their eyes not to look upon a maid," and are always making a fuss about their s-o-u-l. I would rather have a good, plump, hearty heathen, like Aristotle, or Demosthenes, or Fabius Maximus than all the saints from Peter, James, and John (δοκοῦντες στυλοι εἶναι) down to the last one manufactured by the Roman Church—I mean as those creatures are represented in art; for the actual men I have a reasonable respect—they had some spunk in them, while the statues even of Paul represent him "as mean as a *yaller* dog." But let *ngsin-n-n-n* go—I will turn to something else.

This letter indicates how a portion of the autumn of 1839 was spent.

TO WM. SILSBEE.

Westfield, October 15.

Here we are; I say we, meaning George Ripley, Henry Lee, jun., and myself, on a pedestrian expedition of great extent and most uncertain duration, but *here* at all events, and obliged, since we have perishable bodies, to lay by, on account of a violent rain which has continued all night and all day, and threatens to be perpetual. Doleful it is, with the scent of the bar-room on the one hand, and on the other the pattering of rain, the jingling of crockery, the neighing of horses, and the cackling and crowing of little hens and cocks. Yet withal it is not dismal, for we have right fair weather within ourselves, and I have just now, this blessed rainy day, read through Sterne's "Sentimental Journey" and "Peter's Letters to his Kinsfolk," not to mention the fibs we have told one another this morning.

I wish to know if you have read Ripley on the "Latest Form of Infidelity," and what you think thereof. To me it seems excellent, both in design and execution—equally fine in manner, matter, and spirit. The Professor may well thank Heaven that he has fallen into the hands of a Christian man and not the clutches of a Philistine. Some men would have treated him as the giant charitably designed to treat Jack—would have broken every bone in his body. But, after all, the Professor is not to be despised nor abused. He has done a good work, so let him be honoured for that; for there are few scholars who have done *one* good work.

Our party, hoping for a pleasant expedition, design to spend this and the next week in roaming about among the hills of Berkshire county; we should have much pleasure if you were with us. It grieves me to think how much we are separated, when we of old time were so strictly conjoined. Pray write me of your plans, and tell where you may expect to be the next few months. Give my best and most affectionate regards to Charlotte, and the little unshod Carmelite who blesses your arms the greatest part of the time I fear.

TO THE SAME.

September 15, 1840.

Dr. Walker's discourse before the Alumni was exceedingly good, and so far from "prohibiting the banns between Religion and Philosophy," he said matters had gone so far between the two parties already, that the affair could not be winked out of sight (by the old folks); it could not be hushed up in the family, nor was it safe at this stage of the progress to call Philosophy by a bad name and then let him go. He recommended immediate union, as soon as the priest could be got ready.

Now I suppose the parties, for both Religion and Philosophy were in the church, took the hint, and went off to Providence or New York, and were made man and wife with all convenient despatch; for not a word has been heard from either of them since. I suppose they are now making a nuptial tour through the States; for I hear of "ferments" and "excitements" in other parts, which make me suspect the couple are still active. If they do not return to New England for some years I trust they will come back with their arms full of giant babies, who shall build up the shaken walls of the church, and the school, and so revise the work of both parents.

TO MISS E. P. PEABODY.

December 18, 1840

I love to lie a bright day in June, under a tree, while the growing leaves produce new modifications of beauty in shadows on the grass each moment, to look up to the rich clouds and half think, half dream about the manner in which the Infinite created the Finite. But when I get upon my feet, it all becomes a dream again. The idea of something created out of nothing is an absurdity. God created the world—*out of Himself*, so He is still in it, creating every day—not only worketh *hitherto* but *now* likewise. Creation in its essence may not be a profitable subject of contemplation, but some of the aspects of it are infinitely touching I think. At different stages of life I have been amazed at the power and the wisdom that are involved in the creative act. But of later years, as I look more through the surfaces of things, or at least try to do so, it is the beauty and *loving-kindness* of God that strikes me most. I think with you that we can apprehend the creative moment through love, and through that alone. It is this that solves all the mystery ; it cares little for the details of the work, but tells us at once—" Out of the depths of infinite love God drew forth the world. Oh, mortal, whoever thou art, thank God that thou art born ; and take courage, for thou also art a child of infinite love, and all of thy past is working on thy behalf. So fear not ; what though you weep a little while you scatter the seed, and the cold rain of spring drenches and chills you, from this very field you shall fill your bosom with sheaves of satisfaction."

To me this thought, this feeling is enough to wipe the tear from my eye at any time. It is infinite counsel, and infinite comfort. It has been adequate for all the trials I have yet found, and I trust it "will keep me" till the world ends. I often wish I could impart this same feeling to others. But the attempts always remind me of the truth in Plato, "It of all things is the most difficult to find out God, and impossible to communicate Him to others." Yet it has come to me with little *conscious* difficulty. I sometimes try—yes, it is the object of my preaching—to lead all to this same " watch-tower in the skies ;" but they tell me, " Look at the evil, the wretchedness, the sin of the world — the wrongs that patient merit of the unworthy takes," as if I could not not see them all, and feel some of them. I wish you would tell me, my dear Elizabeth, some better method of doing this. You are the all-sympathizer, and must know how to do *this* kindly office also.

TO THE SAME.

Saturday Night.

My VERY DEAR ELIZ.—I deplored more than you could the sad interruption to our talk—I am glad always to see Mr. ——. I respect him much, though he bored me a little then. I got some hints from him which will be useful, I think. The evil was he came when I wanted two things, repose and Elizabeth. He disturbed both. I should have come into your house, Monday, but I did not get into town till four o'clock, had many errands in all parts of the town, came under your window with Alcott, and saw the back of your head at the window, and was besides obliged to go home at eight, for then the carry-all and Aunt Lucy came in. Do not fear that I shall leave or forsake you. I should not commit the unusual sin of writing a sermon Saturday night. But Monday morning I went in quest of a cow ; so there was no sermon. It would not come into shape on Saturday morning, but now it is fortunately all done, but is shockingly poor. It lacks unity, strength, and height and depth, and all dimensions.

Your journal pleases me amazingly. It is *parsemè* with beautiful thoughts, though I had rather tell this to some other than to you. But you criticise yourself with dreadful sharpness. If I had only my own merit, and all your self-condemning modesty, I should expire at once in universal bankruptcy. Nobody would trust me for a shoe-tie. But it is fortunate that such supercelestial self-distrust should be balanced as it is. I need not tell you *how*.

I don't agree with you on the question of the Resurrection. The Berkeleyan hypothesis solves it quite as little as the *Hartleian*, I think. That God should suspend, violate and contradict the laws He has made for no purpose at all, or in such a way as to prove nothing, I find it difficult to conceive; the contradictory accounts puzzle me. Christ comes *through the door that is shut, vanishes* like a ghost, walks with the disciples to Emmaus, and in spite of the wounds in his hands and feet, they do not know him, until he breaks the bread. All these and many more are puzzling circumstances to me.

But the matter itself is of small moment. I am certain of my own immortality. That is enough. I have no doubt that Jesus Christ wrought miracles—though I find it difficult to believe he turned water into wine or fed five thousand with a few loaves. But these things never trouble me. The purple clouds that gather round the setting sun are but the proper accompaniments of the all of light. Still I do not look upon them as the sun, and when I think of him at mid-day the clouds with all their purple are but an insulting thought. I regard the stories of impossible miracles as the refractions of his light in the gross atmosphere of Jewish and Pagan minds.

FROM THE JOURNAL.

BERRY STREET CONFERENCE, 1840.—Last week in May attended the annual meetings of the Unitarians. The following proposition was discussed: "Ought differences of opinion on the value and authority of miracles to exclude men from Christian fellowship and sympathy with one another?" This is the substance. L—— says it smacks of the 12th century to debate such a question. I was not a little horrified to think a doubt could be raised; but men went so far as to ask if it were proper to exchange with one another, if they differed on this question. This is the 19th century! This is Boston! This among the Unitarians! Some good speeches were made by Ripley, Stetson, and Hedge, quite to the advantage of the New School, but the fundamental questions were not touched. I wished to disenchant men of their delusions, but could not. I said nothing. However, they all parted in peace, and with this conclusion, that though there were differences of opinion, there was yet no cause for withholding Christian sympathy—a result they might as well have brought with them as gathered from such a discussion. For my own part, I intend, in the coming year, to let out all the force of Transcendentalism that is in me. Come what will come, I will let off the Truth fast as it comes.

June.—I look upon my office as giving me an opportunity twice a week of addressing men on their dearest interests. The creed of the Church I. have nothing to do with. I wish to make men more moral and more religious. If they think as I do, very well; if they do not, very well also. The rites of the Church do not disturb me much. Baptism I like—it means something. The Lord's Supper I don't like, as it is now administered. It is a heathenish rite, and means very little, I think. Cast away the elements. Let all who will come into a parlour and have a social religious meeting; eat bread and wine, if you like, or curds and cream and baked apples, if you will; and have a conversation, free and cheerful, on moral questions, or simply personal good feelings and prayers. Only let all be rational and real.

I do not believe in the Old Testament or the New, as my Christian fellows do. I know there are not ten churches in New England where I could be admitted, if moral as James and pious as Christ.

About this time Mr. Parker appeared in the discussion which was opened, in 1839, by Professor Norton, in his discourse entitled "The Latest Form of Infidelity." Mr. Ripley undertook a reply, in which he ably controverted Mr. Norton's view of the value of miracles as the exclusive evidences of Christianity, and corrected the Professor's bad translations from De Wette. It was a just vindication of German theologians, and of liberal thinking, from official imputations of infidelity. Professor Norton reiterated his statements in a rejoinder. Then Mr. Ripley, in two letters—the first, an admirable development of Spinoza's metaphysics, the second a full defence of Schleiermacher and De Wette, betrayed his own philosophical culture and thorough knowledge of the subject, and in thus closing his share in the controversy, gave it dignity and value. An anonymous pamphlet appeared about the same time. Mr. Parker's contribution immediately followed, being a pamphlet entitled "The Previous Question between Mr. Andrews Norton and his Alumni moved and handled, in a Letter to all those Gentlemen. By Levi Blodgett." It is an excellent statement of his own belief at the time; and it argues the necessity of putting the evidence for Christianity upon an immutable spiritual foundation.

June 21.—S—— had some good things to say in comparing Plato with Jesus, though I think she assigned him too high a place relative to Jesus Christ—a fault very few Christians commit. We should always remember the different culture of the two, the differing atmospheres they breathed; and still more, that one lived eighty, the other less than thirty-five years. One realised his idea, the other was "soon cut off." Take those three great ideas of each, Man, God, and their relation, and, though Plato were godlike, Jesus is divine.

May, 1840.—Had a long talk with ————. She doubts the infallibility of conscience, under any circumstances—seems phrenologically inclined—denies the will of man. I could shed no light upon the subject at all. She took the ground of *Owen*, that everything is forecast in the mental or physical structure of the man. She will have a *motive* for all things, and makes action the result of the balance of forces inclining this way or that. She will outgrow this. It can only be lived down. I have passed through the same stage, and regard it as I do the chicken-pox—something that must come, and which we are glad is well over, but which confines few persons for any length of time.

May, 1840.—How my own thought troubles me! I have a work to do, and how am I straightened till it be accomplished? I must write an Introduction to the New Testament—must show what Christianity is, its universal and its distinctive part. I must write a Philosophy of Man, and show the foundation of religion in him. In my days of leisure, when I am not hard at work—on a beautiful Sabbath, for instance, or in a moony night, or one filled with stars, when I walk out, this burthen presses me heavily. I must do or die. I sit down to hard work, and then only do I feel free from this tormenting spirit ; at other times I am consumed by self-reproach for the nothings I have accomplished, for the nothing I have undertaken. My heart beats audibly, so that my hand quivers. Hard work only relieves me for the time it lasts. But I must do much hard work before I can approach the *Introduction*. This I am now preparing for. Still harder work must be done before the *Philosophy* can come forth, and much more before the crown of *Theology* can be put on the work. Here is work for digging, for flying, and for resting, still yielding to the currents of universal being that set through a soul that is pure.

June 22.—Saw ———, who, though sick, is strong at his clear heart. I suppose his day and work are over, so that his death would be simply a domestic affair. Oh, that I may live like Dr. Channing and Göthe in this respect, and work on to the end, with spirits only mounting higher.

Heard of a sermon on the New Idolatry, which, if I understand the extracts rightly, is excessive trust in the soul. Now, if this is the most dangerous idolatry in New England, I am glad. I fancy there are very few led away by a false philosophy. But all the clergy are out upon some half-dozen transcendentalists as if they were to set the world on fire. Have not the clergy *always*, from the time of Constantine, preferred the chivalrous office of fighting a few persons who break the trammels of the Church, to attacking robust sins that lead off many men and women? And is not the present position of the conservative clergy *a case in point* ?

Write a sermon on Idolatry. Show that there is as much now as ever. Idols change names. No worship now of Pluto, Neptune, Venus, &c. But show the essence of idolatry, viz., the love of something, *not God*—more than *God*.

The common forms of it—love of money, of show, &c. These are among the wicked. But among the pious, two things usurp the place of God : 1. The Bible ; 2. Jesus Christ. Show how, by showing the common notions. And talk with Dr. Francis about it.

Sept. 23.—Went to Boston to attend the Non-Resistant Convention. Don't agree with them entirely, but like their spirit and upward tendency. Like not their formula of " No Human Government." Think circumstances render it needful sometimes to take life. If a man attack me, it is optional on my part to suffer or resist ; but should he attack my wife, with the worst of purposes, why should I suffer the wicked to destroy the righteous, when I could save her by letting out his life ?

I should deprecate the issue being tendered, but if it were tendered, I have little doubt which course would be revealed to me as the true one.

CHARDON ST. CONVENTION. L— doubts the Convention, fears bad use will be made of truth. *Nous verrons.* Thinks Quincy sincere, disinterested, good. L—— is a beautiful soul.

Dr. C. also doubts the propriety thereof, since it looks like seeking agitation, and fears the opinion of Garrison, Quincy, and Maria W. Chapman. Here again we shall see. I have my own *doctrines*, and shall support them, think the *Convention* as it may. I look on the Church as a body of men and women getting together for moral and religious instruction, on the minister as a moral and religious teacher, and on Sunday as a day set apart from work and common secular vocations. All of them are human institutions. But each valuable—I would almost say invaluable.

Nov. 17, 1840.—Attended the "Sabbath Ministry and Church Convention," of which I shall say nothing, for an account thereof will be published in due time. I will only say that all my friends after the flesh, and some of my friends after the spirit, regretted that I had any agency in calling the Convention.

Dec. 5, 1840.—Work for next week.

1. Write a Sermon on Evil—its power in the world and use.
2. Finish Æschylus.
3. Finish all the "little reading" on hand—to wit, Ozanam on Dante—the Journals, &c.
4. Read all I can find *about* Æschylus.
5. Go to Boston once and see Dr. Channing.

I have solicited an exchange repeatedly with ——, could not get it; with ——, and ——. To ask either of these men again would be a dereliction from Christian self-respect. So let them pass. I feel no ill-will towards any of them. I will try —— soon, for the experiment's sake, and so with others. Their answer decides my course for the future. Let us see! I should laugh outright to catch myself weeping, because the Boston clergy would not exchange with me!

These are brave words, but a soft heart penned them, and infected the page with its own self-distrust.

Last Leaf.—It is the last day of 1840, and I finish this book. To-day I finish Sophocles, with the Trachiniæ, which is scarcely worthy of its author, though the passage on the power of love is "haughty, beautiful, and high." I love and honour this poet. What a portrait of a heroine he gives you in Antigone! But she is hard as marble, she is all over a heroine. She will not mention her lover's name when she dies—not flinch the tithing of a hair from circumstances, and seems to say to them, bind the actual tight as you will, the ideal is winged with freedom.

Oh, Thou Spirit whom no name can measure and no thought contain; Thou to whom years are as nothing, and who art from everlasting to everlasting—I thank Thee that my life still lasts from year to year. I thank Thee that my cup is full of blessings. But I would bless Thee still, if Thou didst fill my cup with grief, and turn my day into night. Yea, O God, my Father, I will bless Thee for whatever Thou shalt send. I know it is all very good. I bless Thee that Thou art still very nigh me, that Thou speakest to my heart from year to year. Thou kindlest my faith; Thou quickenest my love; Thou castest down my fear. When my father and mother forsake me, Thou wilt take me up. Oh, my God, bless me still this coming year. Be not afar off. May I never become false to thy gift. Let my eye be open, my heart true and warm, my faith pure and heavenly. May religion dwell in the inmost sanctuary of my heart. Let it be my daily life, and wherever the years shall find me, may I do my duty, without fear, and so live on—lying low in thy hand and blessed by thy goodness. Amen.

THE PARSONAGE.

CHAPTER VII.

THE decade commencing with 1830 was a memorable period in the spiritual history of the liberal men of Cambridge and Boston. That was the neighbourhood where everything on " tiptoe for the American strand " first planted its foot ; it still is early to welcome the remotest thought from many provinces of human culture. Here, of all American regions, the German language was first received gratefully and with eagerness for the sake of its new literary and philosophic forms. Ingenuous youth were told that it was the natural language of infidelity and spiritual despair, but few of their seniors knew enough of it to misrepresent it, and their mental tendency was distasteful to the new thought which was learning to wield those portentous adjectives, " empirical " and " transcendental." It is not easy to trace to any special cause this new impulse to reconsider the old grounds of faith. A few Unitarian scholars, tired of the English commentators and divines, invited into their study the best thought of other countries ; but there was something else besides liberal scholarship at the bottom of this instinctive combining of many ardent youth, bent upon " New Views," and a " New Church." Mr. Emerson had just begun to draw from the living well of his American genius, which owed as little to France or Germany as Concord River owes to famous transatlantic waters. But he proclaimed the new tendency, and generously nourished and vindicated, but did not originate it. Neither did Dr. Channing, though his preaching implied much, and the moral fervour of his protests against degrading views of God and human nature kindled many a mind. But his lack of wide scholarship indisposed him to encourage the new criticism, and his timidity and fastidious dread of crudeness kept him back from novel speculations. The " Old School " complained that a parcel of fools were rushing in where angels feared to tread. A little Hebrew, with Kueinoel and Rosenmüller, with Yates and Wardlaw, and the sound old Unitarian apologists, with Locke, and Reid, and Stewart, with Butler, Paley, and Watson, no longer appeased these young Hyperions, who meant to travel on the " high *a priori* road."

That was, indeed, an epoch which brought sensitive and aspiring minds at once so close to the great names, which, if mentioned, would present a series of Europe's choicest moments for a hundred years. Imagine a troop of New-England boys, fresh from " up-country " scenes, as they plod along some widening valley, and come suddenly upon a line of beach, where for the first time their feet, that bring down meadow scents to the new mysterious flavour of the sea, touch the edge of that great bosom which heaves with sport and earnest and conceals a myriad unsuspected thoughts. No subsequent deliberate classification of those depths can make them forget the first exaltation of the mind as it struggled to occupy the new horizon.

No doubt it produced some confusion when Leibnitz, Spinoza, Kant, Göthe, Herder, Schleiermacher, Jean Paul, Jacobi, and the rest, sailed all at once into Boston Harbour, and discharged their freight. Here were crops which we had not grown ; they might come in rotation, but as yet the old woods covered their germs. The wharves were littered in a day with the spoils of a century. Distracted critics stumbled up and down, and received a great many tibial bruises in trying to invoice the lot. It was altogether beyond any process of registering. There was no patent thought-distributor to move with untiring facility through this wealth of many-zoned Germany, and sort it for delivery. We all rushed in and helped ourselves.

The somewhat incompetent inspectors withdrew from the scene, condemning the whole importation as impracticable. A few boys, operating with straws and gimlets, were not unseasonsonably whipped by these critical officials. But very soon, and ever since, the persons to whom the freight had been consigned came to claim and to store it. The great intercourse of thought is self-adjusting, and the producing finds the consuming mind.

As if the confusion were not already sufficient, Mr. Carlyle

12

must needs make his first venture westward, about this time, in "Sartor Resartus." His ship was at once pronounced, if a Dutchman at all, a phantom Dutchman, which you might run down to, and hail, and get nothing for an answer. Such was, doubtless, the ill-luck of our admonishers, but other ears gathered with little difficulty a manly and stimulating speech. Mr. Carlyle's Essays were soon republished ; they lent courage and independent direction to many minds, to others nothing but a grotesque idiom. But the youthful hours when thought began to grow are never forgotten : he made us feel glad that we were desiring to know the truth rather than the form, and his electric temperament of spiritual freedom passed helpfully over the expanding mind.

The French also assisted to increase this embarrassment of riches. For, besides Fourier, Leroux, and the writers of the Social-istic school, there came, first, Damiron, then Benjamin Constant, with his theories of the development of religion, Jouffroy, and Victor Cousin, that brilliant expositor of German philosophers, who contributed his famous phrase of the " Impersonal Reason " to the problem of inspiration. And, in America, Mr. Brownson, in the early liberal phases of his preaching and writing, was in-strumental in letting loose among us a great many of the Gallic terms and views.

At first the Unitarians offered hospitality to this great migra-tion of new literary and philosophical forms. Before their pro-testing movement became in turn conservative and sectarian, there was a liberal condition of the body which unconsciously served the purpose of admitting here the speculations whose method and terminology were foreign, but whose substance was really native to men proclaiming the dignity of human nature, and who had repelled vilifying doctrines. The new thoughts should have been, in some form or other, the legitimate deduc-tions of a belief in man's original capacity and freedom. Mr. Emerson began to tread this pre-established path with unbor-rowed power, before the neighbourhood had become much in-fected with the foreign technicalities. But his generous claims in the soul's behalf seemed exorbitant, and they served, with his bold depreciation of historical religion, to set critics and guar-dians on the watch. His influence, though it did not invite, yet helped to welcome the transatlantic speculations to which his own views were persistently attributed.

But this was not entirely just. For it was in the nature of Unitarianism to develope a spiritual philosophy that should claim for the soul primitive notions of God, right, and immortality. Cudworth, the preacher of immutable morality, was the English representative of this tendency. It belongs not only to those who would show the harmony of Scripture with absolute truth, but to those who deny that some doctrines are scriptural, on the ground that they are repugnant to reason. The right of judgment is derived from ideas in the Reason which precede scriptures and doctrines, and subject them to review. The right of judging if a doctrine be scriptural depends upon the capacity to discern if Scripture itself be reasonable. So that the Bible itself is subject to the ideas which the Bible is supposed to embody. It is of no consequence how far criticism may go in this direction after Reason has assumed her right. She herself alone can regulate the extent of her applicability. This is legitimate Unitarianism. And it is also Transcendentalism, properly defined.

Thus there arose a new school of Unitarianism, that sought to found a philosophy, giving to truth her own authority, to the Bible the authority of a record harmonizing with reason, to Christ the authority of displaying what the soul can recognize on its own evidence. And a voice or two was heard to add, "and to reason the right of rejecting everything everywhere that is irrational." This school did not yet deny that the miracles were wrought, but only that they added no authority to things morally and religiously true, because with such things they had no essential connection. Nor did this new school deny generally that some special divine quality supernaturally interpenetrated the Son of Man.

On the other hand, the representatives of the old Unitarianism, which had fought the Trinity and the Atonement on virtually transcendental grounds, now refused to be implicated farther with an independent reason, partly because they were sincerely opposed to its anti-supernatural tendency, and partly because the vagueness and misuse of the new terms disgusted them. They said, very properly, that whoever denies that a miracle is the authority for Christianity, might as well, and soon would, deny that any miracle was ever worked. The semi-supernaturalists vehemently repelled this insinuation; but it was well-founded. For either reason or external authority must rule.

Whoever accepts a premise of either binds himself to all the consequences.

It is certain that the new phrases were very loosely used. The more liberal thought borrowed them instead of growing its own. Such terms, when adopted, should be subjected to a strict survey, for an old ship cannot sail in all waters. The words "transcendental," "intuitive," "immanent," "innate" come down to us from scholastic times, and every epoch of thinking has modified their meaning; any theology can use them if it has the liberty of adjusting what they connote. But a new school cannot assimilate an old term without getting itself thereby misrepresented. When a critic in the interest of Locke, who believes that all ideas are derived from the various sensations of experience, hears the proclamation that perception of truth is "intuitive," that ideas are "innate," that the Word which lighteth every man is "Impersonal," he has all the advantage of *vis inertiæ* in his question, "What do you mean by those words?" To define them is a delicate operation, and the longing for a spiritual philosophy preceded the careful framing of a code of signals that should, without the possibility of misleading, be current everywhere in the great commerce of thought. What is an "innate idea," for instance? The phrase can bear three interpretations:—1st. An original divine mark fully made on the soul, to appear in the sympathetic heat of experience. 2nd. A divine germ, predestined to unfold by gradual stages if the climate be favourable. 3rd. A mere capacity to deduce from the inward and the outward life some absolute conceptions of God and right. But men are not safer in an empirical philosophy because accidents result from the illegitimate and careless handling of abstract words.

Some of the Unitarians, however, thought so; for no possible definition of such phrases as "cognition of absolute ideas," "impersonal reason," "à priori evidence of truth," could pacify their sincere supernaturalism. A few who had good-naturedly assisted at letting in the foreigners, were now aghast at their brogue and uncouthness. The shew-bread began to disappear, and the sacred utensils were handled in a playful manner that boded no good to little sentiments and proprieties, if the new importation were left to run at large. The orthodox began to ask unpleasant questions; and if a Unitarian undertook to pilot "over-soul," or "immanence," or "spontaneity," through Cam-

bridge and Boston, get for them New-England home-spun, and
attempt their introduction in respectable quarters, the watchful
Calvinistic shoulder went up to the ear. To such ominous shrugs a
man is very sensitive when he is just on the point of being admitted
into recognised circles. If he is only an amateur at singularity,
he promptly drops his notion and becomes fanatically conventional.

There were some of these amateurs, who for a time used the
phrases of progress and spiritual freedom with a grand, ingenuous
air, which seemed to extend the patronage of Christianity to
Transcendentalism. They lamented over the formalism of the
Church and the decay of interior religion. Sometimes they
magnificently asked the brethren if their hearts were not large
and tolerant enough to hold Mr. Emerson and all of that
ilk. They were young then, and had a sentimental feeling
for liberty, to which the new phrases lent dignity and picturesque-
ness. They were just baring their breasts with *abandon* to the
universe, and calling to the " over-soul " to come on, when Mr.
Parker's sermon of " The Transient and Permanent," struck their
bellying sails with a sudden dismay, and they were never hoisted
more.

That revolutionary sermon also converted a good deal of lively,
bantering criticism of historical religion into the most inflexible
conservatism. Unitarian scholars had indulged a light way in
private of talking about the miracles, although they really
accepted the greater part of them as facts, and nominally held
them as a basis of authority. But criticism had broken just far
enough with the old reverence to render a jest on Balaam's ass,
the possessed swine, the money in the fish's mouth, not inadmis-
sible on week-days. And men spoke freely to each other of the
Orientalisms of the New Testament, among which they would
sometimes class, not only the Conception and the Star in the
East, but also the Transfiguration and the Ascension. Mr. Parker did not understand this raillery. If he shared the smile, it
was from a strong and ever-deepening conviction that Sunday
was as good a day as Monday on which to expose these unhis-
torical elements.* Fancy his astonishment at the stern and
sudden orthodoxy which seized the liberal circle where he used to
hear this half-considered talk. This must be remembered when

* The specimens which have been collected by Mr. Parker point to private interviews
with the friends whose names are also given, and not to any discussions held at the meetings of Associations or other clerical gatherings.

he is found afterwards hinting at a scepticism which uttered in the study what it was unwilling to utter in the pulpit. It was not really that, but it seemed so to him; for he soon saw how untenable was the assumption of selecting miracles to suit your taste, and preserving one set for banter and another for belief. When the mythological element is once admitted the right of choice expires.

He and his friends were really afloat upon this principle: they without knowing it. What was their perturbation when this island on which they bivouacked and built their crackling, merry fires, began to move off to sea! He might go voyaging in that fashion, but they scrambled for the deck again, and were glad to feel the old ballast underneath.

TO WM. SILSBEE.

April 23, 1841.

I am no Pantheist, nor ever was. My friend —— says " he burns between two fires, Anthropomorphism" (which is the theistical side of Calvinism), "and Pantheism" (which is the religious side of nature, as Coleridge would say if he were here.) Now, for my part, I find a *tertium quid*, and am no more troubled by Pantheism or Anthropomorphism than, at noonday, the evening and morning twilight trouble me. The whole difficulty comes of attempting to get a logical and definite notion of God. The sentiment of religion in a man would naturally come at first to Anthropomorphism, for the human is the highest form known to us; just as an ox, had he religion, would think of God in the form of an ox, counting that the highest. Hence the stories in the Old Testament among the Greeks, Hindoos, &c. Then reason looks at the stars, and says, God is not like a man. It feels God is *infinite*, so it attempts to separate from the idea all that is finite,—1, the human form; 2, passion; 3, memory, &c., and so on with each attribute of the *finite*, till it comes at last to make God nothing but an abstraction, of which even being cannot be predicated. Plato got up so high one day, and Hegel says, "Seyn und Nicht-seyn" are the same thing—no difference between God's *being* and being *not*.

But neither the head nor the heart will subsist on abstractions; so they say the infinite concretizes itself in nature, has no consciousness except through the consciousness of individuals. "God first comes to consciousness in (Adam) man; to *self*-consciousness in Christ, who is the sum total of mankind," says a Hegelian. So God never could say "I," nor distinguish between the divine "me" and "not me," till the birth of Jesus Christ. But with all reverence for philosophy, I would ask, "Who told him this?" I think the instinctive feeling and reason also lead direct to God—God all-wise, all-powerful, all-good—who is the good, the beautiful, the true. But they do not *define* him, except so far as to distinguish the idea of God from all other ideas, either actual or possible. Love, wisdom, &c., in Him who made the stars, must be very different from what I feel and know. Now I bow to this Being and live in him, but I cannot " by searching find out God unto perfection," *i.e.*, perfectly. We see that there is *nothing but the Creator and the Creation*. I feel no desire, as some do, to attempt to simplify the matter still more, and find only a Creator. Creation is to me the glass through which I see God. I can know much about the manifestations of the Creator in the Creation; but can only know of God that He is perfect.

FROM THE JOURNAL.

GOD.—God is in the soul of man, and gives us all the life we live. Reason is not personal, but is a great plane, which cuts the centre of all souls—the larger the soul, the greater portion of the one and indivisible God is intercepted thereby. The life of God is in my soul: it is vain that you tell me of God out of me. The *senses* wish for such a God; they find him, for all they perceive is but the varied deity. Light and beautiful forms are God to the eye, perfumes to the smell, and so of the rest. But the one God, I find and hear of in my soul, all nature is his dress, stars spangle his robe and light is but his garment. Oh, Thou ever-present, I feel Thee evermore! There is nothing where Thou art not. Oh, all in all! I adore Thee, and melt with blissful tears into the deep of Thee!

The following extracts mark the tendency of his thought at this time; how earnest it is, and palpably in the interest of religion :

Christianity is a field on which may be raised the strangest crops—wood, hay and stubble, wheat and beans. The soil remains, the crop varies.

The Christianity which many men embrace is a very poor thing; a belief in the stories of the New Testament. These stories corrupt the truth. None of them rest on evidence. Jesus lived, taught, was crucified. His life was higher, I presume, than any one has ever described it. A great soul lay at the bottom of the Christian movement; men do not tell such stories save of great men. But the miracles—that contradict the natural law—such as the transubstantiation of bread, water, &c., the sending the devil into the swine, the resurrection of dead men, the resurrection of Jesus himself—all these have nothing to do with Christianity. I do not know what to make of them.

But this I feel, that the time is coming when men will wonder quite as much at the Christianity of the nineteenth century as we wonder at that of the ninth century after Christ, or that of the nineteenth century before Christ. The attempt of the times is now twofold, 1, to rationalize Christianity; 2, to Christianize reason. The scholastics began this in the eleventh century. The fathers took Christianity in its *enveloped* state, and *developed* it; so they were *Patres*, as Hegel says. Hence the Church, controversies, synods, and persecution. The scholastics took the speculative Christianity they found in the fathers, the councils, &c., and *methodized* it, and attempted to reconcile it with reason. Scholasticism is the attempt to marry philosophy and religion, to find a principle in man answering to each doctrine of Christianity. They did not first ask, What is Christianity? nor second, What is man? So they did not marry Christianity to philosophy, but only a saucy kitchen wench to fancy. Now is the question, What is Christianity? We are to hunt up the bride, and then, if they will, to marry them. The scholastics were not *Patres* but *Doctores.* We have neither. We are *Scrutatores.* We need, 1. An anthropology. 2. A critical history of religion.

Christianity is progressive, because it is not *positive,* but natural. We may say its main idea is the incarnation, reconciliation, the God-man, union of the absolute and the finite, or a perfect character for all; these mean but the same thing, as I understand it. Christianity, therefore, is the hope of the world, the desire of all nations.

1. Christianity may be considered as *objective* in the whole, and so as a process in God's development of Himself. The supernaturalist is obliged, if logically consistent, so to view it. This was the view which prevailed in the Catholic Church from the Council of Nice to the Reformation, and still prevails. The idea is this—God created the universe, the angels were a part of it—all was perfect; the angels fell, they must be replaced. It was tacitly supposed that God could not create *de novo* angels, so men were made. But they also fell; still the angel's place, and man's place also, was not filled. An instinct of perfection lay in the Divine mind, which led to the restoration of man (and of the angels also, thinks Origen.) He must restore man, so Mosaism as the preparatory step, and Christianity as the completion of the work, *i.e.,* both were phases which God must assume in the process of his self-development. To me it savours of arrogance to decide in matters that are too high for me. "Hardly do we guess aright," &c.

2. Christianity may be regarded as *subjective* as a whole, that is, a phase of human nature in its development. I think this the true notion, if we do not separate the divine too much from the human. If we allow that God still creates as ever, still "worketh hitherto," perhaps this the true view. It is mortifying to human pride to look back and see the crop of errors which have grown on the field of Christian speculation. It serves, however, to quicken one's humility; for each of the *Fathers* in the first age, each of the *Doctors* in the middle age, each of the *Scrutators* in this age, each heretic in all ages, has been certain that he was right. Where they failed, what modest man shall lift up a presumptuous thought? The history of thought teaches us all to be *modest.* The great truths of morality and religion are read us daily in New England or New Zealand by consciousness and faith—we need make no mistake; but when the meddling intellect comes in to do its work, what theologies we form! The Fathers milked the ram, the Doctors held the pail, the Scrutatores are divided on the question to whom the milk belongs.

Anselm, no doubt, thought he had solved all the mysteries of Christianity in his "Cur Deus homo?" Kant, Hegel, and Conradi have thought the same of their systems. But who, alas! shall mould for us the cup in which a single age can drink the water of life?

With most men there is a little of religion, with some there is much; this is only saying that there is more or less of it among men. But thought about religion is quite another thing.

He translates with astonishment a few choice paragraphs of a German book which presents Hegelian-Evangelical views :—

The first point which comes to be considered in this connection is that pure logical or metaphysical one contained in the proposition which stands at the head of Hegel's religious philosophy, viz., that God, as Absolute Spirit, is Triune. In so far as God is spirit, it belongs to His nature to reveal and objectivate Himself ; but it is likewise equally essential that, in this separation, He should remain identical with Himself. There must, therefore, take place a separation in God, without which there would be no process, and therefore no life in God ; but this separation is immediately neutralized in the Divine idea. Here is no serious, deep, penetrating differentiation, but that first attains its rights in the Son, who has proceeded from God, and stands beside Him, as the world, or the finite God, in free subsistency ; but from this separation and divulsion He comes again to unity with God, and returns to the Absolute Spirit which is identical with itself.

Upon this verbal juggling Mr. Parker remarks :—

Here is a subject which has occupied the attention of the greatest minds of the world, from Hierocles down to Hegel. Yet to me the whole question seems to rest on a false position, viz., that Jesus of Nazareth was the Supreme Being. Admit that he was a man—the noblest, best man who ever lived ; admit that if I do my duty as faithfully, I shall be equally accepted by God—the mystery is all over. I am perpetually astonished that men should reason so—on such premises. Still more, that, starting from such premises, they will plunge into the sea of Deity, and tell us the metaphysics, and the physics, too, of God. The history of man's *body* is a series of abuse and war, wrong and suffering. The history of man's *mind*, a story of delusions—brilliant thinking on false assumptions. It is a game that serves to pass the time and sharpen the faculties, but it is played for straws. The victor gains—nothing. It seems, in the history of Theology, as if there was a *tertium quid* between a lie and the truth ; as if the opposite of a lie was also a lie, and not truth ; as if truth and falsehood were the two extremes of a *tertium quid*, and the real way was deemed to be between them both.

There was nothing in his mind or education that could sympathize with the fruitless subtleness of some metaphysical schools. His theology did not need to be shored up by them ; they were alike distasteful to his plain, strong understanding, and to his humanity. It is evident that his late studies were preparing him for the " Discourse of the Transient and Permanent in Christianity," in which a simple intuitive feeling speaks through a well-instructed mind.

That sermon, which conjured bigotry, liberality and amateurship into their proper shapes, was preached at the ordination of Mr. Shackford at South Boston, on the 19th of May, 1841. The occasion passed off without any preliminary stir. The venerable clergyman who offered the ordaining prayer, recognised the heresy, and petitioned that the young incumbent might have a living faith in a Son of God of Divine works and nature. But beyond this the pulpit and the pews made no sign. One person rose during the discourse and retired, whether on account of a badly ventilated building, or a heresy ventilated but too well, remains unknown to this day. After the services a good many clergymen expressed admiration for the discourse, with the qualifications that might have been expected. And to all appearance it was about to be consigned to that limbo of imperfect sympathies whither so many of Mr. Parker's productions had gone before.

He had often preached and written things that were quite as radically defective when tested by any theology that admits the supernatural element. It was not one of his most energetic sermons, by any means, for he had written it during a week of langour and illness. It was diffuse, and too rhetorical. It neither accepted nor rejected the miracles, and the language held towards the person Christ was vague. Its positive merit was a warm and enthusiastic preference for permanent spiritual life to transient theological forms. But Dr. Channing, at least, had enforced the same vital distinction. He, too, would have set free the growing soul from the doctrines of an outworn past, so that intelligence might always preserve its chartered right to build the house for the inner life to occupy. And everybody heartily accepted that tendency which Mr. Parker strove to embody in his sermon.

Still, it was a revolutionary sermon, for its negative portion left some logical inferences to be made from its positive statements, which were not clearly seen at first. If Christ is inspired by means of a law which makes the same inspiration possible to all men, the supernatural distinction of his nature is no longer credible. The denial of miracles and of every exclusive element of divinity, is only a question of time and boldness. Were the Unitarians ready to accept all that lay latent in the discourse, as well as all which was patent for the world to read? And how was their qualified sympathy to be interpreted? When these questions were asked by some orthodox gentlemen, who did not care for a reply, as they intended only to embarrass the Unitarians, and force them to accept or repel Mr. Parker, it became necessary to issue vigorous manifestoe s of belief. Sympathy with one por tion of the discourse was then more firmly expressed by a few, while the majority vigorously denounced its anti-supernatural tendency. Clergymen began to define their theological positions. Necessity drove them into a sudden consciousness of the paramount importance of a Christianity supernaturally revealed and attested. No doubt this had been sincerely deemed important before, but the sermon compelled them to see that there had been too much amiable concession to the excellence of spiritual views. That sermon really created an opportunity to see precisely the reverse, that these spiritual views might become the positive life of a sect which had hitherto only protested against bad doctrines, and that religion, rescued from all kinds of empiricism, might win a sound philosophy, a more ardent piety, a bold and warm philanthropy, at the hands of these men, fresh from their good fight, and eager to reap its glorious advantages. What liberal subjects were languishing then to be organized and led ! What causes of justice and pure morals, and the dear country's vital hope, Anti-Slavery, yearning to be welcomed by the intelligence and spirit of a great religious party ! Instead of occupying this great future, the Unitarians sent a few exiles forth to the whitening fields.

But it is better to attempt a narrative of history than to pick a quarrel with it. Mr. Parker's sermon and its amplification, the "Discourse of Religion," which soon followed, was a peremptory summons to the Unitarians to evacuate their thin didactic lines and come over to him. They fell back in alarm, to select their own position more carefully, and to remain there entrenched. He did not issue an invitation for fraternal co-operation in a reform of theology and a renewal of piety. A tea-party or a picnic may be inaugurated upon those terms, but not Protestantism. He stated the problems of religion, of the Church, and of society in sonorous and uncompromising phrases, and was so possessed by his subjects that he disregarded some points of taste and of religious observance about which people are sensitive. His intuitive beliefs stepped forth fully armed, in revolutionary mien, from the theology which hitherto he had only tolerated. In breaking with it, he displayed all his faults and virtues with a child's sincerity, impetuously rushing forward to claim recognition for his dear convictions ; with strong hand pushing to the right and left what barred his way. Were the Unitarians ready to recognise this new revolution fresh risen, with lustihood and menace, from Lexington Common ? They were not. They did not yield to the more silvery summons of Mr. Emerson. It was a historical necessity that the personality of the appeal should enforce a personality of opposition.

Thus commenced that controversy, the details of which it would be no longer fruitful to recall. It is plain to see why Mr. Parker suffered so much at the sudden loss of scholarly and genial friends, and why he exaggerated the enmity of the genuine Conservatives. It is not wonderful that he should have despised the timidity which could preserve its spurious liberality only during the term of amiable neutrality which his own clear voice broke up for ever. He suffered when old friends refused to exchange with him; he jealously counted the precious names of those who yet remained. His heart was too tender to pass all these things by. He bore it out of the conflict into comparative quiet and the solace of new friendships, but the broken names still hung in it and kept their festering hold. He remembered too vividly, and the old griefs came often straying into his beautiful speech. Charmed hearers felt that the call to pity was an interruption to the inspiring thought. But these passion-flowers never drew malignant sap from the past, of which they were the emblems.

The Unitarians forgot a great many indignant words which their leaders had uttered when the orthodox refused to continue the fellowship of exchange and ministerial intercourse. And their plea was that the old controversy arose from a difference *within the limits* of Christianity, but that the new one was between Christianity and something else. Was not this assuming the very point at issue? And the orthodox never allowed their distinction; but had previously declared that men who denied the Trinity, the Atonement, and Original Depravity were outside of Christianity. If a man is permitted to decide that he is inside anything, he can put his head through his own assumption, and others will appear to him outside.

But this inconsistency was sincerely held, because the Unitarians venerated Christ as a teacher, having discarded him as a person of the Trinity and a sacrificial agent. They struggled to oppose a great authoritative teacher, the Son of Man and of God, to the mysterious doctrines of Calvinism. To construct an adequate idea of such a person, through whom men are to be saved by the more rational process of believing his remedial truth, it was necessary to secure the conditions of infallibility and authority for the truth which is to save. The infallibility was provided in special inspiration, the authority was claimed under miraculous attesting acts. It was objected to Mr. Parker, that without this supernatural basis the idea of a divine teacher could not be maintained. In this respect, then, Unitarianism was quite as consistent as its doctrine.

The newspapers swarmed with notices of the South Boston sermon, written generally in ignorance of the philosophical points which these great religious themes involve. The theological papers exercised their ancient privileges. Editors penned misleading articles, and correspondents sent in contributions of laical piety. A few conservative Unitarians defended Mr. Parker's liberty of prophesying, and in attacking his doctrines did not misrepresent them. Others were not so fortunate.

Divinity students must also splinter their brittle quills against the shaggy breast of this "Orson of Parsons." Some of them lived to know better, and were drawn near enough to feel the beating of that generous heart. Thus, for instance, did one, in discharging his callow petulance, disarm himself and fall a speedy prey to a friendship that led to a better appreciation of the truths involved :—

What, then, has Mr. Parker done for us ? He has with justice annihilated the Transient, but where is the Permanent ? The path he pointed out does not conduct to the goal. We miss the substance for a shadow ; Revelation itself and Holy Writ shrink away at the presence of an Impersonal Reason. Is love to God and love to man, intuition, instinct, the only Permanent ? Can Revelation afford us nothing else ? Where are all our hopes of repentance, regeneration—our assurances of immortality ? And where, too, all this time, is Christ ? Our moorings are all cast loose ! We had already caught a glimpse of the Holy Land—we felt its celestial breath upon our souls—swiftly and sure each little bark was making for its destined haven, when, with one mighty upheaving from some Tartarean depth, we are cast back into the infinite void—into primeval chaos—no Christ, no religion ; only some grim-smiling, sinister Impersonal Reason, brooding over the vast abyss.

It is the divine privilege of youth and a good constitution to get well rid of such perilous stuff as that.

TO DR. FRANCIS.

Away-down East, Aug. 26, 1841.

My most excellent Friend, most sagacious, and wise, and Christian,—I wish you were here to enliven the solitude of the wilderness with your talk and your laugh. But here I am alone among the " salvages." I have been travelling on foot and alone " in these diggins " for several days. Yesterday I walked 35 miles; to-day 22 and rode 18 ; and from these remote quarters of the world I send you a word.

In the history of religions, which do you take to be the true notion: was this the order in which the human race " evolved " itself, viz.—1, Fetichism ; 2, Polytheism ; 3, Monotheism ; or was a part of mankind monotheistic from the beginning ? This involves the question of civilization. Was mankind (or a part of the race) *created* in the civilized state, and have the others *fallen*, or was man created savage, and has he gradually emerged from this state ? The Germans, Eichhorn, Herder, and others, think man had no language at first (following Monboddo in this), but gradually developed the faculty of speech. They, therefore, ought consistently to say man began savage ; his religious progress was 1, Fetichism ; 2, Polytheism ; 3, Monotheism.

Now there is much in history to confirm this latter opinion ; such as the state of theology in the oldest nations at the time of the earliest historical notices. On the other hand, there is much to confound and overthrow this notion, which presents itself very obviously. Besides, all the metaphysical arguments tend the other way, viz., to the notion that *part* of the race at Creation was in a civilized state. What do you think of this idea : that different races were created in different degrees of civilization—some in Fetichism, even in the inferior degrees of it, as it is *now* found in Australia ; others in Polytheism ; and even some in Monotheism ? I feel somewhat interested in this question, but suppose it cannot be solved even *ideally*, much less factically (as the Germans say).

I am writing this in the midst of a great crowd in a tavern reading-room, and there is no little buzzing all around me. It is queer to hear men at the far end of this state talk of going east, and of down east, as if they lived on the Missouri. I asked one of them what he meant by *going* down east. He said, "I once went down among the Blue-noses (*i. e.* into New Brunswick), and there they talked also of going east ; so I went down to the point of Nova Scotia (the very jumping-off place), and even there they talked of going east ! "

The blunt and distasteful way in which he sometimes uttered his criticism, furnished the persons who would not be touched by his real spirit with a convenient reason for avoiding him. Doubtless many who could sympathise with the pure, enthusiastic thought, were disturbed by some of his uncalculating rhetoric. And among his old friends were to be found a few, who, becoming suddenly enveloped in the startling publicity of his views, declared that it was not the light which hurt their eyes, but the rudeness with which he threw the shutters open. They complained of his spirit. That was an unfortunate word to use, for his spirit was the most unexceptionable part of him ; his phrases sometimes misinterpreted it. How common are all the faults of style, how rare is the spirit which counts all the fashions of this world, and of its speech, a little thing compared with seeking truth.

People will speculate upon the possible results of a decided fact if it had been in some respects a different fact. Thus, it is said by his friends, he would have done more good, and by his enemies, more harm, if his temper had been somewhat more diplomatic, and his revolutionary matter couched in cautious phrases. They would tinker the fact, like Alphonso of Castile. Such speculating mends all the world's strong men out of sight. It is the old story of complaining that Luther gets into a great heat with taking the Pope's Bull by the horns, and that Latimer shocks people's sensibilities at Charing Cross. You can have your Luther who fights a good fight, or some other individual good for something else, at whom the Pope and his monks will snap their fingers, if they deem it worth the while. After you have boned your Reformer you might as well boil him, for he is of no other earthly use.

TO MISS C. W. HEALEY.

December 3, 1841.

What you say about touching men's prejudices more gently is true and just. I can only say that while I feel great tenderness towards the preconceived notions of *individuals*, when I am to speak of a mass of doctrines that come between man and God, I think the blow must be strong enough to cut clean through, and let the light stream through the rent. Besides, the sentiments in the South Boston sermon had so long been familiar to me, I had preached them so often with no rebuke, that I was not aware of saying anything that was severe. I thought the sermon would be reckoned tame and spiritless, for it so poorly and and coldly expressed what burned in my heart like a volcano. . . . . . .

Your sympathy is exceedingly precious to me. I never feared the reproaches nor coveted the praise of the hostile or the friendly, but the sympathy of the true-hearted is blessed to me: it is the dew to the herb.

TO HIS BROTHER-IN-LAW, CHARLES MILLER.

12 July, 1841.

You seem to think it *possible* that my *motives* were not good in writing and preaching the sermon which men make such a noise about. Now, I never in my life wrote a sermon with a deeper conviction of its truth or of the good it would do in the world. I wrote what I felt to the ends of my fingers, If you can find anything bad, pernicious, or likely to injure morality and religion, I am very sorry ; but I am certain it contains nothing of that character. The noise which men make, the bad names they call me, the threats they utter, move me as little as they move Monadnock . . . . . Do *you* think I could have any but the *best* of *motives* for this work ? What could I gain but a bad reputation ? Nothing else. No : I felt the difficulties of the common opinions. I wished to show that religion was independent of the foolish doctrines men have piled upon it. I wanted to break the yoke of bondage bound on men's necks, and have done what I could to make men better here and hereafter. The opinions in the discourse are nothing new to me ; not the random thoughts of a young man, but the sober, deliberate convictions, the result of thought and study. The end will be good, no doubt of that ; but the end *is not yet*.

The following alludes to a letter which about this time he addressed to the clergymen of the Boston Association :—

TO MISS E. PEABODY.

June 26, 1841.

Thank you a thousand times for your letters ; your criticisms are also encouraging; nobody knows better than I how numerous my faults are, and certainly none feels them so strongly as I do daily. I know I am quick—sudden and quick in quarrel it may be—particularly after a good deal of intellectual excitement; but in the case you instance you are mistaken entirely. I meant in sober earnest that those people were *wiser* as well as older, and *mean it now ;* not that all are older or wiser, but the leading persons I know to be both older and wiser, so I beg you not to misunderstand me here. It did not occur to me that anyone could misconceive the matter so entirely as to think I would insult a respectable body of people by a sneer after that fashion. Again, the letter was not written quickly, nor until after a good deal of reflection ; and then the original draught was shown to a cool, cautious, delicate-minded man, who said it was good, but *too weak*. He objected to nothing therein. Then Lydia read it, and thought there was nothing amiss in it. Now, my usual hastiness had nothing to do with this letter. But if others' eyes have the mote of suspicion, as yours and Sarah's have *not*, why they will see an innuendo in my wish that they may found a more *liberal* church, and even in my subscription as their "friend in the Christian faith." But, believe me, I should not interweave *inuendoes* or sarcasm in a letter to a Church, though I think sarcasm a legitimate weapon to use in certain cases of argument and fun.

This letter indicates the commencement of that popular sympathy, which was preparing to secure for him a more magnificent hearing than any man ever had in America :—

TO MESSRS. WM. LARNED, S. E. BRACKETT, CHARLES L. THAYER, AND CHARLES ELLIS.

West Roxbury, 26 June, 1841.

MY DEAR FRIENDS,—Your kind and very flattering note came safely to hand, and I have given it the best consideration in my power to bestow. I am thankful for the interest you express in my views of the Christian life. I know of no finite happiness so great as that which attends a successful attempt to set forth the great truths of religion, on which our welfare depends. It is with great reluctance that I conclude it is wisest and best to decline the invitation you have so generously made me. My reasons are chiefly a distrust of my own ability to effect the object you contemplate. Besides, I can still utter my word in the pulpit, and occasionally through the press, and, perhaps, can do what is given me to do better in this than any other way. The subjects you suggest offer a most noble and beautiful theme ; and would to Heaven I were able to discuss them as I feel they *now* require to be treated. The lectures of Dr. Walker, however, will more than supply anything I could attempt with any hope of success.

Believe me, gentlemen,

Very affectionately,

Your friend and brother in the Christian faith,

THEO. PARKER.

This invitation of a few friends who desired to maintain his privilege to speak and to define his own position had important results, notwithstanding his first refusal. He was persuaded to deliver a course of lectures in Boston during the winter of 1841-42. The old Masonic Temple was filled to hear him. The young men walked in from Cambridge, and back again over the long bridge in the darkness, with hearts aflame. All the earnest thinkers came to hear what he had to say, and many a girl who is now a noble mother, and many strong women whose names have since stood for some humanity of letters or of life.

These lectures appeared in the spring of 1842, somewhat more elaborated, in the volume entitled, " A Discourse of Matters Pertaining to Religion."

When this volume appeared, people were puzzled to reconcile the popular warmth and simplicity of the text with the remote and varied learning piled up in the foot-notes. They observed the anomaly "as a curious traveller counts Stonehenge." It led them to suspect an illusion. Had all these leading books, in all languages, been faithfully read and assimilated ? Then, where is the trace of it in the composition ? The terminology is neither German, French, nor Latin. There are no terms : every sentence is a lucid drop. When he states that, in the last analysis, the root of religion is a sense of dependence, you expect a popular re-hash of Schleiermacher. But his speech merely borrows the phrase as a temporary convenience. The word Fetichism, with references to Constant, whose extravagant love of system he really blames, put the critics on the scent of

13

a French theory of development. So also did the sight of
Comte's name, to whom he generally refers to note his disagreement with the Positive Method. The names of Strauss,
Hennell, Baur, Bayle, and Hegel were presumptive evidence
against the genuineness of the volume. The religious newspapers
scorned an infidel dish which caught the drippings of all foreign
kitchens. They supposed that an American could not associate
with the thought of other nations upon terms of equality and
dignified reserve. He would infallibly be sent home in a suit
of foreign livery, of fantastic cut. Though they could not
undertake to read Mr. Parker's authorities in order to trace
the audacious plagiarisms, the fact was assumed by every subservient mind which felt that one volume of Kant would be
quite enough to swamp its own style and carry down its
cherished sentiments. All the pocket-tapes broke in measuring
up against the poor boy from Lexington.

There were errors in this book, no doubt; inaccuracies and
marks of haste. They were duly noticed in the reviews of
the day.

This was a genuine American, who had loves and tastes
which were cosmopolitan, Massachusetts' independent hardihood
without the Know-nothing prejudice. His mind was like the
republican idea itself; it could afford to be hospitable, but
could not afford to be exclusive. Vigour, simplicity, a sensitive heart, a kindling enthusiasm, greatness to welcome great
things and to remain still greater, breadth, homeliness, use, and
the plastic power of natural elements,—these are the New
World's character. He represented it. His mind, in its
prime, was the first thorough democrat. He never Platonized,
Judaized, nor Germanized. The hordes of emigrants found
they were no match for the country. Their obtrusive characteristics were seized by the climate and made over; they
gained protection, but no exclusive immunities, from his self-
relying mind.

He had read all the books which assumed to lead thought in
their respective provinces. He knew perfectly well what had
been said upon all great points. His references indicated
honest study, for careful analyses and estimates crowd the
pages of his common-place books. What a proof of absence of
confusion and surfeit is his simple American style, in which his
home-bred piety and ethical sincerity flow and sparkle! Some

of the pages of this volume are like broad, sweet waters, heated by the summer sun. The foot-notes show below; sharp Kant and stony Hegel, and uncertain Schelling, thin, sinuous grass, and all the waifs of time. In the still shadowy reaches the lily of religion floats.

His style is wonderful for its absence of all taint from scholastic and metaphysical terms. It has other faults, precisely such as the self-grown vigour might be expected to betray; but it steals, begs, and borrows nothing. It has the cant of no school, transcendental or parti-evangelical; no bristling words of Teuton or of Gallic origin. He finds the country language capable of telling his most spiritual thought.

That was the danger, men considered; it would be better if his sentences were subtly involved, and his ideas only half conscious of themselves. And it was alarming that a man of such undoubted piety should be furnished with such an aggressive common-sense. What shall be done for the Church, when a single man can show so clearly how religious he can be without the expense of miracles and mystical formulas? Men of all creeds instinctively saw in him those elements of a revolution, the primitive human right, the possession of weapons, and the defiance of authority.

Aside from private griefs, he enjoyed the struggle which bade him put forth all his powers. Now he stood in a wider horizon, and felt the excitement for which, without knowing it, he had languished. Without it he never would have vindicated his own ability, nor acquired that unrivalled expression and trained courage which made him so formidable in the great questions of the day. The contest came just in time to give humane love for man and for man's ideas, the advantage over scholarship and seclusion.

Duty, freedom, truth, a divine life, what are they? Trifles, no doubt, to Monk Tetzel, to the Leos and the Bembos, and to other sleek persons, new and old. But to a heart that swells with religion, like the Atlantic pressed by the wings of the wind, they are the real things of God, for which all poor temporalities of fame, ease, and life are to be cast to the winds.

He that feareth the Lord, when was he not a prey? He must take his life in his hand, and become as a stranger to men. But if he fall and perish, it is his gain. Is it not the world's? It is the burning wood that warms men.*

* Discourse of Religion : Am. Ed. 1842, pp. 110, 443.

TO DR. FRANCIS.

Feb. 14, 1842.

It is not often I have an hour for a letter, since to write two sermons a week, and spend five days of the week in other matters, and get no Sabbath on Sunday, though it may do well with stronger heads, yet goes hard with mine. I never cared much for the sympathy of other men, and never less than now; but once in a great while I feel it is not altogether pleasant to stand alone, to be viewed with suspicion and hatred. Blessed are the men who can take things as they find them, and believe as the mob believes, and sail in the wake of public opinion. I remember you told me a year ago, he that defies public opinion is like the man who spits in the wind; he spits in his own face. It is so. But what then? Let it be so. Better men have found less sympathy than I. I do not care a rush for what men who differ from me do say; but it has grieved me a little, I confess it, to see men who think *as I do* of the historical and mythical matter connected with Christianity, and who yet take the stand some of them take. It is like opening a drawer, when you expect to find money, and discover that the gold is gone and only the copper is left. This has been my fate very often. I put my finger on a *minister*, and " he ain't there."

TO THE SAME.

March 8, 1842.

You must have thought me a great fool to write so lugubrious a letter the other day. I ask as little for sympathy as any man, and when I mourn it is not on my own account; but I have seen some manifestations in certain persons that, I confess, made me feel sad, not for *my* sake, but *their* sake. I will tell you of this some time, but not write, for *scripta manent*.

But then there are times when I am sick, worn out and shattered, and I have nobody to fall back upon. " Wo unto him that is alone when he *falleth*." Paul could *stand* alone. I often think of those lines of Coleridge, which I trust are not so frequently on your tongue, nor so deeply graven in your memory, as in mine :—

> " There was a time when, though my path was rough,
> This joy within me *dallied with distress*,
> And all misfortunes were but as the stuff
> Whence fancy wove me dreams of happiness:
> For hope grew round me, like the twining vine,
> And fruits and foliage not my own seem'd mine.
> But now afflictions bow me down to earth:
> Nor heed I that they rob me of my mirth.
> But oh, each visitation
> *Suspends*, what nature gave me at my birth,
> *My shaping spirit of imagination.*
> For not to think of what I needs must feel,
> And to be still and patient, all I can,
> And, haply by *abstruse research* to steal
> *From my own nature all the natural man*—
> This was (is) my sole resource, my only plan:
> Till that which suits a part infects the whole,
> *And now is almost grown the habit of my soul.*"

But I will trouble you with no more threnodies, and I know you will forgive me this once.

TO THE SAME.

May 5, 1842.

I should have answered your last long ago, but the book I have in the press ("Discourse," &c.) has demanded from fifty to eighty hours a week of me, for the last six weeks, and I have had sermons to write, and neighbours to visit, and a thousand little "notions" to attend to, so that really I could not gratify my wish to see you or write to you. But this morning I sent the last sheet to the printer, and am now at leisure for a little while; so you may not only hear from me, but peradventure I shall waylay the tome-devourer, like Cacus, in his den, and that before long.

The other day I found a little bit of "literary history matter," which perhaps you have not seen; and as it concerns a favourite book of yours, I will copy it for you. Luther's "Table-talk" "did so promote the Protestant religion in Germany that each church had one of them (a copy of the 'Table-talk') chained in it, on which the Pope and the Emperor caused them all to be burned. Only one of them was afterwards found wrapt up in an old wall, by a German gentleman that pulled down his old house, who, not daring to keep it, for fear of the law against it, sent it to his friend, Captain Henry Bell, in London, desiring him to turn it out of German into the English tongue. The said captain, through business or otherwise, deferring to translate it, one night, between twelve and one o'clock, there appeared to him, then awake, an ancient man standing at his bed-side all in white, with a broad white beard down to his girdle, taking him by the right ear, saying, 'Sirrah, wilt thou not take time to translate this book which is sent thee out of Germany? I will shortly provide thee both time and place to do it in,' then vanished. His fright and sweating astonished his wife; yet, not heeding visions, the book again slipped out of his mind, till warrants from Charles I.'s council-board laid him up in the gate-house in Westminster for ten years, without showing him any cause, five of which were spent in composing the said translation, which was published by the Assembly of Divines."

This is from the "Surry Demoniack; or An Account of Satan's Strange and Dreadful Actings in and about the Body of Richard Dugdale, of Surry, near Whalley, in Lancashire," &c., &c.; London, 1697. Of course, you who own the book of Captain Bell must believe the story, for the translation must have divine authority, such as no translation pretends to except the LXX. Since you are a logician and casuist I will propound a *practical* question growing out of this case; *An liber fallibilis sit ne infallibilis si translator infallibiliter atque miraculose, &c.?* The "Tisch-reden" of honest Martin may be a human book, fallible, to be judged of like other books, and censured when it talks nonsense or contradicts itself. But the "Table-talk" as it comes from the hands of the aforesaid captain, is a divine and infallible production, and as such is not to be tried by "carnal reason." Then a question rises, whether the miraculous character is vested in the letters and points (the single parts) or in the book (the universal), and whether all subsequent editions would therefore be infallible, or only the *Codex Bell* which came from the hand of the captain.

My book will appear about May 20. After that I suppose you will never speak to me except to say, *Apage Sathanas!* So I shall come to see you before.

TO MRS. DALL.

Faithful are the wounds of a friend. I do not love to be admired. I like much better one who sees my faults also, than one who only sees what little excellence I may chance to have. Yesterday I had a note from a stranger, calling me a *wolf in sheep's clothing*, and other gentle titles. To-day comes your note with its womanly tenderness, and its manly rebuke.

But while I thank you for your frankness, I by no means admit the justice of what you say. I am by no means conscious of giving utterance to "an unchristlike sneer or an unkind accusation" in any of my writings, preachings, or prayings. I do not admit the justice of your remarks about *sneering tones*. I never spoke of such as have faith in the Gospel record in terms of sarcasm and abuse, say Mr. —— what he will. If you will read over the passage where I quote the lines of Pope,* I think you will see little to censure. If I sneered at such as still believe in the ordinances, do you think I should still administer these ordinances? I? And invite others to participate in what I publicly administered—that I publicly mocked at! When I quoted these lines, I rejoiced that at God's table there was milk for the maidens, meat for the men. In short, that there was something for all—that man can take such things, water, bread and wine, and by means of association therewith connected, can find them helps in their spiritual progress. I think that in comparison with the great work of forming a Christian character and living a Christian life, all will confess that the " ordinances " are but straws, rattles and childish playthings. I never *mocked* at anything. I am not aware of uttering contumely and reproach. I pray thee, where or when? I have spoken strongly, and I have strongly felt. I feel willing to stand up before men or God, and declare that I am not conscious of having written one line with any unchristian feeling. I knew I should be misunderstood, misrepresented and abused. Once I said, " We whine and whimper in our brother's name," &c.; for that I have been called mocker, yet I wrote that sentence in tears of anguish, in great burnings of heart. I say to you, what I never said before—not even to my wife—that after writing some of those sentences for which I am most commonly abused, I have been obliged to pause, then throw myself on a couch and get relief in tears. I don't know why I tell *you* this, for I do not like to talk of myself. So I beg you never to repeat or show it to any one. But it is in such mood that I have written such pas-

---

* Discourse of Religion, Ed. 1842, p. 261. The lines were applied to the ordinance of the Lord's Supper :—

> "Behold the child, by Nature's kindly law,
> Pleased with a rattle, tickled with a straw ;
> Some livelier plaything gives his youth delight—
> A little louder, but as empty quite."

sages as some men read in coldness or in passion, and then call me an infidel, a heartless man for writing!

He that reads my books twenty years hence—if I am not quite forgotten before that time—will not find in them the abuse, the sarcasm, the contumely, and all that, which so grieves you. At Salem they said I painted the Salem ministers, at Marblehead the clergy of that place, and at Boston it was the "Brethren" that I "abused," and on whom I "poured scorn and contempt." I think some of the brethren ought to fall down on their knees and thank me for my forbearance, that I have not told what I most assuredly have known and still remember.

FROM THE JOURNAL.

May 6, 1842.—To-day I received the last proof-sheet of my "Discourse on Matters," &c. It fills me with sadness to end what has been so dear to me. Well: the result lies with God. May it do a good work! I fear not, but hope. There may be a *noise* about it; it will not surprise me. But I think it will do a good work for the world. God bless the good in it, and destroy the bad! This is my prayer.

May 11.—The life of Dr. Follen is written by his wife. It interests me exceedingly. The character of the man was deep, sensitive, and beautiful. He had a *religious genius:* most of the New Englanders have *moral talent*, but very few have, or understand, what I call religious genius. Henry Ware has much of it, Dr. Channing less.

Oct. 5.—I have to-day heard of the death of Dr. Channing. He has fallen in the midst of his usefulness. His faculties grew brighter as age came on him. No man in America has left a sphere of such wide usefulness; no man since Washington has done so much to elevate his country. His life has been spent in the greatest and best of works. A great man—and a good man—has gone home from the earth. Why, oh! my God, are so many left, when such are taken? Why could not I have died in his stead?

Here is a downright famous letter, which Luther, journeying to Worms, would not have been ashamed of:—

TO DR. FRANCIS.

June 24, 1842.

I trust you have long before this made up your mind to go to Cambridge.* I can't help thinking that the welfare of the denomination depends upon it. It seems to me to be the bloom and fruitage of your life, your going thither and pouring out the learning you have hived up in diligent summers, and drawing from the wells of thought and emotion which you have so long frequented. I rejoice at it most continually. The young men at the school, I learn, are much gratified with the arrangement. I know the intellectual and the liberal party of the clergy—I am sorry it is a small number—will also rejoice at it.

* Dr. Francis had just received an invitation to occupy the Parkman Professorship at the Divinity School.

But there is one thing of some consequence to me, though of little to you, of which I want to say a word or two (I am not complaining of any one, nor writing a Jeremiad to grieve you). The experience of the last twelve months shows me what I am to expect for the next twelve years. I have no fellowship from the other clergy. No one that helped in my ordination will now exchange ministerial courtesies with me; only one or two of the Boston Association, and perhaps one or two out of it, will have any ministerial intercourse with me. "They that are younger than I have me in derision;" they turn the cold shoulder. Well: *Quorsum hæc spectant?* If I stay at Spring Street, I must write 104 sermons a year for about 104 people. This will consume most of my energies, and I shall be in substance *put down*—a bull whose roaring can't be stopped, but who is tied up in the corner of the barn-cellar, so that *nobody hears him;* and it is the same as if he did not roar, or as if he were muzzled. *Now this I will not do.* I should not answer the purposes of life; but only execute the plans of my enemies—of the enemies of freedom of mankind.

I must confess that I am disappointed in the ministers—the Unitarian ministers. I once thought them noble; that they would be true to an ideal principle of right.

*   *   *   *   *   *   *   *

Now this I shall do when obliged to desert the pulpit; because a free voice and a free heart cannot be in "that bad eminence." I mean to live at Spring Street, perhaps with Ripley. I will study seven or eight months of the year, and four or five months I will go about, and preach and lecture in city and glen, by the road-side and field-side, and wherever men and women can be found. I will go eastward and westward, and southward and northward, and make the land *ring;* and if this New England theology, that cramps the intellect and palsies the soul of us, does not come to the ground, then it shall be because it has more truth in it than I have ever found. I am perfectly free of two things—fear and ambition. What I have seen to be false I will proclaim a lie on the housetop; and, just as God reveals truth, I will declare His word, come what may come.

It grieves me to the very soul of my heart's life to think of leaving the ministry (which I *love* as few *ministers* love it) and this little parish. But, if duty commands, who am I to resist? If you have any word of advice to give me I shall be glad; and, in the meantime, rejoice in the new field of usefulness opening its harvest to you. I hope you will teach the young men to be valiant and fear not.

TO THE SAME.

July 25, 1842.

You give me ground to hope you will come over and see me soon; the sooner the better, you know. I see very few persons, especially scholarly folk; and, though I have little claim to the society of such, yet enjoy their visit, perhaps, all the more. But, after all, books, nature, and God afford the only society you can *always* have, and on reasonable terms.

I rejoice in the motto you mention, *Sursum corda.* Many men live on the motto, *Sursum et deorsum,* and so go see-sawing through life.

Here and there one takes sadly the motto, *Omne ferendum*, and lives on.

You will go to Cambridge soon; and I rejoice in your prospect of long usefulness, and the society of men that will appreciate your worth and sympathize with your aspirations. I look forward to a brighter period than you have ever rejoiced in before, when the wine of your life, hoarded and ripened in fruitful years, shall show itself worthy of its *mark*, and quicken the blood of youth, making their pulsations more generous than before. Well: God speed you, and keep and bless you! Farewell!

TO THE SAME.

St. John's, August 9, Down East, 1842.

I am here for the sake of health, strange as it may seem; I do all physical work, but none metaphysical. This is a queer place, an odd, amorphous, undescribable city, in which there is absolutely nothing attractive to any but a native or a speculator. . . . . . .

Don't you know that the charge brought against you by certain of the "brethren" is, not that you have done, written, or said or thought anything specially naughty, but that you are *notoriously the companion of suspected and abandoned persons?* It *is* so. Now I will speak plainly. I do not wish to stand in your way; I will not, knowingly, bring on you the censure (or suspicion) of your brethren. Therefore, after you go to Cambridge, I don't see how I can visit you as heretofore. Certainly Mr. ——, and Br. ——, will say, "It won't do, Francis holds intercourse with Parker! we be all dead men." Now I hope you will consider these things. I might, like Nicodemus, come by night, privately, but it is not my way. I hope neither you nor Mrs. F. will suspect anything unkind in this, for I only write sincerely. To come to other things . . .

May young divinity students heed the sound advice in the letter which follows:—

TO THE SAME.

September 25, 1842.

Mr. Withington of the Divinity School has passed an hour or two with me, and told me what I knew must take place, namely, that the school already wears a new aspect, as it has a new soul; that you stimulate the dull, and correct the erratic, and set right such as have prejudices inclining to narrowness, if not bigotry. I knew that this was *the* place for you; but besides awakening the soul of piety in the youth who are to teach it, there is one work which (you will pardon me for suggesting it) the *wiser* part of the public look to you to perform.

There was a time when *sound scholarship* was deemed essential to a Unitarian minister. I think the denomination has more *first-rate scholars* from the age of Frothingham down to that of Upham than any other denomination, in proportion to our numbers. But among the younger men there is a most woful neglect of sound study of all kinds. A man's library is, in some measure, the index of his mind; and the library of a young minister presents a deplorable picture of our theology; a few reviews, popular histories, Hülfsmittel for New Testament exegesis in *English*, perhaps an unused copy of Kuinoel, works of fiction, show books, and the scum of the press make up the whole, saving a few volumes of sermons. This neglect of sound study has been *excused* by the example of some pious men, and *justified* by the demands of the time, that a man should lecture on intemperance, slavery, &c., visit all the old women in his parish once a week, and retail gossip from house to house.

Now it seems to me that the denomination has a *right* to expect the first *scholar* that has been Professor of Theology since Norton to reform this evil, not only by his example but by his precept, and by the discipline he gives the young men under his charge. The orthodox and even the Baptists are doing much more than we to encourage good scholarship. One of two things I fancy must be done, either, 1, all study of theology must be abandoned; or, 2, it must be studied in a method and with a thoroughness and to an extent which bears some resemblance to the state of other sciences. Theology is contemptible at present in comparison with astronomy, geology, or even the pretended science of phrenology. Even this last pretends to verify its facts and legitimate its principles. Does theology do either? Is not a minister to do both of two things, viz., 1, to teach truth about man and God, and the relation between them; and, 2, to promote goodness? Is the present method adequate to the first object? It seems to me that the whole matter of theology requires to be taken back to the shop and cast over anew. Is not theology in about the same state with us that natural philosophy was in before Bacon? Shall we leave the reformation of it to the orthodox, or do our part?

I hope you will excuse me for what may seem very impertinent, and the intrusion of a boy's advice.

In the winter of 1842-43 he delivered a course of " Six Plain Sermons for the Times," which he prepared at the invitation of friends who desired to hear from him again. They were repeated in seven different places in the vicinity of Boston.

Everywhere I have found a much better reception than I had reason to anticipate. It has been to me a season of no little trial. I have no doubt that good will come out of the great evils of the present day.

April 13, 1843.—Went to Cambridge. Saw W——, who expresses a great horror at the unfairness with which some men have treated me, " who believe just the same thing." I don't understand good ——.

Went afterwards to Medford. Saw Schoolmaster Thos. Starr King— capital fellow, only 19. Taught school three years—supports his mother. He went into Walker's three courses of lectures, and took good notes. Reads French, Spanish, Latin, Italian, a little Greek, and begins German. (He is a good listener.)

Now, he was much sought after, but he was not always found.

FROM HORACE SEAVER.

Boston, January 11, 1843.

REV. AND DEAR SIR,—As chairman of the committee of arrangements for the celebration of Thomas Paine's birthday in this city, on the 30th instant, I am instructed to perform the highly pleasing duty of soliciting the honour of your company at the dinner ; and to say to you, in addition, that it would give the committee great pleasure, as well as many others of your personal friends, if your health and time will allow you to comply with this invitation.

I am, very respectfully,

Your obedient servant,

HORACE SEAVER.

REPLY.

West Roxbury, 14th January, 1843.

DEAR SIR,—Your favour of the 11th instant came in my absence from home, and I now hasten to reply to the invitation you offer me. With the views I entertain of Mr. Paine's character in his later years, I could not, consistently with my own sense of duty, join with you in celebrating his birth-day. I feel grateful, truly so, for the service rendered by his *political* writings, and his practical efforts in the cause of freedom ; though with what I understand to be the spirit of his writings on theology and religion, I have not the smallest sympathy.

I am, respectfully,

Your obedient servant,

THEO. PARKER.

Horace Seaver, Esq.

April 17.—Read " Rousseau's Confessions " and the article upon him in *Biographie Universelle*. Rousseau—a liar ! a thief ! a great knave !—I abhor him. He seems sadly ill-born—one of the creatures that are the sport of destiny. I shall never read his works with much interest after the developments of the " Confessions."

18.—Read Gliddon's "Ancient Egypt." It is a confused mass of valuable matter gathered from the recent works on Egypt. Mr. G. wishes " to run with the hare and hold with the hounds ;" so he professes, apparently, his respect for the Scriptures, and really despises them, it seems to me. His notions about the LXX. and Mas. Heb. text, which he calls the " Masorite Hebrew Version," are highly erroneous.

JOHN WOOLMAN'S JOURNAL.—This is one of the most encouraging books I ever read. What depth of insight into divine things, and not less into human things ! How lowly and meek ! How lofty, too, his aspirations ! What gentle courage—what faith ! He reminds me of Isaac Hopper.

TO REV. INCREASE S. SMITH.

October 10, 1842.

You asked some time ago about De Wette, and the "Introduction to the Old Testament." It is in the press, and about 300 pp. of the first volume are stereotyped. But it goes on slowly. All summer I have been ill, and able to do almost nothing. Had I been well, the book would have been out of the press before now. But I find I can improve it.` What has often been hammered, I take back to the anvil again, to file over the filed, and linger on the manuscript with a superstitious regard for the accuracy of quotations, references, &c. About the first of April, 1843, I think it may see the light.

I am glad you mentioned the mistake in my poor book ("Discourse," &c.) There are several errors—some of them in the notes—in the book, which are lapses of memory, or slips of the pen, or errors of the press. After the last sheets of manuscript went to the press, the excitement that sustained me in the work failed. I was not well enough to look over the book and make a *complete* list of errata, for a few weeks. But a list of six or eight errors was printed in about a fortnight; and some *weeks* later, as friends pointed out a few mistakes, or as my own eye detected them, I printed a more complete list of them. I gave Mr. Stevens two copies of the printed errata, and requested him to give one to you; but I supposed he forgot it, so I send you one.

Brownson's review, I hear, is not vindictive. I have not read it yet, nor looked at it, though it has been in my hands for more than a week. I have lent it to my friends, and when I have a convenient season I *shall* read it.

ECCLESIASTICAL RELATIONS.

January 23rd, 1843.—I attended a meeting of the Association by particular request. It seems that, so early as last September, at a meeting at Putnam's, the Association thought proper to discuss the affairs of myself and my book ("Discourse," &c.) The discussion was continued from time to time. But once, in December, I think, or the latter part of November, some felt a delicacy in discussing such a matter in my absence. Therefore they considered it meet to request me to come and talk the matter over with them in a friendly way. So I came. The Association met at R. C. Waterston's in Temple Street, and what follows is a faithful history of the events that took place.

After tea, which was got through a little after six, ——— * called the meeting to order, and with a considerable degree of embarrassment, stated the business of the meeting. ——— followed him, and also stated the occasion, the circumstances that gave rise to the meeting, viz., that the Association felt a delicacy in discussing me and mine in my absence. He said he, however, and the Association had felt a difficulty in asking me to come; for, first, it was my place without invitation, and second, the invitation might look like a summons. Here the record of the last meeting was produced by Mr. Robbins, and the resolution inviting me was read; it was stated

* The blanks are the same throughout this relation, but they cover the names of half-a-dozen speakers, who, however, never cared to conceal any opinions that referred to Mr. Parker.

that the resolution was worded with great care, and debated on some time before adoption.

These preliminaries settled, —— opened the business by going *in medias res,* stating, however, beforehand that, first, I was not to catechise them, nor second, were they to catechise me. Then he said that he could have no ministerial intercourse with me—though still he hoped to have a friendly and social intercourse. The reason was, the character of the book I had written. That he charged me with two offences. 1. It was vehemently deistical, using the word in the worst sense; and 2. It was not only not Christian, but subversive of Christianity, as a particular religion, for it aimed to dissolve Christianity in the great ocean of absolute truth.

Then —— took up the word, and spoke of ministerial exchanges again, and said also that the book was not the only offence, but the article on the Hollis Street Council,* was also bad, for it reflected on the members of the Association. He confirmed what —— had said relative to the book, but added that the doctrines of the book were not a matter of discussion, and that it had been so agreed at a former meeting.

Then I stated that it seemed there were two sets of offences I was charged withal, to wit, 1. in the book, and 2, in the article on the Hollis Street Council. To each I would say a word, but first of all, I. On the matter of ministerial fellowship. I begged them to consider that I had never complained on that account; never felt an ill-natured emotion—nor uttered an ill-natured word respecting them, or any of them, on that ground. I would, however, tell the result of their refusing fellowship, viz., (1.) Soon after the South Boston sermon, men refused to exchange with me. I had some very curious letters in my hands relative to that affair, which might be printed after my death or before it. Some from clergymen refusing to exchange with me—they agreed to do so before. The result was this—some members of churches in the city asked me to come and deliver five lectures on five subjects. I pleaded youth,—inability,—and refused. They would not be satisfied with the plea. They said, "you are excluded from the pulpits of the Unitarians for no sufficient reason. We want to hear what you have got to say: we can't hear you in the old way, let us try a new one." I consulted two ministers, they said " Go," and I went; delivered the lectures in Boston, and five other places, before some thousands of people, and printed them in a book.

2. In 1842, some young men repeated the same arguments, and called me to come and preach, continually, old sermons every Sunday evening. I thought it better to preach six sermons, such as were needed for the times. I did so in Boston; they saw the result. Others in other places made the same request. I went there also. That was the effect on the public of their treatment of me—on myself it had no effect.

3. I spoke of the article on the Hollis Street Council, and said that it was no wonder different men took different views of that affair. I could not expect them to take the same views as myself.

* Published in the *Dial,* exposing the clerical servility to the prominent interest in Mr. Pierpont's parish.

II. I turned to the book and said: It was curious that a theological book was to be discussed, and we were not allowed to speak on the subjects of the book, and discuss the doctrines on which we differed, or were alleged to differ. (I ought to have said before, that I showed at the beginning that I took the spirit of the resolution, but did not see any good that could result from that meeting.) However, I would avoid touching doctrines so far as it was possible. Then again, as it was said, I was not to be catechised, I would avoid catechising others. Then I proceeded to the 1st charge (under "the book") made by ———— that it was "deistical," and said that I knew but little of the Deists, but so far as I knew anything, there were four classes of them, which were named by Dr. Sam. Clarke, in a book familiar to all of them; but all Deists denied the possibility of direct inspiration from God. Therefore, as inspiration was a cardinal point in my system, and I maintained that all men were inspired just in proportion to their quantity of being, and their quantity of obedience, that I did not come under the caption; or if I am a Deist, I must be put in a class by myself alone—and then it was arbitrary to call me by a name that did not describe my belief. Then I proceeded to the second charge of ————, viz., that the book was subversive of Christianity, &c., and said that though an author's opinion of his own work was of no value to others, yet I sincerely thought it was a most Christian book. Christianity was one of three things: either (1) less than absolute religion, or (2) equal to absolute religion, or (3) absolute religion, and something more. No one, I would assume for argument's sake, would admit the 1st proposition. I affirmed the 2nd, they the 3rd. Therefore, if they would point out the precise quiddity that made absolute religion, Christianity, they would do a great service. That other sects defined the shibboleths of Christianity to their mind, but the Unitarians had no symbolical books, and therefore a young man like myself, and not learned, found a difficulty. I ended by asking ———— to tell just what it was in which Christianity differed from absolute religion. He replied, "But I will remind Mr. Parker, that he is not to catechise me."

Then ———— took up the article on the Hollis Street Council. ———— said that in that article I held up the Council to the scorn and derision of mankind, representing them as a set of hypocrites, and double-dealing knaves: that I called the "result in council" a "Jesuitical document," and as he was one of the Council, and one that drew up the "result," he contended that I had traduced him, representing him as a double-dealing and base man; that I had undertaken to weaken his influence and ruin his character with the world and his own congregation, and so far as my influence went, that I had done so. This kind of charge he continued at length—in language and manner which are peculiar to him.

I then replied that I was not answerable for the inference which other men drew, only for the fact of what I had written. One man said I slandered the brethren in the sermon of "Pharisees;" another in the conclusion of South Boston sermon; and ———— that I held him up to scorn in the article of the Hollis Street Council. I was not not accountable for their inferences.

———— then said, that he did consider that I meant the Asso-

ciation in the " Pharisees" and in the South Boston sermon ; an orthodox gentleman in the country said to him, " You have madded Parker,
and in this way he shows his spite. He is in your confidence, and
knows what you talk about in the Association, and tells your secrets."
To which I observed that as it regards the "spite," and the being
" mad," the facts spoke — the " madding" began in May, 1841 : the
sermon was written December, 1840.

The " Pharisees" spoke of six classes of Pharisees ; nobody complained but the ministers. I should be ashamed to say that I meant
no personalities in either the " Pharisees," or the South Boston sermon.
Then says ————, " since Mr. Parker will not say he did not mean
us—I will take it for granted that he does," &c., &c. He then enlarged
more on the article on the Hollis Street Council. I replied that if
need were, I would condescend to say that I meant no particular and
definite persons or body of men, in either case, but aimed to expose
sin and Phariseeism wherever they were—if in the Association, then
there. But had no individuals before my mind. The letter on the
Hollis Street Council stood on different ground, and there it was plain
who was meant. I had nothing to alter or add to that. Some said,
You called the result in council a " Jesuitical document ;" another, you
brought together a great deal of matter about ecclesiastical councils,
and about cowards, and knaves, and hypocrites. It meant somebody—
I suppose it meant us. I did not read it very carefully, for I disliked
it so much. To be sure, you treated the writers of the New Testament in about the same way, and said the apostle St. James "roars
like a fanatic radical." Then some one said " You quoted the words of
somebody—'Expect no justice of the Council,' as if you endorsed
them." I told them I did not endorse them ; since, as the words of
a great and wise man, they required no endorsement of mine. " But
you applied them as if you expected no justice." I did so then, and
do now. I expected no justice from the Council at the time. When
I wrote I thought the " result," &c., a most Jesuitical document—I
think so still. I then added that I didn't wish to write the article ;
asked others to do so ; they refused. I consulted several persons,
telling them the view I should express (three of them were present—
but I did not say so). They said, " Go on." I wrote carefully, deliberately, conscientiously. I told one clergyman—who had no affinity with
me—a man older than most of them, distinguished for good sense and
piety—what I had said, before I published ; he said, " You are right,
say it in God's name." I read it to another, who had little theological
affinity with me—he said, " Well, it ain't much after all for you to write,
and I have but this criticism to make, that you have been too severe
on Mr. Pierpont, and not half severe enough on the Council." Then
said ————, " Well, Mr. P. can't disown what he has said ; if he is
conscientious, as no doubt he is, we can't ask him to do so. I will
say that I freely and from my heart forgive him, as I hope God
Almighty will forgive me ; but I can never grasp him by the hand
again cordially."

Let us leave this subject and proceed to the book. He then said
that as I asked what was to be added to absolute religion and morality
to make them Christianity, he would add, the miracles, the authority of
Christ, which I did not acknowledge. To this I replied, that I made

Christianity to be love to man and God; and, admitting miracles were performed (for argument's sake), I did not see how they affected the case—making that true and a duty which was not so before, or of authorizing what was in fact true and a duty. But further than that, I did not believe the fact of his working miracles as a general thing. I was by no means certain that the four Gospels came from the men to whom they are ascribed; and, if they did, I could not take their word in the circumstances of the case. I had no philosophical objection to a miracle—in my definition of it—but only demanded more evidence than for a common event. Then some one said, that was enough; it was plain I was no Christian: for Christianity was a supernatural and a miraculous revelation. To which I said, that it might be, but it had not been shown to be such. It seemed preposterous to make miracles the shibboleth of Christianity. Each sect had its own shibboleth. The Trinitarians the Thirty-nine Articles—the Catholics the Church, &c. Nobody accused me of preaching less than absolute morality and religion. If they could exist without Christianity, what was the use of Christianity? So I thought it a mistake to make absolute religion one thing and Christianity something different.

Then some one said, "It is plain we can't have ministerial intercourse with Mr. Parker: he denies the miracles."—Then I said that I didn't think it depended on that, it was only a theological matter at best. The difference began before the article on the Hollis Street Council, before the "Discourse of Religion"—the theological lines were drawn immediately after the South Boston sermon. I had a collection of curious letters on that theme, which I might publish one day. I was at first surprised at the effect that sermon had on the Unitarian ministers. I thought the sermon a poor one—I was sick when I wrote it—read it to a friend before preaching, who said it was the weakest thing I had written for a long time. I looked round to see who would stand by me in the pulpit, and I had not been disappointed in general. I knew the ministers pretty well. But in two —Here somebody interrupted me, and ——— brought me back to the point. Mr. P. says there are two things; I want to hear that. I replied that I had not been disappointed in general; but in two persons I had been disappointed—grievously disappointed. ———'s face fell, for I looked full upon him as I said it. However he soon recovered, or I should have told him that he was not one of the two. Then said ———, "Since Mr. Parker finds the feeling in respect to him is so general, I think it is his duty to withdraw from the Association." Others spoke to the same purpose—I hurt their usefulness, compromised their position, &c. I told them that if my personal feelings alone were concerned I would gladly do so, but as the right of free inquiry was concerned, while the world standeth I will never do so. The matter was then discussed at length. ——— said, if it were a meeting of free inquirers he should very soon withdraw. I showed that theological agreement in all things was not necessary to our union, and quoted the case of Dr. Freeman, for many years a member of the Association, who never exchanged with him. To this ——— replied the case was not in point, for many others of the Association were not Unitarians. "Indeed," said I, "did they say so?" Then ——— said, "But the difference between Trinitarians and Unitarians is a difference in Christianity, the difference between Mr. Parker and the Association, is a difference between no Christianity and Christianity." Then ———— said, they did not deny that I was a Christian man, but only that the book was a Christian book, affirming it, as it was on account of the miracles being rejected. Then it was argued that I should not now be admitted to the Association, when my opinions were known; and therefore that I either had changed my opinions since I came, or came with the opinions not known to the Association: in either case that I ought to withdraw. I replied that I was not examined as to my opinions on admission, and was not asked to promise never to change, If I did them an injury they had the remedy in their hands, and could pass a vote of expulsion at any time; but it was a new thing that the shibboleth of Christianity among the Unitarians was miracles. A few years ago, it was said in the Association, that formerly Christianity was thought to rest on two great pillars,—Jachin and Boaz—prophecy and miracles. Dr. Noyes knocked down Jachin, and George Ripley, Boaz, yet Christianity stood. If I remember right it was ———— who said so. "True," said the Doctor, "I do remember something about Jachin and Boaz; but I did not say that I was one of them who said Christianity did not rest on the two, still less did I say that George Ripley had knocked the miracles down."

So they talked much more to the same effect. At last, a little before nine, Bartol spoke in praise of my sincerity, which some had called in question—spoke many words of moral approbation; so likewise did Gannett, at length, and with his usual earnestness. Then Chandler Robbins opened his mouth to the same purpose. I burst into tears, shook hands with Waterston, and left the room. Going below in the entry, I met ————, who had gone out a little before. He shook hands with me with apparent cordiality—hoped I would come and see him, &c. So the matter ended, and the bells struck nine as I left the house. I ought to mention one thing more, namely, that ————, in course of the discussion, said that I dipped my pen in gall when I wrote, and my razor in oil.

GENERAL NOTE ON THE ABOVE.—I may have mistaken the order in which things were said, and have put in one sentence what was uttered at several times. But I am confident that I have preserved the opinions of each that spoke, and often the language; and also that I have omitted nothing which would alter the character of the discussion.

Soon after this (three or four days) I received a letter from Chandler Robbins.

To which the following is a reply:—

TO REV. CHANDLER ROBBINS, BOSTON.

Plymouth, Sunday Morn., January 27, 1843.

MY DEAR FRIEND,—I thank you truly for your kind note of Thursday last; thank you for your sympathy; thank you, too, for the caution you give me. I can live with no sympathy but that of the Infinite, and His still, small voice saying, "Well done!" but when sympathy—human sympathy, comes, it is truly welcome. You mistake a little the cause of my tears the other night. It was not a hard thing said by yourself or others. All might have said such as long as they liked; I would not have winked at that. It was the kind things said by Bartol and Gannett, and what I knew by your face you were about to say; it was this that made me weep. I could meet argument with argument (in a place where it is in order to discuss "the subjects" of a theological book which is talked of), blow with blow, ill-nature with good-nature, all night long; but the moment a man takes my part, and says a word of sympathy, that moment I should become a woman and no man. If Pierpont had been present, I should have asked him, at the beginning, to say no word in defence of me, but as many of offence as he liked. I felt afraid, at first, that a kind thing might be said earlier in the evening, and am grateful to the "brethren" that they said none such till late.

But to leave this painful theme. I knew always the risks that I run in saying what was hostile to the popular theology. I have not forgotten George Fox, nor Priestley; no, nor yet Abelard nor St. Paul. Don't think I compare myself with these noble men, except in this, that each of them was called on to stand alone, and so am I. I know what Paul meant when he said, "At my first answer no man stood with me;" but I know also what is meant when a greater than Paul said, "Yet I am not alone; for the Father is with me."

If my life ends to-morrow, I can say,—

" I have the richest, best of consolations,
        The thought that I have given,
        To serve the cause of Heaven,
The freshness of my early inspirations."

I care not what the result is to me personally. I am equal to either fate, and ask only a chance to do my duty. No doubt my life is to be outwardly a life of gloom and separation from old associates (I will not say friends). I know men will view me with suspicion, and ministers with hatred; that is not my concern. Inwardly, my life is, and must be, one of profound peace—of satisfaction and comfort that all words of mine are powerless to present. There is no mortal trouble that disturbs me more than a moment—no disappointment that makes me gloomy, or sad, or distrustful. All outward evil falls off me as snow from my cloak. I never thought of being so happy in this life as I have been these two years. The destructive part of the work I feel called on to do is painful, but is slight compared with the main work of building up. Don't think I am flattered, as some say, by seeing many come to listen. Nothing makes a real man so humble as to stand and speak to many men. The thought that I am doing what I know to be my duty is rich reward to me; I know of none so great. Besides that, however, I have the satisfaction of knowing that I have awakened the spirit of religion, of faith in God, in some twenty or twenty-five men, who before that had no faith, no hope, no religion. This alone, and the expression of their gratitude (made by word of mouth, or made by letters, or by a friend), would compensate me for all that all the ministers in all the world could say against me or do against me. But why do I speak of this? Only to show you that I am not likely to be cast down. Some of my relations, 200 or 300 years ago, lost their heads for their religion. I am called to no such trial, and can well bear my lighter cross.

Perhaps I ought to say that, if the Association think I compromise them, and injure them and hurt their usefulness, they have the remedy in their own hands, and in one minute can vote me out of their ranks. At that I will never complain; but so long as the world standeth I will not withdraw voluntarily while I consider rights of conscience at issue. I think, too, that, when I shall have more leisure (as I shall in a few weeks), I shall attend the meetings more frequently than heretofore. To withdraw voluntarily would be to abandon what I think a post of duty.

Excuse this long letter, and believe me,

Truly your friend,

THEO. PARKER,

In the summer of 1843, his translation of De Wette's "Introduction to the Old Testament" appeared. He had so modified the arrangement of its text, by throwing all the bibliography into notes, and introducing illustrative matter from the German sources, that his edition became more convenient than the original. He also judiciously interpolated matter of his own, as in the chapter on the Latin versions of the Bible, the excellent description of the Venetian version, and a continuation of the author's account of the Samaritan Pentateuch. In the books of Samuel and of the Kings, he has several pages to bring out more fully their characteristics. His pen assists materially in clearing up Leviticus. His contribution to Daniel is now acknowledged by most theologians. He finds a historical occasion for the prophecy which Isaiah uttered against Tyre. Occasionally he gives a reason for not agreeing with De Wette, as in Vol. 2, 188, and he boldly shows the mythological elements where the author's pen is disposed to falter.

This was a labour of great service, which was frequently recognized in various quarters by intelligent persons who never before could acquire clear ideas of the composition of the Old Testament, the canon, the Jehovistic and Elohistic documents, and the intention of the various books. A book in English, based upon the latest learning, and carefully treating the Old Testament from the point of historical criticism, and in the interest of no theological party, was a want which this translation met. Later labourers in this field, of more narrow and orthodox tendency, acknowledge still a healthy direction in De Wette's work, and that he opened the way. De Wette afterwards modified a few statements in his "Supplement to An Introduction;" but his original judgment was more sound. A vast amount of valuable information is brought together in these two volumes, in an orderly and scientific way, subservient to the only kind of criticism which can save the Old Testament from the marauding of superstition, and leave it cultivable by simple, reverent human sympathy.

Nothing shows so well the value of De Wette's method of treating the Old Testament, as the attempts of later critics to clear up in a historical way the historical difficulties he finds. Thus the very point in dispute between bibliolatry and reason is surrendered. The Bible must be treated like any other ancient collection of documents. The appeal is made to uninspired sources to defend the authenticity of the so-called inspired books. Nineveh bricks and sculptures, excavators, explorers, Egyptologers, comparative philologers, a more careful investigation of the whole written and monumental past, will doubtless yield many historical confirmations to whatever history the Old Testament contains. It may occasionally discover an actual occurrence embedded in supernatural and legendary stuff. That will be clear gain, for it substitutes a fact for a fancy. Let the smallest relic be carefully hammered out of its conglomerate. The scholars of all creeds ought to countenance this rational tendency. It is not difficult to prophesy the end of it—an extrication, namely, of the historical from the mythological. Ahasuerus, for instance, may turn out to be Xerxes, and the Feast of Purim the commemoration of a real event. So much the better ; we have a historical fact. There may be fewer incongruities in the book of Daniel, but that does not reinforce its mythological element. The horns of its visions will not the less toss and worry the prophecy-mongers of every description, till scholarship rescues the whole book from ignorance. The historical may be everywhere proved and vindicated, so much the worse for the mythological ; its incompatibility will only the more appear.

What an astonishing infatuation is that of some English scholars, who think that the more historical they find the Old Testament to be, the less incredible its supernaturalism becomes !

In the autumn of 1843, Mr. Parker found himself fairly exhausted with the unusual labours and experiences of the two previous years. He chafed as he recorded the days and weeks which had been lost in consequence of illness and depression. Following the advice of friends he left his parish, to prosecute a long dreamed of tour in Europe. Here are extracts from the sermon which he preached just before he started, from the text,

"I have not shunned to declare unto you all the counsel of God." After describing the duties of a minister of religion, he says :—

Such being a minister's function, it is plain there are two several dangers which await him : one, that he becomes over-confident, opinionated, and teaches mere whimsies and spectres of his own brain instead of everlasting truths—in short, that he err through excessive confidence in himself—aspiring to lead where he is only competent to follow. The other danger is, that he succumb to things as they are about him ; take the opinions of his sect, or the public, for truth, and the practice of his neighbourhood, or the public, for religion, and sit down contented to repeat the echoes of his time and place. Then the man becomes a mere thing—with no independence, no self-respect, no power, a mockery set up in a place designed for a man. If a minister consents to hold this place, he may have the greatest original power of thought, fortified with the finest culture and the widest learning ;—what does it all avail him ? Nothing ! He becomes a Prophet of Lies, a blind leader of blind men, fit only to dangle about the tables of rich men. His genius goes from him, his learning becomes of no value, his culture ridiculous. Though born a giant, and armed in the panoply of clerical mail, and master of the most crafty skill to boot, a single shepherd boy with a true heart can bring this boastful champion to the ground and smite off his giant head. The fate of such a man shall be that which is recorded of one who disobeyed God and ate the bread of a liar—he fell by the wayside, and the men that passed by saw there a dead prophet and a living ass.

I have attempted to show that sentiments, ideas, and actions, belonged to religion—that what was at first a feeling got next an intellectual expression and became an idea, then a functional expression and became a deed. Taking Christianity as the absolute religion, I have insisted on Christian sentiments as the foundation of all, on Christian ideas, on Christian works. I have endeavoured to legitimate the sentiments and ideas, and then to apply the ideas to life, in part to criticise existing institutions, and in part to create new institutions thereby. Tried by Christian sentiments and ideas, you know how the popular sentiments, the popular opinions, and the common life must appear. I have shown that these ideas must at length prevail, for they are the ideas of God ; in this connection I have dwelt often on what I call the immanency of God in matter and in spirit, His perpetual presence and activity in the world of matter and the world of spirit, the laws whereof are but modes of His activity, and the results forms of His manifestation. I have shown that there was fate nowhere, Providence everywhere and always. Hence it followed that the material world is inspired by God according to its measure of reception ; that mankind as a whole, and each man in severalty, is also inspired just in proportion to the man's natural ability and his faithful use thereof. From all this it follows, that the providence of our Father in heaven has created a perfect system of optimism, of which we comprehend but little by the understanding, though we have a fore-feeling thereof by the affections and religious sentiment ; that this life was but a small part of the whole, and the evils incident to the present conditions would at last lead to higher good.

I have not taught these results on the authority of any church, any book, any man ; I have appealed only to facts, facts of necessity, facts of consciousness, facts of demonstration, and facts of observation.   I have tried to teach absolute religion on its own authority.

I found less than ten Unitarian clergymen who were willing to exchange with me.   I often said with the melancholy prophet, " Woe is me, my mother, that thou hast borne me to be a man of strife and a man of contention to the whole earth ; I have neither lent on usury, nor men have lent to me on usury, yet every one of them doth curse me."   Fear in the churches, like fire in the woods, runs fast and far, leaving few spots not burned.   I did not know what you would do ; I thought you would do as others did ; there are times which try men, there are men who must not be tried ; I feared that this church might be of that metal ; others had promised more but fled at the first fire. I made up my mind that you might ask a dissolution of our union ; I calculated ts value ; I did not think of begging, I knew I could dig,—

> " For since these arms of mine had seven years' pith,
>   Till now, some ten *years* wasted, they have used
>   Their dearest action in the *furrowed* field."

I knew my hands could win my bread, for they could toil at numerous crafts, and were perhaps better educated than my head; I never thought of being silenced.   The fact that a truth was unpopular was the reason why it should be spoken with a thousand tongues.   In case you had refused to hear my voice, this was my plan, to betake myself for six or eight months of the year to any work which might offer, and the rest of the year to go forth and proclaim the word which was so unpopular in all parts of the land.   If I could not find a place in a church, then I meant to take it in a hall, in a school-house, or a barn, under the open sky wherever a word could be spoken and heard.

But I must bring all this to a close ; what shall I say ?   Has my ministry thus far been a faithful one ?   I cannot judge myself.   In some things it has surpassed my expectations : in others fallen far short of it.   You shall say whether or not I have done good to your hearts, and thereby made your lives better.   If I have deepened your love of truth, if I have helped you to a clearer knowledge of duty, if I have enabled you to bear better the burthens of life, to love man and God, to obey His laws, meekly and reverently to trust therein with a calmness which the world cannot disturb ; if I have persuaded or helped any of you to aspire after a manly character and a divine life, then I feel that I have not laboured in vain.

We have discoursed on the loftiest themes; for six years our prayers have been mingled together.   Here we have assembled for a closer remembrance of one so dear to our heart and the world's heart.   The recollection of these modest walls, of these familiar faces, while they bring tears to my eyes, will bring not less joy to my heart.   May God bless you and keep you, and lift the light of His countenance upon you; may reason guide you; may religion be your daily life, your hope and your portion for ever and ever. Farewell!

FROM THE JOURNAL.

September 5.—To-day I leave home for a year; it had long been a day-dream with me to visit Europe, it now approaches fulfilment. A friend kindly furnishes me the means.

G. R. RUSSELL'S HOUSE.

CHAPTER VIII.

WHILE Mr. Parker was waiting in New York for the ship to sail in which he had taken passage, he made a visit to the city prison called the "Tombs."

The taste which would expend all that architecture on a building so loathsome as a jail is most wretched. Shame that the disgrace of society should be thus arrayed in costly dress, and made to flaunt before the public eye. In New England we hide our jails; for we are ashamed of them, and very justly. You shall go through our shire-towns again and again and never see the jail. I went into the court-house to see justice administered. A negro was on trial in the Court of Sessions for abusing his wife. It seemed to me the place was well called "Egyptian," for the darkness that covered over justice in that place; and "Tombs," for it appeared the sepulchre of equity. This poor negro at trial for a crime showed me in miniature the whole of our social institutions. 1. He was the victim of Christian cupidity, and had been a slave. 2. From this he had probably escaped, by what was counted a crime by his master. 3. He was cast loose in a society where his colour debarred him the rights of a man, and forced him to count himself a beast, with nothing to excite relf-respect either in his condition, his history, or his prospects. Poor, wretched man, what is life to him! He is more degraded than the savage, has lost much in leaving Sahara, and gained infamy, cold, hunger, and the white man's mercy—a prison of marble. Oh, what wrongs does man heap on man!

Here was a man who had got drunk, and was clapped into the "Tombs." His wife and two children were left with no protector. He had waited five days for his trial. This was a hard case, truly. I might have got drunk at the Astor House and have gone to bed every day; the police would take no notice of that. This poor fellow must smart.

He sailed on the 9th in the *Ashburton*. After five or six days of sea-sickness he attacks books again, and makes observations of a practical nature.

There is one thing that disturbs me much at sea; that is, the awful difference between the cabin and the steerage, or the forecastle. If I were in the forecastle, perhaps it would not appear so bad; I might think the men in the cabin deserved their pre-eminence of ease and comfort. Now, I *know* it is not so. Here are 160 poor wretches in the steerage, with almost no comforts, while the 30 in the cabin live in luxury. As the lion in the wilderness eateth up the wild ass, so the rich eat up the poor. Alas! this truth is told us often enough; in great cities it is thundered in our ears each moment, but in that little despotism, a ship, you see the whole thing more clearly, because more compendiously. There must be a cure for this terrible evil. What is it?

Here comes a list of various patent medicines for social ills. But he proceeds :—

The evil lies deeper. I look for relief only gradually, by applying good sense to religion, and religion to life. This is the field in which I design to labour.

I am now to spend a year in foreign travel. In this year I shall earn nothing; neither my food, nor my clothes, nor even the paper I write on. Of course I shall increase my debt to the world by every potato I eat, and each mile I travel. How shall I repay the debt? Only by extraordinary efforts after I return. I hope to continue my present plans in this way.

A. Practical.
  1. To work in behalf of temperance, education, a change in the social fabric, so that the weak shall not be the slaves of the strong.
  2. To show that religion belongs to man's nature, that it demands piety and morality (the inward sentiment, the outward action), and theology (the mediator between the two.

B. Speculative.
  1. To write an introduction to the New Testament.
  2. To write a historical development of religion in the history of man.*
  3. Such other works as may become necessary, *e. g.*, a popular introduction to the Old Testament, in 12mo.

In this way I hope to work out my debt.

Finding that the sea life did not favour reading, he began to gather hints for sermons. There are 37 subjects in all ; one of which is designated by the Italian proverb, " *La farina del diavolo va tutta in crusca* " (The devil's wheat grinds all to bran).

As soon as he lands at Liverpool he begins to visit and observe everything—nothing escapes. All is characterized with

---

* This is the projected work for which he gathered a great amount of material, under appropriate heads—enough for one or two volumes.

a touch ; the warehouses, enormous docks, monuments, beggars in the streets, the markets, with the prices of all the meats and vegetables, clean servants "looking like Methodist ministers," rich churches ; " but I have thought there were two ways of honouring God, one in marble and mortar, the other in benevolence and daily duty.   I love the beautiful like a poet ; but potatoes first and paintings afterwards is my rule ; " factories at Manchester, machines, men, colleges, and curiosities everywhere.   He draws the plans of public buildings, occasionally gets in a Puseyistic profile, unscrupulously strips an evangelical sermon ; seeing Scotus Erigena, " De Divisione Naturæ " on a library shelf, he forgets everything and sits down to read.   In the libraries he is particular to examine as many manuscripts as he can find time for.   He took dinner with Mr. John James Tayler, a Unitarian clergyman, and met Professor Newman.

We talked about various matters of scholarship.   He thought Xenophon gave the truer account of Socrates—so thought Tayler.   I stood out for Plato's account—of course somewhat idealized, else we could not explain the hostility of the Athenians (excited by the orators, who were all sophists), nor for the influence he exerted on the world, then and since then.   Professor Newman did not like Plato; he thought he never did the sophists justice ; that Protagoras was not so bad as Plato made him.   This led to a long discussion of the *functions* of the sophists, and the cause of their origin at that period.   Newman thought they were a sort of private tutor, and not so black as they were often painted.   I added that the state of theology naturally helped form this race of men.   Then we came upon the " Republic." Mr. N. thought it foolish to attempt such a work, which must necessarily be vain.   I defended the scheme as a method of putting forth great thoughts.   This led to a talk about the truths which lay at the bottom of the treatise.   Then we spoke about Aristotle ; his better method of giving an account of the actual.

Professor Newman surprises me.   I know many that I think have more native power than he ; but few of our scholars show such accurate and varied learning—such accomplished scholarship."

Few indeed ; but here is one who meets the scholars of the old world, in England and on the Continent ; knows what they know ; has read as fully, if not as minutely ; and can hold dignified intercourse upon their varied themes—and they, too, bred in the costly force-houses of universities.   It is singular to follow this poor boy, who carries learning back to its seats in Europe.

In the Bodleian, he applies himself to reading some scholastic books not to be found in America.

At Paris, he carries on the same minute investigation, noticing the men and women, the habits of the street and house, as much as the monuments of art. He begins to attend lectures on Arabic, Corneille, Cicero, philosophy of Gassendi and Descartes, law of nature and nations, ancient history, mysticism of the Alexandrine school, unity of the human race, and Italian literature. There is an analysis of every lecture which he hears. He even goes to the Jardin des Plantes, to hear Geoffry St. Hilaire lecture on vultures ; and carries classification, habits, and anecdotes—the whole spoil, home with him. But all these scholar's notes are not in a condition to be published. Pretty soon the journal begins to be written in French, by way of exercise.

In the Spanish Gallery of the Louvre :—

I would that I had a copy of the " Saviour " to hang in my house, to cheer me in my hours of sadness, and inspire me in my moments of happiness. But I am rejoiced to see it here, where all see it.

I saw a Frenchman kiss his horse in the street to-day ; a fine, noble horse it was, too. I also came up and paid my respects, though not with my lips.

He carries off a list of the curious names of streets, to be enquired into at leisure :—*Git-le-cœur, Pic-pus, Tait-bout, Tire-chappe, Brise-miche, Tire-boudin, Chat-qui-pèche, Cloche-perche,* and all the rest.

To Avignon.—Sunday, Dec. 31.—In the morning I strolled out to enjoy the Sabbath awhile, on the *pons ingens et sublicius* which crosses the Rhone, and had myself to myself. At 4 P.M. we started in a diligence for Avignon, and passed the Rhone.

We rode, and rode, and rode on the left bank of the Rhone ; and, at 12, wished one another a happy new year, which awoke separate trains of thought in our heads, and sent us far from the Rhone.

Jan. 1.—We rode all night, and in the morning took a hasty breakfast at a little inn. This is the first day of January, 1844. It is mild as an April day with us. The Rhone is on one hand, the mountain chains come down on the other, bold, naked, and picturesque. Here the plains are covered with mulberry-trees, kept from attaining more than eighteen to twenty-five feet in height, and reared to feed the silkworms ; underneath, crops of wheat are raised, or else, where the trees are far asunder, the whole is covered with vines. Some of them have been pruned already. Some of the towns are beautifully situated. Here the rocks rise up 200 feet almost perpendicularly, and just at their foot the village is built. On the top of the rock are the remains of a wall and towers, which still look imposing at that height. All round in the fields there grows a shrub resembling the box, it is called *buis.* Here, too, the olive grows in perfection ; all the soil seems wretchedly thin and poor, yet on the poorest knolls the clumps of olive-trees offer their perpetual green. In the summer, I fancy, they do not look beautiful, for they have a dusty aspect, and are not *bright* green; but now they give a very cheerful appearance to the fields.

To-day we have passed the place where Hannibal crossed the Rhone, and pushed on towards the Little St. Bernard, where he crossed the Alps. The whole country is to me one of great historical interest, rich with incidents from the times of Cæsar to the Crusades. I regret that all my life I have been so poorly supplied with maps, that much of my historical reading has not half its value, because I could not designate the special place where events happened. I feel the want now particularly.

From Avignon to Arles.—We went to the diligence-office to go to Arles. We had taken our places the day before, and found that we had before us a *chapter of accidents* as follows:—1. The diligence had no *intérieur* (where we had taken the four first places), but only a *coupé* and a *rotond*. 2. There was a large woman, hideously dirty, and *puante* to the last degree, with a squalling *enfant* in her arms, which she ever and anon regaled with the breast, or an apple, for he alternated between the two. 3. After riding about half-an hour, we came to the Durance, which had lost its bridge, in 1840, perhaps, and had not found the whole of it yet; so we had to dismount and be ferried over the blue stream, this took us a good while; we thought it durance vile. 4. I left my *parapluie* in the diligence, at the suggestion of the *conducteur*, and when I went back to take my place, found the great woman, whom we named *Mdme. Fumeau*, had *se mit sur la*, and it was *cassée*; therefore, *voila ma parapluie cassée*. 5. We reached Tarascon, and passed over its long bridge, and got safe into Beaucaire at 5 o'clock; where we had to sit down in a coach-office, with a stone floor and heaps of luggage, and in an atmosphere which would generate onions, to wait till 7 for the coach to Arles. 6. At last it came, and we got in and went to Arles, when, behold! there was nothing at Arles to see, and we were further from Marseilles than before. However, our friends the Scottish lady and gentleman are with us still.

Went to the Cathedral. It contains a curious bas-relief, representing the Passage of the Red Sea. Here the Lord is riding on a horse, and *troubling* the Egyptians; for He rides over them, while Moses and his friends reach *toute de suite* the dry land. The front of the church, about the door, is quite rich in carved stone; a huge figure over the door represents the Almighty, as Ezekiel dreamed of Him, looking like the Devil. Even the Scotchman said, "*It is blasphemy.*" There is a profusion of carving—lions, toads, devils, and angels, not to mention men. It betokens the exuberance of childhood, and belongs to the time when the church was built.

From Arles to Marseilles.—Soon after leaving Salon, we came upon the most beautiful sight we have yet seen in France. The sea was far off in the distance, but before it, and as far as the eye could reach, were plantations of olive and almond trees. The almonds look like large old peach trees. The air was soft, and the sun looked out upon the lovely scene as if to bless the whole. On one side of the road was a rock, extending for miles, with only here and there a trace of vegetation; on the other, this garden of perpetual verdure.

GENOA.—I have seen some handsome women here. In general, there is something quite pleasing in their appearance. I like their covering for the head—a sort of scarf, sometimes of white muslin, elaborately worked; but oftener of gay calico—white ground and violet figures. They hold the ends of this—the hands often crossed on the breast—in a very graceful manner. To-day, as I went early into the Chiesa San Matteo, I saw a most beautiful woman kneeling in the church; her face was much like some of the Magdalens. She might have sat for one. She is the handsomest creature I have seen in Europe.

PISA—DUOMO.—But it is painful to see such a building surrounded by a fringe of beggars. At Genoa—yes, and at London—we see the same thing. The first time I heard the Italian language spoken, it was by blackguards and beggars. Here, at Pisa, the one are more obtrusive—the others more tenacious. As I stepped into the street, I know not how many offered their services—or their caps; one begged for a *crazia*—one said, " *Vuolate un cicerone, por videre il Duomo, Campanile,*" &c. (You can't look at a building, but out comes a knave *to show it*.)

The Duomo and its neighbours seem not to belong to Pisa. Not only do they stand apart from the town, but they have a foreign aspect, and seem, indeed, to have no affinity with the rest of it. However, the *Campanile* has one descendant—illegitimate, but not natural: another tower, which resembles the great one only in its *leaning*. This is like all imitators; they get the prophet's halting step, not his inspiration.

DUOMO.—The effect of the whole building is wonderful. The enormous columns, their great number, the lofty arches, the prodigious dome, the altars, the varied marbles, the curious mosaic beneath the dome, rich with its many hues—all fill one with wonder, though not with the same reverence that steals over you at Notre Dame or Westminster Abbey.

I am surprised at the fewness and smallness of the windows; but the brightness of the Italian sky compensates for this. The stained glass is very rich. The effect of the enormous cross, with John and Mary, in the roof, just over the choir, is marvellous—a mosaic, with a gold ground. I think there are twelve altars in the nave and transepts—all beautiful, all different, and all harmonious. The black and white marbles alternating produce a curious effect.

The best painting, I think, is a Madonna by Allori.

In Florence, he went into the convent attached to the chapel of St. Antonin, called sometimes Del Salviata, " and saw the cell in which Savonarola used to live. It is like all the rest, small—ten feet square, perhaps, and ten feet high. There is a fresco of Beato Angelico, representing the coronation of the Virgin. Here lived that dauntless soul who feared nothing *but wrong and fear;* a soul of fire was in him."

He takes at once the thought of Michael Angelo :—

But the Day and Night, oh, how they strike your soul! The day is dawning—a man huge and brawny, full of lusty life. He is just awakening, " as a bridegroom coming out of his chamber, and rejoicing as a strong man to run his race." Here you do not find ideal beauty—

you never meet it in Michael Angelo, but boldness of thought, and wantonness of unconscious strength. He is the Middle Age all over, as it seems to me, yet he has the profound wisdom that comes of long studying the best models, the profounder wisdom which comes of that inspiration " which rounded Peter's dome." I never see one of his works, from the Young Apollo unfinished in the gallery, to the Fates at the Pitti Palace, without feeling his awful depth and strength. His Aurora is fresh, strong, and full of *rhythm*—you feel this in all his works with the chisel; I can't think his Day was quite finished, but Night bends her head in slumber, and seems, like the Night of the old mythology, to be the mother of all things, who, of her own consent yields to Fate and resigns the field to Day. I do not see the connection these figures have with a tomb or a chapel, but I feel their force.

SANTA CROCE.—This is the great burial-place of the illustrious departed of Florence; here sleep in peace the men that were persecuted when living, and driven from their native land.

He copies the epitaphs, and in some cases the shapes of the monuments.

The first time I visited this beautiful church it was a very sad day, and not knowing what to do, I turned into the home of the departed. While I copied the inscriptions the priests chanted their service, and ever and anon the organ poured out such music as might have fallen from the sky; it was sad, sweet, and soothing to the soul.

It is a little curious that Galileo should be buried in *this* church and have such a monument *here*, for the tribunal that persecuted him had its residence in this very cloister. So the world goes. The conventuals of St. Francis, to whom Urban IV. entrusted the inquisitorial power in Tuscany, meet in the cloister of Santa Croce. Now the Grand Duke of Tuscany is curious to preserve every relic of Galileo, even his finger, kept in the Laurentian Library.

FLORENCE.—I have now visited most of the wonders of this charming place. Let me say that the great paintings of Raphael—the Madonna Della Seggiola, the Julius II., the Leo X., the Fornarina, affect me more than I had ever dreamed of. The first time I went to the Pitti Palace, I did not know what I was to see; all at once my eye fell on the Madonna. What a painting! God in heaven, what a painting! What a genius! I must say the same of the great work of Titian—the Magdalen, and both the Venuses; but the Laocoon, the Venus de Medici, and the Apollo did not fill my mind as I had expected. The statues in general have fallen a little below my imagination, the paintings (I mean the great ones which I knew well by engravings before) have risen above it far; so have the public buildings.

I have visited one or other of the galleries almost daily, and devoted almost all my time to the study of art. I have, however, lost a good deal of time by illness. I have had a bad cold ever since I left Paris; it became at last a violent pain in the region of the right side of the frontal sinus. It came on regularly from 3 to 4 p.m., slight at first, but increasing in violence, till at last it was like the tooth-ache, condensed agony; then it gradually abated and disappeared about 9 or 10. It lasted me about ten days.

We have had a fine lofty situation, No. 1189, Lung d'Arno, with a beautiful prospect far off to the snowy hills.

Feb. 1.—We left Florence with sorrow, and at night reached Livorno, on the way to Naples.

PUTEOLI AND BAIÆ. Mem. The girl near the Cento Camarelle, who *filé'd à la mode antique*, the pretty girl whose teeth Mr. Freeman looked at, and the beauty to whom I gave half a carline, and who knelt down that we might look at her necklace.

All day long we have been on classic ground, ahd a fine day it has been; but what a difference between the ancient tenants of this place and these their successors! Here those old Romans revelled in their Titanic lust, here they poisoned one another, here they framed plans or conspiracies which affected the welfare of a world, and here, too, a scholar wrote immortal words, and a poet said—

"Exegi monumentum aere perennius."

What a mutability in the affairs of men! Mæcenas is forgotten, or remembered mainly as the poet's friend; Baiæ, Puteoli, have perished; the monuments of brass are lost for ever; but the poet lives and will live for many a year (See Carm. iii., Od. xxiv., and the "Beatus ille," which he never wrote in the country, except the four last stanzas.)

Italy is the land of artistic elegance and social deformity. She has taught refinement to all Europe and kept treachery for herself. Oh, when is the great Phidias to come, and carve out of the expectant marble the perfect form of society, and realise in fact the ideal often dimly seen in dreams?

In vintage time, when you throw grapes into the press, by their ow weight they exude their juice, and there runs out a girlish liquor which is sweet, frothy, and will keep two or three days. At the first pressure there comes forth a liquor deeper in colour and more potent in character, which will last half the season, and it is fit for boys' potations and weak men. But it is only the strong pressure that forces out of the grape's reluctant heart that rich and generous wine which keeps good for centuries, bettering by age—the invigorating spirit which fires the heart of hardiest men. So is it with the works of human thought.

At length he approaches Rome, "the widow of two antiquities."

Had no chance to taste the wine of Albano, yet a· "*plenus Albani cadus*" might be forgiven. I had Horace in my hand all the way, and read, not without new pleasure, the Satire II. viii. 13.

Then we came in sight of Rome. Oh, what thoughts it awoke in my heart when first I saw its domes, and rode down the Via Appia!

ROME.—There is no city, except Athens and Jerusalem, so full of recollections to me as Rome. Twice it has been the capital of the world—once, of the Pagan, by physical violence; once, of the Christian, by spiritual violence. She has made a desert about her twice. The memorials of the arts, however, came from the times of the Emperors, scarce any from that of the republic.

Then they only *produced great men*. Compare the two eras in this respect. What great Romans came up after the empire was fixed in Augustus ? How many before.

Wherever the English go they carry with them their pride, their prejudice, their port, their porter, and their pickles. Here they have their national amusements—fox-hunting and horse-racing. When the Americans also become numerous, I suppose we shall have our national amusements—elections and banking.

I love to walk about the streets, or sit in the Forum, and think of the armies that marched out of this little city—the influences that went forth to conquer the world. What traces of these stern giants are written all over the earth. One might, in travelling in the land of giants, come all at once on the footprints of one in the sand ten feet long—and from that judge of the race. So it is with the Romans, but you meet their footsteps everywhere. Yet they *invented* nothing, not even the arch. They borrowed their literature, their art, their religion, but their *arms* they made. But, alas, what a contrast, as one sits in the Forum, and looks on the crowd of beggars and of blackguards. Oh, city of crime from the days of Romulus till these days ! Thou that stonest the prophets ! The blood of martyrs is upon thee from thy earliest to thy latest days.

We went to Sta. Maria Maggiore, which is exceedingly rich, but not imposing. It is not a religious architecture. It seems to me the modern Unitarians would like this style ; it is clear, actual, and the work of logical and demonstrative heads, wholly free from mysticism. It has a continuous architrave over the pillars, which I think is universal in Christian churches.

Mem. The fragments of Christ's *cradle* that are preserved here. In St. John of Lateran is the table on which the Twelve took the Last Supper—the heads of St. Paul and St. Peter—the actual Well of Samaria, between two pillars from Pilate's house at Jerusalem—the stone on which the soldiers casts lots for Christ's vesture—the pillars between which Pilate stood when he told the people to take Christ and crucify him—the column that split asunder at his Crucifixion (very neatly done)—and four columns supporting a slab which shows the exact height of Jesus—*just six feet !*

Here too I saw a hole in an altar—through the marble slab—made in this way ; a priest did not believe in Transubstantiation, so, one day when he was celebrating mass, the wafer whipped through the slab of marble, and left a great spot of blood on the column beneath which supported it. The red spot is still faintly visible. The hole is an inch and a half in diameter !

Really, I think I shall turn Catholic, and be baptised on Easter-day in the baptistery of Constantine, where Rienzi bathed, and where all converted Jews and infidels are baptized.

St. Clement.—This is to me one of the most interesting churches of Rome. It is in the early style of churches, with three naves, a separate place for the presbytery, two pulpits, one for the gospel, one for the epistle. Here too is the seat for the *Episcopus*. All this was constructed by John VIII. Here, says tradition, are the remains of Clemens and Ignatius under the altar in the presbytery. I did not *want* to doubt it ; but what thoughts it brings up to stand over the bodies of Clemens Rom., and Ignatius of Antioch ! Here, they say, was Clement's house—here lived the "true yoke-fellow" of Paul! How it brings home the words of the New Testament to visit these places.

After strolling about all day, to the Baths of Caracalla, the Pyramid of Cestius, the Columbarium of the Freedman of Augustus, &c.,

We went to the prison—the Mamertine Prison, where Jugurtha died, and the conspirators that were with Catiline. Yes, here was Paul a prisoner! The custode shows a spring that spouted up for St. Peter (who was here nine months with Paul), in which he baptized forty-nine soldiers, all of whom became martyrs. There is a stone which records the same event. I drank some of the water. But all nonsense apart, it is something to sit down in the dungeon where Paul was a prisoner!

ARCH OF TITUS.—It wakens deep thoughts to see the sevenfold candlestick of the temple at Jerusalem on the arch of a Roman Emperor. Amongst other things I really thought of Dr. Palfrey's Academical Lectures, with *their* sevenfold golden candlestick. One Pope took great pains to preserve and restore this "*monumentum insigne religionis et artis.*" I don't see how it is a monument of religion; but, as the Pope says so, it must be true.

But I fancy the Romans who took Jerusalem differed a little from the wretches we saw at work to-day in the neighbourhood of the arch. It is a curious spectacle to see the Romans work! However, they begin early, for they rise as the old Romans did.

Sunday, 25th February.—I was ill all night with a headache and feverishness, and all day in a slighter degree. Indeed, my old evils return upon my head. However, in the afternoon we went to the Villa Borghese, a few steps from the gate. It was delightful to hear the wild-birds sing, and gather the wild violet, so modest and fragrant, in a spot where the water trickles all day long. I found, too, some forget-me-nots of a species that I never saw before.

AT THE CAPITOL.—A bas-relief on a sarcophagus attracted me much, but more from the singularity of the conception than the beauty of the work. The story is the Creation of Man by Prometheus, Man's Fate and Death. On the left of the spectator are the four elements out of which man is made : 1. *Fire,* typified by Vulcan with fire beside him. He and a servant are at work hammering iron on an anvil. 2. *Water,* typified by Oceanus with an oar, &c. 3. *Air,* by Æolus blowing a trumpet. 4. *Earth,* by a woman with cornucopia and other emblems of abundance.

Cupid and Psyche embracing, denote the union of soul and body. Aurora, the newness of the world's life. In the centre sits Prometheus, with a clayey-looking, lumpy fellow he has just made, on a block before him, and another in his hand. Minerva puts a butterfly on the head of this latter, to denote the soul's entry into the body. The three fell sisters are there—one writes his destiny on a globe—one looks hard at him and spins her thread—another folds her arms in her robe and regards him. Then you see him lying on the ground—dead; a Love stands over him—I know not for what purpose. The Dawn is flying away in a chariot, to denote the separation of soul and body,

15

and Mercury waits to conduct the soul to its own place. Apuleius*
would have been delighted with it, and Henry More, I fancy, would
have written another ψυχαγωγια if he had seen it—to be read as often
as the first.

Mem. The busts of the Emperors and of the illustrious men. It
makes one feel humble to stand in the presence of such marbles as
are collected in the Hall of Illustrious Men. If one were arrogant, I
would put him there to become humble. Yet the Romans had a very
coarse and materialistic organization. I never find in them (excepting
Virgil) that keen sensitiveness to the beautiful, which belongs to noble
men. Their faces in general have very little that is spiritual, little
that is elevated.

Sunday, March 3.—We were presented to the Pope, with some
other Americans. He stood, in the simple dress of a monk, with his
back against a sort of table, and talked with Mr. Greene, who had
introduced us. He blessed some rosaries which the Americans had
brought. We stayed about twenty minutes. He has a benevolent
face and looked kindly upon us. Talked about the state of Rome—
about the English language in America—about the famous polyglott
Cardinal at the Propaganda—made a sign, and we withdrew.

CATACOMBS.—I know no place that fills one with deeper emotions
in Rome than the catacombs. Here the persecuted when alive found
refuge—when dead found repose for their ashes and bones long tortured.
Here the relatives of a martyr laid down his lacerated body—and in
the *ampullæ* deposited the blood they had piously collected with sponges.
Well : the master died the martyr's death—the servants need not fear
to do the same!

I am confirmed in my opinion that, long before Constantine, the
Church had departed from the ideal simplicity of the primitive state,
so often contended for by Protestants. Indeed, I am now more than
ever persuaded that as Christ gave no form, the first one used by the
apostolic churches was much less simple than we fancy. I shall never
forget the impression left on my mind by this visit. I should like to
come and sit here all night and read the Fathers, Origen's cohortation
to his young converts, urging them to be martyrs,—or something of
Cyprian or Tertullian, or the lives of the martyrs themselves. No
wonder the Catholic Church has such a hold on the hearts of the
world, while she keeps in her bosom the relics of the sainted dead!
Yet, as I walked about here, I could not but think how easy it must
have seemed, and have been, too, to bear the cross of martyrdom,—the
recollection of Christ, of the apostles, the certainty of the prayers and
best wishes of men of earth, the expectations of heavenly satisfaction—
all would conspire to sustain the spirit, and make the man court and
not shun the martyr's death.

ST. PAUL IN THE CORSO.—Perhaps Paul actually lived here and
died here! It is something to stand on the spot where Paul once
stood. I should like to sit here and read his Epistles. Oh, the soul-
stirring man! It is easy to build churches to his memory.

---

* This sarcophagus belongs to the time of Apuleius, who was born in the early part
of the second century. It shows the passage by Neo-Platonism into Christianity ; and
Apuleius himself has a touch of the same in his beautiful story of "Cupid and Psyche,"
which belonged not to him, but came down to him, gradually improving, from older times,
and only owes its Neo-Platonic form to him.

Saw Father Glover, of course a Jesuit, in his room at the Roman College, *i. e.* the College of the Jesuits. He is a good-looking, benevolent old gentleman of sixty to seventy, with a frank English way with him. He is an Englishman. St. Ives introduced me. It was in his room, with a brick floor, a bed, a rough writing-table, a few books, a single window, no fire-place—a cheap place, a divinity student would sicken at the thought of such a place at Cambridge. Yet he is a man famous for his talents and learning, and more and better than famous for his charity and practical Christianity.

I asked him about some doctrines of the Catholic Church, but he would have a controversy; so he had it for a moment or so, but it was all on his side, He thought there could be no religion without believing all that God taught. Of course I assented. God taught the Divinity of Christ; that I did not see proved—so he attacked me for denying that Divinity, and talked as men usually do on that point. However, he desisted at length. Then I asked him,—

1. About Inspiration, or the Catholic doctrine thereof. Inspiration was the Spirit of God acting on the soul of man, and preserving it from all error in regard to the matter in hand. It does not direct the words, but superintends the thought, or substance of what is to be written, so that no error intervenes. No error is in the New Testament when truly expounded. The Holy Scriptures do not require merely an inspired expounder, but an infallible expounder—there is but one such, *i. e.* the Catholic Church. He does not know that anybody has been inspired since the days of the Apostles; may be so, and may be not. Aid is always given by God in proportion to the necessity. Some of the saints have been inspired always. (Dr. Grant said, when the Catholic Church canonized a man, it pronounced his works to be truth with no error by this act. Still, I think there must be limitations to that statement.) Father Glover said the Old Testament was inspired; but it was only a figure of the New Testament, that is, in the main. The Apocalypse was as true and authentic as the other parts of the Old Testament. The Church told him so. (Here I think he was a little mistaken. See Jahn, but, on the contrary, Mühler.) The Apocryphal Gospels might be inspired, but he did not know it, for the Church had not declared concerning them yea or nay. (Here I think him mistaken a little.) The Apocryphal Epistle of Paul was quite like Paul's writings—its doctrines true, but whether inspired or not he could not say.

2. Of Miracles. The Catholic Church works them certainly when there is need. Now there is not the same occasion for this work as in the time of Christ, for then Christianity was preached to the heathens. Now when this is done, miracles always follow, *e. g.* Xavier raised three or four dead to life in the East. Miracles were wrought continually by saints, &c., &c. The liquefaction of St. Januarius' blood at Naples on the 1st of May is a real miracle continually performed. He mentioned the miraculous cure of a young lady in consumption on Conception-day; she lay in a dying state. All at once she said the blessed Virgin had appeared, and told her that she should not die that day, but recover! So she rose and walked about, well as ever! He cited the cure effected by Prince Hohenlohe of a lady in Wash-

ington, U.S.A. He had the printed documents before him. (I knew the case before.) He mentioned a miraculous conversion—a Jew, Ratisbonne by name. One night he knew nothing of Christianity; at 12, raved and blasphemed both God and his Church. At 12¼ he was converted and found to understand Christianity so well that he needed scarcely any instruction! This conversion was quite as miraculous as St. Paul's. Now God only wrought these miracles to attest the truth, *i. e.* the truth of the doctrines of the Catholic Church.

Went afterwards to see Bishop Baggs. Had a long interview with him. He is very courteous, and as free from all cant as one can be conceived to be. Indeed, I have not seen a Catholic who spoke through his nose, or had a hypocritical whine. I never saw one roll up the whites of his eyes. This, though but negative, is no small merit.

1. He said—for I turned the conversation that way—that the Catholic Church was making great exertions in all directions in the way of missionary enterprise, and with great success. Proof, or, rather, sign of it—the young men of all nations in the Propaganda.

2. He said the Catholic Church had never determined whether the infallibility rested in the Pope, or in the General Councils, as the matter of faith. In other words, whether the declarations of the Pope, touching matters of faith, were infallible before they received the assent of a Council, or a Church in general, and independent of that assent or not. Some thought one way, some another; but a man was not a heretic for thinking either way. I mentioned the opinion of Baron von Wessenberg,* which he did not concur in, but said, still, that others shared the opinion, though to him the case was quite clear: (1.) It was not a practical question, or the Catholic Church would have decided it; for during the 1,800 years of the Catholic Church's existence, no one bull of the Pope touching any matter of faith had been without the assent (open or tacit, I suppose,) being granted. Therefore the question is merely speculative. (2.) He thinks that the Pope in other matters, of his private opinion, may err, as any other doctor; yet, in matters of faith, God will infallibly preserve him from mistake. The Gallican clergy were once hostile to the Pope's infallibility, but are now coming round to the Roman side of the question. The question does not concern Philosophy, which the Catholic Church leaves untouched, as far as possible.

3. He said that Galileo was not brought into trouble on account of maintaining that the earth went round the sun, but because he taught that such was the doctrine of the Holy Scriptures, and in this point conflicted with the doctrines already proved by the Church to be true. (Doubt all this, very much.) In matters of philosophy, the Church did not meddle, except they come directly in contravention of the doctrines of the Church.

4. He said, too, that the Church taught that out of the Catholic Church was no salvation. Here he went into a quite able and very clear statement of the scriptural argument for the power of the Catholic Church to bind and loose, enjoin duties, and give absolution for sin. That what the Catholic Church bound on earth should be bound in heaven. Still more; Christ made a distinction—some men

---

* Geschichte der grossen Kirchenversammlungen. Band I.

to be teachers, some not teachers; "Go preach the Gospel," &c.; "they that believe and are baptised shall be saved;" "he that believeth not," &c. Here belief in what they (the teachers) are commanded to preach (that is, of course, the doctrines of the Church), and the reception of baptism (the rite and sacrament of the Church), are made essential to salvation. Strictly speaking, therefore, such as do not come under this rubric are to be damned by the very letter of Scripture. But this letter of Scripture is to be explained by reference to the attributes of God, *e. g.*, justice. Therefore, we are not to suppose that God will damn any one, except for what is his own fault. If he is out of the Church, not by his own fault, he is not to be damned for that. Nevertheless, a man may deceive himself, thinking he is not to blame for his unbelief, while he really is. Still, in special cases, it is not for man to say who is wilfully out of the Church, and therefore to be damned. God only can search the hearts of men and decide this.

He said, very truly, that the Protestants abused the Catholics; that very few persons knew what were their real doctrines—they would not inquire: all of it is very true. Yet, for myself, I have endeavoured always to learn their doctrine from their own writers, and have never wilfully erred in regard to them.

He is in time for the Carnival :—

Notice the beggars in the midst of this festivity, and their hideous deformity. They are sad enough objects at all times—on a festal day what shall we think of them? Men throw flour at each other, and the rich spoil the coats of the rich with what would have gladdened the heart of the beggars! "Whatsoever ye would that men should do to you—." Ah, this is the city where Paul was crucified. God bless men!—they can't crucify Christianity.

We went to St. Peter's, and heard the sweet music at vespers, and smelt the incense. The music is really very fine—the perfection of music; it would stir the heart of a statue to hear it. The children were gathered together (*i. e.* a *few* children) to be instructed. Half a loaf is better than no bread, and I make no doubt the essentials of Christianity are inculcated.

VENICE.—I see the secret of the Venetian colouring here in the actual sky, ocean, houses, and men and women. I rose each morning an hour or more before the sun, and watched that beautiful purple spread itself out in all directions from the point where the sun would rise, and then disappear in the dimmer light of day. The solemn stillness of the horseless city was .broken only by the fishermen going out to sea, their white sails against the purple. The numerous bells only announce the general silence.

Venice is a dream of the sea. Occidental science and Oriental fantasy seem to have united to produce it. A Pagan Greek might say that Neptune, drunk with nectar and Amphitrite, slept in the caves of the sea, and dreamed as he slept. Venice is the petrification of his dream. The sun colours curiously the walls of the palaces and churches. It seems as if their wealth had run over and stained the walls.

VIENNA.—The Strauss music is rich, rhythmic, and graceful. It reminds me continually of Paul Veronese's pictures, examples of a joyous festivity of well-bredness. There is the same colouring in both. But there is music that affects me like Michael Angelo's works, with its grandeur and terrific strength; a great thought strongly carved out in the air, as his in stone.

PRAGUE.—After many inquiries for the *Judenstadt* (Jews' quarter), which I visit in all the towns, an old woman offered to be my *guide de place*; but she spoke a dialect so corrupt, that I could not understand one word in ten. However, she led me to the place. The Jews are as busy as those in Rome—eight or nine thousand of them in all. Some of them are rich. They do business in all parts of the city, but lodge here. There are no gates to shut them in, no soldier to watch them. Alas! for them—they that once dwelt in the fat of the land of Egypt, and went out to a land flowing with milk and honey! Well, they are better off here than anywhere else in Europe.

The old woman put me in the hands of a lad of nineteen, perhaps, who conducted me to the *Alte Friedhof* (Old Cemetery), a small enclosure of half or three-quarters of an acre, surrounded with old houses and old walls, full of dead men's graves. Stone touched stone. There were long inscriptions in Hebrew: the earth was full of Israelitish bones. Old trees, *elders*, grew there to an enormous size. They were the patriarchs of the place. Some of them were a foot thick. The guide said they were more than 600 years old, and I can believe it. Here are the graves of famous Rabbis, of good Levites; of nobles, also, for in this land the Jews sit down with princes. I never saw a Jewish grave-yard before, and this spot made me feel as never before. I have an inborn affection for this mysterious people, for ages oppressed, yet green and living still. I thought of the service they had done mankind—and the reward they got! Abraham, Isaac, and Jacob, Moses and the Prophets, came up to my mind, and He who was the culmination of Hebrewdom, the blossom of the nation. I shall never forget my feelings as I also laid a stone piously on the tomb of a Patriarch who died 1000 years ago, and plucked an elder leaf from the tree that rooted among his mouldered ashes.

The boy showed me a tombstone 1200 years old—so he said; it looked amazingly fresh. I saw the humble shed, with its elliptical block, on which, in a rude coffin, all the sons of Jacob who die in Prague are placed—rich and poor, the Rabbis full of honoured years, and the virgin daughters of Israel—before they are gathered to their fathers. They bury here no more; but they scorn to mingle their dust with that of Christians. No spot this side of Rome or Venice has interested me so much as this.

Went to the famous bridge over the Moldau, from which John of Nepomuck was thrown. Saw the cross, in brass, on the parapet of the bridge, to mark the spot where he was thrown over, and to commemorate the miraculous flames that issued from his body, after his death, while it lay in the water. Numerous statues of John, in various attitudes and actions, are on the sides of the bridge; here and there are bas-reliefs, telling how he converted eight thousand Jews and twenty-five thousand infidels to Christianity. Of course, he was greater than Paul, who could hardly convert *one Jew*. Here was a crucifix of gilt bronze, erected out of the fines paid by the Jews for blaspheming the Christian religion! It stands there to insult them every time they pass the stream! What would Jesus say of them who take his name in vain, could he come back.

Went to the Black Tower and the White Tower, from which there is a beautiful view of Prague. I love to take the *profile* of a town: that of Boston is exquisitely beautiful. But the Middle Age towns are by far the most picturesque. How degenerate and prosy our towns are getting!

I went into a Jewish book-store, and bought a few Hebrew books as memorials of the place and the nation; Hebrew prayers and Hebrew stories—no nation excels them for both—and a little modern Hebrew poetry. The little old man was attentive, and seem pleased that a stranger took interest in Hebrew literature. He had a fine copy of the Talmud, twelve volumes, large paper, for forty gulden!

In Berlin he attended many lectures :—

Heard Werder on Logic. He made a great fuss about *Bestimmtheit*, and was, as I thought, in a remarkable fix himself. When he wanted to touch upon anything very deep, he laid his fore-finger with its tip between his eyes on the organ of individuality, and then gradually drew it down the length of his nose. He goes down so deep, far below the nature of things, that one must take off not only his clothes, but his *Sinnlichkeit*—his memory, his common-sense, imagination, affections, and then he becomes a *blosse Geist*, and is prepared to go down to the deep, deep sea of Philosophy.

Mem. The pudding-faced youth who tried to comprehend the distinction between *Daseyn* and *Realité*, and could not.

This youth is sketched—

Heard Schelling on Offenbarungs-Philosophie. He found a good deal of fault with Kant, but praised Fichte, and said he had done great service to philosophy; thought his "Naturrecht" his best thing; praised the "Way towards a Blessed Life" for its *dialectic* skill, compared it with Hegel's works, which he said were merely mechanical, though he only alluded to Hegel and did not name him; some hissed at the allusion. Then he added that in his (Hegel's) case the work was mere mechanism, the grinding in a mill, and men paid much more attention to the noise of the *clapper* than to the meal which was alleged to be ground. Upon this all laughed.*

Schelling is about seventy, short, 5 ft. 6 in. or less, looks mild, his nose is short and slightly turned up, hair white as snow, an ample forehead, large mouth and pale face, his eyes blue, and have once been very bright, his voice is feeble—he has lost some teeth, so the articulation is

---

* Schelling did not recant, in set terms, his early philosophy of Transcendental Idealism, but was trying to make Evangelical Religion appear to be the same thing. The old philosopher, with his cosmetics and hair-dyes, deceived nobody. His long silence was interrupted by this call to Berlin, with the well-understood object of lecturing down Hegelianism, which was then in its prime. It was a curious piece of legerdemain, during which the Divine Personages and the Church itself, which men had seen Schelling actually swallow in 1800, turned up again quite briskly, saying, "Here we are !"

not very distinct. Audience 150 to 200—the largest by far that I have seen; when one came in after the lecture began, the rest hissed at him. It seems to me a pity he should lecture; the greater part, I am told, come to hear him from curiosity—to see a famous man, and smile at his doctrines. Others come solely to mock at the senilities of a man who is going to " squash the head of the great serpent of scepticism as if it were a Göttingen sausage." He has few that follow his notions here at present, though of course all respect a man who has done so much for philosophy. The Hegelians regard him as the foe of freedom, brought here to keep up the existing order of things.

He also heard Vatke on Psalms iv. v. : Michelet on Logic ; Twesten on the Relation between Faith and Knowledge ; Böckh on the Antigone ; Steffens on Anthropology.

After some delay he obtained permission to visit the public schools of the City of Berlin, which he did in company with Mr. Fay, the American Chargè des Affaires. He heard various recitations, extracted from the teachers all the details of their method, and observed the habits of the boys and girls. The notes are too disjointed for publication.

WITTENBERG AND LUTHER.—We entered the church by the door where Luther put up the 95 theses. I bought a copy of them in the church ; here they are (a pamphlet of 16 pages) ; what a change from then till now ! When shall the work end? At night I walked in front of the door to meditate. The evening star looked down. A few persons went and came. The soft air fell upon my head. I felt the spirit of the great Reformer. Three centuries and a quarter, and what a change ! Three centuries and a quarter more, and it will be said, the Protestant religion did little in comparison with what has since been done ; well, if *this* work be of God! *

Went to Luther's house. Here it is (an engraving). I saw the very room in which he used to write, and think, and work ; the stove which he devised himself, with its reliefs representing the four evangelists and other scriptural characters. There was the seat at the window where he sat with Catherine de Bore, and looked at the evening sky ; there the table at which he sat with Melancthon and the rest. The books are gone, (he never had many), the papers, the man. I went into another room which served for family purposes, and yet another where he lectured. Here are still curious things of his ; his beer-jug ; a glass cup given him by the Elector, and broken to pieces by Peter the Great. Here are some embroideries from the hand of

---

* There is a bronze statue of Luther in the market-place, on which is the inscription :—

> " Ist's Gotteswerk, so wird's bestehen,
> Ist's Menschenwerk, wird's untergehen."

> " Is it God's work, 'twill always stay,
> Is it man's work, 'twill pass away."

Catherine, a face of Luther worked perhaps by her. Here were the impressions of his seal. I bought one, and here is the explanation of it (a printed sheet in German hand-writing, entitled Dr. Martin Luther's Petschafts-Erklärung). I saw the genealogical tree of his family. Six of his descendants still live, at Berlin, Erfurt, Potsdam, and Leipsic, all in humble circumstances. I plucked a few leaves from a linden and a rose-bush that grew in the garden. The guide had great reverence for the reformer *der heilige Dr. Luther*, as he called him. I had heard " stout old Martin " often enough, but here I felt nearer to the man than before. God be praised that he has lived !

We went out of the walls to the spot where he burned the Pope's Bull. It is railed round, planted with shrubs, &c. A young oak grows now in the midst of it; the old oak under which the thing was done was hewn down in the Seven Years' War.

We went to his monument; the pedestal is of polished granite; I only regretted the polish. Beneath the canopy is a fine brown figure of Luther in his preacher's robes, with his Bible in his arms—a grand figure—large, manly, with that peasant's expression, but full of nobleness and commanding faith.

NEAR FRANKFORT.—Went into a little Catholic church, very poor, and very dirty. It had an old brass skillet at the door to hold the sacred water. Some daubs hung up here and there, wretched crucifixes, &c. The stone floor could not have been swept for a year at least; it was like the street itself. There were great cracks in the main door, which was closed, and I could put my hand through in many places. Yet comfortless and unæsthetic as it was, it was affecting. Here some poor man labours on all his life, in celibacy and silence, perhaps a man of genius, no doubt of learning; a little band call him their father. He baptizes, marries, buries them ; tells them of heaven, and perhaps goes there to see the Pope.

FRANKFORT. — Went into the *Jüdengasse*, which is the greatest curiosity in the place to me. It looks like the middle ages. The Jews of Frankfort, I am told, have split into two parties :—1. The old Biblico-Talmudistic Jews, who expect the Messiah ; and, 2. Those who reject the notion of a Messiah yet to come. Strange to say, the Government, which of course has no belief in a Jewish Messiah yet to come, takes the side of the old party and wars against the new school of Jews. What a curious phenomenon this, of the Jews living in the civilization of the 19th century, and sharing so few of its ideas.

In Halle he met Tholuck, and heard him lecture. In Heidelberg, he visited all the notable professors, who received him kindly, and talked at great length with him, and he had very pleasant interviews with the veteran historian Schlosser, and with Gervinus, who was then about thirty-four or thirty-five years of age, and had just been called to that university. He learned to prize highly Mr. Parker's subsequent works, and expressed his warm acknowledgments in 1856, with a hope that a friendship might be cultivated.

Gervinus thinks that the influence of Strauss has passed away; so says Ullmann. I think them mistaken. The *first* influence, that of making a noise, is over, no doubt; but the truth which he has brought to light will sink into the German theology, and mould it anew. Just as the doubts so haughtily expressed in the Wolfenbüttel fragments have done. *Men mistake a cessation of the means for a cessation of the end.* Strauss organizes no party, so there is no obvious action; but his thoughts are not dead—not even inactive, I fancy. They will yet do some work. By-and-bye his falsehood will get separated from his truth, and be forgot. The truth of his book will appear.

He travelled to Tübingen with a very talkative young man, who booked himself as a *Bekleidungs-Kunst Assessor* (a euphuism for journeyman tailor) who was travelling for the *œsthetische Angelegenheiten seines Herzens* (to give his heart æsthetic advantages.)

Went to see Professor Ewald. We sent up our names, stating that we were Americans. He came out and very kindly brought us into his study. He is about fifty, with long hair that hangs about his shoulders. He wore a sort of blouse of calico, with no vest or neckerchief. Has a fine spiritual countenance. He expressed surprise that I in America should know his works; still more that his works upon the Prophets should have fallen into my hands. He complains that the Bible is not studied with freedom; says that the more you study it, and the more freely, the more excellent it appears. He laughed about men fearing for religion lest it failed. I was glad to hear him say that the irreligious tendency of philosophy had received an entire check, and mainly from the higher philosophy itself.

He was glad to hear that I had translated De Wette, for, he said, in ten years it would produce a great change in theological affairs. De Wette was a noble man, but a little too sceptical. Thus in Job he is too sceptical.

Here he heard lectures from Schmidt, Ewald, and Baur. On reaching Bâle, he made the acquaintance of De Wette, who took him to visit various people and places.

Heard De Wette again on the Introduction to Dogmatik. In this lecture he stated that there were no ideas ready made in the human soul, but a tendency to such—laws that necessarily produce them. So the idea of God did not originate in feeling, but in an undetermined tendency which consciousness determines from time to time.

He took us to the library to see some curious MSS.; *e. g.*, the Codex which Erasmus printed the New Testament from—the Codex A of Griesbach—one of Gregory the Great, with a commentary, not yet printed. Some beautiful Hebrew MSS., some of them full of miniatures, remarkably well done, many of them quite like the Old Florentine School. I saw a curious copy of Erasmus's "Laus Stultitiæ," with marginal illustrations from the hand of Holbein, which give me a higher opinion of his genius than all the Eves, Adams and Venuses which he has painted in such numbers. There is one cut representing the Immaculate Conception; the *homunculus* or *corpusculum*, in the shape of a griffin, was entering the mouth of the Virgin. This was quite in the taste of the times. All these were marvellously well done—the ink strong and black as if new.

And here is a very fine portrait of Erasmus. He sits with that peculiar cap and writes. There is a remarkable unity in the whole piece. Erasmus was an *elegant* man in all respects—genteel; all the fineness of his character is pourtrayed here, the cunning mouth, compassed with sharp lips—the nose, slender, delicate—the eyes bright, but cast down, sly, witty.

Here I saw a curious piece of MS. in the handwriting of Erasmus. It was a satire in Latin iambics on Pope Julius II., keen and terrible. It has never been printed.

Took dinner with Dr. De Wette. He was very pleasant. I sat by him at dinner; we talked a good deal about German theology.

De Wette, I learn, has of late years become much more Conservative. Indeed, I think there is not a sound and settled philosophy out of which his opinions have grown. Hence the wavering uncertainty of the man. In youth he was the leader of the enthusiastic young men, the champion of freedom. Now, a life of misfortune has in some sense soured him. Last year, at Jena, all the students came out to receive him; he made a speech, advised them to go home and study their books, and be silent!

He received me quite warmly, and our parting was rather tender—certainly quite affectionate. I do not think my interviews have either raised or diminished the esteem I had for the man.

At Zurich he heard Hitzig lecture on certain points of Hebrew Syntax, and Oken on the Amphibia. After visiting all the famous places of Switzerland, he returned to Bâle, to pass down the Rhine. At Bonn, he stopped to deliver letters, and saw one or two professors. Thence he went to Cologne, through Belgium to Antwerp, where he took the boat for London. Here he made the acquaintance of Hennell, took tea with Carlyle, and met Sterling, who was then " near the skies—a consumption shortening his life." After a brief trip to several places in England, he went to Liverpool, where he was fortunate enough to find Mr. Martineau, and preached for him.

Somewhere in England he met an Episcopal clergyman whose liberal sentiments enticed him into conversation.

I asked him if it were not possible for all classes of Christians to agree to differ about their theological symbols, ceremonies, disciplines, modes and the like, while they fell back on the great principles of religion and morality ; in a word, on religion and morality themselves ; and I told him that I had aimed in my humble way to bring this about.

He said he liked the plan much, and did not see why all could not unite on these principles as they were expressed in the Thirty-nine Articles!

There is hardly ever an attempt at a fine description in the journal in this tour : but all which he saw and heard is briefly characterized in notes and phrases, well equipped with the necessary statistics. He observed the soil, the rocks, the method of culture, and the crops ; collected newspaper scraps, and little engravings of places and edifices ; made with his pen sketches of professors, soldiers, plans of buildings, monuments ; curtly described every man he spoke with. Nothing escaped his cool and simple observation. He found himself at home with each learned man in his own province, and thus saved the talk from evaporating in generalities. No American ever travelled with a better passport.

Sept. 1, 1844, Sunday.—After a most prosperous and felicitous voyage of twelve days, completing the quickest passage ever made, I reached *home*—saw the household, and the blessed Russells, all the four little and live plants in bed. Who shall tell my joy at returning, who the rapture with which I saw old friends !

GARDEN BRIDGE.

CHAPTER IX.

Letters written in Europe—·To Isaac Parker—Dr. Francis—Dr. Lamson, **1844.**

TO HIS BROTHER, ISAAC PARKER, LEXINGTON.

Naples, Feb. 12, 1844..

My dear Brother,—I suppose you have been to meeting to-day, with wife and children in the sleigh, and now sit in your room, with a great fire to keep out the north-westers. To-morrow you will sled wood out of the forest, or the swamps, perhaps. But here we have the verdure of spring. Flowers are in blossom everywhere, roses in the gardens, and oranges hang ripe and golden on the trees. It is a fine sight, too—a tree full of oranges. An apple-tree full of Baldwins, or a peach-tree loaded with yellow *Rare-ripes*, is beautiful; but an orange-tree, with its green leaves and its gold fruit, far surpasses it. Here you see in the fields what we cultivate in hot-houses. The fig ripens its fruit in the open air, the prickly pear grows on the side of all the mountains, and dirty boys sell the delicious hill-side figs in the streets. Every inch of ground is cultivated, not as we cultivate it, but with the nicety of a garden. I have not seen a plough in Italy. Almost all the cultivation is with the hoe and the spade, even where grain is sowed. But their farming tools are a century behind ours. They bring hay to market on the backs of asses, each ass carrying three bundles, or about 300 pounds. In the same way they carry wood, wine, and even *manure*. The harnesses are rudely made, and gall the cattle unmercifully. They put one single ox into the shafts of a cart, and a horse, a mule, an ass, or a *cow* on each side of him: then the driver mounts the cart, and takes the reins, fastened to a ring in the ox's nose, and drives off. It is a queer country in its customs. In all the public-houses men do the *chamber-work* (for the women get into other kinds of work, and so can't be trusted), while you find *women* driving oxen, and even sweeping the streets! Some of the customs are very strange. The Carnival is a sort of holy time: it begins the 6th of January, and lasts till the 22nd of February (this year). During the last week of Carnival, on Sunday afternoon, men dress themselves up in masks—in all sorts of foolish disguises, and walk or ride about the Strada di Toledo, one of the principal streets of the city. To-day we went to see it. The street is about a mile and a-half long, and quite wide. It was full of people, and the windows and balconies of the tall houses were crowded with men, women, and children. In the centre of the street was room left for the procession of carriages to pass, one end of the procession going up while the other end came down. First came private carriages, hackney-coaches, &c., some of them containing maskers, others not; then came an enormous carriage, drawn by four horses, in the shape of a dragon, with head, wings, and tail, as you see in the picture books: it was full of people covered with masques; then came the Prince of Salerno—brother to the king; then a carriage full of men dressed up in the shape of horses, asses, bears, rabbits, &c. Private carriages followed: then came the carriage of the king, with the king himself also in a "fancy dress;" then others of the royal family, nobles, gentlemen, &c. Well, they all threw sugar-plums at one another, and at the people in the streets and at the windows. The king, and some others, threw real sugar-plums, but most of them prefer such as are made of lime or chalk, which hurt a little where they hit. Some one in the king's carriage, when it passed ours, threw a handful and broke the glass of my spectacles. A wagon followed close behind the king to supply him and his companions with sugar-plums when the stock failed, and a barrel would not last ten minutes.

You will think this very absurd conduct, and so it is. It seemed worse than the sports of boys—they are well for boys; but here the whole population of the city spent the afternoon, with the KING at their head, in this foolish frolic. What would they say if the Yankees were half so foolish! Let me give you some idea of the state of the population. There are no *free* schools, and few schools not free. Of course the people are ignorant. Beggars swarm in the streets, yet a most abundant provision has been made for their support, which is *eaten up by the overseers of the funds*, one man, a *nobleman*, making about 18,000 dollars a year out of one establishment, in which he half starves the poor wretches. The taxes are enormous, never less than 20 per cent. of the income, and often 50 per cent. The king, however (they say), is a wise man, and wishes well for the people. I hope he does. Provisions of all kinds are abundant and cheap. Salt is a monopoly of the Government, and could be sold for 18 cents the bushel, but is sold for about 300 dollars. The profit of this necessary of life goes into the *royal* chest. For four cents I can buy ten enormous oranges, or in Sicily I can get forty for the same money.

I have been up to the top of Vesuvius to-day. There is no better way of passing the Sunday here, or, rather, there is no Sunday in Europe, and no day of rest. It (Vesuvius) is just as the books describe it, but it is a most magnificent spectacle, after all. I went so near the centre of the crater that it was necessary to run and escape the large masses of melted stone which fell continually. Some of the little fragments fell on my shoulders, but did no harm. The whole mountain, and, indeed, all the surrounding country is volcanic. Yesterday we went to the ruins of Baiæ, and visited the spot where Cicero had his villa, where Horace wrote his poems, and where Pollio fattened the lampreys with his refractory slaves. But my letter must end. It will be a good while before I shall see you again, so pray remember me to yours. Tell Uncle P., if you see him, that I shall write him by the *next* opportunity So, believe me, your affectionate brother, not at all changed,   **T. P.**

TO DR. FRANCIS.

Oxford, October 18, 1843.

Puseyism is getting forward rapidly; it has already embraced the greater part of the piety, and the learning, too, of the Church ; and men look forward confidently to the time when the Puseyites will all secede in a body as not far distant. Really the rise of this party in the English Church is one of the most encouraging signs of the times. The Old Church is not so dead as men fancied; some are found who say to the fat bishops and easy deans, " Go to the devil with your livings and your rents—your tithes and your distrainings ; let us put life into these old forms which you are humbugging the people withal. We want a revival of Christianity—primitive Christianity, and will *believe* anything and sacrifice all things, but we will have it." Here is Dr. Newman— gives up a rich living out of conscientious scruples ! Dr. Pusey, born of one of the oldest families in the kingdom, who at Pusey Hall keep a horn of gold given them by Canute—a man bred in all tenderness, rides on the outside of coaches, and submits to all manner of hard fare, to save money to give to the poor and promote education, Christianity, and the like of that ! He says a man in good circumstances ought to give up a fourth part of his income for benevolent purposes !—and does it !

*   *   *   *   *   *

When we were at Manchester we went into a very old church, the newest part of it built in 1422. It was very beautiful. We saw where Cromwell's soldiers—for they made barracks of the church—" broke down the carved work." I felt the natural emotions of reverence at treading such ancient aisles, consecrated by the prayers and remembrances of 400 years ; and felt, too, a sort of hatred towards Old Noll, who did such things. But the next day I went to worship in the old church. The organ gave out its beautiful tones ; the sexton, arrayed in a surplice, showed *us* into a handsome pew, but sent an old, tottering, venerable man into a little dirty box. Presently the dean and canons came in, in their robes, preceded by an usher. The dean has a salary of about 25,000 dollars per annum. A fat chough, with a face like George III., got into the reading desk, and "galloped like a hunter through his prayers ; " and another preached a most stupid and arrogant sermon. I could not but think Cromwell did only half his work, and when I was at Oxford I wondered why he never went there with his breaching cannon.

*   *   *   *   *   *

I have been to Kenilworth, to Warwick Castle ; have been in the room where Shakspeare was born, and have stood over his grave—you may judge with what feelings.

*   *   *   *   *   *

I have seen Carlyle twice, taken tea with him on Sunday night; and taken breakfast with Babbage, and had a fine visit ; saw his wonders and heard his wonders. I shall have much to tell you some day.

He wrote thus to Dr. Lamson, after slightly describing the buildings and pictures at Oxford :—

October 18, 1843.

I heard a great bell tolling. I went into the church (St. Mary's), surrounded by colleges, and was told that Mr. Monkhouse, a Fellow of Queen's College, was to preach before the Vice-Chancellor and Fellows. Aha! though I; I am lucky indeed. I shall hear an Oxford sermon—profound, beautiful, eloquent. Here is something to make a plain Yankee preacher blush for himself and his friends. I walked about over the dust of Wallis and Hoadley, and around the monuments of Sir William Jones and other great clerks, till the Vice-Chancellor came, and sundry ushers, with silver wands and golden, and a great flourish.

Mr. Monkhouse read a little prayer, for the University of Oxford, for Queen's College in special, and, in particular, for Queen Victoria and the Duke of Wellington. Then came the sermon, from 2 Timothy, iv., 7, 8. He stated that he should inquire "if Paul were certain of salvation at the time of writing," and on what grounds his hope of salvation rested. 1. Paul "was no common man, he was infallibly inspired," therefore his notion of salvation must of necessity be the true one. Paul did not rely on his own works. No: he knew that God never relied on human means. He gave the apostles this power to raise the dead, &c., but never relied on the apostles to spread Christianity. So Paul did not rely for salvation on his works. 2. There is a twofold doctrine in the text :—1, Hope, 2, Encouragement or Joy. I. Joy. Didn't look as if there was anything to rejoice for; but "*opera Dei sunt in media contraria,*" as Luther said : still Paul was joyful, because he was righteous. A Pagan said "*nisi justus non felix* (or *fortunatus*)." Here he proved from the Old Testament, the Pagans, and the Fathers, that "good men, in general, are happy." Then he showed that "wicked men are not happy," from the case of Haman, and also by citations. II. Hope. Paul had hope of heaven. Here he proved from the New Testament, especially from James and Peter, that Hope was a good thing, and they that had none of it were badly off. He quoted the ancients to the same effect, "*Spes hominum consolatio sola.*" After all that has been said of Hope, the half hasn't been told. Hope never fails; for "whom God hath justified," &c. Paul hoped for a "crown of righteousness." Paul sure of enjoyment now—just as sure of heaven hereafter. No wonder he rejoiced. Before Christ, pain was a bad thing; now it is a good thing—"count it all joy," &c. Trouble is a greater teacher than Reason and Revelation, too. Our great business is to be saved. Salvation depends on justification. Here he fell upon the Antinomians and smote them "hip and thigh." Paul's prize was not for himself alone. So we must not be proud if we are saved, since it don't depend on our worthiness; it is the gift of God. Besides, we may fall from grace, and then, Paul says to the Hebrews, "it is impossible to save such an one."

Application 1. Have faith. David had faith that he could conquer Goliah ; so we. Great religious movement now-a-days. But God never began a work without Satan trying to subvert it. God wrought miracles in Egypt: the Devil tried. God incarnated Himself in Jesus; the Devil possessed many bodies. God inspired the Apostles; the Devil raised up false prophets. God raised up the Reformers; the Devil Anti-reformers. 2. Avoid all lukewarmness.

That is a fair analysis of the sermon.

TO THE SAME.

Lyons, Dec. 31, 1843 ; Jan. 4, 1844.

It is now the last day of the year, and while you are getting ready to preach, I will sit down and write you a letter from this famous old city—the City of Massacres, it might be called—for Antoninus, the illustrious and philosophical, butchered 9000 Christians here at once, as the legend says; and the wretched Terrorists of the Revolution guillotined, and noyaded, and mitrailled, I know not how many. I have seen the bones of the Christian martyrs piled up in a large vault. I have been into the cellar where Polycarp preached the Gospel of Christianity, when it *cost* something to be a Christian (and *meant* something, too), and have stood on the very grave of Irenæus.

I wish you were here, you would enjoy all this even more than I do. Here is a church—that of St. Irenæus, built over the very spot where many of the Christians were massacred; over the very vaults where the early heroes of the faith preached, and where, too, they died. Really, one forgets the Christianity of the Boston Association, the heroes of the Thursday Lecture, and the trials, dangers, and sufferings of Brothers —— and —— (the last things one *ought* to forget, no doubt), and comes back to the time when the world said, "Thou shalt not be a Christian," and the modest man said, "Please God, you lie in your teeth, for I shall be a Christian!" When you stand on the spot where such men perished, with their bones under your feet, you begin to feel the difference between those days and ours.

I began this letter at Lyons; I shall finish it at Arles.

*   *   *   *   *   *

Here is a curious Cathedral, built at a time when Christianity filled the mind of the artist, but before it had taken a peculiar architectural form. Of course there is a struggle between the old form (the Roman architecture, with its round arches and heavy, solid columns), and the new sentiment, which at length shot up into those wonderful buildings, the Gothic churches. Oh, how they fill the heart, those old piles! You feel that they grew up just as the great forests grow; that each age altered them, and took away and added, just as it does in nature. Here, however, the old form prevails, but on the portal the artist has lavished his genius in wanton luxuriance! He has carved out the Almighty over the door, and the angels on the slopes of the sides, and the Last Judgment, with apostles, and saints, and devils *à discrétion*. The whole looks odd enough. It might excite devotion in the Middle Ages; now it only makes one laugh and think of the boys that creep before they walk.

We came here from Avignon, and from Lyons to Avignon, through a very interesting country. Here "Cæsar swam the Rhone, but kept

16

his Commentaries dry" (every school-boy knows they are dry still), and here Hannibal passed the same stream. A whole host of recollections comes up in my mind as I ride along the banks of the Rhone and read Cæsar's own words, and think of what has taken place since he came here, and had a "talk" with the Helvetii in this neighbourhood.

    *   *   *   *   *

Here everything differs so much from home, and I depart so much from my common way of life, that I sometimes doubt if I am the same Theodore Parker that used to live at West Roxbury. I am half inclined to believe that he is a mythological person, and has no real historical existence. But when I come to a college, a book-store, or a Roman temple, and above all to the *Palais des Papes* at Avignon, I believe that I am my old self, not a whit changed.

I hope you preach at Spring Street, in my absence; and if the brethren do not freely exchange with Francis and Ripley, really I shall think it shameful. I care not for myself a *sou*.

TO DR. FRANCIS.

November, 1843.

I heard several lecturers at the Sorbonne—Damiron, amongst others. He lectured about Gassendi. He looks a little like Dr. Lamson, and is about as old. He comes into the *salle*, pours his *eau* upon his *sucre*, and stirs it up; lays an ill-written MS. before him, looks up and says "*Messieurs*," then looks down upon his paper and never raises his nose from his notes once during the *leçon*. He flourishes his left hand continually, while he holds on the text with his right. He has not written out his discourse in full, so he begins, goes back, and begins again, in almost every sentence. His talk is as ragged as that of ——, but not half so rich.

Jules Simon is not twenty-six years old. I went to his *salle* half an hour before the time; it was half full then. By-and-bye, I heard a step at the private door, and the audience clapped their hands. Then entered a finely formed young man, elegantly dressed, with one of the finest countenances I ever saw—pale, with deep, dark eyes; he looks religious, mystic, and philosophic. He lectured on Proclus and his school, on the mysticism of Proclus, its origin and effects. He had no notes, but leaned back in his chair, looked up towards the ceiling, then at the audience, then began. His words were musical, his manner perfect; it was the *beau idéal* of lecturing. He did not quite do justice to Plato, for he went back to Plato to trace the mystical element in Proclus. I never heard or read a *neater* exposition of doctrines than his of Plato's notions of God, though I think them a little erroneous.

Once I heard De Portet lecture on the Law of Nature to four listeners, which was four more than the lecture deserved. I went many times to hear some of the theological faculty, but the knaves did not lecture when they promised.

I heard Lenormant several times. He is the successor, or substitute, of Guizot, and is an able fellow, witty and wise. In one lecture he undertook to prove the "unity of humanity" by demonstrating that all the race descended from one pair. He said he could not prove the fact in one *leçon*, but it was a fact as much to be taken for granted now-a-days as any of the admitted truths of astronomy. Then he pointed out the means of proof, and flourished away with great brilliancy. Again, he lectured on the influence of Christianity upon the institutions of Europe. I heard him discuss quite ably the rise and progress of asceticism in the Church. It was wise and witty, too, what he said. Christianity looked in the face the great problems of the nineteenth century, the problem of *Egalité*, of *Travail*, of *Fraternité*. Cœnobitism, Asceticism, and Monachism were various solutions, not the *real* solution. Christianity is yet to give that in the form of a new society, for which the St. Simonians are in the right to strive. He carried us off to the Thebaid, and gave pictures of the life there, quoting from a translation of Jerome made and printed in the age of Louis XIV.: so he made a contrast between the Christianity of the Thebaid and that of Versailles.

TO THE SAME.

November 20.

Yet, after all, there is a certain unity of character in the French that has its merit. They are always gay; gay in their business, gay in their religion; their churches even have a style that is peculiarly French—at least since the time of Delorme all their architecture has been gay. The Frenchman would "dance before the Lord." Now, John Bull all the week long is spinning cotton, raising potatoes, fatting oxen, and sending ships to the end of the world, He has managed matters so that the income of his Church is £44,000 more than the income of all the other Churches of Europe put together, and so that six per cent. of his whole population receives support from the public purse. All the week long he never thinks of God, nor cares for truth and righteousness; but Sunday comes, and then John is mighty religious all at once. He transports to Botany Bay a man who danced round a maypole, and shuts up an old woman in jail because she sold apples during the hours of service Sunday morning. Here is no *unity*, at the least.

TO THE SAME.

Florence, January 28, 1844.

The effect of the church within—dark, vast, and solemn as it is—must be felt—fancied it cannot be. The rich music of more than a hundred voices (men's and no-men's), joined with the sweet notes of an organ placed high up in the wall, rises and falls upon the ear in tides of harmony that fill the soul with reverence, with zeal, with faith, and waken love of God, just as the south wind of summer when it comes tossing gently the tops of the pines. I love the music and the architecture of Catholicism; its doctrines, its rites, and its general effect, I must say, I *hate* all the more in Europe than I hated at home.

In one church I saw a great crowd of people about a certain door, so I drew near and found the *avviso* setting forth that all persons who on that day visited a particular shrine of the Virgin should have plenary indulgence for forty days. I went with the multitude, so I need not fear for the next six weeks. Indeed, the Pope offers plenary indulgence for all sins—past, present, and to come—to all such as attend five sermons that are to be preached in Holy Week at Rome this very year. I shall hear not only five but fifty, if possible, and so shall be able to "*indulge*" *you* and eight others when I get home, and save them by vicarious atonement; it will be the height of mercy to do so.

* * * * * *

Here, amongst the mummeries, they serve God by ringing bells. I wonder no one ever thought of doing the thing by firing cannon. It seems to me to be peculiarly proper for a military people, and they might find warrant for it in Scripture (as for all other things), only by adopting a slight emendation of the common text, " Praise Him with psaltery," reading (by conjecture) " with saltpetre." Pray suggest it to Dr. Noyes.

* * * * * *

There is one thing which I always admired in the *idea* of the Catholic Church, to wit, its democracy. It (ideally speaking) honours *personal qualities* alone, the real virtues of real men, the apostles, the saints (who are not honoured for accidental qualities, as wealth and fame, but for what are reckoned sterling merits of their own), the prophets (of past times), and Christ himself. The lives of these men are immortalized in stone and brass, and great men and kings are told to kneel down before their relics, or their images, for nothing is so great as goodness. You feel this idea becoming a sentiment in a Catholic church, and it buds out towards an action, and you say, "Fools and blind! damned fools and stone-blind! Why not go and do likewise, honouring virtue by *action*, not with brass and talk?" If a real man were to come and stand in these old churches, over the graves of the noble, with these images of the holy and inspired before the eyes of all his hearers, it seems to me he might make every stone in Santa Croce ring again with eloquence, and every heart burn with love towards man, and faith towards God. Yet, perhaps, he would feel that a marble temple, profuse with silver and gold and precious stones, and cunning handiwork more precious than either, was not the place in which to preach humility, the greatness of the soul, the nothingness of life's poor distinctions. No: the marble devils would grin at him from the arches, and he would fare forth into the free air and predict the destruction of that temple.

Oh, is the time ever to come when men shall be content to honour God by keeping His laws, being good and doing good, when they shall know and feel that the life of heaven is the real service? The longer I live the more my reverence for the real God and the real religion—yes, and the real preacher of it—continues to deepen, widen, and make my heart throb; but at the same time my abhorrence of all false gods and false religions, and false preachers, too, waxes stronger and stronger. I know while men are as now, there must be such things; but I know also that if men are ever to be made better, such things must be warred on, not with earthly weapons, as cunning and spite (the Devil will beat all the saints with them), but with swords of celestial temper, and celestial keenness, too.

I have now had five months' leisure to consider my own position. I feel all its melancholiness, the severity of the task laid on me; but I feel, too, that I must *on, on ;* that the time of rest will never come in my day, and for me ; but, so long as I live, that I must war against the false gods and their priests as false. I have done little hitherto ; if health continues I may, perhaps, do somewhat. I am grateful for this opportunity to pause in the middle of my course and see where I am going. I have done wrong things, no doubt ; but, the more I think of it, the more the general tendency of my path seems to me the true one, and the less do I feel an inclination to turn away or to stand still.

Let me leave this theme. I thank you most heartily for remembering me in absence, and not the less for the good words that you are speaking to the few at Spring Street. Do tell me if "the brethren" exchange with you, and who ; what Ripley is doing, and what the *Examiner* does with that good, sound, modest man, Lamson, at its head. Do you know all his worth ? He is a noble fellow.

I am sorry you should say what you do about yourself. It is not given to many men to taste or even see the fruits of their labour. You *ought* to have the consciousness of having done more than any clergyman of your age, in planting principles that will bear fruit for mankind. If you continue at Cambridge a few years, I know the result will be to impress on the Unitarian sect the spirit of thoughtful and serious inquiry, of the greatest individuality conjoined with the widest toleration.

You speak about your sister's * book. I read some of the " Letters " as they appeared from time to time, and on the passage I read the book anew, and with increased delight. She has spoken nobly a noble word, and may God bless her more and more ! It is a great thing to speak words that sink into the nation's heart. It is not every passing cloud that rains drops into the sea which shall become pearls ; it is only the dews of Heaven which can do that.

TO THE SAME.

Rome, March 18, 1844.

MY DEAR FRIEND,—I owe you many thanks for all your kindness in writing to me when I am a stranger in a strange land. You tell me good tidings also. I am rejoiced to know of the doings of Ripley, Channing, and Brownson. But I hear that the latter has done what he advised the Unitarians to do, " re-establish the *Boston Quarterly.*" I suppose he will devote it to the overturn of the principles established in the first series. I rejoice very much in the *Fourier* movement, not that I accept the statements of F., but because I think our present form of society is irrational and unchristian ; that society makes criminals, and then hangs them ; that trade (in the main) is robbery, and "justice" catches only at petty rogues—never forgiving their offences, gradually makes them worse, and at last hangs them. Men are born in Boston into a condition far worse than that of the Esquimaux. Strong men build their castles by the hands of the weak and out of the property of the weak. The feudalism of money is not so bad as the feudalism of

---

* Mrs. Lydia Maria Child, who had just published the first volume of her brilliantly written " Letters from New York," which was followed by another of like excellence.

birth, nor that so bad as the feudalism of the sword, but too bad to be
borne in a Christian land, it seems to me. I do not believe the Social-
ists see very clearly what they would be at, yet they will help open
men's eyes, it seems to me. Three things are needed to make a complete revolution—the sentiment, the idea, the action. I fancy their
sentiment is not far from right, but if their idea be wrong, so must
their action be. I see no cure for the evil but this, to give each individual clear views of the right, and then leave it to him to do what he
thinks best. A complex evil has a simple cure, it seems to me. England is the richest country in the world, perhaps, but that in which
there is the most misery. It is the paradise of the rich, the purgatory
of the wise, and the hell of the poor. In Italy there is much begging,
but less starving. One million of the English are fine men ; what are
the nineteen millions ?

Now, we, the Yankee nation, are going in just the same way as
the English, and, unless we change our whole system, radically, in
regard to the pursuit of wealth and the pursuit of power, we shall
come to just the same result, and have the Christian feudalism of gold
in Boston as in London. But of this when we meet face to face.

I think I shall become a Catholic, that I may be *Cardinal*, and will
come to Boston, in my red coach, with three footmen on behind—that
is the way they ride here—and will preach a sermon on humility and
contempt of this world, and assure the people at the end that there is
no salvation out of the Church. Here I have seen not a few relics of
the saints, and other worthies, enough to convert a heathen. Let me
name them : the chains of St. Peter ; those of Paul ; the column Christ
leaned on when twelve years old ; the veil which burst asunder when he
gave up the ghost ; the actual well of Samaria (the woman of Samaria,
I suppose, is lost—but, enough could be found here to which the words
of the Fourth Gospel would apply just as well) ; the twenty-eight steps
of Pilate's house, down which Christ was led to be crucified ; and a piece
of the true Cross. Besides these, they have the heads of Peter and Paul.
I wish they were on some of their shoulders. I wonder that they have
not the original " tables of the law " written by the finger of Jehovah,
which Moses broke, or the garments which Elohim made for Adam
and Eve.

They tell a pleasant story about St. Peter. A persecution once
broke out while that Apostle was at Rome. He did as at Jerusalem—
cut and run. But, as he was getting towards Ostia with might and
main, down comes the Lord Jesus from heaven, and alights on the
ground before him. The people can still show the dent where his feet
lighted on the flint. The footprints are actually to be seen at this very
day, marks of the toes and all ! Then, too, I have been into the prison
where Paul was confined—the famous *Tullianum*. They tell you that
Peter was there also ; and point out a spring that started up miraculously on a certain occasion, and Peter baptized forty-nine Roman
soldiers in it, all of whom became martyrs. Apart from the murmurs
of tradition, it makes a man's heart beat a little to stand in the prison
where there is little room to doubt that Paul was once held as a felon.
It carries you back over 1800 years—to the time when Christian was a
name of contempt, and cost a man his life. I went to the place " where
Paul dwelt in his own hired house," &c. You forget the Church, the

Pope, the Cardinals, and think of that man who found Christianity the faith of a few poor fishermen, and left it flourishing in all the great cities of the world. I never felt so near the Apostle as at Rome. I have been to the Catacombs, which interest me more than almost anything at Rome. You know their history, of course. Here I saw proofs enough that some of the alleged "corruptions of Christianity" date back to 107 A.D. The worship of the Virgin can be traced nearly as far; that of the invocation of saints for the dead quite to that very year, I think. Indeed, if I were an Episcopalian, I must needs become a Catholic. You find the ceremony of saying mass, as at present, pretty distinctly traced back to the beginning of the second century; and the Catholics mention a symbol of transubstantiation which shows that it was well known in the second century, and pretty early too. In the Catacombs there are chapels, of course; in the chapels are frescoes painted in the second century (at the latest, in the early part of it), representing the miracle at Cana, in such conjunction with the saying Mass, that it shows a distinct allusion to the transformation of the bread and wine into the body and blood of Christ; at least, they say so. Of course, *I* should laugh at any argument built on such premises, even if I admitted the premises; but many would be overwhelmed by it. In the tombs you find the bottle of blood, which marks a martyr who died a bloody death; and often the instrument of his martyrdom, still sticking in his bones, or laid beside him. Some of the Catacombs have not yet been explored, as they have been filled with earth ever since the time of Constantine (I think), which an inundation of the Tiber deposited there. Therefore, here is no chance for saying, "The monks of the Middle Ages did it!" as some have often said. I should like to sit in this city of graves, and read the Fathers. Here, in Rome, is one Father Marchi, a priest, who has devoted his life to the study of the Catacombs. He went with us, and explained everything; besides that, he took me through a fine collection of Christian antiquities in the Roman College (the great priest establishment), and showed me curiosities without stint, relating to the early Christians, bottles of dried blood of the martyrs, instruments of torture, images of Christ, of the Virgin, &c., &c.

Mr. Shaw sent me a letter of introduction to a young American Catholic here. He introduced me to several Catholics, eminent men and capital scholars, to a D.D., a Bishop, and a Cardinal. I have talked a good deal with them about their *faith*, though I have not disputed, but only questioned. I feared that I might have sometimes done them injustice, but I think I have not. I have found them universally kind, perfectly free from cant; they don't draw down the corners of their mouth, nor talk through their nose, nor roll up the whites of their eyes, and say "O-ô-ô-ô!" There is much about the Catholic Church that I always liked—its music, architecture, paintings, statues. Besides, there is a long list of saints, whom I truly reverence, enrolled on its calendar. The Church is democratic (in the good sense) in appointing its saints. None are made saints except for *personal* qualities; not for wealth, or birth, or power, but goodness. What if they do pray to the saints, as the Protestants say, or through them, as *they* say? The true God, I take it, would as lief be called St. Cecilia as Jehovah; and a true prayer must be acceptable to the true God. I told a Jesuit Father so, the other day ; but he said that was an *odious doctrine*—it justified idolatry.

I love to hear Bishop Baggs talk about the Catholic doctrine. He is one of the most learned men in Rome, and one of the gentlest and kindest of men. I love him much. The Catholic Church practically, I think, cultivates the feelings of reverence, of faith, of gentleness, better than the Protestant Churches ; but I can't think it affects the conscience so powerfully, and 1 know that at present it does not appeal to the reason or practical good sense. How true it is that it takes the whole Church to preach the whole Gospel !—but few men will see it is so. One can't see beyond Unitarianism ; another will not budge beyond the Westminster Catechism, and here a whole Church refuses to go an inch beyond the decrees of the Council of Trent. However, while Bishop B. says, " *Out of the Catholic Church* is no salvation," he adds, " *but none is damned except for his own fault, and many may be in the Soul of the Catholic Church who are not in its Body.*" God only knows who ! I wish I could think better of the priests here. A " divinity student," an American neophyte, said he had known hundreds of priests, and never one who had defiled himself with woman !—that they were far purer in all respects than the Protestant clergy ! But a Roman, also a Catholic, said that about one-tenth were pure, conscientious men ; the rest—here he shrugged his shoulders, and said, " The walls have ears !" About a year ago, in a conventual school for young ladies, seven of them were unexpectedly found in the same state with Rhea Sylvia, but in this case the *deus ex machinâ* was a priest. I asked a *guide de place* one day about the priesthood. He looked over his shoulder, and in bad French, gave me an awful account of them.

Here each person is obliged to take the Communion once a year, and before the Communion to confess and perform any penance that is enjoined : if they refuse they are excommunicated ! This, of course, is adapted to make hypocrites of bad men, and martyrs of good ones. Then, besides, here is an inquisition ; if a Catholic be found uttering heresies he is clapped into the inquisition, when " Heaven help him !" as Uncle Toby said. He is not tortured, but only confined. I am told there are about 400 or 500 in it now. It is close to St. Peter's. They don't prevent freedom of *thought* : a man may think what he pleases, but as Dr. —— said, " *What is the use of talkin' on't ?*" A rigid political censorship is exercised over the press. Austria has a voice in that and a theological censorship. English newspapers are often stopped at the Post-office because they contain *incendiary matter.* If our friend the Heaven-stormer, were to come here, he would find his *Quarterly* in the " Prohibitorum" directly, and himself—anywhere but at ease, I am thinking. If I wanted to convert a fop to Christianity, I think I would send him to Rome ; but if I wanted to put a philosopher in the Catholic Church, I would send him anywhere but to Rome. Nowhere is there more to disgust a thinking man with its doctrines or its practical effects. However, here are also the bright ornaments of the Church, such men as Cardinal Odescalchi, such women as the late Princess Borghese, both of whom spent enormous sums of money and their whole lives in works of mercy. I really believe, that in no place and no Church are such persons more honored than here, in the Church at Rome. When the Princess was to be buried, 500 young men of Rome took off the horses from the hearse, and themselves drew the body to the grave. One day they will make both her and the Cardinal saints. Their doctrine ofthe Communion of Saints is beautiful to the feelings, not like the cold wordy rubric of the Protestants. Here, at Rome, all is in the hands of the priests. Over a lying-in hospital I saw "R.C.A."* The irony of nature is a little sharp sometimes! Here, lottery tickets are sold by authority; the R.C.A. manages that affair also, and once a fortnight there is a drawing, and the apostolical functionary appears in a balcony, and the list of numbers is read off in his presence to the people. You go to the Colosseum; in the centre of it is a cross, and a little tablet states that everybody who kisses that shall receive plenary indulgence for 200 days; another at the entrance states that indulgence for a year and forty days shall be given to all who kiss that! In a beautiful church, that of Sta. Maria Maggiore, is preserved the portrait of the Blessed Virgin by St. Luke. It is in a beautiful chapel, built by the Borghese family, and a Bull of the Pope, in marble, on the wall, tells, that if mass be said in that chapel for any of the faithful who are dead, and have died penitent, they shall be forthwith delivered from purgatory *quibuscunque non obstantibus.*

It is difficult to say what is the present condition of the Catholic Church; they are certainly making great exertions to extend their faith in all parts of the world; the present Pope is a pious and excellent man, I should judge, one that fears God and loves mankind, believing himself fallible as a man, but infallible as Head of the Church, and his character has had an influence on the Church. I should be sorry to see the Catholic Church fall now, for which of the Protestant sects could take its place? Perhaps it will outlive them all, for there is a terrible unity in its system, and it holds to its first principles with remorseless fidelity, while the Protestants feel that their principle of sole reliance on the Holy Scriptures as the only and sufficient word of God and rule of faith, is felt by many to be false, and known to be so by some, and yet they will not admit it, and fall back on absolute religion, taking all tradition (scriptural or non-scriptural) for what it is worth.

But I will not annoy you any more with such talk. Let me go to other things. And, before I forget it, Father Marchi is publishing a work describing the Catacombs—not merely the old but those hitherto inedited; the work will correct the errors of former writers on that subject, and will be a valuable contribution to the history of art, and still more to that of Christianity in a period for which we possess unfortunately but few documents. Cannot it be got for the College Library? When finished it will cost about 60 dollars.

Shall I describe to you the wonders of Rome? No, not I; you must come to know them. I went up to the top of the Capitol soon as I got to Rome. I saw one mountain in the distance, standing by itself, and said to a friend, "*Videsne ut alta stet,*" &c., for then it was covered with snow. Below me were the Seven Hills, not prominent, but made out with a little difficulty; the Forum, a dirty irregular oblong space where the countrymen leave their carts and oxen to bait. The Colosseum is close at hand; the ruins of the Palace of the Cæsars cover the Palatine, and an Englishman has a house on the very top.

* *Romanum Collegium Apostolicum.*

The greater part of old Rome, the Rome of the Republic, is covered with vineyards and gardens!—cabbages and artichokes grow where the pride of the Cæsars once held its dwelling-place! Alas for Rome! She is the queen dowager of the nations. Her power has passed away; but a shadowy respect is still paid to her name, and the recollection of her greatness yet awes the world. I have studied the relics of Pagan Rome, but I cannot tell where it ends and Christian Rome begins. When they baptized the people, they baptized their institutions; alas, I feel that I am in old Pagan Rome still! I was presented to His Holiness the other day. He looks mild and benevolent, has written some books, and is thought a clever man by nature, apart from his infallibility.

Norton's book is as I fancied, but does not he attack the authenticity of the books of Moses? How is the *Examiner* in the hands of L. and G. ? Remember me to Sears when you see him and Stetson. Ever yours, good bye,   T. P.

All your books shall be diligently sought for and duly forwarded. I have made arrangements with a house at Florence for the purchasing Italian books. Write again soon, tell me all the personal gossip and literary and theological news.

TO THE SAME.

Berlin, May 26, 1844.

My dear Friend,—Men, in respect to their mobility, or passive faculty of being moved, may be divided into three classes, viz.: 1, the ductile, who may be led by the hand; 2, the tractile, who can be drawn by the nose; and, 3, the *projectile*, who can be *kicked by the part* which is wanting in cherubs, but fully developed in school-boys—in short, by what the "Secretary of the Commonwealth of Massachusetts," commenting upon Moses, called a *retiring glory.* * Well, in Italy, the Pope thinks the people consist only of the *tractile* and *projectile* classes, so he sets on the tractors (the priests) and the projectors (the soldiers) to conduct affairs. In Austria, the Government proceeds on the supposition that *all* are projectile, and, therefore, has soldiers everywhere, and gives its faithful subjects a sight of its cannons in every little village. At home there are a few who think that mankind are ductile, but the political partisans suppose all the nation to be merely tractile. Nobody, but General Jackson and George III. ever thought we were projectile.

And here I am, in the heart of Germany, in the very spot where the " Geist des Deutschlands " culminates. I have wished you were with me a thousand times here in Europe, but never more than now, for none *deserves* so much to come, and none would enjoy it more, for you have the many-sidedness that receives, the magnanimity that welcomes, and the soul that appreciates all that is good.

Excuse me for saying this *to* you, for I forgot myself and the limits

* "One day," said Dr. ——, " I went out to Cambridge as a delegate for the Society for promoting Theological *Knowledge*, to see what Dr. Palfrey was doing. I had my doubts of his fitness for the station, but I went into the lecture-room. He was expounding Moses (at first I felt like Apostle Philip when he saw *one* reading Esaias). He took that *very difficult* passage, 'Thou shalt not look upon my *face*,' &c., and went on translating, 'But a retiring glory shalt thou see.' I confess I felt ashamed of my doubts, and was myself instructed."

of epistolography for a moment. How you would riot in the *Bibliothek* and smile at the philosophical casuistry one hears lectured forth, and look with wonder on *Hengstenberg* discovering the Trinity in the plural form of Elohim (and also in *Behemoth* I suppose). Berlin is so full of great men that nobody looks at one more than the Parisians look at the giraffe. I believe it is rather a *disguise* here to be a great man. You will say, in your wicked way, that is so everywhere, and in your "Unitarian way" will cite the case of Jesus and Socrates (nobody but the Unitarians ever mention them in the same week you know) as examples; that is true, but here the great men are so common that if —— ever were to come here, he would be thought a very common-place sort of man, fit only to eat beef and cream-cakes. But *revenons à nos moutons*, to the great men again. There are 180 of them connected with the University, not counting the Grimms, who would make a score; then there are Crown Princes, and *Fürsten*, and *Erzherzogen*, and that sort of vermin, in any quantity. I always thought the German philosophers were lean, pale sort of men who "on the barren heath," as Göthe has it, did nothing but think, in short did nothing but think of thinking. It is not so; they look sleek, well-fed, and cosy as other men. Drs. Twesten and Marheineke are plump as partridges. Indeed, I have not seen but one lean man in Berlin, and he was a Yankee. I heard a professor the other day (a sleek man of forty, with a great forehead, and great white teeth, and great black whiskers tied under his chin) lecture an hour or less on *Dagesh forte*, making a slight digression upon *Dagesh lene*, and an episode upon *Chappik*. I thought of your philosophical colleague and wished he had my seat. He would have gone up in raptures, and have been (what has happened to Job and the Prophets) *translated!* But here I am telling you about German affairs and not saying a word about how I got here. Well: then we rode four days and four nights in a diligence to Bologna, from Rome, and then went to Venice—which, by the way, is such a city as Neptune might have dreamed of when a little drunk with ambrosia (and Amphitrite)—thence to Verona, stopping at classical Padua; thence two hundred miles up the valley of the Adige, through the Tyrol to Innspruck. It was delightful to get away from the dark wily character of the Italians to the open faces and blue eyes of the Germans. You feel that you are in *Deutschland* very soon. The horses are well fed, the asses disappear and the priests; the women are seen in abundance. In France and Italy the *femme de chambre* was almost always a *garçon;* there is a certain safety in employing these. But soon as we came to Germany, we found some nice girls to make your bed, move the table, &c., girls with great open blue eyes, rosy cheeks, and well-developed forms. But, alas! I am afraid that the virtue of the Germans is not just what old Roman Tacitus says it was in his day. However, some of the Germans say it was *peu de chose* even then, and he painted an ideal and no actual people solely to shame the shabby Romans and their women.

We went from Innspruck to Munich, saw many festivities—for the King of Bavaria had just given a daughter to the son of the *Erzherzog* Carl of Austria, who in his day is to be *Erzherzog*. Not only that; a wretched son of the said King of Bavaria was just married to the pretty daughter of the Grand Duke of Tuscany; the poor girl was given away in her cradle, and when she grew up had the audacity to love the Duc D'Aumale, but married the stupid Bavarian none the less, for princes no more want love in their wedlock than water in their wine.

This same Bavarian and his Tuscan wife came from Italy at the same time with ourselves, so we also rode through their triumphal arches, and heard the music intended for them. From Munich we went to Ratisbon, saw its lions, Kepler's monument amongst others, the famous Valhalla—you know all about it, I have no doubt, and that Luther has no bust among the heroes of Germany, though the Stolbergs have a place in the national temple. Then we went down the Danube in a steamer to Vienna. Two beautiful days we passed there on that majestic river. The spring was just calling out the individualities of the trees: we had all the varieties of scenery conceivable, from bustling towns to lonely *castles* (so-called by men, by God *robber's dens*), and mountains still covered with primeval forests. I expected to meet old Armenius or Attila at the very least. The Archduke Charles was in the same boat with my humble self, and a small boat it was, too, to contain two such great men, and *we* had, of course, all sorts of honours paid to *us*, as we went along. At Vienna we saw the lions, Von Hammer Purgstall amongst them, and then went to Prague. I saw John Huss's house. A *Schneidermeister* (Boss-tailor), lives in it now, and sundry mantua-makers, wine-dealers, &c. ; the famous university, the grave of Tycho Brahe ; and the place where John of Nepomuck was thrown off the bridge into the river. It is a sacred place now, and John is the patron of bridges —a pretty piece of irony that. We saw the famous *Judenstadt* and the old burial-ground of the Jews. I don't know that Abraham, Isaac, and Jacob are not buried here—perhaps Noah and Adam (Dr. Noyes can tell), were the place old enough. The Hebrew boy, who shows the place and reads the Rabbinical inscriptions into most uncouth Bohemian German showed me a gravestone for the year 600 A.D.! I believe all that the Jews tell me, and they have not lost their national peculiarity. In old times, if a Hebrew were asked for a truth, *he told a story* (at Venice, now, "*parola Ebrea*" means a *lie*). I never see a Jew but I think of Moses, and Noah, and Baal, and Balaam. (By the way, Balaam is the only saint the Romans have taken out of the Old Testament.) I don't feel at all anxious to convert them to the popular form of Christianity, for I think the *nonsense* of the Rabbis is nearly as good as the *nonsense* of the Fathers, schoolmen, and doctors of divinity. To real Christianity, God send that all the world may be converted, though it is just what I think the above-mentioned three classes know little about.

From Prague we went to Dresden down the Elbe ; a beautiful river it is, too, with Bohemian villages and robber's dens (vulgarly castles) on its banks, and nice Saxon towns, with *no cannon* in them ; for the King of Saxony is not an Austrian, so he has faith in something beside cannon. From Dresden we came here, passing through Wittemberg, and at a distance doing reverence to the church where Luther posted up the 95 theses, and where the grave covers his hardy body. I ought to add that in one of the towns we passed by on the Danube, there is a street called "*Dort Hinab*" from this circumstance : once when Luther was there, some enemies wished to seize him, and as he turned to escape, the

Devil (who loved Martin like a brother, in spite of the inkstand) shouted out "Down there!" pointing to a little lane. There is a *fresco* representing the event. Of course, the miracle is a fact, if there is any truth in *Douglas's Criterion* and Leslie's *Short Method.*

Here I am at Berlin, in the third story of the British Hotel. Do you know what sort of a place Berlin is? No? Imagine a sandy plain forty miles square, with one or two nasty rivers trying to get through it, but doubtful all the time that they had taken the right way. In the centre of this plain, and on the banks of the most doubtful of the rivers, imagine a great number of brick houses covered with stucco, and a few churches, &c., of the same material. Then imagine one street sixty or seventy feet wide, and two miles long, with another street two hundred feet wide and one mile long, having four rows of lime-trees in it, a foot walk in the centre, and two carriage ways, one on each side; then add some hundreds of other streets, all straight, and you have a *conception* of Berlin. For the moving part of it, imagine 1000 hackney coaches, the drivers with cows'-tails on top of their caps, 100 private carriages, 400 drags for beer, 150 carts, and wagons for other business, 30,000 soldiers, 1650 students, 180 professors (it will take a day to imagine them all), a King, Baron Von Humboldt, and 270,000 others. Imagine the King with a belly like Uncle Tom Clarke, the students with mustachios, the professors lecturing on *Dagesh lene*, the King "counting out his money," Baron Von Humboldt sleeping on his laurels, and the 270,000 smoking, walking, weaving, making pipes, and getting dinner, and you have an idea of the *personale* of Berlin. I have heard lots of professors since I have been here—Schelling, amongst others. He lectures on the Offenbarungs-Philosophie. I heard him twice. He looks old and feeble, is seventy, his articulation is feeble; he has an audience of 150 or 200: most of them come only from curiosity, or to amuse themselves at the senilities of this *philosophe*. He hates Hegel. In one lecture he took up a certain notion that Hegel had wrapped up in many words, and after disengaging it, said, "Accordingly, when Hegel's doctrine is understood—which seldom happens with many of his followers—it is an absurdity!" He is not professor, but member of the Academy of Sciences, so has a right to lecture, and avails himself of it. The right in a Mem. Soc. Scientiæ is inalienable! His coming here, I should judge, was a failure; Hegelism flourishes like a green bay-tree, full of leaves, and *threatening* fruit. The King don't like it. Bruno Bauer has lost his *Lehrfreiheit* (liberty to teach), so he abandons theology and takes to writing history. I never thought Bruno Bauer was a great man, though he made a great noise; the other Baur, whom Mr. Norton holds in such disesteem, is really a man of *Tiefsinnigkeit* (profundity) and genius too. The other day I heard Werder, a young Hegelian, lecturing on "*Logik.*" The point at issue was "*Bestimmtheit.*"* He got into a great passion and a desperate fix with his *Bestimmtheit*, trying, as I dimly gathered, to discover the *Ur-Bestimmung.* He said, in *Bestimmung* there was *Daseyn* (being) *and Realité.* Hereupon a fat, chubby student, with cheeks like one of your class-

---

* Literally meaning Definiteness; but, in this connection, connoting the essential ground (in reason) of all necessary conceptions.

mates, evidently his Ma's darling, tried hard to conceive the difference ; but after numerous ineffectual attempts gave up in despair. Then said the professor, " In *Daseyn* there is *Etwas real und Anders*" (something real and something else) ; now, "*Etwas ist durch und durch Etwas und nicht Anders ; Anders ist durch und durch Anders und nicht Etwas*."*

He got into quite a dithyrambic mood upon this, put his finger on the organ of individuality, then laid it alongside of his nose, then flourished it in the air. It is no easy thing to go down to the profound of Hegelism. You must take off your *Sinnlichkeit* (corporeity), which is all of many men ; then lay aside your *Vorstellungen* (notions), which is, with most men, like plucking Æsop's jay ; then take off your *Begriff* (conception). Then you are "far too naked to be ashamed ;" in short, you are an *Urmensch* (primitive man), a *blosse Geist* (pure spirit) ; you have then the proper "alacrity in sinking ;" you go down, down, down, and learn that *Seyn* is equal to *Nicht seyn*. Yet, after all my *persiflage*, the hope of the world lies in Hegelism, *so they say*, and the King hates it. So do the ministers. Rosencrantz and Marheineke were going to start a journal, Hegelian, of course ; the King forbade it ; the minister called Marheineke before him and read his instructions, but would not let Marheineke have a copy. Thereupon the "faculty" had a meeting, and decided that this violated their "*Lehrfreiheit*."

I don't know what will come of it. I get this from a Bremen paper, not a Prussian. Men at Berlin know nothing about it. Bettina published a book ; it was *verboten* (forbidden) and *confiscirt* (confiscated) years ago. Then she wrote another, drove up to the King and asked, "May it be published ?" "Yes," said the King. So it appeared with the title "Dies Buch gehört dem König." (This book belongs to the King.) It was worse than the first ; the ministers "kicked," it would not do. Now she prints another, "Clemens Brentanos Laubenkrantz," Charlottenburg, 1844, (Clemens Brentano's Wreath), and will carry it to the King for his *privilege*. She is writing another on the sufferings in Silesia ; a terrible book it is, too, to judge from the pages of the manuscript she read me. She showed me a letter from your sister, and sends thanks. Paulus's "Schelling" † sells here. Schelling tried to have it suppressed, but could not.

I have received accounts of your noble sermons at Spring Street, and thank you with all my might. I am somewhat in doubt that my poor head will be well when I return, for it is certainly in a dubious state now ; but don't tell *this* to any one. You will soon have the Anniversary Week," ‡ and the Unitarian dinner. I send my good wishes to the "Brethren," but learn they are getting rapidly behind-hand in liberality and freedom. Of course, this does not surprise me ; but what will they do with *you* and *Noyes* at the *School ?* Really they are in a pretty "*Bestimmung*" (fix) with a real philosopher in one chair, and a scholar in the other, who denies the inspiration of the Old Testament and the authenticity of many parts of it, declaring too that myths run through the whole of the Gospels ! Really it was a mistake to

---

* Something is out and out something, and not other ; other is out and out other, and not something.

† Written by the famous Rationalist of Heidelberg—since dead.

‡ The last week in May ; devoted to various clerical and philanthropic gatherings in Boston, and to a Unitarian banquet.

appoint both Noyes and you! Better have —— for the Bib. Lit. (he has a *fac-simile* of the first edition of "James' Version," as old Horner would say), and a P.P. for the other chair! Do resign, or become converted. Give my love to the faithful-hearted, and believe me just as really yours as of old, when no ocean "rolled between."

T. P.

I learn that the brethren don't exchange with you! I can hardly forgive it in ——, for he is a wise and good man. I fear that I may get you into trouble by your supplying so excellently (as all say) the pulpit at West Roxbury. God forbid it should be so. Will you, when you meet Brown, beg him to make some arrangements with an English house, if he can; and if he does, let me know before the middle of August, for I shall sail the 19th of August. Tell me all the news of Ripley, Brownson, R. W. E., Stetson, Lamson, Walker, and, above all, Francis. I have bought some books for you that you did not order, because you did not know of them, but to no amount. Adieu.

TO THE SAME.

Auerbach's Keller, 12 June, 1844.

DEAR DOCTOR FRANCIS,—I wonder if a Doctor of Divinity and Professor of Sacred Theology ever received a letter written in Auerbach's Keller, under the influence of the Unmentionable, who guided and directed the outgoings and incomings of Herr Dr. Faust, and was with him when he lay down and when he rose up? I am sure that *you* never did—therefore, in due course of time, if the mails fail not, you shall have that felicity! No doubt you will say I chose the place as one whose inspiration was congenial to my devout notions and theological whimsies! Well, men say Dr. F. (not Dr. Francis, but Dr. Faustus), was inspired by the Devil, but I have sometimes thought that he did nearly as much good as some men, who, it is said, were inspired quite differently. I won't pretend to judge, but I wish some D.D.'s, here and elsewhere, might be inspired by the same *Geist*,—whether it were a blue spirit or a black! Here are pictures of the great scenes of Dr. F.'s life painted, not so very badly either, just over my head. Here is the door out of which he rode on a tun (I take it he signed the pledge here before he went out!) You know the inscription, and I hope it will be a warning to you and to all others, who are willing to eat the Devil's bread. The rhyme states he got for his pains the Devil's reward! so don't you enter into a compact and covenant with that prolific master—pray advise all the students of Sacred Theology never to meddle with such things!

Well; one Martin Luther preached here in Leipsic, though not in Auerbach's Keller—as I now do. He held forth from a high balcony in the street. It stands there still.

Here the relentless hours overtook me, and notwithstanding my sacred occupation, drew me out of the famous Keller, and sent me off to Frankfort A.M. It is now the 20th of June, and I am near, not the tun of Dr. Faustus, but the great tun of Heidelberg. You must know that this tun is not that out of which Dr. Paulus drinks wine and beer, but one quite other and different. But let me not travel away from

Leipsic so fast. I wandered all about it, and a nice place it is too, with its 143 booksellers, its Brockhauses, its Tauchnitzes, its Schneiders, and Fleischers. But there is not a street called after them—not even a steamboat ! By the way, a pious American said, " You see by the very names of things how wicked these Germans are. They call a steamboat a *damdship.* So you see that their ' Atheism ' extends even to small affairs." At Leipsic I thought often of old Homer *—not the poet, but the preacher. I walked in the library of the University, and saw busts of many of his favourites ; grim enough they looked too, as if they were made to write books for old Homer to read, or as if he were made to read books which they should write. Here were *Cocceius* and *Buchenhagen,* and fifty others, whose names I never heard pronounced except by the redactor of Bibles. At last I fell upon " Martinus Geier." He was H.'s particular friend : " Rich, very rich," said H., as he took down once for me a copy of " Geier." Here he was on the canvas, looking a Commentary on the Psalms, and threatening one on the Lamentations.

I have often thought I met Homer in old corners of old libraries— like the 20 Alcove in the former College Library. Here I have had him pursuing the shades of " various readings," and hunting through this and the other unreal " codex." Then I have fancied him in Purgatory, allowed to have a sight of " Tindal's Edition of 1536," yet not allowed to touch it. Then, too, going up to the ghost of great printers—Aldus, Froben, Elzevir, and Stephens—with the shadow of *his* Bible under his arm, trying to find a publisher, seeking rest but finding none. Still further, I have fancied him released from limbo and put in the only heaven he had prepared himself to enjoy, surrounded with forgotten tomes, his favourite " versions " among the rest, and conversing with the kindred spirits, from the eleventh century, who split hairs all their lives, were always labouring, and never came to the truth. Especially would he revel in the company of that great army—" part of the host have crossed the flood, and part are crossing now "—of grave theologians who have expounded the Song of Songs, explained the nature and extent of the sins of Solomon, and given curious conjectures about the Virgin Mary. But let H. go to his own place.

I saw old Hermann here. He looks like Deacon Arnold, who sits at your left-hand on Sundays, and looks up devoutly to catch the words of wisdom that fall from your lips; only the Deacon has the more intellectual face, and the best tempered. Hermann is about seventy-two years old, with little fiery, spiteful eyes that are never still. He is small and thin, has lost his teeth, and therefore does not speak distinctly. It was Sunday when I went to see him with Dr. Flügel. He had not been to church; indeed, I doubt that the *Deutsche Gelehrte* ever go, except to be baptized when they are babes. He had spurs on his feet, for he rides an hour every day in the riding-school. In consequence of this experience in riding, the illustrious man thinks he is peculiarly qualified to write on the equestrian terms in the Greek language. I remember to have seen him praised in some of the journals for his great knowledge of equestrian affairs, " gained," said the *laudator,* " by his daily and praiseworthy habit of riding on horseback." Now,

* Allusion is made to Dr. Homer, of Newton, a clergyman of the old school, whose Calvinism was tempered by a love of book-collecting. For the most part, however, his books were like his doctrines, very venerable and very futile.

if he bathes in a pan every day, he will be particularly able to write on the natatory terms in Greek, and on the naval tactics of the ancients in general. Pray suggest this to Felton, and you will no longer be a "speckled bird," and no jay will ever peck at you!

Hermann talked about America like a book (printed before 1492); about Felton and Woolsey. He thinks Lobeck is a *great* man, though not quite five feet high—that the Aglaophamus is a master-piece. I glory in the honour, which is hitherto peculiar to myself, of having *read it.* I heard Hermann lecture one day on the Trachiniæ, Vs. 1075. He lectured an hour in Latin; sometimes he followed his notes —sometimes spoke with no reference to them. He got into a great heat on a small particle, and destroyed I do not know how many reputations without stint. You would have thought he looked over the author's shoulder, and knew, not only just what he wrote, but just what he meant by what he wrote. How much wiser critics are than authors! I have no doubt that Coleridge said something, for no prophecy is of any private interpretation, whereof he knew not the meaning. Now there will, no doubt, arise critics who will tell future generations just what Samuel Taylor Coleridge meant by his thesis, metathesis, and synthesis.

But let me come to sadder things. I went to Wheeler's grave.* It was a beautiful Sunday afternoon. The roses were all in blossom, and a sweet fragrance filled the whole spot where the dead lay sleeping. In a pleasant little enclosure was the grave of Wheeler—grassy, green. A pan of forget-me-nots was on the head of the grave, all fresh and blooming, bright-eyed and beautiful. The birds sung out a cheerful song. I almost envied him the repose which his body has here. A spirit, pure as his, is, I doubt not, tranquil and blest.

I got your letter—kind, welcome, hearty, as they always are. I need not say how much I thank you for having the courage to go and preach to the good folk at Spring Street. I fear that it may make you more of a *speckled bird,* as I hear the brethren don't exchange with you. Really, I have no patience with them. I do not care for myself, but to refuse to exchange with you at Spring Street is past endurance.

I have seen Ullman and Umbreit, having many talks with both; also Creutzer and Paulus—a noble old fellow is Paulus, eighty-three years old, and hale and flourishing yet, hating nothing but Schelling. He talked an hour to me about German theology.

TO THE SAME.

Zurich, 12 July, 1844.

My dear Friend,—If it were not for the horrible postage of letters I would write you at least once a week, for I see a thousand things, and think of ten thousand which I would gladly tell you of. To-morrow you will send forth your body of youths commissioned to bind and to loose,† and of course with the express understanding that

---

* Charles Stearns Wheeler, graduate of the class of 1837, son of a Lincoln farmer, self-educated, industrious, and filled with scholarly enthusiasm. He was a tutor of Greek at Cambridge, and edited Herodotus with taste and ability. He died at Leipsic some time previous to Mr. Parker's visit.

† Referring to the Annual Visitation Day at the Cambridge Divinity School, when the members of the Senior Class read their Essays before graduating and commencing to preach.

whatsoever and whomsoever they bind shall be bound in heaven, and the rest. Only imagine the youths fagotting for eternity both opinions and passions! By the way, do you believe Jesus Christ ever told his disciples, or anyone else, that *that which they bound on earth should be bound in heaven?* I don't believe a word of it, and think it one of the greatest heresies of the Church (the great parent of heresies) to have told such a story. But of this some other time, or no other time, as the case may be.

Here I am in the great theatre of the actions of Zwingle, with "Zurich's fair waters" spread out before me. I wish you were here to visit the famous places with me, and to talk of famous men, and to speak of our fathers that begat us. Since I saw you (or a letter) I have seen many famous men. At Heidelberg *I saw one Paulus,* who assures me that a third, at least, of the educated men of Germany are Anti-Trinitarian; but they dare not say a word against the Trinity, only to weaken certain modes of proving it. Rationalism, he says, is still the real faith of the nation, *i. e.,* of the educated. Schlosser* says the same, only adding that "my friend Paulus goes too far. To me the Bible is full of *poetry;* it is not truth but poetry: as such I like it. But if I tell the people so, they won't take it as poetry, but to their great loss will reject it altogether; so I call it *Offenbarung* (Revelation), and hurt nobody's feelings." Now, this is worthy of the ——. Pray instruct the hopeful youth in the art of mystification; it will save controversy, and hurt "nobody's feelings." I wish I could have learnt it, and certainly it was not for lack of precept and example that I did not, but from an actual stupidity in myself. But suppose you know your brother is in bondage to a lie, why not let him alone to find it out for himself? Let the blind lead the blind till they fall into the ditch. So far as I can learn, there is precious little faith among the Germans, in the old wives' fables of theology—much less than appears; only the knaves know how to mystify, to save appearances, and so forth. Of course I except such men as Hengstenberg, and in some measure Tholuck, who proves the Trinity *à priori,* and with no help from Revelation. I saw Ullman several times at Heidelberg; he is a pacificator, a *medium-iter* man. One party says $1 + 1 = 2$; another $1 + 1 = 4$. "No," says Ullman, "my dear friends, you are both mistaken, why quarrel? Truth takes the *medium iter,* $1 + 1 = 3$." There may be three parties in theology, viz.—1. That of *midnight;* and 2. That of *mid-day;* and 3. That of *twilight.* I think Ullman belongs the latter class, and stands on the *indifference-point* between day and darkness; yet he is a good man, and I like him much. He is a little *petit maître-ish,* dignified in littleness. Yet he is kind, amiable, fearing a split in *the party* (the *denomination,* as we say), more critical than courageous; in short, a very careful *Geheime-rath,* a *Consistorial-rath.* He tolerates both Strauss and Hengstenberg, and writes treatises on the "Sinlessness of Christ," and the "Reformers before the Reformation," letting alone his pacificatory articles in the *Studien und Kritiken.*

Umbreit is a dapper little man, that expounds the Old Testament, and, wearing fine linen, walks out with the young princes that study (?) at Heidelberg, and fearing to offend them, walks sidewise, with

---

* Professor of History—since dead.

his face towards the object of reverence—their sublime transparencies! I hope *you* will follow a practice so commendable, and recommend it also to the youths. Saw old Creutzer also, and had a long talk with him. He wondering that nobody had translated his *Symbolik* into English. I like the old toothless and skull-capped man very much, though he did not impress me as the thin, eagle-eyed old Paulus did. Paulus is a man of genius; Creutzer of talent, learning, industry only. I saw the Reuchlin-Meldeg, whom they call professor of philosophy here. He looks a good deal like —— or as —— will when he has gone to seed. In short, he is an exaggeration of ——, and keeps his skin so full of beer, that when he opens his mouth, as he often does for self-protection, it goes off like a beer-barrel, pop, fiz, pop! He has written a funny piece of *persiflage*, the *New Reineke Fuchs*; Göthe is the nightingale, Kant the lion, Fichte the eagle, Hegel the bear, and Schelling is Reineke. When the lion died, Reineke got his mane; when the eagle demised, he took his wings, and thus appearing as lion-eagle, taught that the Absolute was the Real and Ideal, adding that the Absolute was in *his* burrow. So then comes a quarrel between him and the bear, and the bear digs him out of his hole, and shows the admirers of Reineke that the Absolute was nothing but an old cloak hung over a white spot on a rock. So off goes Reineke, and digs another hole, and remains in it till the bear is dead. Then he comes out at open day, smelling to see if bear is really no more; goes into bear's den and teaches his old nonsense. But an old eagle (Paulus) sees him, and comes like lightning from his eyrie, screams over him in the sky, soars down, tears off the lion's mane, the eagle's wings he had stolen, and leaves the fox naked, ashamed, and silent! It is a quite pleasant piece of nonsense.

Schlosser is a fine old gentleman, who wrote history for amusement, so he says, equally scorning money and renown. I saw Gervinus, who, they say, has read more books than any man in Germany, except Schlosser. He is about five-and-thirty, has a nice pretty little wife, plump as a partridge, and full of *Geist*. Then he lives in a pretty little cottage, on the banks of the Rhine, in the midst of a vineyard: don't suppose from the proximity that he ever drinks wine; no American would ever read his books if he did; of course he slakes his thirst at the Rhine. Well: Gervinus is just appointed Professor 'of History in Schlosser's place, for Schlosser would rather run away from his *publikum*, than have it run away from him. Of course, you know that Gervinus is one of the seven famous professors driven away from Göttingen. Ewald and the Grimms are of the same clique. They had the impudence to think, and to speak too, upon the powers that be, which of course are "of God," saith Paul, who never interfere with freedom of thought; they however lay a slight embargo on the spoken word, still more on the printed. At Heidelberg, they let a man not only speak after he has thought twice—but before he thinks once, as with us at home.

At Tübingen I saw Ewald, one of the hardest heads in Germany, at least, in the theological camp. But like other hard heads, his is a little wrong, and he quarrels with everybody, inclusive of his bread and butter, which latter proves his wrong-headedness. What is the use of great abilities, if they don't give you bread to your butter? I saw a good deal of Ewald, walked with him, took tea with, &c. I had no letter of introduction, but went boldly up and said, "Sir, I am an American, have read your works, and want to see you." No man that I have seen in Germany strikes me more as a man of genius than Ewald. Yet he is often wrong, I think. He has just published the first part of a History of the Hebrews. I have got it for you. He fears the Catholics; so do all the men that I have talked with, especially do they fear the Jesuits. I think they are right. Ewald represents the condition of things as alarming in Germany—the people have no freedom; no confidence in the Government, which they cordially detest.

Baur is a great hard man—big as Sam Ripley, and looks burly and savage. He is Hegelian all over. I have his History of the Trinity and other books, but he only looks through Hegelian glasses. He is a friend of Strauss, says Strauss is a Christian, that his writings have a deep and radical influence, all the stronger because not much talked of. Tholuck, and others, have told me about the "atheism" of the Hegelians, and that Strauss was no Christian. The talk about atheism is not limited to the circle about Boston. Somebody told me that Strauss was no Christian. "Well," I said, "do you know anything evil of his life?" "Nothing. It is manly, noble, above reproach." "He has had his child baptized, besides. Eh?" "Yes." "Can you say as much in the defence of the Christianity of most cultivated men dignified with that name of Christian?" "No, certainly not. *I did not mean to say anything against the man!*"

I doubt that there is in Germany a university where there is a more able theological faculty. Here is Zeller, a young *Repetent* (such an office exists only at Tübingen—is like that of tutor at Oxford), is thought to be full of promise. You have seen his work on Plato. Here they concoct one of the best journals in Germany. It is Hegelian and new-schoolish of course. But I must not delay too long at Tübingen: we went through the Black Forest, Simmons with us, to Freiburg; saw the famous Munster, but old Professor Hug we did not see. Had it not been so late, I would have gone and told him, as I have a good many Germans, theologians and philosophers, "I have read your book." But the old gentleman had, perhaps, gone to bed, and in the morning I went off before it was decorous to call on the worthy Catholic. At Bâle, of course I saw De Wette, a compact little man, with a rather dry face, a little irritable, I fancy, perhaps something soured by his long disasters. He had not received the copy of my translation which Mr. Brown was to send him. This grieved me much. He is preparing a new edition still, but with no considerable alteration from the last. It will soon appear. During the time I stayed at Bâle, I saw a good deal of him, first and last, heard him lecture, &c., spent an evening with him at a friend's—his wife is away—dined with him at his son's. His functions are not great; he has from twelve to twenty students of theology, and the whole University of Bâle numbers but about sixty pupils! You may fancy that De Wette spends his time more agreeably in the study than elsewhere. But then he has leisure enough to write, and think, and speculate, and print, too. He knew but little of ecclesiastical affairs or theological matters with us. He only knew Norton as one that polemized against him. The light of the seven gold candlesticks, on the back of the

academical lectures, had never gladdened his eye. Even Grey's Key
was known only by name. Wouldn't it be a good plan for the
"body," as Father Briggs says, to send out —— with a lot of Greys
Keys to enlighten the Germans withal? Some of "our excellent
tracts" might also be circulated to advantage. Pray suggest it. Who
knows but it may stay the flood of Rationalism which threatens
to leave sundry dogmas where Grotius says the Ark may still be
seen?

I heard De Wette lecture on the Harmony of the New Testament.
He cut right and left and made no bones of saying that such a passage
was probably *unächt* (spurious), that John knew nothing of it, &c.
"Carpenter's Harmony" would set the Professor right on this
point.

I cannot tell you all the thousand things we talked about in Bâle,
theological and philosophical. Of these at home. Last year or earlier
he went to Halle and Jena, and was received with great enthusiasm by
the professors and students at Jena, he made a speech to them, and
advised them to *study their books*, get their lessons, and keep silent. So
some one told me, which advice they will keep as well as George Fox
the similar advice which some one gave him; but it takes a great deal
of soul to bear up well under exile and long misfortune. Yet De
Wette has never retracted ungenerously anything he has said. The
good men, says Ewald, justified him in all his course at the time of his
exile, but the journals never dared to say one word in his defence. I
think he is a great and noble man. Perhaps no theologian in Germany
has more influence at this moment than he. He is both critical and
mystical, so seems sometimes to waver, and does lean as one or the
other element gets the upper hand. At Bâle I saw some curious
paintings by Holbein, amongst others a schoolmaster's sign-board of
the year 1516. It was not a Massacre of the Innocents, as you might
suppose, but the process of instruction, not without the birch, an
adjunct which has been sacred to pedagogues from the days of Solomon.
Here, too, was one of the most curious and felicitous pictures of Erasmus
I ever saw, and I have seen a hundred, I think. He sat writing; all
about him is exquisitely genteel, yet with no foppishness. There is a
good deal in Erasmus to admire, his exquisite taste, his consummate
skill, the singular refinement and delicacy of his taste is curiously
apparent in the midst of his smutty talk. His handwriting is elegant;
the letters not bold like Melancthon's, nor so feminine as Luther's
(strange contrast with the battles they thunder forth), but graceful
and most elegantly cut. Here are many manuscript letters of Erasmus
never printed, one curious little Latin poem in iambics upon Pope
Julius II. Pray why have not all his letters been published, and why has
no really satisfactory life of the man appeared? But, alas! there is
none of Luther, nor even of John Calvin. Here is, in the library of
Bâle, a copy of Erasmus' Praise of Folly in quarto, with wide margins,
and on each page is a "scrap" by Holbein, beautifully done with a
pen, and just as if made but yesterday, illustrating the text. I remember one illustrating the miraculous conception of the Blessed
Virgin; the *Homunculus* was entering her mouth, the angels applauding
in the meantime. Indeed, I have seen the same thing in churches on a
large scale, shamefully disgusting, and bad almost as the doctrine they

represent. Nothing shows more fully Holbein's genius than these little sportive touches in the manuscript. They have been engraved, but poorly. Stähelin has published his work on Genesis ; De Wette thinks it excellent. I will bring it home, knowing the interest you feel on this special matter. Indeed the poor Books of Moses are fought over with as much violence as Patroclus' body, but the divine Achilles has not come yet to end the strife and rescue the *corpus delicti,* giving it honourable burial.

From Bâle to Bonn. Here I saw Professor Vogt, who married Dr. Follen's sister, Professors Schultz and Schnell, revolutionary men and exiles, all of them. The latter is a terrible fellow ; he has been banished nearly a dozen times from as many different States, and got up perhaps twenty revolutions. He looks like a giant, and keeps always full of beer, now and then running over.

At Geneva I learned all about the Swiss Unitarians. They are going down rapidly, they gain nothing, but lose continually. However, the church in Switzerland has its outer form fixed, but its inner spirit perpetually progressive. Nobody believes the "five points" out of Germany in all Switzerland ; the greater part of the clergy here at Zurich in Bâle and elsewhere, are as much in advance of our Unitarians at home as they are before Dr. Codman. I am rather startled myself at their radicalism in theology. But the influence of Zwingle is one thing and Calvin's another. I have seen Hitzig and Oken—famous men both. Hitzig was surprised than an American had seen all his works at home ; but it was so. Here are letters of Zwingle, and his "Battle-axe" and his Greek Bible.

But I must end ; I hope you will have a little frolic during the vacation and keep strong, rejoicing in your good works.

TO THE SAME.

Brussels, July 29.

MY DEAR FRIEND,—I have remembered that you are probably not in Cambridge, and therefore that my letter will probably reach you as soon by my hands as by "Her Majesty's mails ; " so I shall keep the epistle, and make additions thereto from time to time. Were it not that letters cost dollars, I should have piled up your study-table with them till the stout wood cracked and the legs gave out. All that I see I want to tell *you* of, from the rosy hues of Mont Blanc at sunset and morning to the gossip of German professors. Then, too, such suggestions are made to one's mind by the little angels who people these old places, that I want to talk of a thousand things that never come to me at home. "Home-keeping youths have ever homely wits," says somebody. But it is no more true than its converse, "that home-shunning youths," &c. Yet one does forget old prejudice when he sees new customs ; and though he loves his little village all the more after seeing many other little villages, and great ones too, yet he ceases to think that "Waltham is the finest parish in the world." I have learned that reading books is one thing, and seeing the objects therein treated of quite another—yes, sometimes the opposite. To come to some particulars. I think rather worse of the Catholic Church since I have seen its works and its men, and rather worse also of the Protestants too. The Protestant dungeon is wider, neater, and a good deal newer than the Catholic; then, too, the air is better; the thumb-screws of better workmanship; and the whole apparatus of torture has a more wieldy and scientific appearance—but still there is a dungeon, still there are thumb-screws, and an apparatus for torture.

Bay of Fundy, Sept. 1.

Alas! I have had time to write no more; but I shall soon *see* you again, so God bless you! Ever yours,   T. P.

CHAPTER X.

THE dear friends in his parish joyfully welcomed him back to his work, which he reassumed with equal joy, and a longing for an undisturbed pursuit of his favourite objects.

I thank you heartily for the cordial greeting with which you welcome me back to my home; for your expressions respecting my past labours, and your generous hopes for my future works. The pen you are so good as to send me is almost too beautiful to be used. I shall always prize it highly for the associations connected with it, and as a token of your esteem and friendship. I trust I shall never use it badly, nor in a bad cause. Gratefully and respectfully yours, T. P.

He immediately began to discharge the obligations which he felt had been incurred by this year of enjoyment and repose. Three lectures were prepared for delivery during the winter. Of these, one upon the " Signs of the Times," filled with warm anticipations and a too honest criticism, excited afresh the public interest in him. It also aroused, of course, the old opposition, which had gone to sleep, thinking that his influence ended with his departure for Europe.

FROM THE JOURNAL.

I have, now-a-days, some few struggles with myself to repress indignation at insults, real or fanciful. I must outgrow this.

My real troubles are, that I am short of my own ideals of goodness and usefulness. I feel that I ought to do more for what I receive; but I feel, too, that my head is clay, and requires to be treated as any other earthenware—with carefulness and discretion. I rejoice to write a few lectures; would that I could do more!

In October he received a letter from Mr. Martineau, acknowledging the " Discourse of Religion " and some other publications which he had sent. Mr. Martineau remarks, with creditable perception,—

I am almost angry with you for supposing that I need any answer to the scoffing accusation brought against you. Who that has any insight into an author's spiritual physiognomy, and can apprehend its expressiveness in the smallest degree, could ever attribute a sneer to you?

Mr. Martineau does not deny that the manner in the "Discourse of Religion" is occasionally a little too slashing among the convictions of other people.

But every great writer must put forth what is in him in his own way; and the excess of manly strength is healthier than the scruples of effeminate forbearance.

Mr. Parker preached the Thursday lecture in his turn once more and for the last time in December, from the text, "Have any of the rulers, or of the Pharisees, believed on him?" This sermon sets forth in clear and enthusiastic terms the human nature of Christ, and the relation of simple truth and goodness which he held to his age and to the ages. He had never been so clear before upon the person of Christ. Such clearness involved obnoxious statements, which startled afresh all his brethren who were beginning now to take great care of their conservative theology. And yet when they are repeated, they seem ridiculously out of proportion to the clamour which they raised.

Jesus looked to God for his truth, his great doctrines, not his own private, personal ones, depending on his idiosyncracies, and therefore only subjectively true, but God's, universal, everlasting, the absolute religion. I do not know that he did not teach some errors also, along with it. I care not if he did. It is by his truths that I know him.

No wonder, then, that men soon learned to honour Jesus as a God, and then as God himself. Apostolical and other legends, &c., believe men of these things as they will. To me they are not truth and fact, but mythic symbols and poetry; the psalm of praise with which the world's rude heart extols and magnifies its King.

That God has yet greater men in store, I doubt not; to say this is not to detract from the majestic character of Christ, but to affirm the omnipotence of God. When they come, the old contest will be renewed, the living prophet stoned—the dead one worshipped.

But henceforth Mr. Parker never preached without offending every conventionalism more fatally by his moral tone than by his technical denials. His indignation at the vices of society and the Phariseeism of the Church was too positive, too thoroughly reconstructive. Men will sooner tolerate what they call an infidel theology; for mere negative criticism of Scripture and of doctrine does not put men's livelihood in peril, nor disturb their ease. But when a sensitive conscience cries out with pain, " Woe unto you, Scribes and Pharisees, hypocrites," the sound penetrates and shatters farther than the most persistent depreciation of Moses and the Prophets. The more sublimely the moral sense of an anti-supernaturalist emulates the dreadful indignation of Jesus, the more likely will he be to share his fate. As of old, the theology becomes the pretext for the hatred.

Mr. Parker would not give up his right to preach the Thursday lecture, nor his membership of the Association, because he would thereby ignominiously recede from the principle which liberal thought had hitherto represented. He did not think he had a right to do what nobody had a right to demand. If, therefore, at this juncture a new principle was to obtain control, it must be without his connivance. His right of rotation to preach the Thursday lecture was adroitly cancelled, and nonintercourse would do the rest.

TO REV. CHANDLER ROBBINS, BOSTON.

West Roxbury, 29 Jan., 1845.

My dear Friend.—Your note, which I did not see till five minutes ago, for I have been absent since Monday noon, was as kind as it was characteristic of yourself. I thank you for it, and for the spirit which suggested the motion you made at the meeting. I wonder any one should doubt that I should meet in kindness any kind proposition from the Association : I have no unkind feelings towards any one of them. I had feelings that I thought a little unchristian towards one of them a few months ago; I will tell you how I got rid of them. I never said anything against him ; I said all the good things I knew of him ; I defended him several times, and palliated the severe judgment others pronounced on him. He went on abusing me (so I think it). I avoided, so far as possible, all that he said or printed. At last he did what I think was really a shameful thing, and most unchristian towards me, and now I feel not the faintest sparkle of unkindliness towards him. I met him, not long ago, and shook hands with him, and feel that I have triumphed.

I will meet the committee any time that it is possible for me to see them, and will most cheerfully entertain any proposition they shall make. I think you could not have made a better selection of persons for the work ; for (excuse me for saying it) there are no members of the Unitarian ministry that I prize more highly than these three. Still I don't see what we can do. I don't suppose I shall convert you to my belief; I think you will not in a few hours alter my convictions, deliberately formed, examined and re-examined again and again before they were given to the world. What I wish is, that the Boston Association would fall back on the large principles which I once thought they all entertained—remembering that theology came from the head, and religion from the heart; that while there is only one religion, there may be a great many and quite diverse theologies, each imperfect, yet each helping towards the truth, and that a man may have the Christian religion in his heart and live it, too, who has neither your theology nor mine. I wish they would allow each man the Christian name who claims it and lives a Christian life, leaving the defence of that name and its definition to himself. Then, too, I wish they would treat matters of science (and such I reckon both theological doubts and theological affirmations) as matters of science and not as proofs of a good heart or a bad one. I may have many astronomical errors; they come from my Heart and Will quite as much as any theological heresies; yet no man would refer the first to a wicked heart, nor think to make me orthodox in my astronomy by calling me hard names. I know some of the brethren are offended at that poor sermon of mine at the Thursday lecture. But yet, at the very last meeting of the Association which I attended, a year and a half ago, it was stated to be advisable that the preachers should treat such matters as would disclose their views. I have heard sermons there from some of the brothers that are quite distasteful to me. But I did not feel implicated in a sermon of Mr. Young's or Dr. Pierce's, only in my own. I will not trouble you with more of my hasty scrawls, but will thank you again for all your kindness, and assure you that I shall not tread such a pearl as you offer under my feet.—Believe me, yours truly,

THEO. PARKER.

TO THE SAME.

West Roxbury, 28th Feb., 1845.

DEAR SIR,—I understand that at the last meeting of the Association, the management of the " great and Thursday Lecture" was transferred to the hands of the minister of the First Church, to whom it originally belonged. I do not know what was the design of this movement, but I know well that its effect will be to exclude me from preaching that lecture. I find no fault now with this, though for the honour of the Unitarians I could wish, if that were the design, that it had been effected in a manner not so circuitous : I like directness. I write to ask you—formerly, if not now, the scribe of the Association—to inform me of the facts of the case. Please tell me what was the design of the movement, and " all about it." Don't think I am offended, for I am not, and have no personal feelings in the matter at all. Does the Association make any public statement of the movement they have made ?—Believe me, as ever,

Yours faithfully,
THEO. PARKER.

TO THE SAME.

West Roxbury, 18th Oct., 1845.

DEAR SIR,—Mr. Pierpont told me that you informed him that you once prepared some resolutions, intending to offer them at a meeting of the Boston Association, which resolutions had reference to Mr. Pierpont's leaving the city. I have thought for a good while that his departure from Boston was a sign of the times that ought to be noticed in some way. I meant to ask you to do the very thing you intended yourself to do. I now ask you to do it, *i. e.* to prepare certain resolutions expressing the fact of Mr. Pierpont's faithful and self-denying labours in this city, the troubles which his fidelity and zeal have brought upon him, and also the fact that the Association feels a strong sympathy with him, and an earnest desire for his welfare and usefulness. It seems to me the Association owes this to a man who, for more than twenty years, has been among the foremost in all the great Christian enterprises of the day, and who now withdraws from the city and the state. I beg you to tell me soon if you feel disposed to do this, and also to inform me where the Association will meet the next time, for I wish to be present also. If you decline offering any such resolutions, please send this letter to James Clarke, who, I think, will do it, though I had rather it should come from you. If no one else will do it, I shall feel compelled to undertake it myself.

Very truly yours,
Theo. Parker.

TO MRS. DALL.

West Roxbury, 30th May, 1845.

My dear Caroline,—It is near the end of Anniversary Week, and I wish to write you a word or two. You need not fear that I shall take pains to withdraw from the Unitarians, who are separating from me. I actually attended a meeting of the Boston Association a few weeks ago, to demonstrate to them my existence as a member thereof. I was received as you may imagine. I have attended their conferences and the like, and my opinion is confirmed that, as a sect, they are irretriveably sold to bigotry. The race of scholars is getting extinct among them. I know only four—Francis, Lamson, Frothingham, Noyes. You know what their influence is; the majority can settle questions without the aid of philosophy or learning. I shall expect to see them become more and more narrow for years to come. It seems to be written on the iron leaf of fate, that our progress in theology shall be only by revolutions, not gradual and regular, but spasmodic. I can honour a man who differs from me, who abuses me; but, at the same time that I admit the worth of many of the Unitarians, I must deplore the false and unphilosophical way they go to work in. They confound theology with religion; they then think that theology must be studied, not as a science, in the spirit of freedom, but with fear. So I think they are weaving cobweb, and calling it cloth; and if a man tears asunder their cobweb-trousers in putting them on, they call out "Infidel!" and if he complains that he is cold and naked when he wears them whole, they cry, "Away with him!" It may be this business is always to continue; but to-morrow may bring new things; other and former to-morrows have done so. I trust in the future. In the meantime, I learn to wait, as I have before learned to labour. I beg you to accept my kind salutations, and to be assured that I shall welcome you back to Boston with great pleasure. Remember me tenderly to Mr. Dall, and believe me,

Faithfully yours,

THEO. PARKER.

It was now not a pleasant thing to exchange with him. The Rev. J. T. Sargent, who was a minister at large, and preached to the poor gathered in Suffolk Street Chapel, continued to exchange with him, though dissenting from his views. But the congregation at the chapel liked to hear him. The executive committee of the Fraternity of Churches had the technical right of asking Mr. Sargent not to admit so dangerous a man into that pulpit. It was feared that the poor would be corrupted and misled. They dreaded his influence. What an influence it soon became in Boston, and the region round about, to expose the causes of pauperism and crime, to lift up the hearts of sorrowful men and women, to bring the strong moral help of everlasting truths to a languishing society! He could not preach in the chapel, and Mr. Sargent resigned sooner than take a pledge that he would not exchange with him. Mr. Parker became a minister at large, with seven thousand names upon his private list of men and women who depended upon him for comfort and guidance, to whom he was bound to minister by word of mouth or epistles from his own hand, and with a parish settled in almost every town from East to West, centres of influence and sympathy whither his spirit swiftly ran to bless. How shallow is every technical advantage!

Jan. 17, 1845.—Two members of J. F. Clarke's Society came here this afternoon to state to me that in the Church of the Disciples there was a strong feeling about my exchanging with their minister. They came with the kindest intentions to notify me of the fact—to state, furthermore, that some of the society would abandon the Church if I came. But I think the principle in virtue of which Clarke asked an exchange is true. I feel inclined to live out this principle. *Frisch auf, mein Herz! Frisch auf!* I am shut in, but shut in by God. Shut in for my good. What I can't rejoice in for itself I will welcome as a quickener of humanity and faith.

His next controversial publication was "A Letter to the Boston Association of Congregational Ministers, touching certain matters of their Theology." In a sermon preached to his parish at West Roxbury, he thus explains his object:—

To relieve the brethren from the embarrassment of being held answerable for my opinions while they had no opportunity of showing men how much they differed from me, I address them a public letter. Now, only two possible courses can be conceived: 1. To reply to all the questions. This, I know, they could not do, for there was the greatest diversity of opinions amongst themselves. They could not agree. 2. Such being the case, they could state to me and the public that they could not answer my letter point for point, *because* they were not agreed.

This they ought to have done, and it would have relieved the Association from every appearance of complicity with his opinions, excepting that it might be inferred that where there was so much disagreement with each other, there must be some virtual agreement with him.

What parishes were divided—what sentences were written—what feelings were displayed ! But it will not be profitable to revive the details of the controversy. Several liberal men said from their pulpits that the right of free preaching must be maintained, undisturbed by the application of any doctrinal test. Some valuable discourses were thus preached in favour of righteousness before doctrine. An article in the *Examiner*, by Dr. Gannett, was distinguished for its impartiality and kindliness. He has always sent forth his generous indignation at the first symptom of oppression. There are letters from some of the brethren, testifying to the manly and equable demeanor of Mr. Parker in one or two conferences, which were held in the hope of discovering some adjustment, but which, of course, came to nothing.

TO MRS. DALL.

West Roxbury, 14th December, 1844.

MY DEAR CAROLINE,—I thank you for remembering me in the midst of so much happiness. Yet perhaps it does not seem so meritorious in you ; for your " heart, when filled with love for one, grows bountiful to all." I have no doubt it is so. Most of our common theories about love are foolish ; for they teach that, if you love one, you must forget all the rest. In short, that you can't follow God (or your husband) without hating your father and mother. I subscribe to no such heresy. If I love one dearly, I am all the more likely to love another, or several others, strongly. I thought the wedding service in the church a little too solemn. Serious must all weddings be where the parties are thoughtful ; but I don't like a dirge in a flower-garden. Dr. Lowell's remarks were beautiful. I don't know whether young women on such occasions *hear* all the excellent things said by the minister ; but I know, at my marriage, I thought very little of the fine sentences which Brother Young ejaculated with pontifical gravity.

I don't believe you will do much harm, though you write strong articles in favour of the ministry to the poor. I think you are in the most living portion of the ministry. In Boston, I always thought that the chapels for the poor were the most aristocratic institutions of that blessed city, though they were founded with the noblest intentions and have done no little good. I believe in a *ministry* to the poor; not at all in *chapels* for the poor. Let us have a common temple—" The rich and the poor meet together." The newspapers tell you about Mr. Sargent and the shabby conduct of the committee of the Fraternity of Churches ; at least you will see it in the *Register*. It proves the love of freedom which these " liberal Christians " have at heart.

I was sorry to read what you said about Torrey ;* for I took him to be a noble man. I once met him—I think at the Chardon Street Convention ; he called me an infidel. But I wrote him a letter, since his imprisonment, telling him to play the man, that his position was noble as that of the Christian martyrs. His answer was good, though his mind now and then wandered : for he was sick. I hope you are mistaken.

What can you do to christianize the heart of the slave-holder ? I think there is a great deal of injustice here at the North in the treatment which the strong bestow upon the weak, and am not well pleased with the condition of domestic service in Massachusetts. I was going to say something a little stronger. Still I hate slavery, and can't find the faintest toleration for it. Will your ministrations reach the black directly ? I suppose you must christianize men before you can make them take measures to liberate their slaves. To do that must be very hard work.

I am not doing much externally this winter. I go about and deliver Lyceum lectures, here a little and there a little, and am preparing something for the next winter. I am also getting ready a volume of " Six Lectures on Morality, Theology, and Religion," which will see the light in due time.

Your friend and brother,
Theo. Parker.

TO THE SAME.

West Roxbury, Sept. 21, 1846.

My dear Caroline,—I thank you for your kind letter of the other day, for I am always glad to get a letter from you, though you sometimes ask questions that I cannot easily answer about anti-slavery matters. I can't give you just the information you want ; perhaps I have been obliged to keep such a bright look-out in theological and philosophical matters for several years that I have fallen behind-hand in the literature of the reformers, though I hope not in the spirit of the reforms, or in zeal for their advancement. I suppose you have Jay's books ; they are good reading, as good as anything. Then the articles now publishing in the *Liberator* by W. I. Bowditch are of great value. I believe four numbers have already appeared. Equally good are the articles by Dean Palfrey in the *Boston Whig*, on the slaveholding power. I think you will hardly find more profitable anti-slavery reading for the Society than these afford ; I think some one in

* A clergyman, at that time imprisoned in Baltimore for violation of the Slave Laws of Maryland.

Portsmouth must take the *Liberator* and the *Whig*, and if so, you have the matter at hand. I own few such books, though I have now just borrowed over a bushel of anti-slavery documents, and soon as I am well enough, I mean to read up on the subject The *Liberty Bell* * is a good thing, and I am thankful you mean to write for it. I mean to write something if I can do so.

The Misses Osgood have always been friends of me and mine: noble women are they, and full of intelligence and piety. I fear it will always be the fashion for the Boston Association to speak ill of me until the dust returns to the earth as it was. For myself I care not. It never made me feel the smallest unkindness towards them. It has sometimes saved them from more severe strictures, for I do not like to speak hard against men that try and injure me, lest a little of the old Adam should appear in my own heart. However, in due time, the errors and follies which are personal with me will pass off with me, and the real truth that is in my doctrines will stand free of my follies, and do its work. If I live ten years, and work as now, I hope to do something. But who knows? I have no lack of faith—not belief in the Thirty-nine Articles, in the Creed, or the Catechism, but trust in God. I am content to walk by that. I often find I can *feel* further than I can *see*, and accordingly I rest the great doctrines of Christianity not on reasoning, but reason on intuition.

The Resurrection in its common sense I don't believe. But the soul's immortality I cannot for a moment doubt.

TO REV. JOHN PIERPONT.

West Roxbury, 15th October, 1845.

DEAR SIR,—I called to see you yesterday, but unluckily missed you, and as I shall not, it is probable, have another opportunity to take you by the hand, I will now say a word to you before you leave Boston. None can regret your departure more than I ; we have not been much together ; you have been busy, so have I, therefore I have not seen you so often as I could always have wished. But I have always felt encouraged and strengthened by your example, and that long before I had any " troubles " with my theological " brethren." If you had done as the other ministers, you had been as they are—you would not now be leaving Boston. If you had flattered the follies and winked at the sins of the rich, you would have had, not *your* reward—that you have now—but *their* reward, I mean the reward of the ministers you leave behind. But you have chosen another part, and have your reward, a little different from theirs. You must go in triumph, for you have fought a good fight and a great one. For nearly thirty years you have been foremost in all the great reforms of the day which had the welfare of men for their object ; you have been fearless before force. If others did not help you, you thought that was a reason why *you* should work the more. When your valour was called for, you did

* For a number of years published, by gratuitous contribution of articles from prominent Anti-Slavery persons, for sale at the Annual Fair of the Massachusetts Anti-Slavery Society.

not turn round to remember your discretion. None of the great moral enterprises of the day would have stood where now they stand if you had not raised your manly voice in their behalf. Where would Temperance have been if John Pierpont had been silent? Where many other good and noble causes? It is your zeal for the great cause which Jesus died to serve that now has brought you to your present position. Your reward is with you. The confidence that you worked faithfully and wrought a great work will go with you and bless you to the end of your days. Nothing has happened for years so reflecting disgrace on the Boston clergy as your departure from the city under the present circumstances; but what is their disgrace is your glory. Go, and may God be with you! For *my* sake, for the sake of *many*, I could wish you were to stay; but it is better you should go. I know you will find work enough to be done, and warm hearts to welcome you in doing it. You leave behind not a few to bless you for your toils, and to pray for your future success and welfare. Your memory will live ever in their affections, and their good wishes will follow you wherever you go. I beg you to accept my thanks for all that you have done, and to believe me ever your friend and brother.

TO DR. FRANCIS.

February, 1845.

What do you think of Newman's opinions on the " Parmenides ? " He thinks it was written in mockery of Plato, but has become foisted in with his works. To me it seems a most ingenious piece of *persiflage* of Plato's, to show the absurdity of Parmenides' logic. He shows that you can prove anything by it, for the last paragraph concludes that neither the *one* nor the *many* has any existence. The conclusion is not extant, if Plato ever finished it. Do look over the " Parmenides " and tell me what you think of N.'s opinion, for it is six or seven years since I read it.

I wonder if he never thought that much of our popular theology rests on no better foundation than Hartley's vibratiuncles. It seems to me this is one of our sins, that we rest on *facts of fancy*, and so build a mythology instead of a theology. On an imaginary hook only an imaginary garment will hang. We have woven a good many cobwebs and but little cloth; the cobwebs look imposing at sunrise, glittering with dew, but the *boy* walks through them, and at noon no man can find one of them.

FROM THE JOURNAL.

May 28, 1845.—Attended the anti-capital punishment meeting; nothing remarkable, but as a sign of the times. Soon this sin of judicial murder will be over. Notice the remarkable variety of persons: all conditions were represented there. Saw Mr. Porter, my critical foe, or friend.* I told him that I actually wore a hat and no turban. Saw, too, Mr. Bushnell. Had a very pleasant talk with them about the

---

* Professor Porter, of New Haven, who wrote a kindly and discriminating article in the *New Englander*, July, 1845.

miracles. They do not think miracles a violation of law, or anything like it. They take the ground that God has imparted, or continually imparts, to nature a certain power, so that only certain circumstances take place; new things also follow. Well: here was a remarkable condition of the human race, and so a child is miraculously born, and capable of working miracles all his life. Should the same condition of the human race return, like results are to be expected.

May 30.—What is to come of my position, I know not. Am I to stand always alone, and when I go down shall all this movement end? I cannot believe it. And yet it seems that no man is like to rise up and take my place and help forward my work. Let the truth prevail.

TO DR. LAMSON.

July 19, 1845.

I thank you heartily for your noble address * yesterday. It was just the thing that is wanting. I regard it as laying the corner-stone of a grand and noble edifice of theology. I hope you will not allow it to be spoiled in printing. Do, for Heaven's sake, print strong, very strong, and not let it be spoiled. I liked it more than I can tell you, and think great good will come of it.

Yours in haste.

TO REV. INCREASE S. SMITH.

November 10, 1845.

It would give me great joy to come over to your meeting next Thursday, if it were possible; but consider, all summer long I could not work. I stuck in the ground like a turnip, only I could not perceive that I grew. Now I begin to work again. I can think a little, read and write. I must make hay while the sun shines, for my mind-weather is not to be depended on to last long, certainly not all the year. Then, besides, I am obliged, conscience compelling, to lecture all over the land; on Friday night at Fall River. Further still, I am writing a work on the Reformation, which demands all my spare hours; therefore you see why I hold myself excused. I should be amazingly glad to come and share your hospitality, and enjoy the society of yourself and yours; but when a whole *Garrison* is to take the field, and there is such a stalwart *Smith* there ready to lay on iron strokes, I think it needless that a *Parker* should be called on to beat the bush when the others will capture the game. For me, I prefer to go and labour in places where there is not a *Smith* in the land.

TO DE WETTE.

West Roxbury, 28th September, 1845.

HONORED AND DEAR SIR,—I received from you some time since the sixth edition of your *Einleitung ins A. T.*, which you had the politeness to send me. I am much obliged to you for your kindness. My

---

* "Plea for Theology"—delivered before the Association of the Alumni of the Cambridge Theological School, July 18, 1845. Printed in the *Christian Examiner* for November, 1845.

translation of your work has not produced the effect here which it is yet destined to do. The Liberal party, in fact, are weak; the *so-called* Liberal party, the Unitarians, are partly afraid and partly hypocritical. None of the stout critics had touched it, until recently Moses Stuart, Professor in the Theological Seminary at Andover—a learned man of the *Hengstenberg-Richtung* (tendency)—published a work called " A Critical History and Defence of the Old Testament Canon." In this he refers continually to your views, and of course attacks them; but he always treats them with respect, and entertains a high esteem for yourself as a critic and a scholar. He attacks also Mr. Norton, and treats him with less respect than yourself. Mr. S.'s book will have a wide circulation here, but in Germany it would be considered *ganz unbedeutend* (quite unimportant). Here is a small party who think that Christianity is the Word of God; but the documents connected therewith, like the institutions connected with it also, are to be treated like other documents, criticized, studied, and believed only when they are *probable*. None of our conspicuous theologians belong to this class; a traditionary theology is the curse of the Church in America. But I have strong hopes that to-morrow will be brighter than to-day. In a country where the mind is in general so free as it is here, theology cannot always be kept from becoming a science. I hope much from the introduction of German thought into America, especially from your own writings. I am at present preaching each Sunday to a large congregation of Liberal Christians in Boston.* But I am called a heretic by my Unitarian brothers, who are themselves called heretics and infidels by all the rest. I am also preparing a work on the Protestant Reformation, its causes and its consequences. When that is done, I mean to write a history of the progress of thought in matters of theology and religion from the Reformation to this day. I intend also to prepare, with *your* help, a critical and historical introduction to the New Testament. . . . . If you prepare a new edition of your *Einleitung in das N. T.*, and will send it me, it will be a favour. My translation is printed with stereotype plates, and therefore it is costly to make alterations from one edition to another; but of course I shall in the next edition notice the points in which you have differed from your earlier opinions. When you print a seventh edition I will thank you to send it me.

With sincere desires for your long life and continued happiness, I remain your friend and obedient servant.

FROM THE JOURNAL.

Feb. 7, 1845.—I have just conferred with part of a committee for procuring a place in Boston for me to preach in. I consent for two Sundays, commencing on the 16th, and, if it is possible, to continue to preach for them every Sunday morning for a year. I know not what will come of it. I don't wish ever to leave my Patmos at Spring Street. If the parish will consent, I will continue here and preach half the time, and furnish a substitute the rest of the time.

* See the next extract from the Journal.

The parish consented.

I know not what will come of it, but think only good. God grant it shall be so! There is much to conserve, there is somewhat also to destroy.

16th.—To-day I have preached at the Melodeon, for the first time. The weather was highly unfavourable—rainy, and the snow deep—the streets passable only with difficulty. Still, there was a large audience, mostly of men, unlike most of my audiences. I felt the greatness of the occasion, but I felt it too much to do justice, perhaps, to myself. I felt not at ease in my service. I felt as one that is with some friends, with some foes, with many strangers. It has been a day of struggles. A long, long warfare opens before me! Shall I prove worthy? How much can I do? How much can I bear? I know not. I look only to the soul of my soul, not with over-confidence in myself, but with an adamantine faith in God.

The greeting of some friends did me much good. I love to take a *friend* by the hand. Mrs. —— came into the little room, and took me by the hand. I am a child in some things, I hope I shall always be.

March 3.—I have but one resource, and that is to overcome evil with good—much evil with more good; old evil with new good. Sometimes when I receive a fresh insult it makes my blood rise for a moment; then it is over, and I seek, if possible, to do some good, secretly, to the person. *It takes away the grief of a wound amazingly.* To be true to God, and "that one talent which 'tis death to hide"—this depends on me. To know that I am thus true depends on others, and if they know it not, why that is not my affair, but theirs! Sometimes I wish that death would come and fan me to sleep with his wings: but faith soon stops that murmur, and a " Thy will be done!" is prayer enough for me.

During this winter of 1844–45 he lectured forty times.

At New Bedford I saw some interesting persons. Andrew Robeson I admire, and love as I love few men. I look at him with rapture. He is my ideal almost of a rich man, a Christian man. I speak not of his kindness to me, but of his character, his life. I know not why, but I love better the society of such than the companionship of the most cultivated men. They meet you, and don't dodge.

Sometimes I feel a little satisfied with myself. Then I always know that some mortification is preparing for me; all my swans prove geese soon as they begin to sing.

The old trouble in his head recurred, and he lost a great many days. He called them lost, but they were filled with respectable labour. Still, the physicians reduced him to the smallest amount that was compatible with his peace of mind. He often left his sermon unfinished, and wandered listlessly into the fields. Sometimes he went to see the brave people at Brook Farm.

His preaching in Boston attained a popularity which astonished him. The Melodeon was crowded with a keen, sturdy, and inquisitive audience, many of whom had never before been submitted to the influence of positive religion. His manly piety and powerful assaults upon the conscience, his humor and good sense, above all, the manifestation of his love for man, won them from curiosity into reverence and exalted feelings. He did not believe that he should be able to sustain himself long before such a congregation. He had always been told that he was a mere book-worm, and he loved meditation and seclusion. He was surprised and delighted when he found his words taking a genuine hold upon the people.

Occasionally there was a chance, by exchange with some liberal brother, to preach in another pulpit. He never failed to impress people if they did not know him, or know that he was coming. If they did, the opinion would be divided. An excellent person lingered in Mr. Clarke's vestibule, after one of these sermons, loud in her grateful praises. " Oh, I wish that infidel Theodore Parker could have heard that ! " Yes, indeed, such love to God and man, flowing forth strongly in such lucid speech, found the great want in every unguarded heart.

November 27.—To-day my friends met in Boston to organize more fully, with a view to my settling with them. I would gladly for my own quiet remain always here, but I shall go to Boston and work, if they need me, and wish me. I pray for this only, that I may be greatly good and pious, and thereby greatly useful unto man. If I pass ten years in Boston, labouring at that church, I may do something, it seems to me. If not, why I have done my best, and will not complain.

My chosen walk will be with the humble. I will be the minister of the humble, and, with what of culture and love I have, will I toil for them. I rejoice to see that most of my hearers are from the humbler class of men. If it had been *only* the cultivated and the rich, I should feel that I was wrong somewhere ; but when the voice *comes up from the ground*, I can't refuse to listen to it.

Those aspirations preserved their warmth and purity ; every gift and acquisition was subservient to feed them alone. Did any man, of so strong a mould and of such ardent sensibilities, ever have more innocent ambitions ?

TO DR. JOHN WARE.

West Roxbury, 2nd January, 1846.

DEAR SIR,—I hope you will excuse a stranger for venturing to address you a letter. At any rate, I shall take the liberty. Your memoir of your brother has affected me so deeply, that I cannot forbear expressing my gratitude that you have prepared so noble a memorial of so noble a man. Sir, I knew your brother well. It was my good fortune to be in the Theological School two or three years, while it most fully enjoyed his services. I loved him as I have seldom loved a man heretofore, and perhaps shall never love another. He was not always equal—sometimes was absent, and *seemed* cold. But he drew my heart after him by the very tones of his voice, by his look and his kind way of speaking to a young man. He never flattered. He told truth, and did not wound, even though it was a painful truth. I can't believe any student ever slighted any hint he gave. I treasured up his words as oracles—not Delphic, but Christian. His presence at our religious meetings was the presence of a saint; it was the fragrance of violets in a library; and we felt it. He tuned the most discordant strings.

His lectures, I mean those delivered before the whole school, were nòt professedly religious; but they brought a man step by step to the throne of God, and before he knew it he knelt and prayed. His influence was wholly through his holiness. But that affected all he said and did. His opinions on books we received as from no other man who knew much more of books. I used often to hear Dr. Channing preach in the morning, and in the afternoon your brother, at the chapel. I have heard Dr. Channing, perhaps, preach some of his best sermons; but I could not tell which I liked best, Dr. C. or Henry Ware. One had the magnificence of religious thought, the other had the heavenliness of piety.

Your brother began moderately, with no promise of a great soul-stirring sermon; but gradually he gained greatness of thought, and lovely images, and a sweetness and poetry of devotion and trust in God which charmed your heart away. And then his prayers! I have heard none such. I know nothing to compare them with, public or private, unless it be the music I have heard sometimes in a cathedral, when one little voice begins—like our own thrush in the mornings of May—and softly, gently sings out strains exquisitely tender; then comes another, different but accordant; and then another, and so on till every column, arch, altar-stone seems vibrating with the psalm. His arrow kindled as it rose, and disappeared a flame.

When I left the school I always went to him for advice, criticism, help, and I always found it—found more than I asked. At my ordination *he* laid his hand on my head—and I believe in the imposition of *such* a hand—and prayed words that not only *I* shall never forget, but the people of this church still lovingly remember.

Your memoir brings him back to me just as I knew him. He tells often his own story, and lives again before me. I carried to England and Geneva the tidings of his end, and you know what hearts they were that loved him, and may judge of their grief. He has gone, and your father, too! They were not long separated, now again are together with the Father of us all. They both prophesy after their death, and both will be ever remembered by one who gratefully received instruction and counsel from each.

I am, sir,
      Your obliged servant,
          T. P.

In the year 1845, he opened a friendship with Charles Sumner, which became valuable to both of them, and was ennobled by a mutual sense of fidelity to truth and of suffering in her service. Mr. Parker made a characteristic advance, in an acknowledgment of Mr. Sumner's oration on the "True Grandeur of Nations;" its principles were dear to his heart, and with his customary unselfishness he proffered welcome and admiration.

I hope you will excuse one so nearly a stranger to you as myself, for addressing you this note. But I cannot forbear writing. I have just read your oration on the "True Grandeur of Nations" for the second time, and write to express to you my sense of the great value of that work, and my gratitude to you for delivering it on such an occasion. Boston is a queer little city, the public is a desperate tyrant there, and it is seldom that one dares disobey the commands of public opinion. I know the reproaches you have already received from your friends, who will now, perhaps, become your foes. I have heard all sorts of ill motives attributed to you, and know that you must suffer attack from men of low morals, who can only swear by their party, and who live only in public opinion.
I hope you will find a rich reward in the certainty that you have done a duty and a service to mankind."

A society had been organized at the Melodeon, and he accepted its call in December. His parish made mournful preparations for his departure :—

FROM THE JOURNAL.

The Parish Committee have been here to consult about my leaving the church. It seems worse than assisting at my own funeral—the only *real* calamity that has befallen me in the ecclesiastical way; all the other troubles have been blessings in a mask—this is a sorrow. How can I bear to stand in the dear old familiar pulpit for the last time, and look in the dear old faces for the last time out of that pulpit? But it must be, and soon will be. I cling tenaciously to all I ever loved. I even hate to lose sight of a departing cloud. Well, perhaps this also will be a good—to those dear old friends, to me, to all.

TO THE SECOND PARISH IN ROXBURY.

West Roxbury, 3rd Jan., 1846.

DEAR FRIENDS,—It is with great grief that I write you this note, fixing the second Sunday in February next as the day of resigning my connection with you. Circumstances which I could neither prevent nor foresee constrain me to leave a place which has become dearer to me each year I have filled it—a place in which I had fondly hoped to live long and usefully, and die as I had lived amongst you. I need not say now how painful the separation will be to me, for I think you all know that; I need not say that no personal ambition leads me to this step, for I think you all know the circumstances of this case too well, and know me too well to believe for a moment it is so. If my brethren of the Christian ministry had stood by me, nay, if they had not themselves refused the usual ministerial fellowship with me, then I should have been spared this painful separation, and my life might have flowed on in the channel we have both wished for it. But I bear no ill-will to my brethren. I trust you will bear none ; I hope you may again hear their voices in your own church, and be again instructed by their words. I shall soon cease to be your minister ; I shall never cease to be your friend. I hope long to be your neighbour and fellow-citizen. But wherever I am, I shall always feel grateful for the uniform kindness and forbearance you have shown towards me. There is nothing in all your dealings with me which I could wish otherwise. You have borne patiently with my infirmities, and if I have ever had a new truth to offer, though scholars and clergymen treated it with scorn, you welcomed the word to your hearts, and heard it gladly. When my personal friends forsook me and fell off, you stood by me. Your hearty sympathy has been of more value to me than words can tell. Think not I shall ever forget that. And now I am obliged to leave you. But my heart never shall leave you. My *desire* is to remain still with you ; my *duty* commands me elsewhere. If I am ever able to serve you in any way, I beg you to consider me still your servant, and always your friend. It will always give me pleasure to be of use to you.

With the best wishes for your success, I remain affectionately, your friend and Christian brother.

On January 4, 1846, he was installed over the Twenty-eighth Congregational Society, in Boston, preaching his own sermons—tender, brave, unsparing, and humane—on the True Idea of a Christian Church. That was the first of a long series of discourses, rich with the application of religion to life, through facts, criticisms, and ideas, which made the designation of the " Twenty-eighth Congregational " famous at home and abroad.

Mr. Parker had several times been to Andover for books and conversation with the professors. He knew Professor Stuart, who, acknowledging some publications in the autumn of 1845, addresses Mr. Parker in terms which show a scholarly and magnanimous recognition :—

Accept the accompanying little volume as a small return for your kindness.

As to the liberty which I have taken to controvert some of your opinions, you are the last man to call this in question. You will see, that in drawing the comparison between you and your *non-committal* opponents, I have given you the preference. No half-way measures are consistent in such a case. The Bible is either the word of God, or else it is only a part of the book of nature, standing on the same level with Plato, Plutarch, Cicero, Seneca, and others of the like class. I understand you as taking the latter position, with the modification that the New Testament, in particular, contains a more thorough and explicit morality and religiosity. Mr. Norton will not relish the preference I have given to your views, in comparison with his. I cannot help it; I have only spoken my deep convictions.

I have more hope that you will yet be won over to orthodoxy, than that he will. Not because you are less sincere and ardent in your present views, but because you let Reason have full play, and carry you wherever you think she leads. A thousand things may yet change your views of the nature and necessity of Christianity—things not in your hands, nor mine, but in the hands of Him who has life, comfort, prospects, hopes, convictions even, entirely at His disposal.

What I have said to Mr. Norton, I can truly say to you—*Utinam nostrûm esset!*

In speaking plainly my convictions, which I have felt obliged to do, I hope and trust that I have not transgressed the laws of courtesy. I am, with kind regards, however we may differ in opinion, your friend and obedient servant, M. STUART.

In the summer of this year (1846) he spent the month of July in a journey through Western New York, the White Mountains, and Canada; but of this there is only an itinerary. Rough drafts abound, notes and statistics, hints, anecdotes, for the sermon of merchants, of war, of pauperism, on the state of the nation, material to serve the discussion of slavery, mixed with a great variety of theological and philosophical suggestions. His activity was very manifold for the next five years. The business of lecturing had greatly increased, and his reading had not diminished, as the regular lists of books for every year show plainly enough; and yet his time in Boston was torn to pieces with interruptions. He met them blandly, and his business was more successfully achieved, for obstacles piqued him into great wariness, economy, and system. He used to say that time stretched like india-rubber. Here is an attempt to write a sermon :—

I had been to the Post-Office, had sewed the sheets of my Easter sermon together, and sat down to make a brief of the matter, when— 1, in comes Mrs. K——, to talk over her *connubial* affairs. She stayed till about eleven, when—2, in comes Mr. McKay, and as we talked of various things it was announced that—3. Dr. Papin was downstairs. I went to see him, and—4. R. W. Emerson was coming up the stairs. I left him in the study, and saw the Doctor, who came seeking relief for a poor woman; then returned, and we talked of the *new journal:* saw Carlyle's letter about Margaret. Nos. 3, 4, and 2 successively went away. I was descending the stairs, when, lo !—5 appears, George Ripley, and we talked of the condition of civilization, the prospects of humanity. Dinner came, one hour. Went to see Mr. —— : not at home; visited other people in the afternoon: tea. At half-past seven sat down to the sermon: in a minute came—6, Mr. F. C., wanting to borrow twelve dollars, which I lent him gladly. Then sat down to write: at a quarter past eight came—7, Mr. M——. All chance of work was now at an end, so I gave up, and went down to the parlour. A little before nine came a ring, and then—8 appeared, Mr. ——, who was interested to kill a man that had done a wrong to one of his friends, and brought a letter of defiance. I burned the letter after a long talk, but could not wholly overcome the man's feelings of revenge. At ten he retired, and at a quarter before eleven, I also, to rest—not to sleep for a long time.

The new journal referred to became the *Massachusetts Quarterly Review*, of which he reluctantly undertook the co-editorship with Mr. Emerson and J. E. Cabot. The first number appeared in December, 1847. It proposed to discuss the questions of American society and politics, which were just beginning to assume their great and threatening proportions, of science, and of theology. Mr. Emerson prepared the editorial address, from which this is an extract:—

What will easily seem to many a far higher question than any other is that which respects the embodying of the conscience of the period. Is the age we live in unfriendly to the highest powers; to that blending of the affections with the poetic faculty which has distinguished the Religious Ages? We have a better opinion of the economy of nature than to fear that those varying phases which humanity presents ever leave out any of the grand springs of human action.

In the rapid decay of what was called religion, timid and unthinking people fancy a decay of the hope of man. But the moral and religious sentiments meet us everywhere, alike in markets as in churches. A God starts up behind cotton bales also. The conscience of man is regenerated as is the atmosphere, so that society cannot be debauched. That health which we call virtue is an equipoise which easily redresses itself, and resembles those rocking-stones which a child's finger can move, and a weight of many hundred tons cannot overthrow.

TO A FRIEND.

DEAR FRIEND,—When you come to see me again, don't ask if I am busy, but come in, whether or not. I am not likely to be too busy to see you. If I am, I will tell you frankly.

I want to see you very much. We need a new periodical, for philosophy, literature, theology, religion, and practical morality. Are not you the man to undertake it? If not you, who is? Not ——, who has not the culture, the patience, the stability (in place or idea); not ——, who is too ultramontane for the nineteenth century.

We want a tremendous journal, with ability in its arms and piety in its heart. Cannot you do something for it?

Yours heartily,
T. P.

TO THE SAME.

DEAR FRIEND,—The more I think of it, the more certain I am that —— will not do for our newly-talked-of periodical. He has not the *entireness*, not the firm courage which we want. I admit he has much courage, but not quite enough. Then, too, he is a member of the Boston Association. They would whine round him and choke the life out of him if he undertook, not to say a manly thing, but to let others say it. He is a good man; I honour him, love him, expect much of him : but I don't expect *that which we want.*

We don't want a man of the Middle Ages, but of the nineteenth century, for our work. I have written a letter to Emerson, asking him to undertake the matter. If he will, it will succeed. He is the better man, if he will take hold. He is a downright *man ;* we never had such a jewel in America before. I think him worth two or three of Dr. Channing.

How many young men do you know that could write in such a work ? It should be literary, philosophical, poetical, theological, and, above all, human—human even to divinity. I think we may find help in unexpected quarters.

Come, and let us talk over the matter one of these days.

TO CHARLES SUMNER.

I think we want a new journal, devoted to letters, poetry, art, philosophy, theology, politics (in the best sense of that word), and humanity in general. You know better than I the *North-American Review,* the *Christian Examiner,** &c. They are not *jusqu'au niveau de l'humanité.* They will not be, cannot be. The better minds of the age cannot express their best thoughts therein. If there were such a journal, ably conducted, it would have two good influences : 1. It would strike a salutary terror into all the Ultramontanists, and make them see that they did not live in the Middle Ages—that they are not to be let alone dreaming of the garden of Eden, but are to buckle up and work ; 2. It would spread abroad the ideas which now wait to be organized, some in letters, some in art, some in institutions and practical life. I know you love letters not less than law, and man before both, and so I write to ask you what you think of the matter—how far you would aid in such a work ? Don't suppose I want to be one of the head and front of this movement ; I want no such thing, but not to appear at all. I wrote to R. W. E. to ask him to take charge of such a work. If he fails, what say you to that ?

* In a diary which Mr. Parker kept during his last illness in Rome, is this entry :— "Received, to-day, the *Unitarian Quarterly,* with a notice of my Letter (the Letter from Santa Cruz). What a change in the tone of Unitarian periodicals in a few years !" And he recognized the more liberal character of the *Christian Examiner* under its new management in 1859-60, and was accustomed to say that it was then the best religious periodical in America. He sent a number of it, containing his own article upon Massachusetts, to Moleschott, the distinguished chemist of Zurich, with a note, in which he says :—

"There is an admirable article on Asiatic Civilization in the *Christian Examiner* for July, 1859, written by that very able and enlightened man who wrote those on India and China in 1857-8."

TO THE SAME.

DEAR SIR,—It has been decided in the council of the gods that you must undertake the business of conducting a new review. Remember, now, that you are a mortal, while the gods live on Olympus, and rule the world after the divine sentence of the Fates. Therefore, O mortal, there is nothing for you to do but to set about the appointed work.

I saw Emerson yesterday; he came to my house, and we talked the matter over; thought as I did about it, but "more so;" offered to do his possible in the way of writing, &c., but thought that *you* were the man for editor. He thought we had better talk the matter over at the *Consessus Divorum* presently to be held at Concord, where we could mature the matter.

This review was mainly fed by the voluntary contributions of a few writers in the neighbourhood who were most interested in its principles; * but almost all the labour, and a large share of the writing, fell to Mr. Parker, who was ever ready where he was most wanted, and supplied all deficiencies. Some of his finest compositions appeared in its pages; the biographies of J. Q. Adams and of Dr. Channing, his elaborate criticisms of Mr. Emerson and of Mr. Prescott, and an article on the "Political Destination of America." For three years he kept it from falling to the ground. But there did not exist a sufficient corps of trained and ready writers, who had no interest beyond that of independent criticism, nor a sufficient public, to establish it as an organ of the Liberal School. Such a journal must happen some day; it cannot be deliberately plotted. Mr. Parker went to work in his systematic way and drew up, carefully classified, a list of the subjects which cover the province of such a journal. Some of these he wrote upon, others he offered to friends. Then he prepared a list of contributors under three heads: " A. Certain and valuable; B. Valuable, but not certain ; C. Certain, but not valuable." And not more than one or two names there recorded contradict his estimate.

His enemies used to say that he had a wonderful instinct for depreciation. It was because his common-sense seldom found more in a person than he contained. He deemed it a sacred power, worth developing and protecting from every ignoble disturbance, to judge men with absolute sincerity. He could even bid some of his controversial prejudices stand aside, if any

---

* Extract from a letter to Rev. S. J. May, Aug. 14, 1847. "Dr. Howe keeps still his interest in the work, but *I* thought his name had better not appear among the 'wise master-builders,' lest some should suspect that he was abandoning his duty to the blind who have no eyes, to attend to the blind who have eyes but see not."

matter came to a public judgment. This is different from the prevalent American habits of wholesale eulogy or complete defamation ; and it is the secret of the hatred which he incurred when, to lift pure models and to correct an indiscriminate taste, to rescue the young men from their abject homage to power and talent, he drew his matchless portraits of distinguished names. There are traces of his preparations for these biographical estimates extending for years, careful hoarding of facts, traits, elusive circumstances, distinct references to each characteristic act or speech, correspondence with distinguished contemporaries who could either confirm or contradict a rumor, a most painstaking testing and collecting, ruled by a sad prescience that some day would bring to him the disagreeable duty of clothing these pure facts in speech. He was a self-elected arbiter by character and genius ; courage, jealous conscience, intuitive observation, health, clean hands and a pure heart, were the judicial robes in which he sat. These are certainly essential, though they cannot always be infallible, qualities. They justify one who is ordained to lead and purify the people when he undertakes to exhibit its great men.

He took a pleasure in calculating the forces which result in the direction taken by a public man, the original character, the nature of his education, the associates of his profession, the passions within and the passions without, the worthy acts as well as the doubtful ones, the first great mistake or the first decided sacrifice. Many notes of this description were slowly gathering, under the heads of various distinguished names, from his earliest preaching days ; they were continuing when that and every labour besides was interrupted by the voice which bade a tablet be prepared for him.

TO A FRIEND IN GERMANY.

Boston, June 5, 1847.

My dear Friend,—Your kind and welcome letter of April 10th came to me two days ago, and I write with a very joyful heart to thank you for the kindly estimate which you have formed of my labours, and the hearty words you address to me. It gives me great joy to find a man in Germany who welcomes my books. I feel so much indebted to your country for the efforts so often made for the freedom of mankind, that I rejoice at the thought of paying back to any one a small part of the debt which I owe to the great souls which have risen up in Germany. German literature is well known in this country, and is sowing the land with fruitful seed. When my book was first published in

1842, I sent a copy to the *Wissenschaftliche Kritik*, but I never heard of its reception. A year ago I sent a copy to Wislicenus, and a letter therewith, but never heard from him afterwards, and do not know that he has ever received book or letter. I know your colleague very well bv his writings, and therefore can appreciate your position beside him.

I cannot tell you how it warms my heart to find such a friend at such a distance. I wish I could do something to show my sense of your great kindness towards me, but I must beg you to believe that I am very grateful for your kind opinion of my book, and for your desire to translate it. It will give me great pleasure to introduce my work to the German nation in the German tongue; but though I read German easily enough, it is quite difficult to write, for I think in English. I will send you from London a copy of the third edition of my work, which contains some additional notes not found in the edition of last year. If it arrives in season, you can make use of it; but if not, why it is of no great importance. It has slowly found its way into notice here, but all the periodicals, especially the Unitarian, raised the *Zeter-geschrei* (cry of heretic), which is not entirely ended. I am called infidel, atheist, and other pleasant names of that sort. But if they call the master of the house Beelzebub, it matters little if they treat the household no better.

I had formerly a small parish in Roxbury, but abandoned that a couple of years ago and came to Boston, where I have a large audience of intelligent and noble men and women. I send you a little tract published by the Unitarians themselves, which gives some account of them. What I must add is not much in their favour. They started originally with a protest against the doctrine of the Trinity. They denied the divinity of Christ, but they did not declare the humanity of Christ. So they only affirmed a negative; their history was but the development of a negation, and little more; the protest began amongst a class of cultivated men in the most cultivated part of America; with men who had not the religious element developed in proportion to the intellectual or the æsthetic element. Therefore, they had not the element of piety in their preaching to the same extent as their opponents. Unitarianism always had a worldly character; gradually the opposition of the Trinitarians grew less and less, though the name of Christian is still wickedly denied to the Unitarians by their opponents. The Unitarians formed themselves into a sect, with the regular machinery of a theological party, *i. e.*, officers and missionaries, money and tracts. Then it was necessary for them to publish their symbolical books. But they have not ideas enough to form a theological party; the development of their negations is all that is left for them distinctively as a party. If they would affirm the humanity of Christ, they might become a great sect; but they do not see far enough for that. They declare the paternal character of God, but yet do not (as the Universalists) declare the eternal salvation of all men. They are not now making any advances towards a liberal theology; they stand still, and become more and more narrow and bigoted from year to year.

Yet, among them there are some very noble men who are entirely free, and desirous of further progress. From them as individuals much is to be hoped, but from the sect, as a sect, nothing must be looked for. It is curious to see the distinguished men who have once been Unitarian preachers, but who now preach no longer. Andrews Norton, the best scholar of the party, who, however, devotes himself exclusively to theological pursuits, is narrow, bigoted, and sectarian, but an able man. His chief work is " A Defence of the Genuineness of the Gospels," 4 vols. 8vo. Jared Sparks, eminent as an historian and editor of American State Papers; Edward Everett, formerly Governor of Massachusetts, and American Ambassador to England, now President of Harvard University; George Bancroft, now Ambassador to England, the historian of the United States, a man of great ability and genius as an historical writer; R. W. Emerson, the most original author we have produced in America, a man of wonderful gifts, and the author of some volumes of Essays, which I wish might be translated into German; John G. Palfrey, now a member of Congress, and Secretary of the State of Massachusetts; George Ripley, a sound and philosophical man, who is devoting himself to the doctrines of Fourier. All these men have left the pulpits of the Unitarians. The most prominent scholars in the denomination are Dr. James Walker, Professor of Intellectual Philosophy at Harvard University; Dr. Convers Francis, Professor of Theology at the Unitarian Theological Seminary; Dr. George R. Noyes, also Professor of Theology at the same place; Dr. Lamson; Dr. Gannett; Dr. Dewey, a showy but superficial writer; Dr. Putnam, an eloquent preacher, but nothing more. There is little scholarship and less philosophical thinking among the Unitarians. Some of their members engage in the great moral movements of the day, such as the Temperance Reform, and the Anti-Slavery movement. But the sect as such is opposed to all reforms. However, it has already done a great work in liberalizing the minds of men; the misfortune is that it is not disposed to go on further. However, " *non omnia possumus omnes,*" and others are rising up with nobler ideas than the Unitarians, who go more profoundly to work, and preach absolute religion, not controlled by the traditional authority of men, but resting in the instincts of man, and the primeval revelation which God makes to mankind. The triumph of this liberal movement, I think,i s certain; for every year the people become more and more emancipated from authority, and disposed to think freely, and to allow all others to do the same. Some of the most liberal theologians in the country are not in the Unitarian ranks, but are men of enlarged minds and generous culture. I think the destiny of the sect is to liberalize the mind of the nation in some measure, and then gradually to decay and perish. There is now a powerful movement going on in favour of the most *entire freedom of thought.* This will sweep away all the absurdities of tradition. Some valuable things of tradition will likewise be dropped, and then we must wait till some one goes back and gathers them up. Hitherto our *political* and *industrial* progress has been greater than our advance in literature and philosophy. That was unavoidable. But now intellectual things are getting attended to.

I hail with enthusiasm every great movement in Germany, and feel that the English, the French, the Germans, and the Americans are working together for the common good of the human race. It will be as in the old story of the building of Solomon's Temple; one man hewed a stone at Carmel, one a cedar at Lebanon, each working after the pattern which the great architect had put before him, not one of them having an idea of the work he was building up. At last, on men's shoulders, and upon the backs of beasts, marbles and cedars were brought together, and, 'midst a noise of harmony, the well-hewn material grew into a temple, where the people could worship, and find that God dwelt.

I hope, as opportunity allows, you will oblige me with a letter, which I shall hold very dear. I think I recognize your hand in some articles in the *Halle Allgemeine Zeitung.* Is it not so? Believe me, with the heartiest wishes for your welfare and usefulness.

Most truly, your friend,
THEODORE PARKER.

P.S.—Your *Oster Predigt* gave me great pleasure. I recognize there a noble soul, whose words cannot fall in vain upon the ears of men. I send you also Dr. Baird's book on the various denominations of America. It is an accurate book, and will help your friend, Dr. Fork, also in his work.

The next letter shows the date of his removal to Boston for permanent residence. He was obliged very unwillingly to take this step, which involved a separation from the country scenes that were so dear to him, in consequence of the distance of Spring Street from his new parish, and from the various new duties which beset him in Boston.

TO MRS. DALL.

Boston, 17 Jan., 1847.

MY DEAR CAROLINE,—Here I am in Boston; it is Sunday night, the first Sunday night I have passed in Boston these ten years. But for the trouble of removing the household and my books, I should have answered your letter before now.

What are you driving at? What have I done? *How* is the writer in the *Examiner* generous? How is truth all at once a lie because it gets into my mouth? You talk riddles. I know not what they mean, unless it be that you think I say hard things out of spite. If you will think that, why, you must, and I can't help it; only I protest and say, *such is not the fact.* Why should I forbear to tell the truth when it presses on me to be told? I must speak. Do you think I feel spite against the poor Boston Association? Not the faintest, nor never did I. Nay, nor need I ever. If they, aided by New England rum, drove John Pierpont out of Boston, and thereby disturbed the Temperance movement, why should not I tell the truth, painful though it be to me? I think it is quite Christlike to do so. I know men need to be taught reverence, not fear of men, but reverence for right, truth, justice, reverence for the laws of God, and for God who made these laws. If I lose friends, I can't help it—I must be true to *my truth,* not to *theirs.* I cannot help it, if I lose all my friends. Perhaps I am to have that trial—perhaps to sink under it; who knows?

I will send you my " Sermon of Merchants," soon as I get a little "fixed up." Perhaps that will grieve you yet more. If so, tell me. I prize your friendship all the more for its sincere statement of dissent. I like not to meet a mock concession, but a wall which sends back my words with vigorous rebound. Tell me always my faults; I will thank you for it. Still, it seems queer to me that nobody finds fault when I speak of the fraud of politicians. Nobody finds fault when bigots revile even the sectarians. But when I say a word, never so true and *notoriously* true, about the clergy, straightway a cry is raised! Even you say I use my opponents' weapons. Not so, kind Caroline; I use but my own lawful weapons—Christian weapons.

Believe me, faithfully, your friend and brother,

THEODORE.

TO THE SAME.

Boston, 28th Jan., 1847.

MY DEAR CAROLINE,—Your letter does not make the matter any clearer than before. Either what I say *is true* or *not true ;* either I say it *in a good spirit,* or *not in a good spirit.* I affirm it is true what I say, I affirm that I say it in a good spirit ; of the last I am sure. I know I speak only in a good spirit, in a spirit *wholly good.* The other I believe ; I am confident that what I say is true. As to taking pleasure in saying what you call sarcastic things, I never felt the least pleasure—nothing but pain : if Horace or Juvenal did, it was their affair, not mine. You seem to think when I speak of the clergy, I mean the Boston Association. Far enough from it ; when I mean the Boston Association, I shall say so. Many things I say of the clergy, which belong no more to the Boston Association than to the London Association, but to the clergy.

I should like to know when I ever came out with a flat untruth in regard to men like ——— and others. I never thought of ——— in a sermon. As to the *" good of the clergy,"* I have spoken time and again, till I have been told all round that I exaggerated the matter, and subsequent events have taught me to fear it was true. If I had been writing to a *Sophist,* I should not have made the allusion you speak of as to the abuse which bigots pour upon sectarians. I saw the construction which might be put upon it. I did not think *you* would put that construction on my words. As to sarcasm, I know not what you mean by it. I know of no sarcasm in the sermons under consideration. Censure is not sarcasm. I call sarcasm *malicious irony—a stripping-off the flesh* in wantonness. I plead "not guilty" to the charge. I seldom use *irony* at all ; sometimes I have done it.

I have often cautioned my friends against defending me. The bitterness of my own sufferings has been to see others suffer for me. I am strong and old—older than ever before, at least ; I am broad-shouldered for suffering, and have borne that all my life ; *not to suffer* would be a new thing. But to have others suffer for me, I have not yet got wonted to. I have considered my course again and again in all lights, and I can't see the error you speak of. If it gave me pleasure to say hard things, I would shut up for ever. But the TRUTH, which costs me bitter tears to say, I must speak, though it cost others tears hotter than fire. I cannot forbear. I thank you for your kindly rebukes, not less because I follow not your counsel.

I hope soon to see you, and am truly, your brother,

THEODORE.

TO THE SAME.

Boston, June 2, 1847.

MY DEAR CAROLINE,—I like very much the little book of Munch. It is clear, manly, and popular. The author makes no concealment. He speaks right out. He seems to be a sincere and pious man. I do not like his views on war, and I think he is mistaken sometimes in his exegesis of Scripture; but still I hope the little book will do much good. I suppose he likes the name of Rationalist. I wonder it should be a reproach in New England; but so it is, and poor Mr. —— really seemed afraid the Unitarians might be suspected of the thing, though I think there is not the least danger of that. By the way, do you see how sectarian the denomination is becoming? I find no such sectarianism among the orthodox on Anniversary Week, as among the Unitarians. Our doctrines are so much better than the bulk of theirs, that our sectarianism seems a good deal worse.

The attempt to put down YOUR-*ism* by MY-*ism* is always bad, but in a Unitarian it is ridiculous. The Unitarians have not a sufficient dogmatic basis for a sect, and they do not develope their humanities enough to make their way as a body of working men; so I do not know what will become of them.

I hope they will protect with their ashes the ember truths of time, which the world needs alike for light and heat. We must have a good deal of charity for all men, both conservative and radical.

" Be to their faults a little blind,
Be to their virtues very kind "

is no bad rule for the active or passive part of the world.

Truly yours,

THEO. PARKER.

FROM THE JOURNAL.

Christmas, 1847.—To-day I received from Archdeacon Wolff, at Kiel, the translation of my Discourses, &c. The work awakened such heart-beatings as I have not often had for a cause seemingly so slight. I read the lines of his preface, in which he speaks so tenderly of me, not without many tears. Is it possible that I am to be henceforth a power in the world to move men, a name which shall kindle men to goodness and piety, a name of power? I think little enough of fame. But to be a man who can lead mankind a little onward, that thought would charm me.

Well, at reading that, remembering, too, how I have been treated here, I must confess I wept; and since have felt the better for my tears. God grant I may be more and better as the years go by!

February, 1848.—On Tuesday I attended a funeral of a child, five or six years old; but the parents do not believe in the continuous and conscious life of the soul. It was terribly sad. The friends that I talked with were superficial and conceited. I have seldom attended a sadder funeral. They wanted no form of prayer, but for decency's sake, wanted a minister and an address. I suppose they sent for me as the *minimum* of a minister. I tried to give them the *maximum of humanity* while their hearts were pliant, and they excited by grief. The man seemed a worthy man, humane, but with an unlucky method of philosophy. I see not how any one can live without a continual sense of immortality. I am sure I should be wretched without a *certainty* of that.

In February he went to New Haven and spent two days, very profitably, in the company of the distinguished Professors there, Taylor, and Salisbury the Orientalist, Woolsey, Gibbs, Thacher, and Goodrich.

I stayed with my good friend Noah Porter. Him and his wife I long ago learned to like and since to love. I have seldom enjoyed two days so much as these. I have found these professors kindly and gentlemanly.

He contrasts their treatment with that of more liberal thinkers, and proceeds:—

They all seem to have *liberal methods* and lofty aims. If they have not arrived at conclusions so liberal as the Unitarians, their method is decidedly better. Dr. Taylor loves philosophy and looks for advance in theology. Yet in him I thought I saw the ill-effects of Calvinism. His conception of God was a poor one.

He says most distinctly that in any contest between Reason and Scripture, Reason must be followed: "What in the name of Reason must be followed if not Reason itself?"

TO REV. INCREASE S. SMITH.

Feb. 4, 1848.

The *Anti-Sabbath Convention* is not to be an *Anti-Sunday Convention:* not a bit of it. I think we can make the Sunday ten times more valuable than it is now, only by abating the nonsense connected with it.

I have all along been a little afraid of a reaction from the sour, stiff, Jewish way of keeping the Sunday, into a low, coarse, material, voluptuous, or mere money-making abuse of it. But if we take it in time, we can cast out the Devil without calling in the aid of Beelzebub. The Past is always pregnant with the Future. The problem of the Present is the *maieutic*, to deliver the Past. If the case is treated scientifically, the labour is easy, the throes natural, and the babe is born. The dear old lady, the Past, who is mother of us all, is soon "as well as could be expected," and receives the congratulations of her friends, and is told how well the little sonny looks—exactly like his "ma." So she cossets him up, nurses him, and gives him a Christian name. But if the case is *not* treated scientifically, the labour is long and difficult, the throes unnatural, and the sufferings atrocious; the poor old matron must smart under the forceps, perhaps submit to the Cæsarean operation, perhaps die; and the little monster who thus comes into the world by a matricide, is himself in a sad condition, and will have a sad remembrance all his life of the fact that he killed his mother.

Now, I think that we can deliver the Jewish Sabbath of a fine healthy Sunday, who will remember that he comes of a Hebrew stock on one side, but that mankind is his father, and while he labors for the human race, will never make mouths at the mother who bore him. But if the matter be delayed a few years, I think there is danger for the health of both child and mother.

I hope you will come to the Convention, and will speak, too. I mean to do so, but as I am not a bit of a Reactionist, and share none of the excesses of either party, I suppose I shall be too radical for the Conservatives, and too conservative for the Radicals, and so be between two fires, *cross*-fires, too.

An Anti-Sabbath Convention was held in Boston during the last week of March, 1848. The call for this meeting, written by Mr. Garrison, proposed the creation of a public opinion adverse to the penal laws requiring the religious observance of the Sabbath. This Convention sought to effect their repeal by the State Legislature, so that all persons might observe the day or not, in strict accordance with their conscience. There had been no particular enforcement of the Sunday Law to stimulate this meeting ; it was only another demonstration of the criticizing and protesting spirit which ruled at that period, before all reformatory interests became swallowed up in the magnitude of Anti-Slavery. Prison reform, anti-capital punishment, peace, non-resistance, temperance, and some more transitory subjects, struggled with anti-slavery to possess the public ear. These various meetings for reform were the most vigorous and attractive of all the May Meetings ; they had the best speakers, for they were countenanced by all the earnest and independent men. There was a passion for witnessing the powerful agitation of these great questions, which was not equalled by a passionate practical devotion to them. The causes themselves moved languidly, but so long as they were eloquently advocated there was no lack of audience. In this temper, any call, which involved a point that was debateable, might win a respectable hearing upon its abstract merits alone.

Mr. Parker signed this call, in company with all the prominent reformers of Boston and the State, and there was a two days' discussion of the origin, authority, and use of Sunday. Mr. Parker's speech, prefacing some resolutions, was filled with information : he objected to penal laws to enforce the formal observance of Sunday, but contended that many happy effects flowed from the custom of devoting one day to rest and to purposes of spiritual culture. His resolutions did not pass : they were not quite radical enough for the temper of the meeting. But his speech is remarkable for its common-sense.

Men commonly think they are never clear of one wrong till they have got the opposite wrong. So the Puritans, disgusted with the frivolity which they saw in the Romish Church—disappointed at finding in the Catholic Sunday, in its freedom and its frolic, so little for the direct nurture of religion—went over to the other extreme. That was a time of fanatical reaction against old abuses. There is no great danger of resisting a wrong too powerfully, but there is great danger of going over to the opposite wrong, and contending that that wrong is the right. I would not commit the same fault that the Puritans did, and go to the opposite extreme. If men are fanatical in their notion of keeping the Sunday, I would not be a fanatic and destroy it ; for, if men now are driven by the spirit of reaction against the Puritanic idea of the Sunday, and go to the opposite extreme, why, all the work must be done over again till it is well done.

I heard a man say, that if he had the whole of God Almighty's truth shut up in his left hand, he would not allow a man to unlock even his little finger. That is not my creed at all. I do not believe mankind is in the least danger of being ruined by an *excess of truth.* I have that confidence in truth, that I fear it not under any circumstances ; but I do fear error, whether coming from Churches, States, or majorities, or minorities, in the world.

When, at a later date, the community was vehemently agitated by the penal enactments against the selling of liquor, which passed the legislature notwithstanding a vigorous opposition, he preached a sermon upon the good and bad elements in the Maine * Law. That law prohibited the traffic in all kinds of drinks that intoxicate, affixed a penalty to each case of violation of the law, confiscated the property when it was found on sale, and authorized the destruction of the liquor. All previous laws upon this subject of the sale of liquors were merely regulative. This one was intended to destroy the traffic altogether, though it could not interfere with the use of liquor in private houses. Under its authority, State agents were appointed, who were empowered to keep stores for the sale of liquor for medicinal and mechanical purposes to all responsible persons, that is, to all those persons who were known by the agent not to be habitual drunkards. The name of every buyer, and the kind and quantity of liquor

---

* So called, because the first law of that kind was passed, and partially enforced, in the State of Maine.

he called for, was entered in a book.   The mechanic arts never
required so much spirit for employment in their various processes
as now, and the calls for medicinal purposes showed a sudden
and alarming deterioration of the public health.

This law went into operation in the State of Maine in the
spring of 1851, and was enforced with great vigour.   Steam-
boats were watched, and occasionally overhauled ; railroad sta-
tions were searched, all the dram-shops were closed, hotel bar-
rooms hid their diminished splendour in back-rooms, and the
whole traffic was driven out of sight, not without occasional
disturbances of the peace.   Common carriers contested the right
of the State to invade their parcels and vehicles, and the con-
stitutionality of the law was doubted by many who were not interested in the making or selling of intoxicating drinks.   Practically, little was gained, because the liquor degenerated in quality
as it ran out of sight, and rum-drinkers were poisoning themselves on the sly more rapidly than they did in gilded saloons.
The police occasionally laid a trap to procure evidence against
notorious dealers, and a race of informers began to spring up.
This odious feature, inseparable from the strict enforcement of all
sumptuary laws, increased the clamour of the disaffected, and
provided them with a good deal of magnanimous declamation.
Still, there can hardly be a doubt that a State possesses the
right to abate all nuisances, and seize or remove whatever is
destructive to the general health.   Tainted meat and young veal
are seized ; gambling and counterfeiting apparatus are looked for
by the police.   Bad rum and whiskey are more debasing than
counterfeiters' tools.   And if the State must support the hospitals, asylums, prisons, and almshouses which are so liberally
peopled from the frequenters of the drinking-shops, it might
rationally protect itself in some way against a traffic which
directly increased its burdens.   The whole difficulty lay in the
practical enforcement of a principle that seems abstractly just ;
so difficult, indeed, that it never became organized by permanent
effective operations.   Severity soon relaxed ; the police was, in
general, as unwilling to unearth rum-sellers, as it was in general
willing to help kidnappers, and the law fell into decay.

Mr. Parker had studied well the statistics of intemperance,
and understood and powerfully depicted its immoral effects.   See
his " Sermon of the Perishing Classes in Boston," and " A Sermon of the Moral Condition of Boston."   He never made use

of wine or ardent spirits, except by medical advice, after his
original vigor had become seriously impaired. He saw that the
great movement for total abstinence was saving many souls and
bodies; but he also saw that the question was wider even than
these wide and striking facts, and he treated it in his own way.

FROM THE JOURNAL.

The law seems an invasion of private right. It is an invasion, but
for the sake of preserving the rights of all. Wine is a good thing; so
is beer, rum, brandy, and the like, when rightly used. I think the teetotallers are right in their practice for these times, but wrong in their
principles. I believe it will be found on examination that, other things
being equal, men in social life who use stimulants moderately live longer
and have a sounder old age than teetotallers. I don't know this, but
believe it. I fancy that wine is the best of stimulants. But now I
think that nine-tenths of the alcoholic stimulant that is used is abused;
the evils are so monstrous, so patent, so universal, that it becomes the
duty of the State to take care of its citizens—the Whole of its parts.
If my house gets on fire, the bells are rung, the neighbourhood called
together, the engine brought out, and water put on it till my garret is a
swamp. But as I am fully insured I don't care for the fire, and I con-
tend that my rights are invaded by the engine-men and their water.
They say, "Sir, you would burn down the town!"

FROM A SERMON.

They burnt up a man the other day at the distillery, in Merrimack
Street. You read the story in the daily papers; and remember how
the bystanders looked on with horror to see the wounded man attempting with his hands to fend off the flames from his naked head! Great
Heaven! It was not the first man that distillery has burned up!
No: not by thousands. You see men about your streets all a-fire; some
half-burnt down; some with all the soul burned out, only the cinders
left of the man—the shell and wall, and that tumbling and tottering,
ready to fall. Who of you who has not lost a relative, at least a friend,
in that withering flame?

During the winter of 1847–8, he commenced a series of
Saturday afternoon conversations, which was attended chiefly by
the ladies of his parish, for theological and spiritual discussion.
He also organized a society, with the object of giving the people
to whom he preached an opportunity to practise philanthropy in
the streets and lanes of Boston, whence many a friendless and
tempted girl was rescued by their efforts, and provided with
honest work.

The Melodeon was left in August, 1851, for three or four
months, that some repairs might be made; and the Parish Committee applied for the Masonic Temple to hold their meetings in
for a few Sundays; but this was refused, "on the ground that

it would injure the reputation of the house." This result was
not unexpected by Mr. Parker, who only said, "All things have
their penalty. The jug of Boston is broken in more than one
place."

He spent the time of this enforced vacation in thinking out
new sermons :—

The germs, or thought-cells, have long been floating in my mind. I
hope, for the next five or six years, to have less to do with social, civil,
and political duties, and attend to my function as scholar, philosopher,
theologian, and writer. There is much that I want to do.

He occupied his leisure Sundays with a visitation of the
churches through all the denominations in Boston. This he
did to understand, by personal observation, what the various
clergymen were thinking about, and to note their tendency. He
heard, perhaps, twenty sermons by prominent men :—

Heard Starr King preach on the late Celebration * in Boston. It was
the best service, on the whole, that I have heard in the seventeen
services that I have attended lately in and about Boston.

Many Sundays of his successive summer vacations were thus
spent in hearing the different styles of preaching in the neighbourhood. His criticisms were in no case weakened by too
great partiality for the doctrine which the preachers represented.
Here is a specimen from the journal :—

Last day of my vacation (1856). Heard Rev. Mr. ——, of ——,
preach at the Old South, touching the "brazen serpent"— a silly,
worthless sermon, which, with that of —— last Sunday, makes me
think even worse of the ministry than before, which was needless. The
sermon had nothing of piety or morality ; the prayer scarce any touch
of either. What an admirable opportunity the minister has! An
audience which comes of its own accord to listen to the best words of
a free man on the greatest of themes! What use the minister makes
of it! I sat in the pew of a man who is engaged in the Chinese
(coolie) slave trade! The minister of the Old South Church is one of
the "No Higher Law" men—an advocate of slavery. The building is
historical ; and preached to me of the times that tried men's souls.

Aug. 23, 1852.—Two-and-forty years ago, my father, a hale man, in
his one-and-fiftieth year, was looking for the birth of another child
before morning,—the eleventh child. How strange it is, this life of
ours, this birth of ours, and this death—the second birth. How little
does the mother know of the babe she bears under her bosom—aye, of
the babe she nurses at her breast! Poor dear father, poor dear mother!
You little know how many a man would curse the son you painfully
brought into life, and painfully and religiously trained up. Well, I will

* Visit of the President of the United States, and visit of the Canadians, to Boston,
Sept. 17-19, 1851, to celebrate the Opening of the Grand Trunk Railroad into Canada.

bless you—true father and most holy mother were you to me: the earliest thing you taught me was *duty*—duty to God, duty to man; that life was not a pleasure, not a pain, but a *duty.* Your words taught me this, and your industrious lives. What would I give that I could have added some more of gladness to your life on earth—earnest, toilsome, not without sorrow!

As you look down from heaven, if, indeed, you can see your youngest born, there will be much to chide. I hope there is something to approve. Dear, merciful Father—Father God, I would serve Thee, and bless mankind!

Aug. 12, 1852.—One of the greatest advantages of a clergyman's life is this :—He has all his time devoted to the development and use of his noblest faculties. Men of science all come under this same obligation to a great degree; but they generally are devoted to matters of a purely intellectual discipline, not moral, not affectional, not religious. Doctors of medicine are an exception, and hence their superior *affectional* character; but, then, the sight of death tends, as Dr. B—— says, to make them think man is nothing but a "demnition body," and hence they are prone to materialism and lack *elevation* of intellect; but they have great tenderness of feeling.

They usually associate chiefly with well-cultivated and highly intellectual men. This is of great value to their *intellectual* development, but unfortunate for their *totality of manhood.* There would be no Kants, Leibnitzes (*Lieb-nichts,* a love-nothing, the Hamburghers called him), Voltaires, and Humes, and Hobbeses, with such as live in daily contact with the mass of men, women, and children. The good and ill of these men is apparent, and much comes of their position.

A clergyman must be a rare man to be intellectually great, or accomplish any great intellectual work. Schleiermacher, Luther, &c., had an *exceptional position,* which accounts for their exceptional character. But clergymen have a noble chance for a most manly development, if they will, and do not *herd too much with one another.* Even cabbages and lettuces do not *head* well if they touch. I am deeply grateful for the opportunity I possess, and know how much it increases my debt to mankind, and how it must be paid back.

Oct. 31.—Preached sermon on Mr. Webster—a sad and dreadful day to me: it was so painful to criticize him as I needs must. The preaching of the sermon occupied two and a half hours; it would have required three-quarters of an hour more to preach all that was written. At eleven o'clock, Wednesday, not a line of it was written; at two P.M. Saturday not a line unwritten.

In this short space of time, deducting some interruptions which he mentions, did he give shape and informing power to the materials and suggestions which he had been gathering concerning Daniel Webster for many years.

Nov. 14, 1852.—Preached the last sermon in the Melodeon. It has been a good place to us, and I feel sad at leaving it, though all the elements were hostile. I shall not forget the dark rainy Sundays when I first came, nor the many sad and joyous emotions I have felt there. Still, it was never quite so dear to me as the little church at Roxbury— my earliest one.

APPLE-TREE AND BENCH.

CHAPTER XI.

Exeter Place—The Country—Friendship—Pleasant Traits—Some Letters.

EXETER Place, into which the family moved, is terminated by a huge trellis, substantially built against the end wall of a house. This is covered by creeping plants, which take their rise in a diminutive railed space in the shape of a triangle, with a waterless fountain like an *epergne* in the centre. The end of the lane looks like a theatre-flat which has performed the garden-scene during several highly melodramatic seasons. A Flora stands there, as if for a label, to prevent misconception in the civic mind and to enforce rurality, which she does in melancholy fashion. It was a poor substitute for the woods and fields of West Roxbury. Mr. Parker languished for the natural scenes to which he had been from birth accustomed : next to books, they were essential to his comfort and happiness. He used to anticipate his summer vacations, when for several years the family would return to the house at Spring Street, with childlike delight ; every spring he began to time the blossoming of the shrubs and trees, and to tell over what he should be too late for and what he should find. It was a sore disappointment if he did not get out of town in season for the apple-blossoms, but his favourite walks and secluded spots for prayer and meditation remained to welcome the worshipper, and after he ceased to spend the summers in his old home, his occasional visits there were pilgrimages to a shrine.

Went over to West Roxbury to see the old familiar places—the dear old places! The seat under the willow was there just as I made it; the *Rudbeckia* was in blossom just as I planted it—the *hibiscus* where I set it. But the new proprietor has torn up the *sumachs* that I used to nourish with such care. I got some apples from the tree that I grafted —it was full of porter-apples, rather small, but fair.

Then there were the two favourite spots in the woods—the little *cosy place* under the cedars, where I have spent so many delightful hours : the favourite walk in the woods, with the *houseleek*, the *golden moss*, and the *peppermint* all there ; all the rest had died ; the rose-bush was gone, even the old pine was dead. I planted two peach-stones side by side, touching one another, and they, too, will come to nothing.

I went and gathered my favourite flowers in the old favourite locations, the *Houstonia recurvata*, &c. The trees have grown abundantly, all else looked natural, save the new division of some land; but a deal of sadness comes into the heart on visiting alone the places which are endeared by association with others, such as the rocks in the woods.

These were two large rocks in the precincts of Newton, upon land of the Brackett family. By dint of much heaving with a

THE ROCKS AT NEWTON.

crowbar, and by propping, Mr. Parker had succeeded in converting them into a pair of rude seats ; above them the summer trees whispered to his thoughts.

The dear old pines looked green as ever, and grew finely, heedless of the heads they shade; the tulip-trees have grown very big, and their leaves tinkle as sweetly as ever. The dear old church looked welcome and friendly. How I have loved it, and still love it!—but I hope I shall never preach there again, and get such a touch of the heart-break as the last time.

Here is a spring day during his residence in the old parish :—

May 3.—To-day has been one of those beautiful spring days when mere existence is a pleasure. The sun has been lovely, and a light wind from the south-west played among the pines, like the noise of the sea. As I sat beneath some cedar trees, the birds sang, the winds murmured, the bees hummed, and to show that the scene was human, a symbolical snake, more than six feet long, glided forth in the sun close to me. I felt my skin roughen up into little waves. I love to lie on the ground in such days, and dream under the clouds, and sleep. Beautiful dreams, native to the scene, start up in my slumbers, and when I awake are gone like the spring itself. It is a churlishness towards nature to sit indoors in such weather.

Spring in Boston.—May 19.—It has been one of the beautiful days we sometimes have in May: it is summer come in without singing at the door. The thermometer says 90° in the shade, yet all the morning the weather was perfect. Oh, how bright the sky was, and so deep the blue! Then the grass on the common was so green, the children so happy, and the dogs so delighted with their swim in the frog-pond. It did me good to see such a day; I feel in love with all creatures, and such as I love most I feel quite tender to—I long for their presence; for when I have anything so good as existence to-day I want to share it with one I love.

What a place the city is for outward action! But it is no place for thought, least of all for *poetic, creative* thought. This summer I hope to fill up my little cistern by intercourse with nature. How I long to sit down in the woods on my favourite rock, to gather the *lady's slippers* and *polygalla*—to get a *forget-me-not*, and to swim. Oh, the apple-trees, they are in blossom now! How grateful I feel for them! I hardly dare think how happy I am with them. But there is one thing which affects me more, a blossoming soul, especially a young woman, a girl. I thank God that one dear friend has children, and I can play with the little rogues. I love to have them call me Mr. Parkie—a tender diminutive, which does my dry heart good.

He cannot get out to West Roxbury for a week.

Again have I been cheated out of the apple-blossoms. I never lost them but once before, and that was last year, and I felt as if I lost the whole spring in consequence. But now they are gone again, and I have but had a glimpse of them, so the sweetest of blossoms *I have missed.*

His knowledge of the flowers and trees was extensive : he knew where to find all the lowly beauties of the New England woods and meadows, and could go to fetch them on the very day of their blossoming. "Leave some," he would say, however; "do not take all." In travelling, the aspects of nature challenged observation with his regards for men. He notices the grasses, and the weeds flowering by the hard causeway, the *lapis lazuli* of the lakes, the moraines, the ice-billows of the Mer de Glace, and the veined appearance of the ice itself, the rhododendrons, bluebells, and harebells which contest a patch of soil with the snow. He has an eye for the *Aiguilles*, huge monoliths of nature, and the Alpine church, mimicing them far below with its slender spire. He makes drawings of the roofs, cart-wheels, and women's caps; but his notices of nature never expanded into wilful description; for the commonest objects, which rhetoric makes ridiculous, gave him that sort of pleasure which a child enjoys when he runs to fetch the thing that delights him, or runs to bring somebody else to look. The sublime aspects of mountain scenery escape, in his hands, with a few abrupt word-tracings, mere mnemonics for renewed enjoyment after his return.

But he also went after things which escape through ordinary dredges.

> The quiet farmer tills his field,
> Joying in grass and wheat;
> Not knowing what his meadows yield
> Before my wandering feet.

All his compositions betray this deep and discriminating sympathy with nature. They frequently breathe the freshness of the open country, where shadows, like moods, sweep across the light and are chased by light in turn. You will stumble over little reminiscences of woody brooks, over which he used to hang in the June weather, letting the sinuous ripple fascinate his gaze. Only a boy born in and of the country could run with such clovery feet through the wastes of theology.

My father, a hale man of threescore, laid in the ground his own mother, fourscore and twelve years old. She went thither gladly, with no anguish, no fear, with little pain—went as a tall pine-tree in the woods comes to the ground at the touch of a winter wind, its branches heavy with snow, its trunk feeble, its root sapless, worn out, and old. . . . .
But if he lost a child, it was a sad day, a dark year; for the child perished immature. Sadly in June or July the gardener sees his unripe apples scattered on the ground, disappointing his hopes of harvest.*

---

* Sermons of Theism: "Economy of Pain," p. 309. And see, in "Providence," his minute description of that "great woodland caravansary," the oak-tree, p. 255.

Look up at the stars, study the mathematics of the heavens, writ in those gorgeous diagrams of fire, where all is law, order, harmony, beauty without end ; look down on the ant-hill in the fields some morning in early summer, and study the ethics of the emmets, all law, order, harmony, beauty without end ; look round on the cattle, on the birds, on the cold fishes in the stream, the reptiles, insects, and see the mathematics of their structure and the ethics of their lives; do you find any sign that the First Person of the Godhead is malignant and capricious, and the Fourth Person thereof is a devil—that hate preponderates in the world ? *

No doubt the Bible contained the imperfection of the men and ages concerned in writing it.   The hay tastes of the meadow where it grew, of the weather when it was made, and smells of the barn wherein it has been kept; nay, even the breath of the oxen housed underneath comes down to the market in every load.

Hark! the Bible rustles, as that southern wind, heavy with slavery, turns over its leaves rich in benedictions; and I hear the old breath come up again—"Thou shalt love thy neighbour as thyself."

How much a great man of the highest kind can do for us, and how easy!   It is not harder for a cloud to thunder than for a chestnut in a farmer's fire to snap.

Little boys in the country, working against time, with stints to do, long for the passing-by of some tall brother, who, in a few minutes, shall achieve what the smaller boy took hours to do.   And we are all of us but little boys, looking for some great brother to come and help us end our tasks.

This at my side is the willow ; it is the symbol of weeping, but its leaves are deciduous ; the autumn wind will strew them on the ground. And beneath here is a perennial plant; it is green all the year through. When this willow branch is leafless, the other is green with hope, and its buds are in its bosom.   Its buds will blossom.   So it is with America.

In a sermon upon speculative atheism is this mark of a nice observation :—

Convince me that there is no God—then I should be sadder than Egyptian night.   My life would be only the shadow of a dimple on the bottom of a little brook, whirling and passing away.

In his journal for 1857 occurs the following :

The night spreads her broad soft wings over me and all nature, and I feel inspiration in her presence.   What thoughts of other times come thronging upon me when I have lain, such nights as this, with the soft south-western wind sheeting gently through my half-opened

* "The Popular Theology," p. 107.

window, now listening to the hum of some far-off walker's voice, now letting my feelings take wing to the loftiest, till, lest I forget the body, my charm is pleasantly broken by the sound of an apple dropping softly to the ground.

He took pleasure in animals of every description, and was never tired of watching them. Bears were his especial delight : he said they were great humorous children, with a wary Scotch vein in them. His house was full of bears, in plaster and ivory, and wood, from Berne, and in seal-metal. It was a short and economical way to his heart to fetch him home an odder bear than usual. He once collected materials for an article on bears, and at that time he made the acquaintance of every brute bear between this and the White Mountains.

A French caricature from the Revolution of 1847–48, representing the different characters in the shape of bears, was given to him by Wendell Phillips, and straightway raised conspicuously above his bureau.

TO MISS CATHERINE JOHNSON.

Anti-Slavery Office, New York, 28 May, 1858.

MY DEAR COUSIN KATHIE,—The new bear came the other day—the famous new bear. I assembled all the other bears of the family, introduced them to each other, and left them in their mutual admiration society. You don't know how the little bears rejoiced to welcome this new one ! When the great original bear* came home, and went into the parlor, and saw all the household of bears assembled together and the new bear among them, great was her amazement thereat.

Many thanks for this bear, which, it is thought surpasses all the rest.

For the bears, faithfully,

COUSIN THEODORE.

When he passed through Berne upon his last journey, he spent a great portion of the time in leaning over the pit where the symbolical animals are kept, nor could he be got home to breakfast till he had duly fed them, and exhausted upon them his choicest ursine epithets.

Here is an allusion to another present :—

But the bear,—the *bear*. Why, it is a most admirable specimen of that genus—he stands now, hat in hand—that old slouch hat, such as none but a bear ought to have (I left *mine* at Desor's—I suppose he will wear it when he goes to meeting), and is looking at the brown bear which my wife always carries as one of the Penates of the family.

* "Bearsie" was a pet name for his wife.

Why, it is a perfect beauty; I shall be tempted to seal all my letters, but this to you will have the first stamp, to consecrate the seal.

Here is something upon hens :

FROM THE JOURNAL.

The hen has four notes. 1. She has a *common note*, and in it she speaks all day long to her little charge. She never tires ; cluck, cluck, by sunshine and in rain. Is her brood large, she does not despair. Is it small, she is still faithful in little as in much. So Providence ever watches over all men, great and little, and never wearies.

2. She has also a *special call*. This she uses when she discovers any corn of wheat, an insect, or a worm. The chicks come thronging in to share the bounty. So Providence sends us unusual favours.

3. She has a note of *alarm*. When the hawk or the weasel is at hand she utters a piercing scream; the young ones betake themselves to the nearest shelter.

4. She has a *brooding note*. At night and at noon, and often in the rain or the fierce heat, she calls her little ones under her broad motherly wings. With delicate beak she urges them beneath their shelter, and tucks them in. Then with a low, parental, purring note she lulls them to repose. It has a composing sound. At first they interrupt its tranquillizing monotony with sharp "zip," as one crowds upon the other, but soon all is still and they sleep.

So God broods over all His creatures. The voice of nature speaks softly in its brooding note.

HABITS OF BIRDS.—Wild geese will eat frogs. I saw a couple of tame ones attempt to catch a poor inoffensive frog in the brook to-day. I heard their voracious jaws snap together as they struck at the defence-less croaker, but he skipped away, laughing in his sleeve.

Saw two little birds on a pear-tree eating the little insects that prey on the blossoms. Thus both they and the insects aforesaid aid in consummating the mysterious marriage of the blossoms. I never knew whose matrimony the birds celebrated in their songs before.

He was never able to maintain any respectable sentiment for cathedrals, for the abject rows of the poor and ignorant upon the pavement were so many figures of the total waste in stone of their bread and education, and he believed that the only effect of magnitude and solemnity was to keep stupefied their poverty-stricken natures.

Here is an extract from a letter :—

I should like to look at the cathedrals once more. What grand things they are to look at, and to think of ! But they always struck me as great *tombs*. The men who built them are dead, and the soul which wrought in the builders now works at quite different things ; while the mob of people, and the mob of priests, seem quite unworthy to live in such a huge shell,—a caterpillar in the magnificence of a sea-conch. Pœstum is not deader to Europe, and further behind the civilization of this age, than the mediæval cathedral is behind the life of the more progressive people of New England.

The music has a soul in it; but that now-a-days is often operatic. Yet I love the simple grandeur of some of the great pieces I used to hear in the Italian Churches. There is one—I heard it many times—which seemed to represent the life of man : the top of it light, trifling, foamy, frothy, changeable ; but underneath it all, a great ground-swell of music went on as regular as the psalm of the ocean. It always reminded me of the hymn—

> " Our lives through various scenes are drawn,
>   And vex'd with trifling cares ;
> *While thine Eternal Thought moves on*
>   *Its undisturb'd affairs.*"

But his sympathy for men and women soared far above his feeling for nature, animate and inanimate, and for all the expressiveness of art.

This is the last day of my vacation—for though my preaching is put off another month, my study begins in earnest to-morrow. I miss much that belonged to me at West Roxbury, not to speak of the Human Face. I miss the sweet little spots which were to me my *oratoires* in the fields. There, too, I know every spot where the flowers grow, but here none at all.

This Human Face belonged to a very dear friend, but the phrase becomes impersonal when put on record, expressive of that broad world of kindred people whose horizons enclosed for him the brightening weather of friendship and spiritual delights. " Daylight and Champian" could not show him God's grace so clearly. It seemed to him wonderful what friends could do for a troubled and buffeted spirit.

How soon the memory is clear of disagreeable recollections, of pain, of suffering, of ugly things, and how perpetually do beautiful fancies and dear affections dwell with us ! It is only by effort that I recall the painful things of my life, and when they come back, it is " trailing clouds of glory " that they come. And there is one face in my past life which comes with all the beauty of a new moon, the few hours of her brief sun on a June evening after a shower,—as the moon with the evening star beside her.

1.

> Oh, blessèd days were those,
>   When thou and I together,
> Sought through the fields the wild red rose,
>   In the golden summer weather !

> The lilies bloom'd at morning's glow
>   On the breast of the winding river :
> I brought to thee their purest snow,
>   Less welcome than the giver.

20

2.

There's beauty in the morning flowers,
  And in the noon-day sun;
Time measures out these golden hours
  With the fairest sands that run.

I know not what it signifies,
  But a single look from thee
Comes fresher than the morning skies
  Or noonday light to me.

Oh, people thou my thoughts by day,
  Adorn my dreams by night;
So cheer my sadden'd heart alway,
  By faith when not by sight.

His susceptibility in the society of women to that influence of mind and presence which they have in the society of men whom they attract, was a very decided characteristic. That subjective quality of sex, which the poet calls *Das ewige weibliche* (the everlasting womanly), and which sustains the everlasting difference between woman and man, that draws and piques them both, drew him along, a most willing captive, held and led by all the pure and gentle elements of his own nature.

My companions of choice, and not necessity, are almost all women. I wonder at this; I never willed it so. I have always been intimate with eminent women,—that is, for nearly twenty years; and I number but few eminent men among my acquaintance. Yet in literature, I am no great admirer of the efforts of women. Mrs. Hemans and Margaret Fuller are the only learned women that adorn my book-shelves; among my correspondents, ladies fill a large place. Is it their affection or the beauty of their mind that attracts me to them? The beauty of the person was once a dear attraction, and has lost none of its charms even now. I love to look at a handsome woman. Her beauty has a subtle fascination for me which my weak intellect does not quite understand. I love the subtlety of woman's mind, in striking contrast to my own direct and blunt modes of mental operation. Thus, I love the nimble adroitness of Mrs. H—— and Mrs. A—— much better than the Macedonian-phalanx march of good Miss ——. I like not this dazzling subtlety in men.

Strong is the effect of this diversity of sex; I like the presence of woman, as such. I love to feel the presence of incarnated womanliness.

The other day I met a young woman in the street, and our *eyes met*. I felt a sensation of unspeakable delight which lasted all the morning. I cannot tell why it was, but so it was. It was involuntary delight.

This has been one of my unfortunate days. I went out to Roxbury, but saw not the chief object of my visit. She had gone to visit a sick friend. It makes me better to see her; it is like visiting a shrine which has the gift of miracles, and heals men of sadness, lowness and despair. So I visit my *Madonna Miraculosa* from time to time, and

come home a better man, I hope, certainly with each faculty bright-
ened and enlarged. I barely missed her on the return, for the wagon
was in sight just as I got into the 'bus to come away. But, well, I
shall take as penance and mortification what I receive with sorrow ;
and if angels' visits be few and far between, will make much of the
angel that I missed.

He made the following confession to George Ripley :—

There was a pond a mile off (in Lexington), whither I used to go a-
fishing, but only caught the landscape. I never fished much, but
looked down into the water and saw the shadows on the other side
creep over it, and listened to the sounds from the distant farms. When
I was from six to seven years old, there came a perfectly beautiful
young girl to our little District School ; she was seven to eight. She
fascinated my eyes from my book, and I was chid for not getting my
lessons. It never happened before—never after the little witch went
away. She only stayed a week, and I cried bitterly when she went off.
She was so handsome, I did not dare speak to her, but loved to keep
near her, as a butterfly to a thistle-blossom. Her name was Narcissa.
She fell over into the flood of time, and vanished before I was seven
years old.

TO MISS HUNT.

24th August, 1853.

Dear Sarah,—It is very kind in you to wish me all the sweet and
beautiful things which came in your note. I wish I was worthy of
half the affection you feel for me, and have so often shown.

But I will try to be nobler, and deserve it better.

I believe no man ever was more blessed with the affectionate friendship of men and women than I am. I often wonder at it. For to my
theological and political foes, I appear as one of the most hard and
unfeeling of this world's wretches. But perhaps, there is some " silver
lining " to this ragged cloud, and the dear eyes of some kind women
turn to it, and make sunlight there.

I thank you many times for all the kindly sympathy you have shown
me, and the strength you have given.

So every blessing on you, and good bye. **T. P.**

You forgot to send the customary kisses, but I will call to-morrow,
and take them.

Birth-days and anniversaries seemed as impressive to him as
they do to a child. Every year underscored them afresh with
tender thoughts and holier wishes : the date of his leaving home,
of his sister's death, of his ordination, of his South Boston sermon,
of his settlement in Boston—all the days whose date hope or trial
had deepened, moved his heart with grateful awe at the mystery
of life, as when the great bodies of the sky roll, faithful to a
moment, out of absence into our expecting gaze. So he used to
ask his friends to tell him their birth-days, and some of these he
had set apart for simple observance in his house. In the same feeling
he received the gifts and mementoes of his parish or of friends.

Gifts which he received from members of his parish always drew from him some half-surprised recognition.

Dec. 24, 1853.—Had a family gathering of sixteen persons—all ages, from eighty-five to four. Isaac and I, the last of eleven children.

In the morning, to my great surprise, came a piano. Not one of the company could play on it. But it speaks to me continually of the old sad times, when men who aspired to teach mankind, paid for it with their lives. I will try to be a nobler man, to deserve all the kindness which shows itself more tenderly than in gifts.

What a comfort it is to have about you the mementoes of dear ones when they are absent! I am surrounded by the gifts of tender friends. I wipe my pen on the gift of one ; the pen itself a remembrance of another ; a third gave me the lamp which shines on my writing tonight. The spectacles beside me are the gift of a fourth person ; the little delicate glass-wiper came from a dear old lady ; the portfolio is from one hand now still in the grave ; the *presse-papier* is also a gift ; the knife in my pocket, and the pencil, the basket which holds my letters, the seal I stamp them with, are from a most welcome and dear soul ; even the chair I sit in, and the ornament beside me, is from that fountain of friendship ; the little porcelain vase which holds remembrancers, the sweetest and daintiest flowers in their season, is from the same friendship ; and tender mementoes of affection, there are, too dear almost to name. But what are all these things to the living person ? They are steps in the ladder of love. Affection mounts up, and if the throne be vacant—what emptiness !

I found the wild rose in blossom to-day for the first time this season, and the white azalea, and sent them off to a friend to whom I love to consecrate the first flower of each pretty kind that I gather, and have done so for many a year.

These things are picked up on the field that shook with his polemic tread, across which liberating truths bore their sparkling scorn against oppression. The gentle tokens strew it far and wide.

> " The bravest are the tenderest,
>   The loving are the daring."

Here are lines amid notes of an excursion to the White Mountains :—

> When sunder'd far from one so near
>   My fancy fetches thee ;
>   And to my soul's society
> I welcome thee most dear.
>
> And often as I walk along,
>   The sweetest sense of thee,
>   Comes trickling down my memory,
> And I run o'er with song.
>
> More keen am I for God in prayer,
>   To find myself with thee ;
>   For in that high society,
> Thy spirit seems to share.

No friends ever received such a generous measure of appreciation as his ; yet it was not, as might be suspected, because they were not his enemies, but because the same sincerity which loved them knew also their faults. He spoke of these things to them, like a frank child, and if they proffered the same courtesy in return, in a clear spirit, free from reproach, he was always gratefully surprised.

One day, in quoting the following lines, he adds a commentary which expresses his method of dealing with his friends :—

> " Man muss um gut zu seyn,
> Um jede Pflicht der Menschheit zu erfüllen,
> Nur eine Kunst, die schöne Kunst verstehen,
> In jede Menschenbrust *das Gute nur zu sehen.*"[*]

Now, this is partly true; but let us know the whole that is in man, and then honour him *spite of his faults.* No doubt it is a hard thing to love John and Peter with all their faults. But it must be so.

REQUISITES OF FRIENDSHIP.—I am not exactly perfect myself, but I should be glad to have perfect friends—men without conceivable fault or blemish. Yet, as such are not given on earth, perhaps not in heaven, I am glad to take men as I find them. I don't find it necessary to conceal my friends' imperfections; I like them in spite of their faults, not because they are faultless. I should be sorry if my friends found it necessary to render me perfect before they could love me. I am willing to acknowledge their errors, and still to love what remains unsullied.

In 1859 he writes to a friend :—

Nothing surprises me so much as to find how many persons *love* me, not only in New England, but in Old England, and also in Germany. Rejoice with me.

Though he longed to be on good terms with all people, and had a tender vein which would have betrayed a smaller person into transient, destructive partialities, yet justice meted out all his dealings, and he wanted nothing but conscience to rule between him and his friend.

Oct. 12, 1839. C——'s visit was an April shower to me. It has made me flowery and young again. I cast off my years as if upon a summer's day in the green meadows gathering flowers. He has awakened the slumbering love of song in me. Oh, I love C——! he is so good, so rich, so full of spontaneous fellowship with all that is noble. Yet he is not a man whom the world will use well. So let it be. He that hath the joy of his genius, let the world wag as it will for him.

[*] Would you be good, and fill each human duty ?
One art's enough for that—the finest art—
See but the good in every human heart.

Miss P——— came to spend the Sabbath with us. Her magnanimity almost surpasses conception, or, rather, she has no magnanimity; it is all great-heartedness, and she never dreams that she exercises the virtue of magnanimity.

Her kindness is inexpressible. How much love the divine woman has! It is her life. How disinterested, too! Oh, the perfection of woman's heart—and sometimes the depravity of woman's heart!

What shall I say of ———? I grieve to say what I *must* say. I did not think that religion had softened a spirit naturally so austere, nor that charity had tempered a character so selfish and tyrannical by birth. I did not dream those silken cords had joined her so softly to the sky. But I did dream that considerations of prudence, suggestions of the understanding, not a little experience of the world, and a very subtle mind with considerable insight into first principles, had done the work as well as such agents could effect it. Now I see my mistake. Nor that alone, but my old rule, to which, in her case, I was making a conjectural exception—that religion alone can regenerate a spirit at first ill-born—holds good. After wandering some thirty years in the Saharas and Siberias, the Englands and Egypts of life, finding a sad mingling of earth and heaven, to see one of vast gifts of intellect, great and diversified culture in elegant letters and the arts, of deep experience in the detail of life, one tried by suffering, mind and body —to see such a one giving way to petty jealousies, contemptible lust of power, and falling into freaks of passion, it is ludicrous first, and then it is melancholy.

It is not for me to forgive anything. Thank God, I have no occasion; but it is for me to pity and to mourn. It is for me to show others the only salvation for themselves.

About 1840, Miss Burley told me of the fine genius and finer moral endowments of Mr. Cheney. He made some crayons for her family then, which I admired much. In 1841–2, Mr. G. Russell sat in another artist's room, and heard a conversation in the next apartment relative to the sermon of the " Transient and Permanent in Christianity." One was attacking it and its author; Mr. R., learned that the defender was Mr. Cheney, an artist with fine genius. I was surprised to find an artist who thought enough about religion to venture from the beaten path of theology, and still more to find he was from the heart of Connecticut. In 1842 or 1843, I went and introduced myself, and asked him to make a portrait of Lydia, but he was just going to Europe. I met him in Rome, and we had many good times together. In 1851, I thought that he was to marry E. L., but said nothing until the engagement took place; then I told him of it. It pleased him much that my feeling had indicated what his had told him before. I helped marry them, May 19, 1853. He painted Lydia's and my portrait the following autumn.* Now he is dead. I went to Manchester, Conn., to attend his funeral, to-day (Sept. 12, 1856), my wife's birthday. He was not quite forty-six. A dear, noble man of genius.

Mr. Cheney owed the awakening of his religious life to Mr.

---

* This was a labor of love which Mr. Cheney would insist upon performing.

Parker's influence, which cleared away a good deal of inherited rubbish, and set his pure and lofty soul open to the light. We shall never know all whom he thus liberated, to whom he gave righteousness for doctrine.

When Mr. Desor, the accomplished naturalist, was in America, he was a welcome guest at the house in Exeter Place, for he brought what Mr. Parker always craved, facts, fruitful suggestions, systematic views, a great familiarity with many provinces of science. Seldom has a man better equipped with knowledge, or with a finer capacity for sure and careful synthesis, come from the Old World to lend his talent to the New. But he brought also a pure heart, simple habits, great personal integrity. These qualities were more welcome to the preacher and doer of righteousness than all his scientific attainments, and they became most intimate and dear to each other. It was a dark day to Mr. Parker when Desor felt obliged to return to Europe.

It is pleasant to remember that we, at least, have always appreciated him, have always been friendly to him ; and nothing has ever occurred, in nearly five years' acquaintance and almost four years of intimate friendship, to cause the least regret. He has always been on the humane side, always on the just side. His love of truth, and sober industry, his intuitive perception of the relations of things, his quick sight for comprehensive generalizations, have made me respect him a good deal. His character has made me love him very much. There is no man that I should miss so much of all my acquaintance. I count it a privilege to have known him, and it will be a joy to remember him.

Travellers and exiles from all lands reported themselves early at the house of the man of whose humanity and love for liberty they had heard. Exiles especially, who were generally cultivated and enlightened men, with patriotic reasons for expatriation, received a fraternal welcome. He obtained employment for many, was ready with pecuniary assistance to the extent of his means, and only levied a toll upon the knowledge of the applicants. But they could never smuggle anything intelligible past his scrutiny into the country. Of one he learned the latest speculations of comparative philology ; of another, the state of religion ; of another, curious facts of physiology ; of another, popular statistics ; of another, information concerning professors and public men. He knew how to find, across the disabilities of various languages, the precise *forte* and vocation of all these talented men. Notes of conversations are recorded which were carried on in five or six different languages in the same evening company. But he did not speak any foreign language with fluency.

TO REV. S. J. MAY.

June 17, 1851.—I have just had a letter from Dr. Otto Fock, Professor of Philosophy at Kiel, in Denmark, who wants to come to America. He is about forty years old, learned and able, but, alas! a republican. He cannot live in Germany : the police look after him too sharp. Can we do anything for him here? He is learned and industrious; will *work*. Can we find a place worthy of him? He has written a valuable book—History of "Socinianismus." Perhaps he might write an "excellent t-r-a-c-t" for Father B—, or prove that the Apostle Thomas was a Unitarian, or if not Thomas, then, at least, Jude or Judas.

Besides Dr. F., another German Doctor of Philosophy has written for the same purpose, to find a home in America. He is a philologian, Dr. Lobeck, from Königsberg, a learned man, librarian of the University at that place. He has written some books, and has been an editor of a *Volksbote* (" People's Messenger,") and is a democrat. Do tell me if we can do anything for these noble-hearted men

TO HON. GEORGE BANCROFT.

Boston, March 1, 1852.

DEAR SIR,—I am waiting impatiently for your new book; if it is not the finest piece of historical composition in the English language, I shall never quite forgive you; for then it will not fulfil the prophecy I have often made. But I write now about other matters. There is a noble German *Gelehrte*, Dr. Günther, from Leipsic, about to establish a school for boys, at Newport, and I wish you to send him your little folks. Dr. G. is a very accomplished man—a great *Historiker* and *Philolog*, and a true gentleman. He was one of the Frankfurt Parliament men ; is now in exile, and has been teaching Danish, Swedish, Icelandish, and old Gothic, in Boston this winter. Please remember him, and not forget   Truly yours, THEO. PARKER.

When one or two intimates, who were good listeners, and knew what to expect, came into his study, he would turn towards them from his desk, dropping instantly the care of the moment, to set forth in racy flow, as if the business of the week were to anticipate and enjoy this visit in particular. No matter what lay upon the desk—Welsh Laws—History of Canon Law —a volume of Littrè's Hippocrates—a heap of authorities for an article—or sheets where a sermon was just on the turn of a wave, with whose break the Music Hall should echo,—he would start with the matter which he had in hand, as if you came to see him about it, and thence find his way into a most delightful monologue, which lasted, with occasional runlets from the listeners, as long as they had the hardihood to remain. It was neither metaphysical nor theological, had no didactic malice, and was not oppressively bent upon convincing. You would say it was a reverie, speaking aloud before he knew it, if it were not for the pleased recognition of your presence. As it went on, he would

make such compact and portable statements of whatever subject
happened to be caught up, that you felt for your pencil and note-
book. It seldom failed to draw in his humor, which was an
inexorable common-sense at play, engaged mischievously in stealing the clothes away from some skeleton doctrine, or the rouge
and false teeth from some mediæval spinster of the popular
churches. And it was none the worse for a touch or two of
mimicry, just enough to let a person here and there appear to
color the bigotry or the foolishness,—not to make you despise
whomever you recognized, it was too genial for that, and impersonal, like an improvisatore. If a phantom of some "fee grief"
swept across the surface, and chilled it for a moment, it was soon
gone; you had hardly begun to feel uneasy. It was let out by
his absolute sincerity, which was the only patrol he had around
his wealth and beauty: as ineffective as the broad bright meadows of Conway to repress the mountain streams. And how
you rejoiced that he was incapable of secrecy when some feeling
of Religion, that almost prayed in the deepening voice, some
personal conviction of his own immortality, or of the universal
love which his faith seemed to draw and condense for you in that
book-lined study itself, as if to dim its titled wisdom, took advantage of his life's obedience to endow your morning call.

It was also a good thing to find him in the cars, going to or
returning from his lectures in the East or West. He was never
so deep in his carpet-bag of books as to miss the opportunity for
some gentle and courteous word. He often would approach
women who appeared to be plunged in sorrow, to befriend them
with good words and offices. At the end of one of these jour-
neys he said :—

"Now, I have given up my seat to several women, fed babies with
candy, and made myself agreeable, and nobody but an old squaw with
a load of baskets has recognized it. And she only touched her hat."

He liked to draw bright-looking young men into conversation,
and sometimes in this way has given determining courses to
vague and restless lives. He was very sharp to see who might
be helped in this way. In his carpet-bag he always carried a
little silk bag of comfits for the restless children, and thought it
no loss of time from his book to leave his seat and win them
back to quiet.

It was one of the greatest and most real sorrows of his life
that he had no children. He was capable, as few men are, of

guiding children towards the Blessed Life. He had all which a child needs—love, simplicity, contempt for doctrinal views, wonder and awe for natural marvels, and none for ecclesiastical, an intense sympathy with the "joys of mere living," a genius for truthfulness. He could never conceal that he languished for the society of children.

At one time in our life we need objects of instinctive passion, then objects of instinctive affection. Neither can take the place of the other, and both are needed for the welfare of man. But how many are destitute of both, in the present state of society! I suffer continually from lacking an object of instinctive affection. I want a little *Mites o' Teants*, or *Bits o' Blossoms*.* I nursed my affections for Mr. Russell's little ones, till the affections grew to a great growth. Now there are no objects for them to cling to. So my vine trails on the ground, and earth-worms devour the promise of the grape.

Oct., 1856.—But my immediate help I find in industry—literary and philanthropic work. Yet even with that help, in the pauses of my toil, the sense of loneliness comes over me and fills me with pain. How much worse must it be with women, and especially *the unmarried!* With women the love of children is stronger than with men, and they have fewer external duties to divert their thoughts from their own sadness.

A neighbour, and member of his parish, sends in joy to tell him of the birth of a child. He thus replies, addressing the father and mother :—

I thank you for so kindly remembering me in such an access of new gladness to your hearth and hearts—nay, heart, for there is but *one,* especially at such a time, in man and wife. I have sons and daughters, sympathetically, in the good fortune of my friends. I was expecting to hear of this advent in your family. God bless the little immortal, who comes a new Messiah to cheer and bless the world of home.

Here is another reply, made on a similar occasion :—

It is my lot to have no little darlings to call my own. Yet all the more I rejoice in the heavenly blessings of my friends. The thing that I miss most deeply in coming from Roxbury to Boston is the society of my neighbours' little children, whom I saw several times a day, and fondled, and carried, and trotted, and dandled, in all sorts of ways, as if they had been mine own.

Well : God bless the life that is given, and the life that is spared, and the life which rejoices in them both ! I thank the new mother for remembering an old friend in *such* an hour. So give her my most affectionate greetings, and believe me, happily, yours.

These letters to the Rev. Wm. H. White, his old teacher, now deceased, come from a warm and faithful heart. It need not be

* Pet names for the children of his dear neighbours.

told here in what way, more substantial than by letter-writing, he befriended his teacher's family, and for years supplied a generous culture to his daughter.   And that is only one instance of Mr. Parker's beneficence, out of which pure pleasures flowed for him every year:—

West Roxbury, 26th March, 1846.

DEAR FRIEND,—I found your letter in the Boston Post-Office yesterday, and thank you most heartily for remembering an old scholar who has never thought of you but with gratitude and affection. I supposed you had forgotten me, or I should have sent you my little publications before. I did not know that you would take an interest in one whom you so much befriended twenty-five years ago. But, trust me, I have inquired all about you with the greatest interest. If the *boy* Theodore was affectionate, I think you will find the man is the same old sixpence. I may be "*proud*" and very "*wicked*," for aught I know; I will not say I am not—you shall come and see—but at least I do not forget my old teacher. I passed through your town once, on a rainy day, with three ladies in a coach I did not pass within a mile of your house, to my great disappointment; but I learned of your welfare from one of your parishioners whom I found in the way. Once since I passed, in the Rail Road I think, through Littleton. Otherwise I was never in your town. You inquire after my doings, &c. I have been married almost nine years, but have no children. This is the only affliction of my life almost. But I never complain of that, for I am a singularly happy man. You shall ask my wife if I *love* her—or shall see her, and then guess. I think my neighbours love me—I know their children do. I have been nearly nine years in this place, and think I have but one *enemy* in it—that is a dog whom I never treated ill, but give a bone to now and then. Still, he growls at me, and *bit* me the other day: since that time I have given him over as not to be overcome by me. I think he is the only thing living that owes me a *personal* spite. I had rather have the affection of good plain folks, like my neighbours, than all the fame of Luther and the power of Napoleon. As for my *theology*, it has grown out of *me* as unavoidably as my arm has grown with my body. I think it a Christian theology, and a true one. Doubtless there are errors connected with it: I will gladly cast them away, soon as I find them *errors*. Yet I think there are truths also which will not perish; still, I am but a very humble seeker after truth. That you may judge for yourself, I will leave for you, at Munroe's book-store, a copy of all my works, which I beg you to accept as a humble token of esteem from an old pupil, though it may be an unworthy one. I remember how it grieved me once to get a spot on *your* Latin Grammar (Smith's N. H. Lat. Gram.), on the pronoun *ille, illa, illud,* which you kindly lent me. I hope you will take my gift as a return for the damage I did your book. I wanted to send you the first thing I ever published, and all since, but I feared you would not care for it, and so, through sheer modesty, have been thought *proud.* You ask for my sister—she has passed on where she belonged; so have all my sisters. Out of eleven children, three only are left—my brother Isaac, at Lexington, whom you never knew; my brother Hiram, at Lowell, whom you remember; and *myself*. The red-dish haired girl you mention was only a friend; she became *almost* a sister, but not quite, and has gone I know not where. I have not seen your face since you were at a school-examination in Lincoln. Then you sat down beside me, and did not know me! I cried all night at the thought of it, and weep a little now in sympathetic recollection. If you ever come this way, it will gladden my heart to see you. Next winter I shall live in Boston, and will entertain you hospitably, if you will visit your "dear old pupil,"   T. P.

TO THE SAME.

Boston, 14th March, 1848.

DEAR FRIEND,—It was not I that sent you the sermon on J. Q. Adams, so you have one friend that you did not think of. I sent none of those copies of the sermon. One of these days I think I shall print the sermon myself, in a more full and complete form, and shall then be happy to send it to you. You object to the "Cohasset Rocks;" the words were not in the MS., but I selected the figure at the moment, and for this reason: I once went a-fishing with Mr. Adams (and others) on the Cohasset Rocks. They are large, and extend a long way on the coast, and are much assailed with storms. Everybody at Boston knows the Rocks, and Mr. A. often went down there, and so they were in my mind *connected* with him. I prefer the "Cohasset Rocks" in such a connection to "Gibraltar," because they are an object well known, and the other not well known by the sight. If I were to speak of birds in a sermon, I should not mention the night-ingale and the skylark, but the brown thrasher and the blackbird, for the same reason. I am glad you like the sermon: it is the only pro-duction of my pen that I have heard *praised* more than *blamed*. It has been *popular*, if you will believe it. I know not why, and do not know whether it is to my credit or otherwise, that it is so. You were kind enough to say it had not *my usual faults of style*, or *of thought*. I thank you for the frankness of the statement. I have always been most grateful to persons who made me ashamed and not satisfied. If you tell me what are my usual faults of style and of thought, you will do me a great service. I never sought praise so much as perfec-tion, and shall be very grateful to you if you will do me that kindness. *Fas est et ab hoste doceri*, but my *hostes*, though numerous enough, have done me little good by their criticisms: you were an early friend, and did me a great service once. Why won't you do me a greater one now? Once, when I was a little bit of a boy, in the *old* school-house on the *north* side of the road in Lexington, the first winter that you taught a school there, one of your acquaintance told my sister that you had spoken of me to her at a party the night before. "Well," said I to my sister, "what did he say?" She returned, "He said that he was disappointed in Theodore; they told him he was 'a smart boy,' and he found him a *good* one, and put him upon Latin, but he would not study; he did not get along well, was lazy, and loved play better than his book. He was sorry he had put him into Latin," &c., and I was eight years old, turning to nine. I went off and cried awhile—that I had disappointed *you*, whom I loved with all my might;

but the next day you had to take it, the lesson was the verb *sum*, and
its compounds, in " The N. H. Latin Grammar." I recited six times
that forenoon. It was Saturday, and you heard *me* when I had anything to say, and asked me repeatedly *what had got into me.* I didn't
tell you, but thought *you knew.* The next day my sister, who had seen
what took place, told me that you had never said so of me, but quite differently. Well, the impulse lasted, and I remember well that I repeated
all the rules in the Syntax (I think they were eighty-four) without
prompting or without a question being asked me. So much for your
criticism *then.* Now, I think it might do me *more* good, for certainly I
am quite as humble as then. So let me have the criticism. I sent
you a sermon this morning before receiving your letter, and am truly
your old pupil and present friend,

THEO. PARKER.

TO THE SAME.

Boston, 13th May, 1851.

MY DEAR OLD MASTER,—It was very kind of you to write me such a
nice, good, generous letter the other day. Trust me, your words of sympathy and of esteem are very dear to me, and your words of rebuke, of
caution, of warning are as dear and as much valued. I love most
those that are so sincere as to tell me of my faults, and shall always
value your admonitions as much as when you gave them to me
over a little Latin Grammar, in the little black school-house at Lexington. You have forgotten that you once rebuked me for asking to have
the same thing explained twice. I met, in " Historia Sacra," the word
avulsum, and asked you what it came from. You showed me *avello* in
the dictionary; but the next day, or the next week, I met the same
avulsum again, and asked the same question a second time. You told
me " I showed you that the other day." " I know it, sir, but I have
forgotten it." " You must not forget it again," said you, and showed
me *avello* for the second time. Well, I will try and profit by a rebuke
now as much as then. So if you will always point out my *faults,* while
you commend any excellence you may discover or imagine, I shall rejoice, and will try and mend.

I had hoped to see you at your own house long before this, but much
work forbids; still I hope to see you at mine on Anniversary Week.
With best regards to you and yours, believe me your old pupil and
hearty friend,

THEO. PARKER.

TO THE DAUGHTER.

Newton Corner, 21 Sept., 1853.

MY DEAR MISS WHITE,—I thank you for the tender letter you wrote me
about your late lamented and beloved father. I have been living out of
town all summer long, and seldom see a minister, and never a theological newspaper; and still more, at the time of your father's departure I
was absent on a little journey. After I wrote the letter, as I went in
to Mr. Crosby's to leave the book for your father, Mr. C. asked me if I
did not know that Mr. White was dead. It came upon me with entire
surprise. I knew from his last letter to me that he was ill, but I heard

afterwards that he was better, that he preached as usual, and supposed the sickness was all over. Judge. then. of my surprise when informed of his departure to a fairer world. But my letter was in the post-office, and perhaps already on its way. I could only wait till some one should reply to it.

How much I lament now that I have never been to Littleton to see him! But, in a life a good deal too busy for the delights of friendship, even when friends are within "ten minutes' walk," I never found just the right time when I could go as well as not, but continually put off the pleasure against a more "convenient season." Several days this summer I fixed for visiting him, but something always prevented. Now, the good man has outgrown my friendship. I have always felt a great veneration for him. such as I felt for but few men. He was a most excellent teacher, taking a school at Lexington (my father was the school committee-man who engaged him) when it was in a sad condition, and improving it quite surprisingly. He filled his pupils with a love of study. I know not why, but in a little country school he set me to study Latin. I went through the Latin Grammar, and began to construe " Historia Sacra" the first winter, and finished it the next, and began the Greek Grammar. The school lasted only twelve or thirteen weeks. I shall never cease to be grateful to him for all the kindness he showed me, and the gratuitous interest he took in my studies, for it was no part of his duty to teach a boy Latin.

He lent me his Latin Dictionary, a copy of Young's Latin Dictionary, a book which I lock up to with great respect. This is the only copy of that dictionary that I ever saw; it has long been out of print, replaced by better works, but the old well-worn copy he lent me lives in my memory as a sacred *memorial* connected with the remembrance of one I hold so dear. He taught school for us at Lexington two winters, then he found a better place for the next winter, at Lincoln. I was sick in the autumn after his second winter, and one day, as I was better, and out of danger, one of the neighbours told me that "Master White ain't a-going to keep the school this winter." I turned my face to the wall and wept aloud, and would not be comforted.

He endeared himself to the hearts of all his scholars, and of their parents too. Two years ago, I went up to Lexington to dedicate a new and handsome school-house on the very spot where he first taught, and it did my heart good to recount the valuable services of your father and his successor, Mr. Fiske, also from Lincoln, in the little, mean, and uncomfortable house which was there thirty years before. Some of his scholars were present, and approved the statements; but most of them have already passed on in the road which he has now traversed. I only lament that I never visited him in his own house. From Mr. Emerson and Mrs. Ripley I have often heard accounts of his excellence as a minister, as a husband, and a father, Mr. Pearson also has been abundant in his praise: others that I have seen confirmed to me what I suppose the "daily beauty of his life" sufficiently attested to you. I thank you for writing me the account of his last moments, full of a tender interest and melancholy to me. Yet there is a triumph in the death of such a man. I wish he could have been spared longer, but it is well to die in " God's time," and he rests from his labours. I dedicated the little volume of sermons,* which I wrote about, to him and Mr. Fiske. I am sorry he could not have known it. The dedication was printed before he ceased to be mortal.

Present my kindest consolations to your mother, and believe me, with respect and affection, truly yours,

THEODORE PARKER.

Here is part of a letter to Miss Margaret Fuller, written in 1841 :—

Touching the article (for the *Dial.*) I think I shall finish it before Wednesday, for there are two working days, and still more, two working nights, 'twixt us and that time. My design was to have finished it on Saturday, and then come to perpetrate a long-contemplated visit upon you, Monday evening. But thought would not flow smooth, and I made small progress last week, for my brain was dull (I never write well when Mrs. Russell or Lydia are out of the neighbourhood), and it would not go forward.

Herewith I send you a couple of little bits of verse, which I confess to you, *sub rosâ rosissimâ*, are mine. Now, I don't think myself made for a poet, least of all for an *amatory poet*. So, if you throw the " lines " under the grate in your critical wisdom, I shall not be grieved, vexed, or ruffled; for though I have enough of the *irritabile* in my composition, I have none of the *irritabile vatis*.

FROM THE JOURNAL.

Went to New York to see the Hunts and Apthorps embark for Europe in the *Arago*. It is sad to think of it, but they mean to stay three years (365 × 3 = 1095.. 52 × 3 = 156)! It is appalling to think of. Objects of affection I miss more than all others, and they are also objects of intellectual and other excitement and delight.

A week or two after this he went out to West Roxbury to look up the favourite spots and solicit their refreshment. But another very dear friend was absent from her home for the season, and the visit was a failure :—

> Unheeded grow the precious flowers,
>   No eye woos now their beauty :
> I only came in plaintive hours
>   To strengthen for sore duty ;
>
> But the new sadness of the place
>   Upon my heart is stealing :
> Nature without that July face
>   Will paralyze my feeling.

The departure of his friend has done an injury to all the associations of his old home. The altar remains, but he cannot

---

* Sermons of Theism, Atheism, and the Popular Theology.

muster heart enough to perform the simple rites of friendship :—

> There grows a pale but precious flower
>   In a consecrated spot:
> How oft I've gathered it for thee,
>   And said, " Forget me not!"
>
> But now the gem ungather'd blooms,
>   I pass the symbol by ;
> Why should I take it from the earth ?
>   It will not meet thine eye.
>
> Still grow, O pale and precious flower,
>   In consecrated spot;
> And often as I pass thee by,
>   I'll say, " Forget me not!"

The first letter which follows was written in the railroad
car. He complains of the fatigues of travelling and lecturing,
but these were aggravated by his custom of studying and
writing in the cars. His most formidable article of baggage
was a carpet-bag stuffed with the books which at any time were
occupying his attention. When he was not conversing with
some acquaintance, or a stranger resolved upon a confidential
interview with the victim whose head and face he recognized,
he was drawing knowledge out of his portable library. All
the traction during the journey was performed by himself and
the locomotive.

TO MISS HUNT.

March 12, 1857, Northern New-York Railroad Cars.

DEAR, GOOD SARAH,—If I don't write you now, I shall have no time
for next mail, so this little mite of a pencil scrawl. It won't be worth
much, for I am tired and worn out with over much work and exposure.
Some weeks since, I went to Western New York; travelled from Monday morning till Saturday night, and expected to have a reasonable
dinner each day, and to sleep quiet in my bed at night, and so come
home sounder and stronger than when I went away. " Man proposes
and God disposes." I had *two* tolerable dinners, and one night in a
bed, four nights in railroad cars. I have not recovered from it
since, but have been slipping behindhand more and more each week.

This will be the last winter of my lecturing so extensively (perhaps).
Hereafter, I will limit my services to forty lectures in a winter, and
put my terms, as Chapin does, at F.A.M.E., *i. e.*, Fifty (dollars) And
My Expenses.

This business of lecturing is an original American contrivance for
educating the people. The world has nothing like it. In it are combined the best things of the Church, *i.e.*, the preaching, and of the
College, *i.e.*, the *informing thought*, with some of the fun of the Theatre.

Besides, it gives the "rural districts" a chance to see the men they read about—to see the lions, for the lecture is also a show to the eyes. Now, I think this is one of the most admirable means of educating the people. For ten years past, six or eight of the most progressive and powerful minds in America have been lecturing fifty or a hundred times in the year. Surely, some must dance after so much piping, and that of so moving a sort! I can see what a change has taken place through the toil of these missionaries. But none know the hardships of the lecturer's life. Curtis has a most funny article thereon.

[A long extract.]

This is extravagant for a description of the *instantial* of lecturing ; but, alas! it is below the exceptional cases.

Thus : in one of the awful nights in winter, I went to lecture at——. It was half charity. I gave up the Anti-Slavery Festival for the lecture, rode fifty-six miles in the cars, leaving Boston at half-past four o'clock, and reaching the end of the railroad at half-past six—drove seven miles in a sleigh, and reached the house of ——, who had engaged me to come. It was time to begin ; I lectured one hour and three quarters, and returned to the house. Was offered no supper before the lecture, and none after, till the chaise came to the door to take me back again to the railroad station, seven miles off, where I was to pass the night and take the cars at half-past six next morning.

Luckily, I always carry a few little creature-comforts in my wallet. I ate a seed-cake or two, and a fig with lumps of sugar. We reached the tavern at eleven, could get nothing to eat at that hour, and, as it was a temperance house, not a glass of ale, which is a good night-cap. It took three quarters of an hour to thaw out :—went to bed at twelve, in a cold room, was called up at five, had, what is universal, a tough steak, sour bread, and potatoes swimming in fat. —— wanted me to deduct from my poor fifteen dollars the expenses of my nocturnal ride, and would have succeeded, but I "could not make the change." Afterwards —— wrote to apologise for the omission of supper. " Forsan hæc olim meminisse juvabit," says the hearty young man ; but to graybeards and baldheads a little of *protinus* is worth a deal of *olim*.

Monday last at seven, George and I walked down to the Lowell Depôt, and at eight started for Rouse's Point, two hundred and eighty-seven miles off, sick and only fit to lie on a sofa, and have day-dreams of you, sweet absent ones ! and think over again the friendly endearments that are past, but may yet return. A dreadful hard ride ends at nine P.M., and I find myself in the worst tavern (pretending to decency) in the Northern States. Bread which defies eating, crockery which sticks to your hands, fried fish as cold as when drawn from the lake. Rise at half-past four, breakfast (?) at five, off in the cars at half-past five, lecture at Malone that night, lie all day on the sofa, ditto at Potsdam next day. The third day, leave Potsdam at nine, and reach Champlain (if I get there) at half-past eight, spending ten and a half hours in travelling by railroad ninety-three miles ! Thence, after lecture, to Rouse's Point, and at half-past five to-morrow morning return to the cars which are to take me home.

Next week, three days in the "East Counties,' and the next four

21

days in Central New York. That, I hope, ends the business, bating nine or ten more in April and May.

I have been mending all the time since I left home, but have not taken up all the stitches let down in the last New York expedition.

What a stupid letter—all about myself! Now of better things.

You have said nothing about the *Schatz-Kammer* at Dresden. It is one of the finest collections of jewels in the world, and is worth more than all the railroads and school-houses in the kingdom of Saxony. I should take great delight in studying it anew, with more knowledge of such things now than before.

Do look often at the Christ in the "Tribute Money" by Titian. Did you ever see such an ear as the questioner has? That is a portrait, I take it. Write me always your impressions of all you see and hear.

Much that you say about the aspect of the people—gentle and simple—instructs me a good deal.

What a shame, dear Sarah, you don't read and speak German! Commonly, it is the lone sister who attends to literature. Here her chief delight is in the family baby, who "is nothing but a boy," as Mr. R. says of Bobbie, and so of no great moment. I fear lest the perpetual stimulus offered to this *Bobschen* (small Bob) should not be the thing for him. It is green wood which needs continued puffing at with the bellows—not such kindling stuff as Willie. I wish he was in some good farmer's family for a year or two, to get bottom—material basis. But it can't be. What you write about him is full of interest to us all.

*   *   *   *   *   *

If Eliza wants to read a good philosophical book, she will find it in Kuno Fischer's "Franz Baco," and when you go to Heidelberg, she will see the man, whom I know. She read one of his books at Newton; but he does not know *me*, so I can give you no letter. Oh, how I do wish Bear and I could step over to Germany and pass the summer with you! But it can't be. I trust you will be with the Becks this summer, and next year will drop down into Italy. Well, here is the end of the second sheet. Love to Potamousie;* love to grandmother of one grandchild; love to Lizzie and Robert; love to Sallie—love and something beside. Never fear that my love for you abates, or will or can. Good bye!

THEODORE.

TO MRS. APTHORP.

Boston, Monday Night, 21st September, 1857.

MY DEAR ELIZA,—There is a new moon looking in at my window, or was when I pulled the curtain down; and for you, I suppose it looks down on Pisa, or Genoa, or Florence. How grand the dark, heavy architecture of these old narrow-streeted Italian towns looks in the light of the full moon! I could never tire of Rome or Florence by moonlight, and shall not soon forget how Venice looked in the full moon, in the end of April, 1844. The illumination of a great festival came also at the same time, and the canals swarmed with people in festal dresses. Balloons of light, parti-coloured material hung on all the steeples,

---

* Pet name for the Willie.

whose bells spoke to the ear the same rhythm of sound the lanterns intimated to the eye. I was in Trent once at midnight, and saw the Great Bear hang over the Cathedral, where a famous council once sat so long and with such world-wide significance. Once, too, at full moon, I went to the Colosseum, and stayed till midnight, and heard the owl hoot over the ruins of that terrible amphitheatre of blood, where, oftener than once, 80,000 men and women were brought together to see gladiators butcher one another. Once, too, the last night I was in Rome, I went at full moon to see the arches of the aqueduct which used to water a city of 1,500,000 men—the London of the old fighting world, as London is the Rome of the modern industrial world ; now it is a huge ruin, full of beauty to all lookers on ; also full of wisdom to whoso stops to think of the Whence and Whither of mighty states.

What a dear child you are to take all that pains (for me, too) to hunt up an old book ! These, I take it, are the facts.

It is Ramusio that occupies the corner I spoke of ; in 1844 I had been up to the rooms above the library, and thinking of Sebastian Cabot, looked at books of voyages (I have a weakness for folios), and opened that, and found at the head of the page, or the chapter, the "Navigazioni di Sebastiani Gabotti." Before I could make further explorations, my companions hurried me off to some other place, so I put up the book, and "cast one longing lingering look behind," and saw "Viaggi " on the back, and supposed it was "Viaggi di Giovanni ed Sebastiani Gabotti," or something like that ; the book has haunted me ever since. I have looked in all libraries for it, in bibliographies, asked men well-read in such things, but found no satisfaction. Now it is all cleared up. Keep the book given to you, unless you find an opportunity to send it home by private hand. I have ordered all the Italian books you mention—the new edition of "Marco Polo " I had ordered before in vain. But my friend, Mr. Christern, a German book-seller, was here last night, and I sent again direct to Venice, where he has a friend ; they will go viâ Leipsic, and before the first of January, I shall have them in handsome parchment on this desk, perhaps. Sorry to put you to so much trouble ; but I think it paid for itself by making you acquainted with persons you would not else have met.

Many thanks for it all, and the forty-seven grapes which commemorated the years that have made me *glatz-köpfig* (smooth-headed). It was *glass köpfig*—at least *I* read it so—in my copy, and boggled over it a long time, and looked in dictionaries, and wondered and wondered, but was so stupid as not to think of *glatz-köpfig*. It is a queer piece, with a deal of truth in its *Verfehlte Liebe verfehltes Leben.**

But it is not the deepest truth. No—no—no ! Whoso does his possible best, never fails in *Leben*, but straight out of the deeps of misery and worldly ruin rises in his proper motion up to heaven. Even to the wickedest I think life is no absolute failure. But it is an experiment he could not do without ; one in which he learns what else he had missed. Heine has a deal of the Devil in him, mixed with a deal of genius. Nobody could write so well as he—surely none since Göthe ; that Hebrew nature has a world of sensuous and devotional emotion in it, and immense power of language also. But this genius is lyric, not

* Love that fails in life a failure : the allusion is to a piece written by Henry Heine.

dramatic, not epic; no Muse rises so high as the Hebrew, but it cannot keep long on the wing. The Psalms and Prophets of the Old Testament teach us this; Oriental sensuousness attained their finest expression in the Song of Solomon, and in Heine's *Lieder*. In the latter the idol is veiled in thin gauze; in the former it is without the veil. Much in Heine I hate—much, likewise, I admire and love. The " *Romanzero*."* I never like enough to read. Heine was malignant and blasphemous.

I don't want you to take less pains than you do with anything, only don't get the nettle-rash and the neuralgia, that is a dear child. The old churches, with their cold stone floors, which no sun ever sweeps with his light, the damp, chill air never renewed by a fresh breeze from an open window, are dangerous to American women, with soles of letter-paper on their tiny feet, and oyster-shell bonnets behind the organ of self-esteem on their heads. Let you and S. beware. Your mother has the prudence which needs no caution. I would see all that is worth seeing, and see it thoroughly too, and understand it also. Of course you will learn Italian, and I shall hear your " speech ringing like silver coin falling on marble," as you so poetically describe that at Venice. But Venetian is sweeter than any other Italian. Florentine has more majesty, but less tenderness and grace. The Americans pronounce the vowels better than the English, marking all the delicate variations of their softer sounds, while the British dwell more on the consonants, the *hard peaks* of the language. The Briton says, " The clim-met's rrigrus ; " the American, " The climate is rigōrous." The Venetians drop the consonants, and make a language almost wholly of vowels— thus: " *Bo gioro, Sioe*," for " *Buon giorno, Signore*." There is a little hardness in the Tuscan consonatization (to make a word), but there is dignity and strength. It is the language of man. But, after all, I like the old Latin, so direct, masculine, and concise in its strength, better than even the " *Lingua Toscana in bocca Romana*." For one who knows Latin and French, it is easy to know enough Italian to read and talk it with plainness; but it requires a deal of toil and time to master its subtle beauties. It is the most circumlocutory of all modern tongues : the language of subtlety and finesse.

I long to know what you and S. will think of the *people*. I found them the handsomest of men : I never saw such fine heads, faces, mouths, hands, and feet, as in Central Italy. A good assortment of nationalities was mixed together centuries ago, and now the elements, once conflicting and making homely—as at this day in New England —are blended into one homogeneous mass, which combines various qualities not known before. In Northern Italy you find German faces, German eyes, hair, hands, and feet ; this is partly due to the old Lombard stock, partly to the " *damnate Tedeschi* "—the Austrian soldiers of to-day ; for the military river leaves the stain of its waters on every bank. Doubtless, your and S.'s sharp eyes detected the German face in many a Hebrew mother's baby at Prague, and found *black* eyes

---

* A book of poems in the form of ballads, but not so simple in idea and sentiment. It contains also a prose postscript, half mocking, half serious, in which Heine proclaims his conversion to a belief in a personal deity and personal immortality. His sentiments hardly succeed in escaping from his prevailing irony and *persiflage*.

common in Catholic villages of Saxony or Bavaria, and wondered till you saw the Italian priest. In South Italy you find much of the old Greek beauty in the people. At Rome, look at the *Trasteverini*, and you will be surprised at the odds between them and the other Romans.

I have been prosing away here as if I were preaching; I think you are right in your desire to pay in thought for the delight you get in travel. It is a great bounty that is given you. I felt how much I was adding to the debt I owed mankind, and did not often lay my head on the pillow without counting the cost to the human race of my enjoyment on that day when I had received only, but given out nothing in return. Now, I could learn twice as much as then, as carrying a head " steadier on its shoulders," as you say. Alas, me! my head was always *steady* enough; I wish I had other qualities in proportion to sobriety.

Of course, you won't read much in Italy; but you will go to the theatre, and learn the language with such help as you can get. We went to the theatre at Florence, but only once.

What exquisite culture of the *ground* you find in Italy, but what a *Church*—what monks, and *preti*, and *cardinali*—what a *Pape !* I always like to call the old fellow by the French or the German name, *Pape*, or *Papst*. Rome is a Commentary on Revelations. I fear you missed the Papal visit to Florence; the old fellow will go back to his humble shed of the Vatican, " *nostro humile tapino Vaticano*," with a million dollars in presents. In reading the correspondence of Mabillon, I was struck with the fact that, while the great ecclesiastics do not appear to have any brothers or sisters, they are blest with many nephews who required places in the Holy alone-saving Church of Rome.

Tell me if you hear of any literature that is new or worth notice. Florence is the head-quarters of Italian letters, now. I think no country has such a reserved power of educated gentlemen, fond of literature, art, science, who never print anything; many works are written in the country-houses of these persons which never see the light. How is it possible for a Government to curse a people ! You saw something of that in Germany; more is before you. Tell me what you think of man's relation to the animals in Italy. Tell little Potamousie how much I thank him for his letter in German, every word correct. " He is a precious," as his auntie says, and I think you had better send him home to me; he is only a bother in travelling.

T.

TO MISS HUNT.

Boston, Saturday Night, Oct. 31, 1857.

My DEAR LITTLE MITE O' SARAH, AWAY OFF AT FLORENCE,—It is All Saint's Eve to-night, and my sermon has been long since ended, the last word added at the end, and I have had a little time to gather up my soul for the coming Sunday. I don't like to rush from a week of hard work into the prayers and the hymns of the Sunday without a little breathing time of devotion, so I walk about the study, and hum over bits of hymns, or recall various little tender emotions, and feel the beating of that great Heart of the Universe which warms us all with the life that never dies. I don't know that these are not the richest hours of my life; certainly, they have always been the happiest.

At Roxbury I had a better time for this—more uninterrupted opportunity, I mean. Nature is a continuous oratory, and the pine-trees near, or then not far off, always came to me with their sweet voice full of religious emotion. They did not feel it; I did, for man is the consciousness of nature. In him its facts are ideas, its deeds and habits are laws, and its sounds become the music of a prayer. Here, in the city, one must fall back on his own soul, or, as most men, on some social help of companionship. Mankind makes a world of art in the city to take the place of absent nature. Hence, there are Milan cathedrals, and Duomos of Florence, and St. Stephen's of Vienna. In the Tyrol, or even the White Mountains, you need no such things. When our friend's face is before us, as a grace before and after meat, we need no picture, but when he is afar off, we look on his daguerreotype as a benediction to our daily bread. Hence, the world of religious art, which is only a toy in the fields, a gilt bauble compared to the clover, and the blue-eyed grass, and the dandelion, in the town becomes quite friendly and dear to us.

*   *   *   *   *   *

Well: it is All Saints' Day to-morrow, and as it is the three-hundred-and-fortieth anniversary of the public beginning of the Protestant Reformation, I shall preach of the Catholic and Protestant Churches, the chief theological ideas in which they differ. Last Sunday I spoke of the power of false theological ideas to hinder the welfare and the progress of the individual and the race. Next Sunday I mean to say something of the power of true theological ideas to develope man's possibilities of good. I shall speak historically of what has been done by the best ideas of the Catholic and Protestant Churches, and prophetically of what will be the future of some great truths I now try to set forth.

I take great delight in writing, great also in preaching, sermons on such high themes. The audience seems pleased and looks interested. It is a grand audience to preach to, and it inspires me only to look upon the faces of two or three thousand persons so met together.

But my eyes grow a little dim, dear Sarah, and I see blue suns flitting about the paper, and then green ones; so, for this moment, good night, with a little mite of a kiss to lay under your pillow.

Sunday is gone. Monday has folded her wings, also, and now night broods over the tired city, and the children of toil are beginning to cuddle themselves down under that warm, motherly influence, and sleep off all their cares, at least, for a few hours. What a strange thing sleep is! I think I don't quite understand it, spite of some considerable experience; but I won't inflict a philosopheme upon you.

We got your letters of October 5th, and I have mailed six to Florence. Some of them were directed " Al Illustrissime Signore Robert E. Apthorp." Perhaps the modest man did not inquire for the letters of so distinguished a person. Henceforth the letters shall be to " R. E. Apthorp, Esq." I think they will all come to hand.

What a good soul you are to hunt up the book of " Populari Tos-
cani!" It will have a manifold value—not only its intrinsic, as a book
not known before, but its extrinsic, as the gift of good, kind Sallie.
The bigger work you mention I also took a note of. It is too bulky
for your trunks, and, besides, would have to pay duties, here and there
and everywhere, and be a world of trouble. Moreover, now I know the
title, I can make a long arm, and reach down to Venice or Florence,
and pick it up some day.

Please find the title of such books as *Conti populari*, not so much the
conti villereschi, or *fantastichi*, but rather such as come out of the mouth
of the people in their serious moods.

But I doubt that the Italians have much of this literature in which
the Germans are so exceeding rich. With the Germans, imagination
is diffused among all the people, just as the inventive, organizing, and
administrative talent, which we call thrift, is among New Englanders.
I doubt that it is so with the Italians ; they have been a cultivated people
too long, and when the ground has been ploughed, and harrowed, and
raked over so many times, no sweet little violets and wind-flowers come
up of their own accord, but marigolds, pinks, and passion-flowers grow
in the artificial garden-beds, offensively enriched; while in the lands
where the seed of art is sown, the ground spawns forth its litter of
weeds, ugly and poisonous, too.

You kindly ask for commissions—something to do. Well, this in
general, dear Sarah : drink in just as much health and happiness as you
can all the time, and let it come out in your soul when you return ;
that is the general commission. . . . . . . But there is one thing
more : I should like to be made a cardinal, and have a red hat, and a
red cloak, and a red coach, with six horses, and five great servants to
wait on me to the Music Hall. Now, couldn't you wheedle his Holiness
into making me a cardinal? You know how to get round the Pope.
Tell him what a dear little Pope he is, and that I will be the best car
dinal that ever was in all Boston, from the North End to the Neck.
Then I should so like to go into the anti-slavery meeting in the Melodeon next January, and sit on the platform between Henry C. Wright
and Eliza J. K., with my red clothes on. Why, I should overawe Abby
Folsom. Then it would be so delightful to read the paragraphs in the
Liberator, and the *Standard*, and the *Boston Post*, and to have all the
boys and girls in " South Sthrate " running after me ; and to see the
whole " County Corrrkkk " take off his hat to my red one ! Now, do
tell the Pope how I should like it, and, if he will give it to me, he will be
a dear little love of a Pope, and I will not call him the naughty names
which (the Protestant Christians say) the Bible has got ready for him.

I saw old Josiah Quincy in the street to-day. He has a backbone
which, old as he is, sticks out through his great-coat.

I am applying electricity to my side, and, after thundering so long
against various enormities, I now strike my own sides with lightning
It does me good, and I am mending like a family seamstress.

I sent one fringed gentian to you long ago. Here is another, the last
of the season ; it was on the pulpit Sunday.

So I shall expect my cardinal's hat by the very next steamer after
you receive this letter.

FROM THE JOURNAL.

March 3, 1851.—Seven years ago to-day I plucked violets in Rome, and some of them are still in being to-day with me. Some others are with the one for whom they were plucked.

What an eventful seven years it has been! How little could I, or any one, foresee the course of the next seven years, nor how little that of the forthcoming year, if indeed it be forthcoming! But the good God rules all.

How much of our life depends on *accident*, as it seems—*Providence*, as it is! How much of my life has been shaped and ennobled by one or two persons that I have known! The knowing them was not of my will, but it has changed me much, for good and ill. Men would not see it; God knows it all. So the difference between character and reputation—what men think you, what God sees you! Here is a man who bears a scarlet letter in his heart, that burns and scorches all the day. Here another who bears a crown of glory round his brow within. No man sees it, or either; but God both.

March 22.—It is now just 20 years since I packed up my trunk at Lexington to leave my father's house for ever. It was never *my home* after that. Half of my life has now passed, at home 20 years, and 20 years away from home. All of it has been a *struggle*, all that I have sought for has been sought under difficulties.

23rd, Sunday.—Yet it seems to me that if I live 20 years more I may do something. As yet I have done nothing to justify the hopes my mother formed of me, or I of myself. I might as well have stayed at home, and minded the farm, and been one of the select men of Lexington, surveyor of the highways for one-twentieth part of the town, now and then. What fools we are to think so much of the slate and pencil we cypher with, and so little of the sum we are to cypher out. I might have had just as much to carry to heaven from the farm as from the different *field* I have chosen.

Much weary with the services to-day; for I have been ill many days, not so much from any bodily cause as from one more difficult to cure or to come at. Ah, me! my life is a pursuit of its object under difficulties.

Took tea with Howe, and retired much wearied, and sad, and sick.

There are those who are a continual joy and delight to us. I know one whose presence is to me continual sunshine.

Té spectem, suprema mihi cum venerit hora :
Te teneam moriens, deficiente manu.

Kind Gussie Curtis has just sent me some fringed gentians, the first of the year that I have seen. They have always been consecrated with me, and the dearest flowers that I know, save two or three. But now they will not perform their usual service. I shall carry some to a sick girl.

Feb. 1, 1851, Saturday Night.—All the household are now a-bed, and most are asleep, for it is near midnight. I love to compose my soul a little before I go to rest, and especially at the end of the week look back a little on it. This has not been a happy or a successful week; the fault is my own, which makes it all the worse to bear.   How little do men who look on our faces know what they cover! The good God knows all.   I have no fear of Thee, great Father, for Thou art infinite. But Thy children—I fear their erring eyes.   I can trust the justice of my God, not that of men.

May, 1851.—At West Roxbury in the afternoon.   The *Polygalla pauciflora* just opening; laid some at the foot of my favourite tree in memory of old times—the great oak.

THE WHITE OAK.

CHAPTER XII.

Familiar Letters, to Hon. Charles Sumner, Rev. S. J. May, E. Desor, Peter Lesley, Professor H. D. Rogers, to his Niece, and others.

THESE letters, of a lighter and less formal kind than those in which Mr. Parker deliberately weighed his favourite subjects, follow here more naturally. They are, however, veined with all his qualities of sense and conscience. The pen is still chartered to transmit them. Such letters of mixed play and earnest show a very characteristic mood of his, better than a mere description.

To begin with some specimens of his impromptu notes. A young clergyman writes to him complaining of the number of Sundays, especially of the months which contain five, which he considered an imposition. To this Mr. Parker replies :—

There is *no* peace for the wicked. There is only one place where there is no Sunday. In this world, on *earth*, it is a weekly visitation. *Heaven* is a continual Sabbath. So you see the lot of the ministers who *follow their calling* thither. Only in one place is there no Sunday. I do not like to name it : they say, a great many Unitarian divines have gone thither. *There* is no Sunday, but—a continual Monday, a perpetual *Black Monday*, a great washing-day of souls that will not come clean, scrub you never so tightly !

Will you stay on the earth, there is the Sunday. Will you go to heaven, the inexorable Sunday is still there, and of course, "nulla Dominica sine sermone." If you go to——alas, me ! I dare not hurt your feelings with the *name*, you have not a preach-day, but a wash-day. You are not the *washer* but the *washee*. Here you are not the preachee. Comfort yourself with that. The agony of writing sermons is doubt-less great, but oh, think of the tenfold agony of *hearing* the sermons, of sitting *puncto singulo*, in the worst of situations, to listen, "seized and tied down," not to *judge*, but only *hear*. Rejoice, O —— ! in the strength of your cloth, but know that not yet are you a hearer of sermons.

A contributor to the Massachusetts "Quarterly," had promised an article upon Coleridge, which never got written. His delays are thus vigorously followed up :—

No. 1. MOST EXCELLENT ——. It is known to thee that thee is to write for us a paper on one Samuel Coleridge, and this is to tell thee that we expect that paper from thy pen about the first of July.

No. 2. Thee will not forget thy article on Samuel Taylor Coleridge, which is to be in readiness by the tenth of seventh month. Thy friends will look for it with large eyes.

No. 3. Oh, promising ——, hast thou seen the new little book of thy friend Coleridge? He also was a promising man, and has come upon his resolutions before this time, unless John Calvin lies—which may he!

No. 4 was written just after the procrastinating critic was burnt out of his dwelling.

That's the way they treat the wicked—burn 'em up—burn 'em up! Books and all, babies and all, wife and all! O Lot, that hast fled out of thy Sodom and Gomorrah; I am sorry for thee, and hope there is no *smell of fire* on thy wife and the babies! I sympathize heartily with you, and if you lost your books, will give you some of mine; especially Coleridge. Did you keep your sermons *dry*—as Cæsar *his* Commentaries?

He exchanges with a young friend.

I will come and lecture you out of the year, if you will. The subject shall be what you choose. The Progress of Mankind. I will take tea, and if it storms, pass, perhaps, the night. Somebody said it was cruel of me to let you exchange with me the other day, because it would get you into hot water! If so, I hope you will get out—or the water get cool before spring.

Not long after John Ronge in Germany had exposed the fraud of the Holy Coat at Treves, and had organized a free German Catholic Communion, a similar movement was commenced among the Protestants by Julius Rupp, of Magdeburg, who wanted free parishes and no political church of one recognized confession. His first offence was a letter to the Consistory, in 1844, opposing the preamble of the Athanasian Creed, which pronounces damnation on all who differ from its articles. He attacked in sermons the dogmatism of the Church, and denied several points of doctrine that are deemed essential. Whereupon, the Königsberg Consistory excommunicated him, and he thereby lost his privilege of membership of the great Protestant Association of Germany called the Gustavus-Adolphus Union. A furious war of pamphlets and sermons broke out, and the Pietists demanded the intervention of Government. Mr. Parker thus tells the story of Ruppism to a friend with whom his pen was never very staid.

Rupp was a member of the Boston Association of Ministers in Germany (*they* call it the Gustav-Adolph. Verein) ; he had some notions that were called heretical—*e. g.* he thought a *man* had a right to do his own thinking, and in case he wanted help, might hire a hand on his own account. Then he said, in thinking, a *man* must rest only *in the truth*. Now said the Boston Association, " Brother Rupp, it hurts our feelings to hear you talk so—'taint Christian. It is heathen—it is infidel." So ——, whose German name is Hengstenberg, and ——, who is called Guerike, when he lives at Halle, both of them nice men at hunting heretics and disembowelling them when found, they stirred up the said Boston Association, and got them to *expel* brother Rupp. Still more, they asked the Government to kick Rupp out of his pulpit off there in Magdeburg. But says Rupp, says he, " I won't go, nor stir one step out of my pulpit." So he stayed there : and the King says to Rupp, says he, " What do you want ? " Rupp : " To do just as I'm a mind to." "Well," says the King, " go ahead." So Rupp goes ahead ; his church is a *Landeskirche*, and not a mere *Privat-Gemeinde*,* and so Rupp may come into the *Verein* if he will, and much good may it do him when there !

TO HON. CHARLES SUMNER.

September, 1846.—I thank you most heartily for your noble and beautiful Phi Beta Kappa Address. It did me good to read it. I like it, like it all—all over and all through. I like especially what you say of Allston and Channing. That sounds like the Christianity of the nineteenth century, the application of religion to life. You have said a strong word, and a beautiful ; planted a seed " out of which many and tall branches shall arise," I hope. *The people are always true to a good man who truly trusts them.* You have had opportunity to see, hear, and feel the truth of that oftener than once. I think you will have enough more opportunities yet : men will look for deeds noble as the words *a man speaks.* I take these words as an earnest of a life full of deeds of that heroic sort.

You refer to a passage in the Greek Epigrams about the picture of Philoctetes. By whom is the line ? * I remember it, but cannot turn to it, and as you don't name the author, and my Anthology, though it has eleven volumes, has no *index verborum*, I don't find it.

Many little notes passed between Mr. Parker and Mr. Sumner, upon the subject of books upon law and jurisprudence, for these things were an important element in Mr. Parker's studies. He wanted, principally, the sources of knowledge in

---

* One is a State parish, recognized by Government ; the other is a conventicle, only tolerated.

† From an epigram of six lines, attributed to Glaucus, an Athenian poet.

this province, all codices, and books of historical investigation of the subject, State trials, and the journals in various languages devoted to jurisprudence, and the report of cases. He began these investigations while keeping school at Watertown, and never allowed them to subside. When he came to framing his "Defence," his knowledge of State trials, of the jury, &c., saved him uncounted time and labour. How thoroughly trained he was for all the exigencies of his career!

TO HON. CHARLES SUMNER.

Sept. 20, 1852.

My dear Sumner,—Some day or other I shall publish—if I live, and nothing hinders—a book on the progressive development of religion in the leading (Caucasian) races of mankind. Amongst other topics, treated in one of the later volumes, will be the development of religion in its politico-ethical form, that is, the form of law. Now, I can ascertain the points I need, in the historical development of law, among the classic nations, Greeks and Romans, with their descendants, Italians, French, Spanish, &c., the Slavic nations, and most of the Teutonic, viz., in all the semi-barbarous tribes of that family, and of most of them in their present condition. I am in the way of ascertaining all I wish of the Scandinavians, but I lack the requisite information on the development of law in England. I make it out very well up to the time of the Conqueror. After that I want a little help from you. I wish to understand the complete history of the whole matter, so I beg you to give me a list of authors to be studied. You may go on the supposition that I know nothing of the matter, as the Professor was to do with M. Jourdain; and if you set down works that I knew well twenty years ago, no matter. "Surplusage does not vitiate" in the matter of counsel.

March 21, 1846.—I thank you for the kindly note you wrote me the other day, and which I would have answered before now, but have been so ill that I only have done what was unavoidable. I do not think the sermon * you spoke of worthy of much praise, but yet I have heard so much commendation of it, that I am inclined to alter my opinion. I sympathize most heartily with what you say about the *Nebelwind.* † I know well how *unerquicklich* it is, and among what *dürren Blätter* it *säuselt.*

There are few of the clergy that I respect or esteem. Few of them are intellectually competent to their task, fewer still morally capable of doing any good thing for mankind. Among the more respectable portion of society, religion—using that word in its widest and best sense —is not the leading influence. Of course, therefore, religion is a

---

* The True Idea of a Christian Church.
† Faust : Scene I. The ordinary preached words
   " Sind unerquicklich wie der Nebelwind,
   Der herbstlich durch die dürren Blätter säuselt !"

   Refresh as little as the drizzly wind
   Which rustles through the wither'd leaves of Autumn.

secondary thing in their church—in their minister, &c. Of course they get a minister, and have a church, in which religion is to have little to to. Christianity, therefore, is the last thing they will ask of him, the last thing they will *take* of him, or *tolerate* in him. " Give us," say they, " give us anything but religion—and if you must give us that, give us any religion but the Christianity of Jesus Christ: that we can't bear, nor won't." I don't say this takes place consciously. I have translated the *latency* of such men into *patency*. I don't wonder there is a *Nebel-wind :* the *Säuseln* thereof is, however, applauded, and lulls men to sleep. The fact that no minister of any *famous* church signed the Anti-Slavery Protest,* is to me proof of their deep degradation—the crowning act of their infamy.

Mephistopheles gives some capital advice to a theologian :—

> " Am besten ist's auch hier, *wenn ihr nur Einen hört,*
> *Und auf des Meisters Worte schwört.*
> Im Ganzen—*haltet euch an Worte !*
> Dann geht ihr durch die sichre Pforte
> Zum Tempel der Gewissheit ein ! " †

TO REV. S. J. MAY.

April 24, 1846.—I trust you will attend our annual convention at Berry Street. Alas ! that it should so often be a convention to *bury ;* a convention of the *dead*, though unburied. I wish some of the wiser men would do somewhat to make our meetings more profitable, more alive. I don't think it of much consequence to know that Dr. —— has baptized sixteen children, and Dr. —— added to his church twenty-six children of a little larger growth. Even the detail of " our excellent tracts," and the " great extension of our views " in the " West " or the " North," seems to me no great matter. Cannot something be done and said to stir men's hearts, heads, hands, so that even the drowsy shall go home with hearts beating in their bosoms ? Cannot we set men on and make them take hold of war, slavery, drunkenness, crime, and pauperism, and popular ignorance ? I love theology and philosophy, love them as ways to truth and therefore avenues to human welfare, to goodness and piety. But it seems to me affairs are so managed that the powers of a good many in the denomination are crippled. The best minds are told not to think, or if they do, not to think on theology, still less on reform, but to follow the counsel of Dr. Byends or Mr. Facing-both-ways. We do nothing; nothing in theology, nothing in civilization, *i. e.* in the reforms. If there is an

---

* A protest against American Slavery, in 1845, to give emphatic expression to the feeling of Unitarian ministers. A great many signed it—one hundred and seventy—but *no leading metropolitan minister.*

† Faust : Scene III. Mephistopheles, advising the student who asks about the study of theology :—

> " Here, too, 'tis best, for some one man declare,
> And by your master's dicta swear.
> Upon the whole—the form of words hold fast ;
> Then through the temple-gates you're pass'd
> Securely into certitude.

old woman in the denomination, a *born granny*, we make him, (her, or it,) our oracle, and then at his command drive out of the State such men as John Pierpont—drive them out because they are righteous.

I ask you if this is always to be so, if men like *you* are willing it shall be so, and younger men continue to be disheartened, muzzled, and untimely slain? I speak to a wise man; judge *you* what I say.

Niagara Falls, July 15, 1846.—I actually slipped through Syracuse without seeing Archimedes; I know it seemed unfriendly to do so; it was quite against my will. When I purposed to make this journey, I said to your uncle Sam, "I shall see S. J. M." "And you will preach for him, too," was the answer. So I intended to stand in your place all of last Sunday, but was hindered. Yes, "I have been let hitherto." We got delayed by one accident after another, and having *three women*(!!!) with me I was constrained to pass through Syracuse, stopping only to take a "hasty plate of tea." What made it worse is, that I did all that on the *Lord's* day, or rather, the Lord's *night*, for it was after sunset before we left the town where they make good salt and rejoice in a bishop who hath not lost his savour.

I have not been idle, but I have long been so ill at *head* that I have shunned all intellectual action which I possibly could avoid. I am now travelling wholly for health; I have a most excellent appetite and digestion, but all else is poor enough. I will write you soon after I get home, when I hope to be a deal better.

I wanted to talk over many things with you, this amongst others, (which please not name). I have long been intending to write an anonymous "Letter to the American People touching the Matter of Slavery, by One of the Million." I wanted to ask you about the utility of such a thing, and for any hints that you could give me touching the matter or the mode of treating it. I wished to write *anonymously*, because I have a *bad* name; for though I am baptized Θεου Δωρον (God's gift) I believe most men think me a Devil's child.

I am amazed at the way good men and politicians look at the matter, amazed at their silence. Of course I shall not *condemn* the Church or the State; for though bad enough, they are the best *institutions* we have.

Nov. 13, 1846.—I am weekly astonished at myself, that I can do so well as I do. Dr. Jackson has *caulked* my head with quinine till it is air-tight. I was never better off in my head; I can write a sermon that takes an hour to preach, at one sitting and not leave my chair. Isn't that brave? I don't do so often. It is riding the horse a little too hard, and I am careful now, very careful, for I dread the old fire that threatened to burn my head off. I would lend you sermons, but you could not read them. I have about 1001 contractions, and make a dart into a sentence, and then it goes; I can make it out, but I alone.

TO THE SAME.

I am glad that you preach to the young men; do tell them not to become sectarian; but human as they will, and divine as they can. The Unitarians are getting shockingly bigoted and little; their late meetings were windy, and they meet to ventilate their narrowness;

yet how contemptible must be a sect who only *deny the divinity of Christ*, affirming a denial, their life the *development of a negation!* Anniversary Week had painfully little of the Channing, much of the ——, bating his scholarship, more of the ——, cunning, specious, superficial, and worldly. The Universalists are more human than they; they declare the *fatherhood of God*, and do not stick at the consequences, everlasting happiness to all men. I think they are the most *human* sect in the land. They had an address on temperance, one on slavery, one on war, delivered before their ministers on Anniversary Week!

TO THE SAME.

June 14, 1847.—Would teach me "chirography"! As if my hand-writing was not the best in the world! I am offended. They say that S. J. is a good man; I do not believe it. He offers to teach me chirography! That is an insult, a downright insult; no frequency of repetition makes it less. You must have told other persons of your intention, for several others have intimated similar things; certainly the thought could not be original in so many. I forgive everybody but you. I shall hate *you* for ever.

Alas, me! I am so *well* this year that I shan't take any vacation; so *busy* that I mean to work all summer; so *poor* that I can't afford to travel. So my health, my business, and my poverty make a trinity of reasons against my doing what would be so very agreeable to do. But don't tell anybody of the latter reason, for while there is this world of misery about me in Boston, and some of my own kin leaning a little on my shoulders, and the anti-slavery men wanting money for their work, I grudge every dollar which I pay to the butcher and the baker for myself.

TO THE SAME.

Feb. 16, 1852.—"The Rev. Miss Brown" was to have preached for me yesterday afternoon, but there was a blunder made by "Miss Dr. Hunt" touching the time, and so between the two Doctors we fell to the ground. She was to take up Paul's text, "I suffer not a woman to teach," and pitch into the poor apostle, adding a peril that he never dreamed of, the peril of woman! The apostle escaped, but only for a week. Miss Brown is on his track. Really we must have an "Association of Ministers" that will license maidens as well as men to preach. You must be the *head* of it, must organize it (and write its letters-missive), call it together, &c. There are Sargent, Weiss, perhaps Stetson and Stone, and others. We might make a nice association, with the apostolic power to bind or to loose; we might vote that we alone had the apostolical suggestion, "None genuine unless signed 'S. J. May';" that we are infallible, &c. Then we might license, and do all matters and things pertaining to the function of associated congregational ministers. Do think seriously of this.

Then, about the Indians. I saw ——, and I informed him of your doings. "I was afraid," said the Rev. Divine, "that in the f-ô-ô-ô-ô-lish course he hâs pursued, that he had furgê-otten the Ind-yan! I find he has lawst â-âul of his in-flooence as a minister of the Gê-âwspel."

Still, I told him of all that you had done—the meeting-house that you had built, the school-house, and the double dwelling-house. I told him how you mortified the flesh with a buffalo-robe, making yourself "all things to all men," that you might by all means save a squaw: and he was delighted. So I told him of the dogmatic difference between the Pagan Indians and the Christian Indians; the one called the Great Spirit Ka-ka-gee-ga-wah, and the others Ka-ka-gee-ha-wah. But the practical difference was, that the Pagans made the women do all the work, and the Christians did it themselves. He was yet more delighted, and began to think you were not so bad as he at first thought. Still, "He put himself in opposition to the Govern-ment," said this Christian father. Just as I was coming away, I told him that there was not a young man in your society that habitually drank—even wine: and then I fled.

TO THE SAME.

Thanksgiving Night, 1851.—I expect to be a grandfather one of these days, and then shall be reading Dutch or writing to you (as now) on Thanksgiving Night. But as I am not a grandfather now, and have no children to gather under my roof, I keep this day after rather a dull and mouldy sort, as monks do in their cells, reading Dutch books, or some other light nonsense of that sort—say, Ulphilas' version of the New Testament into the Gothic language, or regaling myself with the pleasing fancies of St. Chrysostom, or the Venerable Bede. Nay, Thomas Aquinas comes sometimes and comforts me on Thanksgiving Day after the sermon. Well: that is enough about myself.

Now a word about S. J. M. When we received his letter here,[*] we did not believe it; we knew him better. We had intelligence by the underground telegraph that Mr. May was the head and front of the mob at Syracuse; that he mounted the horse called in heaven *Steadfast*, and on earth *Immoveable*, took the sword which his venerable father, the colonel, formerly wielded so terribly on election days, and shouted, "The sword of the Lord and of S. J. M.!" "*A bas* Millard Fillmore!" "Down with the kidnappers!" "Give 'em ——! —— 'em!" and rode through the town on the same gallant beast, whose vigour Mr. Bradford and I know very well. Yes, sir, we know who it was that broke the marshal's arm. But we never trumpeted the story around. After the Rescue Trials are all over, and you are acquitted of the crime of treason, we shall publish the true account of your exploits in the *Christian Register*. Then see what they will say of you at the Berry Street Conference. You will never preach the Great and Thursday Lecture again. No, sir. It is doubtful, even, if you ever hear it again!

March 7, 1852.—It grieved us all very much to hear of your misfortune, the downfall of the spire. It was undoubtedly the work of the "Divil," who, as Cotton Mather says, has a particular spite against meeting-houses, and in his capacity of Prince of the Power of the Air,

[*] Concerning the Jerry rescue in Syracuse, on which occasion Mr. May, who was with the slave and the marshal's posse, acted his customary pacific part. But it is suspected that his noble and touching appeals so far influenced the guard as to make the rescue more practicable.

smites them with lightning. As Dr. Franklin has taken the lightning out of his hand, he, poor Divil! has nothing but the wind left to strike with.

Good Friday, 1853. — "If you have tears, prepare to shed them now," for a most melancholy event has "turned up." It is terrible for "The Denomination," and all "interested in *our views*." I mean —*horresco referens*—the

DISSOLUTION OF THE GREAT AND THURSDAY LECTURE!

Oct. 24, 1853.—I was over at Cambridge the other day, and looked in at the Divinity School, and saw several of the *bodies* which were waiting their turn. The operators were not in at the time, so I saw nothing of the *modus operandi*. The Egyptian embalmers took only seventy days, I think, to make a mummy out of a dead man. Unitarian embalmers use three years in making a mummy out of live men. I think at Meadville they do it in less.

Do you know Mr. ——, of —— Seminary? He does the mummy-izing for the Baptists. I saw him last July, when he exhibited the result of his work. Pitch, gum, asphaltum had never done their work better. There stood the mummies, dead and dry as Shishak or Shoo-phoo, ready to be ordained and set up in a pulpit.

I hope you read the *Register* of last week, and an account of the "Annual Convention." What subjects for discussion! "Have we a Litany among us?" Shall we have one? Again: "On what Terms shall Persons be admitted to the Communion?" *i. e.* "on what terms" shall a person be allowed once a month, in a meeting-house, on Sunday, to eat a crumb of baker's bread and drink a sip of grocer's wine, which the deacon has bought at a shop the day before!

What if *nobody* at all is allowed to come to the Communion, will not Christendom be in just as good case at the year's end? Dear me, what a world it is! Drunkenness all round us; covetousness eating the hearts out of society; ministers, with kidnappers, members of their churches, discussing a litany and the terms of admission to the Lord's Supper! Bless me! if the Nazarene were there, at the Worcester Convention, I think he would have made a scourge of *large* cords, and let loose upon the assembly till they had such a stampede among the brethren as one does not often see among the reverend clergy!

Well: the age is leaving these old boys to their litanies, and their communions, and their miracles. What politician, what philanthropist, what merchant (of any head at all), what man of science, cares a pin for all this humbug? Religion rises early every morning, and works all day.

The next letter, of the date March 27, 1854, addresses Mr. May in Hebrew, Greek, Latin, and Russian, and then proceeds, with a grotesque fabrication :—

So much for spelling me in Greek, and calling me learned. You say that you are not so odious as I am. You ——! I never got at the cause of your offence till a few days ago, when it was "*communicated*" by the late—no, the prompt—Dr. Pierce. This is it. You preached a sermon at the " Great and Thursday Lecture," taking Dr. Parkman's place, I think, before a very select audience, such as usually convenes at that place and time. You were in a little bad odour, and wished to show that you had some grace ; and so showed what Mr. Somebody, in " Pilgrim's Progress," says is the first sign of it, viz. a disposition to pick holes in the saints' coats. So you let in upon the faults of the brethren ; and, after enumerating a host of them, thus concluded :—

" Dear brethren, it pains me to say it, but it is true—most of you are so far behind the age, and all ages, past not less than present, that you will hear nothing new till the last trumpet ; then you will not *rise* in time to take part in the first resurrection, and will be up in season only to catch your second death ! And now the Lord be with you ! Amen ! "

After that, the brethren thought you made " havoc of the churches," and doubted that you were a peace-man. They decided that a man who entertained such an opinion of Unitarian ministers could not be a Unitarian himself, and voted " not to ask Mr. May to our pulpits." How many men have extended the hand of the churches to you of late ?

TO THE SAME.

Feb. 11, 1856.

My new edition of the " Discourse on Matters pertaining to Religion " is out, and I will send you twenty-five. I have made some alterations of considerable importance, as I do not now believe that John wrote the Fourth Gospel.

I cannot comprehend the spirit in which that book has been treated by the Unitarians and other liberal Christians. I can now look at it as if you had written it, and not I. I have not looked into it since 1846, till last autumn, when I revised it for the new edition ; and the criticisms made fourteen years ago quite amaze me. How can a man be so stupid and so wicked as to mistake the *drift* and *purpose* of the book ; but they did. Orthodox Professor Porter, in the *New Englander*, did admit and appreciate the religious aim and spirit of the book in a most kind and generous manner. But how the brethren mocked at it !

Well, it did not break my heart ; though I had to go to Europe for a year, and take breath.

TO CORNELIUS COWING, ESQ , WEST ROXBURY.

Paris, Nov. 19, 1843.

My DEAR FRIEND, SQUIRE COWING,—You will say I have not forgotten my own joke, and you will say truly. Here we are in Paris, enjoying French " comfort." We are now in private lodgings, which we entered yesterday for the first time, and we have an idea of French comfort, such as we never had before. The furniture is elegant, a handsome timepiece on the marble mantle, and very dashy urns on each side thereof, full of very dashy artificial flowers ; there is a wardrobe of elegant mahogany, with a great mirror for its door, and everything in the room to match, but, withal, we find it utterly impossible to be warm in our superb *apartement*, so they call it, and the winds keep up such a whistling on all sides of us, that you might think you were in a steam saw-mill.

The good landlady promises to remedy all these inconveniences. To-morrow we are to have a grate and some good soft coal in the fire-place; the doors and windows are to be caulked, and *superb* red curtains are to be hung up in the windows. So, you see, we are to be as comfortable as a fly in a barrel in mid-winter. I know you will be specially interested in what concerns the *drinking* in this good city. Let me tell you that we have dined in half-a-dozen different *restaurants*, and have seen all the visitors take wine with their dinner, each half a bottle. The wine commonly drunk is very red, and about as strong as good lemonade, perhaps as strong as your root beer. Here is a market for wines, the *Halle aux Vins* they call it, on the banks of the Seine, which covers, I know not how much ground, certainly many acres. Here are great "magazines" of wine, and counting-rooms of the dealers in that article. You can't walk for two minutes in any street, without coming upon a "magazine of wines." Yet I have not yet seen a man intoxi-cated, not in the smallest degree. In England you see drinking—coarse, hard, vulgar drinking, and men drunk. I have no doubt that men do get drunk in Paris as elsewhere, but they keep it close from the eyes of the curious. I wish some of those who, in Boston, would like to have Sunday made a day of amusement, might look in upon Paris some Sunday, and see the state of things that goes on there. The shops are open for the most part, all sorts of work are going on as on other days; the churches are open, but there are few persons in them, women for the greater part; in the evening, the theatres, all 26 of them, are open, and crowded too, for the best pieces are then performed. There seems no rest for man or beast; carts, coaches, omnibuses, and all sorts of vehicles are flying about. Now, I have no doubt at all, that the popu-lar way of keeping Sunday in Massachusetts is strict beyond all reason-able strictness. Still, it is better by far than the popular method in Paris. I have no doubt that many in Paris go to the theatre Sunday night for just the same reason that many go to church Sunday night, because they do not know what to do with themselves, and must do something. In America, put a man of a great deal of energy, a rest-less spirit, in some country town, large or small; his business will not occupy all his energy, perhaps. If it does, then he becomes an intense money-getter, nothing else. He thinks money, he works money, he dreams money. Suppose his business does not occupy all his attention, and this may happen from various causes, then he must do one of three things, either become a flaming politician, or else a sectarian enthusiast, who gets up four-days meetings, and "hopes to merit heaven by making earth a hell," or else he will be a drunkard—one of the three he must be. Now, however, the temperance and anti-slavery movements are offering new fields for such men, which they will enter, and where they will go to extremes, I fear, and sometimes I think I see. Now, if we had more of innocent amusement, it seems to me we should have less of several things; viz., less intensity of money-making, less political vio-lence, less sectarian bigotry, and less drinking one's self drunk. I don't wonder that some good men were afraid of amusement, when amusement meant getting drunk; but now the Washingtonians have done their work so nobly, it seems to me we might venture to play a little, "with none to molest or to make us afraid."

Here the Government gives 400,000 dollars a year to support the theatres in Paris, a wise measure no doubt, for if the "surplus revenue" of spirit in the effervescent population of France is not expended in frolic, there will be revolutions and mobs and all sorts of trouble, so the Government find it more politic to pay dancers and musicians and mountebanks, who make the people laugh by their fun, than to pay soldiers who make them sour with powder and cannon shot. Do not you think it would be a pleasant joke for some one to present a resolution in the House of Representatives of Massachusetts that the State pay 40,000 dollars to support the theatre in Boston? I cannot tell you of all that I have seen or heard in Paris. I shall do that in the long evenings that we shall spend together, I trust.

TO PROF. EDWARD. DESOR, NEUCHATEL.

Newton Corner, August 24, 1853.

I have lately been to the White Mountains, where I got this original kind of paper, the bark of the Canoe Birch (*Betula Papyracea*), which I write on as a memorial to such a naturalist as you are. Four of us went together: we walked up on the east side, and down on the west, and spent several days in wandering about the mountain valleys. I found some fine plants, *Eupatorium Album, Arenaria Greenlandica*, &c. This latter I have found on the sea-shore at Gloucester, in the decaying granite, but in a temperature quite different from that at the mountains. How I wished you had been there to explain to us the structure of the mountains as you did one Sunday at Pottsville! I went up Kearsarge Mountain also; it is to the east and south of Mount Washington, 3300 feet high and of conglomerate to the top. Of course, not like the conglomerate which we saw in Pennsylvania. From that you get a fine view of all the principal White Mountains. You see them *en famille* as it were.

I have no news to tell you. Hillard has a book in the press, "Six Months in Italy." We are to have an opera-house in Boston which costs 250,000 dollars. It is next door to the Natural History Building. I found the everlasting "Coast Survey" upon Mount Washington—measuring the height—I expected to meet also the "Nautical Almanac," and the "Smithsonian Institute," but found only Dr. Harris with a *Peranychia Argyrocorna* in his hand, and a box full of bugs which he had caught and impaled on German pins—the cruel entomologist! I fear you will miss the Coast Survey. So I send you a report of their doings that you may read and rejoice.

You will be glad to know that my ten sermons are reprinted in England, and in process of translation at Leipsic, when they will be published as a *Festgeschenk*. I shall send you in a few days another little volume, viz., "Sermons of Theism, Atheism, and the Popular Theology," and along with it the Report on the Geology of Iowa; a nice book is the latter, which I begged for you. If you want any of the things published by Congress, I will try and get them for you.

TO THE SAME.

May 24, 1854.—I will send you a sermon and a speech before long. I should like to see you looking at a lithograph in my parlour; when shall I? We take our sacrament of *Schabzieger* * on Natural History nights; but there is no Desor. So I imitate you, call the *Katz*, tell some imaginary discovery in science, and recall the good old times when I saw you. All send our love; no doubt ―――― would if she were here.

TO THE SAME.

July 19, 1854.—We have not much scientific matter of interest. I hope you have seen Dr. Whewell's "Plurality of Worlds." He admits no habitable spot in *Rerum Naturá* but this little dirty globe—all else is *chips;* no intelligent creature but man, none else possible. Jupiter is all water; Saturn a Scotch mist; and Mercury all smoke. But the book is amazingly well written. Whewell is able and diligent, learned and earnest. I never read a book of his I thought so able, nor one I disagreed with so much. Murchison has an able book—so says Professor Rogers—which I have not seen. So you want a copy of the Census. I have one for you.

Dr. Füster is quite happy just now. He teaches *Französisch* at Newton, the *Lateinisch und Italienisch*, drinks some *dutzend* glasses of *Baierisches Bier* in a day, and thinks the Germans are the *schlechteste Leute.* The good old soul wishes me to send his *love* to you every time I write. Dr. Günther is going to Nebraska, for one does many "thincks" in a new country, as he says. Arthur, his son, has gone already, and Clara, I hope, will go and get a husband. ――――
sends her compliments and her thanks, and has read your pamphlets with great pleasure. She is a dear nice creature, brilliant as a star.

Wife sends all sorts of kind messages, and now, dear good Desor, good-bye.

T. P.

TO THE SAME.

Boston, 24th August, 1854.

We are all well—have just returned from a three weeks' expedition to Vermont. We have been the length of the State, up one side of the Green Mountains and down on the other, travelling chiefly by horses. I am surprised to find no more variety in the *botany* of the State. I find many things at Mt. Washington I seek in vain on the Green Mountains. I made the acquaintance of two half-domesticated bears. They were about three years old, and so tame that I fed them out of my hand with nuts, berries, bits of bread, lumps of sugar. In a

---

* Chap-Sager—Sap-sago, goats'-milk cheese.

week they became much attached to me. I put my hand in their mouths and played with them a good deal every day. They were fastened by a chain twenty feet long to the opposite ends of a beam, which revolved on a pivot: so they could walk about as much as they pleased. Now, this surprised me: they always walked their round from the west to the east by the south—*i. e.*, against the sun's course; this was so when the two walked round turning the beam, or when a single one walked round his own special centre. Do they always do so—and if so, why? Who has written a good treatise on bears? Tell me, do bears pair for life, or, like so many other animals, only for the season?

TO THE SAME.

Indianapolis (Indiana), Oct. 18th, 1854.

DEAR DESOR,—Here I am, a thousand miles from dear old sedate Boston. I come on a lecturing expedition. I am to lecture eleven times, and preach once in Indiana, Michigan, Ohio, and Pennsylvania. I have many things to say about the country and the people. I wish I had you to help me observe and to generalize after the facts are known.

The West, which I have now visited three times, impresses me much with the width of all things; there is a certain largeness to everything —streams, plains, trees, pumpkins, apples, swine (a hog in Ohio, 1854, weighed, alive, 1980 pounds, another 2150), and men. But there is a certain *coarseness of fibre* also noticeable in all things; the wood is coarse-grained, the nuts are big and fat, not nice and sweet, the apples have a coarse texture—all the vegetables and all the fruit.

Did you ever see the fishes of the Ohio? They are the most un-couth-looking monsters I ever saw, save the Roman fishes in the market at Rome. The cat-fish, an ugly-looking devil, with a face like an owl; the spoon-billed cat-fish, looking yet worse; the buffalo, an over-grown sculpin; the reed-horse, and the sucker. One must be hard-pushed to eat one of these wretches. The men look sickly, yellow, and flabby. In Indiana I saw but one rosy-cheeked girl, about eighteen or nineteen. "Were you born here?" "No, sir; in New Hampshire." "I thought so!" I saw 300 or 400 children in the schools at Indianapolis—not a rosy cheek! The women are tall and bony, their hair lank, their faces thin and flabby-cheeked.

What effect is this western climate to have on the human race? It must check the intensity of the Anglo-Saxon character: the fertility of the soil, the dulness of the air, the general enervating influence of the physical circumstances, must deteriorate the human being for a long time to come. Health is poor, activity small in comparison with New England. You are right in your estimate of the American climate on Europeans.

But I fear the West deteriorates Americans quite as much. It is too early to undertake to determine the full character of the Westerners; but this is pretty plain, they will no more have the same energy as the New-Englanders than the Britons have the same as the Norsemen and Danes who went from Scandinavia to England.

There has been a great Baby Show in Ohio; 127 babies were offered for prizes. One received 300, one 200, one 100 dollars, and besides several gratuities were given to others; the prize, of course, was given to the mother. I think Jonathan is the first to offer prizes for the *best baby*. An agricultural society in England, a few years ago, gave £25 for the prize ox and five shillings for the model peasant; but you will see an account of the baby show in the *New York Tribune*.

TO THE SAME.

Nov. 14, 1854.

Dr. Füster is well, but *schlimmer*—poor old soul!—he has only one scholar who pays, and that is myself, studying Polish. I learned Russian, Illyrian, and Bohemian a little, with him, long ago. A young Mr. Krebs studies Latin, &c., but is poor, and pays nothing. The old Pachyderm is in a sad condition. He wants to go back, but fears the priests, and their *Pax vobiscum* (*Nicht den Kaiser nur die Priester!*). He is a good soul, and I love him. He is preparing a course of lectures on German *Philosophie* (!) and *Literatur*. Your beautiful prints adorn my parlor, and remind me of dear old Desor, who is duly remembered also in the Swiss sacrament of cheese. I send you Lyell's "Travels in America," two volumes in one, the two numbers of the *Christian Examiner*, with Agassiz's articles, and another book ("Types of Mankind"), which contains things from him. I am always glad to get such things for you— the Humboldt's "Schriften" delighted my heart. Tell me of any new scientific books: what is a good monograph on bears? Remember me to those at Berne. What has Vogt done lately? Tell me about Johannes Ronge, now in London. He has written a friendly letter to our society. I shall publish a volume of sermons, speeches, &c., next month. Did you ever get the "Sermons of Atheism," &c.? Let me know about the atheists of Germany. Let me see all that you write; if it be about the *Metaphysik* of Echinoderms it will interest me. Mrs. Follen and Aunt Susan keep house in Brookline, all happy. I have attended only one meeting of the Natural History Society, for six months. Poor old Dr. —— is breaking to pieces, but is more and more interested in science. Alas! old age is beautiful in science. Von Humboldt, but sad and ugly in —— and most men. I wish I could talk to you about it. A natural old age is a fair evening, but an unnatural —bah! let me never see it! I will send you an engraving of myself before long in the parcel. I don't know how it will look. Dr. Füster sends love, so would —— but calls it "regards." Hannah sympathizes with your gout, but says "he must always call it rheumatism, never gout." Wife sends all sorts of kindliest remembrances, whereto George, now a "young man" of twenty, adds his.

Good-bye.   T. P.

TO THE SAME.

August, 1856.

I have lately been reading the works of your friend Vogt, viz., "Zoologische Briefe," "Physiologische Briefe," "Thierleben," &c. He has great ability—writes uncommonly well, *for a German*. But his books are to me quite sad, so utterly material and atheistic. There is *Natur*, but no *Geist*. He does not merely deny *a God*, such as יהוה, ZEUS, Odin, Thor, but all God—God *an sich:* there is no *Bewusstsein* to the world, no *Grund* to this *Immerwerden.* So all is *planlos* and *wüst.* Nature looks bad enough from the stand-point of the *altglaubige Lutheraner;* but with them there was a *Gott*, a great capricious force, with a blundering mind. A *Dummkopf* is their *Gott,* but a vast will; so He gave a certain order and unity to the world: it was a *Kosmos,* though the kosmifying principle was only a will, not a mind, still less a conscience and a heart. But to me, Vogt's view of the universe is more unsatisfactory, for he admits no ordering mind or will in the universe; there is no *plan*, no planning. I admire his genius, his knowledge, his power, and his love of freedom. I like the man, but his view of the universe seems to me utterly unscientific. I know he would say that I am only a *Pfaff* (priest), and scoff at any judgment I could offer; but *you* know better. His view of man is also sad. Life so short here, old age so gloomy, so hopeless, *steif*, and *starr* (see Physiol., 1854, pp. 671–680), and no pursuits, no immortality!

While I read his books, I am enjoying a few weeks' vacation in the country. I live in the house of ——, an old lady, seventy-one or seventy-three years of age, a tall, stately, handsome-looking woman,

As I think of Vogt's view of the world, it seems utterly absurd and unscientific. You know that I am as far from all *Pfaffenthum* as Vogt himself; but, with his convictions, I think I would not live at all. I should be worse off than his *Gregara*, or *Diplozoon*, who have no self-consciousness, no general ideas. I should like to know how far his views are shared by the *Gebildete* (learned men) of Germany and France. (Look at his Physiol., 1853, pp. 632–634, 648.)

There are many things in his books which I want to talk with you about, relating to affairs of science. I shall now read all of his works. I own all but the "Mittelländische See" and "Kohlerglaube." But to-day it is a leisure Sunday, and I do not preach. I have been looking at a brand new work, "La Vie Future; par Henri Martin, Membre de l'Institut, Doyen de la Faculté des Lettres de Rennes," and am thoroughly disgusted with it. It is "*approuvé par Monseigneur l'Evéque de Rennes, et Monseigneur l'Evéque de Coutances et d'Avanches*," and is a piece of humbug. I thought well of the man from his "Philosophie Spiritualiste de la Nature," &c., but now have *no confidence* in him. Tell me about him; does he *lie*, or is he so *borné* as he seems?

What a long letter I am writing you! and yet there shall be another on my birth-day, three weeks hence. But do you remember that you and I are to visit Sweden together? No doubt you want to see Lilli; but I, the midnight sun, Upsala, &c. Besides, we must go to the tropics together; neither you nor I have been there. Now, in a few years we shall have settled our political quarrel. You must come over to Boston, and you and I, Howe, Cabot, and others, will go down to Trinidad, and pass the months of December and January in those parts! What do you say to that? Let us see the tropics first. Tell me what books to read on the vegetation of the tropics. I will freshen up my Spanish a little, so as to talk with the natives. Perhaps we could go to the Amazon: to Trinidad we *must*—perhaps in 1858 or 1859.

Now, do you know that you have not yet sent me your book on Echinoderms? Don't say, "It is a *specialité*, and so Parker will take no interest in it;" for if you will write on the religion of the man in the moon, I will study *Selenistic* to be able to follow your researches. Tell me all that you do; how you pass your week-days and your Sundays. What sort of preaching goes on about you? Tell me, also, if there are any good works in any department of human activity. What is Vogt's position (*Stellung*) now-a-days? Is he also professor? How is he treated in Germany? Tell me of any books you want from America, and I will get them for you. And now, good bye, and God bless you!

Yours ever,
THEODORE PARKER.

TO THE SAME.

Staten Island, New York, 24th Aug., 1856.

MY VERY DEAR DESOR,—I am forty-six years old this day, and no wiser, no better, have done no more! But I have a fondness for dear old Desor, who is yet not so old as I, but an old friend. So I must gratify my inclination, and begin a letter here and to-day, but which will not get finished for some time to come. First, let me tell you about myself. I fear you would hardly know me, I am grown so old in look. My head is bald, and my beard is gray. I have a full beard, excepting the moustache. (Beards are common now in Boston as in Berne or in Wien.) I have grown very old within the last three years; too much work and too many cares have done this for me. But I shall mend one day when I take a little leisure, and you and I run down to the tropics and see the Orinoco; I shall recruit straightway, and become young once more. Here and now my life has not enough of sociality, of conversation, and joy in it. What you Germans call *Heiterkeit*, I have too little of. I mix with men chiefly as a teacher, to preach, lecture, or harangue. If I had at twenty-five joined some club of good fellows, and met with them to talk, laugh, dance, bowl, or play billiards once a fortnight ever since, I should be a wiser and a happier man. But let me mend for the future.

I look back with great pleasure on the happy times I have had with you when you used to come to our house. I was a little afraid of you at first, thinking it would not do for me to visit such a *savant* and *Gelehrte* as "M. Desor." But Cabot took me over to East Boston and I saw the crabs and the Echinoderms, and got acquainted with you right well. Few men ever stimulated my mind so much as you, for you not only had the knowledge of details in your sciences, but also the comprehensive generalizations which I value much more, and which so many naturalists lack. From my earliest recollections I have always had a tendency to make general rules and find out universal laws. I remember one example, when I was not quite seven years old. I looked over the lichens on a rock, and the reindeer-moss which grew close by it, and the huckleberry bushes, and then at the nut-trees, which were not far off, and said, "Here, now, is a regular ascent, the rock, the lichen, the moss, the grass, the bush, the tree; and it is so everywhere." I went in and told my mother of my discovery of the scale of things, from the rock to the tree. Gradation seems a general law, *nihil per saltum*, though I had no Latin and hardly English to say it in. Dear me, I *am* growing old, talking so much about myself; but as it is a birthday letter you will forgive its *egotism*.

Well: you had a grand talent for generalization—and helped me much in many things. Now, I miss you greatly, not only affectionately, *as dear, good Desor*, but scientifically, as " Wise Mr. Desor, who looks so deep into things, and so wide too." Well: do you never mean to come back? To live with us, I suppose, never; but surely to visit us?

September 11.—Well: the *Scientific Association* has met at Albany. I could not go, for I must attend to my friends the Hunts. But they had a regular quarrel, and the Cambridge clique say that " My Brother," William B. Rogers, you know, "made all the mischief." But Leslev says the boot was on the other leg. I enclose a slip from the *New York Tribune* which gives a general account of the meeting. Of course you will receive the report by-and-bye, and will smile at the little vanities of great men. I wish you would tell me who has written a good book about *bears*, I know of none. Tell me also about the distribution of sensation in animals. What is the primitive sense— Ur-sense? Is there any animal which has the sense of hearing subject to the will, as we that of sight? I think sight is not volitional with spiders and some other insects. What do you think of Moleschott? Have you heard of Silgeström lately? Tell me what books of mine you have, and I will add what you lack. Is there never to be a *Madame Desor*, a *Frau-professorin*?

Yours, ever,   T. P.

TO THE SAME.

Newton Corner, near Boston, Aug. 8, 1857.

You want to know about your scientific friends, what they are doing. Well, then, here, are a few particulars. Agassiz, Pierce, and Horsford, have been attacking " Spiritualism," not without a good deal of bitterness and violence, and some unfairness in the method of treatment, though they may be right in their conclusions. Somebody offered 500 dollars to any spiritualist, who would do what they all profess they can do, in the presence of a committee of unprejudiced and competent witnesses accustomed to investigation. The attempt was made before Agassiz, Pierce, Horsford, and others, and failed utterly. The *savans* publish the result to the world in insolent and boastful language. But the spiritualists claim that they were unjustly dealt with, were pre-judged before the examinations, and insulted in its process, all of which

I think is true. Felton has been writing in the *Boston Courier*, the wickedest paper in New England now, conducted by a club of inveterate Hunkers, who love slavery, and all manner of injustice, against "Spiritualism," in the style of the sixteenth century. His opponents reply in the same style. Of course *you* will not suppose I believe the *spiritual* character of the few phenomena which have made so much noise. I don't think Dr. Franklin and Dr. Channing have become fools since they left the flesh. Two-thirds of the *mediums*, I think, are skilful jugglers. Mr. Hume, you see is humbugging the Parisians. I don't know whether Napoleon the Little believes in him, or merely *uses* him as the priests the "Virgin of La Salette;" but it is not uncommon for tyrants to be superstitious. Atheists, I mean *practical atheists*, often believe in magic. Spiritualism is doing two good things. 1. It knocks the nonsense of the popular theology to pieces, and so does us a negative service. 2. It leads cold, hard, materialistic men to a recognition of what is really spiritual in their nature, and so does a positive good. But there is a world of humbug, nonsense, and fraud mixed up with it.

I was down at Plymouth a few weeks ago, and while walking on the borders of a large mill-pond, noticed some curious facts. The shores are of fine, delicate sand, and slope down quite gradually. In the night the mill does not run, and the pond becomes full; but in the day, while the mill is at work, the water falls five or six inches, or more, causing the shore line to recede, and leaving a wet belt all round the pond. Of course, this happens with all mill-ponds. But during the night, the wind blew moderately, and produced a quantity of foam on one side of the pond, which lay there in spots when I visited it. But when the foam had disappeared, the sand was covered with those peculiar marks which you find on the old sandstones, and which are attributed to rain-drops. I know your theory as to their origin, if I recollect it aright; and thought this fact might interest you. I am a poor draughtsman, or I should send you a drawing of the indentations which these bubbles make as they perish in the sand. But you can see the same thing for yourself, no doubt. Do you know, you never sent me your remarks on *Old Age*? I am quite anxious to have the work, for I am almost forty-seven (!), and my head is bald and my beard gray.

TO THE SAME.

Boston, 26th September, 1857.

I made a little voyage in a yacht, with a dozen other persons, in August, and had a good time. We went to Nantucket, and thence to New York, and up the Hudson. At Powder Hole, south of Cape Cod, we found the fresh water fill the holes we scooped out of the sand, though they were made within a foot of the salt water. You remember this fact, on the little sand-spits at Chatham, on Cape Cod. I never found it so on other beaches. Do you know of other examples of the same thing? What explanation do you give of the fact?

TO THE SAME.

Williston, Connecticut, August 24, 1858

—— The dear, good old Dr.Wesselhöft died September 7, at 4 A.M. It was his 65th birthday. He has been overworked continually for the last seven or eight years. In the spring he was ill, and went to New-buryport, then to the White Mountains for the summer. He returned to Boston, in the end of July, a little better. But he became worse again. Dropsy of the chest set in ; carbuncles came, one on his leg, one on his neck, and though they yielded kindly to medical treatment, it was too much for him. The morning of September 1st, at 4, he was sitting in his great chair beside his bed, and said to his wife, "Are you getting ready also ? " She asked him what he meant, and he said, "Why, you know you are likewise invited." He then laid his face on the side of the bed, and was immortal.

Neither he nor his friends thought he was likely to die. He was the recognized head of the Germans in Boston, very kind to many who for-got his kindness; for gratitude is the latest-born of all manly virtues, the youngest and fairest. I fear W. leaves little property. His two sons will continue the business, I suppose. . . . . I attended the funeral. Dr. Douai also spoke a *Leichenrede* (funeral address). But an atheist had not much that was *tröstend* (consoling) to offer at a funeral. Dr. W. was a brave, good man.

I hear that you have discovered the remains of an ancient people, squatting on the Swiss Lakes. They must have been Dutchmen—Hol-landers, I mean, to build on piles in Switzerland, as at Java. Do tell me about it. It seems strange that in Switzerland every antiquity has not been sucked dry many years ago, with so many antiquarian mouths pulling at it all the time.

TO PROFESSOR HENRY D. ROGERS, EDINBURGH.

Boston, 29th December, 1857.

MY DEAR MR. ROGERS,—It did me much good to take your excel-lent brother by the hand a few days ago, and to see that he had not suffered so much as we all feared from that boulder which came upon him *in transitu* in England. He bears no marks of it now. Perhaps he will have a new theory of the motion of erratic bodies; but I hope will witness no more such experiments. He told us how pleasantly you were all settled in Auld Reekie, and what a nice time you had both for work and play. I am glad to hear that your book gets on so famously, and will see the light so soon.

What is one man's joy is another's grief; the English make a Pro-fessor of you in Glasgow—alas me ! they also, at the same time, make you a Scotchman, and what Glasgow and Edinburgh gains Boston loses. No part of it will feel the loss more than the little house in Exeter Place, and the few persons therein, whom you so often gladdened and instructed of a Sunday night. But, notwithstanding, we all rejoice in your new honours, and pleasant position, and certainty of useful work.

No doubt you can tell me who Henry Thomas Buckle is ? He has just printed a great book on "The History of Civilization in England;"

Vol. I., a thick 8vo, of near 900 pages. This is only Vol. I. of the Introduction to the work. I think it a great book, and know none so important since the " Novum Organum " of Bacon. I mean none in English. Of course I except the " Principia " of Newton. This is a " Novum Organum " in the department of history—the study of man ; it is a *restauratio maxima.* Nobody here ever heard the name of Henry Thomas Buckle before. If you can tell me, I wish you would ; and also what is thought of the book in that Northern Athens where you dwell. In many particulars it reminds me of the "Vestiges of the Natural History of Creation." I don't always agree with the author, even in matters of " great pith and moment ; " but always think him a great man. His learning also is admirable.

Have you seen Agassiz's book ? . . . . . . I wish you would tell me what you think of it. There are two things I wish in special to hear of, namely—1. About his idea of God in the world of matter. Do any thoughtful naturalists, who of course doubt, and must needs doubt, the ecclesiastical idea of God, find any satisfaction in his God who thus intervenes to create new *genera,* while individuals and species get created without that mode of help ?

2. About his ideas of the distinction on which branch, order, genus, &c., are to be based. How original is he there—how correct ? I thought that part of his work the most valuable of it all, but defer to the judges in such a court. My wife and Miss S. send warm greetings to Professor Rogers, Mrs. Rogers, and to Babie Rogers. Need I also to send mine ?

Yours faithfully,
Theodore Parker.

TO REV. DAVID A. WASSON.

Boston, 30th June, 1856.

My dear Mr. Wasson,—I don't know what to advise you, but yet will try and give my opinions about the matter.

1. If you remain in Groveland, you will satisfy your feelings of affectionate regard for the people who have been with you in times of trial, and stood by you. But you will be tormented with the conviction that it is not the place for you, not large enough to occupy your powers, and will die at last, rather early too, with the bitter thought that you have not done what your talents alike demanded and promised.

2. If you go to Medford, you will try to graft an apple scion into a scrub oak. You will keep grafting, and the more you try the more it won't live. Nobody can do any good to that class of men : they would crucify Jesus if he were to come ; your merits will be a perpetual torment to them. You have only two things which they will appreciate —1, intellectual power ; 2, diligent industry : they will feel one and see the other. But the deep religious feeling which warms you all through, the fair humanity which comes out like a green summer all over your features, *that* they will only make mouths at. I know the Hunker genus right well, and take it the Stand-bys of the parish are unmitigated specimens of that genus.

But there are a few men of a different stamp, and a few young persons also; of them there is great hope. But, alas! for the minister who attempts to settle in such a place. I know few persons in Medford: the Misses Osgood, who are noble women, as extraordinary in their moral excellence as in their deep and wide intellectual culture, and Mr. and Mrs. Stearns, earnest and progressive people; I hear of others of that stamp; one young man I partly know. If the controlling Hunkers would be "translated to a brighter sphere," or would enter the Episcopal Church, where they are cakes of the right leaven, all would go on well.

At Medford you will have these advantages—1, a material competence, regular and certain; 2, time for study; 3, opportunity to obtain books. Harvard College is three miles off, and you could now and then buy a volume; besides 4, occasional communion with literary men, the opportunity for lecturing. All these are admirable things.

3. At Columbus I suppose you will find things much in the rough; earnest, hearty, vigorous men and women, progressive also, but a little coarse, irregular, not cultivated. Columbus is the capital of Ohio, and is not without books; half the year it is filled with the political talent of the State. You will have a permanent circle of able men and women whom you will mould and influence, and ennoble them and their children.

Then flouting men will come and hear you from time to time, attracted by your power, and forced to think by what you say and do. You will be one centre of religious power in that great State, where now is not one. You will work hard, fare hard, and grow to great stature. You will not have the nice culture so easily acquired at Medford, so graceful, so beautiful, so desirable. But strength of manhood, nobleness of life, you will have, it seems to me.

I know you better than you think I do, and let me say there is no minister in New England from whom I expect so much. If you go to Ohio I shall not see you a great deal; if you come to Medford we shall meet often and help each other.

Now, pardon me for writing this long letter, and don't let it influence you; do nothing hastily, be sure of the actual state of things at Medford and Columbus, for I may be misinformed of both. The fact that the Medfordians invited you may be taken as qualifying their Hunkerism, showing that the weather is more moderate.

I must preach for you sometimes, and you for me. God bless you!

THEO. PARKER.

TO PETER LESLEY, PHILADELPHIA.

Boston, Nov. 15, 1857.

MY DEAR MR. LESLEY,—It did me good to see your handwriting again; but I fear there is little to be done this year in the way of lecturing, even on iron. The lecturers hereabouts complain of no work. Some societies have sent out their circulars and cancelled the engagements already made. Others have "suspended" for this season. The way to make yourself known in that line is to send a line to the *New*

York Tribune, and ask it to put your name in its list of lecturers. But I fear little will be done this winter. Labour stops, and all stops.

I wish you lived where I could see you often, and talk over matters of science. Since Desor has gone, and now Professor H. D. Rogers, I am in great want of scientific company.

*   *   *   *   *   *

I wish you would tell me what you think of Agassiz's essay. I wish you would tell me if Agassiz, in Chapter I., removes the difficulty which philosophers find in their way, and which makes atheists of them —so the ministers say. I find more real atheism amongst theologians than amongst philosophers. The former deny the substance of God in the world of things and men, and send us off to some phantom which lives (or stays) at a distance, and now and then "intervenes" by a miracle—this *deus ex machinâ;* they are ready to deny his laws. But the latter deny the existence of that God, and yet admit the immanent reality of a power of thought, will, and execution which fills all space and all time, is ever active, and never needs to "intervene" where He for ever dwells.

*   *   *   *   *   *

TO MISS EMMELINE PARKER, HINGHAM, MASS.

West Roxbury, Aug. 2, 1843.

MY DEAR EMMELINE,—I thank you for your pleasant letter, but beg you not to suppose that I should ever criticize your letters. No, no; write just as you think, just as you feel. A person of real elevation is never an unkind judge or critic. Your letter pleases me very much. I understand the feeling of bashfulness that troubles you, but you must overcome that. Try to forget yourself; don't think that anybody is looking at you, or thinking about you. I have suffered a great deal from the same feeling. I have been to see a person, and got to the door, and found it impossible to ring the bell, and walked away till I got the necessary courage. But I overcame it; so will you. Don't keep thinking about what you are going to say; say it as well as you can. You had better take pains to see other persons, as many as you can, and to talk with them, only don't talk when you have nothing to say, but have something. I know you have enough in you, by-and-bye it will come out; what you want is confidence. Habit will give you this. Mr. Smith will be glad to talk with you; he is a little precise in his ways, but no man has a kinder heart, or a better soul, towards all persons that wish to learn. I hope you take care of your health— that you use air, water, and exercise, not forgetting to sit up straight.

Very truly your friend,

THEO. PARKER.

TO THE SAME.

West Roxbury, Aug. 22, 1843.

MY DEAR EMMELINE,—I thank you for your letter. I like the spirit with which you write. Always write as you think and feel. I knew what the cost would be at Hingham before you went. Mr. Smith has only charged what we agreed upon beforehand. The scruple you have about going to Lexington is nothing. I wish you to go, and shall feel myself the party obliged if you accept of my offer. You will help your mother most effectually in this very way. I think everybody ought to work in some mode or another. You will make the experiment; if you find the mode that Providence designed for you is to work with your hands as before, why you will go back to that, a position, in my eyes, just as honourable as any in the world; if you find it is to work with your head, and keep a school, why, you will continue in that. I have no doubt of your abilities; try, try, and we shall see. I know you will succeed. At Lexington the expense will be less, about two dollars a week, and no charge for tuition. I do not think you can do anything to lessen that cost.

I shall want John, perhaps, to go with you to Lexington on the Tuesday before the second Wednesday in September. I will give you a letter of introduction to Mr. May, the teacher of the school. I will have the bills sent to West Roxbury, and will leave directions about returning the money to Mr. May.

Believe me, very truly, your friend,

THEO. PARKER.

TO THE SAME, WEST NEWTON.

West Roxbury, Oct. 4, 1844.

MY DEAR EMMELINE,—Don't be discouraged about yourself. All will come in its time; I have no doubt you get the lessons well. In a short time you will learn to recite them well likewise. Try to keep composed. Don't think of yourself. I don't mean, don't be selfish, for I know you are not that, but try not to think about yourself more than of another person. Little children are always easy and natural, because they are not self-conscious; they don't think how this will appear, so they always appear free. I expect much of you. I knew you would find Mr. Pierce a little harder, and apparently colder, than Mr. May. But he is quite as good a man, I fancy, and certainly as good a teacher. By-and-bye this appearance will wear away, and you will find the man—the man with a large warm heart—not without imperfections, truly, but with real merits and kind sympathies. I know you did not find any fault with him, but I saw how you felt, as well as if you had written a volume. Take good care of your health, sit up straight, don't go out in the damp evenings without a cloak or a shawl; when you study, be careful not to take a constrained position. Then I would try to be free and sociable with others. I know you used to complain that you did not talk; you will overcome that by-and-bye; not all at once, but naturally and slowly. Of course you must continue at the school, and become a teacher. I doubt not you will be a successful one, valuable to the shy and timid as well as to the forward and bold. I was sorry that I could not get over to Brookline to see you before you went away, but so many persons come to see me that I have no time to go abroad. I have not been to Lexington yet. Well, I know you will always be a good girl, and come out right at the last.

Believe me, always truly, your friend and uncle,

THEO. PARKER.

23

TO ———.

Boston, 23rd March, 1849.

MY DEAR ———,—I should be very sorry to have you suppose I would advise you or any one to marry for anything but the most pure and holy affection. I think that marriage is the great sacrament of life, and I hate to see one profane what God meant to be so holy and beautiful. What I said to John, I said as much in joke as in earnest. Do not suppose I meant you should say, " Well, now this year I will look me up a man, and be married!" It is no such thing. Still, I think a good deal of happiness depends upon marriage; a good deal of a man's happiness, and a good deal of woman's: there may be one or two persons in a hundred to whom marriage would not be a good thing or natural thing, but to the great majority of mankind and womankind it is a desirable thing. But it is very bad to marry one not fit for you; one for whom you are not fit. There are whole marriages, and there are fractional marriages, where only a part of each is married, and the rest remains as single as before. I like not the fractional wedlocks. I have thought that you lived too much by yourself, that you saw few persons, and most of them of not a very elevating character; that you were shutting yourself up in a very narrow circle, where there were few liberal ideas, few liberal sentiments, and that the effect on yourself would be a bad one. At one end of your business is the school-room, at the other end an orthodox meeting-house, with an illiberal man in it, setting forth rather degrading ideas of man, of God, and of the relation between man and God. Now, I don't want to make you discontented with your business. I think any condition is high enough to rear the loftiest virtues in. I think your calling is a noble one; the school-room a beautiful place to develope the mind in; the meeting-house I am not a-going to quarrel with. I only want to introduce a little more variety into your life, to get some new influences to work there. I thought a new scene, new duties, new faces, would effect that, and therefore I felt a little sorry that you did not go to St. Louis; but you know best. I think good books would help you a good deal; I don't mean " Josephus," nor " Baxter's Saints' Rest," nor the " last words and dying confessions of "—anybody, but the real sterling literature of the English nation. If you will read good authors, I never will joke you any more about a husband, for I don't think a husband is one of the things which you *must* have, only *might*. I will help you to any books that you may want; a husband you won't ask me to look up for you.

With best regards to you and all, yours affectionately,

THEODORE.

TO MISS E. M. WHITE.

Boston, 6th May, 1858.

MY DEAR ETTA,—I shan't let the mail go back to-day without taking my thanks for your kind and most welcome note. I am very glad to hear you are well and pleased with your school, teacher, study, &c. I think you could not do better than attend Mr. Briggs's meeting. He is a warm, affectionate man. I hope you will become acquainted with his wife also—a noble woman, of a quite superior character. I hoped to see you at the lecture in Salem, and supposed you were gone from town. You must not be afraid of me; I am not at all formidable, and "won't bite." Perhaps I shall see you at Salem before the term ends, and show you how little reason you have to be timid before me. But I was once quite as diffident as you are now; we all get over such things.

I hope you take exercise in the open air, and so will keep your health firm; many of our young women break down in their studies because they don't know how to live. It is difficult to learn without living first; then the knowledge often comes too late.

When you write to your mother, please remember me kindly to them, and believe me affectionately, your friend,

THEODORE PARKER.

TO MISS E. P. PEABODY.

Friday Morning, 1841.

* * * * * *

But you remember that as Christian tranquillity is the fairest and the costliest fruit on the Christian stem, so it is the last that matures. Even Paul, great-minded and deep-hearted as he was, could not find it till old age. Paul the *aged* alone could say, "I *have fought* the good fight. I have finished my course. I know whom I have served, and am *thereby persuaded* that God is able to keep what I have committed unto him. God hath not given me the spirit of fear, but of love and of a sound mind." Even if you are not yet *triumphant*, I know that you will be. The human will is strong and excellent; but not the strongest nor most excellent; when perfectly coincident with the will of God, I suppose, we are not conscious of any *personal* will. Then the Infinite flows through us and we are blessed. Why should not you be egotistical in your letters? It would grieve me if you were not. Do not fear, in the name of all that is good, to tell me your sorrows. I know by very bitter experience that the full heart finds comfort in communing with others, in telling its sorrows even to one who can only mingle kindred tears, but cannot stay them except with compassion and deeper love. I cannot "wonder" at your sorrow, I only wonder that you bear it; that you do not faint beneath the cross. This disappointment is truly the greatest. Love is its own reward, but when changed to a different feeling,—to one almost *opposite*, there is nothing but Christian faith that can bear it. Oh, the depth of the human heart that can suffer, and suffer, and still live on! Your case is well imaged by Milnes:—

> "They who have sat at heaven's own gate,
>   And felt the light within,
> Come down to our poor mortal state,
>   Indifference, care, and sin;
> And their dim spirits hardly bear
> A trace to show what once they were."

TO THE SAME.

Jan. 7, 1841.

MOST EXCELLENT ELIZABETH,—I have often wished for your criticisms on my sermons, and now I will ask you in all friendliness to send me such strictures as you can make from recollection on the "Sermon of Pharisees." If you will do so, you will really confer a great favour. I write swiftly, though I think slowly, and so many of the literary defects of all my sermons are no doubt the result of haste. But still more, perhaps, arise from the principle of saying the best things I have in the plainest way I can. The good folks of Spring Street are not men of dictionaries, and so I never use a word of Latin origin when I can find one of native birth. Besides, I design to take illustrations from the commonest objects. Hence come words, and things, and illustrations, and allusions, which are not in good taste when viewed from any point except the pulpit at Spring Street. Still farther, in all my sermons there is an excess of metaphors, similes, and all sorts of figures of speech. But this is my nature—I could not help it if I would.

" My mouth I do but ope,
    And out there flies—a trope."

This will not always be natural, but so long as it is, why, I suppose I must dwell in the tropics. Now if you, my good and dear Elizabeth, will be good enough to point out my redundancies and defects, my sins against good taste, and any others you think of, in my sermons in general, and that on Pharisees in particular, you will do me a great kindness, for I will try to mend. I think I can bear any severity which you would be apt to display.

Yours, as ever,

T. P.

TO MRS. DALL, PORTSMOUTH, N.H.

West Roxbury, 4th August, 1846.

MY DEAR CAROLINE,—Many thanks for your kind letter of the 13th instant. It came when I was far off, else I should have indulged myself with an answer immediately. I had a great mind to write you from Niagara, but my good resolution went where many before it have also gone. I know how busy you must be, even if you have all the "help" in the world; for you are in a new place, and a woman like you will find quite work enough in an old one. I rejoice in your active head and noble heart, believing they will find much to do anywhere.

The work you are engaged in is curious as a sign of the times—a reproach to us, and an honor; a reproach, that there should be a class of the poor, that they should find no place in our steepled churches—for the rich and poor do not meet together now-a-days; an honor, that some should devote their lives to the work of enlightening the ignorant and comforting the afflicted, that others should give their money for this work. Still, I must count it a dreadful disgrace to a town of 12,000 people that such a ministry is needed. I don't believe in chapels for the poor, or preachings for the poor; but a minister for the poor I do believe in with all my might, and think it the noblest ministry that we know of in these times. The place and duty of *woman* it is quite impossible for a *man* to define. I suppose each woman must consult her own nature and her own circumstances, and then do the best she can. The present arrangement of society I think a very imperfect one, and I hope it is soon to pass away; a few live in leisure, with a town-house, a country-house, and a house by the sea-side. They have nothing to do, and do it; but, in doing nothing, they multiply the burdens of others, and keep some in perpetual toil, with no chance to cultivate their nature.

What you say of Mr. —— rather surprises me. I had thought him a very good man, and quite remarkable for his skill in turning wood, ivory, and the like. I have heard him spoken of as quite as dry and hard as the wood and ivory he turned in his lathe. But what we see depends as much on ourselves as on what is before our eyes.

I don't believe a woman will arrive at the "Science of Universals" in frying fish; if so, she is the most fortunate *friar* the world ever saw. I must confess, however, that I have found all the real problems of life most happily solved by labouring men and women; not, however, by such as did nothing but fry fish.

I doubt not, a great genius would arrive at much wisdom if shut up in a jail all his life. But most men depend on their circumstances more than on their souls. Set ten women to cooking fish all their lives, and nine of them will know nothing but how to fry, stew, boil, broil, and bake. I query if Mr. —— would have learned more in that way. I think the next time your "help" goes away, you had better send for Mr. ——, and give the baby to me. Perhaps I could learn as much from the baby as he from the mackerel. I think a man who has no children is deprived not only of a solace and a joy, but of a quite important element of his education. I have always noticed this fact in others, and *feel* it in my own case. I wish you all manner of joy in your home and your work. Give my regards to Mr. Dall, and believe me heartily and truly yours, THEO. PARKER.

TO THE SAME.

Oct. 23, 1846.

I don't believe it needful for you and Mr. Dall to think alike; true, it is pleasant, but we can't all think alike, however much we feel alike. I don't believe a tenth part of the folks at the Melodeon agree with me in theology; they agree with me in religion, and in the application of that to life. So we agree! I think I have been true to my own first principles.

Harwood* is a quiet, noble man; I admire him, love him very much. But we differ a good deal in our philosophy, I think. He took in Strauss whole. I have been so long familiar with theological thoughts, that Strauss did not much surprise me, except with his terrible ability.

I should teach the little one positive religion; I mean absolute religion—Christianity. I should use the mythical stories in the Old

---

* Philip Harwood, a noted English writer, of the Liberal school.

Testament, New Testament, and from other sources, as helps. I should present Christ as the model; other good men as helps also, but inferior. I would not teach him what he will wish to *unlearn when he becomes a man*. Write to me always when you will and can, and I will answer as I can. Don't fear with wearying or troubling me. I am not very well; but better than before for a year.

About letters, I am caution itself; I am sometimes afraid of myself, I am *so* cautious. I suppose men take me for rash, but so they *mis-take* me.

Give my regards to your husband, my kiss to your baby, and believe me truly your friend,   THEO. PARKER.

TO MISS ELLEN GROVER, LAWRENCE, MASS.

Boston, Nov. 1, 1853.

DEAR FRIEND,—I fear you underrate the actual value of the Bible, and the literary culture of some of its writers, as well as the deep nobleness of their best productions. But I have no time to speak of that subject at length. I can only refer to the books you wish to hear of, and read.

It strikes me that a history of the Christian Church would be of great service to you. The "Church History" of Neander is a master-piece in its way. In that you will find a good history of the opinions of the Christian Church in various ages, and will see the gradual rise of the Institutions which have done so much both good and ill. But Neander does not complete the work—there are four volumes of his book. The history of the Reformation you will find in Mosheim's "Church History." There is no good work in English that I know on the doctrines, but Hagenbach's is the best (" History of Doctrines," &c.) The Ecclesiastical Histories will give you some account of Mohammed and his doctrines. But you had better read the Koran itself.

There is an excellent translation by Sale, with a " Preliminary Dissertation" of much value. Mr. Merrick's "Life and Religion of Mohammed " (Boston, 1850), will help you much in understanding the opinions and whimsies of the Mohammedans.

I do not know any good book in English on the doctrines of the Catholics. In the "Family Library," there is a nice little book on the History of Philosophy, in two volumes. They are Nos. 143 and 144 in that set. Mosheim's book, on the "History of Christianity in the First Three Centuries," is a valuable work.

Mr. Greg's work on the " Creed of Christendom," is also a work of great merit.

Believe me, your friend and servant,
THEO. PARKER.

TO THE SAME.

. . . . I never take texts out of Shakespeare. I once took a text from the Governor's proclamation, " God save the Commonwealth of Massachusetts! " once from the Declaration of Independence, "All men are created equal." . . . . . .

Religion is the most important of all human concerns, as it seems to me, and requires both the heart and the head. But there is only one *kind* of religion—though there may be very many degrees of it. Religion, I take it, is piety (the love of God) and goodness (the love of man.) one man has much of it, and another little. . . . . . .

TO THE SAME.

Boston, 15th Nov., 1858.

My DEAR FRIEND,—I have mainly recovered from the troubles which have afflicted me a long time, and had a rather alarming look for awhile. It will give me great pleasure to do what you suggest on the first day of the new year. The rings and the flowers shall each have their place in the services of the occasion. This is the way I proceed: —I shall first make a little address of a few words. This part will apply to the special character of the persons, and here the flowers may show their fragrant beauty. Then will come the words of the marriage union—and the rings will appear. Finally, I shall make a brief prayer, I hope suited to the feelings of the parties.

If you will let me know at just what hour you will present yourself with the bridegroom, it will be a great convenience, for January 1st is a pretty busy day with me, and I may have other services of the same nature to attend to.

It gives me great pleasure to learn that you have found you a fitting mate. Long may the highest earthly happiness be yours, and in due time the super-earthly !

Yours faithfully,

THEODORE PARKER.

TO MISS CARRIE H. PRATT, CONCORD, MASS.

Boston, 3rd Sept., 1855.

My DEAR LITTLE CHICKIE,—I was very glad to receive so joyous and hearty a letter from you. Soon as I knew who "Agnes Atherton" was, and saw her cheery face, I knew there was nothing to fear. I rejoice with you in your new-found joy. Love—pure, noble, refined love, brings a new consciousness to us. I know of no delight that is merely mortal, so high, so ennobling, so divine. It transforms all the world to us, when another gives us his heart, and we give him our heart.

I say merely mortal, but this is also *immortal*, a foretaste of heaven. I hope you will find a husband worthy of you, and that you will be worthy of anybody. But you have not told me his name.

I am sorry to have missed you, and hope to see you before long; so when you are in town, let me *see* how this joy has writ itself in your eye. I have just returned from the country, and have no more time for a word, so good bye.—Affectionately,

THEO. PARKER.

TO THE SAME.

Boston, Dec. 14, 1855.

MY DEAR LITTLE MAIDEN,—" The course of true love never did run smooth." So it is writ in many a history. This particular affair may turn out quite different from what it now appears. There are many ups and downs in a courtship. If there were not a true congeniality between you, it is fortunate *he* made the discovery so early : by-and-bye it would be more painful to break off. But be the future what it may, of this you are sure—*the love which filled up the four months with its handsome flowers*, that leaves a mark like the traces in the rocks of New England, which will never be effaced from the character.

I know it is very painful for a young maiden to bear such disappointments, especially for deep-hearted maidens ; but there is a source of strength and comfort in the religious faculties within you, which will never refuse supply in the time of sorest need. Burnt spots in the woods bear the earliest plants, and the most luxuriant and most delicate flowers. So can it be with you. So I trust it will be.

It will always give me pleasure to see you, and hear from you. Truly yours,

THEO. PARKER.

TO THE SAME.

Sept. 12th, 1857.

MY DEAR CARRIE,—I have in young days been often in just such a mood of mind as that you now suffer from, and found none even to tell it to. But do the duty which lies next your hand, and you will find the way plainer to another duty, and also that it is not so difficult to bear any special cross that is laid upon you. There are two kinds of sorrows ; 1st, such as have a real outward cause, and 2nd, such as have only an unreal and imaginary cause. Yours are chiefly of the latter, and perhaps for that very reason the more difficult to endure.

There lies on my desk at this moment a note—it came a half-hour ago—from a European exile. He has been Court Preacher, and a Professor at the University of Vienna, has had large sums of money at his disposal, and lived in elegance and wide charity.

Many persons thronged his doors, so that it was difficult for his servant to arrange the visitors in his ante-chamber. Now he lives in a little, miserable, dirty room in a German boarding-house, with a rum-shop in the cellar, and gives lessons in English to German immigrants at 25 cents the hour. Nobody visits him, and though a good scholar, speaking eight or nine languages, he has no society except the low Germans who frequent the groggery downstairs ! But he does not complain—only looks forward to his departure out of this world, to him so sad. I wonder if you would not bear that sorrow better than the imaginary griefs which now disturb your fancy. Do the day's duty, and thank the good God when it is done: bear the cross and be content that it is no worse.

What is not delightful is disciplinary; I don't know a bitter drop that I should dare say I could have done without in my cup.

Cheer up your little brother. Give my best regards to your father and mother, and believe.me,

Affectionately yours,

THEO. PARKER.

TO THE SAME.

Boston, 9th March, 1858.

MY DEAR CARRIE,—I was sorry to see you no more in Boston this winter. You must not make yourself so much of a stranger for the future, when you are here. But I am glad to hear of your present employment. Trust me, actual duties faithfully done are the best ally against ideal woes. There are sorrows which can't be thought down, nor dreamed down, nor wept down, but which may be *worked down*. The common duties of life are the best training for mankind and womankind. They furnish us just the discipline we need. Education by things is the better part of our schooling; at least it has been so to,

Affectionately yours,

THEODORE PARKER.

TO THE SAME.

North River, Aug. 18, 1858.

MY DEAR CARRIE,—When your letter came to me I was too tired to do anything, but yet obliged to do much; and since I have had no time to write any answer. Now I have a moment of leisure while steaming down the Hudson, and write with a pencil (as you see), and not a pen, for the convenience of the thing.

I shan't *scold* you, having small belief in the good effect of that method of procedure; but I think you quite unreasonable in your unhappiness. Why, really it is wicked for a fine, healthy, rosy-cheeked young maiden, with bright eyes and a good appetite, to be unhappy or sad in circumstances like yours. Think a moment how well you are situated. Father and mother rather over-fond of their only daughter; brothers whom you love, while they return the feeling; a congenial and useful occupation, wherein you learn while you teach; and a world of life before you, where you may shape your course as you like, at least very much as you like.

I would disdain to be unhappy, but would chase off and put to utter rout all thoughts of melancholy. You have read too many works of a romantic and foolish character, and the mind, like the hand, gets "subdued to what it works in," or even *plays* with, continually. I think it is not grateful to allow such dreary feelings as you seem to cherish, if not cultivate.

Your school will soon begin once more, and I trust you will cast all these complainings to the wind. By-and-bye you will find some worthy young man of good principles, good habits, and with a hearty love for you, and then you will wonder you could ever have constructed so great winter out of a cloud which hung only in your own fancy. But if this should not happen (and I make no doubt it will, and *hope* it will), yet you have resources enough within yourself to make you happy. I would not be a piece of last-night hanging in the house, but rather a great piece of a bright to-day, spreading warmth and light all round.

I would devote a considerable part of my leisure to the domestic duties of home, would be skilful in all housework, and famous for making *good bread;* the actual plain duties of life are the best outward medicine for the unreal romantic woes of our day-dreams.

Yours truly,

THEODORE PARKER.

TO THE SAME.

Boston, 10th Sept., 1858.

MY DEAR CARRIE,—Your lot is harder than I fancied, for I thought your occupation was a fixed fact, which would continue, and that Theodore's health was mending, and would finally be restored. It is, indeed, very sad to see a *boy* thus fade away. It is natural the old should die; it is against nature that the young pass off so premature. Still, I see no reason for the foolish melancholy you indulge in, and seem to cherish. I know not how much of it is constitutional, and so beyond your control; still, I fear much of it is wilful and within your own power; this latter you should check at once, and finally make way with and end. It cannot, perhaps, be done by a direct act of the will, but indirectly by the performance of daily duties. The common events of life afford the best opportunities for happiness and noble character. House-keeping, school-keeping, and the like, is the best thing for the majority of women—it is as good as grass for the cattle.

By-and-bye you will find a school somewhere—a common school will not be an unfit place for you to work in ; I would seek the highest I was fit for, and put up with the best I could find. But, for the time, you must, no doubt, stay at home, and do what you can for your little brother. I trust you will find comfort and satisfaction, *but it must come out of your own soul.*

Remember me with kind sympathies to your father and mother, and Theodore, too.

Affectionately yours,

THEODORE PARKER.

TO THE SAME.

Brot Dessus, Canton de Neuchâtel, Suisse, August 14, 1859.

MY DEAR CARRIE,—I learned your brother's death at St. Croix, about a month after his release took place. I always felt a strong interest in him, both because he was the first child born at Brook Farm, and because he was the first ever named after me. But of late years I have been so overborne with all sorts of work, that I have had no time to visit him or his parents, whom I learned to honour and esteem long before he was born or Brook Farm thought of.

The fortitude he showed in his long and terribly painful illness is very extraordinary; still more remarkable is the intellectual activity and application he carried on in the winter. I am glad the poor fellow got his release at length, and in a manner so gentle and painless. The emancipated soul has passed on to another sphere of existence, of which we know not the details, nor cannot know till we enter there, I take it. But resting in the infinite perfection of God, we have nothing to fear, but every good thing to hope for and confide in. No misfortune happens to him who dies; he is but born again. He has taken one step more in the endless progress of the individual, to be joined ere long by his earthly dear ones, who with him will pursue the journey of immortal life. "From glory to glory" is a good word for this perpetual march of the human soul.

I know what consolation the religious heart of your father and mother finds in this, as in other sorrows; for great religious truths have fallen into that deep soil, and bear fruit after their kind. But I wish you would tell them of my tenderest sympathy for them.

I am glad you are busy with the work of the house and the dairy, that you can make good bread (I think it one of the fine arts), and also good butter. We lived (or stayed) ten weeks at St. Croix, and had never a morsel of tolerable bread. There are few American women who can make a decent article; many of them commit the (female) sin against the Holy Ghost continually, by transfiguring good meal into bad bread.

By famous, I meant *eminent*, which is in your power; not *renowned*, which is both undesirable and out of your control. I should rather be eminent for bread and butter, than famous for straddling about on platforms, and making a noise in public meetings, and getting into the newspapers, as many women do.

If you can find a school that you suit, and which suits you, I would take it; but if not, I would make the most of the duty which lies about me at home. By-and-bye you will have that opportunity to be *loved* which you wish for so much, and perhaps in the most attractive of all forms. But I should not lightly esteem the purely affectional love of father and mother for an only daughter, nor cherish romantic nonsense in my head. The river of life is not all foam; indeed, the froth is a very small part of it—one, too, which neither waters the meadows, nor turns the mill, nor adds much to the beauty of the stream.

Books will enliven the else dull hours of winter, and both strengthen and enrich your mind, if you choose them well. There must be a plenty of intelligent people in Concord of your own age to afford you the company you need. I see not why you should not be as happy at home as a young maiden need be. The prose of life is quite as indispensable as the poetry, and about twenty times greater in quantity. The apple-tree is in flower a *week*, in bearing some *twenty weeks*, and besides is still and silent long months, but active all the time.

Remember me kindly and tenderly to your father and mother, and also to your uncle and aunt, the Adams, at Boston, whom I both honour and esteem.

Yours faithfully,
THEODORE PARKER.

TO MR. AND MRS. CROOKER, TISKILWA, ILLINOIS.

Boston, October 26, 1857.

MY DEAR FRIENDS,—Your kind letter came to me last Friday. I thank you for remembering me when so far away, and often think of you, especially when I pass the house you once lived in at South Boston. I did not know that you intended to leave New Hampshire till your letter surprised me with the fact that you were already settled in a place I never heard of before. I am glad to learn that you have escaped the financial troubles which now disturb all the industry of New England. We had never such *hard times*, at least not for thirty or forty years: great factories stop their wheels, little industries cease, and thousands of men are out of employment. Where their bread is to come from I know not! But the nation has brought this trouble on itself by various causes, chiefly, I think, by relying on *bank bills*, which will not do for money in America, any better than potatoes will do for bread in Ireland; but we shall grow wiser by our suffering.

I know how much you must, both of you, miss the intellectual and religious advantages which you could find in New England, but am rejoiced to learn you find so many in Tiskilwa, more than I expected. They will grow up about you, and your own demand for such things and effort to create them, will "help the cause along." Last October at Waukegan, Illinois, I found a congregation of "spiritualists" who had the same hymn-book we use at the Music Hall, and preached to them on Monday. Some time, perhaps, I shall drop down among you and find somebody to listen. Many thanks for the kind words you say about my services at Boston. It is exceedingly pleasant to me to find out that my words in sermon or in *prayer* waken so deep an echo in your hearts; I am particularly glad to hear of the *school*. The manuscript did *you* good to write, and so is not lost even if it never gladden other eyes. Believe me always,

Yours sincerely,

THEODORE PARKER.

Many thanks for the *flowers:* they will blossom anew with me for a long time. Let me hear from you again.

TO THE SAME.

Boston, June 7, 1858.

MY DEAR FRIENDS,—Many thanks for the kind letter from each of you. I attended the meeting of " Progressive Friends " (May 30–31), at Chester county, Penns., and when I came home I found the two welcome letters from you both. I know how many material difficulties attend the settlers in a new country. Money is worth twice as much there as here with us, and landsharks prey upon the people. In ruder days the strong oppressed the weak by *brute violence;* now the crafty do it by *brutal cunning.* But the present is an improvement on the old form, and a yet better time is coming. The nature of man shows clearly that he was made to find his perfect development only in the co-operative industry of a large community. One man is naturally a farmer, another a blacksmith, wheelwright, schoolmaster, captain, sailor, trader, tailor, &c., a poet, a botanist, a preacher. Each one is helpless alone, but all united together become immensely strong. You can't make a carriage wholly of wood, or wholly of iron, leather, or cloth; but if you put all these materials skilfully together, how light, strong, convenient, and handsome you can make it. Now, what we want is, to frame the various human elements together into communities, so that each shall do just what he is fit for; then all will be helped by each— each, likewise, by all. Mankind will come to it at length. But, alas! we have suffered much from the violence of old time, and now suffer a great deal from the cunning of these times, and shall suffer in days to come. But, as you and I learn by trial to use our individual powers, to walk on our feet, not also on our hands, so will mankind, one day, learn to organize men better. The suffering by landsharks, who ask 60 per cent. and take 20 or 40, is like the pain little children feel when they fall in their early stumblings before they can walk erect and well.

I was pained to hear of Dr. Otis's death. I don't believe it is natural for man to die at forty, but I doubt that doctor or wheelwright would wish to come back, even if he could. Death is but a new birth—no baby would wish to go back, no man! I am glad you liked the sermons, and put them to so good a use. I will send you more by-and-bye, if published. I thank you for the handsome flowers. The yellow lady's-slipper grows in New England, but not common; the others I never found here at all. I know how you miss the pine-trees of New England, the streams, the hills, and the rocks, but I hope you find some compensation in the fairer and more abundant flowers, and in the deep, rich, black soil, which yields such wheat and Indian corn. In the Sunday prayers we always remember "the dear ones who are near us, though yet afar off," and the words bring back the special tender memories to each one of us. With hearty regards—which Mrs. P. joins in—

Believe me, yours faithfully and truly,

THEODORE PARKER.

TO THE SAME.

Boston, Nov. 15, 1858.

My GOOD FRIENDS,—Many thanks for your kind letters, which came some days ago. I have been confined to my chamber for several weeks—most of the time to my bed. Now I ride, or walk out a little in fine weather—of which November does not offer much. I preached yesterday, and am better for it.

I am glad to find you are settled so comfortably; that the school thrives and you find delight in it. I think I told you that I began to keep school when I was *seventeen*, and continued the business, more or less, till I was twenty-three. I also loved the little ones the best— they were only objects of affection, and could properly be fondled, and kissed, and hugged. But the large boys and girls, with good minds, were yet the most interesting. I like the business now, and never was without a young girl or two, who could not pay for education, till I came to Boston. Indeed, I have had pupils for a whole year in Boston itself.

I think you must miss the green pines of New England. In the Western States I always feel the absence of rocks and evergreens, to which we get so tenderly attached at home. I shall prize the little bits of cypress you sent me, and keep them always.

I don't wonder you miss the Sunday services of New England. In such a state as Illinois, where all is new and rough,—the people more rude, with fewer opportunities for education or enlightenment, there must be a little home-sickness now and then. But it wears off; for there is an admirable power in man of accommodating himself to the circumstances that he must live with. I am glad you don't forget me, and hope I shall never do what will make me wish you could. I send you some little sermons, which I should have despatched before, had not illness, all summer long, turned off my mind from others to myself.

Believe me, always and truly, your friend,

THEODORE PARKER.

CHAPTER XIII.

TO MISS HEALEY.

West Roxbury, November 29, 1842.

Press of business has delayed my writing before, my dear sister, in answer to your kind and most welcome note. I have been delivering "Six Plain Sermons for the Times" in the Marlborough Chapel, Boston, during the last successive Monday evenings; and as each sermon occupied nearly two hours in the delivery, and only a part was preached, you may suppose the preparation of the said sermons required time and labour. To speak in the style of the Old Testament, they have been a "work of sweat and watching."

Last night completed the course, so to-day I have had little to do but hear a few scholars recite who come to me to be helped in their studies, and to read Mr. Brownson's review of my poor book, which I have not had leisure to study or look at till now. Now I have the evening to answer letters of long date, and yours, my good Caroline, is the first to be answered.

Don't think I shall ever be hurt by persecution or neglect. I think I can stand in a *minority of one*, if need is, and feel no danger, except from an access of pride. I have lived long enough to know that a serious man is not to look to men for his reward. He that sows to the flesh "shall of the flesh reap corruption."

However, I have had the sweetest sympathy expressed from some very true and noble hearts, as you know very well. I am sorry for your position in the midst of what you must needs despise, if you had not a Christian heart still. I think it will be advantageous to you. It will call you away from leaning on external things, and teach you to rely still more on yourself and the invisible supporter of man. Ten years hence, I doubt not, you will rejoice in a depth unfolded by these very circumstances, now so disagreeable. Still more, you will help even the bitter evils about you: a good word, I fancy, never falls idle to the ground. You or I may not live to see it bear fruit, but others will, and rejoice in it. It seems to me that you will yourself be a lesson and a beacon-light of blessings to those very persons whose touch would be pollution. The sound man goes among the sick to heal the sick. It is not agreeable, but useful. If you can't speak all you think, the wisdom which you do speak will supply, I hope, for what you keep in silence. The worst evil, next to separation from your friends, perhaps, I should think would be the presence of *Slavery*. Can you bear it? My soul has been moved with the deepest indignation at the very sight of it for a few days. But if you teach the universal benevolence, the absolute justice of Christianity, you will be an angel of mercy to the oppressed slave. Do write me your experience on this subject of slavery.

I told the affair of the descent of our nations from Adam to some friends the other day, who laughed heartily at the ignorance and bigotry of the good folks, though they thought it must be no laughing matter to you.

What do you do for society? Tell me about your friends, I mean your acquaintance: about "the church," and the "minister," and all that. I wish I could step in daily and cheer you when dejected, my dear girl; but as that cannot be, I hope when your heart is heavy you will remember that you have the sympathy of at least one heart who thinks of you when you know it not. The sympathy of men *whom I knew not*, has often cheered me when I was sad, though I rarely suffer for lack of the communion of kind hearts. I hope you will find better men than the wealthy planters, and will find goodness in men and women, as I know you must in the children.

Excuse my bad writing; I have endeavoured to make it a little more plain than before.

My wife is now at home, and sends her best wishes to you. I saw your mother last night at the "chapel"; she spoke of having favourable news from you lately. I will send you a sermon of mine on the death of Dr. Channing, if you will accept it. Believe that distance does not lessen my sympathy for you, though it forces me to express it on cold paper,

Yours most really,

T. P.

TO THE SAME, AT GEORGETOWN.

West Roxbury, April 4, 1843.

My dear Caroline,—It is a very long time since I received your welcome and interesting letter, so long indeed that I fear you have forgotten me, or what is almost as bad—think that I have forgotten you; but I told you I was a bad correspondent at best; and all winter long I have been journeying and lecturing up and down the land in my capacity of heretic, so that I have scarce had time to write a decent letter to any one. But now I can hold in no longer and must write to you, if to none beside.

We used to hear much of the *gentilesse* of Virginia. I hope you will find some of it in fact as well as fiction. That horrible mildew of slavery!—I hope you do not learn to like it any better than at first.

No doubt God will bring good out of *this* evil as of all others, but that excuses no man for his sin. In time, and I hope in no distant future, we shall be crushed with it no more. Then how men will wonder that it was ever possible! how they will praise all who lifted up a word against it!

I suppose your friends tell you of all the talk and gossip of Boston; but have they spoken of two "Apostles of the Newness," Messrs. Lane and Wright, two transcendentalists of the first water, that Mr. Alcott brought with him? They came to set the world right, and heal its diseases, and supply its wants. One is at Lynn, expounding the doctrine of no property; the other (Mr. L.) with Alcott at Concord, helping that gentleman build worlds; all these are men of a singular elevation of character, not without a little greenness. Their heads swarm with new notions, from some of which good will come: at present they do nothing but abstain from eating flesh.

This winter the Bostonians have had their usual treat of lectures and concerts. Dr. W. at the Odeon was not so interesting as usual, they say. He seems in a strange position between the old and new, holding on to opinions which his philosophy long ago declared *could not be held on to.* Then Mr. Gliddon "confirmed all the stories in the Old Testament" (but does not believe a word of them in private), in his lectures on Egypt. Animal magnetism is fashionable just now, and Dr. B. astonishes everybody with neurology but the "philosophers," who wonder only at his effrontery and the "gullibility" of the public. The Millerites think the great quantity of snow in Boston and the comet together will burn the world up in April. The excellent clergy of Boston are about their old work in their old way, and make more noise in beating the bush than in catching the game; a most manifest hydrophobia of ideas possesses sundry members thereof. I know not what shall cure them except the end of the world. Mr. Brownson has made numerous overturns in the last year, exhibiting curious specimens of "ground and lofty tumbling"; where he stands now I know not, as I have not heard from him for eight days, when he defined his position in public. He seems tending towards the Catholic Church. God bless him, wherever he is! He has a hard head.

But I must close my random letter, with a hope that you will not let my long silence deprive me of a speedy answer. Tell me of all your pursuits, what sorrows you suffer, and what consolation you receive, and all that troubles or comforts you, and believe me, ever

Your friend and brother,

THEO. PARKER.

TO MR. AND MRS. JOSEPH H. BILLINGS, WEST ROXBURY.

Leipsic, 12th June, 1844.

MY DEAR FRIENDS,—It grieves me much to hear of your affliction—so sudden, so unexpected! I little thought the last time I was in your house that it would again so soon become the house of mourning.

But the ways of the All-wise Father you and I cannot scrutinize. We are only to submit; we feel they are right, we know they are good, and lead to a higher and nobler end than we had dared propose for ourselves. I have often thought that they who died in early childhood were to be envied more than lamented. "Of such is the kingdom of heaven," said the great Teacher. You could not wish to call the little one back. He has only gone, as the birds in autumn, to skies more genial and serener days. But the birds come back to our land, where the storm mingles with the serene weather, and must encounter the darkness and the cold. But the spirit that wings its way in innocence from the earth encounters its trials no more. It dwells for ever in the serenity that God appoints for such as die pure as they were born. You and I cannot know just what that untried state of being is into which we enter when we shake off the body. I would not wish to know what God has put out of my reach. But this we all feel, that the Infinite Father who loves each man He has made in his image, will so order the circumstances of the next world, that what is best for each one shall take place.

Do you know what is best for you? No, nor I for me; but the Father for us all. There is a great mystery in death. It will always be serious; but yet, after all the tears we pour upon the cold clay, there is yet a satisfaction in the death of the good—in that of a child. The pure has gone back to the pure: perhaps, at some future period, you will meet that child again; no longer a child, but grown in spirit to a stature of goodness and piety which we think is not possible for human beings in either world. I beg you, my friends, for your sake, for my sake, not merely to dry your tears—for time and the business of the world will gradually dry the eyes that weep—but to look to that everlasting source of consolation and strength; and then, though each bright link that binds you to the earth be broken asunder, you will yet live happy the life of the children of God, who lie low in the hand of the Father, and are always safe and always blest.

I don't know but all this will seem cold to you, while your hearts are yet fresh from suffering; but I could not help writing as I have done. I know your disappointment. I know your heaviness of heart. I need not tell you how much I sympathize with you in your sadness. I cannot avoid telling you of the comfort—the relief which comes also upon the sorrow-stricken heart. It will not be long before you cease to think of your little one as cold and laid in the earth, but you will think of him as a superior being—an angel of the other world.

When I have lost those dear to my heart, they have gradually come to take their place in my affections as beings no longer mortal, but purified above the power of death, and in many a dark and gloomy hour the thought of them has come back, a most welcome guest, to give me strength and peace—to banish the darkness and the gloom. Perhaps our most useful guides are those long deceased from the earth, whom we think of, not as men, but angels. When we think of them, we cannot bear to do a mean thing, lest it grieve them, while it cheats us. I know that worldly families are sometimes led to religion by the fact that they have a relative in the ministry, and they would not wish him to have the reproach of ungodly relatives, though they would have had no disdain of ungodliness themselves : I have seen cases often of this sort. But I have seen cases, too, when the recollection that he had a child in heaven has blessed the man more deeply than he thought for. With a child in heaven he felt ashamed of anything not heavenly ; and so the young lamb, which the shepherd took with gentle violence, and in his arms carried up the mountain to purer air and fresh pasture, gradually brought up all the rest of the flock, which the shepherd could not carry.

I beg you to remember me to your mother and sisters, and all the family. Tell good Mr. Keith that I rejoice as much at his last step as at all the news I have heard this many a day.

Give my regards to all, and believe me truly your friend,

THEO. PARKER.

TO REV. S. J. MAY.

Nov., 1846.

I think Jesus was a perfect man—perfect in morality and religion. A religious genius, as Homer a poetical genius. I can't say there never will be a *greater* man in morality and religion, though I can conceive of none now. Who knows what is possible for man ? If Jesus had lived now, I think he would have been greater; yes, if he had lived to be forty, fifty, sixty, or seventy years old—why not ? I think him human, not superhuman—the manliest of men. I think him inspired directly, but not miraculously; not unnaturally, but naturally—inspired in proportion to his genius and his use thereof. I think God is immanent in man; yes, in *men*—most in the greatest, truest, best men. How much of the excellence of Jesus came from organization, I don't know. Artists are true to nature, it seems to me, and give him an organization exquisitely human—noble, intellectual, and heavenly. But I have seen no full embodiment of the Christ in art—none of *my* Christ, though enough of the Church's Christ. I doubt not, that as men follow the laws of nature, we shall have nobler forms, features, heads, and so nobler men. We have loved force hitherto, and bred *draught cattle* —men for war. May we not one day have a man with the philanthropic genius of a Socrates, the poetic of a Homer, the practical of a Napoleon, and the religious of a Christ ? Even Dr. P. knows not that *it cannot be !*

How did Jesus become so great ? Who can tell ? Why do you turn to peace, to reform, to Christianity, and —— to eating and drinking, and —— to money-making ? What made Homer the poet, Bacon the philosopher ? Much is due to *birth ;* much to *breeding ;* how much to SELF ? Who made us to differ ? I doubt not many men go out of brothels, and jails, and from the gallows, with more merit than I have, and will take a higher place at last in heaven ; for they have better worn *their* birth and breeding than I mine. I think God alone has absolute freewill ; we only relative and partial—a conditional freedom—one foot booted, the other chained—that as we live truly, we get more freedom, and so on. I can't think there was a special opening of the heavens to Christ. Each man's measure of ability is special, and for him ; but the use thereof subject to general laws. Inspiration, I think, comes by universal laws. Just as we obey the laws of our being, *we get inspiration*, it seems to me; a little being *less*, the larger being *more*. I look on Jesus as the *celestial blossoming of man*, the highest fact in our story.

It seems to me there is a progress of man's capabilities here on earth. I don't mean that man changes in his essence, but practically in his potency. We don't find Waldo Emersons among the Choctaws, but among the Yankees. Let the world have peace for 500 years, the aristocracy of blood will have gone, the aristocracy of gold has come and gone, that of talent will have also come and gone, and the aristocracy of goodness, which is the democracy of man, the government *of* all, *for* all, *by* all, will be the power that is. Then what may we not look for? Hitherto our hero has been of force, his symbol the sword or the sceptre of command. It will not always be so. We are now developing the hand, and shall one day the head, and then the heart. All this is conformable to Christianity.

I think Jesus saw the great law of man's nature and taught absolute religion, *i.e.*, religion with no limitations; free goodness, free piety, free thought, and free development of man's consciousness. By the reception of that are we to be "*saved*," and the world saved, and by that process alone.

What men and women shall we not raise up? In prospect of that how little seem all the "sects," from the "Catholic" to the "Unitarian," and how melancholy all the swelling insolence of some hero of a coterie—a saint in long-clothes—a demi-god, who at best can fill a surplice! But how encouraging is it to work! Men tell me of the littleness of men—I see it, feel it; of their folly, stupidity, sin—I feel that, and know it well enough. But I say, Well, we have had a Jesus, and see what comes of that Jesus! I am full of hope; I see each day more good in man than I knew of before, and trust *men* more than ever, and am less often deceived. God is in history, slowly getting incarnated.

TO ALBERT SANFORD, ESQ., BOSTON, MASS.

Newton Corner, Aug. 24, 1853.

DEAR SIR,—The article in the *Massachusetts Quarterly*, on Swedenborg, was written by Henry James, of New York. Emerson, in his "Representative Men," has given the best criticism which I have ever seen of Swedenborg. But that is not adequate to the purpose you refer to. Swedenborg has had the fate to be worshipped as a half-god, on the one side; and on the other, to be despised and laughed at. It seems to me that he was a man of genius, of wide learning, of deep and genuine piety. But he had an abnormal, queer sort of mind, dreamy, dozy, clairvoyant, Andrew-Jackson-Davisy; and besides, he loved opium and strong coffee, and wrote under the influence of those drugs. A wise man may get many nice bits out of him, and be the healthier for such eating; but if he swallows Swedenborg whole, as the fashion is with his followers—why it lays hard in the stomach, and the man has a nightmare on him all his natural life, and talks about "the Word," and "the Spirit;" "correspondences," "receivers." Yet the Swedenborgians have a calm and religious beauty in their lives which is much to be admired.

I shall always be glad to see you and *hear* from you, and am yours truly,

THEO. PARKER.

TO MISS E. PEABODY.

I am glad to be the receiver of your sorrows even, as well as the hearer of your bright and kindling thoughts; though I suppose I can only sympathize with them, not remove them. Still sympathy is not always to be despised, nay, is of itself often a relief; so I pray you send the letter, if you have it still. I lament that your visit to us was so much abridged, in particular as I wanted your opinion on so many matters, and had so much to say that was left unsaid, and to *hear* that is yet unheard. But I trust this is but the beginning of your kindness to us, and that I shall have yet many of those " conversations that make the soul." I am sorry for the disappointment you met with in Boston, but hope you will be more successful some other time.

Miss Fuller's scheme will supply a defect in the system of education most erroneously pursued, which gives no instruction in the art of conversation. It does something to instruct the mind, and fill it with ideas, perhaps occasionally help it to make ideas; but certainly does little to teach the art of correct and felicitous expression. How dull it is to visit most of the ladies of the best circle even in Boston! Their conversation turns on subjects of no consequence, and they are discussed in a spirit and manner fully equal to the subject. It seems to be thought unworthy of a lady to do more, or understand more, than "to suckle fools and chronicle small beer," or perhaps read a magazine or novel that will never excite a thought. Now, Miss F. can do away the foolish notion that this is the chief staple of conversation. She will awaken minds to think, examine, doubt, and at last conclude, and will set them an example of conversation, for she smites and kindles, with all the force, irregularity and matchless beauty of lightning. "Teaching should be inspiration," you say, with deep truth. Hers certainly will be in this respect. But to leave Miss F., have you seen Mr. Norton's address? Is it not weaker than you ever fancied? What a cumbrous matter he makes a belief in Christianity to be! you must believe it is authenticated by miracles, nor that only, but this is the *only* mode in which it could be attested. I doubt that Jesus himself could be a Christian on these terms. No wonder Christianity finds little favour with the learned—who, by the way, he says, alone are able to "ascertain the true character of it, if it rests on the same foundation with the Egyptian and older forms of religion." Did you notice the remarkable mistranslations of the German passages, p. 40, *sqq.*? They are such as no tyro could make, I should fancy. Mr. N. professes a great knowledge of the German theology; if so, he must have got it as Heine says Cousin obtained his acquaintance with German philosophy, being ignorant of the language,—that is, by absolute intuition. I have seen some that thought the book profound, not at all one-sided, just, and, to use the phrase, "just the thing." It will do one good work, will present the subject to the public mind, and now we may have a fair discussion.   " Come," said the old Hebrew warrior to his foe, " come, let us look one another in the face !"

I feel, my dear Elizabeth, that I have made you a very inadequate return for your fine and comforting letter, but trust you will not be discouraged, but try us again, and perhaps we shall do better.   L. sends her thanks and best love, to which Aunt Lucy adds hers ; mine you may be sure of always having. I hope in future you will not fear to "trouble" me with your sorrows, as you did before, but will write freely as you speak. I will send you books and other matters as you desire.

Yours in truth,
THEO. PARKER.

TO DR. FRANCIS.

Boston, May 18, 1847.

MY DEAR FRIEND,—Catch Dr. Francis a-nappin'—know something that he don't know! But it is not so. He only asks the question about the " Evangelium Æternum," as he would pretend to a little child that he (the Professor) can't spell *wall-nut*, just to encourage the little fellow, so I will be the little boy, and will tell Pa that I can spell such easy words as are found in " Mosheim" ! Know, then, most erudite Professor, that you will find an account of this book in " Mosheim," Eccl. Hist., Book III., Pt. II., Ch. ii., Secs. 28, 33, and 34.

In the notes to Murdock's Version (note 2, pp. 6–9) you will find references to the literature. Fleury also gives an account of the book : H. E. Tom. XII., Liv. lxxxiii., sec. 54, and Liv. lxxxiv., sec. 35, *et al*. Some attribute it to John of Parma (*sed male*) ; Mosheim thinks it was falsely ascribed to Joachim (*sed pessime*) ; while Grätze (" Lehrbuch Allg. Literargeschichte aller bekannter Völker der Welt, von der ältesten bis auf die neueste Zeit. II. Band. 2 Abthlg. 1te Hälfte," p. 25) thinks it certain that nobody wrote the book but Joachim himself. However, the *Introductorius* has the wickedest part of the matter —sin lying before the door—and that was written by I don't know whom; but I suppose Engelhardt has settled this matter in his " Kirchengeschichtliche Abhandlungen," for he has a tract, " Der Abt Joachim und das Ewige Evangelium," in which you will find all about it—and everything else. Besides this, Fabricius has something about Joachim in his Bib. Med., &c., Lat., and that very *rare* author Gieseler (Ch. Hist. II., p. 301) has two notes about the book.

The " Everlasting Gospel" I never saw—perhaps no transatlantic eye ever rested on its pages ; but it was published in the year of grace 1554, without the author's name. Cave will tell you something ; and Schroeck, and then one Schmid, which is a proper common name in Germany, wrote a treatise about this terrible Gospel. All these things have been printed, but the " Eternal Gospel" got burnt up by the Pope, and so, as it went to the stake, I suppose it will never come to the press.

I hope you will come and see us to-morrow, though I doubt that you can be allowed a seat among scholars, when you are convicted of such ignorance! How did you get your degree of D.D. and not know all about the "Eternal Gospel"? Why I thought they held an examination and made the candidates repeat all of the Bollandist Lives of the Saints before they gave them the title! What would Dr. G—— say of a *Doctor Divinitatis* who did not know all about the MSS. which the Popes burnt? I don't see the use of having Doctors of Divinity if they don't know everything which is of no use to the world.

Why don't you come and see me? I won't infect you with the plague of heresy, nor examine you in the "Bibliotheca Max. Vet. Pat.," nor in the "Vitæ Sanctorum," but will be always, and as ever, your old and faithful friend,

THEO. PARKER.

TO THE SAME.

12th March, 1852.

DEAR, GOOD DR. FRANCIS,—I have been down to the cold State of Maine or I should have answered your agreeable and instructive letter before. I thank you for the information about the dragon's yoke. Some of the old fellows thought that Miss Cynthia now and then slipped her little neck out of the yoke she commonly wore; in short, that she was not ἀεὶ παρθένος. Old Burrman, after his civil fashion, has collected the learning on this matter in a note upon Claudian, which, as old Dr. Homer used to say, is "very rich." Milton's dragon's yoke is quite modern mythology, I fancy. I like still to connect it with the quaint old palaces at Florence or Pisa, where I think he saw the picture.

* * * * * * *

Really, my good friend, it seems to me you ought to be happy. Think of me, hated, shunned, hooted at—not half a dozen ministers in the land but they abhor me, call me "infidel." I have no child, and the worst reputation of any minister in all America. Yet I think I am not ill-used, take it altogether. I am a happy man. None of these things disturb me. I have my own duty to do, and joys to delight in. Think of these poor German scholars in Boston—poor, companionless exiles, set down in vulgar, Tory Boston, shivering with cold, yet thanking God that it is not an Austrian dungeon. Why, you and I might have "glorified God in the grass-market" if we had lived 200 years ago, or 3000 miles east of New England. I have had quite as good a time in the world as I ever merited, and daily bless God for favours undeserved.

TO THE SAME.

Boston, Nov. 21, 1853.

DEAR DR. FRANCIS,—I thank you heartily for your Servetian contributions; some of them were quite unknown to me. I had a duplicate of Mosheim's "Ketzergeschichte," but I thought you owned it, or I should have sent it Francisward; as it was, the book went to a *young* minister. I fear it is rather rare. I saw lately two copies of Servetus' "Restitutio" advertised in the catalogues, and sent for them post-haste (ed. 1790), but expect neither. Baur's books I had not heard of, but will order forthwith. What a learned thunderbolt of Hegelianism the brave man is! But how do they write *so many* books? Oh, *dura messorum ilia!* Buchat I do not know, but must borrow of your library. Do you know the Wertheimer Bible? What a fool I am!—of course you do. Good-bye.

T. P.

P.S. — Baur has a nice analysis of Servetus ("Dreieinigkeits-geschichte," B. III., p. 46), the best I have seen. Saisset is not so good as one might expect after all that has been written. Why can't you get some of your young men on their graduation day to write a paper on Servetus? At the Unitarian Convention at Worcester some man proposed that a monument be erected to S. One gentleman would give 100 dollars, others objected: "It would *offend* the ortho-dox!" I am afraid it will hurt the feelings of the Jews to have Paul commended.

TO THE SAME.

5th January, 1855.

All you say of S. T. Coleridge is abundantly true. He was a great collection of fragments of precious stone, and had such an influence as no Englishman has used for many a day. His followers will write his books.

"Schuchardt" I must borrow of you by-and-by. Cranach was a noble fellow. I have seen many letters of his in MS. in Germany—some charming correspondence between him and " Dr. Martin "; for. Luther, who wrote everything else, wrote letters also. How fine they are sometimes, though at others coarse as Dean Swift and B——, united! I have a new " Life of Lessing," by Danzel, about 1200 pp. 8vo. It looks rich.

That little book, " Meeting of Bayle and Spinoza," I never saw—only references to it; and I do not know who wrote it. On the " Satyre Menippe" you will find something in *Revue des Deux Mondes*, xxxii. p. 266 sq. 280 sq. It is a queer subject.

I have a little volume, " Literæ Pseudo-Senatûs Anglicani Cromwellii, Reliquorumque Perduellium nomine ac jussu Conscriptæ, a Joanne Miltono. Impressæ anno 1676 " (no place). The editor says he doubted, when the MSS. first came to hand, whether " *illas prœbo potius aut flammis committerem.*" But he spares them on account of their style. " *Est enim forsam dignissimus qui ab omnibus legeretur Miltonus, nisi styli sui facundiam et puritatem turpissimis moribus inquinasset.*" Then follow the well-known Latin letters. I never saw the book before, but doubtless your eye had bored into it long ago.

Do you know Caspar Barthius? I have had his "Adversarium Commentariorum, Libri LX.," &c. (1624), this good while (mine was Sharon, Turner's copy); and Saturday there came his " Juvenilia "

(1605), and "Amabilium" (1612), which seem of the Johannes Secundus school. There is a deal of learning in the "Adversaria."

I hope to see you one of these days, when you have no scholars to teach, and I nothing to do. When shall we have one of those *brood-days* which we have enjoyed so much at Spring Street, or at Watertown?

TO THE SAME.

10th May, 1855.

I have just been reading "Lambruschini, Sul'Immacolato Concepimento de Maria (Roma, 1843, 1 vol. 8vo)," which came yesterday. It is funny to see such a piece of nonsense. You must read it to help your *exegesis*. In Gen. iii. 15, the *Mulier* is *Beata Virgo*, of course; but Cantic. iv. 7 refers to her. *Macula non est in te* declares the Immaculate Conception. The Κιχαριτωμίνη in Origen. VI. Hom. in Luc. means *formata in grazia* (*i. e.*, without original sin). Here is one interpretation from St. Epiphanius, Ps. LXXVII. in Vulgate (LXXVIII. in ours), v. 14: "*Et deduxit eos in Nube diei;*" the *Nubis levis* is *sancta Maria nullo semine humano prægravata!* In 1830, at Paris, it was revealed to an old maid, *ad una Semplice Virginella*, that Mary was conceived without original sin.

I wish you would read the last page of *Huntington's Religious (!) Magazine* for May, and see what an admirable "professor of the heart" you are to have in Cambridge. I think he might as well be made professor of the liver, or the gall, as of that tough muscle.

Did you ever read Sulp. Severus his Epistles? I have just got Le Clerc's edition of "Sulpicius" (1709), and read in them for the first time. There is one to St. Paulinus (Bp., you know), to introduce a cook. It seems the saint's cooks had renounced his kitchen, because they would not provide such mean dinners as he required of them. I wonder if the Bishop of London's cook ever repudiated his service for that reason. And Sulp. sends him a *puerulum ex nostra officinâ*, who knows enough to bake beans, to pickle beets, and make gruel for the monks. He has one fault: he is a *flibustier*, and appropriates the contents of his neighbour's gardens, wood-piles, old houses, and fences. But as there are failings which "lean to virtue's side," he sends him *non servum sed pro servo filium*.

There is a letter to Sister Claudia on the Day of Judgment, and another on being an old maid, "De Virginitate," which he thinks the most glorious condition in the world, "*grande est et immortale . . . . . vivereque contra humani generis legem!*" How much such an old fellow has got to answer for, filling the world with old maids in the name of God! The poor *devotæ* were worse off then than now; they must wear no ornaments. One day, I hope, somebody will write the *true* history of what is called Christianity. What a story it will be!

I have got Wolff, "Lectionum Memorabilium Centenarii XVI." (2 Fol. 1600), one of the greatest books in the world—full of *cuts*. It is equal to the Know-nothings in hostility to the Catholics.

In Pater Balbinus, his account of the miracles of the Mother of God at Wart, in Silesia, he speaks of Copernicus as an author of no reputation or authority: " *Stare cœlum, et volvi terram credidit Coperni-cus, falsus sine dubio et nullius exempli auctor.*" The reason why the astute Jesuit thinks the earth does not move is exquisite—"*nam nihil ad motum pigrius centro !*"

TO THE SAME.

Dublin, N.H., 8th August, 1855.

DEAR DR. FRANCIS,—Here I am rusticating in one of the nicest little towns in New Hampshire or New England. Good Dr. Leonard has written his natural piety all over the town, and in all the people. How much a noble minister may do for mankind in such a town as this! There are 23 copies of the *New York Tribune*, and nearly as many of the *National Era*, taken here. No rum in the town, excellent schools, not 1100 inhabitants, and 1200 dollars devoted every year to schools. I often mention Lincoln, old Dr. Stearns's parish for so many years, to show what a minister may do. Concord is also a good example; but Dublin, I think, will bear the palm from all the rest. But why is it that such cases are so rare ? There is not a town in New England but would rejoice to have such a minister as Dr. L. Why is it that we don't *raise* that sort of minister ?

I got from a foreign catalogue a copy of a rare book ; *you* doubtless know it well, but *I* never saw it before, though I have been hunting for it some years : " Epigrammata Clarissimi Dissertissimique viri Thomæ Mori Brittani pleraque ex Græcis versa (Basileæ, apud Joannem Frobenium, Mense Martio, An. MDXVIII.)." I think it was reprinted in the collective edition of " Op. Mori," and again in 1635 ; but I never saw all of the poems before. One thing pleases me in his iambics, " Ad Candidum, qualis uxor deliquenda." You know what interest he took in the education of women. It appears in this little poem :—

> " Sit illa vel modo
> Instructa literis,
> Vel talis ut modo
> Sit apta literis.
> Felix, quibus bene
> Priscis ab optimis
> Possit libellulis
> Haurire dogmata.
> Armata cum quibus
> Nec illa prosperis
> Superba turgeat,
> Nec illa turbidis
> Misella lugeat
> Prostrata casibus.
> Jucunda sic erit
> Semper," &c.

Next time you are in the library, will you be good enough to ask Dr. Harris to lay aside for me the " Op. Mori," and all the " Lives of More ?" I will take them soon as I return. Of course you have read " Campanella, De Monarchia Hispanica." It was written about

1600. My copy is an Elzevir (Amst. 1653, 16mo) ; it is a nice book, wholly heartless, though he rebukes Macchiavelli for his want of principle. His view of the state of Europe is curious and instructive. He is the first author that I remember who recommends crossing the breed of nations. I ought to mention that the edition of "Mori Epig." was printed from a MS. which Erasmus gave to Beatus Rhenanus, who dedicates it to Bilibald Percheimer. It seems from the preface that Beatus had the gout while it was in the press. I have got Danzel's "Leben Lessing" (3 vols. 8vo !). Have you seen it ? It is dreadfully minute, and I do not like L. quite so well as before. But he was a great man : the book could be written nowhere but in Germany.

TO THE SAME.

Boston, December 16, 1855.

Dear Dr. Francis,—I do not remember to have seen Hallam's works in your library, and it strikes me that they would fill up the place you were speaking of a few days ago. You were one of the lucky men who bought the "Retrospective Review," before it became so dear. I am destitute of it still, but will not pay the fancy price now demanded. Do you know Walter's " Life of Sir Thomas More " (Phil. 1839) ? It is curious, written from the American-Catholic point of view. I doubt that I shall get an edition of Thomas before the public—few would buy him; but I wish it might be done. He was one of the noblest that stood out against the progress of religion in England. How he loved good letters, and the education of women !

Yours, ever,

T. P.

TO THE SAME.

Boston, April 21, 1856.

Dear, good Dr. Francis,—Your last letter came on the 23rd February, and since then, I have not had a moment to write a letter, save unavoidable notes, and have not seen a streak of you even. In Leibnitz, I find reference to a set of men, whom I find nowhere else—nor ever hear from out of his pages. I had quite a list of those old fellows marked down once—the last time I read his chief things—to confer with you about. But some of the powers of darkness blew them off to *limbo* or some other purgatory.

I remember the Ἀποκατάστασις πάντων, but never knew who its author was. That *savant médecin de Hollande*, Dr Beverwyk, is a famous old fellow. He was born in 1594, at (the same place as the Synod of) Dort : but he ought to have been born at Beverwyk, a little Dutch town, which seems named on purpose for his birthplace. But he would not consent, and so made Dordrecht immortal. His book is *intitule* " Epistolica Quæstio de Vitæ Termino Fatali an Mobili " *Dordr.* 1634, *4to et sup.* He discussed the question, as I understand it, whether the day of death is a fatal day, or whether the doctors can stave it off—or perhaps bring it on! He collected the " Opiniones Eruditorum," and his book made a deal of noise in Dort, and (I fear) some of the D.D.'s let fly at him. Three editions of his " Quæstio " got published at *Lug. Bat.*, only one at Dort. Perhaps the bookseller got scared, and did not dare reprint. He wrote also on *Women* (" De Excellentiâ Fœminei Sexûs." Dord. 1636, 12mo). But they say he did not write so much for the race of womankind, as for the *kind woman*, viz., *Anna Maria Schurman!* That last third of her sounds too Dutch—write it Annie Maria Sherman, and suppose he found her so sweet, and so pretty, and so tender, and so dear, that he fell down—his heart full of love to one growing beautiful to all—and wrote " De Excellentiâ Fœminei Sexûs ;" and what a pretty piece of medical gallantry it is! Besides, he wrote in Dutch, "Schat de Geezondheyd," or, " The Treasure of Health," a book said to be translated into many tongues, and of great value.

I have a copy of " Tyndale's Exposition," which I have laid aside for you the next time I shall get out to Cambridge, whither I much wish to go. Do you know that we are to have Hedge back again in the midst of us—as of old? Let us renew the old meetings which were so pleasant from 1837 to 1842, and then broke down and vanished, only not " everlastingly."

Hoping to see you soon, believe me, ever yours,

T. P.

TO THE SAME.

Feb. 22, 1858.

It does me good always to see even your handwriting on the outside of a letter before I open it. How much instruction I have to thank you for, it is only *I* that know! When I lived at West Roxbury and you at Watertown, both of us had more leisure than we are likely to find again, and many and many a good time did I have with you. I have walked in the strength thereof for many a forty days since. So if I don't often see you, don't think I am likely to forget the help I once had from your learning—which none that I know equals—and from the liberal direction of your thought.

I don't remember any rationalistic explanations of the absurdities in the Indian Vedas. It would be contrary to the genius of the people. It seems to me that fancy predominated over all else with them. They revelled in the improbable ; the grotesque took the place which the beautiful takes with us. The scientific-true, it seems to me, they cared little about. I seldom open their works without disgust. Their historians lacked both geography and chronology, " the two eyes of history " ; and their philosophers were *grannies*, I think. Emerson has come upon them *late*, and both exaggerates their merits, and misleads himself by their *bizarréries*. Their conception of God in general was gross enough and unsatisfactory, but they had nothing which, for horror, came up to the Calvinistic God. No heathen, with his "light of nature," could come up to the *Rex tremendæ majestatis* of " Revelation." *Deus Damnator* should be his title : *deus damnator hominum infantumque.*

Grotefend's Θεῖος μέν ὁ Πλάτων, &c., I have seen before, but I can't think where. I have tried to remember while courting sleep, but the old passage does not come. Yet I incline to Cyril of Alexandria. I have hardly looked at him these twenty years, but have a dim remembrance of it in his book against Julian. Yet it may be in Chrysostom, whom it seems like—though he snubs Plato. You remember he says, "*Platonem quippe ejecit* [*Deus*], *non per alium sapientorem philosophum, sed per ignarum piscatorem : ita enim et major clades fuit et splendidior victoria.*" I quote the Latin translation, for I have no Greek Chrysostom. This is from his Fourth Homily on 1 Cor., near the beginning.

*   *   *   *   *   *

That other passage, *delirant homines plectitur ipse Deus*, I don't remember ever to have seen before.* It is funny. What ideas men have of the *Deus !* No faculty of man has made such blunders in its development as the religious. No wonder : it is the greatest of all.

I have many questions to ask you, and shall get more satisfactory answers than I can give. I shall come and take tea with you before long, and we will talk over many things.

*   *   *   *   *   *

TO REV. MR. SENKLER, CANADA.

Boston, 6th March, 1858.

MY DEAR FRIEND,—What a sweet and beautiful letter you wrote me not long ago! I have waited for an opportunity to answer its loving words. It comes now. It is Saturday night. I have finished my sermon. I commonly write it at the beginning of the week and leave a page or two for Saturday night; then, when it is all done, and the last tear shed over it—for I seldom get through without moistening my ink a little in that way—I put all the signs of my week's toil aside, and gird up my soul for the other duties of Sunday, which are also great joys. How can I do it better than by thanking you for the letter you sent me? So kind, so tender—it need not be said so welcome. I read it with great emotion, with devout gratitude. I have just ended a sermon "Of the Soul's Normal Delight in the Infinite God," and wish I could read it to you before I preach it, or send it afterwards; but I can do neither, so only a letter will get forward.

First of all, let me thank you most heartily for pointing out some errors in my books. In the Discourse of Religion, p. 65–66, I did take ἱστίη for ἱστία, the Ionic (though perhaps rare) plural of ἱστίον, and thought the sails were taken by metaphor for the ship. I was misled by the authority of a friend whom I once heard quote the familiar passage and translate it "ship." I think too that I have found the thing in some *scholion* where μῦς was put for ἱστίη, but I can't recall the passage. I have no doubt you are right in making it mean "house" or "family." I shall alter the stereotype plate. The other blunder of putting Cithæron for Taÿgetus I corrected in the stereotyped edition. It furnished an Englishman with a paragraph to this effect :—" Mr. Parker is no classical scholar," &c. It was Cranmer and not Ridley (Ten Sermons, p. 233) and I have been burnt in an orthodox fire for making the slip, and that long after it was corrected in an *erratum.*

---

* Horace has " Delirant reges, plectuntur Achivi."

It is all right in the last edition, stereotyped. I made the best repara-
tion I could to the Archbishop by preaching his funeral sermon on the
300th anniversary of his last trial on earth. The other error, p. 67,
stands uncorrected in the new edition; how I made it I know not.
But a few days ago, or a few nights, when I could not sleep, I was
busy with some mathematical matters, and recalled the well-known
formula of falling bodies, and then remembered that I had in a sermon
once stated it wrong, and meant on the first leisure moment to find the
passage and see if it was still left as at first. You are right in both
the corrections in De Wette, Vol. I. The διστισθέντα for θιστισθέντα is
so in three editions of De Wette. I have not Philo's "Vitæ Con-
templat" to see if it be so there. In Vol. II., p. 32, fourth line from
bottom, there is a greater mistake than you think it; the whole sentence should read, "the name of God in these cases is often a superfluous expletive, and no sign that God has ever interrupted the course
of things." The reference should be to Eichhorn, § 422.

I thank you heartily for calling my attention to these things. The
translation of De Wette cost me a deal of labor. I began it when a
student of theology at Cambridge, 1836, and published it in 1843.
Nobody knows how much toil it cost me. I lived in a little country
village, and had a plenty of time, health, and vigor. It must contain
many errors, and I am sometimes astonished that I did the work so well
as it is. It cost me 2000 dollars to stereotype it; I have received about
775 dollars back again! So adding my interest to my principal—and
that to my outlay for books on that speciality—it makes a pretty little
sum, not to speak of my toil. But if I were to live my life over again
I would do the same. I meant it for a labor of love. It has had no
recognition nor welcome in America—it served the purpose of no sect.
But I must now bid you Good night.

It is Tuesday morning now (March 9th) and the newly-fallen snow
lies six or eight inches deep all around—at least it looks so from my
window. Let me write you a word or two more touching your letter,
so full of kindness. I take great delight in the Greek Classics, which
you are probably yet more familiar with—as your nice criticisms
seem to show. I read Homer, in Pope, before I was eight, and the
greater part of Plutarch's Lives at the same time. Latin and Greek
I learned early, and for many years lived in the noble classic authors
(of course the Bible was made familiar to me in my earliest youth).
Of late years my political duties, contending against slavery, have kept
me away from many favorite pursuits; but I still keep my love of the
classics fresh, and all the best new literature relating to them finds its
way to my table.

It gives me great pleasure to find some of my works meet with your
approbation, and touch and soothe your feeling when so tenderly tried.
Your *mourning* card, which I found at my house the day after you left
it there, told me of some bereavement; weeks later a friend from
Canada related the special form of the affliction. I wish I could have
seen you. But I was ill *all* the spring *and* summer, and fled into the
country to nurse myself up to vigorous health again. Last winter,
1856-7, I had two parishes, one at Watertown, where I preached in
the afternoon, and lectured eighty times in thirteen northern States!
Just a year ago this week I broke down, and I am not quite well repaired

yet. So I do little this winter. I send you by my friend Mr. Phillips a little parcel, containing a sermon "Of Old Age," which I think you never saw. It is the last copy I had. The little pamphlet on " False and True Theology" is only a newspaper report of a long sermon I preached —I have not read it, and don't know how well it is done. The newspaper printed it without asking me. But it seems to have provoked the wrath (or zeal) of some of my ecclesiastical brothers, who held a prayer-meeting last Saturday afternoon; about 40 *men* were present. Here is one of the prayers:—" O Lord, if this *man* is a *subject* of *grace, convert him,* and bring him into the kingdom of thy dear Son : but if he is beyond the reach of the saving influence of the Gospel, *remove* him out of the way, and let his influence *die with him,*" &c., &c. The prayer-meeting was called on purpose to labor with the Lord " for the conversion of that notorious infidel, Theodore Parker." So you see the tyranny of the old theology is about as strong in New England as in Old . . . . . (I was " the boy who sobbed himself to sleep" that is mentioned where you refer.)

I never saw the book of Varenus you speak of. I only know his work on Geography, as Dugdale has translated it. (London: 1724, 2 vols. 4to.) The extracts you so kindly made, are very significant, and wholly new to me. I have several books on Japan, but had only known this one by repute. How easy it would be to teach the Japanese and similar nations both natural piety and natural morality ! How absurd to attempt to impose such unnatural and hideous theology upon the poor creatures who had nonsense enough of their own, before we sent them either Catholic or Protestant Jesuits ! Mr. Browning, in his instructive book on Siam, says the people there think God can't be so wicked as to damn men for ever ! I was glad to learn that our American missionaries made almost no converts to their *theology* (the Siamese had quite as much *religion* as the missionaries we sent them to save their souls). Did you ever read Mr. Halkett's " Historical Notes respecting the Indians of North America," &c. (London: 1825, 1 vol. 8vo) ? He treats of the attempts to convert the savages of your and my neighbourhood ; you can't read the story without tears. I am amazed that men think they serve God by such evil treatment of his creatures. Many of his anecdotes resemble those which you copied out from Varenus. I am now studying the Indians of this Continent, intending to write on their religion, &c., part of a larger work on the Development of Religion in Mankind. Have you seen a remarkable book by Mr. Buckle, " History of Civilization in England" (London: 1857) ? I have hardly space to say how much I am

Your obliged and hearty friend,
THEODORE PARKER.

P.S.—Some ministers refused to ordain a young man because he did not believe in the eternal damnation of babies. The fact led to discussion and *clerical lying* in the newspapers. One of the sermons relates to the pleasing doctrine—Infant Damnation.

TO THE SAME.

Boston, May 6, 1858.

MY VERY DEAR SIR,—Your kind letter came quite welcome and instructive. The account of your training in Cambridge, [England]

makes many things clear to me in the character of educated Englishmen. I love the Greek and Roman classics, especially the first, and in early life read the most admired authors pretty liberally. I wish I could have had the careful training in the languages which you both had and conferred on others. But I learned them almost wholly alone—without help; and though I began Latin at nine, and Greek at ten, I think I never had in both so much help from a teacher as you would bestow on a boy in a quarter, perhaps in a month. Still, I learned to read and master them. Teaching these tongues forced me to a more careful study of them. They have always been a great delight to me, and I try to keep up in the recent literature relating to them, but of late years have fallen a little behind. I see Mr. Gladstone has got out a large work on "Homer and his Times" (3 vols. 8vo). What nice classic culture some of your men have! Had I been born in England or Germany, my predilections for literature and science would have made more difficulties for me to overcome than I have *yet* found in the rude culture of America. By the way, have you seen Rawlinson's translation of Herodotus, with huge annotations? There are to be 4 vols. large 8vo, very thick. He omits *indelicate* passages! I suppose he would in a translation of Hippocrates or Galen. The work seems to me highly valuable. But Baker's edition I have found of great service. The new reprint of it (1856, 1858), Vols. I. and II. (III. and IV. are to follow), contains the latest literature and discoveries. You ask, also, of Cudworth. We Americans printed 1500 copies in 1836 or 1837, and sold them all in five or six years! The American edition is difficult to find, and not worth buying now. The mistakes were not rare. Mr. Harrison has made an edition which leaves nothing to be desired. This is in 3 vols. 8vo, published in London, 1845. I think it costs 45s., but I got my copy in Boston for 4 dollars 50 cents. I think it may be had at Burnham's, in Boston, for that price now. Mr. C. published the original in one volume. It abounds with extracts from Greek and Latin authors; but he did not tell where the passages might be found in his author. Dr. Mosheim, that most laborious man of the most laborious nation, read through all the authors C. had quoted, and made reference to *every passage* in Cudworth's book. He translated the original into Latin; added notes, dissertations, prolegomena, indices, &c., and published it in 2 vols. 4to. Le Clerc introduced Cudworth to the Continent in his courtly and generous way; and then Mosheim taught him the manner and language of the learned, and he acquired a distinction in Germany, Holland and France which he did not have in England itself. The next English edition had Mosheim's references. When I was a youth at college, I wanted to get out an American edition of C., with all of his apparatus: a bookseller had it under favorable consideration, when lo! the other publishers announced theirs as in press. My scheme fell to the ground. But Harrison has done like a man what I fear I might have done like a boy. You ask about Strauss on the New Testament. I think you will admire his masterly scholarship. He handles his text with the acute learning and admirable tact you admire in the English classicists, but I think has *more soul* than they. Strauss's idea of God is quite unsatisfactory to me; so is his notion of a future state. He is a destructive critic, but quite fair, and exceedingly able. He has left theology for literature.

What you say of your ecclesiastical position in England is painfully interesting. We are bred very much so in the United States, in all our theological seminaries. The rawest professor is taken for "learned" by the rawer laymen who appoint him, and by the youth (not less raw) who sit and listen, and say "*Ipse dixit, qui contra dixerit anathema sit!*" I remember, with horror, that I used to sit, and see and hear the professor at Cambridge turn his mill for grinding the toughest or the mouldiest Hebrew or Hellenistic grain into homogeneous Unitarian meal, which we were to knead, leaven, bake, and distribute as the Bread of Life to all who came for food! He was very conscientious; we also. He thought he was teaching; we that we were learning. It was neither one nor the other. He milked the wether and we held a sieve, to use an old figure of Ramus. The first three months of trial showed me the folly of all this method; and that, if I wished to find the bottom of the sea, I must sound with a plummet and a strong line, not with a cork and a hair. I took Eichhorn's "Introduction to the New Testament," and prayed (kneeling) that I might not "be led astray by one whom some called an infidel, while I sought after truth." I think most ministers begin honest; but I fear few of them continue so in a long life. Surely they are not more so than lawyers, innkeepers, pedlers, and shoemakers.

I studied Butler once with much care. But his "Analogy" puzzled me with the same inconsistency you name; yet he still means honestly. His stout affirmation of the rule of right in human nature itself was a great step at that time; yet the admission vitiates the purpose of his "Analogy." If man, by the light of nature, can find out justice and all the rules of conduct necessary for the noblest life, it certainly is rather a low function which is left for Revelation, to come and teach us *circumcision, baptism,* &c.

But I have purposely abstained from writing on the main subject of your letter. Let us *talk* it over when we meet. But "*qui enim tam sim vanus ut eruditum erudire, ipse minime eruditus, præsumam?*" . . . You will find good accommodation at No. 34, Chauncey Street, with the Rev. David Read, formerly a Unitarian minister, now keeper of a genteel boarding-house. The best hotels are Revere House and Tremont House. Please let me know when you will come, and I will secure the rooms for you. With gratitude and esteem, yours,

THEO. PARKER.

I sent you a sermon, with the "prayers" of my brethren on its back. Rev. Mr. Burnham, one of the pray-ers last Sunday P.M., in his sermon, said, "Hell never vomited forth a more blasphemous monster than Theodore Parker, and it is only the mercies of Jesus Christ which now preserve him from eternal damnation."

The common additions of the LXX. have Theodotion's translation of Daniel, which, in III. 1, reads as you find and quote. But, in the true LXX., of which the Cod. Chisianus is the witness, the reading is as I say in pp. 510, but I have it not at hand. See Vol. I., pp. 148, 157; and II., p. 508. I have no copy of the genuine LXX. version of Daniel, but will look at it the first opportunity, and see if I represent it fairly.

25

That word *Rahab* occurs several times in the Hebrew text of the
Bible, where neither the English version nor the LXX. show any direct
trace of it.   The word itself has given rise to no little discussion
among the learned.   Some think it an Ægyptian word imported into
Hebrew.   But I think nobody has yet found it in the Ægyptian
monuments.   There is a verb, *rau-hab*, which means to be fierce, to
rage, to make fierce, &c.   Then the noun adjective, *rau-haub*, means
insolent or proud, perhaps fierce.   The noun *ra-hab* is a little difficult
to make out.   Sometimes it means only violence, fierceness, &c., then
it is the mythological name for Ægypt, then the name of a sea-monster,
we don't know exactly what.   It occurs in Isaiah xxx. where our translation reads "their *strength* is to sit still," where *ra-hab* is rendered
"strength."   The literal translation is "insolence—they sit still."   I
fancy it was a proverb—but as the writer was speaking of Egypt,
which bore the same name mythologically (*ra-hab*), I take it he made a
pun, which is now buried up, and not seen often.   The LXX. don't try
to preserve it, but read ματαία ἡ παράκλησις ὑμῶν αὕτη.   The Vulgate misses
the sense : *superbiæ tantum est, quiesce*.   In Isaiah ii. 9, *Rahab* appears
in the English version, which represents the Hebrew text reasonably
well.   But the Vulgate translated, *numquid non tu percussisti superbum,
vulnerasti draconem ?* while the LXX., like a naughty boy who has
not got the difficult lesson, passes over it as Moses went through the
Red Sea, dryshod, *siccissimis pedibus*, and skips it altogether.   It is
clear *Rahab* is Ægypt in this place, the *dragon* is only a synonym in
the Hebrew parallelism.   In Psalm lxxxvii. 4, we have *Rahab* again
in English translation, where it clearly means Ægypt.   But the LXX.
give the word Ραάβ, and attempt no version.   In lxxxix. 10, we have
Rahab in the English, which seems to mean Ægypt.   But the LXX.
has Σὺ ἐταπείνωσας ὡς τραυματίον ὑπερήφανον.   In Job, *Rahab* appears in
ix. 13.   Our translation calls it the *proud helpers*, the Vulgate renders
it *qui portant orbem*, the LXX. has κήτη τὰ ὑπ' οὐρανόν.   This variety of
meanings shows how uncertain the tradition was which guided the authors
of the Greek and the Latin version.   Ewald, one of the profoundest Hebrew scholars in the world, says, on this passage, in which he renders
Rahab "helpers," that as *Rahab* is the mythological name for a sea-
monster even when it means Egypt, so this verse alludes to a legend,
which relates that once in a great battle God conquered a monster, and
for an example of punishment nailed him up as a constellation in the
heavens, where it should always give light to the world, and tell how vain
it was to resist God.   If this be so, then the LXX. are not far out of the
way with their κήτη ὑπ' οὐρανόν, for (as he quotes Lach's dissertations
on the Oriental names of the constellations to show) κῆτος, πρίστις,
Balena, Bellua, and *Pistrix*, areal so constellations.   I don't know how
far this use of the word would justify the remark you refer to in the
Westminster Review, for I fear we are not well-informed as to the date
of these names.   I have long been satisfied that Job was one of the
most recent books of the Old Testament.   Bating the spurious parts—
Introduction, &c., it is wholly un-Hebrew.   God is not called Jehovah
in the genuine parts, I think, and there is nothing narrow or *Jewish*
in it.   The character of Job is one of the finest pictures of a " gentleman" in the whole compass of ancient literature : certainly few moderns
come up to him.

How the harlot Rahab came by her name I do not know. By the way, she was not a very respectable character to put into the ancestry of Jesus, though she is so abundantly commended by biblical and other writers.

I think you will wish you had not touched on this unlucky subject. But I promise I will never worry you with the matter again; but I do not think she was *justified* by the general or *special* works she is related to have done.

TO THE SAME.

Boston, December 9, 1858.

MY DEAR, KIND FRIEND,—Your warm-hearted letter came a little while ago full of indications of a tender regard and esteem which touch me deeply. I think no man has more generous friends: I wish I deserved them. But I will try. I have not perhaps been so sick as the newspapers represented, and am now a good deal better. I *did* preach the 14th November, and on the text named. It was against the advice of all my friends, and the doctors also; but it did me good and not harm. I treated of Needless Sickness, of Premature Death, and their Causes. I meant it for myself as much as others. Since then I have preached twice, once on the Progress of the Anglo-Saxon People in 300 Years — it was close to the 300th anniversary of Elizabeth's coming to the throne—and once on the Elements of Progress in the American People, and the Duty they have to Do.

This is the short story of my health. I have been singularly able-bodied all my life, and free from sickness. But in February, 1857, after excessive labors, I was exposed in a terrible manner all night, and found myself with a pleuritic fever in the morning. I fought against it for a month, bustling as before. But in March, I was obliged to yield and give up all work. The case was not understood by the doctor, nor treated well. An effusion of water in the chest followed, which it took nearly eight months to subdue, though it did not much interfere with my work. In the meantime a *fistula in ano* developed itself, and last summer produced painful and alarming consequences. I lost twenty pounds of flesh—had a cough, night-sweats, &c. It looked like the conclusion of all things here below. I bought no books, and did not look over catalogues. But I had a surgical operation performed in the beginning of October last, and am now gradually recovering from all the evils which tormented me before. But I had a sad relapse a fortnight ago. I attended a funeral of a little boy drowned by accident, and in getting into the railroad cars, strained and wrenched both my leg—which is lame from the fistula—and the abdomen. This now keeps me from walking, and will trouble me for some weeks perhaps; but if an abscess does not follow, there is nothing serious in it all. I think I shall live to be seventy or eighty, but I shall be more moderate for the future. Pray excuse all this talk about myself. I was much grieved that your visit was so short last summer, and it only tantalized me to see you but a minute.

It was Miss Stevenson who saw your son. She is one of the noblest and most intellectual women I have ever known. She lives with me, and has for ten years.

I am glad you found Tindal. He was a great man, shooting so far before his age. Over one hundred replies were made to his book! I read many of them when a student at college, but they amounted to nothing. Abuse was lavished on him by men not worthy to unloose the latchet of his shoes. I thank you for calling my attention to it again. I have not read him for twenty years or more. Toland wrote "Christianity not Mysterious," which drew a storm about his ears, and made him flee his country (Ireland)!

I have Mosheim's Cudworth (2 vols. 4to.), and will gladly lend it to you. Did you ever read Daillé on the Right Use of the Fathers?—that is at your service too. "Middleton's Inquiry into the Miraculous Powers of the Early Christians," is another book of great note, once making an epoch in ecclesiastical doctrine. Both D. and M. are a little unfair now and then, but right in the main. Mr. Blount, of Oxford, I think, wrote against them both in 1856 or 1857, a great, thick, learned, but uncritical book on the Fathers, which would amuse you; it contains really some good things. . . . . There is a curious passage in Photius' Bibliotheca (No. 232, Hoeshel's edition,) in which he gives an extract from Hegesippus, the earliest Church historian. He was a Jewish-Christian, and hated Paul. He speaks of Paul's, 1 Cor. ii. 9, "Eye hath not seen," &c. Then says, Ἡγήσιππος μέντοι ἀρχαῖός τι ἀνὴρ καὶ ἀποστολικὸς, ... οὐκ οἶδα ὅτι καὶ παθὼν, μάτην μὲν εἰρῆσθαι ταῦτα λέγει, καὶ καταψεύδεσθαι τοὺς ταῦτα φαμένους τῶν τε θειων γραφῶν καὶ τοῦ Κυρίου λέγοντος "μακάριοι οἱ ὀφθαλμοὶ ὑμῶν οἱ βλέποντες," &c. This shows what some of the early Christians thought of Paul! It would astonish the ministers a little, if they could understand what the apostles thought (and said) of one another. I hope sometime to have an opportunity to talk some matters over with you at length. I know you will be pleased with dear old Ralph Cudworth, with his wide comprehensive learning (though he had no *criticism*, and often was wrong in his exegesis, as all men then were), and with his deep fervent religiousness and genial freedom. His sermon before the House of Commons I used to think one of the best in the language. Certainly it would astonish the Commons now! I wonder who wrote the article on Newman in the *Westminster*. It seemed to me cold, but open and manly.

With kindest regards to you and yours, faithfully,

THEODORE PARKER.

TO THE SAME.

Roma, Jan. 22, 1860.

MY DEAR SIR,—I have long intended to write you, and shall perhaps find no fitter place than this to address a scholar from, and, it may be, no easier time to write in—for a consumptive man's days are too uncertain to count on. To a man who looks for the progress of mankind, Rome is one of the most hopeless places in the world, for it is the head-quarters of sloth and reaction; its religion is despotism; the subordination of man to an authority outside of his nature, and even alien to its noblest instincts and reflections; nobody knows how bad the principle of the Roman religion is, and how fatal to humanity are its logical measures, until he comes here and studies, and sees how it works the ruin of the people. But to a scholar who loves letters and a generous culture of the arts, and a philosopher who seeks to learn the great laws that control the welfare of the nation and the individual, perhaps there is not a more interesting spot on earth. The general aspect of all things is sad, the face of the people (thoughtless as they look) is more melancholy than I have elsewhere met with. All seems to respond to the popular chant,—

> "Roma! Roma! Roma!
> Roma non è più come era prima!"

I have four pretty, spacious, and comfortable rooms at No. 16, Via delle Quattro Fontane, on the Quirinal Hill, 140 or 150 feet above the river, which is about 20 feet more above the sea. I live 120 steps from the ground-floor, and yet I am not one of those poor poets that Juvenal speaks of—

> ———"Quem tegula sola tuatur
> Apluvia, molles ubi reddunt ova columbæ."

There is an English family 150 steps up, directly over my head, where he has the advantage enjoyed by that poet,—

> ———"Nam si gradibus trepidatur ab imis,
> *Ultimus ardebit!*"

But I have the sun all day from rise to set, and the whole city lies spread out before me, and the Ciminian Hills over on the Etruscan side of the Tiber, and I sleep secure in my lofty perch.

> "Vivendum est *et hic* ubi nulla incendia, nulli
> Nocte metus."

This part of the city used to belong to the 6th Regio, Alta Semita, and indeed it is the *highest* part of the town : the Pope's Palace of the Quirinal is close beside me, with its unprolific gardens, which look as celibate as the Pope himself has vowed to be. The Temple of Semosanctus (Dius Fidius) seems to have been in this neigbourhood. The Campus Sceleratus was not far off, where they buried the vestals who had more fealty to nature than respect for a conventional vow. The τις ἐντὸς τῆς πόλεως ὀφρὺς γιώδης παρατείνουσα πόρρω must have been the brow of this hill that I live on. Ἐνταῦθα κατασκινάζιται κατάγιιος οἶκος οὐ μίγας ἔχων ἄνωθιν κατάβασιν, &c. ; but pleasanter memories cluster about it. There was a temple to Salus, and I have come here to obtain the blessing if haply I may find it. The temple of Venus Erycina was near by. *Extra Portam Collinam*, Livy says, but within the present walls I fancy, not far from the Via della Porta Pia, the favourite walk of the priests, perhaps not unmindful of the old votaries of Venus, who did not wear cocked hats, and black stockings, and buckles in their shoes when they visited the same place. It seems readers of poetry lived here in old time, for Martial tells his book—

> "Vicini pete porticum Quirini:
> Turbam non habet otiosiorem
> Pompeius, vel Agenoris puella," &c.

That *vicini* I suppose refers to the fact that he lived not far off (on the Esquiline, as my landlord says). I have forgotten the passage that proves it, and have not the author at hand just now, and I never liked him much, the dirty fellow! But enough of this; I don't spend much time in identifying the old localities, which is indeed a most difficult and uncertain work so soon as you come to small details, and I think that a "live dog is better than a dead lion." It is curious to see how polytheism clings to this old heathen place. There is not a church in Rome dedicated to God, only one to Jesus of Nazareth, all the rest are consecrated to the Mother of God, the Virgin (conceived without original sin!), or to some of the saints, whose name is legion. The new Christian mythology drove out the heathen one, but the heathen is much the most interesting. The deities of the Roman heathen and the Roman Christian mythology, I take it, are alike mythological, representative of beings who are purely non-existent, or at least never had the qualities assigned them. Surely Jupiter is a more interesting character than the Deus Pater of the actual Roman mythology of to-day! Jupiter had vices of passion, and acted like the Evil One sometimes; but the Deus Pater is going to damn the greater part of mankind, and shows a disposition that would have made even the old Titan giants shrink with horror only to hear of. Besides, he does little, in these times nothing at all: he created the world, and intends one of these days to knock it all to pieces, but in the pictures he is represented as looking down on the *conception*, or the *birth*, or the *circumcision*, or the *crucifixion* of his only-begotten son, or as cockering him in heaven. So the Son, Deus Filius, is a most uninteresting person, adoring the Father, or blessing his Mother, or (in his human character) hanging his head, whining, and canting. The actual Jesus of Nazareth was none of your *dilettanti* men, but one who took hold of things with a man's grip. But the mythological Christ is a Miss-Nancyish sort of a nobody that I hate to meet, in marble, or mosaic, or oil colours. The Holy Ghost does but two things: he broods over the immaculately conceived Virgin at the conception, and over the only-begotten Son at his baptism; else he is commonly as idle as the crowd that Martial found round Pompey's house.

"Vel primæ dominus levis carinæ,"

to follow his verse. The Roman Christian mythology (and theology) discourages the vice of licentiousness, and so this is better than the heathen, but it encourages bigotry, hypocrisy, cant, and many another vice which the older Mother of Abominations kept clear from. Yet, on the whole, I don't deny that the banished gods of Old Rome were worse, in many particulars, than the new adventurers who have taken their place. But God send us the good time when Pope and Pagan, in fact, as in Bunyan's grand fabling, shall sit down in the same cage, and only make mouths at the pilgrims who pass by on the great highway of mankind! Oh, for a religion which suits the conscious needs of men, and a theology which explains the phenomena of the world, with a God that is adequate to the needs of science and of instinct too! In due time it will all come; but, How long, O Lord? we all say continually. If you could but see the *mere externals* of this city, you would feel like Paul at Athens, when he saw the whole city given to idolatry. He that comes to fulfil must also destroy; and there is no considerable human development possible for Italy but by the destruction of the Papacy. 1, The *temporal power*—the ability to cut men's throats and scourge women's backs—must cease; and, 2, The *spiritual power*—the ability to shut up the truths of nature and science from the eyes of men, and to tie a millstone on the neck of the child, and drown him in the depths of the Dead Sea of theology. To this complexion the Pontifex *Christianus* must come, and then be whelmed in the same stream which righteously drowned the Pontifex *Paganus*. Then what a relief will this be for the more advanced Catholic nations! Even Austria and Spain would warm with new life! And the Protestant nations also would draw a longer breath, and begin to cast *their* idols to the moles and the bats, and to worship the actual God of nature, instead of that hideous spectre which now *glowers* out of the Athanasian and other creeds, intending to damn them and their babies not wet by the fingers of a priest. I said just now that I lived near the Esquiline. On that hill of old time was a place for throwing down the dead bodies of slaves and poor people—which I take it were neither burned nor yet even buried; but, as Horace says (Epod. V. *ad fin.*),—

> " Post insepulta membra different lupi,
> Et Esquilinæ alites."

(See, too, 1 Sat. viii. 8–12). It was something better in Horace's own time, for he says,—

> " *Nunc* licet Esquiliis habitare salubribus atque
> Aggere* in Aprico spatiari, *quo modo tristes*
> *Albis informem spectabant ossibus agrum.*"

The old scholiasts on Horace (Cruquius and Acron) give the true geographical explanation. Well, now, just out of the gate in this neighbourhood is a modern *Campo Santo*, which has 500 pits. One of them is opened every day, and the dead—the *poor* dead, I mean—are pitched into the hole at the top, and tumbled to the bottom "without a grave, unknelled, *uncoffined*, and unknown!" Dead bodies are carried to certain churches and left there; at night the dead-cart takes them to this place, when they are thrown in *naked;* lime is next thrown on them, and, at night, the pit is closed till the time comes to open it anew. In the great Church of Santa Maria Maggiore, not far off, are two tombs, which, with the chapels that are but their adjuncts, must have cost three-quarters of a million dollars!—there is an epitome of *Christian* Rome! You once wrote me about the account of Nebuchadnezzar's statue in the *Greek* Bible! Here is the passage, Daniel iii., from the actual LXX., as contained in the Chigi MS., in the Vatican:—Ἔτους ὀκτωκαιδεκάτου Ναβουχοδονόσορ βάσιλευς διοικῶν πόλεις καὶ χώρας, καὶ πάντας τοὺς κατοικοῦντας ἐπὶ τῆς γῆς ἀπὸ Ἰνδικῆς ἕως Αἰθιοπίας, ἐποίησεν εἰκόνα χρυσῆν τὸ ὕψος αὐτῆς πηχῶν ἰξ, καὶ ἔςησεν κ. τ. λ. You see how much this differs from the *Hebrew* text, as represented by our version, and Theodotion's Greek. I believe I am really getting better here at Rome, where the mercury has not fallen below 25°. I hope this will find you in good health and spirits, and that you will believe me   Yours faithfully,

THEODORE PARKER.

---

* A part of the Agger of Tul. Hostilius is still extant.

TO DR. JOHN RONGE, LONDON.

Boston, May 19, 1854.

DEAR AND RESPECTED SIR,—It was with great pleasure that I received and read your letter of the 27th of April. I was in Europe at the time of your early demonstrations against the Holy Coat, at Treves, and since then have looked on your course with interest and admiration : but for the last two years have heard little of you except that you were at London. I am quite glad to learn that you are so successfully at work. England is a promising field to work in; for freedom is indigenous in the British mind, notwithstanding a certain insularity which often limits her development. It is a glorious time to labor in; there is so much activity of mind and body, and so much intelligence in the people.

I am glad to find that you do not follow the lead of Feuerbach or of his coadjutors. He does a service, but it is purely the destruction of the old, and then he roots up the wheat along with the tares. There are some Germans who accept him as their Coryphæus—atheistic men whose creed is—"There is no God, Feuerbach is his prophet ; a body but no soul ; a here but no hereafter ; a world and no God." They are much to be pitied—for the superstition of the Church, with despotism of the State, has forced their noble natures into this sad conclusion.

It is natural for the bud of new life to crowd off the old leaf, but not good to tear the leaves away before the time.

Here in America the work of liberalizing the minds of men goes on rapidly. Science destroys men's belief in miracles ; history shows the human origin of the Churches and of the Bible, and while the old rubbish gets removed, there is no firm ground-work on which to build up the great temple of true, natural human religion. In all the religious sects of America, there are earnest young men looking for better things—longing for truth and religion. The Germans will do something to correct our superstition. But alas! most of the young Germans here are *Feuerbachianer ;* yet they are more *materialistich* in their theology than in their lives.

Here is a noble man whom you know well, Dr. J. G. Günther; I think he first published your earliest communication respecting the Holy Coat. He speaks of you with enthusiasm. I shall always be glad to work with you on all the good things you contemplate, on both sides of the water ; and wish to make a long arm and take you by the hand with affectionate esteem. I look with eagerness for the books you speak of. The letter you speak of from your society to ours here in Boston will be warmly welcomed by us all.

It is now thirteen years this day since I first drew upon me the wrath of the Churches by a sermon " Of the Transient and Permanent in Christianity." It led nearly all of my personal friends among the clergy to abuse me. But there were noble and independent men who said, " No; let us look at the matter with our own eyes, and see what we may see! " It is to such men that we must both look for the advancement of the true and humane religion.—Faithfully yours.

TO REV. E. J. YOUNG.

Boston, May 4, 1854.

DEAR MR. YOUNG,—I thank you for your kind and welcome letter, which came last night. I reply immediately that you may get the letters of introduction in season. Do not dream that my estimation of a man depends at all upon coincidence of conclusions, theological or political. One thing I prize above all others, fidelity to a man's own sense of the true and just, the lovely and the holy ; then it is of small consequence to me whether the man be a Jew or a Christian, a Catholic or a Tübingen Rationalist. Of course I must love a rich, noble nature more than a poor and ignoble one ; but self-fidelity I put first of virtues. I trust you will study impartially, and decide after your best ability, not unduly influenced by the "Progressionists" or the "Reactionists."

I was sorry that I advised you to go to Berlin, when I looked round and inquired who was there to teach. I think you mention all the men worth much notice, for Twesten, I fear, is too *eng* (narrow) to help you much, and Hengstenberg is a man not likely to have a good influence, intellectually more than morally. I thought Tübingen would be a little too strong meat for a Yankee, though there is the ablest theological faculty in Europe. I look with amazement at the learning and *Fleiss* (industry) of Dr. Baur. I was glad to see what Guerike said in his last book. I will look for Rudelbach's account, which I have never seen. I saw no men in Germany who gave such decided indications of intellectual power, as Baur and Ewald. Ewald was then at Tübingen—the quarrelsome fellow ! I hope you will tell me a good deal about him when you return.

Your father's death took me as much by surprise as it did you. I had a letter from him but a couple of weeks before his decease ; he was ill, but no one thought him dangerously ill. I used to attend your father's meeting ; had once a class in his Sunday-school ; he married me. I had been in his meeting-house but once after the wedding. There was much in your father that I always honored and esteemed. He had no nonsense about him ; was "a scholar, a ripe and a good one," with wide scholarly sympathies, and I cannot bear to think that he is dead. I miss him at the book-stores, at the Athenæum. But the immortal man has gone to his better world !

I am glad to see how you feel about America ; our conduct is more infamous than that of Russia. You will soon hear that we have seized Cuba, I think. There will be work enough for you to do when you return, whether you come back *réactionnaire* or the opposite. Only be faithful to yourself—then you are faithful to your God.

TO H. C. BOSTON.

West Newton, 31st Aug., 1852.

The Law has these disadvantages :—1. That it exercises and develops the intellectual to the detriment of the other and higher faculties ; 2. That it does not allow a very complete and generous development of the intellect itself, especially of the higher departments thereof,—say the reason and imagination,—but only of the understanding. Most of the lawyers that I have known are examples of this defective and vicious development. Indeed, most of the lawyers that I know make a mere money getting trade of their profession, and no science at all; so that with them law is not a *liberal* pursuit, only a head-craft, and they are only *Mechanics at Law*, with little more elevation, and sometimes less than is law to a handicraft.

* * * * * * * The same onesidedness which keeps lawyers from the study of the permanent-abstract of metaphysics deters them from the permanent-concrete of natural science. So they look on the arbitrary statutes of man, which are only a temporary accident of development, as if they were absolute and fixed, as much as the permanent-abstract or the permanent-concrete mentioned above. A statute is a temporary rule of conduct devised to suit the passing emergency. The metaphysician and the naturalist deal with natural laws, which are the constant modes of operation of the forces of the universe; the lawyer deals with those statutes which are the variables of man, while the philosopher deals with these laws which are the constants of God. But the misfortune of the lawyer is that he looks on his human variables as if they were as permanent and as absolutely imperative as the divine constant, the laws of matter or of mind. Hence he loses his natural conscience and gets a fictitious and artificial conscience; loses the conscience of Nature and gets the conscience of Doctors' Commons or of the Old Bailey or of the Supreme Court. The study of science helps to correct this. Yet I fear few lawyers care much for science. Judge Parsons was a man of large scientific attainments. John Pickering also—a quite uncommon man in many respects—was familiar with the highest results of science. Both of these were better lawyers, as well as more complete men, for this scientific development. I know a young lawyer who had to manage a case of damages for injury done to cows by water artificially contaminated, who in preparing for the case set himself to study the entire physiology of the cow, and so understand the effect of poisons upon her. That was the true way for a scientific lawyer to go to work; the rule applies everywhere.

I would not waste my time on mean authors. I would study the masters of poetry before I played with their apprentices, and still more before I played with the lackeys of the apprentices. You see uneducated persons waste a whole evening in silly talk about silly men or women. It is yet worse for an "educated man" to waste his time on silly books; they are always bad company. The books of great men will be good companions.

You need not fear that you shall suffer as a lawyer for what you gain as a man. Reputation for strict veracity, integrity, and honesty would be most eminently valuable to you as a lawyer. It would give you the best kind of business of the best men. I am glad you are to study with Mr. Charles G. Loring,—for I take it his moral character is loftier than that of any lawyer, of his age, in Boston. His personal influence will be good and greatly good. I need not say to you that I think there is no real nobleness of manly character without manly religion—the love of God and the love of man.

TO REV. JOSEPH H. ALLEN.

Boston, Oct. 29, 1849.

MY DEAR ALLEN,—Your very kind and welcome letter came to me some days ago, and I have had no time till this minute to reply to it. You may judge of my business when I tell you that during the first five days after I came in town, fifty persons came to see me : then I have other things to do besides the entertaining of visitors. But it is very kind in you to write me nice letters, and long ones, too, when I am so rare a correspondent, though I would gladly be a frequent one. I liked your book on orthodoxy much. It has a good deal of originality in it. I wrote a little paper on it which you crowded out : I do not like to write on the books of one I hold so dear as yourself, because I always fear that private friendliness may mar my critical justice, or else my justice would seem unkind. I saw S. J. May a little while ago, and he delighted in your book. I asked him to write and tell you what he thought of it, and, still more, to write a little notice of it for the *Quarterly*, which he promised. I saw nothing inaccurate in the book, and admired very much the catholic spirit in which it was written. I understand the course you propose—your lectures, I mean. It seems to me a good one. You omit one man in the early age, the greatest name in the Church for many a day ; I mean old brass-bowelled Origen. He comprehended the liberality of Christianity better than any one for a long time. You cannot fail to make the lectures interesting and valuable, it seems to me ; but they will demand a deal of work. The practical affairs you speak of must take up much of the attention of a minister, for a part of his function is to concretize religion, and *make* the "kingdom come" which he prays for. Getting employment for the needy is a great charity, one of the best at the present time.

There is another that you do not mention—public education : can't you do a little for that also ? Much depends on the minister, and in a few years he can do a great deal, with a good will for the work and some practical good sense. I take it, sentimentalism is the degeneracy of religion. Thought and feeling, idea and sentiment, seem to be the male and female elements in religion, both of them needful to beget actions. What comes of mere thought or mere feeling is poor, and does not grow up or perpetuate itself. I long to see a more real union of various minds in religion. We live now in a state of heathenish isolation, and lose half our strength from want of concert. I see not why there might not be an association of theologians for the advancement of theological science, as well as one of "geologists and other naturalists" for the advancement of natural science. They would quarrel a little at first, as the Neptunists and the Vulcanists were wont to do, but soon the quarrelling would end, and Neptunists and Vulcanists would both by-and-bye cease to exist. They need not call one another Christians if they did not like, only theologians. At present the Unitarians, we think, are the most liberal sect in New England, or, the least illiberal ; but they do not contain all the liberality in the land, or exclude all the illiberality. Dr. —— is more illiberal than Dr. Taylor, of New Haven. I do not attend their conventions, nor would it be desirable in me to do so, even if inclined. They often take pains to have me away from their assemblies, and certainly I would not intrude upon them; and, indeed, I do not like to appear to make them responsible for doctrines of mine which they do not share.

Good will come out of this all. Men are getting to trust reason more, conscience more, affections more, and the natural religious element more. Of course, they rely less on authority, less on the Bible; upon the Churches less, and less on the ministry; but more on man and on God. Reverence for the letter declines, for the spirit thrives and grows strong. I shall always be glad to hear from you, and will be a better correspondent for the future.

I am, yours sincerely,
THEO. PARKER.

TO THE SAME.

Boston, January 29, 1851.

DEAR ALLEN,—I thank you for your kindness in remembering me in your new position. I am so bad a correspondent that I am not at all surprised if my friends forget me, though I do not forget when I do not reply. I have heard good things of you through Mr. Appleton, whom I saw not long ago, and hope you will find a more congenial field to labor in than at Washington, though you must miss many things which you had there. The library of 8000 vols. must come up to you as the "leeks which we did eat in Egypt freely," to the migrators out of that land of "cucumbers," &c.

I should be glad to be rid of the sight of slavery, though the imagination would still haunt me. I know well how much is a mere matter of *latitude;* it is so in all things. How many of the good folks of Boston would have become Protestants if born at Rome, or Christians if born at Constantinople? Why, it is not a great stretch of fancy to conceive of —— born at Constantinople and a Turk, with all the accompaniments of charity, hospitality, and fatalism. So of us all; I feel great sympathy with slave-holders; still, my abhorrence of the thing is not in the least diminished by the remembrance that I have relations of my own name, in the city of Charleston too, that are slave-holders. I hate the thing, while I love the men.

I am glad you ask me if I ever said that my present opinions or convictions *did not give me support in sorrow.* The great points on which I differ from most Christians is this. I believe in the infinite God, who is perfectly powerful, perfectly wise, perfectly just, perfectly loving, and perfectly holy. Of course He must have a *purpose* in creation, a *plan of creation,* both perfect and consistent with his infinite wisdom, justice, love, and holiness. This plan must be adapted to secure the ultimate welfare of each creature He has made, must be perfect in detail as well as in the sum. How, then, can I fail to *find* comfort in every sorrow, even in the worst of sorrows, consciousness of sin? I cannot: I have unspeakably more delight in religion, more consolation in any private grief, personal or domestic, more satisfaction in looking on the present or for the future than ever before, when I trembled at an imperfect God. I never said, never thought, never felt the sentiment imputed to me; quite the contrary.

Now, a word about the philosophical books. I think Ritter is a dull old plodder. I have his books, all of them, one on the "Erkentniss Gottes," not much known in America, nor much worth knowing. Still, let us eat his meat with thankfulness of heart; who else would give us an analysis of Albertus Magnus, of heaps of schoolmen, and write for us *ten volumes* of "Geschichte der Philosophie." I felt the want you complain of, and know not how to make up for it: the best way, perhaps, is to read "Colebrooke" or "Windischman," and "Schlegel on the Indian Philosophy." But you don't get much that is satisfactory. We are a little too early to learn the Hindoo philosophy. Ten years hence it will be easier. Bernouf is at work on something (Hist. Buddhism), that will help a good deal.

But Greece, after all, is the country where spiritual individuality got on its legs for the first time, and though Socrates believed *Helios* was a God, and not a "mass of iron red-hot," yet his contemporaries did common service for us in daring to think: Pythagoras, Anaxagoras, Hippocrates, even Theodorus, did us great service. I am glad you are studying this matter thoroughly, taking notes. The study of the Greek philosophers was a great help to me when in the Theological School; but I was too much of a blunderer to do the work well at that time, and the road was not so well turnpiked as it is now. I honor your spirit, and love your brave, good heart. If I can ever help you by lending a book, you know it will give me pleasure. Why not read Grote's Vol. I. and VIII. in connection with Ritter? Both are of much value in this matter. I shall read your article on "Comte" with pleasure. I could not give you any hints about him, only can say that he is able, dull, materialistic, and ill-natured, and has made a book of sterling merit. But what a pity he can't get out of his more material phrenology!

Remember me kindly to any friends I may have in Bangor.

Yours truly,
T. P.

TO THE SAME.

Boston, May 5, 1851.

DEAR ALLEN,—I have not time to write you a long letter, but will say that I am satisfied from your letter, that I was misinformed about you and your doings and sayings at Bangor. I never named my suspicions to anyone; but all I ask of a man is to be true to his own conscience, and take all pains to develope that conscience. He is to be faithful to *himself*, not to *another man's* self. Still, I admit the possibility of a man's being false to himself, of his violating his own conscience; and I think this is a common occurrence—a very common one with ministers, and, I fear, more common with Unitarian ministers than others. For, as a general thing, the Unitarian ministers have ideas in advance of the Orthodox ministers, while they have, generally, congregations more mammonish, hunkerish, and worldly, than the Orthodox congregations.

Then, I think the ministers take counsel, not of God, but of the congregation, and turn out such men as —— and ——, *et id genus omne*. Now, these men may be faithful to their conscience: it is not for me to say they are not. I never said that of any man.

I have been told that I stabbed everything I ever touched. Once I " stabbed " religion, then Christianity, then Unitarianism, then education, temperance, peace, prison discipline.

Still they all live after their " deadly wound."

Yours truly,   T. P.

TO THE SAME.

Brookline, Aug. 1, 1851.

MY DEAR ALLEN,—I read your paper before I read your letter. It is a grand paper, the best thing you have done as yet. I see in the critical part of it the influence of Comte and Gfrörer, two able helps. I have no criticism to make on that part,—the two first books of your discourse,—only to say that I think there is no man in the Unitarian denomination who would not be honored by writing it. The third part seemed to me not quite equal to the preceding, not conceived with so much vigor, nor expressed with so much scientific sharpness. I don't think it goes quite down to the deeps of the matter. The short of the matter, I think, is this: the old theology, all previous theology, has been bottomed on the idea of an imperfect God, not always imperfect in power, but in wisdom, in justice, in love, or in holiness—commonly in all four. There is a Devil as the Fourth Person of the Godhead in the common theology. In some schemes he is the *First* Person. Hence, there is a personal Devil who is a creation of God. Of course, God must have created the Devil out of his (God's) own substance, so there must have been a devilish element in God at the beginning. Others say there is no personal Devil, but yet must admit the *devilish in God;* for they believe there is absolute evil in the world. Hence, they have a hell, not as a *hospital* built by the Divine as house of care, but as a rack chamber, or torture cellar, built by the devilish as a place of torment and vengeance. Now, I take it that philosophy (physics and metaphysics) is at war with the Devil-god, but not also with the God-god. Philosophy believes in no Devil, neither in God nor out of Him. Hugh Miller finds " footprints of the Devil in the old red sandstone ;" they will turn out very different tracks. The time has come for affirming the infinity of God by his attributes as well as by his essence. Men have said God is infinite in nature (*Seyn*), but denied it when they came to treat of his *function* and *modes of being* (*Daseyn*). The future theology must rest on the idea that God is perfect in power, wisdom, justice, love, and holiness (self-fidelity), then it may be a scientific theology. Sometimes the expression in your writing is vague, and so the thought difficult to grasp. A German writer would not make this objection to you, for he loves the vague clouds he breathes from his own tobacco-pipe. Perhaps Comte is not likely to have a good influence on your style. With these exceptions I like your paper very much, and wish the *Massachusetts Quarterly* were alive to publish it to the world.

I like your scheme of Hebrew lectures. The patriarchs, I think we know very little about. I don't know whether you consider them historical or mythical. I have only one book which you need, that is

Ewald's "Geschichte des Volkes Israel," 4 vols. 8vo. If you like that, it is at your service. Knobel would help you on the Prophets. I have most of the books Mackay refers to in his " Progress of the Intellect."

The misinformation was that you preached "an old Hunker sermon denying the higher law."

Truly yours,

THEO. PARKER.

TO ROBERT WHITE, NEW YORK.

Boston, Feb. 11, 1848.

DEAR FRIEND,—Your letter of the 25th ult. came to me a few days ago, accompanied by J. Dunlary's manifesto. I feel glad that you can approve something which I have written about religion, and also I rejoice to hear of another man who loves the freedom of the truth. I think I understand the doctrines of the Shakers. I am not wholly ignorant of the books they have issued, which set forth their history and their opinions. I have always admired the order, the neatness, the economy, the plenty, and the peace which are so noticeable in their establishments. I rejoice to confess that they have solved the problem of association, at least so far as to show that men can live harmoniously in a community, and thereby make a great saving of time, labor, and all the material things which help to make up the comforts of life. But you will excuse me for my frankness when I say that I think they have made a capital mistake in attempting to nullify the distinction of sex: that is not a distinction of man's making, but of man's finding as God made it. From that distinction there comes the union of one man and one woman, united by the most sacred and most beautiful and endearing ties. Each is a complement to the other. Out of their union grows up the family—each new-born child to them a new Messiah, a new revelation from God. I admire the wondrous ways of God. I reverence his wisdom, I love his love, as I find this everywhere. But I see nowhere more lovely instances thereof than in the very distinction of sex, and the effects which grow out of that cause; yet I think I see the causes which led the founders of the Shakers to renounce all this. I know, too, the history of similar parties in other days, and the doctrine which led them also to renounce marriage.

One thing more let me mention, and that is, the neglect of education in the establishments of your friends. You are a man of cultivation: it is evident the men who transact the business of the societies, and come in contact with the world likewise get some culture. But I have looked with great pain on the countenances of the young men and women that I have seen in Shaker settlements; they look so ignorant, so undeveloped, so clownish, and sometimes stupid and almost animal. Excuse me, my friend, for mentioning these things; think not that I do not honor the much of good that is in your friends, because I point out what seem to me the evils. God gave us many faculties, all good in their place; certainly all good when acting in harmony, and each in its proportion. The problem of life is to tune all these strings to harmony.

Now I think the Shakers found one or two strings a little difficult to tune, and so they broke them off; then they tuned the rest quite well. Still the cords broken off were wanted. So the Shaker music is not yet *the whole human hymn.* Excuse me for writing this long letter, and believe me, truly your friend, THEO. PARKER.

TO THE SAME.

West Roxbury, July 31, 1848.

DEAR FRIEND,—I received the other day a copy of the *Knickerbocker,* which reminded me that I have long been remiss in not replying to your kind letter, received a great while ago. They who are good at excuses are commonly good at nothing else, so I will not try and excuse my silence,—only will break it now, and thank you for that letter as well as other favors, and also for the magazine, and the interesting notice of a visit to New Lebanon. What you said in your last note about the superiority of the domestic economy of the Shakers, I am not only ready but happy to admit. Certainly, you have no menial service—none of your community think work is degrading; while, in society at large, many men are ashamed of work, and, of course, ashamed of men (and women) who work, and make them ashamed of themselves. Now, the Shakers have completely done away with that evil, as it seems to me; that is one of their great merits, and it is a very great one. At the same time, they secure comfort, and even wealth; the only charge that I can bring against them is that of the neglect of marriage. In an argument you would very likely say a great many things against marriage, and all connection between the sexes; but still, the fact remains that God created men and women, and left the perpetuation of the race to the union of the two, doubtless intending that marriage—of one man with one woman—should continue so long as the race should endure.

It seems to me, also, that some of the best qualities of human nature are developed by the connection. I look on it as much a spiritual as a carnal want. It seems to me that the omission of this is the great defect of the Shakers. If they could still preserve the family tie and then have all the other good things, they would have all that the Associationists are contending for. I feel grateful to the Shakers for all they have done, and to you for bringing me better acquainted with them and their opinions. So, believe me, truly, your friend,

THEO. PARKER.

TO THE SAME.

West Roxbury, Aug. 11, 1848.

DEAR FRIEND,—Your kind letter came to me a day or two ago with the communication in the newspaper. I will forward that to the author of the article in the *Quarterly.* I will presently write you about the matter which you refer to—that is, as soon as the hot weather is over, and I have written two pieces which are now on my hands, but only laid away till the Dog-days are past. I have not done it before for this reason, I dislike controversy. You may think it strange that I, who have been mixed up in so much of it, should have no natural appetite therefor, but I have not even an *acquired* taste for it: I always fear that I shall not do my opponent justice. I like to make my statement, to have him make his, and then let the two stand for what they are worth. One thing I am sure of in *this* matter, viz. the entire fairness, candour, and love, of the person who will confront me. If I can be as fair as I know you will be, I shall be glad. I will write it all out as plain as I can. But I suppose the end will be that each of us will be thoroughly confirmed in his own opinions. Differences of temperament, education, &c., make a deal of difference in the conclusions men arrive at. I shall not be able to attend to this, I fear, before October; but then I will do so, only I shall write with no thought of publication. I think it takes all mankind to represent all of the truth that is known as yet, and each particular sect, or party, or class, has some function thereof which no other possesses. I aim to find out all the new truth I can, not yet known by anybody, then to take all I can get from each sect, party, or class of men, and put all together, the new and the old, and set it before men. If men do not then accept it, I proceed to point out the particular truth of each party, and also its particular error; and when that is done, I do not suppose that I am free from errors, nor do I expect that all will come over to my way of thinking. I shall be very glad to write the papers I speak of to you, knowing very well that it can only increase my esteem for you.

So good bye.

Truly your friend,   THEO. PARKER.

TO THE SAME.

Boston, Oct. 7, 1849.

MY DEAR FRIEND,—If I did not know that you are a true man, I should suppose you would think me a very false one for not writing to you on the subject I long ago promised to write on, and which you have been kind enough often to remind me of. But when I am well, I am a busy man, and when ill, a silent one. Now I have a little time at command, and thus proceed to write.

I find that Mr. Dunlary admits that marriage, or the sexual union of men and women, belongs to the order of nature; but if I understand him, he thinks this order of nature has been superseded by a new dispensation, and of course, all the accidents of the order of nature are likewise superseded, and marriage among the rest.

Now, to make out his case, he must (first) show that there has been such a dispensation which thus supersedes the order of nature; or else (second), show that there was a new order which expressly forbids marriage to the persons who accept the new. I do not find that Mr. Dunlary has done either of those two things.

Marriage seems to me as plainly demanded by the constitution of the human body, as copulation amongst animals is demanded by the constitution of their bodies. So long as the human race continues in the body, the body itself is an argument for marriage. Now, it seems to me that if the duties of the body are not fulfilled, the body suffers and deteriorates, becomes a poorer instrument of the spirit (I use this word to mean all that is not body), and so the spirit cannot fully perform its functions.

26

I think this is the case with many who have never married; I think I know some unmarried women who are examples of this.

With men, cases of involuntary chastity seem to be more rare; men finding a satisfaction for the appetite without marriage. Some men there are, and some women, who do not need marriage, to whom it would be irksome.

Perhaps there is one such in 100, imperfect men and women. Now, if this were all, I should very much distrust any mode of religion, or any school of philosophy, which should teach that marriage was to be superseded. I should say, Here is the body, with its organs and its appetites; this is an argument against you, and one straightway from God.

But I go further, and think that marriage is a spiritual affair as well as a merely physical—it is love as well as lust, and a great deal more love than lust. When man is a savage and subordinate to his instincts, the appetite commands him, and the connection of man and woman is chiefly sensual.

But when he is cultivated and refined, the sentiment is more than the appetite; the animal appetite remains, but it does not bear so large a ratio to the whole consciousness of the man as before, while the sentiment of love bears one much greater. It seems to me that love between man and woman resulting in marriage, leads to the development of all the spiritual powers of man, or helps in their development. Out of that comes the society of man and wife, then of parent and child, and so on. So, it seems to me that marriage is more spiritual than carnal.

Now, if it could be shown to me that Jesus of Nazareth taught that marriage and all communication of man and woman ought to cease with religious persons, it would not weaken my regard for marriage in the smallest degree. I should say, "Here is my body and my soul (I mean my affections), the external and the internal evidences of the naturalness of marriage. I cannot resist their testimony." In short, I should not set aside the old dispensation until the body and the affections of man were themselves set aside.

But then, the question comes, *Did* Jesus teach such a doctrine? It is quite difficult to determine with accuracy what was the opinion of Jesus on some points. But, notwithstanding my reverence for Jesus and my love for him, I cannot attach much importance to that inquiry, for if I think that the work (and so the will) of God is against him, I cannot follow him against God.

I know this is no answer to Mr. Dunlary, and I say it only by way of introduction, hoping to hear from you soon. I am, as heretofore, faithfully, your friend,

THEO. PARKER.

TO THE SAME.

Boston, Dec. 31, 1849.

MY DEAR FRIEND,—Soon as I received your last letter, I set myself seriously to work to write an answer in detail, but continued interruption for the sake of other duties renders it impossible that I should be able to do this; therefore I will limit myself to considerations of a more general character, which require less time and space, and will leave the other matter to be talked over when we may meet, as I trust we shall; for a little conversation will do more than a good deal of writing.

I shall take it for granted that, in making man male and female, providing them with instinctive desires for union, and providing no other way for the perpetuation of the race except by such union, God established marriage in the very nature of man's body. I think the spirit of one sex is as incomplete without the other as the body is, and that there is as much a spiritual desire for the spirit of the other sex in men and women, as a bodily desire for the bodies of the opposite sex. Only in most persons it is not so strong.

On these two points I think we do not differ.

Now, the question comes, Did Jesus Christ intend to forbid marriage to his followers? or, allowing it, Did he think celibacy the better state? Before answering that question, it is necessary to look a little at the state of opinion in the world about him on this matter:—

1. The Jews considered marriage necessary and sacred. Celibacy in a man was thought impious, in a woman disgraceful. But afterwards marriage got into worse repute among the Jews, and moralists found it necessary to commend marriage (*See, e. g.* Ecclesiasticus xxxvi. 24 and 26; xxvi. 1, 3, 13, 16, 20, 21; xl. 23; and other passages). At length there grew up a sect which abandoned marriage—the Essenes. They had some excellent ideas, it seems, and had a good deal of influence on the early Christians in many matters.

2. Amongst the heathens, marriage was generally held in esteem, or, at any rate, celibacy was not much allowed or practised. Still, it was sometimes practised as a religious duty, by a caste of men or women: the vestal virgins are examples.

In the offering of sacrifices, it seems early to be thought that what was most valuable to men or most dear, was also the most acceptable offering to God. Hence, the fruits of pastoral life (oxen, &c.), or of agricultural life (wheat, fruit, &c.), and not the spontaneous productions of the earth, were the sacrifice. As the organs of generation were of value in keeping the race in existence and in satisfying the instinct of man, in a fit of religious excitement men mutilated themselves in the name of God (the priests of Cybele are examples of this), and others made a vow of temporary or continual chastity.

3. The Hebrews never had a high idea of woman. Man is created for his own sake, woman to be a helpmeet for him (Gen. ii. 18 and 24). Man is of God, woman only of man and for man. This, also, is Paul's notion (1 Cor. xi. 7, &c.). The common notions of woman in the Old Testament is, that she is a wanton, or a drudge, or a shrew. She lost us Paradise; her heart is "snares and nets": "Any wickedness but that of a woman" was a proverb. Among the heathens there was great wantonness; there was, also, among the Jews, to judge from complaints in the Old Testament, and the numerous words the Hebrew language has for the crime of sensuality.

4. These things being so, it is not at all surprising that some of the Christians thought it was best to cut off that passion altogether which

they found it difficult to regulate; not surprising that they thought they ought to sacrifice their powers of generation, as the vestals or priests of Cybele had done. Especially would this be so among the rigid Christians; and the persecutions tended to make them all rigid. Still more, if men came from the Essenes to Christianity, would they bring their own notions of marriage with them ?

This being the case, I am not at all surprised to find St. Paul speak of marriage as he does. But, yet further, the early Christians thought the world was soon to end in their lifetime, so marriage was not needful to perpetuate the race. So Paul suffers it for such as cannot do without it; but to him it was a mere physical necessity, not at all a spiritual affection, which led to wedlock. I am not surprised to see such language attributed to Jesus as occurs in Matthew, Mark, and Luke, but I do not find reason to believe that Jesus was at all desirous of disturbing the natural order of things in relation to this affair. Still, I think such opinions were attributed to him before the Fourth Gospel was written, for in that Christ is said to work his first miracle at a marriage. It seems to me the author meant to show that Christ sanctioned marriage, and the use of wine, of which Christ makes three or four barrels for the occasion.

Now, if Christ intended to overthrow and supersede the union of the sexes, I think he would not have left it at all ambiguous, but would have said so with great plainness, speaking as distinctly as he did of the Sabbath and of the Jewish institutions, fasts, and the like. Many of the interpretations of Mr. Dunlary seem to me mistaken; e. g. his account of the "abomination of desolation" seems to me wholly a mistake; yet, in other passages he shows a great degree of ingenuity as well as fairness, and I feel much respect for the man. But you see how much time it would take for me to go over the whole matter, text for text; it would require me to write a great book, which I have not time or health to undertake.

I hope you will forgive me for my long delay and neglect; I know you would, if you knew the amount of matter I must attend to.

Allow me to wish you a happy new year, and believe me,

Your friend,

THEODORE PARKER.

TO THE SAME.

Boston, October 20, 1850.

MY DEAR FRIEND,—I was very glad to receive your kind letter of the 13th, and thank you for the kindly interest you take in me and mine. The *Massachusetts Quarterly Review* came to an end directly through the failure of the publishers, though they always found the *Review* profitable to them. It still owes me a little sum of money. But I was never a suitable person to conduct a *Review*. I am the most unpopular man in Massachusetts, and probably am more hated than any person in the State who is not connected with politics.

I shall not write in any periodical; for there is none in America which would accept my articles if I should write, and I am just now too busy with other matters to write in a journal, even if there were one for me.

If I wrote at all, I should prefer the *Westminster Review*, which you so justly praise. I thank you for calling my attention to the article on " Buddhism." I have been studying the subject, but had not seen the paper before. Buddha came in a period of general decline of religion, and recommended great austerity in morals. His followers, for a time, refrained from all sexual action, but they also refused to dwell in houses, to sit on a chair or bench; but they gradually returned to the common practices of mankind. I had not seen the article on " Prostitution " till you called my attention to it; for I have been out of town all summer, and out of the way of the journals. It is able and awful. I know not what is to be done. The industrial feudalism of the 19th century leads to some terrible results. As I look about Boston, I see the ghastly misery of social life, and know not what to do. Last Sunday afternoon I preached at Deer Island, to a congregation of drunkards (men and women), and street-walking harlots, in a sort of hospital. There I saw some 40 to 60 broken-down women of the town, in bed with the venereal disease ! I see daily sights in Boston of awful sin and misery, not the product of lust alone, but of intemperance, ignorance, poverty, and manifold crime, which make me shudder. All that I can do seems like putting a straw into the ocean to stop the tide. But I do not despair of mankind. No, never ! It is better than ever before, and the good God has a remedy for it all.

A history of the gradual development of the sexual element in mankind would be a noble theme. I wish I had either the talent or the time for the work. The passages you quoted from Mill interested me much ; I read his work soon as it appeared. He is one of the few writers on political economy who have a due respect for woman. He at least does not think she is merely to serve as a receptacle for the lust of man.

I hope you will excuse me for not sending you my little speech on Mr. Webster, but I did not know that it would interest you at all; so I beg you to accept a copy, which I send you now. I will send you a little sermon in a few days, and am,

Truly your friend,

THEO. PARKER.

TO THE SAME.

Boston, November 29, 1850.

MY DEAR FRIEND,—The kindness of your letters surprises me as much as their beauty. I thank you for all the generosity of affection which you have always shown for me, and extended even to my writings. At the same time, you have made a deep impression on my heart, and though I have never seen your face, yet your character has made an image of your person in my breast which will not depart from me. I wish it were possible for me to write the book you speak of ; but I live in a noisy city, in " a world where want and suffering are." I have a large parish, and many daily duties which call me early from my bed, which keep me late from it, and give me little time for the studies I most affectionately cherish. I have been at work on a book about Christianity a long time, and it does not approach completion ; so I must despair of doing what you speak of. But it will give me great pleasure to visit the " Shakers " you mention; only, such are my engagements in the winter, that I shall not be able to do so before May. I think then I shall be glad to meet you there.

Believe me as ever,
Faithfully yours,
THEO. PARKER.

TO THE SAME.

Boston, July 15, 1851.

MY DEAR FRIEND,—Your book came in due time, and a very friendly note a few days later—both welcome, as all that comes from that source always is. I happened, accidentally, to be at leisure that day, and so I read your book through directly. Your informant seems to me a little mistaken in the character of the work.

I think it was written by a very licentious person, for the most obscene purpose. He seems destitute of all true reverence for man or God. He is smutty, and vulgar, and low. Sexual passion is always in his thoughts, and so he rifles the Bible, and the classics, and Christian writers, to find matter to his taste. He teaches that the tree of knowledge, which Adam and Eve were forbidden to touch, was the sexual union of man and woman. He does not seem to believe what he teaches. Some of the Christian fathers were of this opinion. It is contrary to the genius of the Hebrew nation, and to their interpretations of their own literature. I know a clergyman who adopts the above-named opinion. He is a queer man, with the most intense passion for women, and the most erratic notions of forbearance. He seems continually desiring what he never dares to do, and is one of the most unhappy of men—lascivious as a goat, abstemious as a hermit, capricious as a monkey, and (now) as irritable as a hornet. He is the only minister I ever met who publicly maintained this opinion.

I hope you have a nice and quiet time this summer. I am now at Brookline, three or four miles from Boston, and in a place where all is green about me; there is no noise, and the quiet, the silence, the freedom from interruption is delightful. I can do twice as much here as I can in the city. In August I shall go off to the mountains of Pennsylvania, and spend a few weeks there in examining the natural history of the place—studying the coal, the rocks, and the plants. I have some friends engaged in the geological survey of the State, and I hope much rest from the change of scene and the change of thought.

Yours faithfully,
THEO. PARKER.

TO THE SAME.

Boston, Sept. 21, 1851.

MY DEAR, GOOD FRIEND,—I had a good time in Pennsylvania, saw the coal country, went about there with my scientific friends, and learned a good deal that was new to me. I am amazed when I think of the material riches which God has stored up in this world, as school-furniture for the human race. For, I take it, these great forces which science slowly brings to light, out of the ground, are, at last, to serve the great moral purpose of human life; to make the mass of men better off, wiser, juster, more affectionate, and more holy in all their life, without and within. But, hitherto, the great results of human science have been for the few, not the many. The steam-ships that weave the two Continents together are palaces for the wealthy man who takes passage in them. But the poor sailor on board them is hardly better off than the Norse seaman, who sailed to Labrador, dressed in bear-skins, 1000 years ago, and they have not so much self-respect.

You might step from the Crystal Palace to St. Giles's parish in London, and what a contrast you would see between the "London labour and the London poor!" The magnificence of luxury is achieved at immense cost!

The men who make the finery of Birmingham and Brussels, of Lyons and Geneva, never wear it. The ass used to carry papyrus to the Roman bath, but himself was never washed! So it is now with the workers and their work. You, the Shakers, I think, have solved the problem of industry with remarkable success. The labour of each blesses all: none is cursed with drudgery, none with idleness, none with poverty, none with the wantonnesss of unearned riches. Now, I think that, some time or another, the human race will solve this dreadful problem, and do without poverty as easily as without war. Then these great forces,—steam, electricity, and a hundred more which no man dreams of yet, will do their higher work of civilizing, moralizing, refining, and blessing mankind. We must work and wait.

I wish I had the time for the book you speak of, but I have already laid out more work than I shall be able to do in my lifetime, I fear. I have made the preliminary studies for them, so that if I should turn off now to other pursuits I should lose too much that has cost me too dear. I am now engaged on a book which ought to have been done long ago, and would have been, but for the Fugitive Slave Law, which kept me contending with the officers of law all last winter. Now I am at work on that, and hope to have it done by next spring, if I am well all the winter.

I have not yet found out the name of the author of the little book you sent me. Still, it seems very obvious to me that the man had no object in view but an obscene one. Of course I may be mistaken. He enters into such wanton details of wantonness as none but a licentious man would do, as I should think. But I should hate to judge any man too severely.

I will yet ascertain the author, if possible. I write on a slip of paper the name of the clergyman I spoke of. I should prefer that no one knew his name but you. He is one of the most self-denying men that I have ever known. His conscience has grown out like a sickly tumor on him, it seems to me. But I respect and honor him. If you took him out of the ministry in ——, I know not what would become of them.

We have just returned to Boston, or I should have answered your kind letter before.—Truly yours,   THEO. PARKER.

TO THE SAME.

West Newton, June 8, 1852.

My DEAR FRIEND,—Your kind letter came to me yesterday, and I was glad to find your handwriting on the envelope, and marks of your kindly soul in the letter itself. I ought to apologize to you for not visiting you at New Lebanon, as I have repeatedly promised; but two reasons prevented—one was the incessant labor to which I have been compelled all the season: no sooner is one thing over but another comes in its place. The next was this: whenever I laid aside the money for the enterprise, some poor person came who needed my help, and I could not say, "No, sir, I can't help you; I want to spend for pleasure the trifle you need for support," so I have been debarred of the pleasure of seeing you and your friends. I hope you will not mention this to anybody, for it is not a fact that concerns the public, and I only mention it that you may see it was no lack of will on my part. Yet, do not think that I am poor—I am rather rich than otherwise—but can always spend my means more profitably than on my personal enjoyments. This season, several scholarly men of this country and other countries have looked to me for a little help, and I could not say nay.

I saw the article in the *Tribune* which you refer to, and liked the extracts from the book. In my lecture, in quoting the Highlander's remark, " *Wherever McDonald sits, there is the head of the table*," I meant to say, the head of the table was where the greatest worth was, and, if the mutton was better than the man, then the platter was the head of the table, not the owner of the mutton. I fully accord with all you say about gentleness—the native kindliness of heart which seeks to comfort and delight others, and which you so well exemplify in your own house. It is before all natural or acquired gracefulness of manner, which, indeed, is nothing without this inner light of good manners. We should agree perfectly on that matter.

In respect to repelling force by force, I should differ from you widely. I respect the conduct of the Friends in this matter very much, and their motives also, but I do not share their opinions. I follow what seems to me the light of nature. It appears to me the opinion of Jesus is made too much of in this particular.

He supposed the "world" was soon to end, and the "kingdom of heaven" was presently to be established. He therefore commands his followers to " *resist not evil* "—not only not to resist with violence, but not at all. In like manner he tells them to "take no thought for the morrow." These counsels I take it were given in the absolute sense of the words, and would do well enough for a world with no future; the day was "at hand" when the Son of Man should come with power and great glory, and give fourfold for all given in charity; and eternal life besides. But the Son of Man (or God) is to use violence of the most terrible character (Matt. xxv. 31–46). Men were not to take vengeance, or even to resist wrong; not to meditate the defence they were to make when brought before a court—all was to be done for them by supernatural power. These things being so, with all my veneration for the character of Jesus, and my reverence for his general principles of morality and religion, I cannot accept his rule of conduct in such matters.

Yet, I think, violence is resorted to nine times when it is needless, to every one instance when it is needed. I have never preached against the doctrine of the non-resistants, but often against the excess of violence in the State, the Church, the community, and the family. I think cases may occur in which it would be my duty to repel violence, even with taking life. Better men than I am think quite differently, and I respect their conscientiousness, but must be ruled by my own conscience; and, till otherwise enlightened, should use violence, if need be, to help a fugitive.

I went up to Vermont last week, to conduct Miss Stevenson to her residence for the summer (at a tavern in Sudbury, Vermont). She would send her greetings to you, if at home.

My wife sends her most kindly greetings to you and yours. I get on slowly with my book; but have a little volume of sermons which will see the light, I hope, in the autumn. I think nobody has written on the subject you speak of. If I can find such a book, I will inform you.

Remember me kindly to all of your family, not forgetting the visitor from New Jersey.

Truly,
T. P.

TO THE SAME.

Boston, March 15, 1853.

MY DEAR, GOOD FRIEND,—I should have written you long ago; but when I came home from New York I had another of the comforts of Job, which seated itself on my right hand, so that I could not write with it. Some indispensable letters I wrote with the left. You would laugh to see them, but give up the attempt to read. Now that is gone, and all its companions, I hope. I was never better than now.

Your old and intimate relative has taken that step in his life which we commonly call death. I doubt not it was a pleasant step for him to take, though painful always it must be for us, the living, to separate from such as go to a higher life. But there are so many beautiful associations which cling to those we love, and come out with all the more beauty when they cease to be mortal, that the departure of a friend is always attended with an exaltation of our spirits if we have faith in the infinite goodness of the great Father.

There are some men whom I pity exceedingly,—

1. Such as have no belief in the soul, eternal life, and look on death as an ultimate fact.

2. Such as only fear a God, but do not know the infinite Father (and infinite Mother) of all souls, and so have nothing on which they can perfectly rely.

I meet both classes of men (the latter oftenest), and I pity them most exceedingly. To one, the grave is only a deep, dark hole in the ground; to the other, it is a hole which leads down to hell.

The popular religion makes death a most formidable enemy—a thing to be shuddered at.

I am amazed at the feebleness of men's faith in God. Death is one step in our progress; birth was a step once. But birth was a death to one form of being, and death is a birth into another form of being. To die in infancy, youth, or manhood does not seem after the true course of nature; but to die in old age,—

  "Life's blessings all enjoyed, life's duties done,"—

that is no misfortune, but a blessing also. My father, when an old man—seventy-and-seven years old—laid down his weary, mortal bones, and was glad to die We wept over his toil-worn hands and venerable head, which we had kissed so many a thousand times; but we were glad that the dear old man rested from his labors, and went home to his God and our God—the earthly father to the Infinite Father and Mother. So shall we all one day be glad to go, and knock with our feeble hand at our Mother's door. "Undo the gate, and let me in," shall we all say, as we go willing and welcome to meet her. I hope you and yours are all well. We send our kindest salutations to you all. My wife and Miss Stevenson admired your daguerreotype, and thought it quite faithful.

Sincerely yours,   THEO. PARKER.

TO THE SAME.*

Boston, January 15, 1855.

MY DEAR, GOOD FRIEND,—It is long since I have seen your kindly venerable face, or even had a line from your hand. I was never so busy as now; all things conspire to make me *solitary* (in my study) one-half the time; and *public* (in some great assembly) the other half. Just now I have scarce time for anything but public duties, and the arrest and "trial" will only aggravate the evil for a little time to come; but by-and-bye it shall be otherwise and better.

I passed through New York in October, reaching at 9 P.M. and leaving at 8 A.M., and again last week, arriving at 3 A.M. and departing at 8 P.M., but had no time to see even you and yours. Mr. and Mrs. Brace were at our house a few days ago, and I promised them to pass the night of my lecture at their house, and I must keep the promise, else I should have the pleasure of stopping with one so very dear to me as yourself, but I shall come and see you and yours.

I thank you most heartily for the 50 dollars, which shall be put in the treasury for the "Friendless Girls," in the manner you suggest. We will send any girls to the Shakers who wish to go; they are usually sent to families in the country, but doubtless we shall find some who will desire the quiet seclusion of the Shakers. I love to see a man who makes his money serve as a ladder towards heaven, whereon he and his fellow-creatures may climb up to higher heights of humanity: the strong man lifting up the weak! What a ghastly vice this of prostitution is! It comes from the false idea that woman is to be the tool of man, not his equal, but slave; but gradually we should outgrow this folly and wickedness, as we have many others.

I am sorry that I do not see more of your son. I am so busy that I seldom go to Cambridge, not twice in six months, and he does not visit us so often as I could wish. By-and-bye he will get better acquainted.

Remember me most kindly to all, and believe me,

Heartily yours,   THEO. PARKER.

---

* See in the Appendix VI., Vol. II., a letter from Mr. White's son, in acknowledgment of the benefit which the father derived from his correspondence with Mr. Parker.

TO REV. DAVID WASSON.

Boston, December 12, 1857.

MY DEAR WASSON,—Many thanks for your kind and welcome letter. I know how much it cost you to write it, and that dims my joy in reading it. You must not write much; you learned to labor long ago, now " learn to wait." I ate my lunch in the railroad station, and thought over all Higginson said in defence of the Irish. I like good *plump* criticism, and need it oftener than I get it; but I think he was mainly wrong, and still adhere to my opinion of the Celtic Irish. In other lectures I have showed at length the good they will do our country; when I give this again I will do so, and name the good qualities of the "gentlemen from Corrrkk," and the poor wretches from Africa.

I take Blumenbach's five races only as provisional—five baskets which will hold mankind and help us handle them. In respect to power of civilization, the African is at the bottom, the American Indian next. The history of the world, I think, shows this, and its prehistoric movements. I don't say it will be always so; I don't know.

You and I do not differ, save in words, about the Greeks. In the emotional element of religion, I think the Shemites surpass the Indo-Germans, and the Jews were at the head of the Shemites. The Phœnicians took to trade, and cared no more about religion than a Connecticut tin-pedlar, who joins any Church for a dollar. Somebody found one of the scoundrels, a mummy now in an Ægyptian tomb, who was circumcised. He took the religion of the place just as the current coin. Religious emotion, religious will, I think, never went further than with the Jews. But their intellect was sadly pinched in those narrow foreheads. They were cruel also, always cruel. I doubt not they did sometimes kill a Christian baby at the Passover or the anniversary of Haman's famous day! If it had been a Christian *man*, we should not blame them much, considering how they got treated by men who worshipped a Jew for God. They were also lecherous. No language on earth, I think, is so rich in terms for sexual mixing. All the Shemites are given to flesh. What mouths they have, full of voluptuousnesss! only the negro beats them there.

The Jews, like all the Shemites, incline to despotism; they know no other government. The Old Testament knows no king, but one absolute; the New Testament is no wiser, if perhaps you bate a line or two which Jesus spoke—and they indicate a feeling more than a thought. The New Jerusalem is a despotism with a lamb for the autocrat; a pretty lamb too, by the way, who gathers an army of 200,000,000 horse, and routs his enemies by the Euphrates, and then comes to Italy and kills men, till he makes a puddle of blood 200 miles wide and three feet deep. (See Rev. ix. 16, and xiv. 20.) In the Old Testament, Jehovah is King, a terrible King too. He is not a constitutional King, but arbitrary. His word is law. There is no proof of anything, no appeal to individual consciousness. With the Greeks, all this was different—Indo-Germanic, not Shemitic. I love the Greeks, especially the authors you name; but for moral helps and religico-emotional helps, I go to that dear Old Testament, for all Æschylus and Sophocles. Do you remember any example of remorse in the Greek literature? The Hebrews had a pretty savage conception of God; but He is earnest, there is no frivolity attributed to Jehovah. He is the most efficient Deity of old times: none of your *dilettante* gods. Beside, He is wholly superior to the material world, while none of the Greeks or Romans got above the idea that, in some particulars, it was more than any deity or all deities.

Get well as fast as you can.   Yours,   T. P.

TO F. E. PARKER.

Boston, April 15, 1858.

MY DEAR SIR,—I send you herewith some rambling thoughts about the Provident Association, and they will gain nothing by *my* name, so I put them on another sheet with no signature. Show them to whom you like—this to none, nor let the writer be known.

I think 70 per cent. of our out-door charity has only a reflex good action: 30 per cent. helps the receiver, 70 *only* the giver. Now we might reverse the proportions: all would bless the giver, but 70 per cent. would also elevate the receiver.

When I first came to Boston, I meant to go into that work of looking after the perishing class. But three things hindered:—

1. Men had a great horror of me.

2. They had no correct ideas as a basis of action, in general or in special, and

3. The slavery question assumed such an alarming shape, proportions, and position that we must turn head and put it down, or turn tail and die—conquer as *men*, or die *niggers*.

So, for twelve years, I have been laboring to diffuse the true idea of man, God, and the relation between the two—of life for the individual, the family, community, nation, church, world; and also fighting slavery in all its forms. I shall never do for the perishing and dangerous classes what I primarily intended. But I will bore you no longer with this sheet, for I am,

Yours truly,

T. P.

SOME THOUGHTS ON THE CHARITIES OF BOSTON.

1. The effect of our in-door municipal charity is excellent, not without some evil, of course, but in the main it works well. I am thereby insured against starvation. It is quite a step in civilization when a nation guarantees its citizens against death by hunger and cold.

A little shame attaches to the recipients of this charity: it ought to be so as a rule; and a little more to their children: that ought not to be so.

The State almshouses, I think, are an improvement on the old mode of treating foreign paupers.

I have altered my opinion after a little observation, and by the results of trial.

2. The effect of our out-door charity—municipal, social, individual, is mainly bad. The *secondary* (or reflex and subjective) action is admir-

able; it blesses the giver. I think of few persons who make an investment for their own sakes which gives so good dividends as what they spend for the poor; what they lay out for others comes to more than what they lay up for themselves.

But the primary (or direct and objective) action is quite bad. I sometimes think it does more harm than good; but this is a little extravagant.

1. This charity is badly distributed, without discretion, conscientiousness, or industry. Most of your visitors lack those three virtues. The want of the least of them is a great fault. No business in Boston requires a more liberal measure of all three. S—— is a capital good fellow, highly useful in his place, truly benevolent, conscientious—most religiously so—and devoted to this work. He is tender and tenacious both—rare metallic qualities to unite in one person. You will not do better than to keep him. But, spite of him, things are as I say.

2. You have to deal with exceeding bad material. The ethnology of pauperism is worth more than a hasty thought, which is all I can give it *now*. (1.) Anglo-Saxon pauperism, American, English, Scotch, is easily disposed of. (2.) German pauperism will give us little trouble. (3.) Jewish pauperism will take care of itself—it is quite inconsiderable, and will be taken charge of by Jewish almsgiving, which is the distributive virtue of that people, as thrift is their cumulative virtue (and an *evil odor* their cumulative and distributive vice, chronic and progressive with the children of Israel). (4.) African pauperism is easily dealt with. The negro is the least acquisitive of all men; his nature is tropical. He is an equatorial grasshopper—not a bee of the Temperate Zone. Still, he is so pliant that we can do with him as we will, if we will justice and charity. (5.) Celtic pauperism is our stone of stumbling. The Irishman has three bad things—bad habits, bad religion, and, worst of all, a bad nature. In dealing with Irish poor, I lay down three maxims:—

(1.) The Irishman will always lie, if it is for his momentary interest. (2.) He will not work while he can exist by begging. (3.) He will steal when he can get a chance, and preferentially from his benefactor. I can recall but *one* instance of a grateful "gintleman from Cork." These vices—lying, begging, stealing, are *instantial* of the genus "Paddy from Corrrck". The opposite is exceptional—of Bridget and John, eccentric individuals. I might add a fourth: Paddy will get drunk if he can find liquor.

Now, the bulk of our pauperism is *Irish*. Suffolk County is " County Cork"; Boston is a young Dublin. What shall we do with this wild Irishism which is yelping around us? I'll tell you a wrong thing we *have* done: we have put the head-quarters of charity near the centre of the Boston Paddy-land! What is the consequence? Ward VII. *squats* in the anteroom of the Provident Aid Society; it passes its mornings there, that by its continual coming it may weary the wisdom of charity into a foolish gift. I would not have the room too near; as the tap draws the idlers, so the till of charity draws Paddies. If it were half a mile off it were better. Bridget and Michael will feel the " swate influence" from the North End to the Neck; but from Franklin Street to Fort Hill, why, it draws all the virtue out of them. We want a new suite of rooms, for which I would give two limits :—1. They should not be in such fatal proximity to the Irish. 2. They should be ventilated well.   The Irish are poisoning our agents with their contaminating nastiness.

Last autumn the benevolent men of Boston said, "There will be much suffering, and then much crime. Let our charity prevent both!" It was religiously meant; it was well done. I think there has seldom been *less suffering* in a winter in Boston, especially in the class of people who seek our relief.   But where you sow alms beggary springs up; as the tare amid *this* wheat there came theft, the exceptional but regular weed amid the instantial crop.   Next autumn and next winter we shall see such demand on our charity as we never knew before. If charity be organized, dependence becomes also an "institution," and beggary is organized beside it.   Ours is a society for the *preventing* pauperism. Why, we are making it a society for the promotion, diffusion, and organization of pauperism!

Now, we want a good, able-bodied, able-minded man as the out-door organizor and supervisor of this work.   He should be a *religious* man, having *piety* without narrowness, *morality* without cant or asceticism; one upright before God and downright before men; and with a theology he believes in, but does not wish to strangle other men withal. I think Rev. Mr. Ritchie, of Roxbury, is just such a man; Capt. Goodwin is perhaps still better.

TO A FRIEND.

Boston, Feb. 6, 1852.

DEAR SIR,—I take the first leisure hour to reply to your note of last Sunday.   Regarding Jesus of Nazareth as a man, there is no reason why we should suppose that he could never be mistaken.   You make a distinction in this matter, and admit that he might come short of the truth through lack of ability to see it, but seem to hesitate to admit that he could be mistaken or wrong in any of his positive teachings.   Yet I think a careful study of the Gospels will force us to the conclusion that he was sometimes mistaken.

There is a little—nay, a very great—difficulty in ascertaining the opinion of Jesus on some quite important matters; for (1) it is not certain that any of the writers reported his exact words ; and (2) the writers disagree so much among themselves.   Thus, there is an immense difference between the first three Gospels and the fourth—a difference in the history and the doctrines.   In the first three there are remarkable diversities of doctrine.   Thus, Matthew represents Jesus as saying (x. 5), "Into any city of the Samaritans enter ye not;" and, again (xv. 24), "I am not sent but unto the lost sheep of the house of Israel;" and Luke puts no such words in the mouth of Jesus, but represents him as sending messengers "into a village of the Samaritans." Of the ten lepers he heals, only one returns thanks, and he a Samaritan (xvii. 16) ; and the model of practical piety that he speaks of (x. 30–37) is also a Samaritan.   Luke had Matthew's Gospel before him when he wrote.   Mark had both Luke and Matthew, yet Mark omits all that Matthew and Luke report about Jesus in relation to the Samaritans. This could not have been by accident. Matthew seems still to have clung to Judaism, hence he gives such passages as that in xxiii. 1–3. Luke was more liberal, and broke away from Judaism, and so never gives such a command as that in Matthew. Notice also the account in Matthew of the sending out the Twelve (x. 1) and that in Luke (vi. 13), and Luke's account of the sending out of the seventy (x. 1–16, and 17–18). Luke is not favorable to the exclusive claims of the Twelve Apostles. Since this is so, I find it difficult to be certain how far opinions have been ascribed to him which he never held, and how far he changed his opinions, and so taught differently at different times. He did the latter it is plain, for in Matthew (v. 17–19) he says he was not come to destroy the law (*i. e.* the law in the Books of Exodus, Levit., Numb., and Deut.), but to fulfil—*i. e.* to keep. He affirms the doctrine of the orthodox Jews, that not a jot or tittle of the law should be altered or repealed till the end of the world (v. 18), and would not have one of the least of the Commandments (of that law in these books) set aside or neglected. Yet, by-and-bye, how differently he speaks of the Sabbath and of fasting, *e. g.* in the same Gospel! How very different are his own doctrines in the Fourth Gospel (*e. g.* John iv. 21–23), and in the Epistle of Paul, who rejects the law which Matthew would have us keep.

If the First Gospel is correct, Jesus believed the end of the world was presently to take place (Matthew xxiv. 3–27, 29–34). Unitarian and other interpreters refer this to the destruction of Jerusalem, I think very unjustly. It is plain from the Epistles that the Christians thought the world would soon end ; Paul, John, and James seem to agree in this. In Peter there is a remarkable passage (2 Peter iii. 3–4, 7–10). All this is enough to show that Jesus was greatly mistaken if Matthew reports him correctly.

Now, I think that Jesus was a greater man than the Gospels represent him. I look on him as a man of vast genius, a great mind, a great conscience, a great heart, and a great soul. I mean that he was a man of great genius—intellectual, moral, affectional, and religious genius ; and of course lived a great life of piety. But when he was a boy I suppose he stumbled in learning to walk ; miscalled the letters in learning to read ; got wrong conclusions in his thoughts. From his very nature as a finite person this must be possible and actual too. When he reached the age of thirty he must have made mistakes in his intellectual processes, and in his moral and religious processes. We always stumble in new things : the greatest men must do so. Kepler, the great astronomer, first discovered the great law in astronomy which governs the planets in the solar system ; but he had made many a wrong hypothesis before he hit the right. From the nature of the case this must be so with any mind except the Infinite God.

Now, I should be much amazed to find a man, with even the vast endowments of Jesus Christ, at that period teaching the idea of the infinite perfections of God, and never saying anything inconsistent with that idea.

But look at the facts, and see what the others teach about God which implies a limitation in his idea of God. He tells men to "*fear* him (God), which is able to destroy soul and body in hell" (Matthew

x. 28). This (with its parallels) is the only place in which Jesus commands men to fear God. And this alone might easily enough be explained away, but in other places the character of God is represented as worthy of fear more than love, *e.g.* Matthew xviii. 23–35 ; xxi. 44 ; xxii. 11–14 ; xxiv. 48–51 ; and xxv. 30. I think in the New Testament there is no indication of the idea that the suffering of the wicked in the next life is for the good of the wicked themselves: it is vengeance, and not medicine, that they smart under. I think the Evangelists believed that Christ taught the eternity of torment in hell, otherwise I cannot explain such passages as Mark ix. 43–48 ; xxv. 41–46 ; Luke xvi. 25–26. Good and holy men try to explain away such passages, and so violate the language they ought to interpret, because the idea of eternal damnation, or of any torment which is not for the welfare of the man who suffers it, is too atrocious for us to accept. This alone shows that Jesus did not conceive of God as infinitely perfect, as it seems to me.

Then : the fact that Jesus believed in a Devil, an actual personal Devil, seems to me abundantly plain, if we can trust his biographers. The account of the Temptation presupposes this existence, and that in the most literal kind. But I pass over that. In that beautiful prayer which is so deep that the world prays it, the petition, " Deliver us from evil," means from *an evil one* (*i. e.* the Devil). The same word is used in the same sense in Matthew xiii. 19. It is he, the Devil, that sows tares in the field, and so is the rival of God (xiii. 38–39). Nay, as " many are called, and but few chosen," so it would appear that he was the successful rival of God, and got more souls than the Father Himself at the end of the world. But it is needless to cite passages to show that Christ believed the actual existence of a Devil and devils (*i. e.* demons) that " possessed" men; the whole thing is so plain and obvious that it needs no argument.

Now, if there be a Devil, absolutely evil, and so eternally evil, then, so far as he has any power at all, he checks the power of God and hinders Him from accomplishing his purpose. So God is not infinite in power. But if there be such a Devil, then God must have made that Devil; and if God made such a Devil absolutely evil, it could only have been out of evil in God Himself. Then, God could not be infinite in wisdom, or in justice, or in love and holiness; for a Being perfectly wise, just, loving, and holy, could not make a being perfectly unwise, unjust, unloving, and unholy. If God be infinitely perfect, then there can be no absolute evil in the world, no evil that does not come to serve a good purpose at the last. You and I stumbled when learning to use our legs in childhood, and got hurt in the fall ; we stumble in learning to use our higher powers, and get hurt by the error or the sin. But the stumble of the child and the sin of the man must alike have been foreseen by God, and are alike accidents of development, requiring no Devil as author of the child's stumble or the man's sin. You and I have outgrown the first form of mistake, and walk erect ; the little hurts we got in our fall made us take better heed. So we shall outgrow the moral stumbling ; and the pain of our error, the smart of our sin, will make us take better heed, and so the suffering be medicine.

I think Jesus had a feeling of the infinity of God, and hence the grand and beautiful words of comfort that he speaks, which are the things that you doubtless value most in the New Testament. Such passages as these, Matthew v. 3–12, 23–24, 43–44 ; vii. 7–12 ; ix. 13 ; xi. 28–30 ; xviii. 11–14, 21–22 ; xx. 25–27 ; xxii. 37–39, &c. &c. The marvellous story of the Prodigal Son, in Luke xv. 11, is a most touching example of the same thing.

I have the greatest reverence for Jesus, the greatest gratitude and love, and feel the vast obligations we all owe to him, perhaps no man more so ; but I love and reverence him for what he *is*, not for what he is *not*. I know how these opinions will shock men, but must take up that cross also, and bear it as I can.

TO A FRIEND.

Oct. 5, 1858.

Many thanks for your interesting letter, with the reminders of numerous friends you. met. Gurowski is a man of great talents, of truly wide and deep historic learning. I know few men that are his equals in respect to these things. He and I have often picked that crow—the diversity of races. He does not satisfy me, nor I him. Perhaps both of us are a little wrong, only I see his error and not mine.

Buckle *did* read many poor books, but it was unavoidable. To cross the Continent, we must go through much poor land, which yields nothing to the artist or the man of science. The charm of Buckle is—his poor books don't hurt him.

Since I saw you, I, too, have had a little journey in an open wagon, with Mr. Lyman. We drove about 700 miles in New England and New York State—the Hudson River Valley. We were in the open air about ten or twelve hours a-day, and saw the farmers and mechanics of the small towns. I saw but one *American* drunk in all the journey ; not a ragged *native*, or his windows stuffed with old clothes. The evidences of industry, thrift, temperance, intelligence, and comfort, were a happy surprise, even to me, though I am pretty familiar with New England. We kept in the small towns, and slept only once in a " first-class hotel " at Albany.

If I were Governor of Massachusetts, I would visit all the gaols, all the asylums, State almshouses, and other public institutions. I would set my mortal bodily eye on them all, and *see*, and *know* how the State's hired men did their work. All the normal schools, likewise, all the teachers' conventions would I visit. Of course I would not neglect the farmers' show, the mechanics' show, or the soldier show. I liked Banks's speech much. We have too much neglected the militia ; we may need the armed men when we little think of it. I hate the armies of Europe—putting the destroyer or the defender before the great creative classes who manage the thought and toil which give us all desirable things.

TO GEORGE RIPLEY.

Boston, Nov. 19, 1858.

My DEAR GEORGE,—What a troublesome correspondent I prove to you ! With this note you will receive the third edition (stereotype) of my translation of De Wette's " Introduction to the Old Testament."

27

It has never received any reasonable notice in America, for it favors the truth and not the prejudice of any sect. It has never had a friendly word said for it in any American journal.

    *   *   *   *   *   *

Let me say a word about the work.

I. Of the Original.

It is the most learned, the most exact, and the most critical introduction to the Old Testament ever made in any tongue. It contains the result of all the critical investigation of the human race on that subject, up to the date of his last edition. Since then no important additions have been made to the science of biblical introduction, except as follows :—

1. The learned researches of Mr. Movers, a German Catholic priest, at Breslau, on the Phœnicians, have shed new light on the Books of Chronicles, Jeremiah, and some other passages in the Old Testament. But what he has adduced belongs more to commentaries than to an introduction.

2. The labors of Mr. Ewald, a man of genius and enormous learning, clear up some dark things in Hebrew history. He gives his conjectures on the composition of the Pentateuch, but he is so subjective and capricious that his works are vitiated by uncertainty. Still, he saw some things which De Wette saw not.

3. Recent researches in Egypt (Lepsius', &c., I mean), may hereafter give some help in biblical introductions, but *not yet*.

4. Light may come out of the Assyrian darkness at Nineveh, and shine on obscure things in the Bible. But it has not reached us yet.

With these exceptions, the original of De Wette bears the same relation to the actual learning of the age as in 1842 and 1843.

II. Of the Translation.

1. I read the original carefully, studied it (beginning in 1836), and the new editions, as they successively appeared till 1843.

2. I translated the work word for word.

3. I read up on the subject thus :—

    (1.) All the previous introductions of the Old Testament, from Simon down to Hengstenberg. That was a labor.

    (2.) All the early Christian writers (Fathers, &c.) who treated of such matters down to Jerome and Augustine; that also took *some* time.

    (3.) I read all the modern works relating thereto—often a weariness.

    (4.) I added from those what I found necessary, to make the matter as clear to the popular audience I hoped to address, as the original was to the learned reader of De Wette himself.

I popularized the original thus :—

    (1.) I translated in the text all the Latin, Greek, and Hebrew (Rabbinical) passages which De Wette put in without translating, and I put the original extracts into the margin. It was a pretty piece of work, you may guess to do into English the awful Latin and Greek of the old choughs who wrote so barbarously!

(2.) I looked over the references to the Bible. Where he said, "comp. Isa. ix. 1, with Jer. xlv. 16," I printed the passages side by side, sometimes in the common translation, sometimes in Noyes's, and sometimes in my own. Thus I made easy and obvious what else were difficult and obscure.

Now, if you will give some little notice of the book, I will consider that you renew the right hand of fellowship once extended me.

Good bye.

T.

TO DR. R. L. HOWARD, COLUMBUS, OHIO.

Boston, April 30, 1849.

DEAR SIR,—Your letter reached me to-day. I cannot suffer any business or any weariness to prevent me from answering it before I sleep. I thank you for the candor with which you write. I confess my work seems to me somewhat fearful; it did so when I began it, and I was often tempted to be silent, for I saw what a revolution would take place, suddenly or slowly, in the popular theology. If my principles were true, I saw that a mountain of rubbish must be swept away; that many reputations, many hopes, many institutions, likewise, were based on that mountain of rubbish, and of course must perish with their foundation. I saw that many men would look on me as the enemy of religion, and so as the enemy of mankind; that some would think that, while I opposed the folly of so much which men had believed in as religion, there was no reality at all for religion. But, at the same time, I had a strong confidence that what was true was also safe; that falsehood was not safe. I thought I could show men that the popular theology had no natural, at least no indissoluble, connection with true religion; that underneath the shifting sands of sectarian theology there lay the eternal rock of religion. I have never been sorry that I undertook the work; indeed, I could not have forborne if I would. I have felt the loneliness which you speak of; that comes from breaking away from early associations and tender ties. But that has long since passed away; still, I do not like to be hated, as I sometimes have been.

I have been compelled to pull down; but I have no delight in that work. It has always been painful. I did it only that something better might be built up in place of what but cumbered the ground before. I saw that religion was natural to man; the infinite goodness of God I could never doubt; the connection between God and man seemed to me so obvious, so essential to the nature of each, that I wondered any man could doubt of these facts. The more I live, the greater religion appears, the more attractive, the more satisfying, the more beautiful. But it seems plainer and plainer that religion is one thing, and the books written about it quite a different thing. At one time the Bible rested on me like a nightmare; I could not bear it nor get rid of it; now that I take a different view of it, the imperfections which I find in both the Testaments no longer disturb me, and the truths I find in both are the more welcome, because I feel free to come and to go, free to examine and satisfy my own mind and conscience, before I accept the conclusions of men who lived in another age and wrote from a different point of view.

I think I understand the circumstances in which you are placed. It requires not a little heroism to do as you seem disposed to do. But who can be contented with a divided heart? You do not lose your sympathy with the religion of your old associates, only with their theology. In all that is real piety, love of God, or real goodness, love of man, you will sympathise with them the more. Still, I suppose men not much enlightened will think ill of you, and speak harshly of your name. Sometimes it requires a little charity to be just to men who, from their ignorance, are unjust to us, but such charity is twice blessed. I hope my poor book will do no harm, but some little good to mankind. It would be a comfort to think that I had helped men in the way to religion, and all it brings; even to have helped a little. I have no doubt committed many errors, which, of course, must do harm. I hope they will be exposed, and left to perish. Now and then, some one writes me a letter like yours, which shows me that I have not spoken in vain; altogether, we may all be grateful for the liberal spirit of this age, which allows men to keep their heads on their shoulders, while these heads are full of thoughts which must work a revolution in the world. But let me not weary a busy man with a letter over-long. I will send the *Review*, as you suggest, and such of my sermons as are still on hand, though I lament that some which I value most are out of print. If I can ever be of any service to you I shall be glad, and am,

Truly your friend,

THEO. PARKER.

TO P. D. MOORE.

It seems to me that the Christian world has honestly made two great mistakes, in common with the rest of mankind: namely,—

I. They consider that God is finite. In our time they do not say so in so many words, yet, when they come to speak of his works and motives, it continually leaks out that they think so. Hence comes the notion of the wrath of God, of vindictive punishment, of eternal hell, of God changing his plans, either directly, as related in the Bible, or indirectly, by miracles, such as are spoken of in the Bible and the religious books of most of the nations. The belief in miracles rests on two things. 1. A Deity who can control the material world; but, 2, a world previously shaped by this Deity in so poor a way that it does not answer his intentions, and he, therefore, must alter it to suit the particular purpose in hand. The alteration is not according to the nature of the thing, as the blossom of the bud, and the fruit of the flower; but against the nature of the thing, as a man born with no human father, an ass speaking Hebrew, and the like. The notion of a miraculous revelation made to man rests on this previous thought, namely, that God had made man so poorly at the first, that he would not ascertain the religious truths needful for the safe conduct of his life, and so God must by miracles supply the defect of nature, that is, He must alter and mend what He made badly at first. The Bible represents the world as not turning out as God expected. The common notion of the Christian pulpit is, that mankind is a disappointment to God; the world is not what He meant it to be. All this comes from the imperfect idea men have of God,—of God as finite.

II. They conceive of religion as something unnatural to man. In human nature there is either too much, something to be cut off, members of the body to be mutilated, as in the Hebrew Church; then of the spirit to be mutilated, as in the Christian Church, where the reason is thought a dangerous thing, and all good Catholics or Protestants are to circumcise that, and cast it from them; or else too little; so something must be added in opposition to human nature. This is a second birth, or a gift of the spirit, which does not mean a development of the original faculties we are born with, but the acquisition of qualities from some foreign source—from God or Christ. Then the deeds demanded in the name of religion are not such as are the flower and beauty of human nature; they are not natural perfections, but things often against nature. The conventional sacraments, which are thought to make a man a " good Mahometan," or a " good Catholic," or a " good Jew," or a " good Calvinist," are things not needful to make him a good man. The man is put down; the sectarian is put up. The consequences of this mistake as to the nature of religion are seen all about us. There are noble men in every sect; but the sects themselves seem to me working with poor tools, and not trying to do the thing most needful to have done. We want men, not Mahometans, Catholics, and Protestants.

I take it, the remedy for these two evils is simply the true idea of God, the true idea of religion, and a life in accordance therewith.

I. God is not finite, but infinite—a Being of perfect power, wisdom, justice, love, and holiness. Doubtless, God possesses other perfections of which we have no idea. We, having no corresponding power of conceptions but these, make up our idea of a perfect being—the infinite Being. Then He must be perfect cause and perfect providence. He must make and administer the universe—including matter and spirit and each creature therein—from a perfect motive, for a perfect purpose, and use a perfect means thereto. Of course, the work would not require alteration and amendment, in whole or in parts. It would require only development. Then all notions of the wrath of God, of the jealousy of God, of his changing his plans, of his hating men, of eternal damnation, and the like, must end at once. Everything is insured against ultimate shipwreck at the office of the infinite God. His hand is endorsed on all that is.

II. Religion is natural to man; I make it to consist of two things, namely, 1st, piety, our consciousness of God and of our relation to Him in its perfect form, this absolute love of God, absolute faith in God, and absolute delight in God; and, 2nd, morality, the keeping of all the natural laws of the human constitution in all the relations of life. Thus, then, religion taken as a whole in the service of the infinite God by the normal action of every faculty of the spirit, intellectual, moral, affectional, and religious; every limb of the body, every power we possess over matter or over men; this religion will appear in all forms of singular or associated action, in the life of the individual, the family, the community, the State, the Church, and the world of nations.

To awaken this idea of God in the souls of men, and to induce them to live out such an idea of religion, that, my dear sir, is a great and noble work; but it will be done by the prayers, the tears, and the toil of earnest and noble men. I wish you much joy in this manly undertaking.

Yours sincerely,
THEODORE PARKER.

TO MASTER WASSERBOHR, AT THE LATIN SCHOOL, BOSTON.

Montreux, Canton de Vaud, Suisse, September 2, 1859.

DEAR MASTER WASSERBOHR,—I was quite glad to hear of your progress at school, and of the welfare of your father and mother and all the family. I often think of your fighting your way along at the Latin School, and overcoming both the difficulties of the Roman and the English languages at the same time. When Mr. Gardner, at your request, put you into a higher class, I hope the additional studies were not too much for you, and that you went on with fresh heart and strong hope. Nothing can be done without regular persistent industry,—

"Labor improbus omnia vincit."

The talent of work is one of the greatest of all; without it no other brings much to pass. At your time of life, two things require to be specially attended to; one is attention, the power of fixing the mind on what concerns it, as steadily as an auger bores into a log; the other is memory, the power of keeping what you get, and reproducing it when needed. These are the two great things you must cultivate now; if you do it faithfully, you will find by-and-bye, that you can master a book by reading it once, and remember all the good things that are in it. Other intellectual powers will come into play later. Of course, the imagination always has work to do. It is a good plan for you before you go to sleep at night, to think over all you have seen, and heard, and done, and thought in the day; that will help to fix the attention, and confirm the memory, and, besides, it has inestimable moral advantages, for you can't fail to ask of all, "Is it right, or is it wrong?" Indeed, education must be of the moral and religious powers, as well as of the intellect: a good scholar, who is also a bad boy, is a shameful monster. Of course, you don't forget your play; few boys do that. But you must take great care to keep good firm health; a sick scholar is a good-for-nothing—about as worthless as a horse with but three legs, who needs propping up at one corner in order that he may stand still.

Remember me to your father and mother, and believe me always,

Your friend,
THEODORE PARKER.

We have some Holsteiners boarding here at the same house with us, intelligent people.

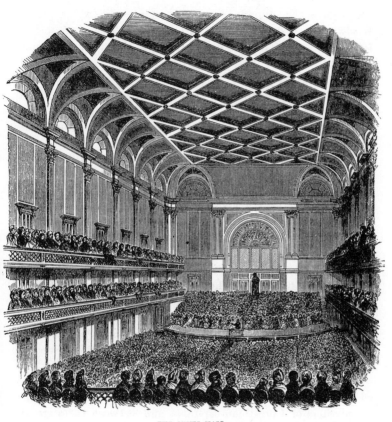

THE MUSIC HALL.

CHAPTER XIV.

Twenty-Eighth Congregational Society—The Music Hall—Preaching—The Fraternity.

THE engraving represents the interior of the Music Hall during the lifetime of Mr. Parker. It is at present (1863) in the hands of mechanics and decorators, who are refitting it for the reception of the great organ which has been built in Germany for the Music-Hall Association, at a cost, as finished in Germany, of 25,000 dollars (£5000). The Twenty-eighth Society is worshipping elsewhere, and will not probably return to the Hall after its re-opening.

The project of erecting a hall in Boston for musical entertainments was the subject of frequent discussion, which had no result, until a committee of the Harvard Musical Association took the matter in hand, and secured the amount required, 100,000 dollars, for the purchase of land and the erection of a building. A vacant lot of ground, known as the Bumstead Estate, and a small adjoining lot, comprising in all 16,642 square feet, with an entrance from Bumstead Place and one from Winter Street, were purchased. The passage way from Winter Street is 15 feet wide and 110 feet long.

The greatest care was taken in elaborating the plans for this noble building. Mr. Snell, the architect, submitted his designs to competent judges, such as J. Scott Russell and Dr. Faraday in England, the former a distinguished architect, the latter a man well versed in all that was then knowable on the difficult point of acoustics. The result was the finest building in America for its special purpose, and stately and convenient for all the objects of a popular assembly.

The main hall is 130 feet long, 78 feet wide, and 65 feet high. In the day-time it is lighted by semi-circular windows on either side, above a cornice that is 50 feet from the floor; by night the cornice of the four walls springs into jets of flame. There is a passage-way in the wall large enough for a man to move along in lighting.

The ceiling is deeply moulded into diamond-shaped spaces, which are flat, and of a blue color. Arches spring to it from the pilasters of Corinthian capitals; and between them are the windows. Two rows of balconies with latticed fronts extend around three sides; there are fourteen doors to each. The floor, covered with oval-backed chairs of stuffed damask, each with its porcelain number-plate, will seat 1500 people: fourteen doors empty the audience into ample corridors. A faint rose-color prevails over the whole interior of the building.

The stage is five feet from the floor, with a level foreground, whence it rises in seven steps, the whole width of the hall, to a gilded screen of wood-work in the centre of one end. At first a small organ that was used in the Melodeon was concealed behind this screen. The stage-steps might accommodate 500 people, and the whole building would comfortably seat 2700.

When the audience was perfectly still, the ordinary voice of a speaker could be heard with ease; but every little sound in the body of the house accumulated so readily as to blur the sentences coming from the stage. The clapping of the two-and-forty doors was sometimes a great annoyance, but generally there reigned a silence so eager and deferential when Mr. Parker preached, that his level, conversational style could be heard with ease ; and it was only towards the close of his services that his speech was sometimes marred by belated or impatient listeners.

On one of the stage-steps stands Crawford's bronze statue of Beethoven, presented to the Association by Charles C. Perkins, of Boston. It was cast at Munich, on the 26th of March, 1855, the anniversary of Beethoven's death, and placed in its present position, with appropriate ceremonies, chief of which was a poem of great vigour and beauty by Wm. W. Story,* on the evening of March 1, 1856. It is seven feet high, of yellow, almost golden, bronze. The head is erect, and the face has a firm, earnest, and inward look. The neck is open, and a large cloak is thrown over the right shoulder. The hands are crossed, lightly dropped before him ; the left holds the score of the Choral Symphony, and the right holds over it a pen. On the score are the first notes of the strain

" Freude, schöne Gotterfunken,"

the opening line of Schiller's Song to Joy, and the first of the Chorus in the Ninth Symphony.

The seal of the Music-Hall Association is a figure of St. Cecilia, with a motto that was furnished by Mr. Parker :—

Cœlo venit aurea dextro,†

which he translated,—

She comes, resplendent, from auspicious skies.

Here is Mr. Parker's prayer on Sunday, March 2, the day after the unveiling of the statue, privately reported :—

O Thou infinite Spirit who fillest the air that is about us, and the ground underneath our feet, and the heavens above our head ; and who Thyself art the Spirit whereby, wherein, we live and move and have our being ; we would draw near unto Thee, who art never withdrawn from us, and feeling Thine infinite presence in our heart and soul, would worship with our morning prayer, that we may serve Thee in our daily, nightly, long-continued flight.

O Thou, who art the life of all things that live, and the being of

* Son of Chief Justice Story, of Massachusetts, and sculptor of Cleopatra, The Sybil, and other noble works, including the bust of Mr. Parker which is given in this Memoir.
† From Manilius : Astronom. Liber N., p. 539.

whatsoever are, we pray Thee that Thine infinite soul may stir us in our poor prayer, and quickened by Thine infinite life, may re-ascend in our aspiring flight to higher and higher nobleness and human growth.

O Lord, we bless Thee for Thy providence, which broods over the world, and blesses it with Thy fourfold year. We bless Thee for the summers and autumns that have gone by; for the winter, whose brilliant garment of resplendent snow has been so broadly spread across the shoulders of the Continent. Yea, Lord, for all the providence whereby in winter Thou preparest for spring, and makest summer to be the porch and entrance for harvests, autumns full of beauty and abounding in fruit.

O Lord, Father and Mother of the ground, the heavens, and all things that are, we bless Thee for Thy loving-kindness and Thy tender mercy. We thank Thee that Thou art kind and large in Thy providence to every created thing; that from Thy hand we take our daily bread, and from Thy cup Thou pourest out to us all things whereby we live and are blessed. We thank Thee that Thou watchest over us in our prosperity, in our distress, and followest the exile from his native land to every home, giving the wanderer Thy blessing, that when despair comes to Thy children's heart, Thou, who knowest their weakness, takest them home to Thyself, and blessest every wanderer with Thine infinite peace, whence no soul shall ever be exiled long.

O Lord, we thank Thee for noble men Thou raisest up in the world; for those great souls who proclaim truth to mankind; for those who reveal justice to the earth, enacting it into laws and institutions, building up Thy righteousness, Thine ever-living truth.

We thank Thee for those great souls to whom Thou confidest the precious charge of genius, blessing them with lofty gifts. We thank Thee for the sons of song, who make sweet music in the hearts of men, and when their own body crumbles to the poor ground, their breath still surrounds the world with an ever-new morning of melody, giving to highest and lowest, and blending all into one magnificent family of souls who are lifted up by the sweet strains of art.

O Lord, we thank Thee also for those sons of genius who, with kindred power, stretch out their plastic hand over the hard elements of earth, which become pliant at their touch. Father, we thank Thee for the creative genius of the sculptor, which folds a kindred genius in brazen swaddling-bands, and so hands down form and lineament, all glorified by art, from age to age.

O Lord, we bless Thee for another power, which is music and sculpture to other faculties; for the poet's kindling eye, whose wide embracing heart is vision and faculty divine, whereby, to listening crowds, he anticipates the spontaneous feelings of our hearts, and makes perpetual in speech the transient feeling of an hour.

O Lord, while we thank Thee for those whom Thou hast blessed with creative genius in the intellectual sphere and moral, still more do we bless Thee for those whom Thou hast gifted with genius for loving-kindness and tender mercy, whose art is the art to love, and who embalm in affection such as are near and dear, and put great, all-embracing arms about the universe of men, lifting up the fallen, refining the low, raising those that are dropped down, and encouraging the sons of men.

O Father, while we bless Thee for the sons of poetry, the children of song, and those great geniuses born for creative art, still more do we bless Thee for the dear fathers and loving mothers, the great philanthropists of the world, who have blessed us with more than music; they make perpetual Thy thought which shall endure when the marble shall perish, and brass exhale as the vapor, unseen and forgotten to the sky.

O Thou, who possessest manifold gifts, we would ask of Thee a double portion of the spirit of love, that while we serve Thee with our hands, while we honor Thee with our mind, while we serve Thee with our conscience, we may serve Thee more nobly still with sweet sacrificing love. May we so love Thee, O Lord, that we may feel Thy perfections in us, Thy truth making us free, Thy law a lamp to our feet, a staff to our hands, and the love which Thou bearest to every mute and every living thing, a great moral inspiration in our souls, bringing down every vain thing which unduly exalts itself, making us of cleaner eyes than to behold with favor iniquity, and setting our affections on things divine.

O Lord, help us to love our brethren everywhere; not those alone who love us with answering touch of joy, but those who evil entreat, and persecute, and defame us. So we may be like Thyself, causing Thy sun to shine on the evil and on the good, and raining Thy rain on the just and on the unjust.

O Father, we ask Thee for that gift all divine which is righteousness, and mercy, and love, in our hearts. May we chastise ourselves for every mean and wicked thing, set our soul in tune to the music of Thine own spheres, and so, hand in hand accordant, journey round the world, blessing without with toilsome hands, and inwardly blessed by the spirit Thou puttest in our souls. Amen.

And here are extracts, privately reported also, from the sermon which he preached on the same day, called " Of the Culture of the Affections :"—

I honour great power of thought, few perhaps more so. I reverence with great esteem a man of genius for art, poetry, science, practical life, with executive power to plan and build. to organize matter or men into forms of use and beauty. When I meet with such an one, spite of me, down go the stiff knees of my veneration. And most spontaneously do I bow to a man of great justice, one of the pillars of righteousness. I know several such, whom the good God has set up here and there in great towns and little, and I take off my hat thereto, with an inward relish of the homage that I pay them, as I shudder a little with delight, as a poetic-minded New-Englander needs must when he first sees a great antique temple of Grecian or Roman art, or when he stands for the first time before the statue of Apollo, which enchants the world, or Olympian Jove,—

> "—— which young Phidias wrought,
> Not from a vain and shallow thought,"

or when he stands before this majestic figure, in which one great American artist, cradled in poverty, has incarnated the lofty lineaments of another great artist, also cradled in poverty, who beforehand had builded for himself a monument more lasting than brass, for he had carved out of the unseen air a figure of himself, which will endure when this brass shall have dissolved itself into gases, and escaped into the sky.

I say, when I meet one of these great pillars of justice, I take off my hat, not without a shudder of that awe, wherewith all men must contemplate the great of life, or the great of art. But if I could have one, and only one, of these three gifts, intellectual, moral, or affectional, I would take the latter.

What delights of affection there are! Love is the great idealizer of man's life. There are many such. Beauty is one, in nature and art. There is music, a common and sweet idealizer; and " the magic harp of David soothes the haunted heart of Saul." There is also the plastic art; and these two are great idealizers, fellow-workers with men in the cause of humanity.

There, my friends, stands a new colleague, whom I welcome to the work of philanthrophy and piety. He is ordained as colleague, pastor with myself. It is a great honour, that I, prosy man as I am, stand at the feet of that incarnation alike of music and poetry; and when I am silent, that majestic brow will speak to you; those eyes, turned upward and inward, will disclose to you the vision through his faculty divine; and when my hand writes not, that still will be to you emblematic of higher thoughts than I can set to music in poetry or speech. That, I say, is one great idealizer; there is a dearer, and that is the *love* which his song represents, and which the sculptor's art would fail to portray.

Francis,* deeply loving his kith and kin, and his immediate friends, like-minded men and women, has yet a great, robust, broad-footed heart which travels out beyond individual persons, leaps over the Atlantic Ocean even, and loves men of diverse tongue, other colour, varying religion, distinctive race—loves even the wicked men who persecute him, and casts the garment of self-denying charity on the shoulders of men who hate him the more abundantly that he loves them.

The New Music Hall was opened for the religious services of his parish for the first time on November 21, 1852.

FROM THE JOURNAL.

What shall befall us, I know not, the next eight years; what will befall the country, what the society, what me? Dear God, Thou only knowest!

---

* Here, as often, some living friend is the hint on which he speaks,—Francis Jackson, now departed into the company of his beloved pastor.

There was a great audience, which made me feel littler than ever. That is the sad part of looking such a crowd in the face. Whence shall I have bread to feed so many? I am but the lad with five barley loaves and two small fishes. Yet I have confidence in my own preaching.

He immediately drew up a " provisional scheme" of subjects to be treated in sermons, to occupy the time till the end of 1856. That is, he anticipated his subjects for four years, and adhered to the scheme in almost every particular. At the same time he began to collect information under the heads of some subjects which required a basis of facts, as for the "Duties and Dangers of Woman," the "Characteristics of America," the "Physical Condition of Nations," some of which were not preached for three years. Among other sermons, he premeditated one for the first Sunday in March, 1855, the 85th anniversary of the Boston Massacre, "On the Ultimate Triumph of the True and Right," which was delivered according to the programme.

FROM THE JOURNAL.

Aug. 24, 1853.—I am this day forty-three years old. I used to think I should live as long as my fathers; but certain admonitions of late warn me that I am not to be an old man. The last three years have made great alterations in my health and vigor. I write and work more with a will than by the spontaneous impulse which once required the will to check it. I neither grieve nor rejoice at the thought of departure. But I will try to keep my affairs in such a condition, that I can at any time go over the other side when summoned, and leave no perplexity.

Work for the year.
    I. Ministerial.
        a. Parish.
        b. The Perishing and Dangerous Classes of Boston.
    II. Non-Ministerial.
        a. Lectures.
        b. Article on Seward. Books upon Slavery. Historical Development of Religion; finish Vol. II. by Sept., 1854, if possible, and have it in print.

Work for September.
    I. Letter to the Unitarian Association.
    II. Lectures.
    III. Paper on Seward.

In the great audience, sometimes of 3000 people, which repaired to the Music Hall every Sunday forenoon, there was a small nucleus of devoted friends who constituted a parish, and from whose ranks came all the reliable workers and representatives of the Twenty-eighth Congregational Society. But their parochial action had nothing formal or conventional : they had recourse to none of the usual methods of preserving an ecclesiastical organization. Rites, conference-meetings, prayer-meetings and lectures gave place to practical attempts at applying the human doctrines of their great preacher. The Sunday service was perfectly simple. The desk raised upon one step, with a vase of flowers at the right hand of Mr. Parker, where his fingers might touch and caress them ; the chair in which he sat, just in front of the choir ; — these, and an assembly of beating hearts, such as Boston never saw before, and will hardly soon see again, furnished forth his occasion. No finical upholstery of liturgies, and chantings, and invocations, and responses ; no fine singing, no prim and well-dressed silence; the costliest things were the flowers and the speech : next to the living souls who yearned for truth, the most imposing thing in the house was a Bible, read with natural joy and reverence. The most impressive thing in all Boston on those famous Sundays was the moral sincerity of the preacher's voice, as it deepened from common-sense to religious emotion, or sparkled into indignation that was not for sale, or softened into sympathy and human pleasure at the Beautiful and the Good.

He read the hymn quietly and evenly ; then went forth the breathing of those prayers, still, natural, and simple, but laden with awe, and falling irresistibly into every heart with all the glad weight of his own joyful feeling.

Some words from a very dear friend and parishioner will be found effective to restore those Sundays. They also help us to appreciate his personal and pastoral relation to those families in the great congregation whom he might call his own :—

Those nearest to him feel that the central heart of his life, his dearest and highest function, has been most inadequately appreciated. Others thought of him as the great theologian, the bold reformer, the accomplished scholar ; he thought of himself as the minister of the Twenty-eighth Congregational Society, the shepherd of a flock of earnest souls who looked to him for help, and consolation, and guidance in all their private griefs and difficulties as eagerly as they listened to his deep and bold lessons on all great public questions. Why he has not appeared in this light to the literary world is plain ; his society was not composed of learned and scientific men, but of simple, practical people, whose life is occupied more with action than expression. I hope to be pardoned if I cannot give utterance to my views of the great value and importance of his pastoral relation without personality ; it is this very close personal relation which I wish to prove and illustrate. Even a friend can speak of his Sunday *Lyceum*, where he harangued a promiscuous audience on all themes of thought, science, or politics, but to Mr. Parker it was far otherwise. He knew that every Sunday a crowd of unknown persons were there to hear him, but to him there was always a central group of well-beloved faces, in whose eyes he read all the trials and struggles of the week. There was his "glorious phalanx of old maids, on whose aid he could confidently rely for every work of charity or mercy." There was his St. M——, her face a constant benediction; his beloved John, "who idealized his life after a day of hard toil by providing for the wants of every poor child in his neighbourhood;" there was the faithful clerk, who was, he said, more important to the society than himself; there were the grey heads, so precious in his sight; the young men, in whom he saw the hope of the country and the world; and the young maidens, in whose culture and well-being he ever felt the most paternal care.

Who can forget how he would come into church, and sit there, partially screened from sight by the desk, and look around on the faces of his congregation? Then he gathered up from the multitude all the joys and sorrows of the week—the tear-dimmed eye of the mourner; the earnest struggling of a soul wrestling with temptation; the new joy of happy lovers, or a mother rejoicing in her firstborn child—all sent up their incense to him, and he gathered their fragrance into his heart, and bore it up to God in his prayer. Nor did he fail to bring his own life into the same holy presence. Who has not at times felt some deep sorrow or penitent tenderness of his own private heart veiled in the universal language of his prayer? Those early days of his ministry at the Melodeon can never be forgotten by those favoured to share them. The dark, dingy building, with its dirty walls and close atmosphere, became a holy temple, for it enshrined a living soul. The cold, rainy Sundays which succeeded one another so constantly could not keep us away. "How could we bear the burden of the week," said many a listener, "without the inspiration of that hour of prayer, of that lesson of wisdom and truth?" The constant offering of flowers on the desk was a beautiful emblem of the faith in and love of nature which so characterized his teachings. As spring advanced, we often first saw the dear remembered friends in field and grove on the desk; the violets and barberry-blossoms, the purple rhodora, the sweet wild-rose, the lilies of the valley (now sacred to us from his last look on them), the fragrant magnolia, the stately laurel, the blue gentian, in its autumn loveliness, all came as offerings from one or another friend. Nothing was too precious or too lowly to be laid at that shrine; and as the great teacher gathered lessons of divine wisdom and truth from the lilies of the fields and the grass of the plain, so did he never fail to point some moral or enforce some lesson of love and truth by reference to these beautiful emblems of God's presence and power. How sacred was his feeling in regard to them, a little circumstance will show. Being called to the country to pay the last tribute of love and reverence to a dear friend, he gathered some blue gentians from the little brook which ran before his old home, and the next Sunday he placed them on the desk, and wrote to his absent parishioner how she, too, was not forgotten by pastor or people in their Sabbath prayer.

But we were speaking of those old days at the Melodeon, dear to us as the first little humble home of boyhood, or the first dwelling of a married pair. We could never have quite the same feeling in the ampler space and more elegant arrangements of the Music Hall, but it made no change in the constant ministry of our friend. How many incidents might be told of those early days, when his words were so strange and new to many! "Well, I never heard before that toads were prophets and grass was revelations," an old lady was heard to mutter angrily as she went out of meeting one day. But to him all beings did preach, and all nature did reveal the truths of the religion he believed and taught.

One of Mr. Parker's noblest efforts was his sermon on John Quincy Adams. The house was densely crowded, and all were held in rapt attention by the tribute, full of glowing heat, and yet of manly truth, which he paid to the great departed. As he spoke of the only blots on the fair fame of his hero, the snow, which covered and darkened the roof, fell with a tremendous crash, which sent a thrill through the audience and preacher. Mr. Parker recovered himself instantly and added, " So may the infamy slide off from his character, and leave it fair as open daylight!" As he closed, the wind, from some unknown cause, sounded through the organ pipes a wild, sweet strain, which seemed, to our excited minds, like an amen from the spirit of the brave old man, who accepted the bold and true words which had been spoken of him.

One tribute of honor we can never bring to Mr. Parker—that which a distinguished lawyer paid to his reverenced pastor.* We could never fail to be reminded of the whole week on Sunday; our errors, our shortcomings, our dangers, our blessings, our hopes, trials, and fears, all came up in review before us, and the words which were spoken for all seemed most special to each one. Once, when preaching on the forgiveness of sin, and showing how the infinite love of God had provided means of recovery for the most guilty soul, a man in the gallery suddenly cried out, " Yes, I know it to be so ! I feel it to be so !" Mr. Parker paused in his sermon and addressed him in words of strong faith and assurance. " Yes, my friend, it is so; and you cannot wander so far but God can call you back."

The special event of the day of which his congregation were thinking seemed to him the appropriate subject on which to give them words of religious advice, comfort, or warning. Sometimes he waited a week or two for the excitement to subside, that he might speak from and to a calmer mood, but he never left such occasions unimproved. In this he resembled the early Puritans, to whom he had, indeed, much likeness. Who does not remember the strength and wisdom of his words on occasions like those of the trial of Professor Webster, the fugitive slave cases, important elections, and the commercial crisis ? He never rested till he had withdrawn these startling facts from the list of exceptional accidents, and shown how they resulted from sufficient causes, and were co-ordinate with the whole providence of the Divine government. He did not suffer us to believe that a man, good

---

* To the effect, namely, that the pastor in question never made allusions to professional or political iniquity, but only to the glittering generality of sin.

and pure in heart, became suddenly a murderer from the force of an untoward circumstance, but showed us how the yielding to minor temptations had weakened the power of resistance to this fatal one. And yet how tender was his pleading and his trust in God for the poor sufferers! Many of us then, for the first time, realized that God had consolation in store, even for such misery.

When the slave Shadrach was arrested, but released by a spontaneous movement of our citizens, the event occurred on Saturday. We were still anxious on Sunday in regard to his final escape. Mr. Parker preached that day an anniversary sermon—the fifth of his settlement in Boston. At its close he said, "When I came among you I expected to have to do and to bear some hard things, but I never expected to have to protect one of my parishioners from slave-hunters, nor to be asked to read such a note as this:—'Shadrach, a fugitive slave, in peril of his life and liberty, asks your prayers that God will aid him to escape out of bondage.' But," he said, "he does not need our prayers. Thank God! we have heard of him safe, far on his way to freedom." I cannot describe the intense excitement of the audience. For a moment there was perfect silence, and it seemed as if our hearts would burst with the pressure of feeling. Then one spontaneous shout of applause re-echoed through the building, and gave us the relief so much needed.

Here let me say that, while Mr. Parker felt the genuineness of such expression when inevitable and fit, he yet very much disliked the habit of applause in church, and kept it in check by remonstrance whenever a disposition to indulge in it appeared. He was a great lover of decorum and order. He always wore at church the plain dark dress which he thought befitting the service. The Bible and hymn-book were laid in their places—everything was in order before he began to speak. But he loved freedom and individuality also, and he would not suffer them to be sacrificed to his own comfort. How gentle was his remonstrance against the noisy slamming of the forty-four doors of the Music Hall towards the close of the sermon! how patiently he took it for granted that only important engagements led people to such a violation of good manners towards those who held their doors invitingly open to them! He said to us once, "I do not like to see people reading books and newspapers before the services commence. It troubles me very much, and I have often been tempted to ask people to abstain from it; but I remember how precious a half-hour's reading was to me often when I was a young man, and I feel that I ought not to ask anybody to give it up for the sake of my comfort when it is not wrong in itself."

So thoroughly conscientious was Mr. Parker in the performance of the duties of his parish, that he never seemed quite reconciled to having Sunday afternoon for his own use, and not devoting it to some special service in their behalf. In vain they assured him that they neither required nor wished it—that one such sermon as his was quite sufficient for a week's digestion, and that they preferred to spend the afternoon hours with their families or in other ways. He tried various plans—occasionally he would hold meetings for free discussion, but, when held in a public place and open to all, some of the trouble-

28

some fleas of conventions were sure to intrude and destroy all quiet and peace. The subject of a Sunday-school often occupied his thoughts, and he made two different attempts to form one. The first effort was to gather in poor and ignorant children from the streets, and teach them reading and the general principles of morality and religion. But the preponderating influence of the Catholic priests over our foreign population, the only class needing this charity, rendered all efforts to keep the children together fruitless. He also attempted a school for the children of the parish. The young men and women professed themselves perfectly ready to assist him in his plans, but generally incredulous of its value or necessity. He took the superintendence of the school himself, always either making some original remarks or reading a story to the children. But a few months' experiment convinced him that the teachers were right, and that this class of children had sufficient direct instruction from other sources. A pleasant incident connected with this school illustrates his considerate thought for others in the most trifling matters. One stormy Sunday, one of the most constant attendants at church and Sunday-school was absent in the morning. The storm was so severe that he announced there would be no school in the afternoon; but feeling that the teacher might come out from a sense of duty to others, though not for her own pleasure, he sent her the following pleasant note : —" The little birdies will be all safely folded under their mothers' wings this afternoon, so you need not wet yours by coming out in the storm."

Another plan for Sunday afternoon was a series of lectures explanatory of the text of the New Testament. In these he gave, in condensed form, the results of all the latest criticism of English and German theologians, as well as his own private interpretation of the text. The information thus given was exceedingly valuable, but the dry and methodical form of a critical analysis did not enchain the attention of a large number of hearers. The attendance was always small, but constant on the part of those most interested ; and he did not complete the course proposed, but continued the lectures only a few years. He thus reviewed the Four Gospels, the Acts, and Epistles, but we believe neither Revelations nor the Old Testament.

On Saturday afternoons, for several years, soon after his settlement in the winter of 1847–48, he invited the ladies of his parish to meet at his house for conversation on themes of moral and religious interest. He always considered the culture of women to be of the highest importance, and often said that a body of highly educated women could do more to elevate a community than any other influence. Nothing can exceed the skill and courtesy with which he conducted these meetings. So thoroughly did he put himself in relation with his pupils, for such they might well be considered, that he often seemed to understand the action of their own minds better than they did themselves. He listened with patient attention to the stammering, diffident expression of thought from any earnest mind, and, placing it in the light of his own vast intelligence, reflected it to her and others in grander proportions and clearer beauty than she had imagined. The subject proposed one winter was the formation of a perfect character, and all the helps to it. Another time it was the gradual development of the religious nature in communities and individuals. Another time it was education in its broader sense. Although he allowed free play to fancy and wit in the illustration of all these themes, he never suffered the conversation to be aimless or profitless and without result ; but at its close he gathered up the scattered thoughts of the company, and wove them into a concise and full expression. This wonderful power was still more strikingly displayed at Mr. Alcott's. For two or three hours the stream of thought would seem to flow at its own wayward will, without direction or aim. No other member of the company, perhaps, could have reported more than sparkling fancies or pithy, orphic sayings ; but Mr. Parker would surprise all by briefly reviewing the whole course of the conversation, placing the remarks of each speaker in their proper relation to those of all the rest, and giving them the pleasing consciousness of having said far wiser and profounder things than they had dreamed of. Little record of these genial and profitable occasions can be made. Surrounded by loving friends and disciples, he could here forget something of the stern battle in which he was forced to mingle, and the whole sweetness and warmth of his nature had free play. We remember once, in speaking of the life of Jesus, the stress which he laid on the mental isolation in which he was forced to live. Although the multitude followed him, not one seems even to have attained to a full understanding of the grandeur and loftiness of his idea. We cannot estimate, he said, what he would have accomplished surrounded by those who could fully receive his mission and work with him. Once he said, " It is the greatest of all blessings to a man to meet his superior."

Speaking of sex in souls, a lady quoted Coleridge's famous remark, that " the man who does not recognise sex in souls has never known what it is truly to love a mother, a wife, or even a sister." " Yes ; I remember that passage well," said Mr. Parker. " I had a profound reverence for Mr. Coleridge, and felt very badly to fall under his anathema, but I never could recognise any sex in souls." The class were often pleased to see the strain of thought which was called forth at conversation reappear in the service on Sunday. Nothing was ever buried in his mind ; all was planted seed, and sure to come up in fresh life and beauty.

His valuable library, now so wisely placed at the service of the citizens of Boston, was always freely open to the use of his parish, as of all other friends ; and the book was always selected for the young borrower with discriminating care, and with words of criticism, or recommendation, which added wonderful interest to the perusal. Yet, I think, he lost much fewer books than most who lend them ; for they were evidently so dear to him, yet so freely loaned, that the most careless did not like to neglect the trust. It did annoy him to have a book kept a long time, and returned *unread ;* but while it was faithfully used he was quite willing to spare it.

While he thus cared for the spiritual and intellectual wants of his parish, he did not forget their claims in suffering and trial ; no, not even when the greatest public excitement demanded his strength and energy. I chanced to be seriously though not dangerously ill at the very time when the slave-hunters were in Boston, in pursuit of William and Ellen Crafts, whom he sheltered and protected in his own home. Although obliged to arm his household, and to watch the door narrowly against a cunning enemy, and taking part in all the exciting discussions, and active exertions of that period, he yet came in person, almost daily, to inquire after his sick parishioner; and soon as he saw the hunted fugitives safely afloat on the free Atlantic, he turned his steps to my sick room, where for the first time I was able to see him. What an atmosphere of health, and strength, and life he brought thither! So was it with all who needed him; he never forgot individual claims, any more than public duties. His power of consolation was great, and never-failing. It is not time, nor occupation, nor forgetfulness, which can console us for a real sorrow. It is only that time and a healthy re-action puts the grief in its right place, enables us to see the great eternal truths which a passing cloud obscured, shows the wise Providence ordering all things well, when all seemed ill to us. Of this, which we must often slowly and painfully learn, his ever-living, ever-acting faith, helped us to consciousness at once. Tender and sympathetic as a mother, he was yet wise and strong, and demanded life and right action from others. Did life seem valueless, because the one who blessed it was gone, he made us feel that all life is one; that this life and eternity are close together, and that we work with those who have passed beyond the veil as truly as if they are here. Trusting wholly in a perfect God, how could he doubt his perfect providence? "No man ever dies when it is a misfortune to him," he often said. His scheme of the universe admitted of no accident; an immanent God must order all things well. He usually prefaced his remarks at a funeral by a statement of the cardinal doctrines of his faith, the two great truths of religion dear to every human heart, and sufficient to sustain it in all trials—the loving fatherhood of the perfect God, and the immortality of the human soul. Often, when some peculiar circumstances in the life or death of the departed one seemed to render all attempt at consolation but mockery, his clear and full enunciation of these truths, and the beautiful application of them to special circumstances, which he never failed to make, seemed to take the sting from death and the victory from the grave.

Not less impressive and beautiful was his performance of the marriage service; always a solemn and touching sight to him. His appreciation of the mysterious holiness and blessedness of the conjugal union and of the joys of the family relation, was so great that his parishioners sometimes complained that he never gave thanks for anything else; and his single friends petitioned that their joys, however inferior, might sometimes be remembered. Yet, perhaps, no one has ever done higher justice to the maiden aunt. Speaking of the struggles of earnest young men to gain education and a wider sphere of life, "it is the maiden aunt often," he says, "who, when father and mother forsake him, like the Lord, has taken him up."

Oh, how little can we tell of what he was to us in his fifteen years' ministry; of what a pillar was taken from us when he was gone! His place standeth desolate, and none cometh to fill it. Days of peril seem before us; where is the warning voice which ever prophesied the storm afar off, but ever spoke words of courage and hope when it was nigh? All the changes and chances of life are yet ours; where is the steady arm on which to lean, the heart to cheer us?

It remains for us, his disciples, his parishioners, to take up his work and carry it on ; not as he could, with the wonderful genius and power which were his alone, but with the same devotion, the same independence, the same unselfish labor for others. When one of his parishioners thanked him for all he had been to him in years past, " I will be more to you hereafter," he said, " than ever before." Few months were given him to redeem that promise by deeds of earthly love and kindness, but will it not surely be fulfilled in the influence of his life and teachings, on, not one, but all who sat at his feet? How little it seemed to him that he had reaped of the vast field of labour, which had opened before him! Let not those who must follow him with slow and patient gleaning, faint because they are few and feeble. Fewer and seemingly more feeble were the hands to which the dying Galilean trusted his truths, but Paul planted, and Apollos watered, and God gave the increase.

In looking back over the fifteen years of Mr. Parker's pastoral life in Boston, we are astonished at its richness and importance, when we remember also his great labors in other connections and other spheres. Great as he was in the pulpit, many a one felt he was more to them in private. We can see no failure, no want in the relation. He was the friend when a friend was needed ; he spoke rebuke, or encouragement, or consolation, or counsel as it was needed ; and, alas ! he did not remit his labors, even when continued at a risk of his precious life " How can I refuse to go ?" he said, when sent for to attend a funeral while very unwell ; and he went, in spite of all entreaty. The last precious hours of strength were all exhausted on Sunday ; when too feeble even to take his meals with the family, he went out to the desk, and spoke with all his whole fervor, though the husky voice betrayed the fearful cost at which we bought the hour. And yet we can hardly mourn or complain at this excessive labour, although its penalty was early death. What generous heart can remember to be always prudent, when the claims are so pressing, and no other hand is ready to work ? He is the faithful shepherd who giveth his life for the sheep.

Here are fragments of sermons, not hitherto printed, which were gathered up from Sunday to Sunday. They are not his best, but still characteristic of him, both by subject and treatment :—

OF THE EDUCATION OF THE RELIGIOUS FACULTIES. *Preached March 9, 1856.*—How great is the power of education in the soul of man, and how strongly is he influenced by the circumstances in which he is placed ! The cradle is the place whereon we stand to move the world, and education is the Archimedes for that universal lift. Take a single example. Look at the history of the Warren Street Chapel in this town, for the last five-and-twenty years. A quarter of a century ago, perhaps less, some wise men made a sacrifice, and by sweet self-denial they built up a little conservatory, wherein they might take and shelter the precious plants which they found in the mire of the streets. How many hundreds, how many thousands, are now honorable, noble, heavenly-minded men and women, simply because they were transferred from the cold, bleak atmosphere of the street, where temptation lay in wait to destroy them, and were set in this green-house of souls, and blossomed into fragrant flowers !

OF THE DANGERS AND DUTIES OF YOUNG WOMEN. *Preached Jan.* 18, 1857.—Oh, young woman, cultivate your mind, shun frivolous reading, poor, weak, silly books, sentimental books.   Read for knowledge some hard book which demands attention, memory, thought; master one good book, no matter what—geography, arithmetic, astronomy, history, what you will; but study it, and know it well, understand one thing certainly.   Read, also, for beauty, what feeds the imagination, fills it with handsome shapes, and wakens noble thoughts.   There are poets, our own or those abroad, who can do this ; some of the present generation, some long passed by. Read, also, for the reason—something that gives you general laws, universal views.   Read for inspiration; you may be poor, and have little time, or rich, and have much, still, there is one humanity and one womanhood in the idle and the active, in the rich and the poor, and the same noble book will speak to each and to all ; and so is America favoured and blessed that the poorest, the activest, can find the book and the time also to read it, if she will.

Next, reverence your own moral instincts ; ask your conscience, *Is it right ?* as well as your heart, *Is it kind ?*   Man is more likely to go astray through self-love, you through the opposite path.   Keep your individuality sacred ; surrender that not to priest, nor husband, nor father, nor mother, nor lover, nor child.   Look to your own moral sense for approbation, not to man nor to woman ; but,—

> "As that pronounces lastly on each deed,
>   Of so much praise in heaven expect your meed."

Be faithful to yourself ! Are you single ? " Come into port greatly, or sail the seas alone with God." Are you wedded ? it will be a part of woman's domestic function to " soothe, and heal, and bless "—aye, she will often be called upon to soothe where she cannot heal, and where she is not suffered to bless ; and the self-denial for the sake of soothing will heal others and bless you, when neither you nor they asked for such result.

Cultivate the religious faculty ; develope the instinctive religious feelings; have reverence for God, not the God of Calvinism—I cannot ask any one to reverence that—but the dear God who made the heavens and the earth, who speaks in your heart, uttering parable, prophecy, and beatitude.   Develope a great piety in yourself, and let this be the central fire to warm, still further, your human affection, spreading it from mother, father, husband, child, clear round to neighbourhood, kinsfolk, all the world.   Let it light your conscience, and give you a general moral rule whereby to find your path.   Let it beautify your intellect, and stimulate your understanding, imagination, reason.   Let it correct that poor temptation to frivolity, peevishness, vanity, discontent.

Remember that all the little every-day duties of woman's life are just as much means to help you as the rougher discipline of man is to aid him in his course.   The little cares, sorrows, and joys, the vexations of the household lot, the perplexities of those careful and troubled about many things, these are the elements to help form the noble woman; only she must have a noble ideal, a noble will. So the artist takes the little chips of many-coloured stone and constructs his grand mosaic of creative skill, a queen, a Madonna, an angel, and the dead stone becomes a living oracle, a moral prophecy of nobleness to come. Grandeur of character is not easy to young women or men ; God be thanked, it is possible to both ! and one noble woman, she is parent of many more ; in her spiritual image and likeness she shall create women and men to the end of time ; aye, people eternity with noble souls, beautiful in their life, and welcome unto God !

OF GRATITUDE AND INGRATITUDE. *Preached March* 8, 1857.— There is to be a *future* of the benevolent emotions, when what is prophecy to-day, instinct in your heart and mine, shall become fact and institutions through all the land. Now, in the walled garden a single handful of snowdrops comes out of the ground and looks up and welcomes the sweet sunshine of March. Everywhere else the ground is dry and frozen, and the trees are leafless and bare. These are a prophecy as well as a beauty, and ere long the snow has run off from all the hills, the frost has come out of the ground, the trees shake down their odorous flowers, the spring is everywhere, summer is coming, and the harvest is not far away.

OF THE ULTIMATE PURPOSE OF HUMAN LIFE FOR THE INDIVIDUAL AND THE RACE. *Preached Sept.* 13, 1857.—Now, the power of moral good in the world is destined to overcome the power of evil. I mean, the constant tendency towards the right, the just, and the true on the part of man, will overcome all the general evil attendant on the experience of human life. God has so created the nature of men that instinctively they long for the triumph of good, pray for it, and presently will, with reflection, devise means, and put their shoulders to the wheel, and so work in conformity with their internal desire, and bring that result to pass. This triumph of good is just as certain as the infinite perfection of God's character. Sure of Him, you are sure that everywhere good will triumph over evil, truth over falsehood, justice over wrong, love over hate, and holiness over all uncleanness, for God's nature is endorsed as security, and lodged as collateral, for the fulfilment of every holy desire that enters into the heart of man.

This triumph of good is for the individual, and for each individual. It comes partly here, for the individual's course begins here ; it comes partly hereafter, for that course ends unseen above. There is no man to whom existence on the whole will not be ultimately a blessing, a triumph of those faculties which lead to good, over such as contingently tend to evil. There is no earthly life that can be altogether a failure, wholly a misfortune. You shall take the worst woman in Boston, foul and loathsome with long-continued wickedness, yet, before her there is a future development in all the grand virtues of humanity. You and I in our weakness cannot but loathe her ; we treat her as the world's vermin. Not so the infinite God, who will never shirk His responsibility. In this poor wretch, likewise, lies the power of good, for she, too, is human; and though they sleep, they are not dead, and the Father and Mother of the universe has so arranged the world of here and hereafter, that some event or some person shall come to her as a saviour, take her by the hand, and say to her, "I say unto thee, arise; take up thy bed and walk!" and the humanity of the wretch shall cast off its filthy garments, and stand on its feet clean and erect. I feel sure that her life here, howsoever mean and abominable it may be, is no complete failure; it is a step towards triumph, a step which she might not have done without.

Look at this fact: in the world of matter no atom is lost, in all the busy changes thereof, of growth and dissolution. No straw, no particle of dust ever flies off from the world's swift wheels. In all that world of starry motion yonder, there is not a movement in vain; all is planned before-hand, and made subject to the scheme of the universe, in the vast designs of God, which hover over it, and penetrate it through. This being so—so much care taken of man's material house—do you believe that God, who made it for man's abode, will take less care of you and me, will save the cradle and spill the baby out? When that material universe is so wisely planned, do you think He will allow a whole human life to be a failure, even that of the wickedest of wicked women?

There are men whose early lives have been spent in the meanest, humblest, and most loathsome toil, who yet rise to great eminence of wealth and station, and, though they crept into social life through the lowest hole, yet go proudly out through its golden gate. So, I doubt not that from the gaol, the brothel, the gallows—from the murderer's den, from the kidnapper's office, from the hypocrite's pulpit, by many a long and winding slope, the soul shall go up into God's highest heaven; for though human charity fail, there is One whose love knows no beginning and no end. Oh, infinite Father and Mother, it is Thou!

Suffering is a merciful angel here, which scourges us to virtue. You and I are thankful for many a stripe in kindness laid on us. Our Father provides the best teachers, and is sure to give us the best education. In what men call hell, Swedenborg tells us, the murderer writhes in his dream of murder, and the covetous in his dream of covetousness. Be sure that the suffering which is before us is only the sinner's porch into heaven—a means to an end.

This triumph is for the race, and of course a great part of it must take place here. The life of individuals is short, that of humanity knows no end. There are fluctuations of people and nations—Ægypt, Judæa, Chaldæa, Syria, were and are not; but though the populous waves rise and fall, the ocean of humanity continues steadfast, and on that great deep the spirit of God moves continually, bringing light out of darkness, changing chaos into creation. As you look on the sum of human history, and on the present condition of men, and see the amount of wickedness in the world, you cannot fail to ask if mankind could not have been created on a little higher plane, with less animal grossness and ferocity, and so human history be not so writ in blood. But presently you remember it is the work of the infinite Creator and Providence, who from His very nature could only do the best of possible things, and you recall the thought, and you content yourself with human nature as He gave it, looking with joy at the signs of past growth and future prosperity, justice, and humanity, and you toil for the progress of mankind, with earnest efforts which you know shall not fail. This triumph of the individual and the race is part of the divine plan and divine providence of God, which underlies all human affairs, which directs Columbus, Franklin, Moses, Jesus, Paul, you and me, to ends we know not of. But it will be brought about also partly by human consciousness, looking before and after, and working for a definite purpose of good. It is the destination of mankind on earth to develope the higher powers, and in such sort that the moral and religious faculties shall control and guide all the rest; then shall the power of evil prove only an instrument of good. You and I, in our short life, are here to achieve this triumph, and mankind collectively in its immense duration; you and I with conscious individualism. This is our work.

My life is valuable to me just as I use my talents and opportunities for the development of my highest faculties, and no more. Simply to have large talents shall avail me nothing; to have small shall be no hindrance. As growth in the highest human qualities is the purpose of life, and all lines providentially converge to this central point, so the question to be asked of each man's life is, " How faithfully have you used your talents and opportunities?" not "How great was your gift?" Money is the pecuniary end of business, office of ambition, knowledge and power the aim of study, and the delight of self or the tickling of others' eyes is the aim of many a beautiful dress or other ornament; but while these are ends to individuals, as traders, office-seekers, scholars, and fops, to them as men and women they are only means and helps to manhood and womanhood—no more. If she will, the young woman's showy dress may be worth as much to her as John Rogers' garment of faggots was to him; if she will not, it is worth to her less than the leafy girdle of a savage woman at Nootka Sound.

I deny not the local, temporary value of ornament, of knowledge, power, and fame, but, after all, their chief value is moral. That is not the best business which gives the most money, nor the best policy which affords the highest office, nor the best school which teaches you the most knowledge; but that which affords the highest development for your highest faculty is the best business, policy, or school. He is the most fortunate who hives up the most character of the noblest kind. If he does it in the sunshine of honor or riches, well; if in the dark, nocturnal storm of disgrace and ruin, still well; it is the hive of sweet character that is the end, not the toil by day or night. By this test we must try fortune and misfortune, forms of government and religion, and ask what men and women they bring forth and rear up. That is not the best farm which gives us the best cotton and sugar, not the best manufactory which best weaves the one into muslin, or changes the other best and cheapest into candy; but that is the best farm or manufactory that raises us the noblest men and women. In the vast variety of human occupations, from that of the naked hunter of New Holland to the astronomer of Cambridge, in the vast variety of human fortunes, God has provided the best circumstances He knew how to provide for the training up of His children. If we use them ill, there comes smart, and harm, and loss, and inward woe, which scourge the nation or the

man. If we use them well, then eye hath not seen, nor ear heard, nor
the heart of man conceived the magnificent welfare and the grand progress which there is before the individual, the nation, the race ; and that
infinite Father and Mother who broods over the world, who breathed
it from his love, and warms it with that same breath, has so tempered
human nature and human circumstances, that at last this result shall
be brought about for the whole of mankind, for each nation, for each
individual, howsoever wicked.   Smarting in that wickedness, there is
heaven over us, and God leading us !

OF THE PRACTICAL CONSEQUENCE OF THE IDEA OF GOD AS IN-
FINITE PERFECTION.   *Preached June* 13, 1858.—A thousand years
ago, your and my Saxon fathers, living in mean hovels, for their
favorite sport had mimic battles, wherein with quarter-staves, or
spears, or swords, men laid at each other in their savage joy, and
were often hurt and sometimes slain.   Looking on that howling
wilderness of amusement, who could have foreseen the time when,
in another land, peopled by other Saxons, in Boston, two thousand
Christian men and women should come together in a theatre, paying
large prices, to see a great scene of ambitious human life, done
into magnificent language by an old English Saxon poet, the chiefest of
his tribe, and that grand poetry enacted into a great drama by a New
England Saxon woman,* who transfigured his thought to life, teaching
how the justice of God comes and torments the murderer, and her who
excited the murder, walking in such ghastly sleep ?   Who, a thousand
years ago, in the rough sports of our Saxon fathers, could have imagined
a Boston audience, thrilled with æsthetic and religious delight at seeing
" Macbeth " fitly enacted by fitting men and women ?

OF THE POWER OF HUMAN WILL OVER OR UNDER ADVERSE CIR-
CUMSTANCES.   *Preached October* 8, 1854.—Here is a woman who sits
spell-bound in her chair.   Her feet are fettered by disease, which
long ago froze every joint and limb : her arms are bound by the
malady, and *embrace* and *caress* are figures of speech, no facts, to her.
A foreign hand must feed her mouth, or wipe a tear away.   But how
large a soul is perched upon that spray, and in that sickly nest finds
room to rear a family of virtues large enough to people a whole
kingdom with innocence, faith, and wisdom, and love !†

OF THE IMMEDIATE AND ULTIMATE CONSEQUENCES, TO THE INDI-
VIDUAL AND TO MANKIND, OF THE PERFORMANCE OF DUTY AND THE CLAIM
OF RIGHT.   *Preached December* 23, 1855. — Here is a woman in
Massachusetts who has travelled all over the North, labouring for
woman's cause.   She bore the burden in the heat of the day ; she was
an outcast from society ; other women hated, and men insulted her,
when defended only by her own nobleness and virtue.   Every vulgar
editor threw a stone at her, picked out of the mud.   Many a minister
laid sore stripes on her with the epistolary whip of Hebrew Paul.   The
noble woman bore it with no complaint, only now and then in private

* This was Miss Cushman.

† This is another picture drawn from the life, and recognizable by all who need to
know it.

the great heart of Abby Kelly filled her eyes with tears; but she never allowed tears to blind her eyes, nor quench the light shedding its radiance along a steep and barricaded path. But when the cause of woman had won something of respectability, and a great convention of women and their friends was summoned in the heart of this common-wealth, they who controlled the matter thought it would not do for their stoutest champion to sit on the platform; she must sit beneath the platform, lest it hurt the cause and peril the rights of woman, to have woman's champion sit in woman's honored place.

His method, already mentioned, of blocking out his time was habitual. Generally whatever was projected was duly performed within the assigned limits. But soon after his coming to Boston, the calls upon him for public and social service of every descrip-tion accumulated in a way that seriously disturbed all his favorite plans of study and composition.

FROM THE JOURNAL.

Sept. 1, 1853.—My vacation is now at an end. I had some knots I wanted to untie, so I went to Nahant to get the sea to help me, not without profit, I hope.

Notice the profusion of life in the sea. Homer calls it barren and boundless, $\alpha\tau\rho\nu\gamma\epsilon\tau o\iota\alpha$ $\kappa\alpha\grave{\iota}$ $\alpha\pi\epsilon\bar{\iota}\rho\alpha$. But how full it is of life! It is lined with green and purple plants, which cover snails, muscles, barnacles, and certain *echini*, and insects innumerable; then there are the fish of countless number, of immense variety. This strikes me more and more, the more I get acquainted with the sea.

Notice the little pools of water in the rocks, the sides and bottom lined with little shell-fish, who live secure in the clear tranquillity, and know nothing of the tide which scours the coasts. But when the ocean is chafed by the storms, and licks out its tongue against the rocks, how all these vanish, and the insects fail!

Sept. 4, 1853, Sunday.—How delightful it is to begin preaching again! It was so pleasant to see the dear old familiar faces, and to read again to those persons the hymns and psalms which I have read them so often, to pray with them also, and feel that many a soul prayed with me. I preached of the nobleness of man's nature.

Sept. 6.—This day my new book appeared, " Sermons of Theism, Atheism, and the Popular Theology " It seems to me so poor and dull now I look it over, to find the printer's mistakes, that I hate to touch it. I was too ill to work well when it went through the press, hence, doubtless, many an error. Well, I meant well, if I have not done so. I wish there was no *fighting* to be done, but, alas! *non veni pacem mittere sed gladium* must be said by every man who would make the world better.

In a few weeks is the following, without a date :—

I have been very dull all this week past, all this, and the last month. The journey did me little good, the old difficulty in my head (or stomach) troubles me ; I know not why, I feel ashamed to be ill, as if I had wrecked an estate. As I lie awake in the night, I feel as if I had done nothing. My idea shames me. I must *be more* and so do more. I have never had either a friend who continually stirred me to nobler activity by *words*, nor a rival who did it by his own *action*. I wish I had both.

Here are some rough notes upon spiritualism, meant for use in sermons :—

Spiritualism.—In 1856, it seems more likely that spiritualism would would become the religion of America than in 156 that Christianity would be the religion of the Roman Empire, or in 756 that Mohammedanism would be that of the Arabian populations.

1. It has more *evidence for its wonders* than any historic form of religion, hitherto.

2. It is *thoroughly democratic*, with no hierarchy ; but inspiration is open to all.

3. It is no *fixed fact*, has no *punctum stans*, but is a *punctum fluens;* not a finality, but opens a great vista for the future. Its present condition is no finality.

4. It admits all the truths of religion and morality in all the world-sects.

Spirits.—1. Man's spirit more interesting than his body to him. Thence, stories of miracles are more interesting than science, for they presume an effect of mind over matter by direct action ; and ghost-stories are more interesting than history.

2. Scholars in America neglect spiritual and turn to material nature. Metaphysics have gone to physics, ethics to political economy, theology to politics.

3. Ministers keep up the old metaphysics and superstitions of spirit, but it is restricted in Protestant countries to the old Bible times, their ghosts, miracles, inspiration, speaking with tongues, &c., but not to our new ones.

4. Life is intensely practical—all work, little account of imagination and fancy, little sport; money-making and dress—no games, no *Volks-lieder* (people's songs), &c. So,

5. The mass of the people take up a popular spiritual metaphysics ; it feeds spiritually, and pacifies the hunger for the marvellous.

But the dangers are,—

1. Those which befall the sincere believers ; moral and bodily derangement.

2. Of insincerity itself.

3. Of a reaction from all this ; libertinism, &c.

And the good is,—

1. Appeals to the immaterial against the material.

2. Destroys the prestige of old things.

3. Removes doubts of spiritual life in some men.

May 18, 1855.—Lectured on slavery, at Wilmington, Del., the first time in a slave state. My theme was, "The Relation of Slavery to the Democratic Institutions of America." Received with much applause, and a vote of thanks at the close.

May 19.—Preached a sermon at the opening of the Meeting House of Progressive Friends, Longwood, Chester County, Pennsylvania, "Relation between the Ecclesiastical Institutions and the Religious Consciousness of the American People." It is fourteen years, to-day, since I preached at the ordination of Mr. Shackford, at South Boston. Since that I have taken no part in church festivals, having no invitation.

20.—Preached again, "Of the Blessedness of True Piety."

And he gave three lectures on the three succeeding days.

In 1858 he again attended the meeting of the Progressive Friends, and delivered four sermons : "The Biblical Conception of God ; " "The Ecclesiastical Conception of God ; " "The Philosophical Idea of God ; " "The Soul's Normal Delight in the Infinite God." These are strong and lofty discourses ; they contain his most unsparing criticism of the popular ideas of God, expressed occasionally in phrases that do not shrink from the plain odiousness of ecclesiastical doctrines, as he saw them all bare and mischievous. For his object was not to show how human nature often proves too much for its beliefs, clothes them in its sentiments, and mitigates their influence with instinctive tenderness, but to show, for human nature's sake, the more important fact, how the beliefs devastate it and continually make war upon its excellence. Sturdy language and an unwincing pen are needed for that operation. Any rhetorician can perform the other useless task.

In no sermons can the essentially *constructive* nature of Mr. Parker's work be more distinctly seen. The criticisms of doctrine are burly workmen clearing the field of its rubbish, that Piety may serenely raise her dwelling there. All the work tends to growth ; it is undertaken in the dearest interests of the soul, and with a motive which the soul's highest faculties alone can worthily represent, to make the law of the spirit supreme in man and in society, to compel the imperfect conception to yield to the perfecting idea, that man may be saved from the license of igno-rance by the freedom of purity and health. Did he undermine venerable doctrines and sentiments ? Of course he did ; and as they sink into a little heap, which just marks the circuit of their former proudness, the glad soul steps over it into the great labors and glories of a world. It is plain that God has this work done for His children as often as it is needed, and when the time comes He does not send a boy upon a man's errand.

The four sermons glow with positive ideas and feelings—with definite religious faith. That makes them so tenacious and intolerant. If he did not see the beauty of holiness so clearly, he could not be so indignant with the sin of ugliness in low conceptions of the infinite God. The fault with Mr. Parker always was that he saw too much, and undertook to tell it. Only two other ways are possible—to see nothing, or to say nothing: and neither of these was his misfortune.

FROM THE JOURNAL.

March 23, 1856.—I find I need more time for my own daily religious meditation, for contemplative internal life. Once I had much, now little. The intense busyness of my late years is not favorable to certain religious joys I once had time for, and still have inclination towards and longing after. So a little more time shall be daily given thereunto.

Aug. 16. Saturday Night.—It is now the third week of my annual vacation. I have been rejoicing in quiet, in idleness, and doing just as I have a mind to. I have read a good deal in Vogt's works, also in works of art, and translated divers little gems, which are in the leaves before this.

But when Saturday night comes, I feel a little uneasiness; solemn emotions of awe, and reverence, and delight, spring to consciousness. I don't feel quiet, but wish I was to preach to-morrow; and on Sunday night I feel a little dissatisfied that I have not preached.

Sept. 9 —To-day, I received from Messrs. Voigt and Günther, booksellers, of Leipsic, B. II., of Parker's *Sämmtliche Werke*, which makes four in all, accompanied with a collection of notices of me and mine, which are mostly quite friendly—more so, indeed, than the books entirely deserve. One, quite pleasing, was a hearty appreciation of the earnest religiousness of the writer. Faults I must have committed, and that in no small number, but I am glad to find that the motive is set down as human and religious.

His activity was very great just after he began to preach in the Music Hall. To the year 1852 belong the "Ten Sermons of Religion," the "Discourse on Daniel Webster," a sermon on leaving the Melodeon, and one, "The Function of a Minister," on entering the Music Hall. He also preached consecutively the six sermons, perhaps his most elaborate ones, upon atheism, the popular theology, and theism. These, with four more, make the volume entitled " Sermons of Theism:" to this he prefixed an historical introduction, which is a good popular exposition of the development of Christian Churches and nations, and of the religious needs of mankind. Nothing can be better than all the statements in these sermons, of the different kinds of atheism, the errors of the popular theology, and its past services, of providence, of evil, of the economy of pain. They are simple and racy, marred by no difficult terms, full of proverbial sentences.

Everything is addressed with warmth and sincerity to the simplest comprehension. Broad facts are displayed without subtlety ; all the essential points and movements of religious history are given without any compromises to rhetoric or popular predilections. There never was a more thorough, yet more religious, attempt to emancipate the common mind from the vices of traditional belief. No wonder such unadorned consciousness of theological absurdities became odious to the strong believers of every creed, who accused him of loose statements and immoral misrepresentation ; of a vague spite against doctrines which he feared to examine, but which in reality he saw uncolored and unclad. A different estimate must some day be made of these great popular utterances of a pious and sensible spirit. The sermons silently do their work among the people, flowing into the minds that are the most accessible by birth or culture to their approaches, and thence making their fertilizing way. Bigots will resist in vain an influence which they style insidious, but which shares the silence and the breadth of every elementary force. The Music Hall is empty ! Men will look in vain for his parish ; it waits in Europe and America upon his printed speech, which addresses, with a rare comprehension of the general intelligence, and in a style born to emancipate the longing of all men for simple religion, and charity, and good works. Delegations of this great parish of mankind sits even in churches the most traditional, listening through the open windows to the sweet voices of the natural world, while the preacher, perhaps himself also listening, vaguely, with half an ear, hums the prescriptive texts, and spins with the old assiduity his doctrinal snares.

It is not easy at once to gauge the precise nature and limits of a man's influence, who has sounded the world's popular systems with the plummet of learning, held by a humane and vigorous hand, and whose primitive sentiments look from above through a broad, pellucid understanding, in which, as in a dry light, things appear to him as they are.   He has not the beneficence of a great organizer of thought, or of imagination; he displays no special knacks of metaphysics, and does not make progress by mining and boring ; the long roll of the orator does not call men together for a day's muster.   His excellence was not merely in the exposition of some preliminary processes of mind.   No processes appear, but instead of them, light and warmth, broad elements of hope, and humanity, and faith.

FROM THE JOURNAL.

Oct. 5, 1858.—The Music Hall opened three weeks ago, and has been filled with quite large congregations. Our course of lectures begins to-morrow. Mr. Sanborn gives the introductory poem.

The course of lectures was that known as the Fraternity Course, which was put forth by a parochial organization of the Twenty-Eighth Congregational Society, established for charitable and philanthropic purposes.   It was very active, and did a great deal of good in a quiet way.   The character of the lectures reflected the free, progressive character of the Society.   Men and women were invited to speak who had something to say upon all the great humane subjects of the day, to which the ordinary lyceums in cities seldom tolerate any direct allusion.   In the country and the small towns, the real questions of society fare better, and the stock subjects of lecturers are heard with indifference.   It is plain that Mr. Parker could not lecture before any of the associations in Boston which annually blossom into a course.   His words were welcomed by great audiences, from the Penobscot to the Mississippi.   But the east wind blew in Boston at the mention of his name.

After the establishment of the Fraternity Course, he had an opportunity to lecture, which he occasionally improved.   We owe to it the admirable Biography of Franklin, which he first preached in a fragmentary form as a sermon, and then presented as a lecture.   It was a favorite subject ; he loved to trace the lives of strong men who grew in an American fashion.   This lecture he elaborated with great care, and wrote it three times over; once, however, in consequence of losing the manuscript on his return from delivering it in South Boston.

There was not a religious society in Boston at the time of Mr.

Parker's last illness that wielded so great a practical and charitable power as the Fraternity of the Music Hall. Its earnest
young men and women took the life of Mr. Parker's great heart
as he poured it into them, and carried it out through Boston
streets, to put it to the lips of the fugitive and the miserable. Is
not that a sacrament for a Church to blossom into, better than a
conventional communion? The bread and wine, and the Christian fraternity, went out for those who needed them. These
true disciples did two things—they showed their faith by their
works, and they showed how faith could flourish without rites
and observances.

The bronze statue of the man whose greatest symphony broke
forth into a song of joy for earth's millions, looked over the
preacher, steadfast as bronze himself, while the warm heart beat
and flowed. An earth must be rugged and solid to contain its
own broad tides. The preacher and the composer were kindred
in sorrows and in moral quality, in love and in scorn; they
built faith upon the essential harmonies of the great world of
nature and of man, and bade the tumultuous passages of life
resolve themselves, with all their low, presageful thunder, into
the triumphant security which only the man who has kept himself like a little child can feel.

In this world there is no end of fine coincidences where
things themselves are fine. The great German stands mutely in
the hall of the great American, while he preaches a universal
doctrine.

" In the mighty realm of music there is but a single speech,"
and that is the speech of all hearts who yearn for the harmonies
of God; deep religious awe, tender dependence, flashing, sarcastic
sincerity, fiery indignation, pure humanity, love that melts all
races, like kindred drops, into one heart, even that heart which
the Father, through all diversities, is striving to create.

Some people say they are not indebted to Mr. Parker for a
single thought. The word "thought" is so loosely used, that a
definition of terms must precede our estimate of Mr. Parker's
suggestiveness and originality. Men who are kept by a commonplace-book go about raking everywhere for glittering scraps,
which they carry home to be sorted in their æsthetic junk-shop.
Any portable bit that strikes the fancy is a thought. There
are literary rag-pickers of every degree of ability; and a great
deal of judgment can be shown in finding the scrap or nail you

29

want in a heap of rubbish. Quotable matter is generally considered to be strongly veined with thought. Some people estimate a writer according to the number of apt sentences embedded in his work. But who is judge of aptness itself? What is apt for an epigram is not apt for a revolution : the shock of a witty antithesis is related to the healthy stimulus of creative thinking, as a small electrical battery is to the terrestrial currents. Well-built rhetorical climaxes, sharp and sudden contrasts, Poor Richard's common-sense, a page boiled down to a sentence, a fresh simile from nature, a subtle mood projected upon nature, a swift controversial retort, all these things are called thoughts ; the pleasure in them is so great, that one fancies they leave him in their debt. That depends upon one's standard of indebtedness. Now a penny-a-liner is indebted to a single phrase which furnishes his column ; a clergyman near Saturday night seizes with rapture the clue of a fine simile which spins into a "beautiful sermon ;" for the material of his verses a rhymester is "indebted" to an anecdote or incident. In a higher degree all kinds of literary work are indebted to that commerce of ideas between the minds of all nations, which fit up interiors more comfortably, and upholster them better than before. And everything that gets into circulation is called a thought, be it a discovery in science, a mechanical invention, the statement of a natural law, comparative statistics, rules of economy, diplomatic circulars, and fine magazine writing. It is the manœuvring of the different arms in the great service of humanity, solid or dashing, on a field already gained. But the thought which organizes the fresh advance goes with the pioneer train that bridges streams, that mines the hill, that feels the country. The controlling plan puts itself forth with that swarthy set of leather-aproned men, shouldering picks and axes. How brilliantly the uniforms defile afterward, with flashing points and rythmic swing, over the fresh causeway, to hold and maintain a position whose value was ideally conceived. So that the brightest facings do not cover the boldest thought.

We are only really indebted to that thought which premeditates and selects the great points for a moving world, and that is always a combination of insight, temperament, and will. The whole man is the thought to which we are indebted. His sentences are not smart traps into which he steps to be held while you look at him. You cannot bag your game in that way, and stock your larder. Probably your whole house would not hold him. In that case, his is not the thought to which you care to be indebted. You will go hunting for other marsh birds, who live by suction, plunging their bills, sensitive to fare, in every pool. Certainly the exigencies of a commonplace-book are not the measure of originality. And as no single thought in any form can be pronounced new, so all thinking which is full of the blood of old thoughts, and beating with nature's primitive pulse, is original. It may be quotable besides; but its originality is movement, direction, sincerity, and power. It is a bold, deep-breathing man who plants the whole of himself forward with each step, sowing all the furrows, not with a gift, nor a view, nor any knacks of mind or fingers, but with the health of his personality, as he lets conscience, intellect, and heart forth in one untrammelled jubilation over nature's beautiful spring day. His audacious looks reflect the climate and the sun. It is his genius to stifle in a close room, and to be well enough to rough it in the open air. We sit inside cramming note-books, putting bugs in spirits, labelling drawers full of fossils and tenantless shells, enriching our cabinet. His cheery voice comes in like the warm, meadow-scented wind, recommending the living and thriving nature outside to us who are cataloguing nature within. If we cannot stand a draught we slam down the window, pitying people in the weather and predicting various ills.

This kind of originality will not respect our preconceptions. It has no time for that. Persons who join exploring expeditions find at first that Nature disdains their city ways; she is very rude, and occasionally there is a touch of contempt in the way she handles them. They bear all this for the sake of getting eventually upon the sky-bounded prairies; there they discover something better than buffaloes and Indians; better, even, than clear-water valleys with distant blue gentian-fringed mountains. They discover a capacity to be on friendly terms with the sincerity of the air and the earth. The disdain is found to be nothing but the unconscious freedom of the weather. So we fare with men whose thoughts emancipate. Not dreaming that our chamber needed ventilation, we set forth some day, and at first find it cheerless sleeping with the ceiling fled off to the stars, while vague perils assail us. It is very shocking to be without our usual conveniences. When the exigencies of the scene dispense with the little delicacies and contrivances of our genteel housekeeping, it is like trifling with sacred subjects. We suspect that something

malignant, under pretence of enlarging our estate, has robbed
us of all that is dear and precious.   If we have made an attempt
to bring with us a cherished utensil, to serve whatsoever turn—
crockery and tinware, to maintain some culinary traditions—one
by one they are sacrificed to freedom of movement, and our course
is marked by household relics. When the pack is well cleared out
how lightsome is the march !   We smile at our old horror, and
enjoy Nature's satire upon impediments.   Nature never means
to hurt our feelings ; she shines and grows ; the brightening weather laughs at the retreating thunder ; the grass has no bad
motive in drenching our feet ; the lightning but emphasizes the
element which the bud and wheat-ear gratefully confirm.

CHAPTER XV.

THE wide influence which the sermons preached in the Music
Hall attained, as they were scattered in volumes or the phono-
graphic reports of newspapers, is shown in a remarkable way by
the letters received by him from all quarters of the world, from
persons of both sexes, and of every estate in life. If they could
be published, they would create the most emphatic endorsement
and guarantee of the fitness of his nature to reach the heart of
mankind, and to feed its inmost longings. He was sought by
young and ardent minds, during the period of transition in New
England, and later in the West, when parties were changing, and
old modes of thought were breaking up. They came to him as
to a master : there was no reservation in the eagerness and
positive abandonment of their hearts to his brotherly society.
People who desired to know what were the facts about theology
and religion, troubled by creeds, just cast adrift from them, and
uncertain where next to go,—soldiers, students, laborers, shop-
keepers, Catholics, Methodists, and members of all sects,—people
with special questions about retribution, God, non-resistance,
miracles, free-will, many who were in distress or uncongenial
circumstances, suffering from intemperance, pining for want of
remunerative labor, and all people who longed to be of service to
their kind ; young converts who had become suspicious of the
machinery which turned them out Church members ; old men,
filled suddenly with profound dissatisfaction at dogmas which
they fancied they believed ; and whole neighborhoods speaking
through their ready writer, who had been put forward to ask
some news of him ; it was as if a great crowd hurried towards

a clear and steadfast voice that hailed them to come over where it spoke, by the only safe and speedy way. What a testimony to the horrors of Calvinism sleeps in these still letters, that were once wet with tears before they came to him—and often afterwards! It was in this way, that his dread of the logical effects of that violent and narrow creed became confirmed. He had documents enough, sealed with the heart's blood of the writers, to bear him out in the strongest things he ever said.

He prized above all other communications of this kind, the awkward and ill-spelled letters of laboring men, through whose grotesque sentences divine desires struggled to reach him, as if with gnarled and calloused hand, to grasp his own large and manly one.

In December, 1857, he writes to a friend :—

I send you a letter, which I count as precious. Here it is—from Minnesota—a curious specimen of our civilization, and the proof of the relation which a thinking scholar may stand in to the great mass of the people. Please return it by-and-bye, or keep it safe against our meeting—which is the better way.

Here it is, a little helped in spelling, perhaps, but not otherwise meddled with :—

Aug. 30, 1857.

Mr. Parker—Dear Sir,—I take the liberty to make you acquainted with a request that has been made to me a number of times, and that is this—to ask what way we may obtain your sermons regular, or such ones as would be adapted to our situation. I came to this place one year ago. I had a town laid out, &c., and commenced operations. We have a flour-mill, two saw-mills, blacksmith-shops. My hotel is most done. I am now living in a log-house, which answers for hotel, church, town-house, school-house, and last spring was used for a fort to keep secure from the Indians. But we are fast completing other buildings for the same purposes mentioned above.

I left Boston last June with my family, and among our library we have two volumes of your sermons, Nos. 1 and 2, and in the absence of our minister, I have taken the liberty to try and satisfy the audience by giving them something from your works, which has had the effect to cause them to ask for more, and to-day I have been requested to give them one more of your sermons, as our Close-communion Baptist is not present, "A Sermon of Old Age."

It is now requested that a part of each Sabbath be occupied in listening to one of your sermons. Now, sir, if you will send to me such of your sermons as in your judgment will suit a frontierman's mind best, I will settle the bill whenever it is presented. You think strange of this way of proceeding, but that may be explained hereafter. There are a number of your hearers in this place. You will not know the signature of this. I have attended your meeting at the

Music Hall but little, from the fact that soon after I heard you preach I moved from Boston to Melrose, which made it inconvenient for me to attend your meeting in the city.

Among the numerous examples of Mr. Parker's influence, let one suffice. It is the story of the beautiful development of a soul, out of poor and ordinary circumstances, and notwithstanding all the discouragements which friends, the Churches, and society so well know how to deploy against the independent seeker. This poor boy tells his life in letters from the Far West. The first two or three are illiterate, without punctuation, and of uncertain spelling, but they improve rapidly, and blossom with all the refinement and fragrance of a religious heart. It is almost like the miles of waving western corn, the miracle of a single season.

"Four years ago," commences the first letter or call of this lad to the strong and famous preacher, "I had the misfortune to lose my left hand by an accident. Since that time, until the winter before last, I went to school where I live. The winter before last, my brothers and friends raised sufficient money amongst them to send me to a school in Wisconsin. While there (1854–5), I saw one of your works, with the title, ' Discourse on Matters pertaining to Religion.' "

The next winter he made a little money by teaching a district school. Part of it he sent to Little and Brown for more volumes of Mr. Parker.

I had several disputes with prominent Church-members, and soon the hue and cry ran through the village that I was a confirmed infidel, and when I would give them arguments that they could not answer, they would ask with a sneer, whether a boy like me—being only twenty-one years old—should attempt to teach ministers. Last week I made a public lecture against Slavery and for Fremont, during which I quoted a passage from the Bible. Since that, the whole town nearly have risen against me, and with pious horror they ejaculate, "An infidel to quote Bible as argument!" Even my brother and friends have turned against me, and I expect in a few days to have no home. I am poor. Last summer I worked out as a day-labourer on a farm, but even that has failed—nobody will receive the infidel —— in their family. If I had the means I would stay here, and alone I would face and tear down their dreadful theology.

He wants to get some employment in Boston, where " I may clasp you by the hand, listen to your noble words, and take example from your manly life." We can imagine what answer the farm-bred preacher sent to this day-labourer with the divine thoughts waking in his soul.

TO MR. H. A. W., MENDON, ILLINOIS.

Boston, Oct. 10. 1856.

DEAR SIR,—You case is a very hard one, but I do not know what advice to give you. It would be in vain to venture to Boston or any of the eastern towns—where the avenues to all kinds of business are more crowded than with you at the West. I feel the warmest sympathy with you, and trust that patient efforts will secure you the victory in the end. There are several modes which men try to overcome an enemy withal; one is to knock him down, another to talk him down, but, I think, the manly way is to live him down. After a little while, farmers will sow the wheat which gives the largest crop of the best kind of grain, and will not care much by what name it is called. If Hebrew wheat only yields ten bushels to the acre, and heathen wheat yields thirty of a better quality, the bad name won't keep the wheat from the fields.

It is always pleasant to try and live down the evil name which good deeds bring on a man. You are always sure of the peaceful victory at last.

Believe me, yours truly,
THEO. PARKER.

THE ANSWER.

DEAR FRIEND,—Allow me to call you so. I received your letter, but words cannot express the delight with which I read it, and the strength that I received from your advice and expressions of sympathy —sympathy on a subject that of all subjects is the dearest to me, but which for many years I have had no one to sympathize with.

Then follows a little sketch of his personal history. The father and mother were English, of the Episcopal Church ; he was the youngest of a large family, which emigrated when he was eleven years old. Three weeks after they reached the West the mother died. "She only knew my wishes and desires, and sympathized with me. My memory still goes back to the time when I sat at her feet and heard of a loving God." The family was decent and moral, but absorbed in the day's work. No one spoke to him to ask if the soul also hungered. But when the "Discourse" fell in his way,—

I had at last found a key to that something. I knew not what it was, lying dormant within me. My relations and friends are pained and angry with me. They ask me why I do not go too, and make money ; they tell me that I have talents and eloquence which, if I will throw away my suicidal notions, will place me in a high position and fill my lap with gold. But you can sympathize with me. I feel like one that has just awoke from a horrid dream. I have found there is something to live for, and that instead of my pocket I have a mind to cultivate. It is as you say, a person with natural talents can live without much effort here in this magnificent country. But consider my situation; I can live here easier than any place that I know of, but I want some one to sympathize with me, not that I am afraid, or have no faith in the truths that I have read, but there is something within me that longs for that twin sister of love. I am a child in feelings if not in body. Ofttimes as I have been reading your manly words, my heart has gone out towards you, and I have longed with an irresistible longing to be near you. And since I have been writing, I have wished that I could be in the place of this letter, and that you could look into my eyes and read me as you can this letter. But if that cannot be now, let me hear from you often. Write brave words to me. And I will endeavour to live down all opposition.

He has caught the Western frankness and intuitive appreciation, which created for Mr. Parker one of his chief consolations. It hailed him unsolicited, from every social rank, as pioneers shout to each other across the prairies, for guidance and good-cheer.

TO THE SAME.

Boston, Nov. 3, 1856.

MY DEAR SIR,—I thank you for your kind letter which I find on returning from your State. I confess I know of nothing which calms, cheers, and strengthens a man so much as a fixed and abiding confidence in God. If I am sure of the cause and providence of the universe, I am sure that all things at last will turn out well. If I am not certain of Him, I am sure of nothing else. The great vice of all the religious systems in the world is this—they do not know the perfect and infinite God, so they have only a poor and imperfect trust in God, and, instead of love, nothing but fear. To my apprehension, religion is natural piety—the love of God—and natural morality, the keeping of the laws He has written on matter and man.

It is not easy to find any wide sympathy with opinions dear to you, for they are yet too new in the world. But the noble man gradually makes a little circle of friends about him who sympathize with his best emotions, and soon the circle grows wider. The history of mankind seems dark as you look back, so much stumbling for so short a walk, but when you look forward you see the signs of triumph for the individual and the race. It is sure to come, and every earnest, good man, put him where you may, will do something to help the victory to draw nigh.

Let me hear from you from time to time, and believe me, truly your friend,

T. P.

The next letter describes his success at inoculating the chief minister and enemy with the " Discourse on Religion." " He has now your sermons on Theism, Atheism, and the Popular Theology, which he has taken without any of his former reluctance, and which, in fact, he seemed anxious to take."

Dear friend, you know not with what joy I read and re-read your last letter, and treasured up your expressions of friendship; and when I think of the terrible opposition that you have braved and are still braving, it gives me a confidence and hope that nothing can subdue.

Now a change has come over the hand-writing, and the arrangement of the sentences. There is a rhythm in the feeling and the style.

When the cold shoulder of contempt is turned towards me, when the finger of scorn is levelled at me, when there is no one to whom I can look for sympathy and instruction in the great truths of religion, I turn to thee with all the confidence of a child to a parent—confident of thy sympathy, confident of thy love. Oh, how I wish, now, while my mind is forming, that I could be near you, and mould my mind after the manliness, the beauty, and all-embracing love of thine! But, with the assurance of God's aid and thy sympathy, I will go forward a seeker after truth, let it come in whatever form it may.

There has come a change over my mind, a calmness, a contentedness, a peace, that I never knew before. I can compare my life up to the present time to a vine without support, crawling along the ground, clasping and clinging to all kinds of dirt and rubbish, but which has at last reached a support, and begun to climb; it looks back on the time and strength it has expended in reaching that support; it looks up though the path seems steep and rugged, and the winds of adversity for the moment arrest its progress. Yet it will only cling the closer, and go on climbing till it dies.

Following this are some questions addressed to Mr. Parker upon immortality, and the future growth of the soul out of its present habits and restrictions.

The next letter is dated two months later, in 1857.

I wish I could express to you on paper my feelings, the joy, the peace, the satisfaction I feel in contemplating the thoughts of the good God in His works. It is not a great while since the thought of God was the most terrible that ever crossed my mind. What hopeless agony I have suffered, as in the dead of night I have thought of the endless hell to which in all probability I was hastening! and yet the grim and ghastly hell of the Christian theology was preferable to its idea of God. But, thank God, it is past, though it is hard to have "Infidel!" hissed in my ears, to have those whom I once considered my bosom friends turn away. Yet I gladly bear it; yes, ten times more, than turn back to my former belief.

I have new thoughts, new objects, new aspirations; everything is new, new heavens, new earth, with no dark future beyond. But I look forward to a future bright, glorious, grand; and I look forward with a peaceful calmness that is surprising to me. There is no fear, for I cannot fear what is good.

My mind is settled as to my future object in life. It is my wish to follow in your footsteps, and preach to others the truths you have awakened in my mind, and, God help me! I will do it faithfully and fearlessly.

This is the emancipation which the broad and humane thought proclaimed, as it won thousands of souls from the slavery of indifference or fear.

The next letter was written in the spring of 1858.

Last summer I worked on a farm, though it may appear somewhat strange to you that a person with one hand could work to advantage as a farmer. Yet, I find that knowledge is power. Last winter I devoted three months to study, but as soon as spring came, the warm sun called me to the open fields. I know not why, but I love to turn the generous soil, to scatter wide the seed, to watch the peering blades as they come forth, and to meditate on the laws of growth and reproduction. The little birds, mate with mate, seem to be full and running over with joyous notes, as they flutter hither, choosing a place to build their nest and raise their young. I love the noble, generous steeds that draw my plough, fleet as the deer, graceful in proportion as nature made them, their spirits unbroken by the whip or spur; but they will come at my call, and look at me with such expression in their large eloquent eyes, that I have often wished they could talk and tell me their feelings. I know they love me, and their love is returned with compound interest.

* * * * * *

I hope I have done something. I have circulated your works to some extent here, and, with one or two exceptions, they have not failed to convince all who have read with them with care.

* * * * * *

For three weeks past there has been here what is called a revival of religion; meetings have been held every day, and the whole town is stirred up in such a manner as I have never seen it before. The farmer has left his plough, and the mechanic his shop, and all joined in the general commotion. I respect any effort that a man makes to approach his Maker, yet I do not see that this way makes their minds any freer, or their ideas of God purer. Last Friday, two ministers came to see me: we had a long talk, which only resulted in making me still stronger in my opinions, and to wonder still more that educated men should cling to doctrines without foundation.

In the summer of 1858 he reported as follows:—

I can see a gradual and steadily advancing inquiry after truth. Much has been done since spring. The books of yours, which I own have been going steadily from house to house, and the desire to read them has been growing stronger every day. I have been thinking lately that we ought to form ourselves into a society, as by that means the bond of union would be closer, and more could be done in the way of distributing books and papers to others. I would like your opinion on the subject.

He had seventeen acres of noble corn planted, during a dry season, part of which he got into the ground on Sunday, because it promised rain on the morrow.

Oh, what a hubbub it caused! Old ladies threw up their hands and eyes in horror. Old gentlemen handled their canes with threatening motives. It furnished a text for four preachers. The young gazed on me with eyes at least a third larger than ordinary. The middle-aged, to a man, have been waiting impatiently for some special interposition of Providence. But, no—I am not stricken with incurable disease, nor is my corn blasted, contrary to their expectations and wishes, and, I suspect, prayers. There is no change in nature, no special providence in their behalf, unless they consider it was the cause of the long-continued and soaking rains.

But the next letter is from another hand :—

Sir, —— has bin sick, is now beter; if i should not recover, I should always think your doctrine right; he wishes a sermon on immortal life.

The explanation follows, in Nov. 1858, from his own hand :—

I was very sorry to hear of your sickness, and sincerely hope that, when you receive this, you will be convalescent. Should you die, it would be a severe trial to me, for thou art near and dear to me. When I stood alone with no one to encourage and advise, I wrote to you. Your answer nerved me for the battle. At the present time, instead of standing alone, I have powerful and influential friends, and the number is slowly but surely increasing. It has been the influence of your letters that has encouraged me to go forward, and should they fail the loss to me would be great. . . . . . .
Frequently while discussing religious subjects with others, they have said that my belief would do to *live* by, but it would not do to die by. The day of trial came. On the evening of the 26th of September, I felt that I could not live till morning. My stand being close to the bedside, while my friends were absent for a few minutes, I with great effort wrote these words on a piece of paper: " I die in the belief in which I live," dated and signed it, and placed it with my other papers. When my friends returned, I told them I thought I was going to die ; and I settled up my worldly affairs. The physician and my friends conversed with me, and tried to shake my belief, but in vain: my reliance on the infinite perfection of God grew stronger ; there was no doubt, no fear, but a peaceful happiness came over me. Gradually I lost all consciousness, my body lost its feeling, my pulse was gone. I lay in that state for several hours, when, contrary to expectation, I rallied ; for a week life hung in the balance. No one could say which way the balance would turn. Part of the time I was conscious, and conversed freely with those that came to see me ; my bed was besieged daily by church members and ministers; daily I was urged to renounce my belief, but daily that belief grew stronger, and the contrast between natural and ecclesiastical religion grew wider and more distinct. At the end of a week, my youth and excellent constitution triumphed.

TO THE SAME.

Boston, Dec. 2, 1858.

My DEAR SIR,—I thank you for the letter you so kindly sent me Nov. 6th, which I have not been able to answer till now, and at this moment but briefly.

I am glad to find that you seem to be permanently convalescent; so likewise am I; but, though a great walker, I cannot yet accomplish more than two miles a day, and use another's hand to save my own when possible. I trust we shall both be entirely well, and that soon.

I am glad you held fast to your faith amid the weakness of disease and the assaults of well-meaning but bigoted men. It required some courage to do that. It gives me great pleasure to find that I have helped any one to learn the road of true religion. Bigotry and fear are the great enemies of the human race. If I can destroy them, and bring up in their stead piety, which is the love of God, and morality, which is the keeping of His natural laws, then I shall feel that I have not lived in vain.

Believe me, yours truly,

THEODORE PARKER.

Mr. Parker highly prized this letter from John Brown, a blacksmith of Rhinebeck :—

TO THE REV. THEODORE PARKER.

Rhinebeck, Dutchess Co., New York, Feb. 4, 1859.

REV. SIR,—It's with sincere heartfelt regret I've being made acquainted, through the public press from time to time, of your severe sickness. Although we differ somewhat materially in our theological views, I have long been an enthusiastical admirer of your talents and virtues as a man, a scholar, and a gentleman. I take this method of conveying to you my heartfelt sympathy and condolence in your affliction; permit me to express a hope it may be of short duration, and that you may be speedily restored to your former good health and usefulness. And in doing so I believe (in fact I know it to be so) I'm expressing the sentiments of hundreds, if not thousands, in the circle of my acquaintance, which is pretty extensive through the State, and particulary in Dutchess Co., where I've resided for the last 25 years.

You'll perceive I've made several mistakes, which you will please pardon, as I am nothing but a poor blacksmith, with a wife and family depending upon my labor for support. In conclusion, accept of my best wishes for your present and eternal welfare, and believe me your sincere friend and well-wisher, now and for ever,

JOHN BROWN.

TO MISS PATIENCE FORD, DORCHESTER, MASS.

West Roxbury, April 18, 1841.

MY DEAR FRIEND,—I have just received your letter and have read it both with pleasure and with pain ; it gives me great *pleasure* to find that a thought which has burnt in my own bosom, finds a warm resting-place in a pious heart. There is no sweeter joy on earth than the thought that you have comforted or strengthened one single human soul ; have made truth brighter and heaven more high. But it gives me *pain* to find you look *to me* for light, when I am so ill-qualified to give it. Out of the depth of your own spirit it will spring up. "A man's mind is sometime wont to tell him more than seven watchmen that sit above in a high tower," said the old wise man. The infinite Parent of truth sheds light, without let or hindrance, down into all souls that look reverently and obediently up to HIM. It seems to me, that if we *always* obeyed the law God has written on our hearts, the decisions of reason, of conscience, and of faith, would be as infallible in their action as the instinct of the bee and the law of gravitation now are. But no man is in this state ; so as the penalty of our disobedience, "we grope for the wall like blind men," and "feel after God if haply we may find Him." We are not *one with God* as Christ was ; so we are in doubt and fear. The best and wisest men feel this the most deeply. *Jesus alone felt none* of it. His obedience was perfect, and so God's truth passed through him as light through the celestial spaces where there is no atmosphere, and was not bent to either side. You ask an explanation of one passage in the sermon. After I preached it, I felt it might be understood to mean something I never assented to. It belonged originally to a course of several sermons, and the others would perhaps explain what was obscure in this. I meant simply that Jesus was not *all that human nature is capable of becoming,* that is, He was not a poet, astronomer, architect, or musician. He did not come to be a Milton, a Leibnitz, a Michael Angelo, or a Mozart. This does not diminish his greatness. I meant to imply that *each* blackbird is all that *any* blackbird or all blackbirds *can be.* But no one man has ever developed on earth *the whole of the capabilities involved and folded up in his nature.*

This was doubtless the case with Jesus. If you wish to learn astronomy or music you do not go to the Gospels, for Christ did not come to teach these arts. I take it, this statement would harm no man's feelings. But, on the other hand, in his own department of morality, religion, a divine life, perfect goodness, I think he was true, perfect, and complete. We can see no limitation to his perfection in this respect. He was all that man can be of goodness and religion. He was all of God there can be in a perfectly good and religious man. So he could say, "I am the way, the light, and the truth." "I and the Father are one," for he thought God's thoughts, felt God's feelings, lived God's will. I never said that man would outgrow Christianity—never thought it possible. To me Christianity is perfect love to man and God. Can mankind outgrow this ? Not even when they become angels. I think St. Paul had this in mind when he says, "we shall judge angels," viz. that Christianity is perfect truth by which even the higher beings are judged. If future revelations of truth are made, they can never supersede the Christian doctrine, for one truth is congenial to all truth. Therefore, if God should create a man wiser, better, holier than Jesus, the revelation this new messenger brought would not destroy the old.

Whether such a being ever will be created, no one can tell but He who possesses the riddle of the world. The counsels of God—no one knows them. I think it becomes Christians to leave the future to Him whose it is. For my own part, I cannot conceive of a being more good, and beautiful, and holy, and true than Jesus of Nazareth. His words judge the world. The higher we think, the holier we live, the more we find in them, the more we admire and love in him. I do not worship Christ, but I love him, and would kiss the hem of his garment. As you say, he is still "the Star of Promise." He has not come, oh, no! It is not the Christianity of Jesus, that most of even pious men assent to. It is still in the world, but not known by the world. The wisest and best have at most only after*thought* what he fore*knew*. In love, and religion, and truth, I think no one has come up to him, and man cannot go beyond the truth, as you so well say. I think we are yet to have a period of real Christianity on the earth; so we all pray, "Thy kingdom come," and often say, "How long, O Lord?" What you say of your experience of one of Christ's sayings is true of all of them. To-day a man says this is Christianity, to-morrow he lives it out, but then he finds Christianity is still above him, for he sees a new meaning with the new eyes his life has given him. "Inasmuch as you have done it unto the least of these, you have done it unto me." What a world of meaning it has! It condemns us all. I thank you, my dear lady, for the confidence you have placed in me, and rest assured that if I can be of service to you in any way, it will give me the greatest pleasure to do so.

I remain yours, in the bonds of Christian love.

TO THE SAME.

West Roxbury, June 15, 1841.

MY DEAR SISTER PATIENCE,—I thank you most heartily for your kind letter. You felt moved, as you said, to help me; and your letter did help me, and that not a little. There are times when the strongest men need help, and if it is so with the strong, how much more is it the case with me, who am only strong when I am weak! Your letters have given me encouragement and new vigor. It is delightful to find one who sympathizes in what is deepest and highest in your own mind, who is true to what is truest in your own heart. In this world, where sinners are so much more common than saints, it is very refreshing to find one who is pursuing an upward path, and asking God, reverently, for more light and higher truth.

I sent you "Fénélon," because I thought it would not have fallen in your way, and I know it must speak to your heart of hearts. A religious book is always understood by the religious heart, and by that alone.

The common people counted John as a prophet, and seem to have heard Jesus gladly; while the *wise men of earth* slew both the prophet and the Savior; so it always is. In "Fénélon" you will find something that you will not like, perhaps. He would *destroy* self, not merely *bring all into subjection* to the law of the Spirit of Life. Did you ever read Dr. Channing's remarks on Fénélon? If you never did, Mr. Hall will be glad to lend them to you; and you will find many good words that came out of a good man's heart, and have already reached other good hearts and made them better.

You must take great delight, I think, in Mr. Hall's pulpit services, and his conversation also. If there are any pious ministers—and *I* think there are many—he is one, and one of the most excellently pious. He does not make the kingdom of heaven consist in meats and drinks, but in righteousness, and peace, and joy in believing. He has an unction from the Holy One, if any have it now-a-days. I rejoice, my dear sister, in the strength of your convictions and the brightness of your inward life.

TO THE SAME.

West Roxbury, July 5, 1841.

MY DEAR SISTER PATIENCE,—Your last letter gratified me much. That alone was worth all the hard things men say in the newspapers. But, as you say, they *cannot hurt* any one. I thank you most heartily for your kind sympathy. It makes me feel strong. It is delightful to get the fellow-feeling of one good religious heart that is full of faith, and tries doctrines by *feeling* of them. I do not care much whether a person agrees with me in opinions or not; that is a very small affair, but if we *feel* alike about the highest things, we can walk together; for we *are agreed.* But now I have time only for a few words. I shall *not* be at home next Sunday; but I shall the *Sunday after that,* when both my wife and I shall be very glad indeed *to give you the right hand of welcome,* if you will come, as you propose.

Very affectionately,
Your brother,
THEO. PARKER.

TO THE SAME.

West Roxbury, September 11, 1844.

MY DEAR SISTER PATIENCE,—I have not time as yet for a long letter, but yet for a few words. I was quite sorry to see you so sad as I thought you on Sunday. I had not then opportunity to speak of it, but you seemed less happy than I was wont to see you. Pray tell me the cause. Is there any occasion in the state of the body? any reason in the state of the mind? or has any trouble you do not outwardly speak of befallen you? I know that you used to welcome angels, whether they were dressed in wedding robes or mourning garments. Then, too, you say in your note—which, like all yours, came in the right time, and was most heartily welcomed—that a dispensation of silence is upon you. Surely not, if you have anything to say. A misfortune, I think it would be to be silent when you were certain you had somewhat to speak of, and felt certain you had something good and true. Be not faithless, but believing. I know God waiteth to be revealed to all such as lie low in His power and reverently look to Him. But He expects them also to reveal what is granted them, not hiding their wisdom in its own beauty, but letting their light shine. Life is one way, speech is another form of our revealing to men what the Great Father reveals to us; such as can speak the truth are in duty bound so to do, as well as live it. After I have got over the hurry of business, and the no less urgent hurry of friendships, I hope you will come up and pass some days with us, and in the meantime will send me more letters.

Yours faithfully,
THEO. PARKER.

TO THE SAME.

West Roxbury, Feb. 7, 1845.

MY DEAR PATIENCE,—I thank you for your kind and seasonable letter. It came, as your letters always came, at the right time. I have delayed a little while my reply, because I have been too much occupied to find time to write any letters but the most urgent: so you will excuse my delay with the same charity you have always extended to me.

What you say of the love of God is true and beautiful. I understand your feelings and your experience—at least I think so. No one can dwell too deeply in the love of God, for it is the noblest sentiment we are capable of feeling, and it leads out to a love of truth, goodness, usefulness, loveliness—for these are among the modes in which we conceive of God. It leads, therefore—in a sound and healthy state of mind—to a life full of truth, goodness, usefulness, and loveliness. But there is always a danger that such as dwell in this sentiment should lose themselves in contemplation, become dreamers, not doers, and so should be abundant in the blossoms of piety and yet bring no fruit to perfection, so that when the Lord comes, seeking fruit, he shall find leaves only. Now there is always a strong temptation for a mystical man—and I think still more strongly to a mystical woman—to dwell amid the sentimental flowers of religion, charmed with their loveliness, and half-bewildered with their perfume, so to say,—a danger lest common sins of the times should not be thought so sinful and injurious as they really are; and lest the man should sit down patient and contented, not heeding his brother's condition, nor helping him out of the ditch into which he has fallen. At a certain stage of religious progress, we lose sight of the human element; we look perpetually at the Divine; we think God does all; we resign ourselves unconsciously to His will, our own will ceases to be. Many stop there, and stop in outward inaction; then they become one-sided, and at length dwindle. But, if a man goes on, he catches sight of the human again, and does not lose the Divine. He serves God consciously, and knowingly lives in obedience to the Great One. He ceases to be one-sided, but loves God with all his understanding and reason, as well as with all his heart. Then, too, though he loves contemplation none the less, he loves action all the more. One

30

lives like a worm in the heart of an apple, fattens and grows, and then flies off; the other not only grows and fattens, but comes out not a moth, but a bee, and visits all the flowers of the garden, culling from all its sweets, carries off honey for other bees, and builds up the comb—the residence of future bees that are to rejoice in his labours. We must not only fly, but, as we mount up, we must take others on our wings, for God gave one more strength than the rest only that he may therewith help the weak! I hope you will one of these days come and see us, and let us talk with you. I had a very pleasant conference with Mr. Hall, the other day. I wish there were more such men in pulpits.

Remember me to your parents and sisters, and believe me, as always,
Truly your friend and brother,
THEO. PARKER.

TO THE SAME.

West Roxbury, 27 Aug., 1845.

MY DEAR PATIENCE,—I did not hear of your affliction until Saturday, or I should have come up to see you instantly. Now I am obliged to go off for some few days, so I fear I shall not see you till next week. I hope you not only sustain yourself with a Christian fortitude, but are able also to comfort your father, whose afflictions are greater than your own; and your sisters, who naturally will look to you for consolation in this hour of sorrow. I know you will be calm, resigned, lying low in the hand of God. I know you will know that all is for the greatest good of her that is gone and those she has left behind. I hope you will be able to cheer hearts which are sadder than your own. They will see more than patience in you, I doubt not, even resignation, cheerful acquiescence in the will of the Great One who always is doing us good, not less when he causes us to weep than when he makes us smile. I beg you to assure your father of my sincere sympathy for him in this loss, and my hope that he will find comfort and peace. Let your sisters see and feel that you are superior to affliction, and you will gradually take away the grief of this sudden wound, and at last heal it. I have time to say no more, for I go presently; so good-bye.
Sincerely,
THEO. PARKER.

TO THE SAME.

West Roxbury, July 10, 1847.

MY DEAR PATIENCE,—I have not had a convenient opportunity to write you before. In your note you do not give me very distinctly to understand why you expect to lose the love and affection of your friend. It seems to me that you may "study the laws of the spirit," and live the life of the spirit, without losing the affection or even the sympathy of your friends. The laws of the spirit may be as well studied in one place or one sphere of life as another. Living itself affords the material of that study, and the study consists in reflecting on the material thus given. But perhaps you are looking for some new form of activity in which to work—I am no judge of that. You must determine that for yourself; but I hope you will not mistake any transient impulse which has its origin in some physical derangement for a serious monition of a lasting duty. I know you will be faithful to your own convictions of duty—my only fear is that you should decide without due deliberation, and without a complete understanding of your own case. Then, of course, the decision will be incorrect, and the result vanity and vexation of spirit. Would not it be well to state distinctly to yourself what it is that you wish to do, and how you wish to do it; then you will know exactly what you are about, and not "fight as one that beateth the air." I know you will be true to yourself, but only fear lest you should not always consult your permanent self, but only a fleeting emotion of the day or the night. If I can ever be of any help to you, you know it will give me great pleasure to be so; so, dear Patience, farewell.

T. P.

FROM MISS PATIENCE FORD.*

Dover, October 14, 1851.

MY DEAR FRIEND,—Moved by an inward impulse I do not resist, I take my pen to address you. It is very long since there has been any communication between us, yet the associations of the past come thronging upon my memory and filling my soul with grateful love. Perhaps we may now meet again upon paper, as there seems an insuperable barrier interposed to our meeting elsewhere. I must speak to you from the inner temple of my being, because it is only from thence I can speak, and it is only of that which you would care to hear. It is a temple of truth and purity, erected for the abode of our Father. God himself superintended the construction, and polished and fitted each stone before it was brought hither, so that "there was no noise of hammer, or axe, or any tool of iron, heard in this house while it was in building." But, oh! the rubbish that had to be removed ere the foundation of this temple could be laid strong and enduring! How much which I thought was pure gold had to be cast aside as base and useless metal, so much so that it seemed at times there would be nothing left upon which to base a superstructure. But the wise Master-builder knew better than I did; and as I earnestly besought Him to permit nothing but genuine material to remain, nought but would bear any test of time or change, He kindly bore away that which I had previously erected with much pains and care, and showed me it was of a crumbling nature, and liable to be swept away by the floods of time and decay. But what is more than all, He has promised to take up his abode in this temple He helped me to rear for his worship, so that now I have nothing more to ask of Him. I have but to put forth every faculty and power he has bestowed upon me, with the full assurance that I am going forward in harmony with the great creative spirit; and, oh! He brought me, when He came to take possession of this inner temple, the key to the outward universe, by

---

* This beautiful spirit passed away in the summer of 1863.

means of which I can penetrate into the very centre and essence of things, and discern of what they are composed. And He also brought other rich and costly gifts, the nature of which it were not possible for human language to describe.

*   *   *   *   *   *

TO PETER ROBERTSON, STONEHAVEN, NEAR ABERDEEN, SCOTLAND.

Boston, April 16, 1849.

My dear Sir,—I thank you for the very kind and affectionate note you sent me on the 10th of the last month. It reached me by the last mail-boat from England, and is very welcome. Such a letter shows me that my words have not fallen idle, nor been spoken wholly in vain. I have lamented from my childhood that such a subject as religion should be involved in such a cloud of superstition. But I thank God that we, live in an age when many men, in all parts of the world, are ceasing to fear God, and learning to *love* him. The old theologies are fast going to pieces ; new systems are taking their place, which rest on a truer idea of God, and a juster appreciation of the nature of man. It is a great and glorious age we live in. I trust that Christianity has great triumphs in store for mankind ; for Christianity is the just and complete action of human nature. We shall do a little towards this good work in America. You in England are contributing to the same end ; so is all the world. To me it is delightful to think that every truth is eternal, and each error is local and temporary. The Christian nations are gradually learning that there is but one religion—that is, in its *internal* form, piety, the love of God ; in its practical development and manifestation, goodness, the love of man. Christianity is free goodness, free piety, connected with free thought. When nations believe this, as now a few individuals believe it, what a beautiful world we shall have—what societies of men and of nations ! I love to look on the great temples which once were built in the name of religion, on the priesthoods and ecclesiastical institutions it has founded. In them I see signs of the power of religion ; and I look forward to the time when religion will be a yet greater power, and will build up, not theocracies, but democracies—when the government is of all, for all, and by all ; when we shall build up institutions to educate all men, so that we shall have a Church without bigotry, a State without despotism of the few over the many or the many over the few, and a society with no want, no ignorance, no crime. It seems to me that our human nature demands this ; that God designs it—and that it must come, not in our day, but far hence. We can do something to help it forward. Wealth is power, wisdom is power, religion is power ; and when mankind have all these three, what great results shall we not accomplish ? It is pleasant to think that each one of us may do a little towards a work so glorious.

I will send you a few sermons which I have published as soon as an opportunity offers. I have long been intending to print a volume of sermons relating to subjects like that which you name, and hope to do so in the coming season. Hitherto I have had so many things to attend to that it has been impossible. It will give me pleasure to hear from you at all times, and to be useful to you in any way.

Believe me faithfully your friend,

THEO. PARKER.

Rakhal Das Haldar, an intelligent Brahmin, now a Unitarian missionary in India, after expressing private gratitude for the awakening of his religious feeling, writes,—

It could not be otherwise than pleasing to you to know that the better portion of the community of this country take an unusual interest in perusing your theological works.

I ought to mention here a fact, that whenever there happens a conversation among my educated countrymen about religious compositions, they unanimously point out those of yours as models. Dr. Channing's sermons are undoubtedly excellent; but they want that energy, that manly boldness, that brilliancy of thought which characterize your sermons.

TO GEORGE ADAMS.

West Roxbury, June 24, 1842.

I cannot tell you how much your letter interested and *encouraged* me. I know there are many whom the Church and the ministers drive into infidelity, by their bigotry and contempt for reason. If I can ever do anything to remove the cloud of darkness which men have collected about the temple of truth I shall rejoice; still more if I can help any one to see the real beauty of true religion. I feel it is a great work which I have undertaken. I know that, so far as the ministers are concerned, I am alone, all alone. But I have no ambition to gratify, and so neither fear the disgrace nor count the applause which they can give me. If I can speak the truth plainly to honest and earnest men, it is all I ask; the result is with the God of all, and you and I have no cause to fear. I have received the ready sympathy of intelligent and religious laymen, and confess that it makes me feel strong, for most men have moments of depression, when a kind word is like rain to the parched grass.

FROM JAMES T. DICKINSON.

Middlefield, Conn., May 21, 1854.

DEAR SIR,—I give below an extract from the private journal of a congregational minister, which, as it relates to one of your books, may interest you. The writer is in "good and regular standing" among the orthodox; was formerly for several years a missionary to the Chinese, is now an invalid, but preaches and lectures occasionally. He is thought, I believe, to be rather peculiar in his notions—somewhat rash and radical, yet, on some points, conservative enough. Some have called him a Swedenborgian, and one man was known to whisper it about that he was a "kind of Atheist." A few weeks since he preached a sermon which contained a number of startling sentences, one of which, as a specimen, I quote :—" Deliver us from that religion which claims to have the love of God, whom it hath *not* seen, while withholding love from the brother, however dark in color or weak in faith, whom it hath seen ; which communes with the orthodox slaveholder, but casts out as unholy Dr. Channing and Theodore Parker, heterodox in creed, but so beautifully, bravely orthodox in life."

Now for the extract :—

" May 21st, 1854.—During the past week I have read Theodore Parker's ' Discourse of Matters Pertaining to Religion.' A great and good book, notwithstanding its want of orthodoxy. It is a strong help to me to find a man standing on the extreme verge of liberal theology, holding so firmly, so *tenaciously*, the one true religion, *love to God and man*. No doubt this is the absolute religion, and Mr. P. deserves the thanks of the world for setting it forth so clearly and beautifully. When *will* men learn that Christianity consists not in saying, ' Lord, Lord,' but in ' doing the Father's will ' ; not in believing a creed, but in living a true life ; not in opinion, but in character ; not in dogma, but in duty ; not in understanding the ontology of Christ, but in possessing his spirit ? When will men see the broad distinction between theology and religion, between formula and righteousness ? Though I dare not adopt a theology so extreme, so different from that so long and generally received, yet I rejoice that others can do so without peril to our holy religion. I still adhere to the idea that Christ is God, ' God in Christ, reconciling the world unto himself ' ; but it gives me great joy to find that a man can be an earnest and noble Christian, while believing Christ was only a man. But remembering Mr. P.'s excellent philosophy, that God is always present and helping in all our goodness, does it not follow that there is in Christ *so much* of God that, *practically*, we come to nearly the same point ? If T. P. were but the Pantheist he is said to be, could he help asserting the divinity of Christ ? Pantheist ! Who, then, is a theist ? who a believer in individual responsibility in sin, if not the man whose energy of conscience and will and word can send forth living, burning thoughts that pervade the continents, making Everett and Cass and Douglass turn pale, Pierce tremble on his four years' throne, breathing into the nation heart and hope ? Noble is the spiritual philosophy of T. P., which brings God back into the worlds of matter and mind, from which materialism and a half-atheistic theology had almost banished him, making him ' immanent,' living, loving, in all nature and all spirit. Baptism, the Lord's Supper, the Church, the Bible, the possible inspiration of all men, creeds, theologies, hold their proper place in this remarkable book, though I should sometimes prefer language less severe and impatient. But we must pardon much to the spirit of liberty. The Luthers are not mealy-mouthed. Against creeds, not even T. P. can invent words too severe. Though wrong, it is natural enough in the orthodox to excommunicate such a man from Christianity, but in the Unitarians it is weak and wicked."

Sincerely and respectfully yours,

JAMES T. DICKINSON.

TO JAMES T. DICKINSON.

Boston, 25th May, 1854.

I am much obliged to you for your kindness in sending me the opinion of your friend, so highly commendatory as it is. I wish I was worthy of half the praise he bestows upon me. But it is a strange state of things which now prevails. Mr. Webster denied that there was any law higher than an Act of Congress. When he stood and looked at the magnificent mountains of Virginia, he scoffed at the thought of a higher law than their tops. And when he came to die, more than a hundred and fifty clergymen preached and printed sermons eulogizing him as a great Christian. The evidence was :—he went to meeting, knew Watts' hymns, and in the Girard will case declaimed in behalf of the Christian religion. But on the other side, all the philanthropists of the age in America are denounced as heretical, unchristian, often as irreligious, and atheistic. *Not to love your brother* whom you have seen seems to be a sign of love of God whom you have not seen.

The great difficulty is, we have not an *idea of God* at all adequate to the wants of mankind; the popular theology does not know the God of infinite perfection. It is a partial and exceedingly imperfect God that all the churches worship. Hence they have a form of religion which is not adequate for the purposes of science, of politics, of philanthropy, or of piety. So the philosophers, the politicians, the philanthropists, and the men of solid piety turn off from the popular forms of religion. The *politicians comply* with it—it is a part of their policy, and means as much as their praise of democratic institutions, which they subvert while they profess to honor ; but this is not to last long.

TO J. P. HAZARD.

I hope good will come from these spiritual manifestations. Indeed, I see two special good things which are getting accomplished by them, viz.; 1. some men who had little satisfaction in any form of religion, who were disgusted with the foolishness taught as " divine wisdom," have found in these phenomena something higher than the mere *material* elements connected with them ; and they rise up thence to nobler forms of internal life, to satisfactory modes of religion. Such as did not believe in the immortality of the soul find a " proof" of it here. 2. These phenomena lead men to think about the miracles of the Bible, to disbelieve and reject them. Thus the old theology of the dark ages is rapidly melting to pieces.

No doubt other good results will follow. But I must confess that as yet I have seen nothing which leads me to believe in the *spiritual* origin of these strange things. I see nothing but the action of faculties not much studied hitherto, and but little understood. Much deceit also I find—deceit and fraud. But the real genuine cases only report to me the action of human faculties not as yet well understood.

TO WM. L. AND WENDELL P. GARRISON.

If you have a vehement desire for a good literary culture, and if a college were the only place which could afford it, I should say, by all means go there and get the coveted pearl in spite of the age of twenty-two. But the case is not exactly such ; a college is by no means the only place to furnish this culture, nor is it at all the best place to help a man of your years and experience of life. The discipline of a college is designed for boys, not for grown men ; so the studies are adapted to the boyish mind, not the manly. What you want, I take it, is (1) a vigorous development of all your intellectual faculties, and (2) competent literary and scientific *information*. Both of these you may obtain without going to college, and without even quitting the regular methodical business at the bank. Here is what I would suggest for your consideration ; to find some good, well educated man to guide you a little in these particulars, in studying such works of science, physical and metaphysical, as you and he may think advisable, in studying such foreign languages as you may need—perhaps French will be sufficient, —and in studying the history of mankind in various countries and in all ages. Some well educated friend would be needed simply to give you the list of books, to tell you the order you shall follow in reading them, and to point out the right method of study. Should you pursue this method, I think in four years, by using only your spare time, you would secure more development and more information than you would in the six years necessary to fit you for college and take you through.

Now a word to the other brother. I am glad to hear of your Students' Temperance Society. It was more needed than in any other part of N. E. Your class seems fortunate in having a little company of noble minded young men in it. I put *you* among their leaders. It is a great thing for any class to have even but a few such in it. * * * *Literature* is a good staff, but a poor crutch, and reform makes but a poor *profession* for any one. The public is naturally jealous of a *professed* reformer, and looks upon him much as it does on a common scold ; no profession probably has more and more terrible temptations. * * * I regret that so much of our best talent is of necessity forced to occupy itself with this matter of slavery, and to take up the time of the people with discussion of what our grandfathers thought they had settled forever, while the great work of organizing society, so that there shall be no idleness and no want, no involuntary celibacy and no prostitution, no drunkenness nor crime, remains almost untouched. * * * *

I hope your friend Hallowell justifies the high hopes formed of him, both in talent and character. Russell and Shaw, in the class before you, I hope will do no discredit to their fathers and mothers—old friends of mine. Spalding I am sure of. * * * *

I should like to step into the A. S. Rooms and see Mr. Wallcut and his green bag, Sam May writing letters, and H. C. Wright covering the desk with one of his hands.

TO THOMAS G. BARNARD, NORWAY, MAINE.

Boston, March 30, 1853.

DEAR SIR,—I thank you for your interesting and welcome letter, which I have just read. It gives me great pleasure to know of such men as yourself, bred by deeply religious parents in the old forms of religion, yet coming out of bigotry into freedom with a continual increase of piety and faith in God. I know some men who cast off the old forms of theology and of church service for the sake of getting rid of the restraints of religion. I always love to find one who grows in morality as he advances also in intellectual freedom.

I know many persons whose history is the same as yours. The Methodist Church does a great deal of good; the Methodist minister,—poor, badly educated, often quite ignorant,—goes amongst men more ignorant than he, and rouses up the religious spirit in their souls, and quickens them with new life. How many thousands of men there are who owe their earthly salvation to the labors of some modest minister of that persuasion? I have great respect for them; but, alas! they find men in fetters; they make men fear; they drive by terror while they ought to draw by love; they make too much of a separation between life and religion. Their idea of God is dark and sad, so are their notions of the next life. But when one comes to the conviction that God is infinite,—I mean perfectly powerful, perfectly wise, just, loving and faithful to himself,—then the great difficulty is over: you do not fear God, you love him; you will not seek to shun his laws, but to keep them, and if you fall away sometimes through the strength of temptation and the weakness of your character, you feel mortified, ashamed, and penitent, and come back full of vigor and resolution anew, and go on your way rejoicing.

I am sorry I did not know you while you were here in Boston, and hope you will continue to grow in all religious and manly excellence.

Truly yours,
THEO. PARKER.

TO A FRIEND, A PHYSICIAN IN UTICA, NEW YORK.

October 2, 1848.

I thank you for the kind things which you say of my writings. I sincerely hope they may do a little to direct the attention of men to the great realities of religion, and help make the earth the paradise which God designed. I see most hopeful signs. Here in Boston and its vicinity there has been a great change for the better in half a dozen years. Men do not insist so much as formerly on what is reckoned miraculous in Christianity. The more I study the nature of man and the history of his progress, the more I am filled with admiration at the genius of Jesus of Nazareth, and with love for his beautiful character and life. He is the greatest achievement of the human races, and Christianity the greatest idea which mankind has thought out as yet; for, take the results of Christianity into account, it is the greatest fact in human history.

But I look on all that has gone before as only the spring-time of religion, the few warm days in March which melt the snow off the most southern slopes of the hills, and only promise violets and roses. The real summer and autumn of Christianity, I think, are a good way off. But they are certain, and every good man, every good deed, every good thought or feeling, helps forward the time.

I am glad you like what I said of Mr. Adams. I certainly studied the matter carefully, and read every line he ever published which

I could find, and looked at every vote he cast. Then I had several times met the old man, and conversed with him.

As you say, he had more justice than kindness, and kindness is the more popular virtue. But justice is far the more excellent. Some men here rate him higher than I do. But my article on him has met with more favour than anything else I ever wrote. It has been circulated very widely, and I hope will do some good work.

When a public man dies, we ought to take warning from his faults and be guided by his merits. It seems an ungrateful work to hunt the one dead fly out of the whole pot of ointment; but if all else be fragrant, it is profitable to detect the cause of the offence which arises from the one ill thing.

TO MISS COBBE, ENGLAND.

May 5, 1848.

MY DEAR FRIEND,—Your letter of April 2nd gave me great delight. I rejoice exceedingly at being able to smoothe the difficulties away which have been thrown in the way of religion, and so your kind letter warmed my heart anew with the thought that I had actually helped one fellow-mortal—one, too, whom perhaps I shall never see. Your history lends additional interest to it all. I know how you must have suffered under that bewildering orthodox theology which you were taught to accept instead of religion, and which you could not receive, still less be satisfied with. We have the same orthodoxy here in America, only, as we think, a little more—as everything is a little more—intense on our side of the water.

I confess to a strong love of that good and true man, Blanco White. His " Memoirs " have brought much comfort to many a man's and woman's heart in America. What I love most is the entire truthfulness of the man, and his entire trustfulness. He felt and he knew the goodness of God, and, loving Him, forgot all fear.

You ask me if Jesus believed in eternal punishments, &c., or why I call myself a Christian if he did. I don't believe he did; I see not how he could. I doubt that even Paul believed it. Why, Jesus is teaching that God loves all men, the sinner as well as the saint. I know there are many passages, some parables, which plainly teach this odious doctrine. Still, I don't believe Jesus taught it, though it was easy for a Jew to misunderstand his words, and long after his death relate such things of him. I cannot ascribe a very high historical value to the Gospels; they rather indicate its facts than tell it. I call myself a Christian because I believe Jesus taught absolute religion, goodness, and piety; free goodness, free piety, free thought. He was, in some things, fettered by the follies of his nation and age, but did men such a service by setting before them the true *method of religion*, that I love to call myself a Christian out of gratitude, but I would not think ill of another who disliked the name; nay, I doubt if Jesus himself would recommend it. I have written you a longer letter than I thought I should at first. If I can be of service to you in any way, it will give me pleasure to do so, and I shall always be glad to hear from you when it is agreeable to you to write. Allow me to subscribe myself,

Sincerely your friend,
THEO. PARKER.

TO THE SAME.

Boston, June 5, 1855.

MY DEAR MISS COBBE,—Your kind letter came to hand in due time, and the book followed it, reaching me a few weeks ago. I did not go to bed till I saw through its whole.* The next day I gave it a more careful study. Let me say I admire the work throughout; the plan, the execution, and all the details. It is a noble work, in many points reminding me of some of the best things in Leibnitz, in others coming close upon Milton in its tone and language. Your learning also surprises me. I am making efforts to have it reprinted here, for it is much needed to counteract the sensationalism of the Locke school, who still occupy most of the chairs of philosophy in New England. It will do good service among our young men and women. If I succeed, you shall have a copy as soon as possible, only the depressed state of the money market makes my success doubtful. In your note you seem to think you and I might differ as to the use of *experiment* in morals. This is my notion: moral experiment furnishes *new facts of moral consciousness*, which else we should not acquire so soon—perhaps never. Still the ultimate appeal is to the *moral element* within us. By experiment alone we can never learn what is (scientifically) just —only what is (empirically) convenient in a special case. I hope soon to have the other part, the "practice of morals."

Be pleased to accept a copy of a new book of mine, though made up of old matter, and believe me respectfully and sincerely yours,

THEO. PARKER.

TO THE SAME.

Boston, December 20th, 1855.

MY DEAR MISS COBBE,—When your book first reached me I submitted it to my friends, Messrs. Little and Brown, who said they would take it up at once on my recommendation, were it not for the deranged condition of the country at that time, they having much capital at risk, and getting but slow sales. I tried another house, and was determined it should be published if I took the risk myself and gave away the edition, for I thought it so valuable. The other house, Messrs. Phillips and Samson, delayed a long time, their reader not liking to take the responsibility of deciding on a book which lay outside of his lines of knowledge. So he delegated the matter to a minister of the Unitarian denomination, a man of nice scholarship and fine character, though quite conservative. In the meantime I was busy making ready for publication the "Defence," which I send you with this letter. But a few days since the reader sent me the note from Mr. Hale, which I enclose, so the book will appear 'ere long. To make it as perfect as possible, I will beg you to send me another copy, with such corrections, emendations and additions, as you see fit to make. The mistake of those writers who copied the strange errors of Mosheim, were first pointed out to me by an acute Catholic lawyer of this city, who wrote a lecture on "Robertson's View of the Middle Ages," detecting that

* The volume written by Miss Cobbe, entitled "Theory of Intuitive Morals."

and other errors; as I looked into the matter I found the whole passage of St. Eligius was given in Schröckh, Kirchengesch, b. xix. p.
438, and in Gieseler K. G. b. i. 123. You refer to Sharrolu's book
ὑπόθεσις ἠθική. I had never read a word of the man, but in a few days
received his De Officiis secundum Jus Naturaê, (Gothæ, 1667, 1 vol.
18mo.) bound up with Puffendorf's de Officio. Is it the same book as
the ὑπόθεσις ?

I send you two or three little sermons which you have not yet seen,
and my defence, which will tell its own tale. I shall print another
volume of miscellanies, and one more of sermons and speeches, as soon
as I find time for the work.

With many thanks for your noble book, believe me, affectionately
yours,

THEODORE PARKER.

TO THE SAME.

Boston, Aug. 11, 1857.

MY VERY DEAR MISS COBBE,—It is more than a year since I wrote
you a line, and my last letter, I think, you never received, for I gave it
as an introduction to one of my friends, who took an Irish wife, and
went to show her parents the new baby. It was Mr. Brace, who has
written some clever books, and is one of the best young men that I
know. He married a Miss Neile, of Belfast, and lives at New York,
busied in picking forlorn children out of the streets of that Gomorrah
of the new world, and placing them in worthy families. So he saves
" such as be ready to perish."

I had no right to expect a letter from you when the last one came,
but as the telegraph announced the arrival of the steamer, I said:
" Now there is a letter from dear Miss Cobbe," and when the letters were
brought up—behold there were many, some from Germany, one from
England, but *none from her*. I felt sure there was some mistake, and
the next morning yours actually came; it had been overlooked the day
before, but I did not think of the heaviness of heart with which you
had been writing. I suppose the sad event—sad to the survivors—has
taken place before this, and the venerable head is laid peacefully to rest,
while the soul has gone home to its Father and Mother. I am the
youngest of eleven children, and of course my parents were old when
I was born; my mother was forty-nine, my father more than fifty. My
father's mother lived with us, and passed on at the age of ninety-two.
She was more than eighty when I was born. My father died at seventy-
seven. So you see old age is familiar to me. I love the venerable
hairs of old persons, not less than the brown locks which curl so hand-
somely about youthful brows. But we don't sorrow for the old as for
the young. It is right and natural that the ripe apple should fall in
Time's autumn night. My grandmother, my father, grown old but
with faculties still bright, were glad to pass further on, taking the next
step in the continuous process whereof birth is the first. We shed
natural tears, and the place felt cold when the shadow of an empty
chair fell on the household fire. But we recognised the fitness of it all.
There are two points of certainty: the infinite perfection of God, the
immortality of man; those are fixed, and the consciousness of them is

not merely a matter of reflective demonstration for the philosophic few, but rather of spontaneous instinct for the sympathetic many. Between these two points hangs the great world of human consciousness, with its hopes, fears, doubts, uncertainties, disappointments, errors, follies, joys, sins, terrors, and unbounded aspirations. But all are supported on these two points of certainty, and I think it is the end of wisdom to *know* this, as it is the beginning to feel it. Sure of my continuance, and sure of God, I fear nothng. There is compensation for all sorrow, and recovery for all sickness of the soul.

Your book came most welcome; it is every way worthy of its predecessor. I read it with joy—not always without tears. I meant to have it republished here a year ago, and took it to my bookselling friends. Two wealthy and excellent houses—Little and Brown, and Ticknor and Co.,—thought well of the work, but said such a book on such a theme would have but a slow sale, and they should make no money by it. Now I am very anxious to have it brought out here, and but for a little trouble in my own finances during one or two years (I have been stereotyping some of my own books, which took all my spare money), I should have taken the risk myself, and spread the work before the American public. I think if I am financially prosperous, that when the work is finished I will stand as godfather, and secure the publisher from any loss, and so honor the Continent with so valuable a birth. A Rev. Mr. Buckingham, a Unitarian minister in Hartford, Connecticut, found a copy by accident in a book-store, and was much delighted with it. He wrote to me to enquire for the author, and has now written a review of it for the *Christian Examiner*, the Unitarian periodical, one of the best journals in America. It will appear about January; I fear not earlier. He says, "she is a fine fellow, though a little old-fashioned." He envied your wide and deep learning, as well he might.

Now let me say a word or two about myself. I have been ill for nearly six months, a thing quite unusual with me, who have not before passed a day in bed since I was twelve years old, which is now thirty-four years. I had a fever, with typhoidal and pleuritic symptoms. For a long time I could not preach, Mr. Phillips, R. W. Emerson, and similar men taking my place. Even now I am ill; feebler than usual, but likely to recover. My wife and I are passing the summer in a charming little country place, seven miles from Boston, where I do nothing but gather wild flowers, swim in the fresh water, sit under trees, and read what takes my fancy. To-day I start with a few friends in a yacht, for a sail along our coasts, to be absent a fortnight. I hope to preach again the 6th September, and be as well as ever. You will receive this about August 24, I fancy, which is my forty-seventh birthday. I wish you would tell me when you were born, that I may keep the day as a festival. So I do with other dear ones. Please grant me this favor, and I shall mark with a white stone one more day in my friendly year.

TO THE SAME.

Boston, Dec. 4, 1857.

My dear Miss Cobbe,—I meant to write this letter so that you should receive it on your birthday; but the relation with the day is still the same, though the time be different. I send you the last number of the *Examiner*, the chief Unitarian periodical, and one of the best, if not the best, in America. It is edited by the Rev. Dr. Hedge, Professor of Ecclesiastical History in the School at Cambridge, and Rev. Mr. Hale, whose note touching your book you received some time since. The article on your "Intuitive Morals," p. 370–84, is written by the Rev. Mr. Buckingham, a man about forty years old, not settled now, but a pleasant preacher and serious, earnest man, with a touch of genius about him it is said. You will see the earnest, progressive spirit that is in him. I hope you will be pleased with the article. Mr. B. saw a copy of your book on a friend's table, was much interested in it, borrowed it, read it, and then wrote me, asking what man (!) had written so noble a book? I put him in the way of the other volume, and he then wrote the article. The last paragraph is by Mr. Hale.

One of these days I will send you the photograph you speak of, if I can ever get a good one. There is a crayon portrait by my friend, Mr. Cheney, now dead, which my intimates like, and a great lithograph which they do not like. I judge neither. The London *Times* says of Lord Brougham, "Nature certainly did not make him a handsome man." I fear the oracle would not be more complimentary to me; but when I get a photograph which is decent, I will certainly send it.

We have been married nearly twenty-one years, and have never a child. We have a moderate little property, partly my wife's inheritance, partly my earnings; a good house, a large collection of books. Her name was Cabot. The family *claim* descent from the famous Giovanni Cabotti, who discovered these parts of the continent. Her domestic name is Bear, or Bearsie; and various symbols of "Beauty and the Beast" appear in the house. As usual, she is nearly the opposite of her husband, except in the matter of *philanthropy*. A young man by the name of Cabot, one-and-twenty years old, lives with us. We have brought him up from infancy; his mother died when he was five or six; he is now in the store of a large West India goods dealer. An unmarried lady, a little more than fifty years old—Miss Stevenson—a woman of fine talents and culture, interested in all the literatures and humanities, is with us. These are the permanent family, to which visitors make frequent and welcome additions.

You are very dear to us all. I ought to say that my wife was born September 12, 1813; and so is three years younger than I. She is tall, with blue eyes and brown hair, a little white beginning to steal in insidiously. My eyes are also blue, my head is bald, and my beard grey. I am five feet eight inches high, and weigh about one hundred and fifty pounds .All my forebears were great, tall, stout men, six feet without their shoes, weighing two hundred pounds and more. My mother was a slight delicate woman, with a fine organization. . . . . So much about ourselves. As my letter is dated *your* birthday, and your last note was on *mine*, and you asked for some particulars about us all, it is not so egotistic as it looks. Now to other things: No. VII. in the *Examiner* is by Dr. Hedge; you will be surprised at the freedom with which it criticises parts of the "New Test."; it has already wakened the wrath of some of the bigots, who have attacked Dr. H. in the *Christian Register*, the Unitarian newspaper of Boston.

Have you seen a quite remarkable book by H. T. Buckle? It is a "History of Civilization in England," vol. i. (pp. xxiv. and 854, London, J. W. Parker). It is one of the most remarkable and instructive books I have seen from the English press in this century. I do not always agree with him, but he is a great man—learned too in many departments of thought. I have read only the first part of his book. Can you tell me who he is, what his antecedents were, and his surroundings. The work is not less significant in its department than the "Vestiges of the Natural History of Creation" in another sphere.

What a terrible time dear old England has in India. Both parties are in the wrong; England has treated India harshly, exploited her. No doubt her native rulers did the same, perhaps in a worse manner, and to a greater extent; but it is more inexcusable in Father Bull to do such an evil thing, for he knows better. But I suppose he will conquer, kill ten men and violate twenty women where the Indians did but one or two, and then celebrate thanksgivings in all his churches. I look with great pride on this Anglo-Saxon people. It has many faults, but I think it is the best specimen of mankind which has ever attained great power in the world. One day I fancy Asia will be divided beween the Russians and the English, and the English people will have the whole of America, South as well as North. I think it *can* be done by no violence or cruelty, but it *will* not be. I wonder what the moral effect of your two recent wars will be in England. Will it make you a nobler people, as trouble did in the sixteenth and seventeenth centuries?

In America we are to have much trouble from the question of slavery. You in England, I think, do not see how slavery corrupts everything. Politics, theology, literature, trade, it is the *bête noire* which threatens to devour all the flock. Every national administration pets and cossets it. The democratic party thinks it is the only American institution worth spreading. Every Irishman in the United States is in favour of slavery, so are all the Jews. The Germans go the other way. So strong is national disposition! No property here is held so sacred as property in *men*. No laws so important as the laws of slavery. There is trouble before us! I care little how soon it comes.

Of course, you know what a sad commercial panic we are passing through in America, as in England. I hope both nations will come out of it wiser than before. I hope your honoured father continues comfortable, and your own health and spirits are as good as your heart. We all send you our love.

FROM D. H. TWEEDY.

Stamfordville, New York, Feb. 10, 1856.

DEAR SIR,—"The world does move." It was very gratifying to me, on the receipt of your pamphlets at the Post-office in our country store, to see the physician, the merchant, and some of my most bitter opponents, each with book in hand, lost to everything else, and to hear them exclaim, "good," "here's a good idea," "just hear this," &c. One said, "these are my sentiments, but I did not know how to express them," &c.

When I gave a home to Stephen and Abby Foster, Parker Pillsbury, &c., those same persons could hardly find language bitter enough wherewith to denounce them and me. But this was not my worst offence: universalists and heretics of all sorts, when travelling, have found a resting-place with us, and occasionally I have dared to question the doctrine advanced by their minister; but now I could not get away without leaving some of those anti-slavery and heretical works with them, and promising to loan the rest at some future time.

The Baptists in our vicinity are holding a protracted meeting; it has continued near a month, only letting off the steam now and then, long enough to establish or confirm their new converts by immersing them in ice-water.

A more interesting and progressive society has been organized in the same village, who meet regularly to read and discuss the merits of your discourses; sometimes they elicit so many comments that but a few pages will occupy a long evening, and we do not consider it lost time, as it induces people to think for themselves, the first progressive movement, and calls forth their ideas another step.

Those meetings are composed of such as have very little sympathy with the churches called orthodox; we have two volumes of your Discourses on Religion, and those you sent me come in play.

So you see we have a counter revival, and the prospect is that we shall make the most converts; and that ours will be of that class who possess the most intelligence.

My wife joins me in wishing you success in your labours for the cause of humanity.

Yours, &c.,   D. H. TWEEDY.

FROM E. H. BOWMAN.

Edgington, Illinois, December 25, 1857.

MY DEAR SIR,—Somewhere in the neighbourhood of a year ago, I took the liberty of addressing you. Although an entire stranger, and destitute of all claims of a personal character on your time and attention, still your kindness did not deceive or rather fail me.

I received the volumes you sent me, and have perused them, not only once, but again. I feel truly grateful; I was like a chick just pipping the shell, so to speak; you kindly assisted me, and very materially expedited the process. You requested me to let you hear from me again. If I have delayed near a twelvemonth, it has not been without reason. In the first place I know "new converts" to any views, party, or sect, are apt to be carried away by enthusiastic feeling and excitement. The novelty wears off by time and the attrition of circumstances. Not claiming any unusual exemption from the frailties of humanity, I deemed it prudent to try myself, and give time for sober second thoughts.

A year is probably a reasonable probation, and on careful retrospect I find myself more and more strongly confirmed in the radical change which has taken place in my views of God and Man, and the relation between the two.

When I wrote to you last, I was quite sanguine as to the possibility of extending such views in my neighbourhood. The observation and reflection of a year have materially moderated that sanguine expectation. I find many good men seem to look on me with a suspicious eye. I cannot get access to their ear. One of my intimate friends, an old-school Presbyterian preacher, who has known me familiarly for thirteen years, and been more conversant with my mental habits than any other man, gives me no chance to broach any controverted subjects. I can scarcely indulge the vanity that he fears an encounter. Being a man of good reasoning powers, close observation, and a *most excellent heart*, he possibly misgives as to the strength of his fortress. Yet he does preach the hardest sermons and doctrines extant. He seems to me sometimes almost desperate, as if his own mind was not satisfied with its meagre fare, yet determined not to acknowledge it, even in his inmost soul. I heard him preach a sermon not long since on the miraculous and divinely-inspired character of the Bible. I could not help pitying him. With solemn earnestness he took the ground that if a single word were untrue then the whole must be false. It looked to me like the desperation of the gambler who risks his pile on a single throw, and that made wildly, with shut eyes. Just as if a single truth of God could be corrupted or negatived by mountains of error. I found men hard to approach. Touch any of their favorite views and they turn fiercely, somewhat like Micah of old—" Would ye take away my gods, and what would we have left ? "

It seems hard to make entrance for a new idea. It took me a good while to progress to where your writings found me, and I believe I am more than ordinarily inclined to think for myself, and assert man's right to personal individuality. I am inclined to doubt the success, to any great extent, of diffusing a correct knowledge of religious truth by efforts directed to *adult minds*. They have generally received their impressions, and become hardened into such shape as the operating forces may give. You cannot change them; the capacity is not there. The advocates of the " popular theology " have imitated the wisdom of the Jesuits, and much of their labor is expended in special efforts upon the mind of childhood and youth. Now, the friends of absolute truth, it seems to me, must imitate the wise example, and spend their efforts in the same field. In adults, far more labor is requisite to pull down error already established, than would be needful to instil truth into the unoccupied minds of children. Teachers of common schools could do more than preachers among adults. The system of Sabbath schools could be advantageously imitated, and made to contribute as actively to the moral and affectional growth of the human soul, as now they do to fetter and confine. I am busy everywhere I go, trying to do good. In my capacity as physician I have access to many. I can help to introduce some knowledge of truth; and the connection between obedience to physical and moral law is so close, that it is impossible to separate the two. I believe the vocation of physician and preacher should be combined, and will be, ultimately. In my address as one of the officers of our county medical society, I took for my theme the relations of our profession to the moral and intellectual progress of mankind. The views which I then presented to my brethren seemed to strike them as novel, and yet, at the same time, to be true. I claimed for our profession that, with all the rubbish of centuries, it still had in it the master-key of human progress. Theology is finished. Law looks to no new truth; it is all learned already, and is now stored up in the musty records of the past. Medical science has man for its subject, and extends to the investigation of every cause that can or does operate favourably or unfavourably on the human organization. We are already on your platform, a simple but sublime one. We investigate fearlessly after truth. We acknowledge practically "no master but God," and accept "no creed but truth."

I feel now more than any other single thing the want of intercourse with those of similar views; "iron sharpeneth iron, so doth the countenance of a man his friend." I can in a small degree begin to comprehend the firmness needed to not only "go alone," but in additon to stem the current of opposition which has its source in ignorance, fanaticism, and intolerance.

On the subject of slavery I do not entirely harmonize with you; I spent several years in the midst of slavery in its mildest form, that is, in Kentucky. Having had my birth and what little education I possessed in a free state, I was disposed to observe closely, and the sum of my observations led me to the conclusion that the dominant race was more legitimately the proper object of pity than the servile. The servile is gradually improving by contact and *amalgamation* with the white race; on the contrary the white race is visibly retrograding.

God's eternal law of right is setting its seal there, in characters so plain that it seems to me, " He that runs may read it ;" just in proportion to the wrong inflicted by the powerful and knowing on the weak and ignorant, is the rebound on the wrongdoer of righteous retribution.

That retribution is, it seems to me, intensified in proportion to the difference in the moral and intellectual development of the races. With this view, I cannot help feeling that the wrongdoers are in need of more pity and commiseration than the enslaved and oppressed Africans. The steady result is the gradual elevation of one race, and the depression of the other until an equilibrium is attained. " God's balances are even."

One of the sources of vitality in slavery is the infusion of new material from the North. Commerce, theology, teaching, and adventure take every year many young men from the free states. A limited view of their own interest converts them to supporters of the "peculiar institution," and in time they " out-Herod Herod."

But I fear I have been trespassing on your time in rather garrulous style, so will stop.

Very respectfully and truly yours,
E. H. Bowman.

I should like to hear from you, if not incompatible with your duties and inclinations, when you may have leisure.

FROM HENRY THOMAS BUCKLE.

59, Oxford Terrace, London, March 27, 1858.

DEAR SIR,—I have delayed several days answering your very obliging letter, in the expectation of receiving the review of my history which you mention having sent to me.

Several numbers of the *Massachusetts Quarterly Review* have been forwarded to me, but not the *Christian Examiner*. However, I will defer no longer thanking you for a mark of attention which I value highly as proceeding from one with whose writings I am so familiar.

That men simply urged by a love of truth should know and communicate to each other without personal acquaintance is a cheering consideration, and thus it has always been in the history of literature, and thus I trust always will be. I will not reply to your objections, partly because I dislike controversy, and partly because it would be impossible to state in the limits of a letter my view of the most important point, namely, the moral and intellectual laws.

I have requested the publisher to send you a copy of *Fraser* as soon as it is issued, which will be on the 1st of April. It will contain a report of a lecture which I delivered a few days since, at the Royal Institution here, and which has made some little talk.

Possibly you may be interested in my view of the too empirical character of English science.

Believe me, dear Sir, with great regard, very sincerely yours,

HENRY THOMAS BUCKLE.

FROM THE SAME.

59, Oxford Terrace, London, April 4, 1858.

MY DEAR SIR,—I have just received another parcel, containing not only the *Christian Examiner*, but (what I value even more) a collection of your own works. By sending these last you have really placed me under a very considerable obligation, as, apart from the interest I feel in whatever you write, such productions are among the best materials I could have for estimating the highest points of American speculation and American knowledge.

My next volume will contain a history of the civilization of the United States, and I shall, perhaps, some day encroach upon your kindness by troubling you with some questions on the subject. The importance of the investigation is only equalled by its difficulty. Before publishing my next volume I shall, if possible, pay a visit to the United States, and the prospect of making your acquaintance will be no small inducement to do so.

You will no doubt have received a letter which I wrote to you towards the end of March.

Believe me, my dear Sir, yours very sincerely,

HENRY THOMAS BUCKLE.

I hope you have received *Fraser* for 1st April, containing my lecture on the " Influence of Women."

FROM THE SAME.

59, Oxford Terrace, London, July 9, 1858.

My DEAR SIR,—Absence from town prevented me from receiving till yesterday your very kind and friendly letter. I certainly shall not venture to write upon the civilization of your noble country until I have visited it, and satisfied myself in regard to many matters respecting which books (as you truly say) supply no adequate information. Indeed in the national character of every really great people there is a certain shape and colour which cannot be recognized at a distance. But, at present, I am exclusively occupied with an analysis of the civilization of Spain and Scotland, which I hope to publish early next year ; and should I fulfil that expectation, I shall hope to visit America in the summer of 1859.

In regard to Scotland, the leading facts are its religious intolerance and the absence of the municipal spirit during the middle ages. The causes of these phenomena I have attempted to generalize.

Spain I have almost finished, but I find a difficulty in collecting evidence respecting the rapid decline of that country during the reigns of Philip III., Philip IV., and Charles II. In investigating the *causes* of the decline (both remote and proximate), I trust that I have not been wholly unsuccessful. In Mr. Ticknor's singularly valuable " History of Spanish Literature " there is more real information than can be found in any of the many Spanish histories which I have had occasion to read.

You mention a book on America by a Pole as being important, but I cannot quite decipher his name. I should be very glad to buy it, and if you would take the trouble to send its title either to me or to your London bookseller, with a request that he should forward it to me, you would render me a service.

I do not like reading at public libraries, and I purchase nearly all the books which I use. I have at present about 20,000 volumes.

I believe you correspond with Mr. Chapman; if so, would you kindly beg him to send me any criticisms which appear in America on my book. You ought to know of some which he would not be aware of.

Sometime ago I received from an American publisher a request that I would write my life; at that time I was very unwell, worn from overwork, and harassed by domestic anxiety. I also thought the form of the request rather blunt; and from all these causes I was induced to return a somewhat curt answer, and one very foreign to my usual habits. But you and I are no longer strangers to each other, and I willingly send you the particulars which you desire for your friend.

I was born at Lee, in Kent, on the 24th of November, 1822. My father was a merchant. His name was Thomas Henry Buckle, and he was descended from a family, one of whom was well-known as Lord Mayor of London in the reign of Queen Elizabeth. He died in 1840. My mother, who still lives, was a Miss Middleton, of the Yorkshire Middletons.

As a boy, my health was extremely delicate, and my parents were fortunately guided by the advice of that good and wise man, Dr. Birkbeck (whose name I believe is not unknown in America), who forbade my receiving any education that would tax the brain.

This prevented me from being, in the common sense of the word, educated, and also prevented my going to college. When I was in my eighteenth year my father died (January, 1840), and left me in independent circumstances, in a pecuniary point of view.

My health steadily improved, and to this moment I had read little except "Shakespeare," the "Arabian Nights," and "Bunyan's Pilgrim's Progress," three books on which I literally feasted.

Between the ages of eighteen and nineteen I conceived the plan of my book—dimly indeed—but still the plan was there, and I set about its execution. From the age of nineteen I have worked on an average nine to ten hours daily. My method was this. In the morning I usually studied physical science, in the forenoon languages (of which, till the age of nineteen, I was deplorably ignorant), and the rest of the day history and jurisprudence. In the evening general literature. I have always steadily refused to write in reviews, being determined to give up my life to a larger purpose.

I have, therefore, produced nothing except the first volume of my "History," and the "Lecture on the Influence of Women."

This, I think, is all you requested me to communicate. Any further information which your friend may require will be much at his service. I should always feel it a pleasure and a privilege to hear from you, and am, my dear sir, yours very sincerely,

HENRY THOMAS BUCKLE.

FROM THE SAME.

Eltham Place, Eltham Road, near Blackheath, July 5, 1859.

MY DEAR SIR,—I have been in town for a few days on business, and found your card on my table in Oxford Terrace. I cannot tell you how much I regret that we should not have met. The great respect which I feel for you as the most advanced leader of opinion in one of the two first nations of the world, would of itself suffice to make me eager for the pleasure of your personal acquaintance.

And when I add to this, the memory of your obliging and friendly letters to me, you will easily believe me when I say how much I have been disappointed at being unable to call upon you, and make arrangements to see you.

But the severest of all calamities has befallen me, and has so prostrated my nervous system that I am now enjoined the strictest quiet.

Your conversation would arouse in me so many associations, and excite me to so many inquiries respecting your noble country, that I feel myself, alas, unequal to meeting you; and, as you might possibly hear from some of my friends in London, I have been compelled to give up all society. In such cases, the more I am interested the more I am hurt. I do not know how long you are likely to stay in England;

but it would give me great pleasure to hear from you, and to be assured that you understand the cause of my apparent inattention. I shall probably remain here until the end of August.

Believe me to be, most truly yours,

HENRY THOMAS BUCKLE.

TO REV. M. A. H. NILES, NORTHAMPTON, MASS.

West Roxbury, March 4, 1845.

MY DEAR SIR,—I thank you for the kind and affectionate letter which you wrote me the other day. I have just received it, and as I shall be absent for a few days I will reply now. I felt a strong interest in you from the much that I heard and the little that I saw of you at Marblehead. You have certainly left a strong impression of yourself on some who were not your parishioners in that place. Mr. F. told me of the peculiar circumstances of your case in that town. I confess I thought you were too far before them for their appreciation; and this is a very peculiar circumstance for a minister now-a-days. The questions that you mention have been to me one of the greatest interest for many years. The relation between man and God, and the inspiration that man can receive through that relation, was a subject of deep interest to me when a child. As a boy, I had reached in sentiment the same results that I now hold as ideas translated out of the unconscious into consciousness. The canonical nature of a book is still of a good deal of importance to me (though not the same as to you, I fancy) for I like to know how near a man stood to that mighty soul of religion which so aroused the world. Still I do not always find the canonical books, such as came from the disciples of Christ, so much better than those of men a little more remote. Thus the Epistle of James is worth more to me than the 1st of Peter, though there is little doubt of the genuineness of the latter, and little evidence for the genuineness of the former.

I think the matter of the Apocryphal Christian writings of the first and second centuries has never been duly inquired into. Mr. Norton has written something which I think is quite shallow, on this matter in his late work. I can't find evidence, internal or external, that the writers of the Bible had a mode of inspiration, or kind of inspiration differing from that of other men. Some of them certainly had a very high degree of it—Jesus the highest—so I think, that was ever attained by man. I don't wonder you do not accept my conclusions, I wonder much more at the kindness with which you speak of them. I must of course have committed errors in reasoning and in conclusion. I hoped once that philosophical men would point out both; then I would confess my mistake and start anew. But they have only raised a storm about my head; and in a general way a man wraps his cloak about him in a storm and holds on the tighter. It would be very surprising if I had not gone to an extreme, and yet I do not think I have (pardon my apparent want of modesty) in this matter; for after looking again and again, reading and talking, I find a flaw in the process. God is infinite; therefore he is immanent in nature, yet transcending it; immanent in spirit, yet transcending that. He must fill each point of spirit as of space; matter must unconsciously obey; man, conscious and free, has power to a certain extent to disobey, but obeying, the immanent God acts in man as much as in nature, only in a higher mode. Hence inspiration. If the conditions are fulfilled, it seems that inspiration comes in proportion to the quantity of a man's gifts and his use of these gifts. I feel in me a something that leads me to reverence, worship, trust, &c. I reckon this a distinct faculty (as much as judgment, reason, imagination, &c.), or, it is the man acting in a special direction; of the existence of this I am sure. I can't analyze it further than this, into a sense of infinite dependence; here the subject and the predicate seem identical, and the analytic process ends with me; others may be more skilful. I think Brownson sometimes merely splits hairs, with no very certain desire to get at the truth. Now I think that as the man developes, he finds as facts given in his consciousness, an idea of God; where this idea is fully unfolded, that it is the idea of a Being of infinite power, wisdom, and goodness; but we are not content with that, but add various human appendages thereto, and thus generate what I call a conception of God (I tried to find better terms to express this difference, but could not). The idea represents an objective Being corresponding to it exactly, viz.:—The God who is of course not only all our idea represents, but much more; while the conception of God, added to the idea, has no objective reality corresponding to it. Jesus, Jupiter, Mars, &c., denote conceptions of God purely subjective, with various limitations; there is no objective reality that corresponds thereto. But when I speak of the infinite God, I speak of an objective reality, in whom I live, and move, and have my being. In short, we create our conceptions of God in our own image.

About miracles, I agree with you that it is a question of fact, to be settled by historical evidence only. I believe in something extraordinary in the case of Jesus; his healing of diseases is special, but not miraculous. I think miracles are entirely possible. I think God can manifest himself in a thousand ways that he never did reveal himself in, and I can't say that he won't to-morrow. But I see God much more in what I understand than in what I am ignorant of. *Omne ignotum pro miraculo habetur* is an old proverb, but *Optime notum optime adoratum* suits me better. The deeper I look into nature and man, the more do I see a certain orderliness, a lawfulness; not the action of fate, but of the immanent God. And the further I look the deeper is my admiration, and the more absolute is my trust. I say with Thomas, "My Lord and my God!" I beg you to write me often; but do not speak to me with so much deference, as if I were some great man; for I know that I am a very humble one; and if ever you can make it agreeable to come to West Roxbury, you shall find a prophet's chamber and hospitable hearts to give you a welcome.

Believe me, truly, your friend and brother,
THEO. PARKER.

TO THE SAME.

West Roxbury, April 16th, 1845.

MY DEAR FRIEND,—I thank you for your kind letter of the 9th, and having now a little leisure, I will reply to some of the points you refer to. I hope, however, we shall sometime have an opportunity to confer together with the living voice, for in that way we shall the more readily come to an understanding. I am, like yourself, an humble seeker after truth. I learn a little one year and a little the next; but the vast ocean of truth spreads out before me, immense and unvisited. I feel often a sense of imperfection; yes, always, and sometimes the sad consciousness of positive sin. My ideal hovers far over my head, while the melancholy fact of my life foots it humbly through the dust. I suppose it must always be so; for with progressive beings the ideal of to-day must be far above the attainment of to-day. It is indeed the prophecy that to-morrow is to fulfil, or some to-morrow. I can say also with Paul, "The good that I would," &c. It is one thing to see the right, another to will the right. It is not easy to account for this abnormal state, in which a man introduces a contradiction into his consciousness, and voluntarily keeps it there. To explain it I think we must look far away into the future destinies of the man, just as to explain the caprices of a little child—its preference of the showy before the substantial—you look forward to the maturity of that child, and find that the feelings of infancy are but a trifle compared with the rational moral action of a full-grown man, living in his normal state. Can't we in this way get at some nearer solution of the problem of sin? I confess it seems so to me. Many men, I think a great many theologians, make mistakes in this matter; quite as absurd as it would be in a physician who should suppose that the child of four years was always to remain a child of four years. Of course there is then no explanation of its conduct, its tendencies, or its instincts.

About the matter of intercourse with God, I think this doctrine of His immanency in spirit, or in space, follows from the very idea of God as infinite. Of course he transcends creation (spirit as well as matter), so that his existence and action are not limited either to this, or by it. I suppose that all the action of the creatures who have no freedom is, in a word, the action of God; for they are tools of God, not self-moving artists. But I think he has given man a certain degree of freedom—not absolute freedom, which he alone can have, but relative freedom—so that, compared to God, we are bound, but compared to nature we are free; in virtue whereof we may, up to a certain point, do wrong, abuse the powers that are given us. In that case we act by the strength God has given, but not in the direction he commands. If we do this ignorantly, it is an error, a mistake; if consciously, wilfully, it is a sin, and we have brought a contradiction into our consciousness. In each case we suffer; in the first negatively, by the loss of the satisfaction that would come from conscious obedience; in the second, positively also, from the remorse that we have brought into our soul.

Now I think that God has placed in the world checks to disobedience, such as (1) negative—the loss, or at least the absence, of the satisfaction that comes of obedience—a state of uneasiness and discontent; —positive remorse, grief, and also the outward obstacles which come from the world of nature or the world of man, and resist what is not in harmony with God; which hurl a despot from his throne, which arrest the thief, the glutton, the miser in his course of sin. If you conclude that man ends with the body, these checks are inadequate; but I regard death as another check also; and, if that is not enough, I doubt not the same love that guides us here has other means yet in store, and will at last reclaim us all; and incentives to rectitude, such as the satisfaction one feels from simple virtue, the sense of wholeness, of unity of consciousness, the being one with God, all of which come directly from the various degrees of our obedience. Then, too, I think that death also must be a still further help in the way of perfection; for, as God orders the material world with perfect wisdom and infinite goodness, so must it be with the spiritual world. His world is one great system of optimism; of this I feel sure as that $1+1=2$.

My notion of forgiveness is this,—that by a perfect law each conscious departure from the right (for that only is sin) is followed by painful consequences that we call God's justice; that these painful consequences will gradually lead to repentance, change of life, obedience; that then we feel a unity of consciousness, once more a sense of restoration to God. This also is effected by the action of the same laws working jointly with ourselves, and this we call God's mercy; yet it is the same thing in different parts of the progress. All this, I think, we can learn with no miraculous or abnormal action of God.

It seems to me that our notions of interposition, mediations, and the like, come from the notion that God is purely extra-mundane, and not also intra-mundane (using mundane as the sum total of creation, material and spiritual both). But if God be immanent, and be the mover of all, then the interposition is not occasional and rare, but continual. I think the notion that there is only an *omnipotentia operatica* (in virtue of which God is in my garden only as the watchmaker is present in my watch) and not an *omnipræsentia essentialis*, has been productive of much evil, very much. It leads to all those notions of God's interfering, sending messengers, &c., which fill so large a place in popular theologies, and make the whole spiritual world a piece of mechanism, cold as clockwork, and dead as brass, in which God has nothing to do, but now and then sends some one to wind up the weights or alter the pendulum—a mechanism which all the rest of the time gets along very well without God! This to me is awful!

Now, about inspiration of the Bible. I believe all truth is divine, and from God, *in ratione originis* (for he is the author of it, he is the body of the truth if you will) but none peculiarly divine *in ratione acquisitionis*. Antecedent to all experience, it would have been as probable that God should make his communications in one way as another, but with the experience that in all matters, excepting such as pertain to religion, He communicates with men in a regular manner, through the normal exercise of their faculties, it becomes probable that the same rule holds good in religion also. At least the opposite is not to be assumed outright. I look at such things historically, and cannot settle matters of fact *à priori;* and looking in this way, I don't find evidence which makes it probable to me that God, even in his communication with men, departed from this normal method. I doubt not that He can do so, I don't know but He will to-morrow, but I don't find that He has hitherto.

To meet great emergencies I don't find that God makes use of new means, or new modes of means, but only more of what is regular and normal. Thus, there was a time when there were not more than 1000 men on the earth, and possibly some of them found it hard to get enough to eat, &c. They would have said, " When the earth contains 10,000 men we shall all starve." That is what the Malthuses would have said. "No!" said some pious man, " God will rain down bread from Heaven." But when there are 10,000, 10,000,000, or 10,000,000,000, neither prophecy comes true ; the nations do not starve, and the regular mode of production continues still sufficient. So I find in great emergencies of philosophy, &c., there is no departure from the common mode. I doubt not that God is no less the Providence of the world in all affairs of politics, science, &c., as in affairs of religion ; yet, to produce great results, I find that Solon and Washington, that Aristotle and Newton, that Homer and Shakespeare come regularly into the world, receive aid through their faculties, and produce the results we see. I don't find that they had anything differing in kind from what belongs to you and me ; but only a greater quantity of the same powers. I take it this rule holds good in the religious history of men. I think God raises up men with a great religious genius, so to say, who differ from you and me as Homer or Newton differ from us ; not in kind of faculties, not in the mode of receiving truth, but in degree only. Men have pretended that Homer had miraculous aid from the muses and Phœbus Apollo ; that Numa held communications with Egeria. It was thought that Wallenstein could be shot only with a silver bullet ; and the Indian who "had seventeen fair fires" at Washington with his rifle, concluded " he was not born to be killed with a bullet!" Yet I think there was nothing miraculous in these cases.

Now, these great religious geniuses, I think, come in the plan of Providence, take men by the hand, and lead us on in civilization upwards towards God. They help us to see for ourselves. But for Christ, what would you and I have been ? Surely vastly less than we are now. All the providential men before Jesus helped the race on towards him. They are παιδαγωγοι (child-leaders) to conduct us to the Διδάσκαλος ! You may call these men mediators, it matters not to me. Jesus is certainly the medium through which millions of men have gladly come to God, only I don't think He stands between us and God, so that we must go through Jesus to come to God.

Now, about the Miracles and the Resurrection, I don't reject these things à priori, but simply because I find so little historical evidence in their support. I must have more evidence to support a statement at variance with all my experience than I demand to support what agrees with my experience. In the case of the New Testament Miracles, I don't find adequate evidence ; but this circumstance does not make me think any writer of the New Testament designed to deceive, still less that Christ was a deceiver. Among such a people, under such circumstances, it would be quite surprising to me if such a religious teacher had arisen and had not been popularly believed to work miracles ! About the immortality of the soul, I think, as Justin Martyr says, in that remarkable fragment of his work, πέρι ἀναστασιῶς, that the Resurrection was no proof of that doctrine, for it did not need a proof, as it had been taught before by Plato and Pythagoras. I find abundant proofs of the soul's immortality. I have no more doubt of it than of the fact of my present existence. But long before I abandoned the resurrection of Jesus I saw that it had nothing to do with this doctrine. I don't believe in any outward criterion of spiritual truths.

It seems to me the conscience of you and me is the Lydian stone, with which we are to try the gold of truth. I doubt not that God will make at last this existence of ours a blessing to each one of us, even to the worst of sinners, for I can't think of Him otherwise than as a kind father, who leads the human race by the hand, and will lead us all home at the last, losing none of his little ones, neither you nor me. To believe the eternal damnation of any one of the human race is to me worse than to believe the utter annihilation of all ; for I take it the infinite damnation of one soul would make immortality a curse to the race; and the fact that immortality has seldom been taught so that it would be a blessing to mankind to have the doctrine true, is the main cause why some reject the beautiful doctrine of Christ on this point at this day. I know but a little ways, but when my knowledge ends my trust in God does not end. My knowledge is finite, and very little, but my faith in God is absolute ; and just as I distrust the traditions of men, does my faith in the truths of God, in His goodness and love, become deeper and more strong. I fear you will find this long letter wearisome and unsatisfactory, my dear brother, but I hope we shall some day have a chance to confer face to face, and more fully.

Truly your Brother,   T. P.

TO MR. JAMES B. PATTERSON, DAYTON, OHIO.

Boston, Feb. 28, 1855.

DEAR YOUNG FRIEND,—I am the person whom you met in the cars, and parted from at Albany. I sought you in the cars, but in the dim light I failed to find you. I took a good deal of interest in the bright young face, looking so pure and hopeful, and thinking that some five-and-twenty years ago I was on the same road that you are now. I am sorry that you have met with the " misfortune " you refer to. It certainly casts a shade over a young man's prospects for the moment, not for the day. You have a good start thus far, and seem to have laid the foundation well. It will be no misfortune in the end that you must get your own education. It will bring out the deep manly elements at an earlier period; will make you more thoughtful when you would else have been more gamesome and playful. If you are a teacher you can find much time to study by yourself. I began to teach when seventeen years old, and continued it for four winters, working at home on my father's farm in the other parts of the year. I always found from eight to ten hours a day for study, beside the work hours in school; then I taught a high school for three years more, and kept far ahead of the class in college of which I was a (nominal) member. You can do all that, and perhaps more.

Perhaps it will be well to pursue the same studies you would have taken at college ; with the addition of such as belong to your calling as teacher, or you may perhaps teach till you accumulate money enough to go through the college at a later date. No good thing is impossible to a serious and earnest young man with good abilities and good moral principles.

But above all things be careful of your health ; your success depends on a sound body. Do not violate the laws which God writes in these tables of flesh.

Let me know where you go and what you find to do, and I will write you again when more at leisure.

Truly your friend,
THEO. PARKER.

TO THE SAME.

Boston, Jan. 7, 1856.

MY DEAR SIR,—Your note came a day or two since, and I take the earliest opportunity to answer it. I replied at once to your former letter, but it miscarried, I suppose. I have often wondered why I did not hear from you. Please send me any newspaper that contains communications from you, with a mark on the article to draw the eye thither. I hope you are well paid for your fifteen hours work in a post-office, otherwise it is waste of time. I thought you would be a lawyer. You may easily be a distinguished one, and, with a little more effort, a noble man in the calling of a lawyer, which is a quite different thing. I hope you will try for that also.

The love of surpassing others is a common but dangerous quality. Love of absolute excellence (ideal perfection) is one thing, love of excelling others is quite another ; not a noble quality at all, but only an expansion of selfishness: it is vulgar and low. I trust you will avoid that utterly. Set a high mark of intellectual and moral and religious character that you will reach, the other things will take care of themselves. If I were amongst low men, I would try not to be low ; if among high ones, to be as high as possible. Always be yourself, not another man's self.

But I have not time to write you a sermon, so I send one or two that are printed. Let me hear from you as you have inclination, and believe me,

One of your friends,
THEO. PARKER.

One more letter must suffice to close a chapter which, after all, can only vaguely reproduce the extent and method of Mr. Parker's influence :—

FROM PROF. GERVINUS.

Heidelberg, Dec. 29, 1856.

HONORED SIR,—Mr. Apthorp has sent me from Dresden your letter of the 18th August of this year, as he tarries there longer than he thought. The lines from your own hand are so precious to me, that I hasten thankfully to reply. The announcement in your letter that we already have the pleasure of *personally* knowing you—in fact, without being aware of it—took me not disagreeably by surprise. When we saw you at our house in 1844, it was, in fact, before we knew *who Parker was*, for it is only since the German translation of your writings that we have become acquainted with you, American books are so seldom sent to us. And, unfortunately, so many people pass through this little gathering-point of the great routes, that the interesting visitors rejoice us less in the mass of indifferent ones; but that *you* should have been lost to us in this manner, disturbs us greatly. It must, however, humiliating as it is, be confessed. My wife, who is an enthusiastic admirer of yours, was in a sort of despair.

We rejoice every day at the happy idea of Herr Ziethen to translate your works. I hope that, gradually, this will have wide and deep results. We possess your liberal stand-point in theory, in learning, in the schools; we have it in the broad circle of the world, among all people of common sense, but we repel it from the place whence it ought to be taught and planted, so that morality and religion might not disappear *with* obscurantism. Everybody among us knows how it stands with the religious convictions of the majority, only the pulpit does not dare to say it; that is the domain of official hypocrisy. Consequently the calling of the clergyman has been altogether corrupted; let sermons sound ever so high, the whole profession is one of the most despised in Germany. I hope that the impression of your discourses will be favourable to a practical theology among us. I can remark how much they have improved the orthodox themselves. I do what I can to circulate them, in order to make propaganda of the theologians.

To this end, the communications which you have twice sent me are invaluable. I read them with joy and edification. It is a pity that all efforts towards a more rational theory of divine things among us must have only a preparatory significance. We shall have no rational Church until we have a rational State. In this respect, a great apathy now reigns since the failure of 1848; but there is a deep and powerful fermentation, and I venture to predict that the next attempt, which may come late, but certainly will come, will not pass so fruitlessly away. Political storms must free us from a good deal of literary choke-damp, before anything can come out of us. The blessing of our literary revolution of the last century has become a curse, just as Luther's theology did one hundred years after him. I strive with my own scribblings to demonstrate this to my good countrymen, and I shall frequently recur to this theme in the "History of the Nineteenth Century."

You say generous things about this book, which make me feel very proud. But the humanitarian tendency which you discover therein is rather a German one than peculiar to myself. An exclusively partizan history-writing will not be possible here for a long time. I confess that I hold deliberately to the old-fashioned faith that history should be free from all partizanship, except for the universal facts of reason and progress. Whether such a principle can be steadily maintained, after a stable government has been founded, in which parties will strive to rule, is very doubtful to me. It is one advantage of the political disability in which we find ourselves, that the historian can sustain himself upon a height of humanity which he will be obliged to relinquish as soon as earnest talk begins among us concerning a nation, parties, and a state.

Pardon my pen for rambling so. But may I hope that you will embrace future opportunities to communicate with me? You may be assured that you will thus lend a great pleasure to our home. My wife joins her sincere regards to mine.

Faithfully, your obliged

GERVINUS.

END OF VOL. I.